Original Intent and the Framers' Constitution

Leonard W. Levy, whose *Origins of the Fifth Amendment* was awarded the Pulitzer Prize in history, is formerly Earl Warren Professor of Constitutional History at Brandeis University and Andrew W. Mellon All-Claremont Professor of Humanities and History at the Claremont Graduate School. His other writings, many of which have also won awards, include *The Palladium of Justice, Blasphemy, The Establishment Clause, Freedom of the Press from Zenger to Jefferson, Legacy of Suppression*, and *Jefferson and Civil Liberties*. Mr. Levy lives in Ashland, Oregon.

Original Intent and the Framers' Constitution

LEONARD W. LEVY

IVAN R. DEE
CHICAGO

Library of Congress Cataloging-in-Publication Data:
Levy, Leonard Williams, 1923-
  Original intent and the framers' Constitution / Leonard W. Levy.
  p. cm.
  Originally published: New York : Macmillan, c1988.
  Includes bibliographical references and index.
  ISBN 1-56663-312-5 (alk. paper)
  1. Constitutional law—United States—Interpretation and construction.
  2. Constitutional history—United States.   3. Judicial review—United States—
History.   I. Title.
  KF4552 .L485 2000
  342.73'029—dc21   00-043037

To Elyse
the best

Contents

Preface

"Tis funny about th' constitution," said Mr. Dooley, the philosophic Irish bartender created by Finley Peter Dunne. "It reads plain, but no wan can undherstant it without an interpreter." The Supreme Court is the official and final interpreter of the Constitution, but from the beginning of its history, disputes have raged about how it should interpret the Constitution. In its very first constitutional decision the Court provoked a controversy on the question whether its judgment faithfully adhered to the intentions of the Framers of the Constitution. For several decades after the ratification of the Constitution the fading memories of those who had attended the Philadelphia Constitutional Convention supplied the main evidence of the Framers' intent. Even when those memories were fresh, the Framers disagreed vehemently about what the Convention had meant or intended, as the controversy in 1791 over the chartering of the Bank of the United States showed. Not until the publication of Madison's Notes in 1840 did a source become available for original intent analysis.

The Court has professed to favor a constitutional jurisprudence of original intent since the first decade of its history. More accurately, the Court has invoked the authority or intent of the Framers whenever it suited the Justices. Half a century ago a scholar who wrote a pioneering study of the Supreme Court's use of "extrinsic aids in constitutional construction" concluded: "Whenever the United States Supreme Court has felt itself called upon to announce a theory for its conduct in the matter of constitutional interpretation it has insisted, with almost uninterrupted regularity, that the end of constitutional construction is the discovery of the intention of those persons who formulated the instrument or of the people who adopted it."[1]

The term "original intent" (or "original intention") stands for an old idea that the Court should interpret the Constitution according to the understanding of it by its Framers. In most cases original intent should be followed when clearly discernible, and it is always entitled to the utmost respect and consideration as an interpretive guide. The Constitution lacks the eloquence and passion of the Declaration of Independence, although the majestic opening of the Preamble, "We the People," summons forth the still radically democratic idea that the government of the United States exists to serve the people, not the people to serve the government. That is fundamental to the Framers' original intent, as is the related idea that government in the United States cannot tell us what to think or believe about politics, religion, art, science, literature, or anything else; American citizens have the duty as well as the right to keep the government from falling into error, not the other way around. That marvelously wise principle, too, is part of original intent. Lincoln summarized it best when he said that this nation was conceived in liberty and dedicated to the proposition that all people are created equal.

Liberty and equality are the underpinnings of the Constitution, the essential ingredients of the philosophy of natural rights that the Framers passed on to posterity and, alas, no longer has the respect it once mustered. Much that is part of original intent still commands our loyalties, our admiration, and our affection: government by consent of the governed; majority rule under constitutional restraints that limit majorities; a bill of rights that applies to all branches of government; a federal system; a tripartite system of government with a single executive, a bicameral legislature, and an independent judiciary; an elaborate system of checks and balances that limits the separation of powers; representative government; and elections at fixed intervals.

If this book were written from the standpoint of one interested primarily in a principled constitutional theory, it would be very different. But I have not written as I teach my course on the Foundations of American Constitutionalism. I have written it in the context of the contemporary controversy over original intent.

Original intent as constitutional theory is rarely if ever at issue in real cases decided by the Supreme Court. When the Court employs original intent, it refers to the understanding of the Framers respecting a particular provision of the Constitution that is imprecise. In real cases the meaning of the provisions involved in litigation is not clear. Indeed the Constitution tends to be least clear when most involved in litigation; that is especially true of rights as compared with matters of structure. Some of the most important clauses of the Constitution are vague, ambiguous, or, paradoxically, too specific in meaning. The most important evidence of original intent is the text of the Constitution itself, which must prevail whenever it surely embodies a broader principle than can be found in the minds or purposes of its Framers. For example, they had political and religious expression in mind when they framed the First Amendment, but its language contains no restriction. They probably did not mean to extend the rights protected by the Sixth Amendment to "all" criminal prosecutions, but the text says "all" and deserves obedience. They had black Americans uppermost in mind when they designed the Fourteenth Amendment, but its expansive expression applies to all, not only to all races but to people of all religions, creeds, and national or ethnic backgrounds, regardless of legitimacy, sex, or alienage.

Conversely, if two centuries of constitutional government have resulted in wider understanding than the text itself suggests, that is, if the meaning of the text has become expanded beyond its literal phrasing, the text takes second place. Thus, although the Framers did not include "words" as well as "persons, houses, papers, and effects" in the Fourth Amendment and although eavesdropping was commonplace in the eighteenth century, words seized by wiretapping and electronic eavesdropping come within the amendment's protection against unreasonable search and seizure.

Similarly, the right against compulsory self-incrimination protected by the Fifth Amendment seems, literally, to apply only in "criminal cases," but the text applies with equal force to nonjudicial proceedings such as grand jury and legislative investigations, to administrative proceedings, and even to civil cases in which questions are posed that might, if truthfully answered, raise a threat of criminal jeopardy. Notwithstanding some advocates of a jurisprudence of original intent, the Constitution cannot be interpreted literally, if only because it is murky at important points. Were it not, the real cases would not keep arising.

Until recently, original intent had no political coloration. Both liberals and conservatives, especially among judges, have relied on original intent to add respectability to their opinions. But, constitutional historians, among others, do not respect judicial versions of history. Clinton Rossiter, a great constitutional scholar of conservative proclivities, censured politicians and scholars as well as judges when he said that most talk about original intent "is as irrelevant as it is unpersuasive, as stale as it is strained, as rhetorically absurd as it is historically unsound." He added that "men of power who know least about 'the intent of the Framers' are most likely to appeal to it for support of their views."[2] Perhaps because original intent has severe limitations as an instrument of constitutional adjudication in real cases and ought not be taken too seriously, the *Encyclopedia of the American Constitution* has no article on the subject. That set of books covers constitutional events through the close of the Court's work in July 1985.

At that time, as we shut our editorial doors, Edwin Meese III, then attorney general of the United States, castigated the Supreme Court in a sensational speech before the American Bar Association for opinions that he disliked, and he demanded that the Court abandon decisions based on its views of sound public policy. The Court, Meese declared, should give "deference to what the Constitution—its text and intention—may demand." In answer to his question, "What, then, should a constitutional jurisprudence actually be?" Meese asserted, "It should be a Jurisprudence of Original Intention." Such a jurisprudence, he added, when "aimed at the explication of original intention would produce defensible principles of government that would not be tainted by ideological predilection."[3] In 1986 Robert H. Bork, then a judge of the United

States Court of Appeals for the District of Columbia, argued that judges who do not construe the Constitution in accordance with the original intent of its Framers "will, in truth, be enforcing their own morality upon the rest of us and calling it the Constitution."[4] The present Chief Justice of the United States, William H. Rehnquist, has professed similar views. Conservatives, political and judicial, have sought to preempt original intent as their exclusive bulwark and as the only proper foundation for constitutional interpretation. They give the impression that original intent analysis would legitimate their own constitutional views on controversial questions, and they ignore the extent to which original intent would undermine their own positions. Their assumption that the Supreme Court's versions of history are accurate seems naive. A state jurist with a good eye for the meretricious remarked that people who take seriously the Supreme Court's "historical scholarship as applied to the Constitution also probably believe in the Tooth Fairy and the Easter Bunny."[5]

To say that the Supreme Court should decide constitutional questions in accordance with the intent of the Framers is comparable to saying that the Court has a Tom Sawyer mentality, especially with respect to its devotion to principle. In *Huckleberry Finn*, Tom and Huck set out to rescue Jim. Tom, always the romantic who remembered the adventure stories he had read, knew that the proper way to rescue a prisoner was by digging him out of his prison with a case-knife. They dug and dug for many hours, until they were dog-tired and had blistered hands, yet they had scarcely made any progress. Tom admitted that they would have to use picks "and *let on* it's case-knives." He declared that Huck, being ignorant, might use a pick without letting on, but that would not do for himself, Tom, because he knew better. "Gimme a case-knife," he ordered. Huck handed him one but Tom threw it down and said, "Gimme a *case-knife*." Huck finally caught on and handed Tom a pick; Tom took it and set to work. Huck marveled, "He was always just that particular. Full of principle."[6]

The Supreme Court, also full of principle, uses Tom Sawyer's "case-knife" when it credits original intent for its decisions. Whatever picks it uses as its grounds of decision, it stays respectful of the Constitutional Convention. James Madison, James Wilson, and Gouverneur Morris might, like Moses, be astounded at interpretations attributed to them as the source. On arriving in heaven, Moses did not understand what God was doing and was told that in the future a man named Rabbi Akiba would explain. Moses asked to see Akiba and was transported to the future. He listened to Akiba's discourse on the law but it mystified him; he could not follow Akiba's arguments. Moses felt comforted, however, when one of Akiba's disciples asked the master how he knew the meaning of the law on a certain subject, and Akiba responded, "It is a law given unto Moses at Sinai."[7] The process of seeking original intent is elusive, if not illusive, because the fundamental text may be ambiguous and vague, or overarches a particular situation. In a sense the text, whether Constitution or Talmud, is always unfinished even as it is perpetual; and subsequent teachers or judges must expound its meaning. Their exposition can be a legitimate extension of the original, because the text fixes not only a system but an ongoing process. E. L. Doctorow, the novelist, examined the Constitution as a sacred text whose judicial readings are equivalent to priestly commentaries, and he concluded: "It is in the nature of a sacred text, speaking from the past to the present and into the future in that scriptural voice that does not explain . . . to shimmer with ambiguity and to become finally enigmatic, as if it were the ultimate voice of Buddhist self-realization."[8] A Constitution of this sort does not allow original intent analysis to be dispositive or even meaningful in real cases that raise quite specific questions. Rossiter concluded his book on the Constitutional Convention by affirming, "The one clear intent of the Framers was that each generation of Americans should pursue its destiny as a community of free men." Even if some intent is discernible in a case before the Supreme Court, it is probably so general that no one disputes it and it cannot serve to settle the question.

"Original intent" is not a well-chosen term but it is commonly used and widely understood to mean what the Constitutional Convention understood or believed about the Constitution. Intent, intention, and intendment may be distinguished but I do not find the distinctions fruitful in a discourse meant for nonlawyers. Intent may refer to motive, to purpose, even to reasons, but I think that the commonplace usage of intent, in the context of the debate about the "original intent" of the Framers, refers to what they meant. Nevertheless, "intent" is unsatisfactory because it implies a single or uniform frame of mind, or purpose, or understanding on the part of the Framers of the Constitution and even of the ratifiers of the Constitution. "Original intentions" would have been a far better term.

I try to avoid the nomenclature used in the law reviews to describe the contending scholars in the original intent controversy. "Interpretivist" and "noninterpretivist" are probably most common. Generally an interpretivist is one who believes that courts should stay as closely as possible to the text of the Constitution, to original intent if ascertainable, to principles and purposes derived from the Constitution, to history, and probably to precedents and conventional rules of construction. I regard myself as an interpretivist or, at least, a "broad interpretivist" rather than a "narrow" one. On the other hand, I share much of the skepticism, but little else, of the "noninterpretivists." They believe that interpretation based on interpretivist values or norms is unrealistic in the sense of not accurately describing what the Supreme Court is doing. That is true. But noninterpretivists rely on values and norms that go quite beyond anything the text or history can provide; they tend to stress current values, usually their own, which they find in some philosophy or alleged consensus of which they approve, and they insist that judges ought to decide accordingly; or they complain that the Court decides on the basis of bias that is wrong because it is not their bias. The term "noninterpretivism" is silly because "noninterpretivism" is more interpretive than "interpretivism," though it purports to interpret something other than the Constitution. Noninterpretivists are really saying, "The Constitution should be interpreted to enforce my policies rather than yours." Interpretivists are also called "intentionalists" and "originalists," and on occasion in my final chapters, I lapse into these terms when following or characterizing an argument made by one who uses the terms as his own. Originalist and intentionalist seem to be self-evident in meaning. I suppose the opponents of originalism are unoriginalists or plagiarists and the opponents of intentionalists are unintentionalists or accidentalists. In short, I avoid the jargon because it misleads and sounds even sillier than it is.

A book on original intent must necessarily be a book on the judicial process and judicial review, because "original intent" signifies a way for courts, the Supreme Court in particular, to interpret

the Constitution. Most of this book, however, is about selected
provisions of the Constitution as understood by the Constitutional
Convention. As the table of contents indicates, I have made no
effort to be systematic in covering the provisions of the Constitution. I have chosen provisions that I think are interesting and
important, that I know most about, and that are frequently litigated.
I have restricted myself to the original Constitution and the Bill
of Rights in my chapters on what the founding generation understood the document to mean. The concluding chapters ask whether
a constitutional jurisprudence of original intent, as advocated by
Chief Justice William H. Rehnquist, ex-Judge Robert H. Bork, and
former Attorney General Edwin Meese III, is realistic and viable.
Until those concluding chapters I try, on the whole, to depict
original intent on various subjects without regard to subsequent
developments.

Judicial reasoning has always fascinated me. The life of the
law combines logic and experience, blended with a spice of insight.
A story that I have told elsewhere bears repeating here because it
concerns the blend of logic, experience, and insight that produce
reasoned judgment. Telling the story a second time exposes me to
condemnation by Voltaire's followers. He was once invited to participate in an orgy and did; on a later occasion, when invited again,
he declined, saying, "Once a philosopher, twice a pervert." The
story, however, is of a wholly different character. It concerns Jews
who lived outside the ghetto communities of nineteenth-century
Russia. Such Jews could not travel without official permission. After
months of negotiation, an old Jewish scholar who lived in Odessa
got permission to travel from Odessa to Moscow. He boarded the
train, and after one stop a young man got on and sat down opposite
him. The old scholar looked at the young man and said to himself:

> He doesn't look like a peasant, and if he isn't a peasant, he probably
> comes from this district. If he comes from this district, he must be
> Jewish because this is a Jewish district. But, if he's Jewish, so where
> could he be going? I'm the only one in the district who has permission
> to travel to Moscow. To what village would he not need permission
> to travel? Oh, just outside Moscow there's the little village of Moz-
> haisk, and to Mozhaisk you don't need permission. But who could
> he be visiting in Mozhaisk? There are only two Jewish families in

the whole of Mozhaisk, the Linskys and the Greenbaums. I know the Linskys are a terrible family, so he must be visiting the Greenbaums. But who would undertake a trip at this time of year unless he were a close personal relative? The Greenbaums have only daughters, so perhaps he's a son-in-law. But, if he's a son-in-law, which daughter did he marry? Esther married that nice young lawyer from Budapest. What was his name? Alexander Cohen. Who did Sarah marry? Sarah married that no-goodnik, that salesman from Zhadomir. It must be Esther. So, if he married Esther, his name is Alexander Cohen and he comes from Budapest. Oh, the terrible anti-Semitism they have there now! He probably changed his name from Cohen. So what's the Hungarian equivalent of Cohen? Kovacs. But, if he's a man who changed his name from Cohen to Kovacs, he's a man who shows a basic insecurity in life. However, to change his name because of anti-Semitism, a man would need status. So what kind of status could he have? A doctor's degree from the university.

At this point the old scholar got up, tapped the young man on the shoulder, and said, "Dr. Alexander Kovacs?" "Why, yes," said the young man, "but how did you know?" "Oh," replied the old scholar, "it stands to reason."

It also stands to reason that I should have written this book. I have been writing about original intent, which I used to think of as original understanding, since 1960, when *Legacy of Suppression* was published. *Origins of the Fifth Amendment, Emergence of a Free Press,* and *The Establishment Clause* are also preoccupied with original intent. Summaries of those books appear in the appropriate chapters on the same subjects in this book. I hereby acknowledge my appreciation to Oxford University Press for permission to draw upon materials in *Emergence of a Free Press*.

CHAPTER ONE

The Framers
and Original Intent

*J*ames Madison, Father of the Constitution and of the Bill of Rights, rejected the doctrine that the original intent of those who framed the Constitution should be accepted as an authoritative guide to its meaning. "As a guide in expounding and applying the provisions of the Constitution," he wrote in a well-considered and consistent judgment, "the debates and incidental decisions of the Convention can have no authoritative character."[1] The fact that Madison, the quintessential Founder, discredited original intent is probably the main reason that he refused throughout his life to publish his "Notes of Debates in the Federal Convention," incomparably our foremost source for the secret discussions of that hot summer in Philadelphia in 1787.

We tend to forget the astounding fact that Madison's Notes were first published in 1840, fifty-three years after the Constitutional Convention had met.[2] That period included the beginnings of the Supreme Court plus five years beyond the entire tenure of John Marshall as Chief Justice. Thus, throughout the formative period of our national history, the High Court, presidents, and Congress construed the Constitution without benefit of a record of the Convention's deliberations. Indeed, even the skeletal Journal of the Convention was not published until 1819.[3] Congress could have authorized its publication anytime after President George Washington, who had presided at the 1787 Convention, deposited it at the State Department in 1796. Although the Journal merely revealed motions and votes, it would have assisted public understanding of the secret proceedings of the Convention, no records of which existed, other than the few spotty and jaundiced accounts by Convention members who opposed ratification.[4] The Convention had, after all, been an assembly in which "America," as George Mason of Virginia said, had "drawn forth her first characters," and even Patrick Henry conceded that the Convention consisted of "the greatest, the best, and most enlightened of our citizens."[5] Thomas Jefferson, in Paris, referred to the "assembly of demigods."[6] The failure of the Framers to have officially preserved and published their proceedings seems inexplicable, especially in a nation that promptly turned matters of state into questions of constitutional law; but then, the Framers seem to have thought that "the original understanding at Philadelphia," which Chief Justice William H. Rehnquist has alleged to be of prime importance, did not greatly matter.[7] What mattered to them was the text of the Constitution, construed in the light of conventional rules of interpretation, the ratification debates, and other contemporary expositions.

If the Framers, who met in executive sessions every day of their nearly four months of work, had wanted their country and posterity to construe the Constitution in the light of their deliberations, they would have had a stenographer present to keep an official record, and they would have published it. They would not have left the task of preserving their debates to the initiative of one of their members who retained control of his work and a proprietary interest in it. "Nearly a half century" after the convention, Madison wrote a preface to his Notes in which he explained why he had made the record. He had determined to preserve to the best of his ability "an exact account of what might pass in the Convention," because the record would be of value "for the History of a Constitution on which would be staked the happiness of a young people great even in its infancy, and possibly the cause of Liberty throughout the world."[8] That seems to have been a compelling reason for publication as soon as possible, not posthumously—and Madison outlived all the members of the Convention.

Madison also explained how he managed to keep such detailed notes. He was present every day and never absent for more than "a casual fraction of an hour in any day," so that he heard every speech. He sat center front so that he could hear everything, and every evening he wrote out his daily notes.[9] He told a friend that the labor "almost killed him" but he determined to finish the task, and he did.[10] Given his exertion, the importance of the record, and his own explanation of why he made it, why did he not publish it?

No injunction of secrecy bound him. The Convention had immediately adopted a rule of secrecy: "That nothing spoken in the House be printed, or otherwise published, or communicated without leave."[11] But the rule applied only while the Convention was in session. As George Mason explained to his son, the Convention had adopted the rule as a precaution against misrepresentation "until the business shall have been completed," when the final product might have a shape quite different from initial proposals.[12] Secrecy also served the same function as the Convention's habit of meeting in the Committee of the Whole: one might speak candidly with political impunity and still reserve a right to change one's mind. None of those considerations prevailed, however, after the Convention had adjourned and the Confederation Congress had submitted the draft of the Constitution to the states for ratification. If Madison's Notes had been published at that time, both the voters who chose delegates to their state ratifying conventions and the members of those conventions would have performed their tremendously important civic duties more knowledgeably. Delegates were chosen on the basis of whether they favored or opposed ratification, and, like the voters, they deliberated on the basis of the text of the Constitution with no knowledge from its Framers of how it was framed, or which of its provisions represented consensus or compromise, or what its Framers understood its various clauses to mean. Its Framers, however, may have believed that the publication of their proceedings could have damaged the prospects of ratification by revealing the conflicts among the delegates. Those revelations might have hurt the political fortunes of some of the Framers and might have exacerbated sectional differences as well as differences between large and small states. The Convention even refused to publish its journal for fear that, as Rufus

King of Massachusetts said, "a bad use" would be made of it "by those who would wish to prevent the adoption of the Constitution."[13]

The ratification controversy triggered a torrent of pamphlet and newspaper literature, much of it of an extraordinarily high caliber, including works by members of the Convention, those opposed to ratification as well as those who supported ratification. But much of the Anti-Federalist literature was trash based on hysterical assumptions or on political calculations intended to deceive and incite fear of the Constitution. Anti-Federalists persistently expressed exaggerated fears about the way in which the new government would abuse its powers if the Constitution were ratified. In North Carolina, for example, Henry Abbot frenetically predicted, in his state's ratifying convention, that the treaty power would be used to make Roman Catholicism the established religion of the country,[14] and Major William Lusk warned the Massachusetts ratifying convention that the "Inquisition may be established in America."[15] In his own ratifying convention Madison heard Patrick Henry prophesy that the United States would "extort confession by torture," perpetuate "the most tyrannical and oppressive deeds," and send taxgatherers into everybody's homes to "ransack, and measure, every thing you eat, drink, and wear."[16]

The Convention had invited some of this sort of thing, of course, by its double blunder: it had omitted a bill of rights and, worse, had provided explicit protection of just a few rights, thereby provoking the fear that all the rights that had been omitted were in jeopardy. But the blunders were not sinister, as the record of the Convention could have shown; without that record, friends of the Constitution, including those who signed it in Philadelphia, were driven to some arguments that were rather preposterous, and others that were quite lame, to explain away their failure.[17] The debates in Philadelphia turned out to be of slight interest or significance during the ratification controversy; even members of the Convention debated ratification in tracts published under pseudonyms and argued for or against the text on its merits, without relying on the Philadelphia story.

Not even James Madison and Alexander Hamilton as the authors of *The Federalist*, writing as "Publius," relied on their authoritative experience as Framers. In their essays they speculated about what the Convention "must have" intended, as if they did not know from first-hand experience.[18] *The Federalist* #37, which purported to "survey . . . the work of the Convention," did not mention or ascribe to the Framers any intentions or understandings of any significance. Rather, Madison predicated his essay on the principle that the meaning of the Constitution must emerge in the course of time and as a result of experience, however difficult the inherent ambiguities of language made that task.

Not once during his long public career as a congressman, party leader, secretary of state, or President, not even as an elder statesman, did Madison rely on the authority of his Notes. The state papers connected with his name, including the Virginia Resolutions of 1798 and the great Virginia Report of 1799–1800, contain no reference to the Notes or to the intentions of the Framers. Madison rarely referred to the Convention for the meaning or intent of the Constitution.[19] When he did, he subordinated original intent to other considerations, as when he said that the sense of the Constitution would be found "in the proceedings of the Convention, the contemporary expositions, and, above all, in the ratifying conventions of the States."[20] On one occasion when he referred to "the intention of those who framed" the Constitution, he corrected himself and added, "or rather, who adopted" it, meaning its ratifiers.[21] Madison also relied on the text of the Constitution, the ordinary rules of the common law applicable when construing a document, and the history of the time. Nor was he alone in that practice. It was the customary basis of analyzing constitutional issues, as the debate in the First Congress on the removal power showed.

That was the first debate in the House of Representatives on a constitutional question. Eight of its members, including Madison, were, as he always remembered, "fresh from the Convention which framed the Constitution," and there were "a considerable number who had been members of the State Conventions which adopted it. . . ."[22] During the discussion of a bill for establishing the Department of Foreign Affairs, the House debated a motion to make the head of that executive branch, who was appointed by the President with the advice and consent of the Senate, removable by the President alone. On June 16 and 17, 1789, congressmen made extemporary speeches on that issue with an elegance, profundity of analysis, and elaborate complexity that would grace the pages of *The Federalist* or of a Supreme Court opinion delivered after much deliberation. The occasion loomed momentously to the debaters. Madison declared in his first remarks on the issue:

> The decision that is at this time made will become the permanent exposition of the Constitution and on a permanent exposition of the Constitution will depend the genius and character of the whole government. It will depend, perhaps, on this decision, whether government shall retain that equilibrium which the Constitution intended, or take a direction towards aristocracy, or anarchy, among the members of the government. Hence, how careful ought we to be to give a true direction to a power so critically circumstanced! It is incumbent on us to weigh, with particular attention, the arguments which have been advanced in support of the various opinions with cautious deliberation. I own to you, Mr. Chairman, that I feel great anxiety upon this question. I feel an anxiety, because I am called upon to give a decision in a case that may affect the fundamental principles of the government under which we act, and liberty itself. But all that I can do, on such an occasion, is to weigh well every thing advanced on both sides, with the purest desire to find out the true meaning of the Constitution, and to be guided by that, and an attachment to the true spirit of liberty, whose influence I believe strongly predominates here.[23]

The only allusion to original intent that Madison made during the course of the debate came in his remark that the Convention could not have contemplated the incongruity contended for by those who did not wish to vest the removal power exclusively in the President, despite the fact that the Constitution empowered him to exercise the executive power and to take care that the laws be faithfully executed. The few references to the Convention by other speakers were as casual, incidental, and unsubstantial.[24] Notwithstanding the sophistication of the constitutional arguments, original intent simply did not matter. Members of the House who had attended the Convention divided on the issue; none invoked the authority of the Convention as he recalled it. No one asked those who had been in Philadelphia what the Convention had thought of the issue, which the Constitution left unresolved; no one asked Madison to check his Notes to determine whether they might offer some illumination. This state of affairs characterized other debates in Congress on other constitutional issues. The founders of the national government and its early officers simply did not think in terms of the original intent at Philadelphia.

That fact stands out in the great debate of 1791 on the constitutionality of the bank bill. Congress proposed to charter the Bank of the United States, which, despite its name, was a private corporation. The bill raised the question whether Congress had the constitutional power to charter a corporation. If original intent had any significance, the answer to the question should have been clear and decisive. At the Convention, Madison had proposed, for the consideration of the Committee of Detail, that Congress be empowered to "grant charters of incorporation in cases where the Public good may require them, and the authority of a single State may be incompetent."[25] Nearly a month later, after the committee had failed to act on the proposal, Madison renewed his motion for consideration by the Convention. Three delegates spoke on the issue. Rufus King thought that the power, being divisive in nature, would set the states against each other, while in Philadelphia and New York, where bank charters had provoked political controversy, the power would be construed in terms of banks; elsewhere it would suggest mercantile monopolies. James Wilson disagreed. He wanted Congress to charter canals in order to facilitate communication with the frontier and saw nothing in the power that might excite political parties.[26] George Mason, however, expressed a fear of monopolies; he moved to restrict the power to canals only. The Convention, by a vote of 8–3, then voted down a motion restricted to canals, and, Madison recorded, his main motion on the general power to charter corporations, "fell of course, as including the power rejected."[27] That ended the matter in the Convention.

When the question arose in the House of Representatives four years later, Madison spoke against it at length, offering reasons of policy and especially interpretations of the Constitution calculated to show that Congress lacked the power to enact the bill. He also observed in passing "that a power to grant charters of incorporation had been proposed in the general convention and rejected."[28] That was the only occasion that Madison, while in public service, ever referred to the intent of the Convention. Five years later he spoke of the incident as if acknowledging an impropriety, and he read to the House the remarks in rebuttal by Elbridge Gerry, "who had himself been a member of the Convention, . . . protesting, in strong terms, against arguments drawn from that source."[29] Gerry observed that Madison had invoked the "sense" of the Convention, but, Gerry asked, "how is this to be obtained?" He favored "applying proper rules of interpretation" rather than depending on memories of participants, because memories "would probably vary, as they already had done." In any event, the opinions of those who spoke "are not to be considered as the opinions of the Convention."[30] Madison apparently agreed. No one else during the bank debate referred to the Convention or to original intent, except John Vining of Delaware. Vining summarily dismissed original intent as the "opinion" of 1787, which he thought had become obsolete, "not a sufficient authority . . . for Congress at the present time to construe the Constitution."[31] Members of the House conducted the debate by analyzing the text of the Constitution according to the usual rules of interpretation. The bill, which the Senate had voted for unanimously, passed the House 39–20. Thus, Madison's view, the view of the Convention, suffered overwhelming defeat. Politics, rather than original intent, prevailed. And politics may have taught Madison that original intent did not matter.

President George Washington, who had presided at the Philadelphia Convention, felt uncertain whether to sign the bill or veto it, and so he sought the opinions of others. Attorney General Edmund Randolph, another member of the Convention, urged a veto. Secretary of State Thomas Jefferson, who had been in Paris when the Convention met, wrote the classic state paper employing narrow construction of delegated powers, and he recommended a veto. Jefferson's memorandum to Washington benefited from Madison's advice, and Madison even let Jefferson use his Notes of the Convention's debates. Although Jefferson relied mainly on the "established rule[s] of construction," he added:

> It is also known that the very power now proposed *as a means* was rejected *as an end* by the Convention which formed the Constitution. A proposition was made to them to authorize Congress to open canals, and an amendatory one to empower them to incorporate. But the whole was rejected, and one of the reasons for rejection urged in debate was that then they would have possessed a power to erect a bank, which would render the great cities, where there were prejudices and jealousies on the subject, adverse to the reception of the Constitution.[32]

Secretary of the Treasury Alexander Hamilton, another Framer, confidently supported the constitutionality of the measure, which he had proposed. He disagreed with Jefferson's reliance on what had happened at the Convention because the precise nature of the proposition that was defeated and the reasons for its defeat were "not ascertained by any authentic document, or even by accurate recollection. As far as any document exists, it [the Journal] specifies only canals."[33] In effect, Hamilton capitalized on the fact that Madison's Notes had not been published. Hamilton elaborately relied on constitutional construction or logical analysis of the text to prove that Congress had the legitimate authority to enact the bill, and he contended that no extratextual aids should be employed: "The Secretary of State will not deny," he declared, "that whatever may have been the intention of the framers of a constitution, or of a law, that intention is to be sought for in the instrument itself, according to the usual & established rules of construction." Accordingly, he concluded, if the power to charter a corporation might be deduced from the text itself, "arguments drawn from extrinsic circumstances, regarding the intention of the convention, must be rejected."[34] That accurately stated the truth of the matter for the founding generation.

How, otherwise, could we explain Madison's casual reference to the Convention? But there is no way to explain, except on policy grounds, his tightly controlled explication of the necessary and proper clause and of the so-called general welfare clause, on the one hand, and on the other, his eagerness to have Congress support what was called the "magnetic theory." He wanted the United States to subsidize a scientific expedition to Baffin's Bay in the hope that by throwing "valuable light on the discovery of longitude," it would aid navigation. Congress thwarted him because the money he wanted was needed elsewhere, and, anyway, ships could navigate without knowing whether the magnetic theory explained compass deviations. The point is that Madison supported an expenditure justifiable only upon a breathtaking interpretation of the general welfare clause, at the same time that he opposed justifying the charter of the bank under the same clause.[35] Madison, like Hamilton, adeptly manipulated the text to reach a preconceived result.

Under the circumstances, the president might have been perplexed. After Hamilton's argument and statement that no authentic proofs existed to show the Convention's intent on the bank issue, Washington summoned Madison to hear firsthand the arguments opposed to the bank bill and, as Madison recalled, "listened favorably" to Madison's views without committing himself. Washington even requested and received from Madison a veto message in case he should decide against the bill, but he signed it.[36] The message, incidentally, contained no reference to the Convention or its intent.

Given the differences of opinion among Framers on the bank issue, original intent may not have been as discernible as it seemed in this case, or it may not have mattered significantly. More likely, the constitutional text lent itself to reinterpretation in the light of policy preferences by the administration in power. When the bank's charter expired twenty years later, and the United States fought the War of 1812 at considerable cost, without its financial services, experience taught new constitutional lessons. In 1816 Congress chartered a second Bank of the United States, at the instigation and support of the Madison administration. Three years later, in the monumental case of *McCulloch v. Maryland,* the Supreme Court sustained the constitutionality of the act in an opinion by Chief Justice John Marshall (who had been a ratifier of the Constitution). Once again, original intent counted for nothing. If Marshall had consulted the Journal of the Convention, he would have had to explain his way around it. He ignored it.[37] Indeed, he never cited the Journal. In *McCulloch* his astoundingly broad interpretation of congressional powers dismayed even Madison, who declared that the Constitution would not have been ratified if the people had known that the United States possessed nearly illimitable powers.[38]

The one point on which nearly everyone agreed, during the bank controversy, was that the Constitution should be construed according to conventional rules of interpretation. For all their disagreements, Hamilton and Jefferson concurred on that point— interpretation of the fundamental text, as Hamilton said, according to the "usual and established rules of construction," or, as Jefferson said, according to "the established rules of construction." The fact that they arrived at contradictory results suggests that those rules were made of the same waxy substance as the text itself, enabling judges, Jefferson bitterly complained, to twist it as they pleased into any shape.[39] In his *Commentaries on the Constitution*, Justice Joseph Story later discoursed on the rules of construction for some sixty pages, without convincing his Jacksonian colleagues.[40] The rules of constitutional construction are comparable to those of statutory construction, which a current federal judge has called "a total jumble." "Karl Llewellyn," Frank Easterbrook wrote, "listed them in *The Common Law Tradition*. Playing the role of a legal Isaac Newton, he showed that for every rule there is an equal and opposite rule. Statutes in derogation of the common law are strictly construed, but remedial statutes are liberally construed. It turns out that every remedial statute is in derogation of the common law, so the judge has discretion aplenty."[41] Rules of construction in effect free, rather than fetter, judicial discretion. Edward S. Corwin, when the foremost constitutional scholar in the nation, wrote incisively: "In brief, alternative principles of construction and alternative lines of precedent constantly vest the Court with a freedom virtually legislative in scope in choosing the values which it shall promote through its reading of the Constitution."[42] Hamilton, Jefferson, Madison, Gerry, and Washington, among the Framers who disagreed with each other on the constitutionality of the bank, were as skillful as judges in employing rules of construction to reason their way from unquestioned premises to foregone conclusions. Their rules of construction did not provide a particular result. The rules, rather, provided a way of clothing a policy preference in a respectable rationale, giving the guise of objectivity to a highly subjective task. *McCulloch v. Maryland* and the reaction to it from Madison, Jefferson, and Spencer Roane showed how impersonal rules could be used to reach results that could be passed off as the consequence of duty, not choice.[43]

Following the first bank bill, the most significant event involving original intent occurred during the controversy in 1796 over Jay's Treaty, which the Senate had already ratified. That treaty obligated the House of Representatives to appropriate monies to implement certain provisions, and the House, controlled by the opposition party, decided that it had a duty to determine whether the treaty should be carried out. It therefore requested President Washington to make available for its deliberations all executive records concerning the making of the treaty. Administration supporters regarded that request as an unconstitutional violation of the treaty-making powers of the president acting with the advice and consent of the Senate. In the course of the debate, William Vans Murray of Maryland, a loyal Federalist, thinking that the original intent of the Convention would support his party's position, wondered why Madison had not informed the House about the Convention's intent on the issue.[44] Albert Gallatin of Pennsylvania, second to Madison as the leader of the opposition, expressed surprise that years after the Convention Murray should have inquired about original intent or what he described as "the doctrines and constructions of those persons who had framed and proposed the Constitution, opinions given in private, constructions unknown to the people when they adopted the instrument."[45] Gallatin believed that the text of the Constitution provided the answer to the question whether the House had an obligation to appropriate monies called for by a treaty. The only opinions about the meaning of the text that Gallatin endorsed were those of the members of the state ratifying conventions who favored ratification, because they alone, acting on behalf of the people, adopted the Constitution, and so, "their intentions alone might, with any degree of propriety, be resorted to."[46]

President Washington refused to comply with the House's request for executive records, even though that request had the support of a huge majority. He made explicit what Murray had implied: the original intent excluded the House from participation in the treaty-making process. Speaking as one who had been a member of the Convention and who knew the principles that bottomed the Constitution, Washington insisted that the power of making treaties "is exclusively vested in the President," with the advice and consent of two-thirds of the Senate, and, he added, the state ratifying conventions understood that. If proofs other than the "plain letter of the Constitution itself" were needed, Washington added, "they may be found in the Journals of the General Convention," which he had just deposited with the Department of State. The Journal showed that the assent of the House was unneeded, because the Convention had rejected a proposition that no treaty should be binding until "ratified by a law."[47]

Washington's message angered Madison, who remembered that the President had ignored original intent in 1791 when the bank bill was at issue. Madison informed Jefferson in Virginia that according to his memory the Convention had entrusted its Journal to its president, who was to keep it "sacred until called for by some competent authority." Madison asked Jefferson to read his Notes to check his recollection.[48] According to the Notes, the Convention had resolved that Washington should retain the Journal "subject to the order of Congress, if ever formed under the Constitution."[49] What surprises us is that Congress never asked for the Journal and did not authorize its publication until 1818.[50]

Madison replied to Washington on the floor of congress. The president had misunderstood the position of the House. No one, Madison declared, argued that the House's assent be required for the ratification of treaties. The House's resolution, rather, had limited the power of the House over treaties "to cases where Treaties embraced Legislative subjects, submitted by the Constitution to the power of the House," as in the case of appropriations. Madison then turned to the message. On the question of the intent of the Convention, he stated that members of the House who had been members of the Convention did not expect an appeal to the proceedings of the Convention "as a clue to the meaning of the Constitution."[51] Nine years had passed since the Convention, he complained, and he had not a single note with him to assist his memory. No one who had been a member of the Convention had an obligation to answer queries concerning his views in Philadelphia in 1787 or "the intention of the whole body; many members of which, too, had probably never entered into the discussions of the subject." Moreover, members of Congress who had attended the Convention disagreed on the subject at issue. Senators who concurred in ratifying the treaty put a different sense on the matter than he did.[52] At that point Madison recalled that he himself had once simply referred to the Convention's intent, when the bank bill had been under discussion, and others had criticized him for it. He read some of that criticism to the House, adding that there had not been a single instance "in which the sense of the Convention had been required or admitted as material in any Constitutional question."[53] Members of the Supreme Court who had attended the Convention, he noted, had not been called on for the meaning of the founders when the question before the Justices dealt with the suability of the states—an allusion to *Chisholm v. Georgia*.[54] Madison then criticized Washington's use of the Journal of the Convention.[55]

His main argument, however, emphasized the irrelevance of original-intent analysis:

> But, after all, whatever veneration might be entertained for the body of men who formed our Constitution, the sense of that body could never be regarded as the oracular guide in expounding the Constitution. As the instrument came from them it was nothing more than a dead letter, until life and validity were breathed into it by the voice of the people, speaking through the several State Conventions. If we were to look, therefore, for the meaning of the instrument beyond the face of the instrument, we must look for it, not in the General Convention, which proposed, but in the State Conventions, which accepted and ratified the Constitution.[56]

This was an extraordinary, even an inexplicable position for Madison to take in view of the political cacophony and partisanship that characterized the ratifying conventions of the states, and above all, in view of the fact that the proceedings of those conventions were so incompletely and poorly reported. Indeed, Madison in 1796 believed that only the ratifying conventions of Pennsylvania, Virginia, and North Carolina had published their proceedings; and the only published proceedings for North Carolina covered its first convention, which rejected the Constitution. That Madison knew the records of only two conventions that ratified subverted his theory about deriving original intent from their records.[57] The proceedings of two other state conventions, Massachusetts and New York, had also been published,[58] but other convention records, excepting skeletal journals, did not exist; moreover, all records had gaps and, as Madison conceded, inaccuracies. Of his own state's record, he said that it "contained internal evidence in abundance of chasms and misconceptions of what was said," and Virginia's record of its ratification proceedings was probably the best of all.[59] Compared to Madison's Notes of the Federal Convention, the most striking features of the Virginia convention's debates were the raving suspicions of Patrick Henry and the political need for a bill of rights to quiet the apprehensions of the people. Discerning original intent from only the state ratifying records is nearly impossible, because we have incomplete and unreliable accounts from less than half the states, and Madison could not have really believed that it was possible. Elbridge Gerry accurately asserted that the "debates of the State Conventions, as published by shorthand writers, were generally partial and mutilated. . . ."[60] Without a record of the state debates, ratifier intent cannot be ascertained.

Justice Joseph Story made the definitive rejection of ratifier intent in his *Commentaries on the Constitution:*

> In different states and in different conventions, different and very opposite objections are known to have prevailed; and might well be presumed to prevail. Opposite interpretations, and different explanations of different provisions, may well be presumed to have been presented in different bodies, to remove local objections, or to win local favor. And there can be no certainty, either that the different state conventions in ratifying the constitution, gave the same uniform interpretation to its language, or that, even in a single state convention, the same reasoning prevailed with a majority, much less with the whole of the supporters of it.

Story continued by observing that the terms of a document may have differently impressed different people. Some drew conclusions that others repudiated. Some thought about it cursorily and others profoundly. Some may have understood its terms too strictly, others too broadly. Story added that not even the members of the Philadelphia Convention understood the Constitution in the same way. "Every member," he wrote, "necessarily judged for himself." And in the state conventions, the well-known "diversity of construction" given by different people "in different conventions" required an emphasis on the point that no such thing as a unified "Framer" or ratifier intent existed. The result is that we must always bear foremost in mind a crucial fact: "Nothing but the text itself was adopted by the whole people."[61]

In response to the argument by Jefferson that we should conform as much as possible to ratifier intent, Story retorted:

> Now, who does not see the utter looseness, and incoherence of this canon. How are we to know, what was thought of particular clauses of the constitution at the time of its adoption? In many cases no printed debates give any account of any construction; and where any is given, different persons held different doctrines. Whose is to prevail? Besides; of all the state conventions, the debates of five only are preserved, and these very imperfectly. What is to be done, as

to the other eight states? . . . What is to be done, as to the eleven new states, which have come into the Union under constructions, which have been established, against what some persons may deem the meaning of the framers of it?

Story also raised the question whether the views of the authors of *The Federalist* are to be followed—and they conflicted with each other and also changed their minds—or the differing views by others expressed at the time. If we are also to consider the opinions of the voters, as well as the Framers, he asked, "can we know those opinions?" And how are we to gather what Jefferson called the "probable meaning" of statesmen and others who left conjectures from scattered documents, private papers, and table talk? And when probable meanings turn out to be understood differently by different people, "what interpretation is to be followed? These, and many questions of the same sort, might be asked. It is obvious," Story concluded, again, "that there can be no security to the people in any constitution of government, if they are not to judge of it by the fair meaning of the words of the text. . . ."[62]

Madison, believing or professing to believe in ratifier intent, thought that to ascribe an "ascendancy" in expounding the Constitution according to the "*intention* of the [Philadelphia] *Convention*" was an "error" for two reasons. First, he mentioned "the difficulty of verifying that intention"—a consideration that applies with far greater weight to the deliberations of the state conventions; then he offered his standard contention that "if the meaning of the Constitution is to be sought out of itself [not derived from the text] it is not in the proceedings of the Body that proposed it, but in those of the State Conventions which gave it all the validity & authority it possesses."[63]

Madison died at eighty-five, having outlived every other person who attended the Convention of 1787, yet he never altered his low opinion of original intent, if defined as the intent of that Convention. Madison, in fact, profoundly believed in original intent, if it is understood as the meaning to be derived from the people acting through their ratifying conventions. As he put it, he concurred in "resorting to the sense in which the Constitution was accepted and ratified by the nation. In that sense alone it is the legitimate Constitution."[64] How he divined that sense, or whether he did, is not clear, except in one regard, and for him it outweighed all others: The Union must survive. After his death a note headed "Advice to my Country," found in his papers, said "The advice nearest to my heart and deepest in my convictions is, *that the Union of the States be cherished and perpetuated*."[65] He must have had the Union in mind when referring to the importance of the legitimating state ratification conventions. He could not possibly have meant that one should turn to the records of the two or three state conventions with which he was familiar, to find an explanation of some phrase or provision, such as the "executive power," or the contract clause, or the full faith and credit clause, or the exceptions clause of Article III.

One must be familiar with Madison's thought to understand that when he spoke of "the intentions of the parties" to the Constitution[66] or the supremacy of the views of those who gave the Constitution its "stamp of authority,"[67] he meant the people of the United States acting through their state conventions; when he spoke of the intention of "those who made the Constitution" or of its "authors," he meant those who ratified it, not those in Philadelphia who framed it.[68] So too, one must be familiar with his thought to understand that when he spoke of the supremacy of their views, he did not mean that one turned to those views for an explanation of specific or particular clauses of the Constitution. When he said that the debates of the Convention could have "no authoritative character,"[69] he did not mean that the debates lacked significance when one construed the meaning of the Constitution; he intended, rather, that as a matter of fundamental political theory, the consent of the governed, who alone were sovereign, was the force that legitimated the Constitution. As he put the point: "But whatever respect may be thought due to the intention of the Convention, which prepared & proposed the Constitution, as presumptive evidence of the general understanding at the time of the language used, it must be kept in mind that the only authoritative intentions were those of the people of the States, as expressed thro' the Conventions which ratified the Constitution."[70]

Madison did not trouble to spell out what everyone knew: the Convention of 1787 had exceeded its instructions from the Confederation Congress. Congress had adopted the original suggestion of the Annapolis Convention, which authorized a convention to meet in Philadelphia "for the sole and express purpose of revising the Articles of Confederation" to render that document, the existing "federal constitution," adequate to the exigencies of government and the preservation of the Union; the Convention's charge obligated it to recommend those revisions to the Confederation Congress and to the state "legislatures."[71] To be sure, the existing government, without approving or disapproving of the Constitution, in effect endorsed the Convention's scrapping of the Articles of Confederation; Congress's endorsement consisted of its having unanimously agreed to transmit the Constitution to the state legislatures "to be submitted to a convention of Delegates chosen in each state by the people thereof in conformity to the resolves of the Convention made and provided in that case"—ratification by the conventions of nine state conventions, rather than unanimously by the state legislatures.[72] But because the Convention had violated its commission, Madison always insisted that "the legitimate meaning" of the Constitution must be sought "not in the opinions or intentions of the body which planned and proposed the Constitution, but in the sense attached to it by the people in their respective State Conventions, where it received all the authority which it possessed."[73]

If the people of the states, acting through their elected representatives, had authorized the Philadelphia Convention to frame a new constitution, original intent would have possessed a cachet of legitimacy. If the existing Congress, which represented the people of the states, had commissioned a new constitution, original intent would have mattered. A constitutional convention was becoming the only proper means used by a free people to propose their fundamental law, which created government and subjected it to systematic and regularized restraints, obedience to which subordinated that government to the sovereign will that alone could create government. Legislatures, however, had framed most of the first state constitutions. At the Philadelphia Convention, Oliver Ellsworth of Connecticut declared that since the framing of the Articles of Confederation, "a new sett [sic] of ideas seemed to have crept in. . . . Conventions of the people, or with power derived expressly from the people, were not then thought of. The Legislatures were considered as competent."[74] But the idea had quickly spread that the body that formed a constitution possessed the power to alter it, and that a constitution alterable by a legislature offered no security against government's encroachment on the rights of the people. In 1780 Massachusetts ratified a state constitution that was framed by a constitutional convention, the first in the history of the world to be authorized by the people to create a new government subject to their approval. New Hampshire copied the procedure when revising its constitution in 1784, and that procedure, which alone accorded with democratic political theory, became common.[75] Given the failure of the Philadelphia Convention to abide by its instructions, which authorized only a revision of the Articles of Confederation, original intent as Framer intent could have no legitimacy; opponents of ratification could also depict the Constitution as the product of a renegade body.

The Constitution's supporters rejected such contentions by reverting to the proposition that popular ratification legitimated the Constitution, notwithstanding the intent of its Framers. Thus, James Wilson, next to Madison the most influential member of the Convention of 1787 and the foremost advocate of its adoption in his home state of Pennsylvania, answered the charges of Anti-Federalists by explaining:

> [T]he late Convention have done nothing beyond their powers. The fact is, they have exercised no power at all. And in point of validity this Constitution proposed by them for the government of the United States, claims no more than a production of the same nature would claim, flowing from a private pen. It is laid before the citizens of the United States, unfettered by restraint; it is laid before them to be judged by the natural, civil, and political rights of men. By their FIAT, it will become of value and authority; without it, it will never receive the character of authenticity and power.[76]

That was always Madison's position, too. It constituted an orthodoxy of the time.

Madison meant the same thing whether he referred to the sovereign authority as the people of the states[77] or the people of the United States, who could act as a constituent body only through state conventions. Thus, when he minimized the opinions of the members of the Convention in a letter of 1821, his purpose was to emphasize, by comparison, the obligation of everyone to support the Constitution "in its true meaning as understood *by the nation* at the time of its ratification."[78] Similarly, he spoke of the meaning of the Constitution as "ratified by the nation."[79] So too in his "Detached Memoranda," when discussing why the meaning of the

Constitution should be sought in the state ratifying conventions rather than the Philadelphia Convention, he declared that those state conventions were the "authoritative bodies that made it law, or rather through which the Nation made it its own Act. It is the sense of the nation therefore (wch ratified) not the sense of the General Convention" that should be consulted. Thus, he regarded the state conventions as "the true keys to the sense of the Nation," that is, of the people of the Union.[80]

But the sense of the nation was not easily discovered or discoverable, not even as to major allocations of power, let alone as to the meanings of particular clauses. So Madison argued in *The Federalist* #37. He believed that to allocate authority between the federal and state governments and between the three branches of the federal government created problems that perplexed even statesmen, jurists, and philosophers. The Constitution necessarily contained ambiguities. It reminded him of laws that had been framed with the greatest technical skill and passed in fullest deliberation, yet remained "more or less equivocal, until their meaning be . . . ascertained by a series of particular discussions and adjudications." Words stated ideas imperfectly, giving them an "unavoidable inaccuracy" that increased with the complexity and novelty of a task such as strengthening the Union. Madison offered various reasons for "vague and incorrect definition," any one of which resulted in obscurity of meaning. The Convention, he concluded, "must have experienced the full effect of them all."[81]

How then was the meaning of the Constitution to be fathomed? Madison believed that experience fixed meaning in doubtful cases but that meaning was not fixed forever. He would have preferred a static Constitution, and he resisted, even deplored, certain changes in meaning. He probably had in mind the Hamiltonian financial system, the Sedition Act, and overbroad judicial opinions such as those in *McCulloch v. Maryland* and *Cohens v. Virginia* when he said that deviations from the "fair construction of the instrument have always given me a pain," and he wished that innovations based on overbroad constructions would cease; but he knew that change was inevitable.[82] He would have preferred to believe that the Constitution speaks for itself according to the usual and established rules of interpretation, for which intention cannot be substituted. And he advocated that whenever possible the language of the Constitution should be construed according to the people's understanding as evidenced by "contemporaneous expositions."[83]

But he understood that just as words changed in meaning, so did the Constitution. "It could not but happen, and was foreseen at the birth of the Constitution," he declared, "that difficulties and differences of opinion might occasionally rise in expounding terms and phrases necessarily used in such a charter," especially as to the powers in the federal system. Practice would settle some doubtful matters, and the meaning of the Constitution, to the extent that it depended upon judicial interpretations, would emerge from decisions over a period of time.[84] Madison conceded that experience had caused him to change strong opinions on some matters. For example, he once thought that the Constitution prohibited Congress from chartering a bank, but he had been compelled to change his mind, because the sovereign will had expressed itself by acquiescence in a course of exposition that altered the original meaning of the Constitution. Popular understanding simply had overruled his previous views of the matter. When an authoritative, uniform, and sustained course of decision or practice received "public sanction," Madison believed that the Constitution evolved in meaning, and the old must give way to the new.[85] When the words that composed a text altered in their meaning, "it is evident that the shape and attributes of the Government must partake of the change to which the words and phrases of all living languages are constantly subject. . . . [O]ur Constitution is already undergoing interpretations unknown to its founders. . . ."[86] Similarly, he observed: "Some of the terms of the Federal Constitution have already undergone perceptible deviations from their original import."[87] Those were not facts that he applauded; rather, he personally disapproved but understood and acquiesced.

He rejected interpretations unknown to the Constitution's founders or its ratifiers if those interpretations significantly altered the federal system by expanding national powers at the expense of the states or significantly expanded state powers at the expense of the nation. Thus, President Madison vetoed a national roads and canals bill in 1817 because the Constitution did not authorize such an enactment under any of the enumerated powers or under supposed general powers, especially not the "general welfare" clause. Congress's interpretation of that clause, according to Madison, made it more than a power to tax and spend in connection with expressly delegated powers. According to Madison, Congress's interpretation would render "nugatory" the careful enumeration of Congress's powers and "would have the effect of giving to Congress a general power of legislation" to pass laws for the general welfare and common defense in place of the Constitution's restriction of congressional powers. Madison added that the roads bill also violated the Constitution because the possession by Congress of virtually unlimited powers would exclude the judicial authority of the United States from participating in the definition of the boundary between the powers of the nation as opposed to the states. Questions relating to the general welfare, he reasoned, "being questions of policy and expediency, are unsusceptible of judicial cognizance and decisions." He supported judicial interpretation of the Constitution.[88]

The evolutionary cast of his thinking about the changeability of the Constitution derived in part because of his distrust of Congress and his willingness to accept Supreme Court opinions as the "final resort" in matters involving constitutional interpretation.[89] Madison could refer to congressional experience as a factor in constitutional interpretation when that suited him, but he believed that Congress respected popularity and public opinion far more than it did the Constitution.[90] He preferred judicial to legislative interpretation of the Constitution, especially in matters involving the demarcation between national and state powers. In the abstract he claimed to believe that a continued course of legislative action, accepted by the people, took on the color of constitutionality; but despite a continued course of congressional enactment of road bills, Madison believed that only an amendment to the Constitution could authorize such legislation. On the other hand, when Congress passed a measure whose constitutionality he opposed, Madison accepted it as constitutional if it received judicial approval. As a member of Congress, he had opposed an excise tax on horse-drawn carriages and had contended that it was unconstitutional, but when the Court gave is imprimatur to that statute, he changed his mind. As he said, the carriage tax, "which was generally regarded by those who opposed the Bank as a direct tax & therefore unconstitutional . . . did not receive their acquiescence until [sic] these objections were superseded by the highest Judicial as well as other sanctions."[91]

To Spencer Roane, Virginia's chief justice who repudiated the supreme appellate authority of the Supreme Court in cases arising under the Constitution, Madison wrote that Congress more likely than the Supreme Court might encroach on state powers. He thought that Congress could probably control judicial excesses, but scarcely a remedy existed against the danger of legislative usurpations such as the Alien and Sedition Acts or a national roads bill. As a remedy for the abuses of power invited by the necessary and proper clause, Madison favored amendments to the Constitution rather than intrusive legislative interpretations. "I cannot," he wrote, "join in the protest of some against the validity of all precedents, however uniform & multiplied, in expounding the Constitution, yet I am persuaded that Legislative precedents are frequently of a character entitled to little respect, and that those of Congress are sometimes liable to peculiar distrust."[92] The judicial power of the United States, he informed Roane, "must be admitted to be a vital part of the System," especially in cases arising under the Constitution. "A liberal and steady course of practice," he added, "can alone reconcile the several provisions of the Constitution literally at variance with each other . . ."—and he did not mean a course of legislative practice. In an unusual reference to the Constitutional Convention, Madison, who was upset by congressional usurpations of power, reminded James Monroe that in 1787 some Framers had recommended a Council of Revision, which would have vested in the Supreme Court "a qualified negative on Legislative *bills*." His point was that such a judicial control over Congress on constitutional matters would have given greater stability to the exposition of the Constitution, and it "would have precluded the question of a Judiciary annulment of Legislative *Acts*."[93]

Similarly, when Madison censured the Supreme Court's promiscuity in expounding the necessary and proper clause, he did not oppose the results in *McCulloch v. Maryland* or the Court's powers; he opposed its endorsement of nearly unbounded congressional powers. Indeed, he criticized Marshall's *McCulloch* opinion because it undermined judicial review. Madison believed that a definite connection should exist between the enumerated powers and the means employed by Congress to implement them. According to Madison, Marshall had substituted for that definite connection a legislative discretion or expediency for which "no practical limits can be assigned." By so doing, the Court had relinquished "all controul on the Legislative exercise of unconstitutional powers," because when the expediency of means and their constitutionality became indistinguishable, only Congress could be "Judges of the expediency. The Court," he added, "certainly cannot be so." He reasoned that the moment that a question concerned "mere expediency or policy," it went "beyond the reach of Judicial cognizance."[94]

Madison supported the Supreme Court's interpretation of the Constitution against that of the states as well as against that of Congress. He consistently argued that "an appellate supremacy is vested in the Judicial power of the U.S."[95] To Jefferson, who had become a crabbed localist, forever carping against the Court, Madison wrote that the Philadelphia Convention had "intended the Authority vested in the Judicial Department as a final resort in relation to the states" in all cases arising under the Constitution. Otherwise the supremacy of the United States over the states could not be maintained. Knowing that Jefferson had incited and encouraged John Taylor and Spencer Roane in their attacks on the Court's supreme appellate power, Madison emphasized the paramountcy of the Court's interpretations of the Constitution. He insisted that "the prevailing view of the subject" when the Constitution was adopted and the view of the nation that continued to prevail was the view to which he subscribed.[96] The need for a uniform interpretation of the supreme law of the land also persuaded Madison to accept the Court's constitutional decisions, even if he disagreed with them. Short of amending the Constitution to overcome judicial excesses, the alternative consisted of each state's having a different interpretation of the Constitution as well as of the laws and treaties of the United States. He thought that such differences in the meaning of the supreme law of the land "must be destructive of the common Govt. & of the Union itself." As long as the Constitution remained as it was, stability of government required that the Court's decisions "must be acquiesced in."[97] Despite some unpopular decisions and overbroad opinions by Marshall that Madison himself criticized, he believed "that, with but few exceptions, the course of the judiciary has been hitherto sustained by the predominant sense of the nation."[98] The aged Madison summed up his views on the necessity of judicial review to determine the meaning of the Constitution, as follows:

> With respect to the supremacy of the Judicial power on questions occurring in the course of its functions, concerning the boundary of Jurisdiction between the U.S. & individual States, my opinion in favor of it was as the 41 No. of the Federalist shews, of the earliest date; and I have never ceased to think that this supremacy was a vital principle of the Constitution as it is a prominent feature in its text. A supremacy of the Constitution & laws of the Union, without a supremacy in the exposition & execution of them, would be as much a mockery as a scabbard put into the hand of a Soldier without a sword in it. I have never been able to see, that without such a view of the subject the Constitution itself could be the supreme law of the land; or that the uniformity of the Federal Authority throughout the parties to it could be preserved; or that without this uniformity, anarchy & disunion could be prevented.[99]

Although Madison mentioned everything from impeachment to constitutional amendment as ways of checking judicial "usurpations," he also considered "usurpations" by Congress as equally or more serious, to be overcome by amendments, should the nation so desire.[100] But Madison disliked amendments to the Constitution, especially as ways of resolving controversies between the nation and the states "in cases of Judicial cognizance." Resorting to amendments, he wrote to Jefferson, "would be a process too tardy, too troublesome, & too expensive; besides its tendency to lessen a salutary veneration for an instrument so often calling for such [judicial] interpositions."[101] Definition of the meaning of the Constitution through judicial interpretation constituted a major means, for Madison, of keeping the Constitution enduring and vital. He accepted constitutional interpretation by the Supreme Court as a force for stability, and when compared with Jefferson, Roane, and Taylor, he was flexible in matters of constitutional interpretation.

His flexibility, however, seems stunted when compared to Marshall's. Madison certainly condemned the "fallacy," as he put it, "in confounding a question whether precedents could *expound* a Constitution, with a question whether they could *alter* a Constitution."[102] He never sought to present a systematic analysis of constitutional change, nor did he reconcile the view that a consistent and accepted course of precedent could reverse original intent, as in the case of congressional chartering of a bank, with the view that precedents could not alter the Constitution. His thinking on the subject shows unresolved ambiguities, with a pronounced tendency to acquiesce eventually in change, even though he yearned for a "consistent and stable" interpretation of the Constitution based on the "sense" of it by the nation at the time of ratification.[103] When he took that position, which made him seem to be a foe of constitutional evolution, he had convincing reasons for stressing consistency and stability. He usually had in mind the need to maintain a strong Union in which the federal government remained supreme. He also emphasized the virtues of stability when rejecting some novel states' rights position such as the supposed unconstitutionality of protective tariff acts or nullificationist interpretations of the compact theory of the Union. That is, he sounded orthodox, anchoring himself most firmly in 1787–1789, when the change under consideration would have weakened the Union or lessened established national powers. On the other hand, he sometimes resisted change when confronted by novel expansions of national power that, in his opinion, found no justification in the text of the Constitution, in expositions of it at the time of its ratification, or in the opinions of the Supreme Court. Although he finally swallowed the constitutionality of the carriage tax as an indirect tax, because the Supreme Court had so ruled, he discovered nothing to support the constitutionality of a congressional appropriation for roads and canals.[104] Accordingly, he assumed a fixed Constitution when he opposed a congressional act in support of national roads, just as he assumed a fixed Constitution when he opposed state rejection of the final authority of the Supreme Court or when he opposed state acceptance of a disunionizing theory of compact.[105]

Without doubt he prized stability, not change. He invariably extended his loyalty to the proposition that a "stable and known Constitution" could have no foundation if "all the authoritative interpretations" did not settle its meaning.[106] Those authoritative interpretations to which he referred included the intentions of its Framers and ratifiers, contemporary expositions, opinions of members of the First Congress and decades of experience with acts of

Congress, Supreme Court decisions, and presidential opinions. In effect, Madison's understanding of "authoritative interpretations" possessed built-in evolutionary considerations based on experience.

Throughout his career, as Madison effectively applied his theories on how to construe the Constitution, he stressed the conditions existing at the time of its framing and ratification, contemporary exposition, and subsequent usage. That was the context he generally established as a basis for analyzing the text. His masterful essay late in life on the constitutionality of the protective tariff shows how varied were the sources that he considered when confronting a constitutional issue.[107] In that essay he spun complex inferences from two clauses of the Constitution that seemed appropriate. First he asked whether the power of Congress to impose duties required the raising of a revenue, which was not the object of a protective tariff, and second, he asked whether the power of regulating commerce extended to restrictions or prohibitions of foreign commerce and to the governance of manufacturing as a part of interstate commerce. In search of answers, he examined economic tracts and the press to determine the condition of American manufactures in 1787; he also examined the intentions of those who "framed, or, rather, who adopted the Constitution," relying especially on the debates in the Massachusetts ratifying convention and other sources of the time, including *The Federalist*. He particularly emphasized the deliberations of the First Congress, which he lauded for knowing the meaning of the Federal Convention. He additionally pointed to forty years of experience with protective tariffs and the fact that every president from Washington to Jackson concurred with Congress, thus buttressing his argument that a uniform and long-continued practice settled meaning. The one source the aged Madison did not use to augment his elaborate argument was his Notes.

That he did not use his Notes is jarring, because he considered as his most important argument the fact that the Convention had been called to remedy defects in the existing government, which could not protect American manufactures. Evidence from his Notes might have been appropriate. Indeed, he himself in 1787 had advocated protection of domestic manufactures.[108]

Madison neither published nor used his Notes. Although the state ratifying conventions legitimated the Constitution, that fact did not diminish the value of the Philadelphia debates as the basis for understanding original intent. Madison simply did not care about it, and never adequately explained why. Nor did he reveal why he failed to rely on the Notes in developing his own arguments. He did, however, suggest why he failed to publish the Notes during his lifetime: he believed that after all members of the Convention had died, the Notes "will be read with less personal or party feelings. . . ."[109]

On the issue of publication, the most we have from him is a letter of 1821 in which he offered two reasons for his belief that "it might be best to let the work be a posthumous one." First, he wrote, delay of publication would allow the meaning of the Constitution to be settled by practice; he did not explain why its meaning should be settled without the benefit of as full a knowledge of the intentions of its Framers as possible. Second, he wrote, delay of publication prevented a knowledge of "the controversial part of the proceedings of its framers" from being misused; he did not wish the record turned to an "improper account."[110] His remarks of 1821 may have cryptically referred to the slavery issue, but we do not know why he believed that misuse of controversy could not be corrected or would be damaging at all. In the same year he spoke of the "delicacy attending . . . a use of them" (his Notes) at such "an early season."[111] Apparently he believed that the Notes would provide ammunition to the political opposition—in an earlier time, those who supported Hamilton's program or the Sedition Act, later those who opposed Jefferson's Embargo Acts or "Mr. Madison's War," still later those who endorsed Calhoun and state sovereignty.

There is no explaining, however, why Madison lacked confidence in the capacity of the public to support the best policies when exposed to all arguments. Presumably Madison believed, with rare exceptions such as that of the bank, that his own views on constitutional matters corresponded closely with those of the Framers, especially on great issues such as the nature of the Union, the distribution of powers within the federal system, and the supremacy of the Supreme Court over state courts in cases of conflict. If so, that would make even more perplexing his failure to rely on or publish his Notes. His primary explanation is unsatisfactory: What the Framers intended at Philadelphia paled to insignificance compared to the intentions of those who ratified the Constitution. His secondary explanation makes better sense: When public understanding endorses a course of judicial and political practice, the meaning of the Constitution changes.

CHAPTER TWO

President and Congress: Foreign Policy and War Powers

We the People of the...

riginal intent and subsequent understanding contrast starkly on questions dealing with control of foreign policy. Although original intent is indiscernible or ambiguous on many matters of constitutional importance, that intent holds no mysteries as to control of foreign policy. The Framers intended the Senate to be the principal architect of foreign policy. Had original intent prevailed, we would speak of the imperial Senate, not the imperial Presidency. The Framers simply did not intend the President to be an independent and dominating force, let alone the domineering one, in the making of foreign policy. They meant, rather, that the President should be the Senate's agent and, in matters involving war powers, the agent of the Congress, in the sense of being the branch of government empowered to carry out or conduct policies formulated by the legislative branch. The Framers meant, at the most, that the President should be a joint participant in the field of foreign affairs, but not an equal one.

The evidence is abundant and easily obtainable to show that the Framers intended Congress to control the making and conduct of war, the Senate to control foreign policy, and the President to control the ceremonial functions of representing the nation in its foreign relations, personally or through diplomats. That evidence consists mainly of the records of the Philadelphia Constitutional Convention supplemented by such "contemporaneous expositions" as *The Federalist*.[1] Despite that evidence the original intent of the Framers became irrelevant in the sense that it did not shape developments or even constitute a yardstick by which to judge departures from an original norm. The dynamics of government and the force of personality ultimately had a greater influence than formal empowerments; politics as well as law has its claims.

The Framers separated powers among the three branches of the national government but gave each, especially the legislature and the executive, a share of each other's province as a means of keeping all checked and balanced by the others. In *The Federalist* #51 Madison observed that a way to thwart the aggrandization of powers by any branch was to give to each "the necessary constitutional means, and personal motives, to resist encroachments of the others."[2] The Framers devised a system that built "opposite and rival interests" within the government itself. They separated powers but also, quite deliberately and systematically, blended them and, in effect, stepped back to let different branches fight it out for control. "Ambition," Madison wrote, "must be made to counteract ambition. The interests of the man must be connected with the constitutional rights of the place."[3]

Thus, the Constitution creates tensions and invites conflicts among the branches as part of the system of checks and balances. Separation of powers may suggest hermetically sealed departments, but the Constitution certainly does not mark out exact boundaries for each branch nor give to it exclusive control over all dimensions of its responsibilities. Fearing the accumulation of different kinds of power in a single branch, the Framers believed that a way to prevent a dangerous concentration of power was by *not* keeping the branches "totally separate and distinct."[4] They believed that without a "partial mixture" of powers and a partial control of one branch by another, separation could not be preserved. They condemned only "too great a mixture" or "an actual consolidation of the different powers."[5] As Madison explained, "unless these departments be so far connected and blended, as to give each a constitutional control over the others, the degree of separation which the maxim requires as essential to a free government, can never in practice, be duly maintained."[6]

Of the three branches, Madison thought that the legislature was the one most to be feared in a republican system of government. The legislature represented the people, had the only "access to the pockets of the people," and tended to draw "all power into its impetuous vortex."[7] The Framers believed that Congress would predominate over the President to such an extent that the executive, which was naturally weak in a republican government, had to be "fortified." In order to keep the Congress bitted and bridled, the Framers divided it into two houses with different tenures of office, different constituencies to represent and be elected by, and different "principles of action, as little connected with each other as their common functions . . . will admit." Beliefs about the dominance of Congress, the natural weaknesses of the executive, and the need to check powers in order to maintain a separation are all evident in those deliberations of the Constitutional Convention that touched the control of foreign policy and the war powers.[8]

Although the Convention failed to face major questions about that control until late in its deliberations, the matter arose early and unexpectedly in connection with the introduction of the Virginia Plan. One provision of that plan recommended that a national executive should be established "and that besides a general authority to execute the National laws, it ought to enjoy the Executive rights vested in Congress by the Confederation."[9] Under the Articles of Confederation, no executive branch existed and no executive "rights" or powers were identified as such. The government of the United States consisted of a unicameral legislature, which possessed all the powers of the government, including the powers of "determining on peace and war," sending and receiving ambassadors, entering into treaties and alliances, fixing rules governing captures and prizes, granting letters of marque and reprisal in peacetime, appointing officers for the armed forces, and making rules for the governance of those armed forces.[10]

Given such an amplitude of powers touching on war and foreign affairs, the proposal of the Virginia Plan to vest in a national executive the executive powers of Congress, which were not named, seemed frightening and provoked hostile remarks about the executive. Charles Pinckney of South Carolina asserted that he favored a vigorous executive "but was afraid the Executive powers of the existing Congress might extend to peace & war," and if delegated to a new executive would make that office an elective monarchy, which he called the worst of its kind.[11] Clearly Pinckney wanted Congress to retain powers over "war and peace." Roger Sherman of Connecticut differed because he considered the executive "as nothing more than an institution for carrying the will of the Legislature into effect. . . ."[12] James Wilson of Pennsylvania sought to appease Pinckney's fears by pointing out that "the Prerogatives of the British Monarch" did not properly define the executive powers. Those prerogatives, he declared, included some that were of a legislative nature, among them "war & peace."Indeed, the only powers that Wilson considered to be "strictly executive" were enforcing the laws made by the legislature and the choice of officers not to be appointed by the legislature. Wilson agreed with Sherman that the executive was an agent of the legislature, which should continue to control war and peace. John Rutledge of South Carolina also opposed vesting power in the executive over war and peace. Indeed every speaker who addressed the issue shared that opinion, including Madison who declared that the executive powers did not by definition include war and peace.[13]

When the Convention failed to agree on whether the executive should be a single or plural office, Madison observed that they should first fix the extent of the executive powers. The Convention accepted his proposal to vest in the executive the power of carrying out national laws and making such appointments not otherwise vested in Congress, but the delegates could agree on nothing else concerning the executive. No one spoke for an executive with powers stronger than Madison had proposed.

Wilson's reference to the "prerogatives of the British Monarch" alluded to what the delegates most feared about executive authority in the field of foreign affairs. In his discussion "Of the King's Prerogative," Sir William Blackstone described not the king's personal powers but the powers of the English executive branch or "the executive part of government."[14] It included the exclusive power of sending and receiving ambassadors, making treaties and alliances with foreign nations, "the sole prerogative of making war and peace," the power to issue letters of marque and reprisal, the power of being "first in military command," and, generally, representing the nation in all matters concerning "this nation's intercourse with foreign nations."[15] Every one of these powers, regarded in England as executive in nature, became part of the legislative authority under the Articles of Confederation, and even the finished Constitution of 1789 regarded only two of these powers as belonging to the President exclusively: receiving ambassadors and commanding the armed forces. Blackstone described the model that the United States had rejected. Not even Alexander Hamilton embraced that model in his astonishing speech to the Convention on June 18.

Hamilton's long oration, supposedly five to six hours in the delivery, extolled the "excellence" of the British constitution. He proposed an indirectly elected single executive who held office for life, and argued that no good executive "could be established on republican principles."[16] This was the same speech in which Hamilton described the House of Lords as "a most noble institution," and he almost urged the extinction of the states. As he said in an understatement, he "went beyond the ideas of most members," and knowing that the Convention would not support him, he did not propose anything in the form of a motion.[17] His sketch of a constitution is, nevertheless, extremely significant. Despite the fact that the Convention seemed to go on as if he had never spoken, his recommendations on war and treaty powers had a profound influence. Moreover, his recommendations are important for what he did not say.

He did not say that the executive should enjoy the prerogatives of the English crown; and, he did not propose to empower the executive to control foreign policy or decide on war. The supposed apostle of nearly unbridled executive powers urged that the Senate should have "the sole power of declaring war, the power of advising and approving all Treaties, [and] the power of approving or rejecting all appointments" excepting department heads. The executive appointed the department heads; nominated all other officers including ambassadors, subject to Senate approval or rejection; executed laws passed by Congress; directed wars "when authorized or begun"; and made treaties "with the advice and approbation of the Senate."[18] Some of the crucial clauses of the finished Constitution closely approached these recommendations of Hamilton. Clearly, however, he envisioned no exalted role for the executive with respect to war and treaty powers. His executive would have had important powers, none of them held exclusively, excepting the appointment of the heads of the treasury, state, and war departments. With that exception the Senate shared those responsibilities, which were as much legislative as executive, according to Hamilton's scheme.

Far from showing an intent to establish a powerful executive to control foreign affairs or the making of war, the Convention failed to attend to those matters during its first two months. On July 26, it appointed a Committee of Detail to frame a constitution that conformed to the decisions made up to that point, and the Convention adjourned until August 6. In the interim the Committee of Detail acted as if it were a miniature constitutional convention.

The committee included some of the wisest heads. Its chairman was John Rutledge of South Carolina, a future member of the Supreme Court. James Wilson of Pennsylvania and Oliver Ellsworth of Connecticut were also future Justices. Edmund Randolph of Virginia and Nathaniel Gorham of Massachusetts rounded out the committee. They had little to work with concerning the powers of the executive. After two months, the Convention had decided only that there should be a national executive, still unnamed, to consist of a single person chosen for six years "with Power to carry into Execution the national Laws," to appoint officers "not otherwise provided for," and to veto legislative enactments. He was to be paid a fixed compensation and was subject to removal from office by impeachment and conviction.[19] The Committee of Detail also had the benefit of a plan submitted by Charles Pinckney, which authorized the executive to "carry into execution the national laws."[20] No one had yet used the phrase "executive power"; later exponents of an imperial Presidency would ascribe to that phrase an inherent authority comparable to the royal prerogative in matters of foreign policy and the making of war. The Constitutional Convention halfway through its deliberations probably was unanimous in the opinion that the executive power extended to the enforcement of existing law. That is, the executive power was fundamentally ministerial in nature and nearly devoid of discretion and leadership. The Committee of Detail did little to alter that understanding.

The committee made the first attempt, excepting Hamilton's,

to differentiate legislative and executive powers. It had to. Its working drafts show a listing of powers under each of those categories. Significantly, the committee never considered assigning to the executive any role in the making of war or of foreign policy. As it considered various drafts of a constitution, the committee finally concluded that the executive, "whose stile shall be 'The President of the United States of America'," should have the particular powers recommended by the New Jersey Plan, a nationalistic small-states proposal that had been rejected in favor of the Virginia Plan. The Virginia Plan had recommended that the executive should have "authority to execute the laws" plus the undefined executive powers exercised by Congress under the Articles of Confederation.[21] The New Jersey Plan had empowered the executive "to execute the federal acts," appoint lesser officers, "direct all military operations," and call out the power of the Union not against foreign enemies but against states that recalcitrantly failed to obey federal laws.[22]

In its final report to the Convention, the Committee of Detail urged that the President should be authorized to address the Congress on the state of the union and recommend measures for its consideration. He received no "executive power" in express terms but was commanded to execute faithfully the laws of the United States—which is what the Convention understood "executive power" to mean. He could appoint inferior officers, those whose appointment had not been provided for elsewhere in the document, and he had four other explicit powers: to grant pardons, be commander-in-chief of the armed forces, receive ambassadors, and correspond with the state governors.[23] Except for the authority to "receive" ambassadors, a ceremonial function on the part of the President representing the nation, he had no authority to determine on war or to make treaties or conduct foreign policy or even to appoint diplomats. The legislature received sole power "To make war; to raise armies; To Build and equip fleets" and even "To call forth the aid of the militia, in order to execute the laws of the Union, enforce treaties, suppress insurrections, and repel invasions. . . ." And the Senate was delegated sole power "to make treaties, and to appoint Ambassadors, and Judges of the supreme Court."[24] No imperial Presidency was in making as of August 6, when the Committee of Detail reported to the Convention.

On August 16, the Convention reached the recommendation by the Committee of Detail that Congress shall have the power "to make war." Charles Pinckney objected to the involvement of the House of Representatives, because it would proceed too slowly, would meet too infrequently, and be too large. He thought that the Senate alone should have the power to make war. Pierce Butler, Pinckney's colleague from South Carolina, disagreed because some of the same objections pertained to the Senate. He preferred to vest the power in the President. No one else in the Convention spoke for that proposal, then or later. Madison and Elbridge Gerry of Massachusetts jointly moved to substitute the word "declare" for the word "make," thus proposing that Congress shall have the power "to declare war." They explained that the purpose of the motion was to allow the President "to repel sudden attacks." They believed that repelling attack was an executive power, because it required no legislative deliberation, and that the President could move swiftly as commander of the nation's armed forces. Several delegates expressed unease at the thought of allowing the executive in a republic to exercise a prerogative power, whether declaring or making war. The Convention then defeated the motion by a vote of 4–5. The record on this matter is unclear. Apparently Rufus King of Massachusetts asked for a reconsideration; he stated that to allow the Congress "to make war" involved it in an executive function, namely "to conduct" a war decided upon by the legislature. Another vote was taken on the motion to substitute "declare" for "make," and it passed, 8–1.[25]

The decision of the Convention to empower Congress to "declare" rather than to "make" war indicated no shift in the Convention's attitude toward the executive. After the convention had adjourned, Roger Sherman of Connecticut continued to speak of the power of Congress to "make" war, as if no difference existed between "make" and "declare."[26] The change in wording took nothing from the Congress and added nothing to the President. The Committee of Detail had already recommended that he be the commander-in-chief. Repelling attack and "conducting" a war, in the literal sense of "leading" or "guiding," were executive functions.[27] The commander-in-chief clause, which the Convention adopted ten days later without discussion, imported no grandiose breadth of powers. The Framers made the President the commander-in-chief because he could act swiftly, maintain responsible civil authority over the military, and decide "on priorities and command" in the military conduct of a war first decided upon by Congress.[28]

On August 23, the Convention considered for the first time the recommendation of the Committee of Detail that the Senate "shall have power to make treaties." Madison reported himself as having stated that because "the Senate represented the States alone" and for other "obvious" but unnamed reasons, "it was proper that the President should be an agent in Treaties."[29] The statement is as fascinating as it is brief. The word "agent" meant a "deputy," one who represents and acts for another. By recommending that the President should be an agent for the Senate in the making of treaties, Madison recognized that treaty making involved executive functions exercised in subordination to the Senate. He may have been analogizing from the experience of Congress under the Articles of Confederation. Although it had possessed sole treaty-making powers it had created an executive officer, the Secretary of Foreign Affairs, to assist in carrying out Senate policies during treaty negotiations.[30]

After Madison's brief but striking remark about involving the President in making treaties, Gouverneur Morris of Pennsylvania declared that he had doubts about involving the Senate at all; he would be satisfied, though, with an amendment that tacked onto the motion: "but no Treaty shall be binding on the U.S. which is not ratified by a law."[31] Ratification by law meant the enactment of a statute. Morris, that is, indirectly added the House of Representatives to the treaty-making process by requiring that the House ratify the Senate's action. As different as the Madison and Morris statements were, each revealed considerable unease with empowering the Senate alone to make treaties.

Yet the two men had previously supported the Senate's exclusive role in treaty making. As delegates from large states, they had strongly opposed "the Great Compromise" of July 16, which gave the states equal representation in the Senate.[32] That compromise saved the Convention from breaking up, but the large-state delegates took their defeat hard; they had wanted proportional representation in both houses, giving control to their states. Equal representation meant that they had lost control of the Senate, and they feared that it would become a battle ground in which states' rights interests, sectional interests, and economic interests would prevail over the national interests, as they understood the national interests. The remarks by Madison and Morris on August 23 showed their dissatisfaction with the idea that the Senate as constituted should decide on the terms of commercial treaties.

Wilson of Pennsylvania, supporting the motion offered by his colleague, Morris, sought to attract votes by warning that an unchecked Senate might sell out the interests of some state or section. Without the House of Representatives being involved in treaty making, he stated, "the Senate alone can make a Treaty, requiring all the Rice of S. Carolina to be sent to some one particular port."[33] The suggestion conjured up images of the Senate compacting with some foreign power to abandon western interests in navigation on the Mississippi or the fishery interests of New England. John Dickinson conceded that equal state representation in the Senate, which he supported, gave to the "little States . . . an *equal* share in making Treaties," and he endorsed Morris's motion to amend. The discussion almost got derailed, however, by delegates who wondered whether one house should be able to ratify the acts of the other. In the end, as Randolph observed, no one had spoken for the motion as it came from the Committee of Detail, yet Morris's motion lost badly. Madison wondered aloud whether both houses should be jointly responsible for commercial treaties while "the President & Senate" should jointly make treaties of peace. No one commented on the suggestion. The Convention, unable to reach a decision, then voted to send the entire matter back to the Committee of the Whole for further consideration.[34]

After more than three months of deliberations, the Convention had failed to settle numerous important issues, among them the power to control the making of treaties. Accordingly, as August ended the Convention agreed to the creation of a "grand committee," as one delegate put it.[35] The committee was charged with the responsibility of making recommendations on "such parts of the Constitution as have been postponed" and on parts of reports not acted on. It has been known, therefore, as the Committee on Postponed Parts, consisting of eleven members, one from each state—hence "grand"—and loaded with heavyweights, among them Madison, Gouverneur Morris, King, Sherman, and Dickinson. The chairman was David Brearly, the chief justice of New Jersey.[36] His

committee worked speedily and made many major recommendations, including the electoral college for the choice of the President.
Its recommendation on foreign affairs and war soon proved to be
acceptable to the Convention:

> The President by and with the advice and Consent of the Senate,
> shall have power to make treaties; and he shall nominate and by and
> with the advice and consent of the Senate shall appoint ambassadors,
> and other public Ministers, Judges of the Supreme Court, and all
> other Officers of the U—S—, whose appointments are not otherwise
> herein provided for. But no Treaty shall be made without the consent
> of two thirds of the members present.[37]

As early as June 18, Alexander Hamilton had recommended:

> The supreme Executive . . . to have the direction of war when au-
> thorized or begun; to have with the advice and approbation of the
> Senate the power of making all treaties; to have the sole power of
> appointment of the heads or chief officers of the departments of
> Finance, War and Foreign Affairs; to have the nomination of all other
> officers (Ambassadors to foreign Nations included). . . . The Senate
> to have the sole power of declaring war, the power of advising and
> approving all Treaties, the power of approving or rejecting all ap-
> pointments [except department heads].

Brearly's committee obviously found wisdom in Hamilton's recommendations to involve the President in foreign affairs and major
appointments.

On September 5, the day after the committee made its recommendation on the treaty power and power of appointments, it
recommended that Congress should have the power to issue letters
of marque and reprisal, and the Convention voted unanimously for
the proposal.[38] Such letters died in international law during the
nineteenth century, but the fact that the Convention located that
power in Congress after vesting diplomatic powers in the President
reveals the Convention's conviction that the President should have
no role in the determination of war. At the time, letters of marque
and reprisal authorized private citizens to make war against foreign
nationals to avenge injuries not redressed by their governments.
As Blackstone said, the power to issue such letters "plainly derived"
from "that other of making war; this being indeed only an incomplete state of hostilities, and generally ending in a formal denun-

ciation of war."[39] Thus, the involvement of the President in diplomacy in no way detracted from the legislative nature of the power to make or begin war, whether or not it was declared or complete.

Making the President a party to treaty making constituted a striking change from all that had preceded yet did not in any way indicate a new understanding that the President should become the architect of foreign policy. Madison on August 23 had suggested that "the President should be an agent in Treaties," and Brearly's committee in effect accepted his suggestion as a way of checking the authority of the Senate.[40] Nevertheless, the inclusion of the President in the treaty power thrust him in a position of leadership. He could act independently but could not accomplish anything; neither could the Senate. It could advise and consent; but only the President could make a treaty, even if he required concurrence. "Make," however, might have signified merely that no treaty had been executed until signed by the President. And "advice and consent" was a formula intended to signify that the President was dependent on the Senate. Indeed, "advice and consent" had two sets of meaning of long standing, both of which conveyed a limiting force to the powers of the President. The first was legislative, the second councilmanic in nature.

As to the first, English history shows that from the late seventeenth century, no bill could become a law unless it received the endorsement of both the Parliament and the crown. The endorsement consisted of a prefatory formula stating that a bill was enacted or made by the king "by and with the advice and consent" of the two houses of Parliament. To say, "Be it enacted by the King . . ." indicated that without the king no bill could be made a law. After 1689, however, Parliament became supreme and the king's involvement ceremonial. "By and with the consent" of Parliament became, that is, a way of designating the legislative process. The use of that formula in the recommendation by Brearly's committee, which the Convention adopted, connoted the legislative nature of treaty making in the minds of the Framers. Their phrasing no longer conveys that. Today, when we read that the President shall have power to make treaties, by and with the consent of two-thirds of the Senate, we see a text that makes the treaty power essentially executive in character, especially as to leadership and initiative. The Framers, however, saw the treaty-making power as essentially legislative in character, an original meaning that we retain through Article VI of the Constitution, the supremacy clause, which makes the Constitution, laws in pursuance thereof, and *treaties* the supreme *law* of the land. A treaty once made or signed by the President becomes law, or as John Jay stated, once made, treaties "are to have the force of laws."[41] Hamilton expressed the point most directly in *The Federalist* #75 when he said that although the power of making treaties was a shared one, between President and Senate, the treaty power "will be found to partake more of the legislative than of the executive character. . . ."[42]

The second or councilmanic meaning of "advice and consent" applies to the President's appointment powers. The clause used in connection with appointments is not the same as the clause used in connection with treaties. The President makes treaties by and with the advice and consent of the Senate, but he "shall *nominate,* and by and with the Advice and Consent of the Senate, shall appoint. . . ." As to appointments, then, the Constitution assigns an initiative to the President, not so as to treaties. In either case, however, the Constitution obligates the Senate to give advice and consent. Advice, with respect to appointments, loses some of its legislative character; the Senate does not share a deliberative and policymaking power with the President in the case of appointments as much as it exercises the advisory powers of a privy or executive council. In New York, the state of Alexander Hamilton who initially recommended an advisory capacity for the Senate in treaty matters, the state constitution empowered the governor to make appointments "with the advice and consent" of the executive council.[43] In Massachusetts, whose constitution provided the best model for the office of President, the governor exercised his extensive appointment powers "by and with the advice and consent of the council."[44]

Although the legislative character of treaty making was more pronounced in the case of treaties than in that of appointments, advice and consent in both instances signified a two-stage process. "Advice" required the Senate's involvement in foreign policy decisions and negotiations as to treaties, and its recommendation of a slate or a job description as to nominations. In neither case was the Senate meant to be a pro forma instrumentality for endorsing decisions reached by the President alone. "Consent" indicated ratification. "Advice and consent" indicated a deliberative involvement followed, in cases of agreement, by ratification. In effect the Framers made the treaty power and the appointment power concurrent powers, shared by the two branches.

The Convention's debate on the Brearly committee's treaty proposal suggests no major switch in previous positions. After that proposal had been introduced, Wilson worried about the Senate's excessive powers, which he said included, still, the power "to make Treaties which are to be the laws of the land. . . ." Gouverneur Morris, his colleague who was a member of the Brearly committee, disagreed. He referred to the "agency" of the President, to suggest a check on the Senate; and, denying that the committee had augmented the Senate's powers, he said, quite extraordinarily, "If they are to make Treaties as the plan now stands, the power was the same as in the printed plan," that of the Committee of Detail, allowing no role for the President.[45] The colloquy between Wilson and Morris did not indicate an understanding that the President's entrance in the treaty-making power portended a substantive change in position from the Committee of Detail to the Brearly Committee. During the next two days, on September 7 and 8, the Convention considered the treaty-making power. The debate began with a motion by Wilson to authorize the House of Representatives as well as the Senate to give advice and consent to the President in treaty making. Wilson's motion lost overwhelmingly, and the committee speedily accepted the role of the President.[46] It then unanimously adopted the clause on appointments, before returning to the final provision of the treaty-making clause.

That clause required a two-thirds assent of the Senate. Wilson favored a simple majority, and King, a member of the Brearly committee, observed that a majority might be sufficient because the President's involvement constituted enough of "a check" on the Senate. Madison, also a member of the Brearly committee, complicated matters by making two motions, which showed no enthusiasm on his part for expanding the President's role. The first motion restricted the two-thirds majority requirement to commercial treaties; it passed—for the time being. The second motion authorized a two-thirds majority of the Senate to make treaties of peace "without the concurrence of the President." Madison feared that the President's stake in a war might tempt him to impede a treaty of peace.[47] Gouverneur Morris replied that the President's

involvement in the treaty power was "harmless"—hardly a revelation of a fear that the President would dominate the exercise of
that power. He believed that the President's participation was
valuable because the President "was the general Guardian of the
National Interests."[48] That unique remark urged no expansion of
presidential powers, only the retention of his role in making all
treaties.

Elbridge Gerry was the one who showed that Madison was
mistaken. "In treaties of peace," he reminded, "the dearest interests will be at stake, as the fisheries, territories, &c." Accordingly,
treaties of peace, like commercial treaties, required a greater rather
than a lesser proportion of votes, in order to allow a geographic
section to protect its interests. Madison's second motion lost 8–
3.[49] Hugh Williamson of North Carolina, who was also a member
of the Brearly committee, in effect asked for a reconsideration of
matter decided by Madison's first motion. Williamson disapproved
of a mere majority of the Senate deciding on treaties of peace that
affected territorial rights.[50]

The Convention agreed to reconsider the entire issue of a two-
thirds majority. Morris, who supported Madison, did not help their
cause by asserting that "the two great objects of the Union," fisheries and navigation of the Mississippi, might be injured as a result
of the greater difficulty of making peace by a two-thirds vote, rather
than a simple majority. Williamson's reply suggests, once again,
that the Brearly committee's addition of the President to the treaty-
making power did not seriously alter the situation, for he remarked
that "Treaties are to be made in the branch of the people," that is,
the Senate would make treaties. Gerry improved on the point by
observing that a majority of the Senate, where the states had an
equal voice, might represent only one-fifth of the people"; accordingly, a two-thirds majority was all the more needed. When Gerry
added that two-thirds was the number in the Articles of Confederation, Nathaniel Gorham, his Massachusetts colleague, remarked
in effect that under the Constitution, an additional protection existed: "The President's consent will also be necessary in the new
Govt."[51] It was the last remark about the President and the treaty
power. Gorham, like others, seemed to have believed that although
the Senate gave its advice and consent to treaties made by the
President, the President was the one who gave consent. Nothing

that was said indicated that anyone thought that the President would have an important independent role in treaty making. The Convention, at last, adopted the two-thirds requirement as the Brearly committee had recommended it.

On the same day the Convention appointed a five-member Committee of Style to put the Constitution in final shape. William S. Johnson of Connecticut, the newly appointed president of King's College (Columbia), served as chairman of a powerful committee, which included Madison, Hamilton, Gouverneur Morris, and King. Morris and his colleague Wilson, who was not a member of the committee, did most of the work, composing a preamble, restructuring the paragraphs, and giving a literary finish to the language.[52] The committee placed in Article II, which deals with the executive power, the paragraph on the power of the President to make treaties and appointments with the advice and consent of the Senate.[53]

On September 15, two days before the Convention finally adjourned, it took up Article II and gave its consideration only to the pardoning power and the power of appointing minor executive officers. No one commented on the fact that the treaty power had been shifted from the article on the Senate to the one on the President. No one thought that the new placement of the treaty power suggested an enhancement of presidential power.[54] The members of the committee, except its chairman, had been among the most active delegates in the evolution of the clauses dealing with the relationship of President and Congress in the fields of foreign policy and war powers. Consequently, the placement of the two clauses bearing the formula "by and with the advice and consent of the Senate" had no substantive significance. In 1787 Madison, Hamilton, King, and Morris were not advocates of an independent Presidency, let alone an imperial or prerogative Presidency. They believed that the Presidency constituted an independent branch, but they did not mean that the chief executive was in business by himself or that he could take significant action in foreign affairs without having the concurrence of the Senate; they expected the Senate to dominate the making of foreign policy as much as Congress controlled the making of war.

What supporters of the Constitution meant in this matter received definition with considerable accuracy by the authors of *The Federalist*. John Jay, one of the authors, had not been one of the

Framers, but no one was closer than he to their thinking. He had been the principal author of New York's first constitution and its first chief justice, and he became the first Chief Justice of the United States. In 1788, when he wrote *The Federalist* #64, he was the nation's most experienced diplomat. He had served in the Continental Congress as its president and as a member of its committee of correspondence with foreign powers; he had been minister to Spain and a member of the American commission that negotiated the 1783 Treaty of Peace with Britain. When he wrote *The Federalist* #64, he was Secretary of Foreign Affairs for Congress. More than anyone, Jay would have known firsthand the fecklessness of Congress and of American foreign policy under the Articles of Confederation; as the foremost executive officer of the Confederation in the field of diplomacy, he would have been best able to evaluate the Constitution as the basis for a viable government, and he would have been most likely to interpret executive powers broadly in matters involving foreign policy.

Jay approved enthusiastically of the joint responsibility vested by the Constitution in the President and Senate. He thought that members of the lower house of Congress held office too briefly and that the House itself was too large to serve effectively in treaty making. The senators and President, however, were "best qualified" to wield that power and most likely to do so for the public good. He liked the continuity of the Senate and the six-year term of office. Senators would have "sufficient time to become perfectly acquainted with our national concerns, and to *form* and *introduce* a system for the management of them." In short, he expected the Senate to make foreign policy. But he thought that the President would be best suited to conduct that policy. The negotiation of treaties, he explained, sometimes required secrecy and dispatch. The Convention had done well, he wrote, in structuring the treaty power so that the President in negotiating them must act by the advice and consent of the Senate, yet he "will be able to manage the business of intelligence in such manner as prudence may suggest." As to the management of that business, Jay observed that the secrecy and dispatch needed for negotiations "are those preparatory and auxiliary measures which are not otherwise important in a national view, than as they tend to facilitate the attainment of the objects of the negociation." In other words, the Senate shaped the policy or the "objects of negotiation," and the President carried out the policy by managing the negotiation. As Jay summarized the matter, "the constitution provides that our negociations for treaties shall have every advantage which can be derived from talents, information, integrity, and deliberate investigations on the one hand [the Senate], and from secrecy and dispatch on the other [the President]."[55]

In *The Federalist* #69, Hamilton analyzed the powers of the President in comparison to those of the royal prerogative. Anti-Federalists had trumpeted the charge, without explaining the basis for it, that the President was no better than an elected monarch, who might abuse his powers so as to imperil liberty. The President's authority as commander-in-chief seemed to them to be most intimidating.[56] Hamilton systematically compared the prerogative of the British executive office with the President's limited powers, to refute the allegation. In so doing, he agreed that the authority of the President as commander-in-chief "would be nominally the same with that of the King of Great-Britain, but in substance much inferior to it." The President, he explained, merely directed the armed forces, while the King's power "extends to the *declaring* of war and to the *raising* and *regulating* of fleets and armies; all of which by the Constitution under consideration would appertain to the Legislature." The President exercised the treaty power provided that he had the advice and consent of the Senate, while the king of Great Britain was the sole representative of his nation "in foreign transactions" and of his own accord could make all treaties and alliances. The crown appointed ambassadors, while the President shared that power with the Senate. Hamilton contrasted the crown's "sole power" with the Constitution's "concurrent power."[57]

In *The Federalist* #75, where Hamilton discussed the treaty power, he emphasized the peculiar "intermixture of powers" that resulted from "the union of the executive with the senate." Refuting the assertion of some that the treaty power belonged to the executive, Hamilton declared, "For if we attend carefully to its operation, it will be found to partake *more of the legislative* than of the executive character, though it does not seem strictly to fall within the definition of either of them." That seems to indicate that Hamilton believed that the Senate would propose foreign policy; the President would execute it. In the management of foreign negotiations, he wrote, the President was "the most fit agent [deputy] in those transactions," while the importance of foreign policy and the "operation of treaties as laws, plead strongly for the participation of the whole or a part of the legislative body in the office of *making* them." But to have entrusted the Senate alone to make treaties, he added, "would have been to relinquish the benefits of the constitutional agency of the president in the conduct of foreign negotiations." He ended by referring to a "joint possession" of the treaty power, but the direction of his essay revealed his expectation that the Senate would make foreign policy, despite the language and placement of the treaty-making clause, and that the President would be the Senate's agent in carrying out that policy in the course of negotiations with foreign nations.[58]

The proponents of ratification widely shared the opinions of Hamilton and Jay. Robert R. Livingston, a signer of the Declaration of Independence, informed the New York ratifying convention that under the Constitution, Congress would have the same power of making war as it had under the Confederation; like others he did not understand the power to "declare" war as any different from the power to determine on or make it.[59] In Pennsylvania, Wilson answered Anti-Federalist charges that a despotic Senate would be corrupt and unchecked. The President, he argued, checked the Senate. That body could make no treaties or approve of any "unless the President of the United States lay it before them." The Senate could not even vote on an appointment unless the President made a nomination. "So that if the powers of each branch are perverted," he argued, "it must be with the approbation of some of the other branches of the government. Thus checked on each side, they can do no one act of themselves." He added that with respect to the Senate's "power in forming treaties, they can make none, they are only auxilliaries to the President." Objections against the Senate's powers, he added, came with bad grace from those who preferred the Articles of Confederation to the Constitution; under the Articles the legislature possessed all the powers of the United States.[60]

In North Carolina ratificationists had to refute charges that the President, not the Senate, would be all-powerful, so they magnified legislative powers. James Iredell, soon to become a Justice of the Supreme Court, corrected Anti-Federalist misstatements by observing that although the President was commander-in-chief, he was subject to the check of Congress, which possessed the powers to decide on a war and raise armies.[61] The approach of William R. Davie, a signer of the Constitution, differed markedly. He preferred, he said, that the President should possess exclusively the power of making treaties, because he would be elected by the people and would "have their general interest at heart." The Constitution, he regretted, did not provide for the President's exclusive power because the "little states" would not accept a union in which they did not possess "an absolute equality in making treaties." Thus, the Senate possessed "the power of making, or rather ratifying, treaties."[62]

In South Carolina, Pierce Butler, who had been a member of the Brearly committee more accurately portrayed the President's treaty-making power as a check on the Senate's, so that a "balance" prevailed.[63] But General C. C. Pinckney, also a Framer, asserted that "a few members" of the Convention had desired the President to possess the treaty power exclusively. That assertion, despite Pinckney's statement, cannot be substantiated except as to Pierce Butler. "At last it was agreed," he reported, "to give the President a power of proposing treaties, as he was the ostensible head of the Union, and to vest the Senate (where each State had an equal voice) with the power of agreeing or disagreeing to the terms proposed." Thus the President and Senate were "joined" as one body "in whom we could with safety vest the diplomatic authority of the Union."[64]

The remarks of Davie and Pinckney, even of Wilson, suggest that some Framers preferred a major role for the President and a minor one for the Senate in exercising "the diplomatic authority" of the nation. In view of what they said during the ratification controversy, to depict that authority as mainly legislative in character and the President as the mere implementer of Senate policy seems to be an exaggeration. But the records of the Convention show that only one delegate at the Convention, Butler of South Carolina, proposed that the President should possess the treaty power exclusively; the records show, too, that no delegate preferred a more important role for the President in foreign affairs than for the Senate. James Francis Mercer of Maryland should not be quoted out of context or incompletely. He arrived in Philadelphia after the Committee of Detail had reported its plan and objected that the Constitution was "objectionable in many points"; he wanted it understood that he did not like it and "would produce a better one." He remarked that "the Senate ought not to have the power of treaties. This power belonged to the Executive Department." But, in the next sentence he added that no treaty should be final or become the law of the land "till ratified by legislative authority."[65] Mercer irascibly left Philadelphia after having attended the Convention only during the eleven days from August 6 to August 17; he later opposed ratification.

Anti-Federalists like Mercer could be found on any side of an issue. The President, they dolefully warned, would be a king or a minion of the Senate. He should have a council; the procedure for electing him was bad; his term was too long or he should not be eligible for reelection; his pardoning power was dangerous; a plural executive was preferable; the commander-in-chief might use the army for tyrannical ends. On and on they ranted. But Anti-Federalist objections against the President were more manufactured than real, surely with respect to the power to control foreign policy or involve the nation in war. Congress, after all, possessed the power to declare war, and Anti-Federalists made nothing of the fact that "declare" was less than "make" or "determine on." Major Anti-Federalist productions, including the *Letters of a Federal Farmer* and the "Brutus" essays, had nothing critical to say about the Constitution's provisions on diplomacy, wars, and treaties. Some Anti-Federalist tracts that revealed profound distrust, such as the charge by "Centinel" that the President would become a king, had no meaty discussion to support the charge.

Anti-Federalists also complained that the President was too weak. He might nominate, but only the Senate could approve, forcing him to nominate to satisfy their choice; he could make a treaty, but only in conformance with Senate wishes, or they would reject it.[66] More commonly, Anti-Federalists proposed that the House of Representatives should be a party to the process of advice and consent, or they expressed a fear that treaties would abrogate state constitutions and state laws. But they did not disagree that the Senate had a crucial role, probably a decisive one, in the making of foreign policy, and that Congress possessed war powers. Anti-Federalists cared little about war and treaty powers, compared with their concern that the national government would swallow up

the states or that Congress had nearly unlimited, undefined powers. The lack of a Bill of Rights also figured in a major way in their
protests. State sovereignty and personal liberty were at risk, in
their opinion, and they doubted that so large a republic could
survive. They did not, however, expect the new government to
operate very differently from the way the Framers predicted, as
to the making of foreign policy and the decision for war or peace.

One scholar, Charles Lofgren, who has studied the power to
decide on war, examined all the recommendations for amendments
to the Constitution proposed by the various state ratifying conventions. He found that only one of seventy-seven dealt with the
power of Congress to declare war; New York wanted a two-thirds
vote.[67] If one also looks at those recommended amendments on
the questions of treaties, about as little evidence of dissatisfaction
turns up. Virginia wanted a two-thirds majority of the whole number of the Senate, not just of those in attendance, to ratify commercial treaties, and a three-fourths majority of all members of
both Houses for making treaties involving territorial or navigational
rights or fisheries.[68]

Scholars who have studied Anti-Federalist thought pay scant
attention to foreign policy or war powers, because the Anti-Federalists had so little of substance or disagreement to say about the
subjects. They and the Federalists shared a consensus on the meaning of the text in that regard, though not necessarily on how it
should have been framed.[69] If the Anti-Federalists believed that
the Framers intended the President to dominate foreign policy,
that intention would have become a major focus of Anti-Federalist
attack.

James Wilson's exaggerated statement, that the Senate would
be "only auxiliaries" to the President's treaty power,[70] was intended
to appease Anti-Federalist fears of the Senate. At the Convention
Wilson had favored Senate domination, checked by the House not
by the President. In the long run his exaggeration at the Pennsylvania ratifying convention proved to be a reliable prediction
about the locus of the power to make foreign policy. But the consensus of 1787–1789 operated effectively for a remarkably long
time. It disintegrated briefly in 1793 when Hamilton completely
altered his opinion by championing the power of the President to
declare neutrality without consulting, let alone advising with and

obtaining the consent of, the Senate. In effect Hamilton was the first to make a sustained argument that the President had plenary authority in the field of foreign affairs and by virtue of an inherent executive power could do whatever he wished so long as the Constitution did not clearly limit him.[71] Madison demolished that argument by showing that the Constitution had rejected the British theory of executive prerogative and by quoting *The Federalist* against Hamilton.[72] Hamilton's position was destined for acceptance by Presidents in the twentieth century but it was not accepted in its time or at any time before Lincoln's aggressive exercise of powers.

Words and actions of the founding generation that have been drawn upon to support the imperial Presidency in foreign affairs and his use of armed force in the absence of a declaration of war have been taken out of context and twisted in meaning. In 1790, for example, Jefferson as secretary of state asserted, "The transaction of business with foreign nations is Executive altogether. . . . Exceptions are to be construed strictly."[73] Jefferson was merely discussing the power to send and receive ambassadors, not the power to make foreign policy. Similarly, John Marshall's 1800 declaration, "The President is sole organ of the nation in its external relations, and its sole representative with foreign nations,"[74] meant nothing more than that only the President communicates with foreign nations; he is the organ of communication. In 1936 the Supreme Court misused the Jefferson and Marshall statements to support a historically fallacious opinion that the President possesses inherent powers to make foreign policy.[75] Hamilton himself in 1798 agreed that the quasi-war with France did not trigger inherent presidential powers to authorize reprisals for attacks, but he could repel attacks without congressional approval— a statement in keeping with the original intent at Philadephia.

In *Talbot v. Seeman* (1801), one of Chief Justice Marshall's earliest decisions, he declared, "The whole powers of war being by the Constitution of the United States vested in Congress, the acts of that body alone can be resorted to as our guide in the enquiry."[76] President Jefferson, in the absence of congressional authorization, refused to take aggressive action against the Barbary pirates who had proclaimed their hostility to the United States, but he dispatched the navy as a show of force. Justice Joseph Story's *Com-*

mentaries on the Constitution (1833) also sustained the position taken by Jay and Hamilton in *The Federalist*.[77]

Nowadays, leading supporters of a constitutional jurisprudence of original intent are advocates of inherent presidential powers in the field of foreign relations, a stance that sheds light on either their ignorance or their hypocrisy. The obsolescence of original intent does not necessarily invalidate the wisdom of what the Framers meant.[78]

CHAPTER THREE

Judicial Review
and Judicial Activism

*T*he law, constitutional law included, is cluttered with un-
truths that convention charitably describes as legal fictions. One
of these fictions, particularly popular with conservatives (not that
liberals do not subscribe to legal fictions of their own liking) is that
conservative jurists have eschewed judicial activism. The most activist judge in our constitutional history, Chief Justice John Marshall, cloaked himself in the fiction that "Courts are the mere
instruments of the law, and can will nothing."[1] Conservatives, who
tend to romanticize Supreme Court history and to portray as sa-
tanical the modern Supreme Court, would like us to believe that
the subjectivity of the Court used to amount to little, because the
Justices, out of respect for the traditions of the bench, suppressed
their own policy preferences and impersonally decided as the law
told them to, without exercising private discretion. They did not
legislate; they merely discovered and applied the appropriate law
to the case at hand. They did not compel government to do what
it opposed doing; they simply kept government within limits prescribed by the Constitution. They respected and enforced original
intent whenever it was clearly discernible. They did not hold acts
of government unconstitutional except in clear, even unavoidable,
cases; their failure to exercise the supreme judicial power in such

cases would have meant a judicial failure to honor the Constitution above an act in conflict with it.

Such views have often received expression from members of the Senate Judiciary Committee when examining the qualifications of someone nominated by a President for appointment to the Supreme Court. A ritual usually characterizes such hearings. Almost invariably some Senator Claghorn will inquire of the nominee whether he or she, if confirmed, means to use judicial office for legislating new public policies for the nation, or, like a good Justice, means to show loyalty to the revered tradition of merely finding and announcing the existing law of the matter. The nominee, as if the script had been rehearsed, soberly forswears all intentions to make law or legislate in any way, and Senator Claghorn, whose name has also been Eastland, Thurmond, McClellan, Ervin, Hatch, and Hruska, approvingly endorses the candidate's judicial temperament. The customary colloquy usually includes a round of congratulations as everyone disdainfully repudiates judicial activism. The 1987 hearings on the nomination of Robert H. Bork were a model of congressional scrutiny, comparatively free of the usual malarkey.

A lot of malarkey receives currency nowadays about the differences between Supreme Court decisions of the Court's classic early years and its decisions in recent constitutional history. In the good old days, we are told, the Court used to be merely proscriptive; but it has become prescriptive.[2] That formulation, even if true, by no means proves that the Court is more activist than it used to be. But it is a misleading formulation, because it ignores the prescriptive dimension present in what were supposedly merely proscriptive decisions. When, for example, the Court ruled that certain state acts conflicted with the contract clause, the Court required the states to do what they strenuously opposed: honor their legislatures' fraudulent land grants and grants of tax exemption for corporations, despite subsequent sovereign decisions to rectify mistaken public policies by revoking such grants.[3] Similarly the Court made Congress countenance a compulsory racism that it regarded as repugnant to public policy as well as contrary to the Thirteenth and Fourteenth Amendments.[4] When the Court held the income tax unconstitutional, it forced Congress to allow the great fortunes to go untaxed and to raise the nation's revenue from consumers until a constitutional amendment superseded the judicial decision.[5] And, the Court forced the United States to suffer the existence of manufacturing monopolies and various other "reasonable" restraints upon interstate commerce by great corporations, notwithstanding the language of the Sherman Act, which explicitly condemned *all* conspiracies and combinations in restraint.[6] Similarly, the Court required the states and the United States to allow the production and shipment of oil produced in excess of quotas that were calculated to conserve a national resource and increase the price of its sale.[7] Judicial legislation, or judicial policymaking, is creaky from age. As Benjamin Hoadly, the bishop of Bangor, observed in 1717, "whoever hath an absolute authority to interpret any written or spoken laws, it is he who is truly the lawgiver, to all intents and purposes, and not the person who first write or spoke them."[8] President Theodore Roosevelt boldly asserted that the "chief lawmakers in our country may be, and often are, the judges, because they are the final seat of authority. Every time they interpret contract, property, vested rights, due process of law, liberty, they necessarily enact into law parts of a system of social philosophy; and as such interpretation is fundamental they give direction to all lawmaking."[9] In fact, judicial activism has characterized the Supreme Court from its early history; indeed, the Court's earliest constitutional decisions of note reflect a rampaging judicial activism.

Chisholm v. Georgia (1793), the first constitutional case decided by the Court, is exhibit number one. The case involved the question whether a state could be sued in the Supreme Court by a citizen of another state without its consent. Nothing said at the Philadelphia Convention answers that question, but the text of the Constitution seems to extend the judicial power of the United States to "controversies . . . between a state and citizens of another state." But that provision of Article III, understood in the context of the ratification controversy, seems not to mean what it says. The reason is that after opponents of the Constitution condemned the clause because it derogated from state sovereignty, advocates of ratification explained that it meant only cases in which a state had given consent or had initiated the suit as plaintiff.

In New York, "Brutus," who may have been Judge Robert Yates, a Framer who walked out of the Convention in protest against its subversion of state sovereignty, wrote the best and most detailed Anti-Federalist analysis of the federal judicial power. In the course of his discussion he lambasted the clause in question as pernicious and destructive not only of the sovereignty of the states but of their treasuries. They would, he argued, have to redeem depreciated paper money at face value, when sued in federal court by out-of-state citizens. By this means, he concluded, "judgments and executions may be obtained against the state for the whole amount of the state debt."[10] James Winthrop's "Agrippa" letters in Massachusetts and the letters of "Federal Farmer" in Virginia, the most popular of all Anti-Federalist tracts, attributed to Richard Henry Lee, made arguments similar to that of "Brutus."[11]

Alexander Hamilton responded to Brutus in *The Federalist* when he declared: "It is inherent in the nature of sovereignty, not to be amenable to the suit of an individual *without his consent*. This is the general sense and the general practice of mankind; and the exemption, as one of the attributes of sovereignty, is now enjoyed by the government of every state in the union."[12]

In the Virginia ratifying convention a major debate, pitting George Mason and Patrick Henry against James Madison, John Marshall, and Edmund Pendleton, focused on the clause. Mason, expressing concern that the clause opened Virginia to all sorts of claims, asked, "Is this state to be brought before the bar of [federal] justice to be arraigned like a culprit, or private offender?"[13] Madison, rejecting Mason's reading of the clause, declared: "It is not in the power of individuals to call any state into court. The only operation it can have, is that, if a state should wish to bring a suit against a citizen, it must be brought before the federal court."[14] Henry ridiculed the argument "that the state may be plaintiff only" as a perversion of the text's language.[15] Pendleton, unlike Madison, sought to defend making the state suable in federal court at least in certain uncommon cases where justice could not be had in state courts[16]; Mason discredited Pendleton's reasoning, spurring Marshall to represent the fundamental Federalist position on the clause. "I hope," Marshall said, "that no gentleman will think that a state will be called at the bar of the federal court. . . . It is not rational to suppose that the sovereign power should be dragged before a court. The intent is, to enable states to recover claims of individuals in other states. I contend this construction is warranted by the words."[17] In short, Marshall, like Madison, and Hamilton, construed the text as embodying the Convention's intent to include only cases in which the state brought suit as plaintiff.

On the Supreme Court only Justice James Iredell agreed. Chief Justice John Jay, who had been the third author of *The Federalist*, disagreed with its two major authors and with the construction of the words given by Marshall. To Jay the words were free of all ambiguity and left no room for making exceptions of cases not brought by a state as plaintiff. Justice John Blair, one of the three Virginians who had signed the Constitution in Philadelphia and who supported it at the ratifying convention in Richmond, ruled that by ratifying the Constitution a state had accepted Article III and "has in that respect given up her right of sovereignty." Blair believed that to refuse jurisdiction of a case in which a state is a defendant would be to renounce an authority vested by the Constitution.[18] Justice William Cushing of Massachusetts, who had been a ratificationist in his state's convention, construed the text as Blair had. Justice James Wilson, another signer of the Constitution who had advocated ratification in his state's convention, delivered an astonishing opinion on a question that he found present in the case: do the people of the United States form a nation? He censured "haughty notions" of state sovereignty, asserting that the people of the United States had formed the Union and had vested the Supreme Court with jurisdiction over the state of Georgia. By the strictest language, he concluded, the clause extended to the case before the Court.[19] In his state's convention, Wilson had passingly praised the clause, not there attacked, because it provided a tribunal in which the parties might stand on equal footing.[20] Wilson believed that as to the purposes of the Union, Georgia "is not a sovereign state."

A Massachusetts newspaper, commenting on *Chisholm*, reminded readers that when opponents of ratification had criticized the clause because it had made a state suable as a party in actions for debt, "this was denied peremptorily by the Federalists as an absurdity in terms," but now they said that the Court's reasoning "has made that to be right which was, at first, doubtful or improper."[21] Congressman Abraham Baldwin, a Framer, later observed that the suability of the states was not "talked of or believed, till it was declared by the judge to be the meaning of the Constitution."[22] Governor John Hancock of Massachusetts called a special session of the state legislature, which recommended an amendment to the Constitution consonant with the original intent of the Constitutional Convention. Other states denounced the decision; Georgia's House went the furthest by urging death by hanging, without benefit of clergy, for anyone convicted of the felony of executing the Supreme Court's order.[23]

The panic in the states, which expected suits threatening to empty their treasuries, was matched by congressional opposition to the decision. The day after the Court rendered it, an amendment was offered in the House of Representatives that became the Eleventh Amendment; it provided that the judicial power should not be extended to any suit brought against a state by citizens of another state or of a foreign country. The phrasing of the Eleventh Amendment proved to be flexible enough for the Court to practice its inferences and handy rules of construction in such a way as to circumvent the amendment's plain language.[24] But nearly a century after *Chisholm* the Court agreed that it had decided that case wrongly,[25] and the fact remains that the Court's first constitutional decision conflicted with statements of Framers in 1788 and provoked an amendment to the Constitution to make it conform to a general understanding throughout the nation.

Three years after *Chisholm v. Georgia*, in 1796, the Supreme Court decided *Hylton v. United States*, a case that reveals the slight worth of original intent analysis yet is of considerable importance in the history of judicial review and of monumental significance in the history of the capability of the United States to raise a revenue effectively.[26] In *Hylton* the Court passed on the constitutionality of an act of Congress for the first time. The case obligated the Court to expound the meaning of the direct taxes clause of Article One, section nine. The clause provides that no capitation "or other direct tax" be imposed except in proportion to the population of the states; all duties, imposts, and excises, by contrast, must be levied uniformly, that is, at the same rate. In *Hylton*, the so-called Carriage Tax Case, Congress had imposed a uniform tax of $16 on all carriages (horse-drawn coaches), despite protests from the Democrats, including Madison in the House, that the tax should have been apportioned among the states according to the census.[27] Apparently considerable confusion existed as to the difference between direct and indirect taxes. What seemed clear was that the two kinds of taxes were allocated differently. When Congress levied a direct tax it fixed the total amount of money it intended to raise, so that in a state with 10 percent of the nation's population, the parties taxed (carriage-owners) would have paid 10 percent of the total. Thus, if a tax on carriages were a direct tax, the amount raised in two states of equal population would be the same, but if one state had twice as many carriages as the other, the tax rate in that state would be half as great. The contention in this case was that the carriage tax was unconstitutional because it was a direct tax uniformly levied.

The case seems to have been contrived to obtain the Court's ruling on the constitutionality of Congress's tax program. To meet the requirement that federal jurisdiction attached only if the amount in litigation came to $2,000, Hylton deposed that he owned 125 carriages for his private use, each of which was subject to a $16 tax; if he lost the case, however, his debt would be discharged by paying just $16. The United States paid his counsel, Alexander Hamilton, who defended the tax program he had sponsored as secretary of the treasury. Notwithstanding the farcical aspects of the case, its significance cannot be overestimated: If a tax on carriages was indirect and therefore could be uniform, Congress would have the utmost flexibility in determining its tax policies. As Justice Samuel Chase said, "the great object of the constitution was, to give congress a power to lay taxes, adequate to the exigencies of government."[28]

Three members of the Court that decided *Hylton* had been at the Philadelphia Convention in 1787: Chief Justice Oliver Ellsworth and Justices James Wilson and William Paterson. Ellsworth, having just been appointed, took no part in the case, although his brethren might have consulted him on his recollections of what the Framers meant by the direct taxes clause. Wilson, having decided the case on circuit duty, chose not to render a full opinion; he simply signified his belief that the carriage tax was constitutional. Thus the only opinion by a Framer came from Paterson's pen. Justices William Cushing, Chase, and James Iredell had been members of the ratifying conventions of their states. What might Paterson and his brethren have concluded if they had had access to the records of the Philadelphia Convention and of the state ratifying conventions? What could they have remembered? Very little, even though the term "direct taxes" appears twice in the Constitution.

Article I, section 2, provides that representation and direct taxes shall be apportioned among the states on the basis of their populations, counting only three-fifths of their slaves, and the ninth section of the same article refers to "capitation and other direct taxes." What did the Convention understand by direct taxes? When the Convention considered the recommendation that only three-fifths of the slaves should be counted in determining the amount to be raised in each state by direct taxes, Rufus King of Massachusetts, according to Madison's Notes, "asked what was the precise meaning of *direct* taxation?" And, wrote Madison, "No one answered."[29] As late as September 14 the only direct tax clause that the Convention had adopted referred to representation and the three-fifths rule. The related clause, recommended by the Committee of Detail, provided that no capitation tax should be laid except in proportion to the census. But three days before the Convention completed its work and adjourned, George Read of Delaware moved to insert the ambiguous words "or other direct tax" in that clause describing how capitation taxes should be levied. The motion was seconded and adopted without discussion or dissent by any delegate.[30]

Does the silence of the record indicate the existence of a consensus on the meaning of direct taxes? That is not likely because Read himself stated that the object of his motion was to make sure that capitation taxes be regarded as direct taxes: "No capitation or other direct taxes. . . ."[31] Given the need felt by Read to prevent anyone from considering a capitation tax as an indirect tax and the fact that King asked the central question to which no one replied, the assumption that an understanding of the meaning of direct taxes existed appears to be questionable, but not meritless. In the first place, Hamilton's plan of union, which otherwise had no influence whatever except to make nationalists like Madison and Wilson appear to be moderates, contained a provision that taxes on lands, houses, and other real estate, as well as capitation taxes, should be proportioned among the states on the basis of population. Although that provision did not use the term "direct tax," it did show Hamilton's understanding that taxes on land should be levied in the same way as capitation taxes.[32] The day after the Convention adjourned, the three North Carolina delegates who had signed the Constitution transmitted it to the governor of their state with a letter that explained the direct tax clauses. They observed that direct taxes meant land and poll taxes, so that Congress would count five blacks as three, to the benefit of slaveowners; the same three-fifths rule benefited landowners in the South who held large and comparatively unsettled tracts.[33]

The debates in the states during the ratification controversy and the enormous pamphlet and newspaper literature added nothing to the understanding of direct taxes. In *The Federalist*, both Hamilton and Madison used the term as if their readers would understand it.[34] At two points, however, Hamilton specified what he meant. In *The Federalist* #21, he described imposts, excises, and, generally, all duties on articles of consumption as indirect taxes, while he termed as direct taxes those "which principally relate to lands and buildings."[35] In *The Federalist* #36, Hamilton again distinguished taxes on articles of consumption from taxes on real property—on houses and lands.[36] The voluminous sources add nothing to that distinction.

In *Hylton*, Justice Chase revealed confusion when he said that he thought that some taxes could simultaneously be both direct and indirect, but he endorsed the principle that direct taxes included taxes on land and on people. He joined the judgment of the Court that the carriage tax was constitutional. He did not have to decide, he said, whether the Court had the power to void an act of Congress, but if it had that power he would exercise it only in "a very clear case."[37] Iredell construed the text of the Constitution by a practical rule of construction: The only taxes that could be apportioned and therefore were direct taxes were taxes on population and on land.[38] Paterson delivered the most important opinion. Without referring to his personal recollections as a Framer, he nevertheless spoke with authority when he remarked that the Framers of the Constitution contemplated only taxes on land and capitation taxes as direct taxes. He explained that the direct tax clauses were devices to provide fairness to southern landholders and slaveholders, who, in the absence of the three-fifths rule, might have to pay steep taxes on the whole number of their slaves, and who might have to pay comparatively more than landowners elsewhere if land were subject to taxation on the basis of its acreage rather than its value. Paterson also relied on the authority of Adam Smith's *Wealth of Nations* for his understanding of what the term "direct tax" meant. But, like Chase and Iredell, he also employed rules of construing the text as well as authorities like Smith and the intent of the Framers.[39]

Hylton proved, therefore, to be a case in which original intent played a small part, although that intent can scarcely be discerned from the proceedings of the Convention or from the state ratifying conventions. By legitimating an act of Congress the Court in effect suggested that it had the power to hold such acts unconstitutional. Having faced the question whether Congress had authority to levy a uniform tax on carriages, the Court would have had no alternative but to void the act if it had found that the tax on carriages was a direct tax. That, however, is an inference; the Court did not claim the power of judicial review. On the whole, *Hylton* shows a remarkably restrained Court, with little signs of judicial activism.

The British War Debts Case, decided at the same term of the Court in 1796, displayed a monster of judicial activism in the rhetoric and reasoning in the Court's main opinion, by Justice Samuel Chase, who also gave a constructive interpretation of Article VI, the supremacy clause.[40] *Ware* established the fundamental principle of constitutional law that a state act may not violate a national treaty. An act of Virginia during the Revolution sequestered sterling debts owed by Virginians to British subjects and provided that such debts be discharged on payment (in depreciated currency) to the state. The Treaty of Paris of 1783 demanded that creditors should meet with no lawful impediments to the recovery of full value in sterling, and Article VI of the Constitution made treaties of the United States the supreme law of the land. Ware, a British subject, brought an action in a federal court seeking payment from Hylton, a Virginian. The prewar debts of Virginians to British creditors exceeded $2,000,000, then an enormous sum. Justice James Iredell, on circuit, ruled that the treaty did not revive any debt that had been discharged, and on the writ of error from the circuit court, the future Chief Justice, John Marshall, counsel for Hylton, argued that a United States treaty could not annul a statute passed by a sovereign state. He also denied the authority of the Supreme Court to exercise judicial review by questioning the validity of a state law; that authority, he contended, must be "expressly given by the constitution." He further contended that the state could extinguish the property of creditors because "the law of property in origin and operation, is the offspring of the social state; not the incident of a state of nature."[41]

Iredell persisted in his opinion expressed below, but Justice Chase, supported by the concurring opinions of the remainder of the Justices, declared that the supremacy clause (Article VI), operating retroactively, nullified the state act, thereby reviving the sterling debt. Chase cloaked his opinion in extremist nationalist doctrine that twisted history: "There can be no limitations on the power of the people of the United States. By their authority the state constitutions were made . . . and they had the power to change or abolish the state constitutions, or to make them yield to the general government, and to treaties made by their authority."[42] A treaty, he ruled, could not be supreme law if any state act could stand in its way; the treaty and the Constitution, which was the "creator" of the states, "prostrated" state laws that conflicted with them. Such views coming from anyone reinvented the past; that Chase subscribed to those views added a dose of irony, because he had been opposed to ratification of the Constitution on the ground, he said in 1788, that "The National Government will in its operation and effects annihilate the State Governments."[43] The Union, as Lincoln contended, might be older than the states, because the Declaration of Independence, a document of the Continental Congress signed by Chase, called the states into existence; but Justice Chase's hyperbole was about as true as his earlier prediction that the national government would annihilate the states. Chase's rhetoric and the pro-creditor decision of the Court intensified Jeffersonian hostility to partisanship on the federal courts. The decision's imperishable principle of the supremacy of national treaties survived its origins in part because the Jay Treaty went into operation within a week, and it provided that the United States should assume the payment of the controversial debts.

A few years later, the Justices of the Supreme Court, presiding over federal prosecutions as circuit court judges, enforced the Sedition Act of 1798 against Jeffersonian writers. Chase, who became the most vindictive of the judges, had opposed ratification of the Constitution only a decade earlier, in part because it did not protect liberty of the press. "The Constitution gives no power to Congress

express or implied to abridge or take away the liberty of the press,"
he argued, but without a bill of rights to restrain Congress, "They
will have the power," and exercise it at their discretion.[44] Advocates
of ratification agreed that Congress had no power to act on the
press, and after the Bill of Rights became part of the Constitution,
the prohibition of the First Amendment ("Congress shall have no
power to abridge the freedom of the press") seemed to prevent the
exercise of a discretion that Chase had said he feared. But in the
prosecutions under the Sedition Act, Chase, Paterson, and their
brethren arrived at the extraordinary conclusion that somehow the
First Amendment, which absolutely denied power, vested authority to punish critics of the government. The Sedition Act prosecutions, which James Morton Smith has described in gripping
detail,[45] constitute another specimen of judicial activism gone amok
in the early history of the Supreme Court.

In 1798, the year that Congress passed the Sedition Act, the
Supreme Court expounded the meaning of an ex post facto law.
Original intent analysis seems especially suitable for an understanding of the two ex post facto clauses of the Constitution, one limiting
the states and the other Congress. Although the term "ex post
facto" resonates a technical meaning derived mainly from English
antecedents, the understanding of the generation that framed and
ratified the Constitution is the source of that meaning. In *Calder
v. Bull* (1798), a case of first impression decided by the Supreme
Court in 1798 and still the leading case, history dominated three
of the opinions rendered seriatim by the four Justices who participated.[46] One of those three was by William Paterson, who had
been among the most influential members of the Constitutional
Convention; another was by James Iredell, who had been "the
outstanding supporter" and "ablest defender" of the Constitution
in North Carolina[47]; and the third was by Samuel Chase, a signer
of the Declaration of Independence who had opposed Maryland's
ratification of the Constitution in that state's ratifying convention.
The three agreed that ex post facto laws comprehended criminal
cases only and did not apply to civil cases or cases that affect
property rights.[48] All three men seem to have been mistaken.

The issue in *Calder* was whether the ex post facto clause
extended to a state legislative act that had voided a probate court
decree and granted a new hearing, at which the party that had

won the decree lost the property she claimed as hers. More broadly the question was whether legislation that operated retroactively against one's civil interests encroached on the ex post facto clause. Paterson, the Framer, made no reference to his recollection of the debates of the Constitutional Convention. Chase, who gave the fullest opinion, covered all the arguments made by Paterson except one based on a rule of construction. Paterson's construction of the term "ex post facto" depended in part on the significance he found in the placement of the ex post facto clause in Article I, section 10, which imposed prohibitions on the states. Those prohibitions included the coining of money, the emitting of bills of credit, and the making of anything but gold or silver a legal tender in payment of debts; other prohibitions, grouped together after a semicolon, barred state bills of attainder, ex post facto laws, laws impairing the obligation of contracts, and the granting of any title of nobility. Contrary to Paterson "the arrangement of the distinct members of this section" does not "necessarily" prove that "the framers of the Constitution . . . understood and used the words . . . as referring to crimes, pains, and penalties. . . ."[49] The placement of the clause against titles of nobility shows that Paterson was wrong. Moreover, the ex post facto clause appears in a list of prohibitions only one of which, bills of attainder, is criminal in character. Indeed, the clause sits between the bill of attainder clause and the contract clause, suggesting that ex post facto laws can involve crimes such as bills of attainder *and* civil matters such as contracts.

Chase as well as Paterson sought to find the meaning of the ex post facto clause in a rule of construction, namely, that the interpretation of one clause in a text should not make another clause superfluous. He insisted that to construe the clause as a guarantor of rights vested by existing law would make "unnecessary" the Fifth Amendment's eminent domain or taking clause, which provided for just compensation when private property is taken for a public use. Similarly, he insisted that the contract clause and the clause insuring specie payment for debts would also be "unnecessary" if the ex post facto clause applied in civil cases.[50] He was certainly right about the contract clause; members of the Constitutional Convention had opposed its inclusion in the Constitution precisely because the ex post facto clause made it unnecessary; they believed that the ex post facto clause applied to civil matters. Chase was

wrong about the specie payment clause because it prevented prospective as well as retrospective legislation, and he was wrong about
the takings clause because it provided for an explicit guarantee in
the exceptional case when government, without enacting retroactive legislation, must take private property for a public use. Moreover, property rights can be adversely affected in various ways that
do not touch contract rights, a fact that allows for the possibility
that the ex post facto clause had a civil meaning in cases involving
property rights others than those vested by contract.

The authority of Sir William Blackstone's *Commentaries on
the Laws of England* helped determine the views of the Court,
and the authority of *The Federalist* exceeded even that of Blackstone, according to Chase. But in *The Federalist* #84, which Chase
failed to quote, Hamilton had merely called ex post facto laws
"formidable instruments of tyranny," because they created enemies
"after the commission of the fact, or, in other words, the subjecting
of men to punishment for things which, when they were done,
were breaches of no law. . . ." At no point did "Publius" say or
suggest that ex post facto laws did not concern civil matters or
concerned criminal matters only. As a matter of fact, neither did
Blackstone, the oracle of the common law whom Paterson quoted
out of context as follows:

> There is a still more unreasonable method than this, which is called
> making of laws *ex post facto*, when after an action, indifferent in
> itself, is committed, the legislators, then, for the first time, declares
> [sic] it to have been a crime, and inflicts a punishment upon the
> person who has committed it. Here it is impossible, that the party
> could foresee that an action, innocent when it was done, should be
> afterwards converted to guilt by a subsequent law; he had, therefore,
> no cause to abstain from it; and all punishment for not abstaining,
> must of consequence be cruel and unjust.[51]

Blackstone said no more about the subject. He did not include a
section on ex post facto laws, as one might expect. He did not cite
common law decisions on ex post facto laws, nor did he rely on
the English history of those laws. He surely did not conclude that
ex post facto laws could not extend to civil matters. Moreover, he
referred to ex post facto laws in the context of a discussion of "laws
in general" and in connection with the point, which we associate
with the rule of law, that government is obliged to regulate our

conduct by enforcing laws already enacted and thus knowable; that we are not accountable except under existing law is a point equally applicable to civil matters. Nothing in Blackstone or in the common law of England limited the meaning of ex post facto to criminal matters only. In short, Blackstone's *Commentaries* merely showed that he referred to ex post facto laws in the context of discussing harsh laws generally; nowhere did he discourse on ex post facto laws systematically or as a subject for its own sake.[52]

Justices Paterson and Chase also relied on the authority of four state constitutions for the definition of ex post facto laws. Two of those four, Delaware and Massachusetts, did not use the term "ex post facto," although they clearly censured as oppressive any laws that punished actions not criminal when made, and they did not censure retrospective laws involving civil matters.[53] Similarly, Maryland and North Carolina, in identical language, after condemning retrospective laws that made criminal any acts that were innocent when committed, concluded: "wherefore no *ex post facto* law ought to be made." Pennsylvania in a revised constitution of 1790 and South Carolina in its revision of the same year added an ex post facto clause, apparently copied from the United States Constitution, which used the term without in any way referring to criminal matters.[54]

No member of the Supreme Court referred to New Hampshire's constitutional provision of 1784, which explicitly referred to civil matters: "Retrospective laws are highly injurious, oppressive and unjust. No such laws, therefore, should be made, either for the decision of civil causes, or the punishment of offences."[55] The New Hampshire provision belies the Court's insistence that the only meaning of ex post facto laws was one involving penal matters.

That Iredell should have excluded civil matters from the scope of ex post facto laws was inconsistent with earlier views that he, like other ratificationists in his state, had expressed on the subject at the North Carolina ratifying convention of 1788. At that convention Timothy Bloodworth had argued against ratification in part because the Constitution banned state laws allowing payment in paper money for debts; he feared that the ban might be applied "*ex post facto*" with the result that the Constitution could destroy the state's currency laws.[56] Bloodworth had spoken immediately after Stephen Cabarrus, a ratificationist, had argued that the clause prohibiting the states from emitting bills of credit would not affect the state's existing currency, because it had no retrospective operation; moreover, Cabarrus added, the Constitution could not injure the state's currency laws because it explicitly prohibited ex post facto legislation by Congress.[57] Iredell, answering Bloodworth, agreed with Cabarrus by revealing his understanding that ex post facto laws extended to civil matters. The bills-of-credit clause, declared Iredell, operated prospectively only and therefore could have no effect on paper money "now actually in circulation. There is an express clause which protects it. It provides that there shall be no *ex post facto* law."[58] Archibald Maclaine, "the Hotspur" of the ratificationists, also believed that the retrospective operation of any law or constitution would be "contrary to the universal principles of jurisprudence" even in civil matters.[59]

So, too, Justice Paterson, like Justice Iredell, had applied the ex post facto concept to civil matters prior to the *Calder* case. In 1795, when charging a federal jury in the district of Pennsylvania, Paterson, as a circuit court judge, did not for a moment doubt that the Constitution's prohibition of state ex post facto laws extended to statutes disturbing land titles, though on the facts of the case he instructed the jury that the state had not violated the clause.[60]

We do not know why Iredell and Paterson changed their minds about ex post facto laws. *Calder* had the effect of clearing the way for a congressional bankruptcy act that had a retroactive operation. Despite *Calder*, congressional opponents of the bankruptcy act, which was purely civil in nature, described it as a prohibited ex post facto law, and when the opposition mustered a majority to repeal the act in 1803, only three years after its passage, those who sought vainly to save it insisted that it was not an ex post facto law. No one in the debates of 1799–1800 or 1803 stated that ex post facto laws did not apply to civil matters; and no one cited *Calder*.[61]

Calder's having narrowed the reach of the ex post facto clause increased the difficulty of Chief Justice John Marshall in explaining the decision in *Fletcher v. Peck*.[62] The statute by which Georgia had repealed the Yazoo land grants might have been voided as an ex post facto law except for *Calder*. Notwithstanding the fact that the case involved no crime, Marshall buttressed his shaky opinion, based primarily on a novel interpretation of the contract clause, by giving the impression that the repeal act was also void as an ex post facto law. But the doctrine of *Calder* withstood subsequent doubts.[63] In 1854, in the first case involving the ex post facto clause following publication of Madison's Notes, a unanimous Supreme Court merely declared without any proof: "The debates in the federal convention upon the Constitution show that the terms 'ex post facto laws' were understood in a restricted sense, relating to criminal cases only, and that the description of Blackstone of such laws was referred to for their meaning."[64] In this 1854 case the Court based its judgment on a misunderstanding of original intent, without more.

The evidence from Madison's Notes on the framing of the ex post facto clause does not bear out the Court. The subject first arose at the Convention on a motion to prohibit Congress from enacting a bill of attainder or an ex post facto law.[65] Gouverneur Morris of Pennsylvania thought that a precaution was essential as to bills of attainder but not as to ex post facto laws. Madison's Notes do not include Morris's explanation, if he made any. Oliver Ellsworth of Connecticut declared that everyone understood ex post facto laws to be void, but he did not explain what anyone understood such laws to mean. James Wilson of Pennsylvania also opposed the inclusion of a ban on ex post facto laws but said nothing to indicate his understanding of them. The first speaker to support the ban was Daniel Carroll of Maryland, who declared that experience should be a guide; the states, he warned, had passed ex post facto laws. Wilson then observed that people did not agree on what ex post facto laws meant. Nevertheless, Hugh Williamson of North Carolina favored the ban "because the Judges can take hold of it." Nothing else said on the subject clarified the Convention's understanding. It voted 7–3 for the proposal.[66]

The subject arose again a week later when Rufus King of Massachusetts urged a contract clause to limit state power to violate private contracts. George Mason of Virginia objected that King's motion would tie the hands of the states in certain emergencies, prompting Wilson to reply: "The answer to these objections is that retrospective interferences only are to be prohibited."[67] In view of the fact that King's motion sought to protect contract rights, Wilson's remark showed an understanding that ex post facto laws extended to noncriminal matters. Madison understood Wilson to mean just that, for Madison inquired, "Is that not already done by the prohibition of ex post facto laws, which will oblige the Judges to declare such interferences null & void."[68] John Rutledge of South Carolina then urged as a substitute for King's motion: "nor [shall any state] pass any bill of attainder or ex post facto laws."[69] Madison transcribed that motion as a prohibition on state "retrospective laws," thus showing his belief that ex post facto laws comprehended civil matters. The Convention voted 7–3 for the motion.

On the next day, however, John Dickinson of Delaware observed that on examining Blackstone's *Commentaries*, he "found that the terms 'ex post facto' related to criminal cases only; that they would not consequently restrain the States from retrospective laws in civil cases, and that some further provision for this purpose would be requisite."[70] The Convention continued as if he had not spoken. However, on September 14, when the Convention was winding up its work, Mason moved to strike the ex post facto clause from the limitations on acts of Congress. He "thought it not sufficiently clear that the prohibition meant by this phrase was limited to cases of a criminal nature," and he favored the power of any legislature to enact ex post facto laws in civil cases.[71] Adding to the confusion, Gerry then seconded Mason's motion, because, unlike Mason, he wanted the prohibition to extend to civil cases. The Convention defeated the motion. We do not know whether a general understanding existed that ex post facto laws were limited to criminal cases as Dickinson misunderstood Blackstone to mean, or whether the Convention believed that the clause should extend to civil cases. So ended the debate on the subject.

Clearly no evidence from Madison's Notes shows that Dickinson spoke for the Convention when he offered his understanding of Blackstone. Indeed, we are left with only a murky understanding of the Convention's intent. It surely meant the prohibition of ex post facto laws to include criminal matters; we do not confidently know whether it meant the prohibition to extend to civil matters, though some members shared that belief with Mason and Madison.

For example, Roger Sherman and Oliver Ellsworth of Connecticut, the latter a future Chief Justice, when transmitting a copy of the Constitution to the governor of their state, wrote: "The restraint on the legislatures of the several states respecting emitting bills of credit, making anything but money a legal tender in payment of debts, or impairing the obligation of contracts by ex post facto laws, was thought necessary as a security of commerce. . . ."[72] The phrasing shows that they regarded any retroactive law as an ex post facto law. That was scarcely an unusual view; indeed, it may have been the predominant view. In the preceding year, 1786, Pierce Butler and Charles Cotesworth Pinckney, both of whom would represent South Carolina in the Constitutional Convention, used the term "ex post facto" in state debates to apply to laws having nothing to do with crimes. Pinckney condemned as an ex post facto law a legislative resolution that prevented the state auditor from reimbursing old military expenses, and Butler censured as an ex post facto law a legislative effort to alter the value of paper money.[73]

Newspapers in Pennsylvania, New Jersey, Maryland, Virginia, and Massachusetts published articles criticizing as ex post facto laws a variety of retroactive legislation affecting debts, contract, legal tenders, bankruptcy, and land titles.[74] "Centinel," a leading Anti-Federalist of Pennsylvania, alleged that certain rich men had embezzled millions in public funds and that the ex post facto clause protected them from having to make restitution. "Centinel," who equated ex post facto laws with any retrospective laws, believed that their enactment sometimes was necessary to advance the public's interest.[75] In Massachusetts a writer in Boston's leading newspaper declared that the ex post facto clauses of the proposed Constitution justified its ratification. The state constitution, he observed, has such a clause that related to criminal prosecutions but it was "silent as to any ex post facto laws which relate to property, and civil prosecutions; though it must be confessed that such laws are as much against the nature of government as those relating to crime. The federal constitution has accordingly guarded against such laws, and clearly, because some states, of which our own is one, have not observed such a restriction."[76]

During the ratification controversy, remarks on the power to pass ex post facto laws were few in number, but rarely did anyone state that such laws did not apply to civil laws or extended only to criminal matters. New York's ratifying convention, apparently without debate, was the only one that commented on the Constitution's ex post facto clause. New York resolved that the prohibition extended only to laws concerning crimes; the mover of the resolution revealed his purpose by having initially proposed that the ex post facto clause should not be construed "to prevent calling public defaulters to account. . . ."[77]

New York wanted defaulters, who owed money to the state, to be civilly liable and therefore sought to restrict the meaning of ex post facto laws to criminal matters in order to retain the lawful authority to enact civil legislation imposing liability for damages, without the power of the state being diminished by an overbroad interpretation of the constitutional ban. In Virginia's ratifying convention George Mason, Patrick Henry, and other anti-ratificationists argued that the ex post facto clauses of the Constitution meant that states and debtors would be forced to pay paper money debts in gold and silver, and that the old depreciated continental dollars would also have to be redeemed at face value, "shilling for shilling," thus enriching the few against the many. Henry and Mason opposed the ban on ex post facto laws precisely because those laws extended to civil matters.[78] Randolph replied that ex post facto laws were, like attainders, "engines of criminal jurisprudence."[79] Madison mumbled something on the subject which could not be heard.[80] Randolph admitted that "taken technically" ex post facto laws related solely to criminal cases and that Madison, when unheard, had said, "it was so interpreted in the Convention"—a reference to Dickinson's remark.[81] Both Randolph and Madison preferred to emphasize other arguments, such as that any claims against the United States would be as valid as they were under the Articles of Confederation but not more so. Madison, who was concerned about getting enough votes for ratification, did not acknowledge that he too had thought that retroactive civil legislation constituted ex post facto laws.

Edmund Pendleton, a strong ratificationist who presided over the Virginia ratifying convention, also kept his silence on the matter. Four years later, as chief justice of the state's highest court, he declared in a judicial opinion that ex post facto laws "destroy rights already acquired under the former statute, by one made subsequent to the time when they were vested."[82] Clearly Pendleton and his judicial brethren believed that ex post facto laws comprehended civil matters.

On balance, the evidence seems to show that the Constitutional Convention did not have a clear understanding that ex post facto laws applied to criminal matters only; indeed, we have only Dickinson's misstatement of Blackstone as the evidence for that view, and that sole piece of evidence was what Madison and Randolph referred to by their remarks about the fact that ex post facto laws had been interpreted "technically" at the Convention so as not to apply to civil matters. Paterson's opinion in *Vanhorne's Case* and Pendleton's in Virginia a few years earlier were no aberrations. Contemporary exposition suggests that the Supreme Court's opinions in *Calder v. Bull* against the extension of ex post facto laws in noncriminal cases was more innovative than it was an accurate reflection of the opinions of the Framers and ratifiers. Indeed, but for Dickinson's misreading of Blackstone and the statement of the New York convention, which, like Dickinson, desired retroactive civil legislation, the history of the framing and ratification of the ex post facto clauses simply do not bear out the opinions in *Calder v. Bull*. The Court in that case reinvented the law on the subject. In doing so the Court did not rely on original intent, and when it reconfirmed the basic doctrine of *Calder* in 1854 and claimed to be relying on original intent, it rested exclusively on Dickinson's remark; having found what it sought the Court ignored all else.

CHAPTER FOUR

Marbury v. Madison
Judicial Activism
Run Amok

$\mathscr{T}$he judicial activism of *Calder* appears modest compared with the rampaging activism of *Marbury v. Madison*, decided in 1803.[1] *Marbury* is probably the most glorified and certainly the most celebrated opinion in American history.[2] It is also one of the most flagrant specimens of judicial activism and, from the standpoint of judicial craftsmanship, resulted in one of the worst opinions ever delivered by the Supreme Court. Hardly a latitude or a longitude of Marshall's *Marbury* opinion lacked an inexactitude or an ineptitude. As a matter of judicial politics, however, it ranks among the craftiest in our constitutional history, and as a symbol of judicial review it ranks as the most important.

The United States Code today empowers the Supreme Court to issue a writ of mandamus in cases "agreeable to the usages and principles of the law."[3] Yet, *Marbury's* fame derives from Chief Justice John Marshall's exposition of the doctrine of national judicial review, which the Court in that case exercised for the first time in the sense of holding unconstitutional an act of Congress that authorized the Supreme Court to issue writs of mandamus in cases authorized by "the principles and usages of the law." History has restored the act that Marshall held void. That was no ordinary act of Congress and no ordinary Congress had passed the act. The Court in *Marbury* ruled unconstitutional a provision of the Judiciary Act of 1789, the cornerstone of the judicial system of the United States by which Congress gave life to Article III of the Constitution.[4] The Congress that did so was the First Congress of our history, meeting in its first session. The act originated in the Senate, eleven of whose original twenty members (from the ten states then represented) had been delegates to the Constitutional Convention—not a likely group to frame an unconstitutional act.[5] The House of Representatives that passed the act included another eight Framers plus twenty-six members who had been delegates to the state ratifying conventions. Of the ninety-two senators and representatives who composed the First Congress, fifty-one, a majority, had been members of either the Philadelphia Convention or the various state ratifying conventions.[6] In 1926, Chief Justice William Howard Taft, writing for the Court, explained the great authority of the First Congress this way:

> What, then, are the elements that enter into our decision of this case? We have first a construction of the Constitution made by a Congress which was to provide by legislation for the organization of the Government in accordance with the Constitution which had just been adopted, and in which there were, as Representatives and Senators, a considerable number of those who had been members of the Convention that framed the Constitution and presented it for ratification. It was the Congress that rounded out the Constitution itself by the proposed first 10 amendments which had in effect been promised to the people as a consideration for the ratification. It was the Congress in which Mr. Madison, one of the first in the framing of the Constitution, led also in the organization of the Government under it. It was a Congress whose constitutional decisions have always been regarded, as they should be regarded, as of the greatest weight in the interpretation of that fundamental instrument.[7]

The principal draftsman of the Judiciary Act of 1789 was Oliver Ellsworth, assisted mainly by William Paterson, both major Framers. Ellsworth served as Chief Justice of the United States immediately prior to Marshall. Paterson served as an Associate Justice when the Court decided *Marbury*.

The case can best be understood only in the context of the

conflict between the Jeffersonians and the Federalists. Albert Beveridge, the author of the monumental four-volume biography of Marshall, insisted that the case must be understood in the context of the great debate in the Senate on judicial review, when the Judiciary Act of 1802, repealing the Judiciary Act of 1801, was at issue.[8] The context should be even broader, in order to understand why the opinion oozed politics and spewed Marshallian misrepresentation; but *Marbury* has transcended its origins in the party battles between Federalists and Republicans, achieving mythic status as the foremost precedent for judicial review. For the first time the Court held unconstitutional an act of Congress, establishing, for posterity if not for its own time, the doctrine that the Supreme Court has the final word among the coordinate branches of the national government in determining what is law under the Constitution. By 1803 no one doubted that an unconstitutional act of government was null and void, but the question not then resolved was: Who is to judge that the act is unconstitutional? For posterity, what *Marbury* settled was that the Court should be the judge and, as a matter of abstract judicial doctrine, if not of reality, that the Court had ultimate authority over Congress and the President. In fact Marshall did not make that claim, and President Jefferson repudiated it.

Actually, the historic reputation of the case is all out of proportion to the merits of Marshall's opinion for the unanimous Court. Indeed it is an opinion of slight merit, distorted reasoning, and galloping activism. On the issue of judicial review, which made the case live, he said nothing new, and his claim for the power of the Court occasioned little contemporary comment. The significance of the case in its time derived from its political implications and from the fact that the Court appeared successfully to censure the executive branch. Marshall's most remarkable accomplishment, in retrospect, was his massing of the Court behind a poorly reasoned opinion that section 13 of the Judiciary Act of 1789 was unconstitutional. Though the Court's technical competence was not evident, its judicial politics—egregious partisanship and calculated expediency—was exceptionally adroit, leaving no target for Republican retaliation beyond frustrated rhetoric.

Rising republican hostility to the United States courts, which were Federalist to the last man as well as Federalist in doctrine and interests, had passed the threshold of tolerance when the Justices on circuit duty enforced the Sedition Act.[9] Then the lame-duck Federalist administration passed the Judiciary Act of 1801 and, a week before Thomas Jefferson's inauguration, passed a companion act for the appointment of forty-two justices of the peace, a preposterous number, for the District of Columbia.[10] These measures prompted the new President to believe that the Federalists "have retired into the judiciary as a stronghold . . . and from that battery all the works of republicanism are to be beaten down and erased."[11] The new Circuit Court for the District of Columbia sought in vain to obtain the conviction of the editor of the administration's organ in the capital for the common law crime of seditious libel.[12] The temperate response of the new administration was remarkable. Instead of increasing the size of the courts, especially the Supreme Court, and packing them with Republican appointees, the administration simply repealed the Judiciary Act of 1801, thus restoring the situation that existed before its enactment.[13] On taking office Jefferson also ordered that the commissions for the forty-two justices of the peace for the district be withheld, though he reappointed twenty-three, all political enemies originally appointed by President John Adams.[14]

Marbury v. Madison arose from the refusal of the administration to deliver the commissions of four of these appointees, including one William Marbury. The Senate had confirmed the appointments and Adams had signed their commissions, which Marshall, the outgoing secretary of state, had affixed with the great seal of the United States. But in the rush of the "midnight appointments" on the evening of March 3, the last day of the outgoing administration, Marshall had neglected to deliver the commissions or was unable to do so. Marbury and three others sought from the Supreme Court, in a case of original jurisdiction, a writ of mandamus compelling James Madison, the new secretary of state, to issue their commissions. In December 1801 the Court issued an order commanding Madison to show cause why it should not grant the writ.[15]

A congressman reflecting the Republican viewpoint said that the show-cause order was "a bold stroke against the Executive," and John Breckenridge, the majority leader of the Senate, thought the order "the most daring attack which the annals of Federalism have yet exhibited."[16] When the debate began on the repeal bill, Federalists defended the show-cause order, the independence of the judiciary, and the duty of the Supreme Court to hold void any unconstitutional acts of Congress.[17] A Republican paper declared that the "mandamus business" had first appeared to be only a contest between the judiciary and the executive but had become a political act by the Court to deter repeal of the 1801 legislation.[18] In retaliation the Republicans passed the repealer and altered the terms of the Court so that it would lose its June 1802 session and not again meet until February 1803, fourteen months after the show-cause order. The Republicans hoped, as proved to be the case, that the Justices would comply with the repealer and return to circuit duty, thereby averting a showdown and a constitutional crisis, which the administration preferred to avoid.[19]

By the time the Court met in February 1803 to hear arguments in *Marbury*, which had become a political sensation, talk of impeachment was in the air. A few days before the Court's term, Federalists in Congress moved that the Senate should produce for Marbury's benefit records of his confirmation, provoking Senator James Jackson of Georgia, an administration supporter, to declare that the Senate would not interfere in the case and become "a party to an accusation which may end in an impeachment, of which the Senate were the constitutional Judges."[20] By no coincidence, a week before the Court met, Jefferson instructed the House to impeach John Pickering, a United States District Court judge in New Hampshire, and already Federalists knew of the plan to impeach Justice Samuel Chase.[21] Jefferson's desire to replace John Marshall with Spencer Roane was also public knowledge. Right before Marshall delivered the Court's opinion in *Marbury*, the Washington correspondent of a Republican paper wrote: "The attempt of the Supreme Court . . . by a mandamus, to control the Executive functions, is a new experiment. It seems to be no less than a commencement of war. . . . The Court must be defeated and retreat from the attack; or march on, till they incur an impeachment and removal from office."[22]

Marshall and his Court appeared to confront unattractive alternatives. To have issued the writ, which was the expected judgment, would have rivaled the papal bull against the moon; Madison would have defied the writ, exposing the Court's impotence, and the Republicans might have had a pretext for retaliation based on the Court's breach of the principle of separation of powers. To have withheld the writ would have violated the Federalist principle that the Republican administration was accountable under the law. The *New York Post,* Alexander Hamilton's newspaper, reported the Court's opinion in a story headed "Constitution Violated by President," informing its readers that the new President by his first act had trampled on the charter of the people's liberties by unprincipled, even criminal, conduct against personal rights.[23] Yet the Court did not issue the writ; the victorious party was James Madison. Marshall shrewdly exhibited him and the President to the nation as if they were arbitrary Stuart tyrants, and then, affecting judicial humility, Marshall, in obedience to the Constitution, found that the Court could not obey an act of Congress that sought to aggrandize judicial powers in cases of original jurisdiction (originating in the Supreme Court), contrary to Article III of the Constitution.

The Court was treading warily. The statute in question was not a Republican measure, not, for example, the repeal of the Judiciary Act of 1801. Indeed, shortly after *Marbury,* the Court sustained the repeal act in *Stuart v. Laird* (1803) against arguments that it was unconstitutional. In that case the Court ruled that the practice of the Justices in sitting as circuit judges derived from the Judiciary Act of 1789, and therefore derived "from a contemporary interpretation of the most forcible nature," as well as from customary acquiescence.[24] Had the Court applied the same rules of construction when it decided *Marbury* six days earlier, it would have sustained the constitutionality of section 13 of the Judiciary Act of 1789. Ironically, that was the section of the statute whose constitutionality was at issue in *Marbury,* not that the bench and bar realized that fact until Marshall delivered his opinion. The offending section, passed by a Federalist Congress after being drafted by Oliver Ellsworth, one of the Constitution's Framers and Marshall's predecessor, had been the subject of previous litigation before the Court without anyone having thought it was unconstitutional. Section 13 simply authorized the Court to issue writs of mandamus "in cases warranted by the principles and usages of law," and that clause appeared in the context of a reference to the Court's appellate jurisdiction, not in the context of the reference in section

13 to original jurisdiction. Marshall's reading of section 13 as an augmentation of the Court's original jurisdiction was contrived in the extreme. Even so, the Court in 1794 had accepted jurisdiction of and decided an application for a mandamus in a case of original jurisdiction; it had denied the writ in that instance only because the applicant had no legal right to it,[25] not because Congress had acted unconstitutionally or because the Court lacked jurisdiction.

Marshall's entire argument hinged on the erroneous point that section 13 unconstitutionally extended the Court's original jurisdiction beyond the two categories of cases, specified in Article III, in which the Court was to have such jurisdiction. But for those two categories of cases, involving foreign diplomats or a state as a litigant, the Court has appellate jurisdiction. In quoting Article III, Marshall omitted the clause that directly follows as part of the same sentence: the Court has appellate jurisdiction "with such exceptions, and under such regulations as the Congress shall make." That might mean that Congress can detract from the Court's appellate jurisdiction or add to its original jurisdiction. The specification of two categories of cases in which the Court has original jurisdiction was surely intended as an irreducible minimum, but Marshall read it, by the narrowest construction, to mean a negation of congressional powers. If the exceptions clause is construed in the light of a draft version of the Committee of Detail, which composed the final version, the intent was to enable Congress to switch the Court's appellate jurisdiction to its original jurisdiction. "But this supreme jurisdiction," the draft version stated, "shall be appellate only, except in those instances, in which the legislature shall make it original."[26]

In any event, section 13, contrary to Marshall, did not add to the Court's original jurisdiction. In effect it authorized the Court to issue writs of mandamus in the two categories of cases of original jurisdiction and in all appellate cases. The authority to issue such writs did not extend or add to the Court's jurisdiction; the writ of mandamus is merely a remedial device by which courts implement their existing jurisdiction. Marshall grossly misinterpreted the statute and Article III, as well as the nature of the writ, in order to find that the statute conflicted with Article III so that he could avoid issuing the writ without appearing to buckle before political enemies. Had the Court employed the reasoning of *Stuart v. Laird* or the rule that the Court should hold a statute void only in a clear case, giving every presumption of validity in doubtful cases, Marshall could not have reached his conclusion that section 13 was unconstitutional. That conclusion allowed him to decide that the Court was powerless to issue the writ, because Marbury had sued for it in a case of original jurisdiction before the Supreme Court.

Marshall could have said, simply: this is a case of original jurisdiction but does not fall within either of the two categories of original jurisdiction specified in Article III; therefore we cannot decide: writ denied, case dismissed. Section 13 need never have entered the opinion, although, alternatively, Marshall could have declared: section 13 authorizes this Court to issue such writs only in cases warranted by the principles and usages of law; we have no jurisdiction here because we are not hearing the case in our appellate capacity and it is not one of the two categories in which we possess original jurisdiction: writ denied, case dismissed. Even if Marshall had to find that the statute augmented the Court's original jurisdiction, the ambiguity of the exceptions clause in Article III, which he neglected to quote or mention at the crucial point, justified sustaining the statute.

Holding section 13 unconstitutional enabled Marshall to refuse an extension of the Court's powers and award the judgment to Madison, thus denying the administration a pretext for vengeance. Marshall also used the case to answer Republican arguments that the Court did not and should not have the power to declare an act of Congress unconstitutional, though he carefully chose an inoffensive section of a Federalist statute that pertained merely to writs of mandamus. That he gave his doctrine of judicial review the support of only abstract logic, without reference to history or precedents, was characteristic, as was the fact that his doctrine swept way beyond the statute that provoked it.

If Marshall had merely wanted a safe platform from which to espouse and exercise judicial review, he would have begun his opinion with the problems that section 13 posed for the Court; but he reached the question of constitutionality and of judicial review at the tail-end of his opinion. Although he concluded that the Court had to discharge the show-clause order, because it lacked jurisdiction, he first and most irregularly passed judgment on the merits of the case. Everything said on the merits was obiter dicta and should not have been said at all, given the judgment. Most of the opinion dealt with Marbury's unquestionable right to his commission and the correctness of the remedy he had sought by way of a writ of mandamus. In his elaborate discourse on those matters, Marshall assailed the President and his cabinet officer for their lawlessness. Before telling Marbury that he had initiated his case in the wrong court, Marshall engaged in what Edward S. Corwin called "a deliberate partisan *coup.*" Then Marshall followed with a "judicial *coup d'état,*" in the words of Albert J. Beveridge, on the constitutional issue that neither party had argued. In no other case in our constitutional history has the Court held unconstitutional an act of Congress whose constitutionality was not at issue; no one argued against its constitutionality.

Charles Lee, the former attorney general of the United States who argued the case for Marbury, had defined several questions presented by the case, and the first was whether the Supreme Court could award the writ.[27] Marshall deliberately reversed the sequence of the questions, making Lee's first one the last one to be dealt with. Lee also argued that "Congress is not restrained from conferring original jurisdiction in other cases than those mentioned in the constitution." And, he showed that the Court had previously considered mandamus cases in such a way that "the power of the court to issue writs of mandamus was taken for granted in the arguments of counsel on both sides, and seems to have been so considered by the court."[28] In the face of Lee's strong argument, Marshall delivered an evasive opinion that failed to face and consider matters that undermined his own position. He simply twisted and contorted the case to fit his needs. Certainly the Constitution did not dictate the decision.

The partisan *coup* by which Marshall denounced the executive branch, not the grand declaration of the doctrine of judicial review for which the case is remembered, was the focus of contemporary excitement. Only the passages of the opinion on judicial review survive. Cases on the removal power of the President, especially concerning inferior appointees, cast doubt on the validity of the obiter dicta by which Marshall lectured the executive branch on its responsibilities under the law. Moreover, by statute and by judicial practice the Supreme Court exercises the authority to issue the writ of mandamus in all appellate cases and in the two categories of cases of original jurisdiction. Over the passage of time *Marbury* came to stand for the monumental principle, so distinctive and dominant a feature of our constitutional system, that the Court may bind the coordinate branches of the national government to its rulings on the supreme law of the land. That principle stands out from *Marbury* like the grin on the Cheshire cat; all else, which preoccupied national attention in 1803, disappeared in our constitutional law. So too might have disappeared national judicial review if the impeachment of Justice Samuel Chase had succeeded.[29]

Marshall himself was prepared to submit to review of Supreme Court opinions by Congress. He was so shaken by the impeachment of Chase and by the thought that he himself might be the next victim in the event of Chase's conviction, that he wrote to Chase on January 23, 1804: "I think the modern doctrine of impeachment should yield to an appellate jurisdiction in the legislature. A reversal of those legal opinions deemed unsound by the legislature would certainly better comport with the mildness of our character than a removal of the judge who has rendered them unknowing of his fault."[30] The acquittal of Chase meant that the Court could remain independent, that Marshall had no need to announce publicly his desperate plan for congressional review of the Court, and that *Marbury* remained as a precedent. After *Marbury* the Court considered and sustained the constitutionality of acts of Congress in many cases. Considering that the Court did not again hold unconstitutional an act of Congress until 1857, when it decided *Dred Scott v. Sandford*,[31] sixty-eight years would have passed since 1789 without such a holding, and but for *Marbury*, after so long a period of congressional immunity against the invalidation of legislative measures, national judicial review might never have been established; that is, the Supreme Court might never have claimed and exercised the power to hold unconstitutional acts of Congress.

Even so, *Marbury* does not really live up to its reputation as the great case of first impression that provides the foundation of judicial review over the other branches of the national government. In *Dred Scott* the Court ruled that Congress had no power to outlaw slavery in the territories. In *Marbury* the Court held unconstitutional an act governing the Court's issuance of an unusual writ in cases of original jurisdiction, which are extraordinarily rare. The difference between the two cases, with respect to the sort of judicial review that they involved, was vast. In *Dred Scott* the Court asserted finality of judgment in a matter involving public policy for the nation on the most significant issue of the time; in *Marbury* the Court claimed that it could not accept an enhancement of its own jurisdiction in a matter involving the way it performed its duties within the province of its own department. Thus even as to the issue of judicial review, for which *Marbury* is supposedly the trailblazing precedent, its mythic reputation bears no relation to the narrow scope of review that the Marshall Court actually exercised. And, although Marshall's theoretical statement of judicial review outstripped his actual exercise of it in *Marbury*, he claimed neither finality of power nor the authority of the Court to bind President and Congress. The mythic *Marbury* and the real *Marbury* inhabit different constitutional galaxies.

Compared to the issue presented by *Stuart v. Laird* decided six days after *Marbury*, that famous mandamus case presented a trivial issue, other than the one Marshall contrived on the constitutionality of section 13. Charles Lee argued both cases. In *Marbury* he contended that the Court should issue a writ ordering the delivery of Marbury's commission as a justice of the peace. Lee raised no constitutional issue in that case. In *Stuart* he asked the Court to hold unconstitutional a major measure of President Jefferson's administration, one that was of immense political importance at the time. The judicial offices at stake in *Stuart* were not petty as they were in *Marbury*. Federal justices of the peace had a tenure of only five years and emoluments that consisted only of small fees. *Stuart*, however, involved all the United States circuit judgeships in the nation, posts created by Congress with lifetime tenure and annual salary; in 1802 Congress abolished these circuit judgeships, eradicating the jobs of sixteen sitting judges, all of whom had received lifetime appointments, had been sworn in office, and had performed their high judicial duties.

The position of circuit judge had been created in 1801, when the outgoing Federalist Congress had passed a judiciary act that introduced an acutely needed and long overdue reform: it established circuit judgeships to staff courts formerly consisting of a federal district judge and a member of the Supreme Court. Since 1789 Supreme Court Justices had ridden circuit, an excessively arduous task, which required them in many instances to review their own circuit decisions on appeal.[32] That reform act of 1801 authorized the appointment of sixteen circuit judges. Unfortunately politics saturated the reform. Congress did not enact the bill until after the Federalist party had lost the election of 1800, although the Justices of the Supreme Court had requested the reform since 1789. And, President John Adams appointed only Federalists to the sixteen positions.[33] The Circuit Court for the District of Columbia promptly sought the common law indictment of the editor of the capital's Jeffersonian newspaper for the crime of seditious libel.[34] And the last-minute selection of various minor officials authorized by the statute, including marshals and justices of the peace, earned the derisive sobriquet of the "midnight" appointments. Finally, the statute contained a provision that spitefully reduced the size of the Supreme Court from six to five when a vacancy should occur, thus preventing the incoming President from filling it. Understandably the Judiciary Act of 1801 enraged the Jeffersonians whose first major business was its repeal.

The repeal of 1802 obligated the Supreme Court Justices to return to circuit duty. Both Marshall and Chase believed that the repeal act violated the Constitution,[35] but Marshall cannily realized that defiance of the 1802 act of Congress could tempt the administration to impeach the recalcitrant Justices. To Justice William Paterson, Marshall wrote, "This is [a] subject not to be lightly resolved on. The consequences of refusing to carry the law into effect may be serious."[36] Soon after, Marshall recommended that the members of the Court should return to circuit duty, and they complied.[37]

Ultrafederalists, including a few of the displaced circuit judges, devised test cases challenging the constitutionality of the repeal act of 1802. That was how *Stuart v. Laird* originated. In that test case the Fourth Circuit Court had entered a judgment, but before it could be executed Congress abolished the court. When the case was continued it appeared on the docket of the old (pre-1802) Fifth Circuit Court over which Marshall himself presided. Lee argued before Marshall that the Judiciary Act of 1802 unconstitutionally "annihilated" the Fourth Circuit Court, but because the act was void, that court still existed and should decide the case, rather than the Fifth Circuit Court. Marshall rejected Lee's argument, holding that the practice of Supreme Court Justices serving as circuit court members had been settled by custom. On the appeal, Lee repeated his contention that the act of 1802 was "unconstitutional" because the circuit judges had a lifetime tenure that the Constitution protected; its objective was preservation of the independence of the judiciary "to shield them from the attack of that party spirit which always predominates in popular assemblies."[38] Lee supported his argument by invoking *The Federalist* #78 and speeches by James Madison and John Marshall at the Virginia ratifying convention on the reasons that federal judicial tenure was not dependent on Congress.

Unlike *Marbury*, where Marshall's opinion for the Court took over 9,000 words of exposition, Paterson's opinion for the Court in *Stuart* disposed of the case in about 500 words. He made two points. First, nothing in the Constitution limited Congress in transferring jurisdiction from one inferior court to another; and, second, the Justices of the Supreme Court could sit as circuit judges, without having a special commission to do so, because they had in fact done so "commencing with the organization of the judicial system," and that "affords an irresistible answer, and has indeed fixed the construction. It is a contemporary interpretation of the most forcible nature . . . too strong and obstinate to be shaken or controlled. Of course the question is at rest, and ought not now to be disturbed."[39]

Thus ended the case, in a perfunctory way, without the Court having faced the question raised by Lee about the incapacity of Congress to abolish the positions of sitting judges who held the same tenure as Supreme Court Justices. Original intent about the independence of the judiciary yielded to political considerations: The Court sustained the statute, unmentioned in Paterson's opinion, as speedily and quietly as possible to placate a hostile legislature. Congress needed only some pretext to convict the members of the Supreme Court on impeachment charges, thereby allowing the possibility that President Jefferson would appoint Spencer Roane as the new Chief Justice and pack the remainder of the positions with Jeffersonians, just as Washington and Adams had packed the Court with Federalists. Accordingly, the Court in *Stuart* heeded the old adage that he who fights and runs away lives to fight another day. It refused to hold unconstitutional an act of doubtful validity, while in *Marbury* it held unconstitutional an act of undoubted validity. To the extent that national judicial review rests on *Mar-bury* it rests on rubbish, notwithstanding the imperishable lines of Marshall's opinion on the supremacy of fundamental law and the indispensable need to respect constitutional limitations. Those imperishable lines do not, however, prove Marshall's thesis. In any case, the opinion in *Marbury* rested on original intent not at all. Nor did judicial review over Congress rest on original intent.

CHAPTER FIVE

Was Judicial Review Intended? The State Precedents

Marbury v. Madison raised one of the most important questions about original intent: Did the Framers understand that the Supreme Court would exercise the power to hold unconstitutional acts of Congress or of the President? The Constitution makes no explicit provision for that power. On that point no controversy exists, although scholars engage in keen disputes about whether the Constitution implies judicial review. If the Framers intended it, perhaps they failed to provide for it, because there was no need to. The reference in Article III to "the judicial power of the United States" might have been sufficient, if judicial review was a normal function of courts at the time. If it was, how did it originate? Those questions are of interest in view of the fact that legislative supremacy characterized the English system; as Blackstone said, no power on earth could undo an act of Parliament, except another act. Judges, he wrote, were not free to reject an act, however unreasonable, "for that were to set the judicial power above that of the legislature which would be subversive of all government."[1]

The legitimacy of judicial review as measured by the original intent of the Framers merits investigation, because it raises the question of the Supreme Court's role in a political democracy, a topic that could scarcely be more controversial. Much of the literature about the Supreme Court reflects the principle of the gored ox. Attitudes toward the Court often depend on whether its decisions are agreeable. More reflective commentators, however, seek to transcend their own policy preferences and confront the basic and most perplexing questions that speak to the legitimacy of judicial review, its function and character in cases of constitutional law, and its harmony with democratic principles of government. But the usual response to an inquiry about the legitimacy of judicial review is an expression of disinterest in a matter long settled by practice, or, an acceptance of the inquiry and a rummaging through the wisdom of the past for a lineage that will authenticate either some present vision of the role of the Supreme Court in a political democracy, or some theory of the function of judicial review and of the nature of the judicial process. The question whether judicial review was originally intended, in other words, is usually a dowsing rod to guide the wellsprings of judgment on whether the Court should have the power that, in loose and sometimes mischievous phrases, has resulted in "judicial supremacy," or "judicial policy-making," or "judicial legislation." The scope of that power, the conditions for its exercise, and the criteria for judging its practice have also attracted considerable attention. All these considerations should relate to, if not derive from, the principles of limited government and the need to maintain regularized restraints upon government power. Historical experience provides explanations.

The legitimacy of judicial review rests on history, not on the words of the Constitution or of the Framers during the 1787–1789 period. Judicial review was a historical outgrowth of the constitutional theory of the era of the American Revolution. *The Federalist* #78 and Marshall's *Marbury* opinion were, significantly, arguments from general principles. Andrew C. McLaughlin, one of the masters of constitutional history, wrote that judicial review is "the last word, logically and historically speaking, in the attempt of a free people to establish and maintain a non-autocratic government. It is the culmination of the essentials of Revolutionary thinking, and, indeed, of the thinking of those who a hundred years and more before the Revolution called for a government of laws and not of men."[2]

That judicial review was "the natural outgrowth of ideas that were common property when the Constitution was established" was also asserted by Edward S. Corwin, another constitutional scholar of eminence. "In short," he wrote, "we are driven to the conclusion that judicial review was rested by the framers of the Constitution upon certain general principles which in their esti- mation made specific provision for it unnecessary . . ."[3]

Corwin and McLaughlin were thinking of the theory of limited or constitutional government according to which an act of govern- ment in excess of its powers, which are held in subordination to a supreme law, is void. The difficulty with this theory is that it does not account for the definitive power of the judiciary to interpret finally the supreme law, nor does it account for the binding effect of court decisions on equal and coordinate branches of the same government. Articles III and VI of the Constitution, together with the Judiciary Act of 1789, established or made inevitable judicial review by the Supreme Court over the acts of the states, the subordinate agencies within the federal system, but not over the President and Congress. On the other hand, if judicial review was a normal function of courts at the time of the establishment of the national government under the Constitution, there was no need for specific provision. Charles Beard, Edward Corwin, Andrew C. McLaughlin, Charles Warren, Charles Grove Haines, and Raoul Berger head a list of distinguished scholars who believed that ju- dicial review was so well known and normal a function of courts that it was taken for granted by the Framers.[4]

One difficulty with this view is that the evidence is so sparing. If judicial review was a normal function of courts at the time of the Constitutional Convention, we might expect to find a considerable number of precedents in which legislation was invalidated on ground of repugnance to some higher law, either natural law or the written provisions of some constitution. The entire colonial period is with- out a single precedent. Although Virginia county courts announced in 1766 that the Stamp Act was unconstitutional, there was no case before those courts; their statements were gratuitous.[5] Many real precedents might be expected after the establishment of thirteen state governments, each with its own judiciary, but the striking fact is that there were so few. The various books and articles that have been written to exhume the precedents include mythical cases, which bring to mind the entries in *Appleton's Cyclopaedia of American Biography* with its forty-seven lives of men who never existed. The most influential and exhaustive of all works on the precedents is *The American Doctrine of Judicial Supremacy* by Charles Grove Haines. "By 1775," he concluded,

> the principle had taken such a firm hold upon the minds of lawyers and judges that decisions were rendered in rapid succession in which was maintained the authority of courts, as guardians of a fundamental law, to pass upon the acts of coordinate departments. This authority was steadily asserted after the colonies became states, and by an irresistible process was made one of the prime features of the new federal system established by the Constitution of 1787. The state cases in which the American doctrine was first announced, and which were accepted as precedents in its development and extension, have an important role in the legal history of the United States.[6]

A "precedent" in this context refers to a case in which a court actually held a legislative act unconstitutional.

It is something of a letdown to discover that Haines lists only seven state precedents for the period 1776–1787, a number hardly warranting the confident statement that judicial review was such a widely practiced, normal function of American courts that no provision for it had to be made in the Constitution. But there is an additional problem concerning these seven precedents. Several of them are spurious, while others fudge the facts somewhat like William James when he was a young instructor assisting a lecturer on the physiology of the heart. The lecturer used a turtle's heart supporting an "index straw" which projected an enlarged moving shadow across a screen to show the heart beat. To James's consternation, the turtle's heart failed to function, jeopardizing the demonstration. "There was no time for deliberation," he recalled, "so with my forefinger under a part of the straw that cast no shadow, I found myself impulsively and automatically imitating the rhythmical movements which my colleague had prophesied the heart would undergo. I kept the experiment from failing . . . and established in the audience the true view of the subject."[7] Haines also supplied a finger to demonstrate the "true view of the subject," or, more likely, did not realize that someone else had done so.

What is interesting about several of the spurious precedents, as distinguished from the mythical cases, is that the court decisions were either deliberately or mistakenly misrepresented for the purpose of discrediting the judges. The Constitution was framed at a time when the Blackstonian concept of legislative supremacy was dominant. As the judge himself said in *Rutgers v. Waddington*, one of the alleged precedents, if the legislature "think fit *positively* to enact a law there is no power which can controul them . . . the judges are not at liberty, although it appear to them to be *unreasonable*, to reject it; for this were to set the *judicial* above the legislative, which would be subversive to all government."[8] Haines included cases in which disappointed parties, in an effort to inflame opposition to the court, alleged baselessly that it had voided an act. *Holmes v. Walton*, decided by the New Jersey Supreme Court in 1780, was such a case. The Framers could not have taken the misrepresentation for the fact because David Brearly, one of the delegates to the Constitutional Convention, had been chief justice of the court that decided the case.[9] And Brearly knew that the people of his state did not take judicial review for granted as a normal function of courts.

In *Holmes v. Walton*, the first state "precedent" for judicial review, the state's high court supposedly struck down a state trading-with-the-enemy act that provided for trial by a six-man jury; a jury of that size supposedly violated the state constitution. In fact, New Jersey had employed six-man juries in cases of small amounts (six pounds) from colonial times and twelve-man juries in all other cases. Because the property involved in *Holmes* had substantial value, Holmes was entitled to a trial by a jury of twelve; but the trial judge, for reasons unknown, allowed him only a six-man jury. Holmes therefore had no reason to object to the statute's constitutionality, and he did not; he contended, rather, that he was denied a right to trial by a twelve-member jury. The high court upheld his claim. The constitutionality of the act was not at issue, and the court gave no opinion, not even in obiter dicta, on whether it had the power to void an act for unconstitutionality.

Soon after the appellate decision, which allowed Holmes a new trial, disaffected citizens of his locality alleged in a petition to the state assembly that the state's supreme court had held the seizure act void. The legislature supported the court, however, by enacting a new measure providing that in any suit exceeding six pounds, trial by jury meant a trial by a jury of twelve. Somehow a mistaken view of the case originated and survived, making *Holmes* a "precedent," however inauthentic, for judicial review.[10]

The next supposed precedent for judicial review was *Commonwealth v. Caton*, decided by the highest court of Virginia in 1782.[11] The state's 1776 constitution authorized the governor to grant pardons except in impeachment cases. A statute on treason deprived the governor of his pardoning power and vested it in the general assembly. Caton, having been sentenced to death for treason, claimed a pardon granted by the lower house, though the upper house had refused to concur. The court had only to rule that the pardon was not valid, because of the conflict between the two houses.

Call's unreliable report of the case, a reconstruction made forty-five years later, indicates that the court considered the constitutionality of the statute and that seven of the eight judges were of the opinion that the court had the power to declare an act of the legislature unconstitutional, though the court unanimously held the act constitutional. In fact, only one of the eight judges ruled the act unconstitutional, one held that it had no power to so rule, and another, George Wythe, a future Framer, declared that the court had the power but did not need to exercise it in this case; he decided that the pardon had no force of law because it was not in conformity with the disputed act, which he found constitutional. A majority of the court, including Chief Justice Edmund Pendleton and Chancellor John Blair, another future Framer, declined to decide the question whether they had the power to declare an act unconstitutional. Only Wythe and Richard Cary, in obiter dicta, stated that the court had that power. Writing to Madison a week later, Pendleton reported, "The great Constitutional question . . . was determined . . . by 6 Judges against two, that the Treason Act was not at variance with the Constitution but a proper exercise of the Power reserved to the Legislature by the latter. . . ."[12] The legitimacy of the case as a precedent for judicial review is, therefore, valueless except to the extent that it shows that the concept of judicial review was entering the judicial consciousness.

Rutgers v. Waddington, decided by the Mayor's Court of New York City in 1784, provoked the state legislature, sensitive to slights on its sovereignty, to condemn the court in the mistaken belief that it had invalidated a statute.[13] *Rutgers* was the first case in which the constitutionality of a state act was attacked on ground that it violated a treaty of the United States. The Trespass Act allowed Elizabeth Rutgers, who fled New York when the British occupied the city, to sue for the value of rents lost while her property was held by British merchants under military authority. The statute barred defendants from pleading that military authority justified the "trespass" under acts of war and the law of nations. The Treaty of Peace, however, canceled claims for injuries to property during the war. Alexander Hamilton, representing the defendants, expressly argued that the court should hold the Trespass Act unconstitutional, because it violated the treaty. Arguments of counsel should not be confused with judicial decisions, and Hamilton's argument did not rely on the normality of judicial review; indeed, he was inviting a judicial precedent.

Chief Justice James Duane, for the court, declared that the state constitution embodied the common law and that the common law recognized the law of nations. Duane also declared that the union of the states under the Articles of Confederation constituted "a fundamental law," according to which Congress had exclusive powers of making war and peace: ". . . no state in this union can alter or abridge, in a single point, the federal articles or the treaty." His logic having led him to the brink of holding the Trespass Act void, Duane abruptly endorsed the prevailing Blackstonian theory of legislative supremacy and asserted that "to set the judicial above the legislative . . . would be subversive of all government." Duane then declared that the legislature had not intended to revoke the law of nations and that the court had to expound the statute to give the legislature's intention its effect, whereupon the court emasculated the statute. The judge then decided that for the time the property was held under military order, acts done according to the law of nations and "buried in oblivion" by the treaty could not be redressed by the statute: Rutgers could not recover for trespass.

Technically the court had construed the act to conform to the treaty and the law of nations, but the court's construction of the statute defeated the legislature's purpose. As a result, there were mass protests, the governor called a special session of the legislature, and the legislature angrily resolved that the adjudication was "subversive of all law and good order": if a court could "dispense with" state law, "legislatures become useless." Despite impeachment threats, a motion to remove the judges failed. But a public meeting adopted "An Address to the People," which angrily accused the court of having "assumed and exercised a power to set aside an Act of the State." The "Address," severely condemning judicial review and a pamphlet report of the case, circulated widely.

Trevett v. Weeden, a Rhode Island case of 1786, is the best known of the alleged state precedents for judicial review.[14] The state's highest judicial tribunal did not hold a state act unconstitutional but did construe it in a manner that left it inoperative. The case arose under a force act passed by the legislature to compel observance of the state paper-money laws; anyone refusing to accept paper money at par with specie was triable without a jury or right of appeal "according to the laws of the land" and on conviction was subject to a 100 pound fine and costs or be committed "till sentence be performed." Trevett filed an information before the state chief justice charging that Weeden refused tender of paper money at face value. James Varnum, representing Weeden, argued that the force act violated the right to trial by jury, guaranteed by the unwritten state constitution, which was fundamental law that limited legislative power; the legislature could make laws "not repugnant to the constitution" and the judiciary had "the sole power of judging those laws . . . but cannot admit any act of the legislative as law, which is against the constitution." This argument by counsel did not receive the court's endorsement.

The court refused to decide the issue, ruling that it lacked jurisdiction. Its judgment was simply that Trevett's complaint "does not come under the cognizance of the Justices . . . and it is hereby dismissed." Orally, however, some of the judges, according to the newspaper accounts, declared the force act "to be repugnant and unconstitutional," and one of them pointed out that the phrase in the act, "without trial by jury, according to the laws of the land," was self-contradictory and thus unenforceable.

The governor called the legislature into special session, and the legislature summoned the high court judges, as if they were offenders, and demanded an explanation of their reasons for holding an act "unconstitutional," and "unprecedented" judgment that tended "to abolish the legislative authority." Judge David Howell, the court's main spokesman, defended judicial review and judicial independence before the legislature. Although he summarized Varnum's argument that the act was unconstitutional, Howell insisted that the legislature had confused the argument and the judgment, for the judgment was just that the complaint was not "cognizable."

The legislature, unconvinced by the court's technical distinction, recognized that the judgment made the paper-money laws unenforceable; in effect the court had exercised judicial review, which the legislature deemed subversive of its supremacy. Judge Howell, by contrast, had claimed that if the legislature could pass on the court's rulings, "the Legislature would become the supreme judiciary—a perversion of power totally subversive of civil liberty." Anticipating a motion to unseat them, the judges presented a memorial demanding due process of law. Varnum and the attorney general supported them, arguing that they could not be removed except on a criminal charge. The motion to remove the judges failed, and the legislature even repealed the force act but revenged itself on the judges by failing to reelect four of the five members when their annual terms expired, and by ousting Congressman Varnum and the state attorney general. Varnum published a one-sided pamphlet on the case, giving it publicity even in Philadelphia while the Constitutional Convention met. Although the pamphlet popularized the doctrine of judicial review in Rhode Island, no judge in that state endorsed the doctrine for about seventy years after.

The Ten Pound Act Cases, about which little is known (we do not even know the names of the litigants) are especially notable as the first instances in our history of a state court's holding unconstitutional an act of a state legislature.[15] An inferior court sitting in Portsmouth, New Hampshire, in 1786 and again in 1787 voided the "Ten Pound Act," which had been passed in 1785 for the speedy recovery of small debts. Our scanty knowledge of the cases derives from newspaper reports and legislative records. The act of 1785 allowed justices of the peace to try minor civil cases, involving sums less than ten pounds, without juries. The state constitutional guarantee of trial by jury extended to all civil cases except those which juries customarily did not try. New Hampshire practice had previously allowed a justice of the peace to try a case without a jury if the sum amounted to less than two pounds. After the court ruled that the act conflicted with the right to trial by jury, petitions to the state legislature demanded impeachment of the judges. The house, by a 3–1 majority, voted that the act was constitutional, but the judges courageously stood by their initial decision and reaffirmed it in another case. Following the failure of a motion to impeach the judges, the house capitulated and repealed the Ten Pound Act.

Bayard v. Singleton, decided in 1787 by the supreme court of North Carolina, was the first reported state case in which a judicial tribunal held a legislative enactment unconstitutional.[16] This and the Ten Pound Act Cases are the only authentic examples of the exercise of judicial review carried to its furthest limit before the circuit work of the Justices of the Supreme Court of the United States in the 1790s. During the Revolution, North Carolina had confiscated and sold Tory estates; to protect the new owners, the legislature enacted that in any action to recover confiscated land, the courts must grant a motion to dismiss the suit. Bayard brought such a suit, and Singleton made a motion for dismissal. Instead of granting the motion, the high court of the state delayed decision and recommended a jury trial to settle the issue of ownership. The court seemed to be seeking a way to avoid holding the act unconstitutional and hoped that the legislature might revise it. The legislature summoned the judges before it to determine whether they were guilty of malpractice in office by disregarding a statute. The legislature found no basis for impeachment but refused to revise the statute.

On a renewed motion to dismiss, the court held the act void, because "by the constitution every citizen had undoubtedly a right to a decision of his property by trial by jury." In defense of judicial review, the court reasoned that no statute could alter or repeal the state constitution, which was fundamental law. The court then submitted the case to a jury. The committee of the legislature that had heard the charges against the judges included Richard Dobbs Spaight, a vehement antagonist of judicial review, and William R. Davie, co-counsel for Bayard; shortly after, both men represented North Carolina at the Constitutional Convention of 1787. James Iredell, later one of the first Justices of the Supreme Court of the United States, also represented Bayard. Iredell published an address, "To the Public," in 1786, anticipating the doctrine of *Bayard v. Singleton,* and his correspondence with Spaight on judicial review best reflects the arguments at that time for and against the power of courts to hold enactments unconstitutional. Spaight's position, that such a power was a "usurpation" by the judiciary, accorded with the then prevailing theory and practice of legislative supremacy. Iredell's raised a standard for the future.[17]

Such are the pre-Convention precedents, few as they are. Taken as a group, the spurious as well as the legitimate, they scarcely show that judicial review was a normal function of courts. On the contrary, they show that it was nowhere established, indeed that it seemed novel, controversial, and an encroachment on legislative authority. Its exercise, even when imagined, was disputed and liable to provoke the legislature to retaliation. If the Framers intended judicial review, would they have omitted a provision for it, allowing it to rest on so precarious a foundation? They might have, on the supposition that an explicit provision might not have aided the cause of ratification, but the thought lacks evidentiary basis. Louis B. Boudin, who did much of the spadework in exposing the fraudulent character of some of the precedents, and William W. Crosskey, who followed his lead, observed that the precedents tended to arise in certain types of cases—those in which the legislatures had interfered with the normal jurisdiction of the courts or the trial procedures by which they normally did business. Such cases, in Madison's phrase, were "of a Judiciary Nature," as was *Marbury v. Madison.* Judicial review emerged, in other words, mainly in cases relating to the province of the judicial department or trial by jury. The precedents, though revealing a growing familiarity with the concept of judicial review, tend not to show that the courts could pass on the constitutionality of the general powers of the legislatures. As Corwin concluded, in his last word on the subject, "the case that could be made for judicial review in 1787 on either the ground of proved workability or of 'precedent' was a shadowy one at best."[18] Do the records of the Constitutional Convention support that view?

CHAPTER SIX

Development of Judicial Review

*K*ipling in his *Just So Stories* described how the alligator gave the elephant his trunk. Charles A. Beard in his *Supreme Court and the Constitution* (1912) told how the Framers of the Constitution gave the high tribunal its power of judicial review even over acts of Congress. Children find the story about the elephant enchantingly believable. Scholars and jurists read Beard's tale and say, "just so." But history has not really settled whether judicial review was originally intended, because decisive evidence cannot be marshaled to prove what the Framers had in mind any more than history shows that judicial review was a normal function of courts at the time of the Constitutional Convention. The evidence seems to indicate that the Framers did not mean for the Supreme Court to have authority to void acts of Congress.

The problem of legitimacy begins with the fact, which needs repeating, that the Framers neglected to specify that the Court was empowered to exercise judicial review. If they intended the Court to have the power, why did they not explicitly provide for it? Since 1787 when Richard Dobbs Spaight, one of the Framers, angrily denounced judicial review as "usurpation,"[1] the cry that judges have usurped the power has echoed down the corridors of time. In 1924 Professor Felix Frankfurter exasperatedly declared,

"Lack of historical scholarship, combined with fierce prepossessions, can alone account for the persistence of this talk. One would suppose that, at least, after the publication of Beard's *The Supreme Court and the Constitution,* there would be an end to this empty controversy."[2] The charge of usurpation most certainly cannot be proved; it is without merit. The difficulty is that the legitimacy of judicial review in terms of original intent cannot be proved either; it may forever remain obscure, a seductive issue to those who would lift the veil.

In Beard's self-congratulatory preface to a reissue of his book in 1939, he declared that he had "settled" the great controversy over the legitimacy of the Court's most awesome power. The book had been favorably cited many times by expert witnesses before the Senate Judiciary Committee's hearings on the Roosevelt court-packing plan, and the committee itself seemed to accept the book as authoritative. "The ghost of usurpation," Beard announced, "was fairly laid. Whatever controversies may arise in the future over the exercise of judicial power, it is not likely that the historic right of the Supreme Court to pass upon acts of Congress will again be seriously challenged." As Alan F. Westin wryly observed in his introduction to a 1962 reprint of the book, despite Beard's prophecy the "ghost of usurpation" continued to clank its chains through legislative chambers, historical meetings, and publishing houses. Since the first edition of 1912, said Westin, several dozen books and perhaps a hundred articles "have persisted in treating this as still a debatable proposition, and not all of the commentators can be dismissed as incompetents or outraged partisans deprived of reason."[3]

"Judicial review is a matter of inference,"[4] wrote Edward S. Corwin, Beard's sharpest and most formidable critic, though never one to endorse the charge of usurpation. One might add that inferences and insights will lead to any conclusions required by presuppositions. Beard's thesis on judicial review, as a matter of fact, was a foil for a book that he published in the following year: *An Economic Interpretation of the Constitution* (1913). Chapter 4 of Beard's 1912 volume, on "The Spirit of the Constitution," foreshadows his 1913 volume. In Beard's opinion, judicial review over Congress must have been intended because it was part of the system of checks and balances by which the Convention "safe-

guarded the interests of property against attacks by majorities.
. . . This very system of checks and balances, which is undeniably
the essential element of the Constitution, is built upon the doctrine
that the popular branch of the government cannot be allowed full
sway, and least of all in the enactment of laws touching the rights
of property." He concluded that it was incumbent upon opponents
of his thesis "to show that the American federal system was not
designated primarily to commit the established rights of property
to the guardianship of a judiciary removed from direct contact with
the popular electorates."[5] Divination, or reading the minds of the
Framers from a very incomplete and extraordinarily ambiguous
record, may be an intriguing pastime; but it lacks empirical warrant.

The record of Corwin's vacillations testifies to the confusing
and inconclusive nature of the evidence. In an unsympathetic review of Beard's book, published in 1913, Corwin argued that of
the twenty-five Framers who, Beard claimed, supported "some
form" of judicial review over Congress, only eight did so in the
Constitutional Convention. Although the idea of judicial review
was challenged by only four members, "yet popular discussion
previous to the Convention had shown their point of view [oppo-
sition to judicial review] to have too formidable backing to admit
of its being crassly overridden."[6] Corwin concluded that the question was an open one when the Convention adjourned. Within a
year, however, he was substantially in Beard's corner. In a little
book that produced no new evidence whatever, Corwin asserted
that the Convention undoubtedly did intend judicial review over
Congress: ". . . it cannot be reasonably doubted." His 1913 figure
of eight rose in 1914 to seventeen.[7] By 1937, however, it had fallen
to only "five or six," and in blunt language Corwin declared, "The
people who say the framers intended it are talking nonsense"—to
which he hastily added, "and the people who say they did not
intend it are talking nonsense." In the same vein he remarked,
there is "great uncertainty."[8] A close textual and contextual examination of the evidence will not result in an improvement on
these propositions. In Corwin's book of 1938, *Court over Constitution*, his final word on the subject, he counted only five Framers
who accepted the idea of judicial review at the Convention, uncertainly included another, and added three others who previous
to the Convention had supported judicial review but who did not

reveal themselves in Philadelphia. The correct figure, by my count, for in-Convention statements showing approval of judicial review over Congress is six: James Wilson of Pennsylvania, Hugh Williamson of North Carolina, Rufus King of Massachusetts, and three who opposed the Constitution: Edmund Randolph and George Mason of Virginia, and Elbridge Gerry of Massachusetts. Even Raoul Berger's grossly inflated figure of "possibly thirteen," which included opponents of the Constitution, falls far short of a majority of the thirty-nine signers, let alone a majority of the fifty-five delegates who attended the Philadelphia Convention.[9]

Beard, to sum up charitably, saw what he wanted to see, and Corwin was not consistently sure what he saw. Wishful thinking and confusion also characterize the eccentric studies made by Louis B. Boudin,[10] William Winslow Crosskey,[11] and Raoul Berger. They destroy credibility in Beard's work, and lend little to their own. The value of their work on judicial review and the Constitutional Convention, like Corwin's final statement in 1938, is that it inspires an unredeemed skepticism. That means at the least that my figure of six, given above, may be wrong.

Raoul Berger's work, as the most detailed and by a scholar who was familiar with Corwin, Beard, Crosskey, and others, merits special consideration. In his *Congress v. The Supreme Court*, Berger counted eleven, possibly thirteen, Framers who at the Convention endorsed judicial review. His tally is unreliable because it is grossly inflated. He distorted or misunderstood what people meant, took statements out of context, and accepted the slightest evidence as conclusive proof if it suggested a favorable attitude toward judicial review. He failed to distinguish whether the eleven or thirteen favored judicial review over acts of the national government, or only over acts of the state governments, or just over government acts encroaching on the work of the judicial department. Accordingly, Berger's analysis, although fascinating and based on good research, is untrustworthy because he had such a strong propensity to see in the evidence proof of what he wanted to find.

Even a skimpy review of the remarks of Madison and Hamilton will suggest how treacherous is any generalization about their commitment to judicial review. Here, for example, is a complete sentence from a speech by Madison on July 23, 1787, wrenched out of context to give the misleading impression that Madison supported judicial review over Congress: "A law violating a constitution established by the people themselves, would be considered by the Judges as null and void."[12] The full context of the statement shows that Madison was referring to the possibility that state judges would declare unconstitutional a state act in violation of the federal Constitution. Moreover, the state act to which he was referring was an act of secession. On August 27, 1787, when the Convention considered a proposal to extend the jurisdiction of the Supreme Court to cases arising under the Constitution, Madison expressed doubt about "going too far" and advocated that jurisdiction over such cases be "limited to cases of a Judiciary Nature. The right of expounding the Constitution in cases not of this nature ought not to be given to that Department."[13] What Madison meant by "cases of Judiciary Nature" is not clear, but he seems to have meant cases involving the special province or jurisdiction of the Supreme Court. *Marbury v. Madison,* which turned on the power of the Court to issue a writ of mandamus in a case of original jurisdiction, was a case of "a Judiciary Nature."

During the ratification controversy Madison asked what remedy existed if Congress exercised unwarranted powers. In the last resort, he answered, the people provide the remedy by electing a new Congress that will annul any unconstitutional acts. Till then the remedy depended on "the executive and judiciary Departments, which are to expound and *give effect* to the legislative acts. . . ." Clearly, any remedy that gives effect to a legislative act should not be misconstrued as a judicial declaration of unconstitutionality.[14] In 1788, Madison said that neither the state nor federal constitutions provided a means of settlement for the case of a disagreement in expounding the law; the courts, usually the last to decide, might stamp a law with its final character by refusing to execute it: "This makes the Judiciary Department paramount in fact to the Legislature, which was never intended and can never be proper."[15] That opinion is not an endorsement of judicial review. On June 8, 1789, however, when advocating the Bill of Rights in the First Congress, Madison declared:

> If they are incorporated into the Constitution, independent tribunals of justice will consider themselves in a peculiar manner the guardians of these rights; they will be an impenetrable bulwark against every assumption of power in the Legislature or Executive; they will be

naturally led to resist every encroachment upon rights expressly stipulated for in the Constitution by the declaration of rights.[16]

Yet, eight days later, in a debate on the President's removal power, after acknowledging the duty of the judiciary to expound the laws and Constitution, Madison again rejected judicial review: ". . . but I beg to know upon what principle it can be contended that any one department draws from the Constitution greater powers than another, in marking out the limits of the powers of the several departments." No provision had been made, he contended, "for a particular authority to determine the limits of the constitutional division of power between the branches of government."[17] Madison believed that Congress, even just the House of Representatives, could properly construe the Constitution's meaning and that a legislative decision on a clause of doubtful meaning would become an enduring exposition of the Constitution.[18]

Charles A. Beard, incidentally, did not use either the first of the Madison quotations given above nor the one on the Bill of Rights which is the only one that would justify his assertion that Madison's belief "in judicial control over legislation is unquestionable." Madison "was in no little confusion," Beard added.[19] Edward S. Corwin was in no little confusion too. In 1914 he was certain that Madison "had espoused the doctrine of judicial review in unmistakeable terms,"[20] but in 1938 Corwin, "for good and sufficient reasons," pointedly omitted Madison's name from a list of Framers who had endorsed judicial review in 1787.[21]

Raoul Berger counted Madison as an advocate of judicial review over acts of Congress. What surprises even more is that Berger found a pattern of consistency in Madison's statements at the Convention, in *The Federalist,* and at the Virginia ratifying convention.[22] But, Berger declared, "What Madison said *in the Convention* rather than his subsequent statements seems to be controlling."[23] Berger, however, misconstrued Madison's out-of-context remark about judges holding void a law violating a constitution. Berger also found proof of his viewpoint in a statement by Madison explaining his reason for wanting to ally the judges with the executive in exercising a veto power. But the veto power has nothing to do with judicial review, and Madison had merely said that a judicial veto power would give the judicial department "an additional opportunity of defending itself agst. Legislative encroachments."[24] To

Berger the word "additional" necessarily implied a previously existing power to determine unconstitutionality, although Madison's statement simply did not deal with unconstitutionality; it did refer to a check against "unwise and unjust measures." At most the statement implied a judicial power to void acts against the judicial department, that is, encroachments by the legislature against the judiciary.

The one declaration made by Madison at the Convention in favor of judicial review does not even appear in Berger's review of Madison's Convention statements. He remarked on August 28 that judges would hold unconstitutional state violations of the ban on state ex post facto laws.[25] Without doubt Madison favored judicial review over state acts, a matter wholly different from review of congressional acts. In a federal system of government, a uniform and harmonious interpretation of national law is essential. If the Supreme Court could not exercise judicial review over the states, the ex post facto clause and all other clauses of the Constitution might have as many interpretations as there are states. Despite his support of judicial review over the states, Madison never made a comparable statement favoring review of congressional acts. He did not even make a comparable statement about the Court holding unconstitutional a congressional violation of the ban on congressional ex post facto laws.

Hamilton contributed greatly to the ratification, not to the framing, of the Constitution. His views on judicial review are significant, however, because his *Federalist* #78 is second only to Marshall's *Marbury* opinion as the classic utterance on the subject. Beard simply quotes at length from #78 to demonstrate Hamilton's commitment to judicial review over Congress. It is not irrelevant, though, to recall that Hamilton offered to the Convention a complete plan for a new constitution, no part of which remotely provided for any sort of judicial review.[26] He spoke for about five hours, revealing his innermost convictions about an ideal plan of government without suggesting judicial review, and he did not recommend it or discuss it at any other time during the Convention. In *The Federalist* #33, where he discussed the necessary and proper clause, which anti-ratificationists regarded as vesting carte blanche powers in Congress, Hamilton asked who was to judge if Congress "should overpass the just bounds of its authority." Not once in his answer did he allude to the Supreme Court. Congress in the first instance and the people in the last would judge. In the same essay Hamilton discussed the supremacy clause of Article VI, with the provision that laws made in pursuance of the Constitution shall be the supreme law of the land. Having raised the question whether laws not in its pursuance constitute the supreme law, he said only that they would deserve to be treated as "merely acts of usurpation"; he made no reference whatever to the judiciary. In *The Federalist* #16, however, where Hamilton discussed state obstruction of national law, he endorsed judicial review but only by state courts over the usurped authority of state legislatures whose enactments obstructed national authority. He did not even endorse review by the Supreme Court over state acts, let alone review by that court over acts of Congress.[27]

How then is *The Federalist* #78 to be explained? It was a response to Robert Yates's "Letters of Brutus," an anti-ratificationist series that sought to discredit the Constitution by magnifying the powers of the federal judiciary into an engine for consolidating national powers at the expense of the states.[28] *The Federalist* #78, in other words, was an attempt to quiet the fears stimulated by Yates. Turning Yates's argument against him, Hamilton tried to convince his readers that the Court's power was intended to hold Congress in check, thereby safeguarding the states against national aggrandizement. Several other advocates of the Constitution, such as Oliver Ellsworth and John Marshall, sought in the same manner to allay popular apprehensions that Congress might exceed its powers, especially in the absence of a bill of rights to protect the people.[29] Their remarks, like Hamilton's in *The Federalist* #78, seem to be evidence of shrewd political tactics rather than the Framers' intention to vest judicial review in the Supreme Court over acts of Congress.

On the other hand, the Framers were by no means all of the same mind. James Wilson, probably in the Philadelphia Convention and certainly in the Pennsylvania ratifying convention, believed in judicial review, even over acts of Congress.[30] Hamilton tailored his opinion to suit the occasion. As counsel in *Rutgers v. Waddington* (1785) he requested a court to nullify a state act, but when he proposed the constitution of his dreams, in 1787, he made no allowance for judicial review. In the next year, however, to

quash Anti-Federalist alarms about Congress posing a danger by
exceeding its powers, he composed for *The Federalist* #78 a brilliant exposition of the authority of the Supreme Court to hold
unconstitutional an act of Congress. Madison, by contrast, probably
opposed judicial review over Congress, at least during the period
of the framing and ratification of the Constitution.

Major advocates of ratification who had not been at Philadelphia, including John Marshall and Edmund Pendleton, could have
meant what they said about judicial review and could also have
found saying it as much a matter of expediency as an expression
of principled opinion. Marshall's view on judicial review certainly
fluctuated. As counsel in *Ware v. Hylton* (1796) he denied the
Supreme Court's authority to hold unconstitutional an act of a state,
in the absence of an explicit constitutional provision for judicial
review; but at the Virginia ratifying convention he advocated judicial review over Congress as a check on its illegitimate use of
power. In *Marbury v. Madison* he exercised that power, although
he soon seemed ready to abandon it for a congressional check on
the Supreme Court, in return for congressional abandonment of
impeachment of the Justices. Major opponents of ratification like
Patrick Henry and Elbridge Gerry simply were not trustworthy
witnesses; we are not likely to find original intent by looking at the
opinions of those who were against the Constitution and stood to
gain from misrepresenting and defeating it. As Jefferson said shortly
after his first inauguration as President, the Constitution should
be interpreted according to the "meaning contemplated by the
plain understanding of the people of the United States, at the time
of its adoption,—a meaning to be found in the explanations of those
who advocated it, not those who opposed it, and who opposed it
merely lest the constructions should be applied which they denounced as possible."[31]

Two provisions of the Constitution may imply an intent by the
Framers to empower the judiciary to exercise judicial review. One
is the "arising under" clause of Article III, and the other is the
supremacy clause of Article VI. Marshall relied on them when he
advanced the doctrine of judicial review. He also relied on the oath
binding judges to support the Constitution, but members of both
houses of Congress and the President take the same oath, as do
all government officials. Articles III and VI no more vest judicial

review than does the oath. Article III provides: "The judicial power shall extend to all cases, in law and equity, arising under this Constitution, the laws of the United States, and treaties. . . ." Article III does not describe that judicial power or its nature but does describe the kinds of cases the federal judiciary has jurisdiction to decide. The evidence for believing that Article III somehow vests judicial review derives not solely from its forced construction but also from remarks by three important individuals in their state ratifying conventions, although not by anyone in the Philadelphia Convention. The three ratifiers were James Wilson, who had been a member, and John Marshall and Edmund Pendleton, who had not.[32]

In the Convention the "arising under" clause, like the reference to the Constitution itself in Article III, came under consideration very late in the deliberations, and came in the absence of any concern for judicial review.[33] The argument that Framers intended judicial review arose in the context of a discussion of the veto power, which is of a political rather than a judicial nature; and, the discussions of Article III, dealing with the judiciary, were devoid of references to judicial review. But three Framers, Hamilton, Madison, and Davie, during the ratification controversy construed the "arising under" clause of Article III as a means of enforcing the Constitution against the states and not as a license to the Supreme Court to hold acts of Congress unconstitutional.[34]

Article VI provides that the Constitution, "laws made in pursuance thereof," and United States treaties shall be the supreme law of the land, binding the judges in every state, notwithstanding anything to the contrary in the state constitutions or state laws.[35] By this provision the Framers obviously intended to require state courts to enforce supreme federal law. However, nothing said at the Convention in connection with Article VI remotely shows an intent to empower the Supreme Court to hold acts of Congress unconstitutional. Indeed, as a means of fulfilling that purpose, the supremacy clause is extraordinarily inept. It does not even bind federal judges to enforce the supreme law of the land. As an empowerment of judicial review over Congress, Article VI achieves too much by indirection.

It also makes acts of Congress "in pursuance of" the Constitution part of the supreme law of the land, but, presumably, not those acts not in pursuance thereof. And, Article VI, according to this strained argument, somehow empowers the Supreme Court, which Article VI does not mention, to decide which acts are in pursuance and which are not. But Article III has already extended the judicial power of the United States to "all" cases arising under the Constitution and to all laws of the United States, whether or not in pursuance of the Constitution. The "in pursuance" interpretation therefore seems superfluous or wrong. To make sense or to empower judicial review, the clause should appear in Article III, whose subject is the judicial power of the United States.

Moreover, the argument derived from Article VI assumed that "in pursuance" means consistent with or not in conflict with. And, without doubt, as Raoul Berger proved, a few members of the state ratifying conventions understood it to mean just that.[36] But Berger did not attempt to wrest from Article VI a judicial power to hold acts of Congress unconstitutional. Moreover, "in pursuance thereof" does not necessarily mean "consistent with." Crosskey showed that its meaning, at least its main meaning, in the eighteenth century was "done in consequence of" or "in prosecution of," as Samuel Johnson's famous dictionary proved; so did the use of "in pursuance" in the Articles of Confederation.[37]

A reasonable construction of the Constitution aimed at proving judicial review is that Articles III and VI taken together authorize, by implication, a judicial power to void state acts that conflict with the supreme law of the land and, perhaps, acts encroaching on the judicial branch's conventional way of discharging its duties. These clauses must be stretched to yield such results. Their natural meaning simply does not warrant the conclusion that they vest judicial review, certainly not judicial review over Congress. If the Framers had intended judicial review, they would not likely have deliberately used so ambiguous and backhanded a formulation as the supremacy clause's binding of just state judges to laws made in pursuance of the Constitution.

The Judiciary Act of 1789, enacted at its first session by the First Congress, after originating in a Senate dominated by Framers, proves that the Framers probably intended judicial review not of acts of Congress or of treaties but of state acts. Review of the coordinate branches of the national government may be termed *national* judicial review; review of the acts of the states, the subordinate agencies within the federal system (subordinate as to the purposes and powers of the national government) may be termed *federal* judicial review. In a federal system, federal judicial review is necessary for a uniform interpretation of the supreme law of the land throughout all the states. Section 25 of the Judiciary Act explicitly provided for federal judicial review. Given the need for such uniformity, given the fact that the First Congress enacted Section 25, and given the fact that Ellsworth in conjunction with Paterson had drafted it, Section 25 undoubtedly conformed with the intent of the Philadelphia Convention. In three categories of cases the Supreme Court could review a state decision and "reverse or affirm." The three were review of state decisions that (1) voided a United States treaty or statute; or (2) upheld a state act despite a claim that it conflicted with the supreme national law; or (3) denied a right or privilege claimed under that national law. In each of these three categories, section 25 apparently authorized the Supreme Court to "reverse or affirm."[38]

Major scholars, including Beard, Corwin, Haines, Warren, and Berger, have assumed that the choice given to the Supreme Court to "reverse or affirm" constituted Congress's recognition that the Supreme Court had the legitimate authority to hold an act of Congress unconstitutional.[39] The logic is simple enough: a state court, confronted by a case that raised a question of the constitutionality of an act of Congress, might decide against its constitutionality, and the Supreme Court, on review, might affirm the state court decision, thus striking down the act of Congress. And, if the Supreme Court could approve of such a state court decision, the Supreme Court could strike down the act independently of the state court. This view of the matter, resting wholly on the face of the statute, ignores the fact that nothing in its legislative history except a remark by Gerry, who opposed the Constitution, shows an intent to empower the Supreme Court to exercise national judicial review; and the construction, however logical or grammatical, ignores the remainder of section 25, which deals with the means of enforcing Supreme Court judgments against state courts and, in particular, refers to "proceedings upon reversal." The point is that Congress did not intend that the verb "affirm" should refer to the cases described in all three categories of cases. On the basis of experience with the Articles of Confederation, the Framers and the members of the First Congress expected that states would fail to comply with their obligations under national law and might even disobey it. At Philadelphia in 1787 the Framers seriously considered proposals, first suggested in the Virginia Plan, to coerce disobedient states by the use of military power and to allow Congress to veto state laws contravening "the articles of Union." Federal judicial review proved to be the appropriate means of correcting state acts against the Constitution, and section 25 had as its object the definition of those categories of cases in which state court decisions should be reviewed by the Supreme Court in order to give effect to the supreme law of the land.

If Congress by Section 25 intended national judicial review, the legislative history of the statute would reveal that; it does not. And the statute should have revealed that intent somewhat less indirectly. Indeed, using the "reverse or affirm" language of section 25 to vest so great a power seems clumsy, inept, and even devious. But no conspiracy was afoot. If Congress had intended national judicial review, it would not have made the exercise of the most formidable judicial power dependent upon a state court's first having held an act of Congress to be unconstitutional. The same Judiciary Act created the United States district and circuit courts, which had jurisdiction of cases arising under United States statutes, yet Congress did not authorize them to hold such statutes, or any authority exercised under the United States, to be unconstitutional. Activating the greatest power of the Supreme Court only after a state rejection of national law invited that rejection and diverted the drives for strengthening the Union that resulted in the framing and ratification of the Constitution.

If the verb "affirm" applied to all three categories of cases that arise in state courts and are reviewable by the Supreme Court, the Supreme Court might affirm a judgment in which a state court held unconstitutional a United States treaty or a presidential act. Construing section 25 to empower state courts to make such decisions is simply ahistorical. It also creates a problem in construing the supremacy clause of Article VI, or, at least, a problem for those who understand that clause to imply national judicial review. The supreme law of the land consists of the Constitution, laws made in pursuance of it, and "all treaties made, or which shall be made, under the authority of the United States"—not all treaties made in pursuance of the Constitution. One does not have to believe in an illimitable treaty-making power, or a power so great that it could alter the Constitution, in order to reject the notion, insupportable by the legislative history of section 25 or by history painted on a larger canvas, that Congress authorized the state courts and the Supreme Court to hold unconstitutional a treaty negotiated with another nation by the President and confirmed by the Senate. If "affirm" did not apply to treaties, "affirm" did not necessarily apply to all parts of all three categories of cases defined in section 25. If "affirm" did not apply to treaties, it did not necessarily apply to acts of Congress.

Section 25 does not have the clarity of phrasing that it should have had with respect to the predicate of a complicated subject. But the next sentence refers, twice, only to grounds of reversal, not affirmations, and to means of executing reversals, thus showing that the statute aimed at remedying state court judgments against the supreme law of the land. The verb "affirm" could have applied to state court decisions in the second and third categories of cases, because a state court might correctly have decided that the proper law in the case before it was not governed by the supreme law of the land or because some national right or privilege claimed by a party did not exist or did not belong to the party. Affirming such state decisions remained consistent with the purpose of section 25 to enforce national law. One chooses, in the end, between the literal text, the face of the statute that defies history, or a statute that enforced national supremacy, in cases involving acts of the President, the Congress, and United States treaties, at the expense of some misplaced or wobbly phrasing in its verbs.

Nevertheless, judicial review rapidly emerged in the United States, a fact that adds retrospective significance to the few authentic precedents, even to the scattered judicial dicta, the legislative misunderstandings, and lawyers' arguments. Together they reveal, even if only in a shaky way, the growth of a novel idea destined for transformation into a major institution of American government. Federalism hastened the emergence of judicial review, supported by section 25 of the Judiciary Act. The explicit authorization of judicial review in the Judiciary Act constituted an official answer to the question left unanswered by the constitutional theory of the American Revolution: Who decides whether an act of government conflicts with the fundamental law? To be sure, the Judiciary Act recognized only federal judicial review, which the federal system promptly produced as its inevitable by-product, given the fact that the Constitution also created a judicial branch of government that had no precursor under the Articles of Confederation. Still unanswered was the question who decides whether a conflict exists between the fundamental law and an act of the new national government.

On the one hand, the creation of a tripartite system of national government contributed immeasurably to the emergence of judicial review because it established a supreme and independent national judiciary. On the other hand, every state had a judicial branch, but in no state was judicial review regarded as a usual power of courts, not even in New Hampshire and North Carolina, where in 1786 and 1787 the state courts made the first square holdings of unconstitutionality despite vehement protests; and, *Trevett v. Weeden* notwithstanding, judicial review aborted in Rhode Island for many decades.

Edward S. Corwin concluded that until the Constitutional Convention of 1787, "judicial review as a workable institution was still *in ovo*."[40] He believed that the Convention favored federal judicial review to curtail state legislative powers exercised at the expense of adequate national powers or that trenched seriously on private economic rights. According to Corwin, judicial review somehow developed as a result of "the Convention's growing comprehension of the principle of the *separation of powers* in relation *to a written constitution regarded as law*," and he assumed that judicial review of acts of Congress would develop "by the same token."[41] It did develop but not by the same token and not inevitably or necessarily as a result of the separation of powers in relation to a written constitution.

As Corwin pointed out elsewhere, the Blackstonian principle of legislative supremacy characterized American constitutional theory and practice from the time of the Declaration of Independence to the Constitutional Convention.[42] Every state constitution recognized the principle of separation of powers but as of 1789 only the constitutions of New York, Massachusetts, and New Hampshire had checks and balances that mitigated legislative supremacy. Of all the states, Massachusetts by its constitution of 1780 most perfectly endorsed and actually institutionalized a system of separation of powers with strong checks and balances, and in that respect it became a model for the Constitution of the United States. But judicial review scarcely developed in Massachusetts until well into the nineteenth century despite its written constitution, its tripartite division of governmental powers, and its provision that the state government possessed the authority to make all laws "not repugnant or contrary to the constitution."[43] During fifty years of reported decisions, the acts of the Massachusetts legislature, with the exception of two private resolves, passed the gauntlet of the state's high court unscathed.[44]

At the national level, however, the separation of powers and federalism speedily resulted in federal judicial review. The Justices of the Supreme Court serving with federal district judges as members of the circuit courts established the principle that a United States treaty has supremacy over state laws. In 1791, 1792, and 1793, the federal judges on circuit duty held unconstitutional state laws that adversely affected the interest on debts owed to British creditors and that created impediments to the recovery of debts, contrary to the Treaty of Paris of 1783 between the United States and Great Britain.[45] The full appellate bench of the Supreme Court rendered a similar decision in 1795.[46]

In 1792 Chief Justice John Jay and Justice William Cushing, on circuit in Rhode Island, held unconstitutional a Rhode Island stay law that extended by three years the time a debtor had contracted to settle with his creditor. A Providence newspaper reported that the judges held that the stay law conflicted with the Constitution under which "the individual States are prohibited from making laws which shall impair the obligation of contracts. . . ."[47] What is more remarkable than the decision of the federal court is the fact that a year earlier, in 1791, the Rhode Island legislature, which had so vehemently rejected what it took to be an exercise of judicial review in *Trevett v. Weeden*, refused to approve of a petition of a debtor who had relied on the state's notorious legal tender laws. The legislature declined to interfere because it recognized the fact that the state's ratification of the Constitution in effect had abrogated its paper-money laws, so that only specie could be tendered in payment for debts.[48] Therefore, when the federal circuit court held the Rhode Island stay law void

in 1792, the legislature docilely accepted the judgment by voting
that no individual should be exempted from arrests and attachments
for private debts for any period beyond his contracted obligations.[49]
Thus Corwin correctly concluded that federal judicial review developed especially to curtail state powers exercised at the expense
of national powers or of protected private economic rights. Almost
from their conception, the federal courts brushed away state conflicts with federal treaties and enforced constitutional limitations.

Hayburn's Case of 1792, widely regarded in its time and by
many historians as the first case in which a federal court held an
act of Congress unconstitutional, demonstrates clearly the connection between separation of powers and national judicial review. It
also added essential ingredients: party politics and the sanction of
public opinion. In 1791 Congress enacted a law requiring the federal circuit courts to rule on the validity of pension claims made
by disabled Revolutionary War veterans; the findings of the courts
were to be reviewable by the secretary of war and by Congress.
The United States Circuit Court in the District of New York, presided over by Justice James Iredell, addressed letters to President
George Washington explaining why they could not execute the
statute in their judicial capacities, but out of respect for Congress
they agreed to serve voluntarily as pension commissioners. In the
Circuit Court for the District of Pennsylvania, Justices Wilson and
Blair, both of whom had attended the Constitutional Convention,
confronted a petition from a veteran named Hayburn. They decided
not to rule on his petition, and they also explained themselves in
a letter to the President. They would have violated the Constitution
to have ruled on the petition, they wrote, because the business
directed by the act of Congress was not of a judicial nature and
did not come within the constitutional authority vested in the federal courts under Article III. They also objected that the statute
empowered officers of the legislative and executive branches to
review court actions, contrary to the principle of separation of
powers and judicial independence which that principle supported.[50]

Hayburn's Case, therefore, involved no justiciable issue. It
presented no suit, no controversy between parties, and, technically, no "case," and none of the federal courts rendered judicial
decisions under the controversial act of Congress. They reported

to the President their refusal to decide judicially. Clearly the judges thought the act was unconstitutional, and as clearly they did not hold it so; technically they decided nothing on ground that if they did, they, not Congress, would be acting unconstitutionally.

Washington transmitted the judicial letters to Congress, and Hayburn himself, the disappointed veteran, applied to Congress for relief because the federal court had "refused to take cognizance of his case." Representative Elias Boudinot, a New Jersey Federalist, briefed the House on the facts of the case and said, not inaccurately, that the judges "looked on the law . . . as an unconstitutional one." Someone, perhaps Boudinot, declared that this was the first instance in which a court of justice had declared a law of Congress to be unconstitutional. Consequently, according to the tantalizing remark of the reporter of the proceedings, the issue "produced a variety of opinions with respect to the measures to be taken on the occasion." Whether anyone censured or favored national judicial review is a matter the reporter neglected to state. We know only that a committee was appointed to investigate the situation after the House conducted a "debate" on the subject and that William Vans Murray, a Maryland Federalist, vainly urged the enactment of a law that would provide some regularized means by which the federal judges should give official notice of their refusal to act "under any law of Congress, on the ground of unconstitutionality."[51] But Murray's motion died and the committee never reported. In 1793 Congress revised the statute, providing for an altogether different procedure for the relief of pension-seeking veterans.[52]

The novelty of the issue excited public interest, introducing a force, probably the decisive one, that explains the acceptance of national judicial review: party politics. At the least, the refusal of the judges to enforce the pension act discomfited the Federalists and gratified their opponents, the emerging Democratic party led by Madison in the House. Deeply disturbed by the enactment of Hamilton's economic measures, Madison welcomed whatever might halt the "unconstitutional career of Congress." To Governor Henry Lee of Virginia he reported that the federal judges had "called the attention of the Public to Legislative fallibility" by pronouncing the pension act to be "unconstitutional." No advocate of national judicial review, Madison added that the judges "may be wrong in

the exertion of their power—but such an evidence of its existence
gives inquietude to those who do not wish congress to be con-
trouled. . . ." He added his suspicion that their "inquietude is
increased by the relation of such a power to the Bank Law in the
public contemplation, if not their own."[53] The prospect of the possibility that the act of Congress chartering the Bank of the United
States might be declared unconstitutional bottomed the restrained
glee of the Democrats.

The independence of the judicial branch alarmed the Federalists. Congressman Fisher Ames of Massachusetts "censured"
the decision "of our judges . . . as indiscreet and erroneous." What
worried Ames was the possibility that the example of the judges
would "embolden the States and their courts" to stake out claims
to power and oppose Congress.[54] Meanwhile, the anti-administra-
tion newspapers praised the federal judiciary for a precedent that,
they hoped, would lead to a judicial voiding of Hamiltonian legislation. Philip Freneau's National Gazette, the Democratic paper
in Philadelphia, established with Jefferson's blessing, wrote that
every lover of liberty found gratification in the judicial invalidation
of an act of Congress, because it promised protection of the people's
rights against legislative and executive "oppression." Moreover,
Freneau wrote, "an independent judiciary affords a just hope that
not only future encroachments will be prevented, but also that any
existing law of Congress which may be supposed to trench upon
the constitutional rights of individuals or of States, will, at convenient seasons, undergo a revision; particularly that for establishing a National Bank. . . ."[55] Another Jeffersonian newspaper in
Philadelphia informed its readers that because of "the spirited sentence passed by our Judges on an unconstitutional law," the ultrafederalists in and out of Congress "talk of nothing but impeachment!
impeachment! impeachment!"[56]

The Federalists, although apprehensive about judicial review,
did not move impeachment charges or reject national judicial review. Several important Federalists, Fisher Ames included, had
openly expressed support of national judicial review during the
debate on the President's removal power in 1789.[57] From 1789
until the Democrats controlled a majority of the national legislature, the Federalist stance on national judicial review tended to
be supportive, when not noncommittal. Federalists exuded con-

fidence that the Court would sustain any measure challenged in Congress by its opponents on constitutional grounds. The *Annals of Congress* for the 1790s do not yield a single instance in which any member of either house or of either party indicated a belief that the Court had no power to hold unconstitutional an act of Congress. Although some members, like Madison, believed that each branch of the national government could rightfully decide matters of constitutionality for itself, meaning that the judicial branch could not finally bind either the executive or the legislative branch, no one denied the authority of the Supreme Court to declare unconstitutional an act of the other branches, except, possibly, a treaty duly made by the President with the advice and consent of the Senate. During the 1790s the party of the "outs" favored national judicial review in the hope that the Court would hold against the legitimacy of acts of Congress whose passage the minority, despite their arguments against its unconstitutionality, could not prevent. A Federalist congressman, Samuel Smith of Maryland, once sarcastically remarked, "Whenever a Gentleman [of the opposition] is at a loss for an argument, the Constitution is brought forward."[58]

During the 1791 debate on the bill to charter a national bank, some opponents of the bill, arguing its unconstitutionality, acknowledged the power of the judiciary to void an unconstitutional act of Congress.[59] In 1795, during the debate on the carriage tax measure, William B. Giles of Virginia, Madison's lieutenant in the House, warned that opponents of the tax would bring a test case in the hope of securing a decision against its validity.[60] And as Charles Warren wrote in his history of Congress and the Constitution, when the Court sustained the tax measure, "Virginians and other followers of Jefferson complained of the Court for its *failure* to hold this Act of Congress invalid."[61] During the debates on the Sedition Act in 1798 and in the prosecutions under that statute, Democrats persistently invited the federal courts to declare the legislation unconstitutional if it passed. As Nathaniel Macon of North Carolina stated, he "could only hope that the Judges would exercise the power placed in them of determining the law an unconstitutional law, if upon scrutiny they find it to be so."[62] In 1801, as Federalist control of the federal government approached its end, Macon remarked that if members of his party, according to the Federalists, were "always crying out against the unconstitutionality of every Act they do not approve," the reason was that members of his party believed that the Constitution limited the government, while the other side "never questions the constitutionality of anything."[63]

The Democrats did not oppose national judicial review until 1802 when, in power, they debated the repeal of the Federalists' Judiciary Act of 1801; by 1802 the Democrats had become utterly disillusioned with the federal judiciary, which they criticized because it had become so politicized that it was not independent. To the Democrats the judiciary had consistently revealed itself to be untrustworthy, that is, in favor of the constitutionality of all Federalist sponsored measures passed by Congress and tested in the federal courts. The Justices of the Supreme Court had not only shown themselves to be excessively nationalistic and hostile to state interests; they had not only proved to be pro-English and pro-creditor; they had also proved themselves to be egregiously partisan. Presiding over the Sedition Act trials while on circuit duty, the Justices of the Supreme Court had sustained the constitutionality of that infamous act and sought guilty verdicts in every prosecution against supporters of Jefferson.[64] Federalists who previously had been lukewarm toward national judicial review or noncommittal lost themselves in an orgy of rapturous devotion to it after Jefferson came to power, when the constitutionality of the measures that might be tested before the Supreme Court would be those of the new administration.[65]

The Framers of the Constitution could not possibly have anticipated in 1787 that party politics and public opinion would become major forces in shaping the emergence of national judicial review. During the ratification controversy in 1788–1789, supporters of the Constitution who had never before advocated or endorsed judicial review found a practical political need to do so, thus reassuring voters that the Constitution provided a remedy for usurpations of power by the national government. The demand for a bill of rights during the ratification controversy also quickened the spread of national judicial review. When, in 1788, Madison wrote to Jefferson in Paris, defending the Constitution's omission of a bill of rights and expressing skepticism about the practical value of "parchment barriers,"[66] Jefferson replied that one argument in favor of a bill of rights "which has great weight with me" was "the legal check which it puts into the hands of the Judiciary." And Jefferson praised the values of an independent judiciary "kept strictly to their own department" and consisting of men not swayed by public clamors.[67] Madison echoed that idea in his imperishable speech of June 8, 1789, in the First Congress, when he urged amendments to the Constitution consisting of "the great rights of mankind." He argued that "independent tribunals of justice will consider themselves in a peculiar manner the guardians of those rights; they will be an impenetrable bulwark against the assumption of power in the legislative or executive; they will be naturally led to resist every encroachment upon rights expressly stipulated for in the constitution."[68] During the ratification controversy others, besides Jefferson, had made the same point, including Robert Yates, Samuel Adams, John Hancock, Luther Martin, Patrick Henry, and Richard Henry Lee, all Anti-Federalists.[69]

The reality of the federal system and of the need for one supreme law throughout the land speedily accounted for the emergence of federal judicial review. Similarly the realities of political partisanship had as much to do with the growth of national judicial review as did abstract theories of constitutionalism. However inadequate may be the evidence for the Framers' intendment of national judicial review, a remarkable convergence of forces and ideas constituted a pressure cooker for its speedy development. Federalism, the Bill of Rights, separation of powers, arguments appeasing public fears about usurpations of power by Congress, a *written* constitution, higher-law theories, and, above all, politics explain judicial review.

The records of Congress during its first decade show that the parties, with little consistency or adherence to principle, argued the constitutionality of bills they liked and the unconstitutionality of those they disliked. Public policies abhorrent to those out of power generated the hope that the judiciary would reaffirm constitutional limitations that aborted those policies. Thus, the Democrats as well as the Federalists, wrote Charles Warren, "were united in one sentiment at least, that under the Constitution it was the Judiciary which was finally to determine the validity of an Act of Congress." Nor did they endorse some limited form of judicial review that would operate in cases of a departmental or judiciary nature only. Democrats, for example, wanted the Supreme Court to strike down as unconstitutional the Bank Act, the Carriage Tax Act, and the Alien and Sedition Acts.[70] Warren, a conservative historian who adoringly depicted the history of judicial review in his Pulitzer Prize winning trilogy, *The Supreme Court in United States History*, summarized his study of the opinion of Congress on judicial review during the formative first decade in the following words, which hostilely designate the Democrats or followers of Jefferson and Madison as "the Anti-Federalists":

> A review of the contemporary writings and journals from 1789 to 1802 clearly demonstrates that it was frequently the Anti-Federalists who supported the right of the Court to pass upon the constitutional validity of legislation, because they felt that it was the great guarantee of protection to State and individual rights against Congressional invasion, and that only in this manner would the power of the Federal Government be curbed; they welcomed the Court as a needed check upon Congress; and it was in the writings of two strong Federalists, Zephaniah Swift of Connecticut and Richard Dobbs Spaight of North Carolina, that the chief attack was made on this form of judicial powers.[71]

And yet, the power of the Court to hold unconstitutional an act of Congress remained unused, even unasserted, by the Supreme Court. As late as 1800 Justice Chase observed that although an act of Congress in direct opposition to the prohibitions of the Constitution was void, "yet it still remains a question where the power resides to declare it void." The general opinion of the bar, he added, supported judicial review, and "some of the Judges have individually in the Circuits decided that the Supreme Court can declare an act of Congress to be unconstitutional and therefore invalid. . . ."[72] In short, the path to *Marbury v. Madison* remained wide open and it was never shut off by the people of the country after Marshall in that case decided the question mentioned by Chase.

Long acquiescence by the people and their representatives has legitimated judicial review. As Charles L. Black wrote, it was "not imposed by self-annointed fiat on an unwilling people."[73] Despite periodic and sometimes intense attacks on the Court by Congress or the White House, judicial review has survived unscathed for nearly two centuries. Even the brief and unique encounter with Congress's controlling power over the Court's appellate jurisdiction during Reconstruction was only a glancing blow.[74] Within a year or so, the Court handed down a series of decisions holding unconstitutional statutes that made greenbacks legal tender, exceeded the commerce power, and taxed state instrumentalities.[75]

Judicial review would never have flourished had the people been opposed to it. They had opposed only its exercise in particular cases, but not the power itself. The people have the sovereign power to abolish it outright or hamstring it by constitutional amendment. The President and Congress could bring the Court to heel even by ordinary legislation. The Court's membership, size, funds, staff, rules of procedure, and enforcement agencies are subject to the control of the "political" branches, which are periodically accountable to the people at the ballot box. Judicial review, in fact, exists by the tacit consent of the governed. Original intent had almost nothing to do with it.

CHAPTER SEVEN

The Contract Clause

*O*riginal intent analysis of the contract clause of Article I, section 10 (no state shall pass any law impairing the obligation of a contract), does not quite resemble the empty page describing the sex life of a steer; but, scarcity of evidence makes the inquiry hardly more productive. Almost no one cared about the contract clause either at the Constitutional Convention or during the ratification controversy. Those advocating ratification and those opposing it could not have been more apathetic than they were about the clause. That the states under the Articles of Confederation enacted a variety of laws interfering with the obligations of contracts—laws authorizing payments in kind rather than in money, stay laws, legal tender laws, installment-payment laws, laws abrogating court decisions in contract cases, and laws repealing vested rights—is as familiar a fact as is the fecklessness of the Confederation Congress.[1] Most writers condemned such laws as the ruination of commerce, the oppression of the honest, and the cause of fraud and injustice. That was probably the predominant sentiment even among those who became Anti-Federalist.[2]

Shortly after the Convention adjourned, Madison informed Jefferson in Paris that the injustice of state laws of this sort "had been so frequent and so flagrant as to alarm the most stedfast [sic] friends of Republicanism. I am persuaded I do not err in saying that the evils issuing from these sources contributed more to that uneasiness which produced the convention, and prepared the public mind for a general reform, than those which accrued to our national character and interest from the inadequacy of the Confederation to its immediate objects."[3] In short, Madison believed that the weakness of the national government constituted a less important reason for the making of the new Constitution than state interferences with private contracts. In one of his contract clause opinions, Chief Justice John Marshall recalled:

> The power of changing the relative situation of debtor and creditor, of interfering with contracts . . . had been used to such an excess by the State Legislatures as to . . . destroy all confidence between man and man. The mischief had become so great, so alarming, as not only to impair commercial intercourse and threaten the existence of credit, but to sap the morals of the people and destroy the sanctity of private faith. To guard against the continuance of the evil was an object . . . and was one of the important benefits expected from a reform of the government.[4]

Notwithstanding the widespread concern in 1787 about state laws that violated private contractual relationships, the Constitutional Convention did not even raise the subject until three weeks before it adjourned. Indeed the Convention might not have done anything about framing a contract clause but for the fact that the Confederation Congress enacted the Northwest Ordinance on July 13, 1787, about a month and a half after the Convention had begun its work. The second article of the great ordinance declared: "And, in the just preservation of rights and property, it is understood and declared that no law ought ever to be made or have force in the said territory, that shall, in any manner whatever, interfere with or affect private contracts, or engagements *bona fide*, and without fraud previously formed."[5]

A month and a half later, on August 28, 1787, the Constitutional Convention speedily agreed to prohibit the states from coining money, emitting bills of credit, or making anything but gold and silver a legal tender in payment of debts. Rufus King of Massachusetts then proposed the inclusion in the Constitution of "the words used in the Ordinance of Congress establishing new states, a prohibition on the States to interfere in private contracts."[6] Strangely enough, the proposal evoked so little interest that it failed, although it touched off a concern that led to the adoption of the ex post facto clause.

Gouverneur Morris, responding first to King's motion, said, "This would be going too far." Explaining that many laws could affect contracts, he advocated that the best policy would be to let the judicial power of the United States provide protection in cases within federal jurisdiction, and otherwise allow the majority to rule within the states.[7] Roger Sherman, too, opposed the motion because the prohibitions on state power, which the Convention had already adopted, would suffice. James Wilson, however, said that he favored King's motion, and Madison wavered. The contract clause might be useful, Madison thought, despite its "inconveniences," but granting to Congress a power to veto state laws would be far better. George Mason then opposed the motion, because occasions might arise that required a state to interfere with contracts. Wilson replied, "The answer to these objections is that *retrospective* interferences only are to be prohibited." Rutledge then moved as a substitute for King's motion that the states could pass neither "bills of attainder [n]or ex post facto laws," and the Convention adopted Rutledge's motion by a vote of 7–3.[8]

And so died the proposed contract clause—until the Committee of Style made its report on September 12. By that late date the Convention was winding up its work, and the delegates were eager to return home. They had lost their patience for controversy, despite the existence of unresolved substantive issues, and with slight changes they followed the recommendations of the Committee of Style. For inexplicable reasons, that committee had included in the prohibitions on the states a clause against state impairment of the obligation of contracts.[9] The committee's version covered far more than the contract clause in the Northwest Ordinance, which applied only to private contracts made in good faith and without fraud. Morris, who had opposed King's motion, headed the Committee of Style, which included King himself, Madison, Hamilton, and William S. Johnson of Connecticut. No member of the committee had evinced concern for a contract clause broader than the one proposed by King. We know nothing about the deliberations of the Committee of Style, nor do we know whether it meant to recommend a clause broader than King's or merely meant a terser version of it. In view of the Convention's defeat of King's motion, the committee did not likely intend more than he. In any case, the Convention on September 12 hastily refused to consider a belated proposal for adding a Bill of Rights,[10] and two days later reached Article I, section 10. The delegates, voting by states, unanimously rejected a proposal to strike the ex post facto clause, rejected a declaration on behalf of liberty of the press, accepted the contract clause without discussion or vote, ignored Elbridge Gerry's proposal to add a similar clause limiting the power of Congress, and summarily ended its deliberation on the matter.[11] Thus, original intent analysis of the contract clause shows the Convention's monumental indifference, ill-considered judgment, and inconsistent approval, without deliberation of a substantive change by the Committee of *Style*.

Expectations to the contrary, the contract clause inspired neither passionate onslaughts from spokesmen for debtors' relief nor vigorous defenses from its proponents. Luther Martin of Maryland, a member of the Convention who opposed the Constitution, informed his state legislature in a widely circulated pamphlet that he had voted against depriving the states of the power, sometimes necessary during times of economic crisis, to close the courts, authorize installment payments, or pass bankruptcy acts.[12] Whether Martin thought the clause had merely a retroactive operation or also a prospective one, he did not say; nor did he say whether he believed that the clause applied only to contracts between private individuals or also to public contracts—those to which a state was a party. In any event, no one in Maryland seemed much concerned about the clause.

In Connecticut, which was just as indifferent, two Framers, Roger Sherman and Oliver Ellsworth, reported that the Convention had believed that the security of commerce required that no state should impair the obligation of a contract "by *ex post facto* laws," thus revealing their understanding that the clause prohibited only certain kinds of retrospective legislation.[13] The language of the clause itself, however, did not rule out its prospective application, as Chief Justice Marshall noted in his only dissenting opinion in a constitutional case.[14] Moreover, the prospective application of the clause would have made sense in view of the fact that the ex post facto clause very likely was meant to apply to noncriminal matters; that would have made the contract clause superfluous unless it was meant to have a prospective application. But the evidence for that surmise is nearly nonexistent.

In North Carolina Archibald Maclaine, arguing for ratification, quoted Article I, section 10, and observed, "Now, sir, this has no retrospective views. It looks to futurity."[15] Surely the prohibitions in section 10 against bills of credit and against making anything but specie a legal tender had a prospective operation. The "futurity" of the contract clause may have been so self-evident as to require no comment, and none was made but by Maclaine. No one in North Carolina, or elsewhere, supported or opposed Maclaine's view. Whether the contract clause operated only as to contracts that preexisted such state legislation as might be made, or whether it also applied to any contracts entered into after the enactment of such legislation was simply not an issue in the Convention or in the states during the ratification controversy. On the other hand, the Convention, one might infer, had adopted James Wilson's view when he answered those who had opposed King's motion for a contract clause. Wilson said it would operate retrospectively only, and at that point the Convention voted to ban state ex post facto laws. Whether or not such laws extended to noncriminal matters, they had only a retroactive operation.

In Virginia, Patrick Henry, who always imagined the worst, argued that depreciated continental dollars would have to be paid off at face value, if the Constitution were ratified, because "a law called *ex post facto*, and impairing the obligation of contracts" could not be passed. Citizens would not be able to seek relief from taxes needed to pay off speculators who held paper money, "because of that clause. The expression includes public contracts as well as private contracts between individuals."[16] Ordinary rules of construction supported Henry's reading of the clause; nothing in it excludes contracts to which a state is a party, any more than anything in it excludes its prospective operation. Nevertheless, Edmund Randolph, as one who had attended the Convention, answered that the contract clause had nothing to do with the value of continental dollars, first because Congress, rather than the states, had contracted to pay the debt, and second because the clause addressed private contracts.[17] Much the same thing happened at the ratifying convention in North Carolina. James Galloway, opposing ratification, darkly warned that the contract clause would enrich speculators in public securities, which, although depreciated in value, would have to be redeemed in specie at face value.[18] William F. Davie, who had signed the Constitution, spoke for the Convention in reply: "The clause refers merely to contracts between individuals."[19]

Davie and Randolph correctly construed the clause, according to the preponderance of the evidence, which is slight. The Northwest Ordinance, the model for the clause, explicitly referred to private contracts, as had King when he moved the inclusion of the contract clause. In New York, Hamilton in *The Federalist #7*, spoke only about state laws "in violation of private contracts," and in #44, Madison agreed when he spoke of restoring confidence between citizens and endorsed the Convention's "bulwark in favor of personal security and private rights."[20] "Brutus," a New Yorker who confronted "Publius," disapproved of the Constitution but applauded the contract clause because it prevented "fraud in the debtor against his creditor."[21] In Georgia, a citizen of Savannah signing himself as "Tullius," although a supporter of the Constitution, wanted the state legislature speedily to enact an installment-payment law to relieve debtors, before the Constitution went into operation. "A Planter," Edward Telfair, who had supported the Constitution in Georgia's ratifying convention, recommended a different remedy, because, he said, the contract clause would have a retroactive effect. Both Georgians construed the clause only in terms of private contracts.[22] In South Carolina, Charles Pinckney, a Framer, construed the clause the same way, as did David Ramsay, the historian, who supported ratification in his state's ratifying convention.[23] In Pennsylvania, Peletiah Webster, an extraordinary publicist, also wrote about the contract clause, in a pamphlet that circulated in New York and Massachusetts as well as in Pennsylvania, as if it applied only to private contracts.[24]

Private contracts, however, have had a petty business in the constitutional history of the contract clause. Original intent analysis of the clause is a subject of arcane antiquarianism, because it had been so irrelevant to the development of constitutional law. If the Supreme Court had construed the clause as its Framers and ratifiers understood it, it would never have become the most significant of all constitutional provisions until displaced by the due process clause at the close of the nineteenth century. Probably no more than half a dozen major contract clause cases have involved private contracts.[25] Benjamin F. Wright, in his book on the history of the clause, found that in its first 150 years the Supreme Court held state acts unconstitutional on contract clause grounds in 134 cases, of which only fourteen involved statutes that "regulated the debtor–creditor relation in a fashion at least similar to the stay, installment, and commodity payments acts of the years preceding 1787." Indeed, Wright declared, "Had the Supreme Court adhered to the intentions of the Framers the contract clause would never have attained a position of great legal or economic importance."[26] Because of a rampant judicial activism, the clause became the basis for a startling expansion of judicial review; it became the repository of the judicial doctrine of vested rights and of judicially inferred higher-law limitations on legislative power; and it became the link between constitutionalism and capitalism.[27] In 1914, when Brooks Adams wrote, "The capitalist, as I infer, regards the constitutional form of government which exists in the United States, as a convenient method of obtaining his own way against a majority," the contract clause still vied with the due process clause to prove his thesis.[28]

The primacy of the contract clause during the first century of our constitutional history derives from the fact that in *Fletcher v. Peck*,[29] the first contract clause case decided by the Supreme Court, Chief Justice Marshall for the Court held that the clause extended to public contracts. With scarcely an exception, major contract clause doctrines emerged in cases involving a state as a party to the contract. In the formative cases, for example, the Marshall Court held that a state grant of lands is a contract,[30] a state grant of tax exemption or of tax preference is a contract,[31] and a state grant of a corporate charter is a contract.[32]

The precursor for the Marshall Court's contract clause opinions was a 1795 opinion by Justice William Paterson in the 1795 case of *Van Horne's Lessee v. Dorrance*. That was a well-reported circuit court case in the district of Pennsylvania, memorable because of Paterson's extraordinary charge to the jury, instructing them that a state act had unconstitutionally violated property rights.[33] The opinion of Paterson, a major Framer, reflected a judicial activism running wild. That opinion, too, may be read as a road map of the direction that constitutional law would take as a law of judicially implied limitations on legislation adversely affecting property rights. In lucid nonlegal language, Paterson spelled out judicial presuppositions and constitutional principles that were to become orthodox for well over a century. In discussing "What is a Constitution?" and analyzing the legislature's authority to pass its act divesting land titles, Paterson joined together the doctrines of judicial review and vested rights. Prefiguring *Fletcher v. Peck* (1810) as well as the basic principle of *Marbury v. Madison* (1803), Paterson invoked both a higher-law concept and the contract clause against the statute (no state shall impair the obligation of a contract).

Having declared that "it will be the duty of the Court to adhere to the constitution, and to declare the act null and void" if the act exceeds the legislature's authority, Paterson discoursed on the relationship between fundamental law and the rights of property. He found such rights inalienable, their preservation a primary object of "the social compact." Property, when vested, must be secure. For the government to take property without providing a recompense in value would be "an outrage," a "dangerous" display of unlimited authority, "a monster in legislation" that would "shock all mankind." To divest a citizen of his freehold even with compensation was a "despotic" power to be exercised only in "cases of the first necessity." The reason was that the Constitution "encircles, and renders [a vested right] an holy thing. . . . It is a right not *ex gratia* from the legislature, but *ex debito* from the constitution. It is sacred. . . ."

Paterson informed the jury that courts must hold unconstitutional any legislative encroachments on sacred property rights even in the absence of a written constitutional limitation on legislative powers. He relied on "reason, justice, and moral rectitude," "the principles of social alliance in every free government," and the "letter and spirit of the constitution." The letter, in this instance, turned out to be the clause in Article I, section 10, of the Constitution, prohibiting a state law impairing the obligation of a contract. Contrary to the Framers' intent,[34] Paterson assumed, first, that the contract clause extended to contracts to which the state was a party; second, that a state act recognizing a property interest of the original claimant was a contract within the protection of the contract clause; and third, that the divestiture of the titles, even with compensation, violated the clause. Paterson's exposition, widely circulated in pamphlet form, was a textbook exposition of social compact theory, constitutionalism, higher-law limitations, judicial review, courts as bulwarks of property rights, and the contract clause.

Not original intent but the rules of construction allowed the broad view of the contract clause, and nothing except an arrogant activism justified Paterson's reliance on extraconstitutional or higher-law considerations and his reading his prejudices into the "spirit of the constitution" as a basis for judicial review. The same Justice, like the other members of the Supreme Court, found nothing un-constitutional in the Sedition Act of 1798, despite the original intent not to empower Congress to act on the subject of the press and despite the explicit prohibition of the First Amendment.

In crucial respects Marshall's transforming interpretation of the contract clause in *Fletcher v. Peck* in 1810 was a replay of Paterson's opinion. Marshall relied on the higher law as well as the contract clause, as had Paterson. The Chief Justice also relied on rules of construction to achieve his trailblazing contract clause doctrines; that is, he disdained original intent. In *Fletcher,* for example, he observed that the Constitution uses the "general term contract" without distinguishing between executed and executory contracts, though a state law can impair the obligation of only an executory contract. That Marshall included executed contracts within the protection of the clause is not surprising in view of his finding that a continuing obligation exists, on the part of the grantor, not to reassert a right to the land that it had granted.[35] Nevertheless, to rely on the contract clause as the basis for holding unconstitu-tional the state act repealing a land grant was so extraordinary that even Marshall recoiled with uncertainty.[36] Although the case pos-sessed no criminal dimension, he flirted with the thought that the repealer somehow "had the effect" of an ex post facto law and even of a bill of attainder. And in the end he vaguely declared that the state "was restrained either by general principles which are com-mon to our free institutions" or by unspecified "particular provi-sions" of the Constitution. On such flimsy, uncertain reasoning the Court transmogrified the contract clause.

Justice William Johnson, a South Carolinian whom Jefferson had appointed to the Court at his first opportunity, in 1804, con-curred separately. He refused to ground his opinion on the contract clause because he found no continuing obligation that the state act could have violated. But he did not hesitate, he said, "to declare that a State does not possess the power of revoking its own grants. But I do it on a general principle, on the reason and nature of things: a principle which will impose laws even on the deity."[37] Johnson's opinion, then, constituted a specimen of the most unbridled judicial activism, characterized by his imposing his moral concepts on the spirit of the Constitution as the basis for invalidating an act of government. No textual basis existed for Johnson's opinion, nor for part of Marshall's opinion for the Court. And where a textual basis did exist for Marshall's opinion, be it contract clause, attainder clause, or ex post facto clause, his judicial activism seemed bounded only by comparison with Johnson's.

Within two years of *Fletcher* the Court lost its doubts about the inclusion of public contracts and extended the clause even to such contracts that limited the sovereign power of taxation.[38] In the great *Dartmouth College* case of 1819, when the question was whether corporate charters came within the protection of the contract clause, Marshall daringly conceded that original intent did not matter much. He spoke to the issue of original intent because counsel for the college had argued, accurately:

> The mischiefs actually existing at the time the constitution was established, and which were intended to be remedied by this prohibitory clause, will show the nature of the contracts contemplated by its authors. It was the inviolability of private contracts, and private rights acquired under them, which was intended to be protected; and not contracts which are, in their nature, matters of civil police, nor grants by a state of power, and even property to individuals, in trust to be administered for purposes merely public.[39]

In reply, Marshall declared:

> It is more than possible that the preservation of rights of this description was not particularly in the view of the framers of the constitution when the clause under consideration was introduced into the instrument. . . . It is not enough to say that this particular case was not in the mind of the convention when the article was framed, nor of the American people when it was adopted. It is necessary to go farther, and to say that, had this particular case been suggested, the language would have been so varied, as to exclude it, or would have been made a special exception.

He concluded with a hard rule of construction: when the words of the Constitution are general, the case comes within it unless the result is so "absurd, or mischievous, or repugnant" that the Court must make an exception.[40] Obviously, rules of construction, which are as malleable as beeswax, merely rationalize a preexisting viewpoint rather than point the way of reaching a result, especially if the result sought by the Court cannot possibly have a basis in original intent. Judicial subjectivity, not the dictates of the Constitution's text, explains the Court's constitutional law, whether it was construing the text as in *Chisholm* and *Calder,* or holding unconstitutional an act of Congress as in *Marbury v. Madison,*[41] or voiding a state act as in *Fletcher.*

One among the many lessons disclosed by *Marbury* is that the unconstitutionality of an act may be the product of a frenetic judicial imagination or of an unrestrained judicial activism. Ellsworth and the First Congress had not framed section 13 of the Judiciary Act unconstitutionally, and no one had thought so until Marshall loosened his fantasies to find a way out of a political dilemma. In the 1800 case in which Justice Samuel Chase said that the issue of national judicial review remained unresolved, Justice Bushrod Washington declared that the presumption must always be in favor of the validity of a law "if the contrary is not clearly demonstrated," and Justice Paterson insisted that "to authorize this court to pronounce any law void, it must be a clear and unequivocal breach of the constitution, not a doubtful and argumentative implication."[42] And James Iredell had previously observed that although any act against the Constitution is void, "the authority to declare it void is of a delicate and awful nature." Consequently the Court "will never resort to that authority, but in a clear and urgent case."[43] Yet all members of the Court joined Marshall's *Marbury* opinion, as unclear a case as could be invented.

From its earliest years the Court has behaved irresponsibly, acting without regard to original intent or indifferent to it, except perhaps where that intent buttressed the preferred result. And from the earliest years the Court has not felt bound by the Constitution. The Justices have freely gone beyond the text to the wild, blue heavenly yonder in search of extraconstitutional doctrines that would do the job when the Constitution seemed inadequate to the task. Witness Justice Paterson calling on the higher law and the spirit of the Constitution in *Van Horne's Lessee v. Dorrance;* witness Marshall doing the same in *Fletcher v. Peck,* where Johnson went even a step further by cutting himself off from the Constitution altogether. Jefferson complained that Justices twisted the Constitution into whatever shape they wished; he did not mention that his own appointee stood in the judicial vanguard, holding aloft the standards of judicial creativity, judicial legislation, and judicial subjectivity.

Calder v. Bull (1798) held aloft the same standards, even apart from the Court's questionable interpretation of the ex post facto clauses. Justice Chase, discoursing on the "very nature of our free Republican governments," explained that a legislative act that conflicted with "the great first principles of the social compact, cannot be considered a rightful exercise of legislative authority." Chase then paraded a few imaginary horribles that he condemned as "against all reason and justice," and, to boot, against the "genius, the nature, and the spirit" of our system of government.[44] Justice Iredell made the correct rejoinder in his opinion in the same case, when he said that the Court should not hold any act unconstitutional merely because "it is, in their judgment, contrary to the principles of natural justice." His reason was the right one: "The ideas of natural justice are regulated by no fixed standard; the ablest and the purest men have differed upon the subject. . . ."[45]

Nevertheless, the Supreme Court in a case of 1815 held unconstitutional a state act on grounds of natural justice or higher law. That case involved an act made in the aftermath of disestablishment of church and state in Virginia. The state confiscated certain glebe lands belonging to the Episcopal Church and sold them, using the proceeds for charity. The lands in question having been granted as gifts to the church by private persons, no contract existed and therefore no contract clause issue existed either. Justice Joseph Story for a unanimous Court held the confiscation act void, offering as the sole grounds: ". . . we think ourselves standing upon the principles of natural justice, upon the fundamental laws of every free government, upon the spirit and letter of the constitution. . . ."[46] Story did not mention which letter, and that, of course, is the point. The Court had transcended the Constitution, imposing upon constitutional law some standard of morality that had no textual underpinning. Judicial subjectivity can have no expression

more extreme. For that very reason and because a text-based doctrine is more usable as a precedent, the Court speedily read its
natural law presuppositions into the contract clause as the basis for
holding void state measures that offended the Court's sense of
propriety, at least when property rights were at issue.

Nowadays it is fashionable among conservatives to blame the
Warren Court or the Burger Court for decisions one dislikes and
condemns as activist or result-oriented. Judicial activism and result-
oriented jurisprudence have a long history, so far as judicial precedents of the Supreme Court are concerned. Those who praise the
conservatism of the Court of an earlier time and criticize the modern Court employ a double standard or do not know what they are
talking about. From its earliest years, from *Chisholm* through the
great constitutional cases of the Marshall Court, the Supreme Court
played fast and loose with the Constitution, reaching the results
preferred by the policy choices of the majority of the Court.

CHAPTER EIGHT

Why We Have
the Bill of Rights

The Bill of Rights consists of the first ten amendments to the Constitution. The traditions that gave shape and substance to the Bill of Rights had English roots, but a unique American experience colored that shape and substance. "We began with freedom," as Ralph Waldo Emerson wrote in "The Fortune of the Republic."[1] The first charter of Virginia (1606) contained a provision that the colonists and their descendants "shall have and enjoy all Liberties, Franchises, and Immunities . . . as if they had been abiding and born, within this our Realm of England. . . ." Later charters of Virginia contained similar clauses, which extended to legal rights of land tenure and inheritance, trial by jury, and little else. But the vague language was repeated in numerous other charters for colonies from New England to the South, and Americans construed it handsomely. As the Continental Congress declared, Americans believed that they were entitled to all the rights of Englishmen, their constitutional system, and their common law.[2] American experience with and interpretations of charters eased the way to written constitutions of fundamental law that contained bills of rights.

Freedom was mainly the product of New World conditions, the English legal inheritance, and skipping a feudal stage. Because of America's postfeudal beginnings, it was unencumbered by oppressions associated with an *ancien régime*—a rigid class system dominated by a reactionary and hereditary aristocracy, arbitrary government by despotic kings, and a single established church extirpating dissent. "America was opened," Emerson wrote, "after the feudal mischief was spent, and so the people made a good start. We began well. No inquisition here, no kings, no nobles, no dominant church. Here heresy has lost its terrors."[3] Americans were the freest people, therefore the first colonials to rebel. A free people, as Edmund Burke said, can sniff tyranny in a far-off breeze— even if nonexistent. American "radicals" actually believed that the Stamp Act reduced Americans to slavery. They resorted to arms in 1775, the Continental Congress believed, not to establish new liberties but to defend old ones.[4] In fact, they did establish many new liberties but convinced themselves that those liberties were old. That was an English custom: marching forward into the future facing backward to the past, while adapting old law to changing values. Thus Magna Carta had come to mean indictment by grand jury, trial by jury, and a cluster of related rights to the criminally accused, and Englishmen believed, or made believe, that it was ever so. That habit crossed the Atlantic.

So did the hyperbolic style of expression by a free people outraged by injustice. Thus, James Madison exclaimed that the "diabolical Hell conceived principle of persecution rages," because some Baptist ministers were jailed briefly for unlicensed preaching.[5] By European standards, however, persecution hardly existed in America, not even in the seventeenth century, except on a local and sporadic basis. America never experienced anything like the Inquisition, the fires of Smithfield, the St. Bartholomew's Day Massacre, or the deaths of over 5,000 nonconformist ministers in the jails of Restoration England. Draconian colonial statutes existed but were rarely enforced. Broad libertarian practices were the rule, not the exception.

On any comparative basis civil liberty flourished in America, a fact that intensified the notoriety of exceptional abridgments, such as the hanging of four Quakers in Massachusetts in 1659 or the 1735 prosecution of John Peter Zenger for seditious libel.[6] Although a stunted concept of the meaning and scope of freedom of the press existed in America until the Jeffersonian reaction to the Sedition Act of 1798, an extraordinary degree of freedom of the press existed in practice in America, as it did in England.[7] And nowhere did freedom of religion prosper as in America.

The predominance of the social compact theory in American thought reflected a condition of freedom, and like the experience with charters, contributed to the belief in written bills of rights. The social compact theory hypothesized a prepolitical state of nature in which people were governed only by the laws of nature, free of human restraints. From the premise that man was born free, the deduction followed that he came into the world with God-given or natural rights. Born without the restraint of human laws, he had a right to possess liberty and to work for his own property. Born naked and stationless, he had a right to equality. Born with certain instincts and needs, he had a right to satisfy them—a right to the pursuit of happiness.[8] These natural rights, as John Dickinson declared in 1766, "are created in us by the decrees of Providence, which establish the laws of our nature. They are born with us; exist with us; and cannot be taken from us by any human power without taking our lives."[9] When people left the state of nature and compacted for government, the need to secure their rights motivated them. A half-century before John Locke's *Second Treatise on Government*, Thomas Hooker of Connecticut expounded the social compact theory.[10] Over a period of a century and a half, America became accustomed to the idea that government existed by consent of the governed, that the people created the government, that they did so by a written compact, that the compact reserved their natural rights, and that it constituted a fundamental law to which the government was subordinate. Constitutionalism, or the theory of limited government, was in part an outgrowth of the social compact.

In America, political theory and law, as well as religion, taught that government was limited. But Americans took their views on such matters from a highly selective and romanticized image of seventeenth-century England, and they perpetuated it in America even as that England changed. Seventeenth-century England was the England of the great struggle for constitutional liberty by the common law courts and Puritan parliaments against Stuart kings. Seventeenth-century England was the England of Edward Coke, John Lilburne, and John Locke. It was an England in which religion, law, and politics converged to produce limited monarchy and, ironically, parliamentary supremacy. To Americans, however, Parliament had irrevocably limited itself by reaffirmations of Magna Carta and passage of the Petition of Right of 1628, the Habeas Corpus Act of 1679, the Bill of Rights of 1689, and the Toleration Act of 1689. Americans learned that a free people are those who live under a government so constitutionally checked and controlled that its powers must be reasonably exercised without abridging individual rights.[11]

In fact, Americans had progressed far beyond the English in securing their rights. The English constitutional documents limited only the crown and protected few rights. The Petition of Right reconfirmed Magna Carta's provision that no freeman could be imprisoned but by lawful judgment of his peers or "by the law of the land"; it also reconfirmed a 1354 version of the great charter which first used the phrase "by due process of law" instead of "by the law of the land." The Petition invigorated the liberty of the subject by condemning the military trial of civilians as well as imprisonment without cause or on mere executive authority. Other sections provided that no one could be taxed without Parliament's consent or be imprisoned or forced to incriminate himself by having to answer for refusing an exaction not authorized by Parliament.[12] The Habeas Corpus Act safeguarded personal liberty, without which other liberties cannot be exercised. The act secured an old right for the first time by making the writ of habeas corpus an effective remedy for illegal imprisonment. The only loophole in the act, the possibility of excessive bail, was plugged by the Bill of Rights ten years later. That enactment, its exalted name notwithstanding, had a narrow range of protections, including the freedoms of petition and assembly, free speech for members of Parliament, and, in language closely followed by the American Eighth Amendment, bans on excessive bail, excessive fines, and cruel and unusual punishments. As an antecedent of the American Bill of Rights, the English one was a skimpy affair, though important as a symbol of the rule of law and of fundamental law.[13] The Toleration Act was actually "A Bill of Indulgence," exempting most nonconformists from the penalties of persecutory laws of the Restoration, leaving those laws in force but inapplicable to persons qualifying for indulgence. England maintained an establishment of the Anglican Church, merely tolerating the existence of non-Anglican trinitarians, who were still obligated to pay tithes and endure many civil disabilities.[14]

In America, England promoted Anglicanism in New York and in the southern colonies but wisely prevented its establishments in America from obstructing religious peace, because immigrants were an economic asset, regardless of religion. England granted charters to colonial proprietors on a nondiscriminatory basis—to Cecil Calvert, a Catholic, for Maryland; to Roger Williams, a Baptist, for Rhode Island; and to William Penn, a Quaker, for Pennsylvania and Delaware. The promise of life in America drew people from all of Western Christendom and exposed them to a greater degree of liberty and religious differences than previously known. James Madison, whose practical achievements in the cause of freedom of religion were unsurpassed, said that it arose from "that multiplicity of sects which pervades America."[15]

But a principled commitment to religious liberty came first in some colonies. Maryland's Toleration Act of 1649 was far more liberal than England's Toleration Act of forty years later. Until 1776 only Rhode Island, Pennsylvania, Delaware, and New Jersey guaranteed fuller freedom than Maryland by its act of 1649, which was the first to use the phrase, "the free exercise of religion," later embodied in the First Amendment. The act also symbolized the extraordinary fact that for most of the seventeeth century in Maryland, Catholics and Protestants openly worshipped as they chose and lived in peace, if not amity. The act applied to all trinitarian Christians but punished others; it also penalized the reproachful use of divisive terms such as heretic, puritan, papist, anabaptist, or antinomian.[16] The Maryland act was a statute, but the Charter of Rhode Island, which remained its constitution until 1842, made the guarantee of religious liberty a part of the fundamental law. It secured for all inhabitants "the free exercise and enjoyment of their civil and religious rights" by providing that every peaceable person might "freely and fullye hav and enjoye his and theire owne judgements and consciences, in matters of religious concernments. . . ."[17] Thus, the principle that the state has no legitimate authority over religion was institutionalized in some American colonies, including those under Quaker influence.

Massachusetts, the colony that least respected private judgment in religious matters, was the first to safeguard many other rights. Its Body of Liberties, adopted in 1641, was meant to limit the magistrates in whom all power had been concentrated. As John Winthrop observed, the objective was to frame limitations "in remarkable resemblance to Magna Charta, which . . . should be received for fundamental laws." The Body of Liberties was, in effect, a comprehensive bill of rights. In comparison, the later English Bill of Rights was rudimentary and the liberties of Engishmen few in number. Among the guarantees first protected in writing by Massachusetts were freedom of assembly and of speech (at least in public meetings), the equal protection of the laws, just compensation for private property taken for public use, freedom to emigrate, the right to bail, the right to employ counsel, trial b jury in civil cases, the right to challenge jurors, restrictions on imprisonment for debt, speedy trial, no double jeopardy, and no cruel or excessive punishments. In addition to traditional liberties, such as trial by jury in criminal cases, and Magna Carta's principle of the rule of law, the Body of Liberties also protected some rights of women: widows received a portion of the estate of husbands even if cut off by will; physical punishment of women by their husbands was prohibited; and daughters received a right to inherit if parents died intestate and without male heirs. Servants, slaves, foreigners, and even animals received humane consideration.[18]

The Body of Liberties was a statute but the Charter or Fundamental Laws of West New Jersey (1677), which was probably the work of William Penn, functioned as a written constitution because it began with the provision that the "common law or fundamental rights" of the colony should be "the foundation of government, which is not to be altered by the Legislative authority. . . ."[19] The liberty documents of England limited only the crown, not the legislature. The principle of limiting all governmental authority was written into Penn's Frame of Government for Pennsylvania in 1682, a document which extensively enumerated rights that were to last "for ever," including for the first time a ban on excessive fines, a guarantee of indictment by grand jury in capital cases, delivery to the accused of a copy of the charges against him, and assurance that a jury's verdict of not guilty was final. Penn's charter carefully particularized the rights of the criminally accused.[20] Americans were learning that charters of liberty must assure fair and regularized procedures, without which there could be no liberty. Vicious and ad hoc procedures had been used to victimize religious and political minorities. One's home could not be his castle or his property be his own, nor could his right to express his opinion or to worship his God be secure, if he could be searched, arrested, tried, and imprisoned in some arbitrary way.

The case of Sir Thomas Lawrence in 1693 illustrates. Secretary of Maryland, a judge, and a member of the governor's council, Lawrence broke politically with the government and denounced it. Summoned by the council for examination, he was accused of having a treasonable letter. On his refusal to produce it, the council had him searched against his protests, found the letter, convicted him of unspecified crimes, deprived him of his offices, and jailed him without bail. Lawrence appealed his conviction to the Assembly on the grounds of having been forced to incriminate himself by an illegal search, of having been convicted without trial by jury without knowing the charges against him or the names of his accusers, and of having been denied bail and habeas corpus "which is the great security of the lives & Libertyes of every English Subject." The Assembly vindicated English liberties by supporting Lawrence on every point, found all the proceedings against him illegal, and freed and restored him.[21]

The American colonial experience, climaxed by the controversy with England leading to the Revolution, honed American sensitivity to the need for written constitutions that protected rights grounded in "the immutable laws of nature" as well as in the British constitution and colonial charters. To the English, the Americans had the wrong ideas about the British constitution. English and American ideas did differ radically, because the Americans had a novel concept of "constitution." The word signified to them a supreme law creating government, limiting it, unalterable by it, and paramount to it. A town orator of Boston announced that Independence offered the people a chance of reclaiming rights "attendant upon the original state of nature, with the opportunity of establishing a government for ourselves. . . ." "To secure these rights," Jefferson declared, "governments are instituted among men."[22]

The Virginia constitution of 1776, the first permanent state constitution, began with a Declaration of Rights that restrained all branches of government. As the first such document it contained many constitutional "firsts," such as the statements that "all men" are equally free and have inherent rights which cannot be divested even by compact; that among these rights are the enjoyment of life, liberty, property, and the pursuit of happiness; and that all power derives from the people who retain a right to change the government if it fails to secure its objectives. The declaration recognized "the free exercise of religion" and freedom of the press, and included clauses that were precursors, sometimes in rudimentary form, of the Fourth through the Eighth Amendments of the Constitution of the United States. Inexplicably, the convention voted down a ban on bills of attainder and on ex post facto laws and omitted the freedoms of speech, assembly, and petition, the right to the writ of habeas corpus, grand jury proceedings, the right to compulsory process to secure evidence in one's own behalf, the right to counsel, and freedom from double jeopardy. Although religious liberty was guaranteed, the ban on an establishment of religion awaited enactment of the Virginia Statute for Religious Freedom in 1786.[23]

Pennsylvania's bill of rights was more comprehensive than Virginia's. Pennsylvania omitted the right to bail and bans on excessive fines and cruel punishments, but added freedom of speech, assembly, and petition; separated church and state; recognized the right of conscientious objection; protected the right to counsel in all criminal cases; secured the right to keep arms; and guaranteed the right to travel or emigrate—all constitutional "firsts." Pennsylvania also recognized that "the people have a right to hold themselves, their houses, papers, and possessions free from search and seizure," in contrast to Virginia's prohibition of general warrants.[24] Delaware's bill of rights was the first to ban ex post facto laws and the quartering of troops in homes during peacetime; Maryland added a prohibition on bills of attainder.[25] Vermont's contribution was the first to outlaw slavery and the first constitutional provision for just compensation in cases of eminent domain.[26] Connecticut and Rhode Island retained their charters as their constitutions, while New Jersey, Georgia, New York, and South Carolina protected some rights in their constitutional texts but had no separate bills of rights and no noteworthy innovations.

Massachusetts, the last of the original states to adopt a constitution (1780), contributed the most to the concept of a bill of

rights. It had the most comprehensive bill of rights and was the
first to secure citizens against "all unreasonable searches and seizures," the formulation closest to that of the later Fourth Amendment. Massachusetts was also the first state to replace the weak
"ought not" found in all previous bills of rights (e.g., "the liberty
of the press ought not be restrained") with the injunction "shall
not," which Madison later followed. Most important, Massachusetts
was the first state that framed its fundamental law by a specially
elected constitutional convention, which exercised no legislative
authority (and submitted the document to the towns for popular
ratification).[27] In every other state before 1780, legislatures, sometimes calling themselves conventions, wrote the fundamental law
and promulgated it. Theoretically, a bill of rights framed by a
legislature could be changed by ordinary legislation, a fact deplored
by Jefferson as a capital defect in Virginia's model.[28] The procedure
first adopted by Massachusetts was copied by New Hampshire
when it revised its constitution in 1784, with the first guarantee
against double jeopardy; thereafter the Massachusetts procedure
prevailed.[29]

The framing of the first constitutions with bills of rights ranks
among America's foremost achievements, the more remarkable because they were unprecedented and they were realized during
wartime. Nevertheless, the phrasing of various rights and the inclusion or omission of particular ones in any given state constitution
seems careless. Why so few states protected the rights against
double jeopardy and bills of attainder, and why so many omitted
habeas corpus and freedom of speech, among others, is inexplicable
except in terms of shoddy craftsmanship. Even so, the existence
of eight state bills of rights with constitutional status invigorated
Anti-Federalist arguments that a bill of rights should be appended
to the Constitution of 1787. The state ratifying conventions produced about seventy-five recommendations, providing Madison
with an invaluable list from which to create the proposals that he
submitted to Congress.[30]

Congress itself supplied a final precedent, the Northwest Ordinance of 1787, which planned the evolution of territories to state-
hood. The ordinance was the first federal document to contain a
bill of rights. To extend "the fundamental principles of civil and
religious liberty," Congress included articles that were to remain

"forever . . . unalterable," guaranteeing to territorial inhabitants habeas corpus, trial by jury, representative government, judicial proceedings "according to the course of the common law," and, as an additional assurance of due process, an encapsulated provision from Magna Carta protecting liberty and property from being deprived except "by the judgment of . . . peers, or the law of the land." The ordinance also included articles protecting the right to bail except in capital cases, enjoined that all fines should be "moderate," and prohibited "cruel or unusual punishment." Another article provided a federal precedent for still another provision of the Bill of Rights: just compensation for property taken for public purposes. The ordinance also protected the sanctity of private contracts, outlawed sex discrimination in land ownership, banned slavery, and provided for religious liberty. Thus the federal as well as colonial and state experience with written instruments to safeguard rights enhanced the claim that a bill of rights should bridle the new national government.[31]

The Bill of Rights did just that: it was a bill of restraints on the United States. Congress submitted those restraining amendments to the states for ratification on September 25, 1789, and the requisite number of state legislatures ratified them by December 15, 1791. The triumph of individual liberty against government power is one of our history's noblest themes, epitomized by the Bill of Rights. Yet James Madison, justly remembered as the "father" of the Bill of Rights, privately referred on August 19, 1789, to the "nauseous project of amendments." He had proposed the Bill of Rights, in part, because "It will kill the opposition everywhere . . ."—a suggestion that party politics saturated the making of the first ten amendments.[32] Thomas Jefferson, who must have been profoundly gratified by the ratification of the amendments, which he had urged, was the secretary of state who officially notified the governors of the states that ratification was an accomplished fact: he had the honor, he wrote, of enclosing copies of an act "concerning certain fisheries," another establishing the post office, and "the ratifications by three fourths of the . . . States, of certain articles in addition and amendment of the Constitution. . . ."[33] The history of the Bill of Rights from its rejection by the Philadelphia Constitutional Convention to its belated ratification is not as passionless, because the omission of a bill of rights in the original

Constitution had been the most important obstacle in the way of its adoption by the states.

The omission of a bill of rights was a deliberate act of the Constitutional Convention. The Convention's work was almost done when it received from the Committee of Style copies of the proposed Constitution and the letter by which the Convention would submit it to Congress. The major task that remained was to adopt, engross, and sign the finished document. The weary delegates, after a hot summer's work in Philadelphia, were eager to return home. At that point, on September 12, 1787, George Mason of Virginia remarked that he "wished the plan had been prefaced by a Bill of Rights," because it would "give great quiet" to the people. Mason thought that with the aid of state bills of rights as models, "a bill might be prepared in a few hours." He made no stirring speech for civil liberties in general or any rights in particular. He did not even argue the need for a bill of rights or move the adoption of one, though he offered to second a motion if one were made. Elbridge Gerry of Massachusetts then moved for a committee to prepare a bill of rights, and Mason seconded the motion. Roger Sherman of Connecticut observed that the rights of the people should be secured if necessary, but because the Constitution did not repeal the state bills of rights, the Convention need not do anything. Without further debate, the delegates, voting by states, defeated the motion 10–0.[34] Two days later, after the states unanimously defeated a motion by Mason to delete from the Constitution a ban on ex post facto laws by Congress, Charles Pinckney of South Carolina, seconded by Gerry, moved to insert a declaration "that the liberty of the Press should be inviolably observed." Sherman laconically replied, "It is unnecessary. The power of Congress does not extend to the Press," and the motion lost 7–4.[35] Three days later the Convention adjourned. Two months later James Wilson of Pennsylvania would report to his state ratifying convention that "so little account was the idea [of a bill of rights] that it passed off in a short conversation, without introducing a formal debate or assuming the shape of a motion."[36]

In the Congress of the Confederation, Richard Henry Lee of Virginia moved that a bill of rights, which he had adapted from his own state's constitution, be added to the Constitution. Lee was less interested in the adoption of a bill of rights than in defeating the Constitution. Under the Articles of Confederation amendments recommended by Congress required ratification by all the state legislatures, not just nine state ratifying conventions. Lee's motion was defeated,[37] but it showed that, from the start of the ratification controversy, the omission of a bill of rights became an Anti-Federalist mace with which to smash the Constitution. Its opponents sought to prevent ratification and exaggerated the bill of rights issue because it was one with which they could enlist public support. Their prime loyalty belonged to states' rights, not civil rights.

Mason, the author of the celebrated Virginia Declaration of Rights of 1776, soon wrote his influential "Objections to the Constitution," which began, "There is no Declaration of Rights. . . ." The sincerity of Mason's desire for a bill of rights is beyond question, but he had many other reasons for opposing the Constitution. Almost two weeks before he raised the issue of a bill of rights on September 12, he had declared "that he would sooner chop off his right hand than put it to the Constitution as it now stands." A bill of rights might protect individuals against the national government, but it would not protect the states. He believed that the new government would diminish state powers and by the exercise of its commerce power could "ruin" the southern states; the control of commerce by a mere majority vote of Congress was, to Mason, "an insuperable objection."[38] But the lack of a bill of rights proved to be the most powerful argument against ratification of the Constitution in the Anti-Federalist armory.

Why did the Constitutional Convention omit a bill of rights? No delegate opposed one in principle. As George Washington informed the Marquis de Lafayette, "there was not a member of the Convention, I believe, who had the least objection to what is contended for by the advocates for a Bill of Rights. . . ." All the Framers were civil libertarians as well as experienced politicians who had the confidence of their constituents and the state legislatures that elected them. Even the foremost opponents of ratification praised the makeup of the Convention. Mason himself, for example, wrote that "America has certainly upon this occasion drawn forth her first characters . . . of the purest intentions," and Patrick Henry, who led the Anti-Federalists in Virginia, conceded that the states had trusted the "object of revising the Confederation to the greatest, the best, and most enlightened of our citizens." Their liberality of spirit is suggested by the fact that many—Protestants all and including the entire Virginia delegation—made a point of attending divine service at St. Mary's Chapel in Philadelphia. As Washington recorded in his diary, "Went to the Romish church to high mass." How could such an "assembly of demigods," as Jefferson called them, neglect the liberties of the people?[39]

On July 26 the Convention had adjourned until August 6 to permit a Committee of Detail to frame a "constitution conformable to the Resolutions passed by the Convention." The committee introduced a number of significant changes, such as the explicit enumeration of the powers of Congress, and without recommendations from the Convention, decided on a preamble. Edmund Randolph left a fragmentary record of the committee's decision that the preamble did not seem a proper place for a philosophic statement of the ends of government because "we are not working on the natural rights of men not yet gathered into society" but upon rights "modified by society and interwoven with what we call . . . the rights of states."[40] According to American revolutionary theory, the natural rights to which Randolph referred were possessed by individuals in the state of nature, which existed before people voluntarily contracted with each other to establish a government whose purpose was to secure their rights. In the state of nature, when only the law of nature governed, the theory posited that—as the first section of the Virginia Declaration of Rights stated—" all men are by nature equally free and independent, and have certain inherent rights, of which, when they enter into a state of society, they cannot, by any compact, deprive or divest their posterity; namely, the enjoyment of life and liberty, with the means of acquiring and possessing property, and pursuing and obtaining happiness and safety."[41] Because the adoption of the state constitutions ended the state of nature, there was no need to enumerate the rights reserved to the people—or so the Framers of the Constitution reasoned.

On the other hand, they recognized that the existence of organized society and government required the affirmation of certain rights that did not exist in the state of nature but that served to protect natural rights. Trial by jury, for example, was unknown in the state of nature but was necessary for the protection of one's life, liberty, and property. Accordingly, the Framers recognized a

class of rights "modified by society," just as they recognized that
the legitimate powers of government that did not belong to the
central government of the Union could be called "the rights of the
states." The principal task of the Convention was to provide for an
effective national government by redistributing the powers of government. Thus the Committee of Detail, when enumerating the
powers of Congress, began with the power to tax and the power
to regulate commerce among the states and with foreign nations
(the two great powers which the Articles of Confederation had
withheld from Congress) and ended with an omnibus clause that
granted implied powers: "And to make all laws that shall be necessary and proper for carrying into execution the foregoing powers,
and all other powers vested, by this Constitution, in the government of the United States, or in any department thereof." That
"necessary and proper" clause was the most formidable in the array
of national powers, therefore the most controversial, and the one
most responsible, later, for the demand for a bill of rights to ensure
that the United States did not violate the rights of the people or
of the states.

The Committee of Detail, again on its own initiative, recommended some rights ("modified by society"), among them trial
by jury in criminal cases, a tight definition of treason to prevent
improper convictions, a ban on titles of nobility (a way of guaranteeing against a privileged class), freedom of speech and debate
for members of the legislature, and a guarantee that the citizens
of each state should have the same privileges and immunities as
citizens in other states. In addition, the committee introduced the
clause guaranteeing to each state a republican form of government.
In the minds of the Framers, many provisions of the Constitution
had a libertarian character: the election of public officials, the representative system, the separation of powers among three branches
of government, and the requirement that revenue and appropriation measures originate in the House of Representatives—a protection of the natural right to property and a bar against taxation
without representation. During the controversy over the ratification of the Constitution, when the omission of a bill of rights was
the major issue, many Framers argued, as did Hamilton in *The
Federalist* #84, "that the Constitution is itself, in every rational
sense, and to every useful purpose, a Bill of Rights."[42]

All the rights recommended by the Committee of Detail eventually found their way into the Constitution, but Charles Pinckney believed that the committee had neglected several others that also deserved constitutional recognition. On August 20 he recommended "sundry propositions," including a guarantee of the writ of habeas corpus, which protected citizens from arbitrary arrest; an injunction that the liberty of the press should be "inviolably preserved"; a ban on maintaining an army in time of peace except with the consent of Congress; an explicit subordination of the military to the civil power; a prohibition on the quartering of troops in private homes during peacetime; and a ban on religious tests as a qualification for any United States office.[43]

None of these provisions secured what theoreticians regarded as natural rights. The freedoms of speech and conscience were natural rights, but the liberty of the press was distinguishable as a right that did not exist in the state of nature. If liberty of the press was a natural right in eighteenth-century thought, the convention acted consistently when voting that its protection was unnecessary. The ban on religious tests, though protecting the right of conscience, was another example of what Randolph had called a right "modified by society," not preexisting it. Significantly, Pinckney had not recommended a protection of freedom of religion or of speech. Without debate or consideration the Convention referred his proposals to the Committee of Detail, but it made no recommendations on any of them.

On the floor of the Convention, Gerry moved that Congress should be denied the power to pass bills of attainder and ex post facto laws. The motion passed with hardly any discussion. Bills of attainder were legislative declarations of the guilt of individuals and legislative imposition of criminal penalties, without the usual judicial proceedings. No instrument of the criminal law was more dreaded or violative of the fair procedures associated with trial by jury than a bill of attainder, the most expeditious way of condemning political opponents. Ex post facto laws in the field of criminal law were nearly as notorious and as unfair, for they were legislative acts that made criminal any conduct that was not a crime at the time committed, or acts that retroactively increased the penalty for a crime or changed the rules of evidence in order to obtain a conviction. With little debate the Convention also placed prohibitions on the power of the states to enact bills of attainder and ex post facto laws. Some delegates, including George Mason, opposed the ban on the latter because they did not wish to limit the power of the states to enact retroactive legislation in civil cases, and they insisted, against the supposed authority of Sir William Blackstone's *Commentaries,* that ex post facto laws included civil legislation as well as criminal. The Supreme Court in 1798 would settle the matter in favor of the Blackstonian interpretation.[44]

Bills of attainder and ex post facto laws, being legislative enactments, came into existence after the people had compacted to form a government. Banning such enactments, therefore, constituted a means for the protection of natural rights, but the bans did not protect natural rights as such. The same may be said of protecting the cherished writ of habeas corpus as a device for ensuring the personal liberty of an individual wrongfully imprisoned. After the Convention unanimously adopted the Committee of Detail's recommendation for a clause on trial by jury in criminal cases, Pinckney urged the Convention to secure the benefit of the writ as well, and by a vote of 7–3 a habeas corpus clause was adopted.[45]

Pinckney also moved a prohibition on religious tests, which the Convention summarily adopted by unanimous vote. In so doing the Convention demonstrated a rare liberality of spirit, because all of the Framers except those who represented New York and Virginia came from states whose constitutions discriminated against some religious denominations by imposing some religious test as a qualification for public office. In Pennsylvania, for example, a state whose constitution contained the broadest guarantee of religious freedom and a provision that no man acknowledging God should be deprived of any civil right on account of his religion, the oath of office required an acknowledgment of the divine inspiration of the New Testament. A Jew from Philadelphia petitioned the Constitutional Convention not to frame a similar oath of office, which would impose a civil disability upon him. Unitarians, Deists, and Catholics suffered from various religious disabilities in many states. By prohibiting religious tests, the Convention showed a greater regard for religious liberty than most states; yet the Convention did not protect religious liberty itself.[46]

Thus, all the protections written into the Constitution were means of vindicating natural rights, but no natural rights were constitutionally protected. The overwhelming majority of the Convention believed, as Sherman succinctly declared, "It is unnecessary." Why was it unnecessary, given the fact that the Convention recommended a new and powerful national government that could operate directly on individuals? The Framers believed that the national government could exercise only enumerated powers or powers necessary to carry out those enumerated, and no provision of the Constitution authorized the government to act on any natural rights. A bill of rights would restrict national powers, but, Hamilton declared, such a bill would be "dangerous" as well as unnecessary, because it "would contain various exceptions to powers not granted; and, on this very account, would afford a colorable pretext to claim more than were granted. For why declare that things shall not be done which there is no power to do? Why, for instance, should it be said that the liberty of the press shall not be restrained, when no power is given by which restrictions may be imposed?"[47]

Hamilton expressed a standard Federalist position, echoing other Framers and advocates of ratification. Excluding a bill of rights from the Constitution was fundamental to the constitutional theory of the Framers. James Wilson, whose influence at the Convention had been second only to that of Madison, led the ratificationist forces in Pennsylvania and several times sought to explain the omission of a bill of rights. The people of the states, he declared, had vested in their governments all powers and rights "which they did not in explicit terms reserve," but the case was different as to a federal government whose authority rested on positive grants of power expressed in the Constitution. For the federal government, "the reverse of the proposition prevails, and everything which is not given, is reserved" to the people or the states. That distinction, Wilson argued, answered those who believed that the omission of a bill of rights was a defect. Its inclusion would have been "absurd," because a bill of rights stipulated the reserved rights of the people, while the function of the Constitution was to provide for the existence of the federal government rather than enumerate rights not divested. Like Hamilton and other Federalists, Wilson believed that a formal declaration on freedom of the press or religion, over which Congress had no powers whatsoever, could "imply" that some degree of power had been granted because of the attempt to define its extent. Wilson also insisted on the impossibility of enumerating and reserving all the rights of the people. "A bill of rights annexed to a constitution," he added, "is an enumeration of the powers reserved. If we attempt an enumeration, everything that is not enumerated is presumed to be given. The consequence is, that an imperfect enumeration would throw all implied powers into the scale of the government; and the rights of the people would be rendered incomplete."[48]

Civil liberties, the supporters of the Constitution believed, faced real dangers from the possibility of repressive state action, but that was a matter to be guarded against by state bills of rights. They also argued, inconsistently, that some states had no bills of rights but were as free as those with bills of rights. They were as free because personal liberty, to Federalist theoreticians, did not depend on "parchment provisions," which Hamilton called inadequate in "a struggle with public necessity"; it depended, rather, on public opinion, an extended republic, a pluralistic society of competing interests, and a free and limited government structured to prevent any interest from becoming an overbearing majority.[49]

The fact that six states had no bills of rights and that none had a comprehensive list of guarantees provided the supporters of ratification with the argument, made by Wilson among others, that an imperfect bill of rights was worse than none at all because the omission of some rights might justify their infringement by implying an unintended grant of government power. The record was not reassuring: the states had very imperfect bills of rights, which proved to be ineffective when confronted by "public necessity," and the state governments did in fact abridge rights that had not been explicitly reserved.

Virginia's Declaration of Rights, for example, did not ban bills of attainder. In 1778 the Virginia assembly adopted a bill of attainder and outlawry, drafted by Jefferson at the instigation of Governor Patrick Henry, against a reputed cutthroat Tory, one Josiah Philips, and some fifty unnamed "associates." By legislative enactment they were condemned for treason and murder, and on failure to surrender were subject to being killed by anyone. At the Virginia ratifying convention, Edmund Randolph, irked beyond endurance by Henry's assaults on the Constitution as dangerous to personal liberties, recalled with "horror" the "shocking" attainder. When Henry defended the attainder, John Marshall, who supported ratification without a bill of rights, declared, "Can we pretend to the enjoyment of political freedom or security, when we are told that a man has been, by an act of Assembly, struck out of existence without a trial by jury, without examination, without being confronted with his accusers and witnesses, without the benefits of the law of the land?"[50]

The Framers of the Constitution tended to be skeptical about the value of "parchment barriers" against "overbearing majorities," as Madison said. He had seen repeated violations of bill of rights in every state. Experience proved the "inefficacy of a bill of rights to those occasions when its control is most needed," he said.[51] In Virginia, despite an explicit protection of the rights of conscience, the legislature had favored an establishment of religion, which was averted only because Madison turned the tide of opinion against the bill.[52] As realists, the Framers believed that constitutional protections of rights meant little during times of popular hysteria; any member of the Constitutional Convention could have cited examples of gross abridgments of civil liberties in states that had bills of rights.

Virginia's bill was imperfect not just because it lacked a ban on bills of attainder. The much vaunted Declaration of Rights of Virginia also omitted the freedoms of speech, assembly, and petition; the right to the writ of habeas corpus; the right to grand jury proceedings; the right to counsel; separation of church and state; and freedom from double jeopardy and from ex post facto laws. The rights omitted were as numerous and important as those included. Twelve states, including Vermont, had framed constitutions, and the only right secured by all was trial by jury in criminal cases. Although each one also protected religious liberty, five either permitted or provided for establishments of religion. Two states passed over a free press guarantee. Four neglected to ban excessive fines, excessive bail, compulsory self-incrimination, and general search warrants. Five ignored protections for the rights of assembly, petition, counsel, and trial by jury in civil cases. Seven omitted a prohibition of ex post facto laws. Nine failed to provide for grand jury proceedings, and nine failed to condemn bills of attainder. Ten said nothing about freedom of speech, while eleven were silent on double jeopardy. Whether omissions implied a power to violate, they seemed, in Federalist minds, to raise dangers that could be prevented by avoiding an unnecessary problem entirely: omit a bill of rights when forming a federal government of limited powers.

That the Framers of the Constitution actually believed their own arguments to justify the omission of a bill of rights is difficult to credit. Some of the points they made were patently absurd, like the insistence that the inclusion of a bill of rights would be dangerous, and on historical grounds, unsuitable. The last point most commonly turned up in the claim that bills of rights were appropriate in England but not in America. Magna Carta, the Petition of Right of 1628, and the Bill of Rights of 1689 had been grants wrested from kings to secure royal assent to certain liberties, and therefore had "no application to constitutions . . . founded upon the power of the people" who surrendered nothing and retained everything. That argument, made in *The Federalist* #84 and by leading ratificationists as sophisticated as Wilson and Oliver Ellsworth, was so porous that it could persuade no one. Excepting Rhode Island and Connecticut, the two corporate colonies that retained their charters (with all royal references deleted), eleven states had framed written constitutions during the Revolution, and seven drew up bills of rights; even the four without such bills inserted in their constitutions provisions normally found in a bill of rights.

To imply that bills of rights were un-American or unnecessary merely because in America the people were the source of all power was unhistorical. Over a period of a century and a half America had become accustomed to the idea that government existed by consent of the governed, that people created government, that they did it by written compact, that the compact constituted fundamental law, that the government must be subject to such limitations as are necessary for the security of the rights of the people, and usually, that the reserved rights of the people were enumerated in bills of rights. Counting Vermont (an independent republic from 1777 until its admission to the Union in 1791), eight states had bills of rights—notwithstanding any opinion that such bills properly belonged only in a compact between a king and his subjects. The dominant theory in the United States from the time of the Revolution was that the fundamental law limited all branches of the government, not just the crown as in England, where the great liberty documents did not limit the legislative power.

When Randolph for the Committee of Detail alluded to the fact that "we are not working on the natural rights of men not yet gathered into society," he referred to the framing of the state constitutions. The constitution of James Wilson's state began with an elaborate preamble whose first words established the proposition that "all government ought to be instituted . . . to enable the individuals who compose [the commonwealth] to enjoy their natural rights . . . ," and whose preamble was followed by as comprehensive a "Declaration of the Rights of the Inhabitants" as existed in any state. Yet Wilson repeatedly informed Pennsylvania's ratifying convention that rights and liberties could be claimed only in a contract between king and subjects, not when "the fee simple of freedom and government is declared to be in the people."[53] Governor Randolph merely exaggerated at the Virginia ratifying convention when he claimed that the Virginia Declaration of Rights "has never secured us against any danger; it has been repeatedly disregarded and violated." But Randolph's rhetoric became unpardonable when he declared that although a bill of rights made sense in England to limit the king's prerogative, "Our situation is radically different from that of the people of England. What have we to do with bills of rights? . . . A bill of rights, therefore, accurately speaking, is quite useless, if not dangerous to a republic."[54] At the Constitutional Convention, Randolph had been able to distinguish natural rights from some rights modified by society.

That supporters of the Constitution could ask, "What have we to do with a bill of rights?" suggests that they had made a colossal error of judgment, which they compounded by refusing to admit it. Their single-minded purpose of creating an effective national government had exhausted their energies and good sense, and when they found themselves on the defensive, accused of threatening the liberties of the people, their frayed nerves led them into indefensible positions. Any Anti-Federalist could have answered Randolph's question, Wilson's speeches, or Hamilton's *Federalist* #84, and many capably did so without resorting to Patrick Henry's grating hysteria. "Centinel," who answered Wilson in a Philadelphia newspaper, declared that the explanation for the omission of a bill of rights "is an insult on the understanding of the people."[55]

Abroad, two wise Americans serving their country in diplomatic missions, coolly appraised the proposed Constitution without the obligation of having to support a party line. After receiving a copy of the document in London, John Adams wrote a short letter to Jefferson in Paris. The Constitution seemed "admirably calculated to preserve the Union," Adams wrote, and he hoped it would be ratified with amendments adopted later. "What think you," he asked, "of a Declaration of Rights? Should not such a Thing have preceded the Model?"[56] Jefferson, in his first letter to Madison on the subject of the Constitution, began with praise but ended with what he did not like: "First the omission of a bill of rights. . . ." After listing rights he thought deserved special protection, starting with freedom of religion and of the press, Jefferson dismissed as campaign rhetoric Wilson's justification for the omission of a bill of rights and concluded: "Let me add that a bill of rights is what the people are entitled to against every government on earth, general or particular, and what no just government should refuse, or rest on inference."[57]

Adams and Jefferson in Europe were much closer to popular opinion than the Framers of the Constitution who had worked secretly for almost four months and, with their supporters, became locked into a position that defied logic and experience. During the ratification controversy, some Federalists argued that the Constitution protected basic rights, exposing them to the reply that they had omitted the liberty of the press, religious freedom, security against general warrants, trial by jury in civil cases, and other basic rights. If the Framers intended to protect only the rights arising from the existence of society and government and unknown in a state of nature, they were inconsistent. First, they protected only some of the nonnatural rights; the first ten amendments are crowded with such rights which the Framers neglected. Second, any reader of John Locke would realize that the clause in Article I, section 10, prohibiting the states from impairing the obligation of contracts, protected a natural right. At the close of Chapter 2 of *Second Treatise of Government*, Locke wrote that the "promises and bargains" between two men on a desert island or between a Swiss and an Indian in the woods of America "are binding to them, though they are perfectly in a State of Nature to one another. . . ."[58] Oddly, the Convention had failed to adopt the contract clause when it was proposed; the Committee of Style inserted it into the Constitution, and the Convention, without discussion, agreed to the clause in its closing days. The inclusion of one natural right raises the question of why all others were excluded. The contract clause, of course, operates only against state infringement, and raises the additional question of why the Convention failed to include a comparable prohibition on the United States.

Natural rights, in accordance with American theory and experience, required protection in any government made by compact. At the Convention, Madison declared that the delegates had assembled to frame "a compact by which an authority was created paramount to the parties, and making laws for the government of them."[59] Some of the states, when formally ratifying the Constitution, considered themselves to be "entering into an explicit and solemn compact," as Massachusetts declared.[60] During the ratification controversy, publicists on both sides referred to the Constitution as a compact. Chief Justice John Jay, who had been one of the authors of *The Federalist*, observed in *Chisholm v. Georgia* (1793) that "the Constitution of the United States is . . . a compact made by the people of the United States in order to govern themselves."[61]

The new compact created a government whose powers seemed intimidating. Article VI established the Constitution, laws made in its pursuance, and treaties of the United States to be the supreme law of the land, anything in the state constitutions to the contrary notwithstanding. That struck many Anti-Federalists as dangerous, because they thought it superseded their state bills of rights and authorized laws repugnant to personal rights.[62] Most Anti-Federalists believed that enumerated powers could be abused at the expense of fundamental liberties. Congress's power to tax, for example, might be aimed at the press and was thus, in the words of Richard Henry Lee, "a power to destroy or restrain the freedom of it."[63] Others feared that taxes might be exacted from the people for the support of a religious denomination. According to Patrick Henry, tax collectors unrestrained by a ban on general warrants might invade homes "and search, ransack, and measure, every thing you eat, drink, and wear."[64]

The necessary and proper clause particularly enraged advocates of a bill of rights. They saw that clause as the source of undefined and unlimited powers to aggrandize the national government and victimize the people, unless, as "An Old Whig" declared, "we had a bill of rights to which we might appeal."[65] "A Democratic Federalist" wrote: "I lay it down as a general rule that wherever the powers of government extend to the lives, the persons, and properties of the subject, all their rights ought to be clearly and expressly defined, otherwise they have but a poor security for their liberties."[66] Henry warned that Congress might "extort a confession by the use of torture," in order to convict a violator of federal law.[67] Numerous opponents of ratification contended that Congress could define as crimes the violation of any laws it might legitimately enact, and in the absence of a bill of rights, accused persons might be deprived of the rights to counsel, to indictment, to cross-examine witnesses against them, to produce evidence in their own behalf, to be free from compulsory self-incrimination, to be protected against double jeopardy or excessive bail, to be exempt from excessive fines or cruel and unusual punishments, and to enjoy other rights traditionally belonging to accused persons. Such an argument was, invariably, advanced as one among many refuting the Federalist claim that a bill of rights was unnecessary.

If a bill of rights was unnecessary, Anti-Federalists asked, why did the Constitution protect some rights? The protection of some rights opened the Federalists to devastating rebuttal. They claimed that because no bill of rights could be complete, the omission of any particular right might imply a power to abridge it as unworthy of respect by the government. The argument that to include some rights would exclude all others boomeranged. The protection of trial by jury in criminal cases, the bans on religious tests, ex post facto laws, and bills of attainder, the narrow definition of treason, and the provision for the writ of habeas corpus, by the Federalists' own reasoning was turned against them. Robert Whitehall, answering Wilson on the floor of the Pennsylvania ratifying convention, noted that the writ of habeas corpus and trial by jury had been expressly reserved, and in vain he called on Wilson to reconcile the reservation with his "favorite proposition." "For, if there was danger in the attempt to enumerate the liberties of the people," Whitehall explained, "lest it should prove imperfect and defective, how happens it, that in the instances I have mentioned, that danger has been incurred? Have the people no other rights worth their attention, or is it to be inferred, agreeable to the maxim of our opponents, that every other right is abandoned?" Stipulating a right, he concluded, destroyed the "argument of danger."[68] Surely, Anti-Federalists said, their opponents might think of some rights in addition to those protected. The ban on religious tests could have reminded them of freedom of religion. Did not its omission, by their reasoning, necessarily mean that the government could attack freedom of religion?

Patrick Henry cleverly observed that the "fair implication" of the Federalist argument against a bill of rights was that the government could do anything not forbidden by the Constitution. Because the provision on the writ of habeas corpus allowed its suspension when required for the public safety, Henry reasoned, "It results clearly that, if it had not said so, they could suspend it in all cases whatsoever. It reverses the position of the friends of this Constitution, that every thing is retained which is not given up; for, instead of this, every thing is given up which is not expressly reserved."[69] In his influential *Letters of a Federal Farmer*, Richard Henry Lee observed that a clause of the Constitution prohibited Congress from granting titles of nobility. If the clause had been omitted, he wondered whether Congress would have the power to grant such titles, and he concluded that it would not under any provision of the Constitution. "Why then by a negative clause, restrain congress from doing what it had no power to do? This clause, then, must have no meaning, or imply, that were it omitted, congress would have the power in question . . . on the principle that congress possess the powers not expressly reserved." Lee objected to leaving the rights of the people to "logical inferences," because Federalist principles led to the implication that all the rights not mentioned in the Constitution were intended to be relinquished.[70]

Far from being dangerous, a bill of rights, as "A Federal Republican" stated in answer to Wilson, "could do no harm, but might do much good."[71] Lee, discoursing on the good it might do, observed that a bill of rights would assist popular "education," because it taught "truths" upon which freedom depends and which the people must believe as "sacred."[72] James Winthrop of Massachusetts, writing as "Agrippa," explained another positive value of a bill of rights. It "serves to secure the minority against the usurpations and tyranny of the majority." History, he wrote, proved the "prevalence of a disposition to use power wantonly. It [a bill of rights] is therefore as necessary to defend an individual against the majority in a republick as against the king in a monarchy."[73]

In sum, the usually masterful politicians who had dominated the Convention had blundered by botching constitutional theory and making a serious political error. Their arguments justifying the omission of a bill of rights were impolitic and unconvincing. Mason's point that a bill of rights would quiet the fears of the people was unanswerable. Alienating him and the many who agreed with him was bad politics and handed to the opposition a stirring cause around which they could muster sentiment against ratification. The single issue that united Anti-Federalists throughout the country was the lack of a bill of rights. No rational argument—and the lack of a bill of rights created an intensely emotional issue because people believed that their liberties were at stake—could possibly allay the fears generated by demagogues like Henry and principled opponents of ratification like Mason. Washington believed that even Mason's "Objections" were meant "to alarm the people."[74] And, when Anti-Federalists in New York demanded a bill of rights, Hamilton alleged, "It is the plan of men of this stamp to frighten the people with ideal bugbears, in order to mould them to their own purposes. The unceasing cry of these designing croakers is, My friends, your liberty is invaded!"[75] The Anti-Federalists capitalized on the Federalist blunder, hoping to defeat the Constitution or get a second convention that would revise it in order to hamstring the national government.

In Pennsylvania, the second state to ratify, the minority demanded a comprehensive bill of rights similar to that in their state constitution. Massachusetts, the sixth state to ratify, was the first to do so with recommended amendments. Only two of the recommended amendments, dealing with jury trial in civil suits and grand jury indictment, belonged in a bill of rights. Supporters of the Constitution in Massachusetts had withdrawn a proposed bill of rights on the supposition that Anti-Federalists would use it as proof that the Constitution endangered liberty. Maryland would also have recommended a bill of rights, but the Federalist majority jettisoned it when the Anti-Federalists tried to insert curbs on national powers to tax and regulate commerce. Nevertheless, Federalists grudgingly accepted ratification with recommended amendments to ward off conditional ratification or the defeat of the Constitution. New Hampshire, whose approval as the ninth state made ratification an accomplished fact, urged the adoption of a partial bill of rights after the new government went into operation. Virginia and New York, whose ratification was politically indispensable, followed suit with more comprehensive recommendations. North Carolina was the fourth state to ratify with a bill of rights among its recommendations. But the states also recommended crippling restrictions on delegated powers.[76]

Thus, the Constitution was ratified only because crucial states, where ratification had been in doubt, were willing to accept the promise of a bill of rights in the form of subsequent amendments to the Constitution. State recommendations for amendments, including those of the Pennsylvania minority, received nationwide publicity, adding to the clamor for a bill of rights. Every right that became part of the first ten amendments was included in state recommendations except the clause in the Fifth Amendment requiring just compensation for private property taken for public use.

James Madison was one of the Federalists who finally realized that statecraft and political expediency dictated a switch in position. At the Virginia ratifying convention in June of 1788 Madison had upheld the usual Federalist arguments for the omission of a bill of rights, but finally voted to recommend such a bill in order to avoid previous amendments. He later conceded that the Constitution would have been defeated without a pledge from its supporters to back subsequent amendments. In Virginia, Madison's own political position deteriorated because he had opposed a bill of rights. The Anti-Federalists, who controlled the state legislature, elected two of their own, Richard Henry Lee and William Grayson, as the state's first United States senators. Madison faced a tough contest for election to the House of Representatives, and he feared that the Anti-Federalists might succeed in their call for a second constitutional convention. He needed to clarify his position on a bill of rights.[77]

Although Madison had periodically apprised Jefferson, in Paris, on ratification developments, he had not answered Jefferson's letter of December 1787 supporting a bill of rights. On October 17, 1788, the eve of his campaign for a House seat, Madison faced the issue. He favored a bill of rights, he wrote, but had "never thought the omission a material defect" and was not "anxious to supply it even by subsequent amendments"; he did not even think the matter important. Still agreeing with Wilson that the delegated powers did not extend to reserved rights, Madison also worried about the difficulty of adequately protecting the most important rights; experience proved, he asserted, that a bill of rights was a mere parchment barrier when most needed. Government, after all, was the instrument of the majority, which could endanger liberty. "What use then . . . can a bill of rights serve in popular Governments?" Its political truths, he conceded by way of an answer, could educate the people, thereby inhibiting majority impulses.[78]

Jefferson's reply of March 15, 1789, had a profound influence on Madison, as Madison's great speech of June 8 would show. An argument for a bill of rights that Madison had omitted, wrote Jefferson, was "the legal check which it puts into the hands of the judiciary." Jefferson believed that an independent court could withstand oppressive majority impulses by holding unconstitutional any acts violating a bill of rights. The point was not new to Madison, for he himself, when defending a ban on ex post facto laws at the Constitutional Convention, had declared that it would "oblige the Judges to declare [retrospective] interferences null and void."[79] As for the point that the delegated powers did not reach the reserved rights of the people, Jefferson answered that because the Constitution protected some rights but ignored others, it raised implications against them, making a bill of rights "necessary by way of supplement." Moreover, he added, the Constitution "forms us into one state as to certain objects," requiring a bill of rights to guard against abuses of power. As for the point that a bill of rights could not be perfect, Jefferson replied with the adage that half a loaf is better than none; even if all rights could not be secured, "let us secure what we can." Madison had also argued that the limited powers of the federal government and the jealousy of the states afforded enough security, to which Jefferson answered that a bill of rights "will be the text whereby to try all the acts of the federal government." That a bill of rights was inconvenient and not always efficacious did not impress Jefferson. Sometimes, he replied, it was effective, and if it inconveniently cramped the government, the effect was short-lived and remediable, while the inconveniences of not having a bill of rights could be "permanent, afflicting, and irreparable." Legislative tyranny, Jefferson explained, would be a formidable dread for a long time, and executive tyranny would likely follow.[80]

Jefferson's arguments, however persuasive, would have been unproductive but for the dangerous political situation, which Madison meant to ameliorate. Four states, including his own and New York, had called for a second convention, whose purpose, Madison feared, would be to "mutilate the system," especially as to the power to tax. Lack of that power "will be fatal" to the new federal government. Madison correctly believed that many Anti-Federalists favored an effective Union on the condition that a bill of rights bridle the new government. His strategy was to win them over by persuading the first Congress to adopt protections of civil liberties, thereby alleviating the public's anxieties, providing popularity and stability for the government, and isolating those Anti-Federalists whose foremost objective was "subverting the fabric . . . if not the Union itself."[81]

In the First Congress, Representative Madison sought to fulfill his pledge of subsequent amendments. His accomplishment in the face of opposition and apathy entitles him to be remembered as "father of the Bill of Rights" even more than as "father of the Constitution." Many Federalists thought that the House had more important tasks, such as the passage of tonnage duties and a judiciary bill. The opposition party, which had previously exploited the lack of a bill of rights in the Constitution, realized that its adoption would sink the movement for a second convention and make unlikely any additional amendments that would cripple the substantive powers of the government. Having used the bill of rights issue as a smokescreen for objections to the Constitution that could not be dramatically popularized, they now sought to scuttle Madison's proposals. They began by stalling, then tried to annex amendments aggrandizing state powers, and finally depreciated the importance of the very protections of individual liberty that they had formerly demanded as a guarantee against impending tyranny. Madison meant to prove that the new government was a friend of liberty; he also understood that his amendments, if adopted, would thwart the passage of proposals aggrandizing state powers and diminishing national ones. He would not be put off; he was insistent, compelling, unyielding, and, finally, triumphant.

On June 8, 1789, he made his long memorable speech before an apathetic House, introducing amendments culled mainly from state constitutions and state ratifying convention proposals, especially Virginia's. All power, he argued, is subject to abuse and should be guarded against by constitutionally securing "the great rights of mankind." The government had only limited powers, but it might, unless prohibited, abuse its discretion as to its choice of means under the necessary and proper clause; it might, for example, use general warrants in the enforcement of its revenue laws. In Britain, bills of rights merely erected barriers against the powers of the crown, leaving the powers of Parliament "altogether indefinite," and the British constitution left unguarded the "choicest" rights of the press and of conscience. The great objective he had in mind, Madison declared, was to limit the powers of government, thus preventing legislative as well as executive abuse, and above all preventing abuses of power by "the body of the people, operating by the majority against the minority." Mere "paper barriers" might fail, but they raised a standard that might educate the majority against acts to which they might be inclined.[82]

To the argument that a bill of rights was not necessary because the states constitutionally protected freedom, Madison had two responses. One was that some states had no bills of rights, others "very defective ones," and that the states constituted a greater danger to liberty than the new national government. The other was that the Constitution should, therefore, include an amendment, that "No State shall violate the equal rights of conscience, or the freedom of the press, or the trial by jury in criminal cases." He argued that the states would more likely abuse their powers than would the national government "if not controlled by the general principle, that laws are unconstitutional which infringe the rights of the community." He thought that "every Government should be disarmed of powers which trench upon those particular rights" of press, conscience, and jury trial. The amendment was all the more needed, he asserted, because some of the states did not protect these rights in their own constitutions. As for those that did, a "double security" could not reasonably be opposed. When Congressman Thomas Tucker of South Carolina moved to strike the proposed restriction on state powers, Madison carried the House by a two-thirds majority after he argued that this was "the most valuable amendment in the whole list."[83]

To the contention that an enumeration of rights would disparage those not protected, Madison replied that the danger could be guarded against by adopting a proposal of his composition that became the Ninth Amendment. If his amendments were "incorporated" into the Constitution, Madison said, "independent tribunals of justice will consider themselves in a peculiar manner the guardians of those rights; they will be an impenetrable bulwark against every assumption of power in the legislative or executive; they will be naturally led to resist every encroachment upon rights expressly stipulated for in the constitution. . . ."[84]

Although many Federalists preferred to give the new government time to operate before amending the Constitution, supporters of Madison exulted, largely for political reasons. Hugh Williamson of North Carolina, a signer of the Constitution, informed Madison that the Anti-Federalists of that state did not really want a bill of rights. William R. Davie, who had been Williamson's colleague in the Convention, gleefully reported to Madison that his amendments had "confounded the Anties exceedingly. . . ." Edmund Pendleton of Virginia wrote of Madison's amendments that "nothing was further from the wish of some, who covered their Opposition to the Government under the masque of incommon zeal for amendments. . . ." Tench Coxe of Pennsylvania praised Madison for having stripped the Constitution's opponents of every rationale "and most of the popular arguments they have heretofore used."[85]

Notwithstanding the support of correspondents, Madison's speech stirred no immediate support in Congress. Indeed, every speaker who followed him, regardless of party affiliation, either opposed a bill of rights or believed that the House should attend to far more important duties. Six weeks later Madison "begged" for a consideration of his amendments, but the House assigned them to a special committee instead of debating them. That committee, which included Madison, reported in a week. It added freedom of speech to the rights protected against state abridgment, deleted Madison's reference to no "unreasonable searches and seizures," made some stylistic revisions, but otherwise recommended the amendments substantially as he had proposed them. The committee's report was tabled, impelling Madison on August 3 to implore its consideration.[86]

On August 13 the House finally began to consider the reported amendments, and in the course of debate it made some significant changes. Madison had proposed to "incorporate" the amendments within the text of the Constitution at appropriate points. He did not recommend their adoption as a separate "bill of rights," although he had referred to them collectively by that phrase. Members objected, however, that to incorporate the amendments would give the impression that the Framers of the Constitution had signed a document that included provisions not of their composition. Another argument for lumping the amendments together was that the matter of form was so "trifling" that the House should not squander its time debating the placement of the various amendments. Ironically, Roger Sherman, who had insisted that the amendments were unnecessary, deserves the credit for insistently arguing that they should be appended as a supplement to the Constitution instead of being interspersed within it. Thus, what became the "Bill of Rights" achieved its significant collective form over the objections of its foremost proponent, Madison, and because of the desire of its opponents in both parties to downgrade its importance.[87]

The House recast the free exercise of religion clause and its allied clause banning establishments of religion, improving Madison's original language. The House also confined Madison's broad phrasing that no person should be compelled to give evidence against himself in criminal cases. On the other hand, the House restored the extremely important principle against unreasonable searches and seizures, which had been dropped by the committee. In another major decision the House decisively defeated Gerry's motion, for the Anti-Federalists, to consider not just the committee's report but all amendments that the several states had proposed; the Anti-Federalists thus failed to intrude crippling political amendments. Finally, the House added "or to the people" in the recommendation by Madison that the powers not delegated to the United States be reserved to the states. On the whole, the House adopted Madison's amendments with few significant alterations during the course of its ten-day debate on the Bill of Rights.[88]

In the midst of that debate Madison wrote a letter to a fellow Federalist explaining why he was so committed to "the nauseous

project of amendments" which some of the party supported reluc-
tantly. Protecting essential rights was "not improper," he coolly
explained, and could be of some influence for good. He also felt
honor-bound to redeem a campaign pledge to his constituents,
mindful that the Constitution "would have been *certainly* rejected"
by Virginia without assurances from its supporters to seek subsequent amendments. Politics, moreover, made proposing the
amendments a necessity in order to beat the Anti-Federalists at
their own game. If Federalists did not support the amendments,
Anti-Federalists would claim that they had been right all along and
gain support for a second convention. And, Madison wrote, the
amendments "will kill the opposition everywhere, and by putting
an end to disaffection to the Government itself, enable the administration to venture on measures not otherwise safe."[89]

Madison had, in fact, upstaged and defeated the Anti-Federalists. That is why Congressman Aedanus Burke of South Carolina
cried sour grapes. During the debate on what became the First
Amendment, he argued that the proposals before the House were
"not those solid and substantial amendments which the people
expect; they are little better than whip-syllabub, frothy and full of
wind. . . . Upon the whole, I think . . . we have done nothing but
lose our time, and that it will be better to drop the subject now,
and proceed to the organization of the Government." The private
correspondence of Senators Lee and Grayson of Virginia reveals
the explanation for the attitude of their party toward a bill of rights.
A few days after Madison had introduced his amendments, Grayson
complained to his mentor, Patrick Henry, that the Federalists meant
to enact "amendments which shall effect [sic] personal liberty alone,
leaving the great points of the Judiciary, direct taxation, &c, to
stand as they are." Lee and Grayson had failed in their effort to
have the Senate amend the House's proposals by adopting the
Virginia ratifying convention's recommendations on direct taxation
and the treaty and the commerce powers. Lee then regretted the
original Anti-Federalist strategy of opposing the Constitution unless revised by the addition of a bill of rights and other amendments.
He sorrowfully informed Henry that "the idea of subsequent
amendments, was little better than putting oneself to death first,
in expectation that the doctor, who wished our destruction, would
afterwards restore us to life." Later, after the Senate had approved

of the amendments that became the Bill of Rights, Grayson reported, "they are good for nothing, and I believe, as many others do, that they will do more harm than benefit."[90]

The Senate, which kept no record of its debates, had deliberated on seventeen amendments submitted by the House. The Senate killed the one proposal Madison thought "the most valuable": protection against state infringement of speech, press, religion, or trial by jury. The motion to adopt failed to receive the necessary two-thirds vote, though by what margin is unknown. The Senate also weakened the House's ban on establishments of religion. Otherwise, the Senate accepted the House proposals, although the Senate combined several, reducing the total number from seventeen to twelve. The first of the twelve dealt with the relation of population to the number of representatives from each state, and the then second would have prevented any law going into effect increasing the salaries of members of Congress until after the next election.[91]

The House adamantly refused to accept the Senate's version of its ban on establishments. A conference committee of both houses met to resolve their differences. The committee, which included Madison, accepted the House's ban on establishments but otherwise accepted the Senate's version. On September 24, 1789, the House voted for the committee report; on the following day, the Senate concurred, and the twelve amendments were submitted to the states for ratification.[92]

Within six months nine states ratified the Bill of Rights, although of the twelve amendments submitted for approval, the first and second were rejected. The four recalcitrant states by mid-1790 were Virginia, Massachusetts, Connecticut, and Georgia. The admission of Vermont to the Union raised the number of states needed for ratification to eleven. Connecticut and Georgia refused to ratify. Georgia's position was that amendments were superfluous until experience under the Constitution proved a need. Connecticut believed that any suggestion that the Constitution was not perfect would add to the strength of Anti-Federalism.[93]

In Massachusetts, Federalist apathy to the Bill of Rights was grounded on a satisfaction with the Constitution as it was, and the Anti-Federalists were more interested in amendments that would strengthen the states at the expense of the national government. Nevertheless, the Massachusetts lower house adopted all but the first, second, and twelfth amendments, and the upper house adopted all but the first, second, and tenth. Thus both houses of the Massachusetts legislature actually approved what became our First through Seventh and Ninth Amendments. However, a special committee dominated by Anti-Federalists urged that all amendments recommended by Massachusetts should be adopted before the state concurred in any amendments. As a result, the two houses never passed a bill promulgating ratification of eight amendments.[94] Jefferson, the secretary of state, believed that Massachusetts, "having been the 10th state which has ratified, makes up the threefourth [sic] of the legislatures whose ratification was to suffice." He wrote to a Massachusetts official, asking for clarification. The reply was, "It does not appear that the Committee ever reported any bill." In 1939 Massachusetts joined Connecticut and Georgia when they belatedly ratified on the sesquicentennial anniversary of the Constitution.[95]

Ratification of the Bill of Rights by Vermont, in November 1789, left Virginia the last state to act.[96] Its ratification as the eleventh state was indispensable, although the hostility of its Anti-Federalist leaders presaged a doubtful outcome. Senators Grayson and Lee reported to the Virginia legislature that they transmitted the recommended amendments "with grief." They still hoped for a new constitutional convention that would devise "real and substantial Amendments" to "secure against the annihilation of the state governments. . . ." Patrick Henry vainly moved to postpone consideration of the Bill of Rights. The victims of a dilemma of their own making, the Anti-Federalists sought to sabotage the Bill of Rights. The Federalists of Virginia, however, eagerly supported the Bill of Rights in the knowledge that its adoption would appease public fears and stymie the amendments supported by the Anti-Federalists. Virginia's lower house, controlled by the Federalists, acted quickly, but the opposition dominated the state senate. Not all Anti-Federalists were implacably opposed. Some respected George Mason's opinion. When he had first heard of Madison's amendments he had called them "Milk and Water Propositions," not "important & substantial Amendments." But Mason changed his mind, saying that they gave "much satisfaction," though he still wanted other amendments, including one that prevented commercial regulations by mere majority vote of Congress.[97]

Virginia's senate, as Edmund Randolph reported to Washington, postponed consideration of the amendments, "for a majority is unfriendly to the government." As a member of the lower house reported to Madison, the senate inclined to reject the Bill of Rights, not because of opposition to its guarantees but from an apprehension "that the adoption of them at this time will be an obstacle to the chief object of their pursuit, the amendment on the subject of direct taxation." For that reason, Randolph reported to Washington, the Federalists meant to "push" the Bill of Rights; passage would "discountenance any future importunities for amendments."[98]

Virginia's senate at the close of 1789 rejected what became the First, Sixth, Ninth, and Tenth Amendments, at least until the next session, thereby allowing time for the electorate to express itself. The Anti-Federalists still hoped to drum up support for "radical" amendments, as Lee called them. The senators in the majority also issued a statement grossly misrepresenting the First Amendment (then the third). Madison confidently believed that this Anti-Federalist tactic would backfire, and it did. For the senators' statement was not only inaccurate on its face; it came from men who with a single exception had opposed separation of church and state. Madison expected the ratification of the Bill of Rights, which he believed would eliminate the opposition to the new government, and give it a chance to operate with the confidence of the public. Jefferson made his influence felt on behalf of the Bill of Rights, and the Anti-Federalists grudgingly gave ground before public opinion. On December 15, 1791, after two years of procrastination, the senate finally ratified without record vote, thereby completing the process of state ratification and making the Bill of Rights part of the Constitution.[99]

The history of the framing and ratification of the Bill of Rights indicates slight passion on the part of anyone to enshrine personal liberties in the fundamental law of the land. We know almost nothing about what the state legislatures thought concerning the meanings of the various amendments, and the press was perfunctory in its reports, if not altogether silent. But for Madison's persistence the amendments would have died in Congress. Our precious Bill of Rights, at least in its immediate background, resulted from the reluctant necessity of certain Federalists to capitalize on a cause that had been originated, in vain, by the Anti-Federalists for ulterior purposes. The party that had first opposed the Bill of Rights inadvertently wound up with the responsibility for its framing and ratification, while the people who had at first professedly wanted it discovered too late that it not only was embarrassing but disastrous for their ulterior purposes. The Bill of Rights had a great healing effect, however; it did, as Mason originally proposed, "give great quiet" to the people. The opposition to the Constitution, Jefferson informed Lafayette, "almost totally disappeared," as Anti-Federalist leaders lost "almost all their followers." The people of the United States had had the good sense, nourished by traditions of freedom, to support the Constitution and the Bill of Rights.[100]

CHAPTER NINE

The First Amendment: The Establishment Clause

*A*lthough the Framers of the Bill of Rights did not rank the rights in order of importance, some are more precious than others. A right that has no superior is the first mentioned: freedom from a law respecting an establishment of religion. The First Congress recommended twelve amendments to the states, which failed to ratify the first two: as a result, the proposal that originally stood in the third place became the first, a fact swollen with symbolic significance. At the very least, establishments of religion summon historical memories associated with religious persecution. Equality for all opinions on the subject of religion and for the free exercise of religious conscience cannot exist in the presence of an establishment of religion. The classic establishment of religion denoted a legal union between a state and a particular church that benefited from numerous privileges not shared by other churches or by the nonchurched or unbelievers. An uncontested and incontestable fact that stands out from the establishment clause is that the United States cannot constitutionally enact any law preferring one church over others in any way whatever.

Does the establishment clause permit government aid to religion? Do the views of Chief Justice William H. Rehnquist have any historical validity? In 1985, he declared that the "well accepted meaning" of the establishment clause is that it merely prohibited the establishment of a "national religion," which he defined as the official designation of any church as a national one. The clause also "forbade preference among religious sects or denominations." But it created no wall of separation between government and religion, not even between church and state. "The Establishment Clause," Rehnquist added, "did not require governmental neutrality between religion and irreligion, nor did it prohibit the federal government from providing non-discriminatory aid to religion."[1]

The language of the establishment clause provides few sure conclusions. If, taken literally, the clause creates no wall of separation, neither does it refer to a national religion or to the concept of preference; it does not permit government preference for religion over irreligion, let alone of one religion or church over others. It does not even restrict itself to laws banning establishments of religion, because it applies, more broadly, to laws "respecting" establishments of religion. Therefore, a law that falls short of creating an establishment, whatever that might be, comes within the constitutional prohibition if it concerns an establishment or is a step in that direction. But the clearest proposition about the establishment clause is that it limits power by placing an absolute restriction on the United States: "Congress shall make no law. . . ." Reading an empowerment from that is about as valid as reading the entrails of a chicken for the meaning of the establishment clause or for portents of the future.

The clause was added to the Constitution because the unamended text not only placed religious liberty in jeopardy; it seemed to allow for the implication that Congress might exercise powers not prohibited and might, therefore, create an establishment of religion—or so the Constitution's opponents claimed. To the supporters of the Constitution, such reasoning was specious because the proposed new national government would possess merely limited powers, and none had been granted on any subject that would be the concern of a bill of rights. If no power existed, it could neither be exercised or abused. Of the many statements of this argument,[2] the best known is that of Alexander Hamilton in *The Federalist*, where he concluded simply: "For why declare that things shall not be done which there is no power to do? Why, for instance, should it be said that the liberty of the press shall not be restrained, when no power is given by which restrictions may be imposed?"[3] Thus, James Wilson of Pennsylvania, in response to the contention that the rights of conscience had no security, asserted: "I ask the honorable gentleman, what part of this system puts it into the power of Congress to attack those rights? When there is no power to attack, it is idle to prepare the means of defense."[4] Similarly, Edmund Randolph of Virginia declared that "no power is given expressly to Congress over religion," and he added that only powers "constitutionally given" could be exercised.[5] Madison said, "There is not a shadow of right in the general government to intermeddle with religion."[6] And Richard Dobbs Spaight of North Carolina maintained: "As to the subject of religion. . . . [n]o power is given to the general government to interfere with it at all. Any act of Congress on this subject would be a usurpation."[7] Wilson, Randolph, Madison, and Spaight had attended the Philadelphia Convention. Their remarks show that Congress was powerless *even in the absence of the First Amendment,* to enact laws on the subject of religion, whether in favor of one church or all of them, impartially and equally. In 1790, before the ratification of the First Amendment, Madison opposed the inclusion of ministers in a list of occupations to be covered in the first census bill. He reasoned that "the general government is proscribed from interfering, in any manner whatever in matters respecting religion; and it may be thought to do so in ascertaining who, and who are not ministers of the gospel."[8]

The ratification controversy yielded no evidence that reveals the understanding at that time of the term "establishment of religion." Some states, however, proposed amendments that included a ban on establishments. New Hampshire, the ninth state to ratify, was the first to urge an amendment on the subject: "Congress shall make no laws touching Religion, or to infringe the rights of Conscience." That proved to be as concise and perfect a statement of the matter as could be devised, and, indeed, most clearly revealed the meaning of what would become the equivalent clauses of the First Amendment.[9] Virginia, New York, North Carolina, and Rhode Island also recommended an amendment on the subject. Virginia, copied verbatim by North Carolina, and Rhode Island, urged that "no particular religious sect or society ought to be favored or established, by law, in preference to others," and New York expressed the same thought.[10] In each of these four states, opponents of ratification urged amendments as a price of Union. The Constitution nearly failed to be ratified because it had no bill of rights. New Hampshire, the necessary ninth state, ratified by a vote of 57–46, but the votes of Virginia and New York were still indispensable. Virginia ratified by 89–79, New York by 30–27. North Carolina at first rejected the Constitution, and Rhode Island barely ratified, 32–30, even after Congress had recommended the Bill of Rights to the states. The point is, in part, that advocates of ratification swallowed recommendations for amendments whose language they did not necessarily approve.

Moreover, the language of Virginia and New York by no means implied that Congress should have power to favor religion so long as no sect received preference over others. A page of history is worth a volume of logic here. Parsing the nonpreferential language of the proposed amendments on establishments holds no key to understanding. In the first place, Patrick Henry and his followers in Virginia, who were responsible for the language of the amendment, had no intention of augmenting the powers of Congress; they opposed any federal authority over the subject of religion, which they believed to be exclusively within state jurisdiction. They surely did not favor an expansion of the tax powers of Congress, and they did not want Congress to enact an assessment on behalf of religion generally. Virginia had defeated a proposal of 1784 that authorized a state tax for the benefit of religion, allocating each person's money to the Christian church of his choice.[11] Virginia did not intend for the United States a power that it denied even to itself. Its proposal of 1788 against laws preferring one sect above others did not represent the state's position, which is best found in its great Statute for Religious Freedom of 1786. It placed religion wholly on private, voluntary support.

As a matter of fact, the constitutions of Pennsylvania, New Jersey, North Carolina, Delaware, and New York used the language of no preference, yet all five, including the three that had never supported any kind of establishment of religion, relied on private support of religion.[12] In other words, they believed that a constitutional provision insuring no subordination of one sect to another, or providing no preference of one over others, banned government aid to religion. Rhode Island, which failed to frame a state constitution, had never had an establishment of any kind, and as a stronghold of the Baptists, most vehemently opposed government aid to religion, state or federal; yet Rhode Island expressed that position in the language of no preference of one above others. Massachusetts, by contrast, maintained an establishment of religion by its constitution of 1780, yet endorsed the principle of no preference. Several towns that opposed an establishment of religion believed that the principle of no preference required private support of religion.[13] When the Baptist leaders of Massachusetts sought to separate church and state, they relied on the language of no preference, oblivious to the possibility that a subsequent generation, ignorant of history, might twist that language to make it yield government support of religion on a nonpreferential basis.[14] No one in the United States during the generation of the Framers advocated a federal power to promote, assist, or support religion. Religion was a topic that only the arts of voodoo might transmogrify from exclusive state jurisdiction into the subject of a federal power. And no state that banned laws preferring one sect over others ever regarded its ban against preference as an authority to enact laws assisting religion generally or all sects without preference to any.

The history of the drafting of the establishment clause by the First Congress will not make sense to anyone who fails to understand Madison's objective in introducing the amendments that became the Bill of Rights. Its "great object," he said, was to "limit and qualify the powers of Government" to prevent legislation in forbidden fields such as religion. He declared that the goal of "restraining the Federal Government" could be achieved by insuring that "the abuse of the powers of the General Government may be guarded against in a more secure manner" than in the unamended Constitution.[15] As Madison succinctly informed Jefferson, the Bill of Rights was not framed "to imply powers not meant to be included in the enumeration."[16]

When Madison introduced his amendments, the clauses on religion read that no one's civil rights should be abridged "on account of religious belief or worship, nor shall any national religion be established, nor shall the full and equal rights of conscience be in any manner, or on any pretext, infringed."[17] In one respect that constituted a vast improvement over the final version of the First Amendment's clause on religious liberty, which merely guarantees

against a law "prohibiting the free exercise thereof." A literal interpretation destroys the original intent, which was to preserve religious liberty from diminution. But the reference to no prohibition
in the free exercise clause and to no abridgment in the free press
clause gives the impression that the Framers deliberately allowed
for the infringement of religious liberty and sought only to prevent
its abolition. The point is that the clauses of the First Amendment
cannot be taken literally. They do not mean what they say nor say
what the Framers meant.

The establishment clause as introduced by Madison surely did
not mean that the United States could pass laws on religion short
of creating a national religion, that is, short of a federal preference
of one religion or church over others. By "national" Madison meant
an act of the national government, any act. Indeed, his next proposal safeguarded the rights of conscience against state acts, which
the Senate defeated. In any case, a House select committee omitted
the word "national." It is not part of the First Amendment, and it
should not be construed, à la Rehnquist, as if it were still a part
and as if the ban against a "national religion" authorized nonpreferential assistance to all faiths. Madison nevertheless continued
to employ the phrase "national religion," raising the question of
whether he favored nonpreferential aid to religion.

He did not. He had led the fight in Virginia against the "general
assessment" bill of 1784, which would have imposed taxes to subsidize religion. Madison did not oppose that bill because it referred,
too narrowly, to Christianity, and no one for or against the bill
thought that its extension to Hinduism, Islam, Judaism, and other
religions would remedy any defects. Madison opposed the bill
because he opposed any kind of establishment of religion, regardless of how inclusive or exclusive. Proponents of the bill declared
themselves to be on the side of God, because they praised religion
and its many benefits. Madison replied that the question was not
whether religion was a good thing but whether establishments of
religion were good for religion, and he decidedly thought not. He
did not believe that religion needed government support any more
than government needed religious support. He argued, in his famous Memorial and Remonstrance against Religious Assessments,
that religion was not an "engine of civil society," that the establishment contemplated by the bill differed from the Inquisition

"only in degree," not in principle, and that any establishment violated freedom of religion, injured religion, corrupted government,
and threatened public liberty.[18]

Madison, in fact, had an exquisite sense of the separate jurisdictions of religion and government, and he shared Jefferson's belief
in a high wall of separation between the two. He spoke of a "perfect
separation" and believed that "religion and Government will exist
in greater purity, without . . . the aid of Government." As for the
phrase "national religion," he used it to describe the use of public
funds for the support of interfaith invocations and benedictions,
congressional and military chaplains, and a law incorporating a
church in the District of Columbia, all of which he believed to be
unconstitutional. His antagonism to government-assisted religion
was extreme, even as to trifling matters.[19]

Madison rarely used the phrase "establishment of religion."
He almost always misquoted the First Amendment as if it outlawed
"religious establishments," a revealing usage. A religious establishment is a church, a church school, or any religious institution,
and such an establishment implies no government aid or involvement with religion, as does an establishment of religion. That Madison, Father of the Constitution and of the Bill of Rights, misquoted
the establishment clause as he did, even in official documents when
he was President, shows that he understood it to mean that the
government had no authority to legislate on the subject of religion
or on matters concerning religion.

Madison's influence notwithstanding, he did not compose the
establishment clause by himself or determine its meaning. When
his proposed amendments emerged from a House select committee, the religion clauses stated: "No religion shall be established
by law, nor shall the equal rights of conscience be infringed." The
House briefly debated these recommendations without clarifying
their meaning. No one suggested that the United States had the
constitutional power to pass laws about religion. Disagreement
existed about the best way to say that it had no such power; saying
so in some way would satisfy the popular clamor for an amendment
that specifically opposed establishments of religion and favored
religious liberty. Samuel Livermore of New Hampshire recommended that "Congress shall make no laws touching religion, or
infringing the rights of conscience." The Committee of the Whole

adopted this motion, but it apparently did not accommodate those who believed that something specific had to be said on the subject of establishments of religion. When, therefore, the House took up the report of the Committee of the Whole, a motion made by Fisher Ames of Massachusetts passed, with the result that the proposal that went to the Senate said: "Congress shall make no law establishing religion, or to prevent the free exercise thereof, or to infringe the rights of conscience."[20]

The Senate conducted its debate without reporters present and left a record of only motions and their disposition. On one day the Senate defeated three motions phrased in the language of no preference. One said that Congress should not establish "one religious sect or society in preference to others," another that it should not establish "any religious sect or society," and the third that it should not establish "any particular denomination of religion in preference to another." These narrowly phrased motions allowed the semantic implication, however baseless, that nonpreferential federal aid to religion seemed to be the object of those who supported such motions. Such a view, which has no historical backup, ignores the fact that the Senate defeated these motions. It was seeking a way to limit a nonexistent power, not a way to enhance or even vest power.[21] Moreover, the language of no preference often seemed appropriate to those who believed that religion should rest on merely voluntary support. Elder John Leland, the great Baptist minister who was the only person to fight establishments of religion in Virginia, Connecticut, and Massachusetts, strongly believed that because Christ's kingdom is not of this world, government should have no jurisdiction over it. When he sought to frame an amendment terminating the establishment in Massachusetts, he used the language of no preference; he would have been astonished to learn that such language could be stretched to allow government assistance to all sects without preference to any.[22] The Senate, when drafting the amendment that became the First, consistently defeated no preference motions and adopted the House motion.

Six days later, however, the Senate changed its mind and substituted for the House version one that read: "Congress shall make no law establishing articles of faith or a mode of worship, or prohibiting the free exercise of religion. . . ."[23] This was overly narrow language, because South Carolina was the only state that had an establishment of religion that prescribed articles of faith; in five other states whose laws as of 1789 authorized establishments of religion, public taxation for religion constituted the principal feature of an establishment, rather than articles of faith. The South Carolina provision of 1778 was scrapped when a new state constitution of 1790 omitted all reference to an establishment of religion and guaranteed free exercise for everyone.[24]

Despite the narrow language of the Senate, the complexity of the matter demands recognition of the fact that a Baptist memorial of 1774 had used similar language, opposing prescribed articles of faith or forms of worship, in order to achieve, in the minds of its Baptist sponsors, endorsement of the idea that government and religion should be kept separated. As a matter of fact, the foremost Baptist champion of religious liberty in Massachusetts, Isaac Backus, supported ratification of the Constitution in the belief that the United States had no power at all in religious matters, and in his three-volume *History of New England*, he misquoted the First Amendment by stating, approvingly, that "Congress shall make no law, establishing articles of faith, or a mode of worship, or prohibiting the free exercise of religion. . . ." That is, he regarded the Senate's language as sufficient to condemn the establishments of religion then existing in Massachusetts and Connecticut.[25] As Monsignor Thomas Curry has said in his brilliant analysis of the original meaning of the establishment clause, "[e]ighteenth-century American history offers abundant examples of writers using the concept of preference, when, in fact, they were referring to a ban on all government assistance to religion."[26]

The House adamantly refused to accept the Senate's version of the religion clauses. Differences on several of the proposed amendments required a joint committee of the two houses to negotiate a compromise. A strong committee of three members from each house, including four men who had been influential Framers (Madison, Roger Sherman, Oliver Ellsworth, and William Paterson), drafted the language that we know as the First Amendment. Both houses adopted it and recommended its ratification by the states.

Several facts clearly emerge from the legislative history of the establishment clause. The United States had no authority prior to the First Amendment to enact laws about religion; only the states held that power. The amendment did not increase the legislative power of Congress. Congress seriously considered alternative readings of the establishment clause and rejected every phrasing that logic could construe as more narrow than the final version. The Livermore-New Hampshire alternative, the broadest restriction of power, failed because it did not mention an establishment. Another fact may be added: the meaning of an "establishment of religion" remains uncertain after an analysis of the legislative history. Whatever such an establishment was, the nation's legislature faced an absolute ban concerning it.

The states ratified the Bill of Rights but left nothing to clarify the meaning of an establishment of religion. We have no debates, newspaper items, tracts, or personal correspondence that provide clues, except in Virginia, where the evidence is utterly misleading. The state senate, narrowly dominated by Anti-Federalists who took orders from Patrick Henry, voted 8–7 to postpone a decision on the recommended amendments. Virginia's Anti-Federalists understood that if the Bill of Rights became part of the supreme law, no chance would remain for a second constitutional convention or for the passage of the amendments crippling the national judicial, tax, and commerce powers. The eight state senators, who had consistently voted in support of taxes for religion, issued a patently false public statement contending that the proposed religion clauses neither protected freedom of religion from violation nor prevented Congress from levying taxes for the support of religion; they even alleged that it would benefit one particular sect over others.[27] Their statement conflicted with the language of the amendment at issue. Finally, the Virginia senate, unable any longer to explain its opposition to a Bill of Rights, ratified.

What then was the understanding in 1789 of the meaning of the term "an establishment of religion"? Doubtless, any union of state and church comparable to the familiar European establishments of religion came within the prohibition of the First Amendment. Such establishments of religion had weak counterparts in the tidewater towns of the southern colonies before the American Revolution. Where such an establishment existed, attendance upon its services was supposed to be compulsory, unless the government indulged the open existence of dissenters. But only the official creed of the established church could be publicly taught, and only its clergy had civil sanction to perform marriage services and other sacraments, or could allow them to be performed. Only clergymen of the established religion received stipends paid from religious taxes imposed on everyone, regardless of faith, and only the churches of the establishment were built and maintained by those taxes. Dissenters, even if tolerated, suffered from the imposition of various civil disabilities, such as exclusion from universities and disqualification for office, whether civil, military, or religious. Their orphanages, schools, churches, and other religious institutions had no legal capacity to bring suits, hold or transmit property, or receive or bequeath trust funds. According to William Tennent, a Presbyterian minister of South Carolina, in which the Church of England (Episcopal) had been established, Protestant dissenters were merely tolerated as if they stood "on the same footing with the Jews," unmolested but unequal.[28] Except in Rhode Island, second-class citizenship also characterized non-Congregational Protestants in the New England colonies, where for all practical purposes the Congregational Church enjoyed the preferences of the established church. By banning laws respecting an establishment of religion, the First Amendment meant, indisputably, that Congress could make no law concerning the sort of establishment that characterized Lutheran Sweden, Anglican England, Roman Catholic Spain, or Presbyterian Scotland.

The question is whether an establishment of religion signified anything other than a church with preferred status or official privileges? In fact, Europe's post-Reformation model of an establishment of religion was barely known in America, if at all, by the time of the American Revolution. The term "establishment of religion" came to have a far broader meaning in America than it had in Europe. To begin with, American establishments had never been as powerful or as discriminatory as their European counterparts. Tennent may have felt merely tolerated in Anglican Charleston, but further west in Carolina Anglicans were few in number, their clergy was almost nonexistent, all churches were equal in fact, and discriminatory laws had no real operation. By the time of the American Revolution, the interior of the southern colonies had been populated with Scotch-Irish Presbyterians and various German sects and denominations. A bewildering multiplicity of religions existed in the middle colonies, none of which had ever endured an establishment of religion. And in New England, outside of Rhode Island where state and church had always been separated, Congregationalists reaped the benefits of an establishment not because their church was by law established but because a nondescript establishment of Protestant ministers on a local town basis operated in favor of the overwhelmingly numerous Congregationalists. But nowhere in New England was the Congregational Church established by name.

The American experience with establishments of religion was unknown to eighteenth-century Europe. As a matter of fact, at the time of the framing of the Bill of Rights, every one of the six states that still maintained an establishment of religion in the United States had *multiple* or *general* establishments of religion. An establishment of religion had come to mean government support, primarily financial, for religion generally, without legal preference to any church. For all practical purposes, and surely for all legal purposes, the states that authorized establishments in 1789 established all the churches within their borders.

New York's colonial history of church–state relationships provided the first example of an establishment of religion radically different from the European type, an establishment of religion in general—or at least of Protestantism in general—and without preference to one church over others. After the English conquered New Netherlands in 1664, the "Duke's Laws" made provisions for the regulation of churches in Long Island. Any church of the Protestant religion could become an established church. In a sense, of course, this was an exclusive establishment of one religion, Protestantism; but the system involved a multiple establishment of several different Protestant churches, in sharp contrast to European precedents, which provided for the establishment of one church only.

Under the "Duke's Laws," every township was obliged publicly to support some Protestant church and a minister. The denomination of the church did not matter. Costs were to be met by a public tax: "Every inhabitant shall contribute to all charges both in Church and State." A local option system prevailed. On producing evidence of ordination "from some Protestant bishop or minister," the minister selected by a town was inducted into his pastorate by the governor representing the state. In other words, this was an establishment of religion in which there was a formal, legal, official union between government and religion on a non-preferential basis and without the establishment of any individual church. In 1683 the New York Assembly enacted a "Charter of Liberties" that adopted the Long Island system of multiple establishments and extended it to the whole colony.[29]

Following the Glorious Revolution of 1688, the English government instructed its governors of New York to implement an establishment of Anglicanism there.[30] In 1693 a recalcitrant legislature, composed almost entirely of non-Anglicans, passed "An Act for Settling a Ministry & raising a Maintenance for them" in the four southern counties. The law called only for "a good and sufficient Protestant Minister" and nowhere mentioned the Church of England.[31] The royal governors and most Anglicans asserted that the statute had established their church; but non-Anglican New Yorkers disagreed. Thus, in 1695, the legislature declared that the 1693 act allowed the selection of a "Dissenting Protestant Minister," that is, a non-Anglican one, although the governor refused to permit this.[32] A few years later, Lewis Morris, a prominent Anglican, wrote: "The People were generally dissenters [and] fancied they had made an effectual provision for Ministers of their own persuasion by this Act."[33]

In 1703 and 1704 Anglicans, assisted by the governor of the colony, gained possession of the church and parsonage in the town of Jamaica, Long Island. These buildings had been erected at public expense, and the town had chosen a Presbyterian minister. The Anglicans' action set off a long and bitter controversy. The Presbyterians refused to pay the salary of the Anglican minister because, as the Church of England townspeople reported, "they [the Presbyterians] stick not to call themselves the Established Church."[34] In 1710 the Presbyterians managed to seize and retain the parsonage, and in 1727 they brought suit for the recovery of the church, which the provincial court, in an unreported decision, awarded them.[35] For much of the remainder of the colonial period, Anglicans managed to pry a minister's salary out of the reluctant inhabitants, but not without constant complaints and a further attempt, defeated by the courts in 1768, to withhold the minister's salary.[36] Elsewhere on Long Island, the inhabitants supported the non-Anglican town ministers chosen by the majority. Brookhaven certainly supported such a minister, and given the scarcity of Anglicans and Anglican ministers in the colony, most towns had to reach their own accommodations with the ministers of their choice.[37]

In the 1750s the organization of King's (later Columbia) College provoked a controversy over the nature of New York's establishment. Anglicans demanded that they control the new school because they enjoyed "a preference by the Constitution of the province."[38] Non-Anglicans rejected both claims. A young lawyer, and a future Framer of the Federal Constitution, William Livingston, denied that the Anglican Church was exclusively established in the colony. He insisted that the establishment "restricted no particular Protestant Denomination whatsoever," and that the people were to choose which ministers to establish.[39] Here again is evidence that the concept of a multiple establishment of religion was understood by inhabitants of colonial New York. Although New York Anglicans claimed an exclusive establishment of their church, a large number of the colony's population understood the establishment set up by the act of 1693 not simply as a state preference for one religion or sect over others, but as allowing public support for many different churches to be determined by popular vote.

Massachusetts, the major New England colony, proclaimed no establishment of the Congregational Church by name after 1692. That year the legislature provided for an establishment of religion on a town basis by simply requiring every town to maintain an "able, learned and orthodox" minister, to be chosen by the voters of the town and supported by a tax levied on all taxpayers.[40] By law several different denominations could benefit from the establishment. Because Congregationalists constituted the overwhelming majority in nearly every town, they reaped the benefits of the establishment of religion. Except in Boston, where all congregations were supported voluntarily, the law in effect made the Congregational Church the privileged one, which unquestionably was the purpose of the statute, and non-Congregationalists, chiefly Episcopalians, Baptists, and Quakers, were for a long time taxed for the support of Congregationalism. However, in the few towns dominated by a non-Congregational denomination, as the Baptists did in Swansea, the official established church represented that denomination.[41]

The growing number of dissenters, however, forced Congregationalists to make concessions. In 1727, Episcopalians won the statutory right of having their religious taxes applied to the support of their own churches.[42] Connecticut passed a similar act on behalf of the Episcopal churches in the same year.[43] In 1728 Massachusetts exempted Quakers and Baptists from taxes for the payment of ministerial salaries. Thereafter, each denomination was respectively exempted from sharing the taxes for building new town churches.[44] Tax exemption statutes on behalf of Quakers and Baptists were periodically renewed, so that members of these denominations were not supposed to pay religious taxes for the benefit of either Congregational churches or of their own.

Because of complicated legal technicalities, as well as outright illegal action, frequent abuses occurred under the system of tax exemption, which also prevailed in Connecticut. In Massachusetts and Connecticut many Quakers and Baptists were unconscionably forced to pay for the support of Congregational churches, and even Episcopalians who lived too far from a church of their own denomination to attend its services were taxed for support of Congregational ones. Abuses of both the letter and the spirit of the law did not alter the basic fact that after 1728 the establishments of religion in both colonies meant government support of two churches, Congregational and Episcopal, without specified preference to either.

Prominent Congregational spokesmen understood that they did not constitute an exclusive establishment. Cotton Mather wrote that "the Person elected by the Majority of the Inhabitants . . . is . . . the King's Minister," and, he continued, the minister elected by each town was the official minister and as such entitled to its taxes.[45] Benjamin Colman declared: "If any Town will chuse a Gentleman of the Church of England for their Pastor . . . he is their Minister by the Laws of our Province as much as any Congregational Minister."[46] In 1763 Jonathan Mayhew explained that Massachusetts had not established a single church, but rather "protestant churches of various denominations." He understood that "an hundred churches, all of different denominations . . . might all be established in the same . . . colony, as well as one, two, or three."[47] Thus, three of the most prominent New England ministers of the eighteenth century specified that in Massachusetts an establishment of religion was something other than an exclusive preference for one church. Massachusetts, and Connecticut to a lesser extent, maintained not an exclusive but a dual establishment of religion.

New Hampshire's law allowed a multiple establishment. Down to the middle of the eighteenth century, the town system of establishment operated to benefit the Congregational Church exclusively. But New Hampshire did not systematically require the payment of rates by dissenters nor concern itself with the support of their ministers. Quakers, Episcopalians, Presbyterians, and Baptists were exempt from supporting the local established church, which was usually Congregational. In some towns, however, Episcopalians and Presbyterians were authorized to establish their own parishes and to use town authority to collect taxes for their churches. By the eve of the Revolution, the pattern of establishment had become bewilderingly diverse. Some towns maintained dual establishments, others multiple establishments, with free exercise for dissenters.[48]

In the wake of the American Revolution exclusive establishments of religion inherited from the colonial period collapsed. States that had never had establishments renewed their barriers against them, except for Rhode Island, which did not adopt a new state constitution. New York, denying that it ever had a preferential establishment, placed religion on private, voluntary support, as did New Jersey, Delaware, and Pennsylvania. Nowhere in America after 1776 did an establishment of religion restrict itself to a state church or to a system of public support of one sect alone; instead, an establishment of religion meant public support of several or all churches, with preference to none. The six states that continued to provide for public support of religion were careful to make concessions that extended their establishments to embrace many different sects.

Three of these six states were in New England. Massachusetts adopted its constitution in 1780. Article III of its Declaration of Rights commanded the legislature to authorize the "several towns, parishes, precincts, and other bodies politic, or religious societies, to make suitable provision, at their own expense, for the institution of the public worship of God, and for the support and maintenance of public Protestant teachers of piety, religion, and morality." The same article empowered the legislature to make church attendance compulsory, and it authorized the towns and parishes to elect their ministers. In addition, the article stated: "And all moneys paid by the subject to the support of public worship, and all the public teachers aforesaid, shall, if he require it, be uniformly applied to the support of the public teacher or teachers of his own religious sect or denomination, provided there be any on whose instructions he attends; otherwise it may be paid towards the support of the teacher or teachers of the parish or precinct in which the said moneys are raised." A final clause provided that "no subordination of any one sect or denomination to the other shall ever be established by law."[49] That clause against preference proves that constitutionally speaking the several churches of the establishment were on a nonpreferential basis. Clearly an establishment of religion in Massachusetts meant government support of religion and of several different churches in an equitable manner. Congregationalists continued to be the chief beneficiaries of the establishment, because they were the most numerous and resorted to various tricks to fleece non-Congregationalists out of their share of religious taxes. But the fact remains that Baptist, Episcopal, Methodist, Unitarian, and even Universalist churches were publicly supported under the establishment after 1780.[50] Massachusetts did not separate church and state until 1833.

In New Hampshire the state constitution of 1784 also created a statewide multiple establishment with the guarantee that no sect or denomination should be subordinated to another.[51] As in Massachusetts, all Protestant churches benefited. The multiple establishment in New Hampshire ended in 1819. Connecticut, like Rhode Island, did not adopt a constitution during the Revolution. Its establishment of religion was regulated by the "Act of Toleration" of 1784, which was in force when the Bill of Rights was framed. The statute empowered each town to choose which minister to support and guaranteed that no sect was to be subordinated to any other. Those who did not belong to the church representing the majority were exempt from paying toward its support as long as they could prove membership in a different church and that they contributed to the support of their church. Baptists protested against the system but participated in it and benefited from it. The establishment lasted until 1818.[52]

In Maryland, Georgia, and South Carolina, "an establishment of religion" meant much what it did in the New England states that maintained multiple establishments. In Maryland, where the Church of England had been exclusively established, the constitution of 1776 provided that no person could be compelled "to maintain any particular place of worship, or any particular ministry," thus disestablishing the Episcopal church. But the same constitution provided for a new establishment of religion: "Yet the Legislature may, in their discretion, lay a general and *equal tax*, for the support of the Christian religion; leaving to each individual the power of appointing the payment over of the money, collected from him, to the support of any particular place of worship or minister."[53] "Christian" rather than "Protestant" was used in Maryland because of the presence of a large Catholic population, thus insuring nonpreferential support of all churches existing in the state. In 1785 the Maryland legislature sought to exercise its discretionary power to institute nonpreferential support, but "a huge uproar arose against the measure," and it was denounced as a new establishment and decisively beaten.[54] In 1810 the power to enact a multiple establishment was taken from the legislature by a constitutional amendment providing that "an *equal* and *general* tax or any other tax . . . for the support of any religion" was not lawful.[55]

Georgia's constitution of 1777 tersely effected the disestablishment of the Church of England while permitting a multiple establishment of all churches without exception: "All persons whatever shall have the free exercise of their religion; . . . and shall not, unless by consent, support any teacher or teachers except those of their own profession."[56] "This, of course, left the way open for taxation for the support of one's own religion," says the historian of eighteenth-century church–state relationships in Georgia, "and such a law was passed in 1785,"[57] although similar bills had failed in 1782 and 1784. According to the 1785 law, all Christian sects and denominations were to receive tax support in proportion to the amount of property owned by their respective church members, but it is not clear whether this measure even went into operation. What is clear is that an establishment of religion meant government tax support to all churches, with preference to none. The state constitution in effect at the time of the framing of the Bill of Rights was adopted in 1789. Its relevant provision declared that no persons should be obliged "to contribute to the support of any religious profession but their own," thereby permitting a multiple establishment as before. In the state constitution adopted in 1798, however, Georgia separated church and state by a guarantee against any religious taxes and by placing the support of religion on a purely voluntary basis.[58]

South Carolina's constitution of 1778 was the sixth state constitution providing for a multiple establishment of religion. Article XXVIII elaborately spelled out the details for the maintenance of the "Christian Protestant religion" as "the established religion of this State." Adult males forming themselves into any religious society of a Protestant denomination were declared to be "a church of the established religion of this State," on condition of subscribing to a belief in God, worshipping him publicly, regarding Christianity as "the true religion," and accepting the divine inspiration of the Scriptures. Pursuant to this law, Baptists, Independents, Methodists, and Anglicans qualified as "Established" churches. The state also specifically guaranteed that "no person shall, by law, be obliged to pay towards the maintenance and support of a religious worship that he does not freely join in, or has not voluntarily engaged to support."[59] In 1790 South Carolina adopted a new constitution with no provisions whatever for public support of religion.[60]

The constitutions of North Carolina and Virginia did not provide for an establishment of religion of any kind. In 1776 North Carolina banned state support for religion and disestablished the Church of England.[61] By contrast, Virginia's constitution of 1776 was noncommittal on the subject of an establishment. At the close of 1776, the Church of England was for all practical purposes disestablished in Virginia. But the statute of 1776 that initiated the end of the exclusive establishment expressly reserved for future decisions the question of whether religion ought to be placed on a private, voluntary basis or be supported on a nonpreferential basis by a new "general" assessment.[62] The indecision continued until 1785, when public opinion turned against a general assessment. Madison's "Memorial and Remonstrance" acted as a catalyst for the political opposition to the assessment bill, but the religious opposition to it from evangelicals was decisive, resulting in the election of a legislature with an overwhelming majority against it. The new legislature let the bill die unnoticed, and by a vote of 67–20 enacted instead Jefferson's bill for religious freedom with its provision against government support of religion.[63] Had the assessment bill in Virginia been enacted, it would simply have increased the number of states maintaining multiple establishments from six to seven. Indeed, there were seven states with multiple establishments as a result of the admission of Vermont to the Union in 1791, whose vote was counted to determine whether enough states had ratified the Bill of Rights.[64]

Clearly the provisions of these seven states show that to understand the American meaning of "an establishment of religion" one cannot adopt a definition based on European experience. In every European precedent of an establishment, the religion established was that of a single church. Many different churches, or the religion held in common by all of them, that is, Christianity or Protestantism, were never simultaneously established by any European nation. Establishments in America, on the other hand, in both the colonial and the early state periods, were not limited in nature or in meaning to state support of one church. An establishment of religion in America at the time of the framing of the Bill of Rights meant government aid and sponsorship of religion, principally by impartial tax support of the institutions of religion, the churches.

In no state or colony, of course, was there ever an establishment of religion that included every religion without exception. In three of the seven multiple establishments existing in 1791, the establishment included only Protestant churches, and in the other four, all Christian churches. In effect all Christian churches of each of the seven states were establishments of religion. Christianity or Protestantism may signify one religion in contrast with Judaism, Buddhism, Hinduism, or Islam. But no European establishment of religion included all the churches within national boundaries; all European establishments of religion denoted a single state church, that is, the church of one denomination. No member of the First Congress came from a state that supported one church or an exclusive establishment of religion; no such example could have been found in the America of 1789. Their experience told the legislators in 1789 that an establishment of religion meant not just state preference for one religion but also nonpreferential support for many or all. At the time of its ratification in 1791 the establishment clause prevented the United States from doing what half the fourteen states then permitted—giving government aid to religion on a nonpreferential basis. From a broader standpoint, the establishment clause was also meant to depoliticize religion, thereby defusing the potentially explosive condition of a religiously heterogenous society. By separating government and religion the establishment clause enables such a society to maintain some civility among believers and unbelievers, as well as among diverse believers. Above all, the establishment clause functions to protect religion from government, and government from religion.

CHAPTER TEN

The First Amendment:
The Free Press Clause

$\mathcal{A}$lmost two months after the Constitutional Convention had begun its deliberations, Charles Pinckney of South Carolina recommended "sundry propositions" to supplement a partial list of rights that had been proposed by the Committee of Detail. One of Pinckney's propositions urged that the liberty of the press should be "inviolably preserved."[1] He offered no explanation, as if the meaning of "liberty of the press" was self-evident.

The Convention adopted Pinckney's proposal for a ban on religious tests as a qualification for office and his guarantee of the writ of habeas corpus, but did nothing about liberty of the press or his other propositions. On September 12, when the Convention was drawing to a close, a motion to include a bill of rights was defeated. A couple of days later, Pinckney renewed his earlier proposal for a free press clause. Sherman replied, "It is unnecessary. The power of Congress does not extend to the Press." Pinckney's motion lost, and three days later the Convention adjourned.[2]

The Convention had made a massive mistake by having proposed a Constitution that protected a few rights but omitted most. Moreover, Roger Sherman to the contrary, the Constitution empowered the United States to make laws that might infringe upon particular liberties. The power to tax, implemented by the ominous necessary and proper clause, could even be used to destroy a free press and might be enforced by general warrants enabling the government to ransack homes and businesses for evidence of criminal evasion of the revenue laws. Some opponents of ratification, who were either fools or demagogues, wildly hinted at abuses of the treaty power. They predicted that the United States would make a deal with the pope, establish a national church, revive the Inquisition, and torture suspects.[3]

Equally absurd were arguments by ratificationists as sophisticated as James Wilson, Alexander Hamilton, James Madison, and Oliver Ellsworth, to the effect that a bill of rights would be un-American, because government here derived from the people who retained everything not surrendered, and would be "dangerous" because any right omitted was lost. Throughout the nation, freedom of the press became a topic for grand declamation, but nowhere was the insistent demand for its constitutional protection accompanied by a reasoned consideration of what it meant, how far it extended, and whether any circumstances justified its limitation. The rhetorical effusions of Anti-Federalists yield no definition of any freedoms, later protected under the First Amendment, and the newspapers, pamphlets, and state ratification conventions offer as little illumination.

The remarks of the members of the Constitutional Convention who either decamped or refused to sign, are representative. Of the fourteen, Elbridge Gerry, George Mason, Robert Yates, John Lansing, Luther Martin, and Edmund Randolph published explanations of their rejection of the Constitution. None showed any serious concern for the omission of a bill of rights or the guarantee of a free press. Not one of them endorsed the principles of the Zenger case, namely, that truth should be a defense to a charge of libel and that the jury, not the court, should judge the criminality of the statements made by the defendant. Not one person who refused or failed to sign the Constitution argued the value of a broad scope for political discussion, or rejected restrictions on the press that existed in the common law or state laws. Mason, for example, regretted not only the absence of a bill of rights but also the absence of benefits of the common law, which allowed prosecutions for harsh criticism of the government, its policies, or its officials.[4] Yates, the likely author of the "Brutus" essays, a major Anti-Federalist series, failed to mention liberty of the press.[5]

The ratification controversy in Pennsylvania, where the Anti-Federalist press published voluminously against ratification, reveals how stunted was the thinking about a free press. Opponents of the Constitution frequently urged a guarantee that liberty of the press "ought never to be restrained," which echoed verbatim the language of the state's constitution. Those words should not be taken as a guarantee of a broad freedom, because even Sir William Blackstone, the oracle of the common law, had declared that the absence of "previous restraints upon publications" ensured that "neither is any restraint hereby laid upon freedom of thought or enquiry." He added that publicizing "bad sentiments destructive of the ends of society is the crime which society corrects."[6] In Pennsylvania, too, the language of no restraints meant no prior restraints: one could publish without fear of censorship but might be criminally convicted for aspersions on the government. The 1782 case of Eleazar Oswald, the rambunctious Philadelphia printer, showed that the state supreme court believed that the state constitutional guarantee of a free press was compatible with prosecution for seditious libel, and in 1788, Chief Justice Thomas McKean of Pennsylvania sentenced Oswald to a month in prison plus a fine, after holding that Blackstone's views controlled the meaning of the free press clause.[7] In 1797, McKean ruled:

> The liberty of the press is, indeed, essential to the nature of a free State, but this consists in laying no previous restraints upon public actions, and not in freedom from censure for criminal matter, when published. Every freeman has an undoubted right to lay what sentiments he pleases before the public . . . but take the consequences. . . .[8]

Thus, in Pennsylvania, whose constitutional provisions of 1776 and 1790 were the most libertarian in the nation as to freedom of speech and press, the crux of the common law on criminal libels remained in force.

Anti-Federalists reiterated that the United States would have the power to legislate against libels of the government, or prosecute such libels under common law even if Congress had not enacted a statute. Yet they merely proposed a free press guarantee, despite the fact that the state's free press clause accommodated Blackstone's views. Similarly, the Anti-Federalists urged a free press clause to prevent a tax on the press, despite the fact that in Massachusetts a free press clause had not prevented enactment of a stamp tax on newspapers or prosecutions for seditious libel.[9] At the Pennsylvania ratifying convention, Wilson insisted that although Congress had no power to pass laws against the press, liberty of the press meant "no antecedent restraint on it," that "every author is responsible" if he attacked the government, and that the proper proceedings would be by a criminal prosecution in a federal court.[10] No one argued that a free press clause would thwart such prosecution or supersede the common law of criminal libels, and no one urged that truth should be a defense to a charge of libel or that the jury should have the power to return a general verdict in libel prosecutions. Nevertheless, the Anti-Federalist members of the Pennsylvania convention urged the addition of a free press clause in language that improved on the state's version. The Pennsylvania minority substituted "shall" for the namby-pamby "ought" that had been conventional ("shall not be restrained by any law of the United States") and used phrasing broad enough to preclude federal prosecution, because "any law" applied to common as well as statutory law.[11]

Richard Henry Lee of Virginia and Melancthon Smith of New York shared the belief that a federal free press clause would prevent Congress from taxing the press. Lee, whose Anti-Federalist tract was probably the most widely read in the country, also shared with Smith the remarkable view that Great Britain provided a model for the legal protection of freedom of the press.[12] Patrick Henry had an even more complaisant view of the matter. Although he raged frenetically against all sorts of imagined oppressions that would result from ratification, he told the Virginia ratifying convention that as to liberty of the press, he need say nothing, because members of Congress would not infringe the "palladium of our liberties."[13] That he was sarcastic does not alter the fact that he contributed nothing to an understanding of freedom of the press.

On the ratificationist side, almost no Framers had yet revealed their understanding of the meaning of freedom of the press. Ben Franklin was one. In 1758 he had managed Pennsylvania's case before the Privy Council when two men appealed their conviction by the provincial assembly for "highly reflecting" on the government by the publication of seditious libels.[14] In 1789, in an essay on the licentiousness of the press, Franklin urged the use of the cudgels to break the heads of those who used the press for libels.[15] He did not then endorse prosecutions for criminal publications, but he never in his long active life criticized the law governing the press. William Livingston, a signer from New Jersey, had been the author of a youthful essay in which he wrote that anyone who published "any Thing injurious to his Country" should be convicted for "high Treason against the State."[16] In 1784, however, he criticized the doctrine that truth magnified a libel, but not the doctrine that words can criminally attack a free government.[17] Roger Sherman framed a bill of rights in 1789, with a provision that safeguarded the right to express one's sentiments "with decency," a conventional formulation of the time that ruled out libels—personal, obscene, blasphemous, or seditious. Similarly, Sherman's proposal that the government should have no power to "restrain the Press" was straight out of Blackstone, and meant no prior censorship.[18] James Wilson supported truth as a defense but otherwise endorsed Blackstone's views on the press.[19] Hugh Williamson of North Carolina was the only other Framer who troubled to indicate his understanding of freedom of the press when, in 1788, he invoked England as a model for that freedom.[20] Williamson's friend, James Iredell, who had not been at the Convention, masterminded ratification strategy in their state. Iredell, soon to become a member of the original Supreme Court, agreed with Williamson.[21] Before the ratification of the Bill of Rights, Madison never indicated his dissent from prevailing views. His libertarian interpretations of freedom of the press came later, at the earliest in 1794 and then, fully, during the Sedition Act controversy.[22]

Jefferson, also an advocate of ratification but not a Framer, thought about freedom of the press more than most of his contemporaries. His opinions on the meaning and scope of the freedom of the press reveal the limitations of his time. He once remarked that he did not care whether his neighbor said that there are twenty gods or no God, because "It neither picks my pocket nor breaks my leg."[23] But in drafting a constitution for Virginia in 1776 he considered proposing that freedom of religion "shall not be held to justify any seditious preaching or conversation against the authority of the civil government."[24] And in the same year he helped frame a statute on treasonous crimes, punishing anyone who "by any word" or deed defended the British cause.[25] Apparently, political opinions could break his leg or pick his pocket. What, then, did Jefferson mean by freedom of the press? He, like his contemporaries, supported an unrestricted public discussion of issues, but "unrestricted" meant merely the absence of censorship in advance of publication; although no one needed a government license to express himself, everyone was accountable under the criminal law for abuse of the right to speak or publish freely.

Jefferson never protested against the substantive law of seditious libel, not even during the later Sedition Act controversy. He directed his protests at that time against national as opposed to state prosecution for verbal crimes. He accepted without question the dominant view of his generation that government could be criminally assaulted merely by the expression of critical opinions that allegedly tended to subvert it by lowering it in the public's esteem. His consistent recognition of the concept of verbal political crimes throughout the Revolution continued in the period of peace that followed.

His draft constitution for Virginia in 1783 proposed that the press "shall be subject to no other restraint than liableness to legal prosecution for false facts printed and published."[26] He wrote this as an amendment to the state's free press clause. His amendment explicitly opened the door to criminal prosecutions. Yet he framed that amendment after considering the contrary opinion of his neighbors and constituents, who favored exempting the press from prosecution for any signed opinion or news. Jefferson singled out for prosecution "false facts," or "falsehoods," as he initially phrased his provision, in the face of a more liberal recommendation.

Jefferson endorsed prosecution again in 1788 when urging Madison to support amendments to the new federal Constitution, including a guarantee for freedom of the press. "A declaration that the federal government will never restrain the presses from printing anything they please, will not take away the liability of the printers for false facts printed. The declaration that religious faith shall be unpunished," he offered as added assurance, "does not give impunity to criminal acts dictated by religious error."[27] Publication of false facts on political matters seemed the equivalent of an overt crime resulting from a misguided religious conscience. Unlike Blackstone, however, Jefferson implicitly opposed the persecution of accurate information.

Jefferson received a copy of Madison's proposed amendments to the Constitution in 1789. He was disappointed not to see the adoption of his recommendation on the press. He liked the proposal on the press, he said, but would be pleased to see the following revision: "The people shall not be deprived or abridged of their right to speak or write or otherwise to publish anything but false facts affecting injuriously the life, liberty, property, or reputation of others or affecting the peace of the confederacy with foreign nations."[28] One can imagine how free the press would have been during the controversies over Jay's Treaty or the Louisiana Purchase, had Jefferson's recommendations prevailed and been taken seriously.

Significantly, neither Jefferson himself nor anyone else in the United States, prior to 1798, extended his "overt acts" test to freedom of political opinion. Jefferson had devised that test when seeking a way to ensure the free exercise of religion. In his Statute of Religious Freedom, which became law in Virginia in 1786, he declared that

> to suffer the civil magistrate to intrude his powers into the field of opinion, and to restrain the profession or propagation of principles, on supposition of their ill tendency, is a dangerous fallacy, which at once destroys all religious liberty, because he being of course judge of that tendency, will make his opinions the rule of judgment, and approve or condemn the sentiments of others only as they shall square with or differ from his own; that it is time enough for the rightful purposes of civil government for its officers to interfere when principles break out into overt acts against peace and good order. . . .[29]

The overt-acts test applied, in Jefferson's words, only to "opinions in matters of religion," although its principle should have been as relevant in cases of political opinion, and had been specifically extended to such cases by many English theorists.

Virginia's legislature did not extend the overt-acts test to proscribed political utterances. In the same year that it enacted the Statute of Religious Freedom, the legislature passed a law that penalized advocacy that a new state be carved out of state's boundaries without the legislature's consent.[30] The statute did not bespeak broad understanding in Virginia that freedom of political speech and press included a right to express any principle that did not "break out into overt acts." On the contrary, Virginia embodied the bad-tendency test of utterances by failing to distinguish mere words from the overt criminal act of attempting by unconstitutional means to erect a new government within the state's territory.

Virginia reenacted the same statute in 1792, when it also passed an "Act Against Divulgers of False News."[31] The new act of 1792, which covered printers and others who misinformed the people, showed that the legislature believed that it could regulate the press without restraining it in violation of the state's free press clause. Virginia's public law accepted prosecutions for criminal words, and, in the later words of a member of the Assembly, "it is known to the people that in a prosecution for libel in Virginia, under the state laws, you can neither plead nor give in evidence the truth of the matter contained in the libel."[32] In other words, Virginia even rejected the bedrock of the Zenger case, that truth is a defense.

No state got rid of the common law concept of seditious libel. No state gave statutory or constitutional recognition to the overt-acts test embodied in the preamble of Virginia's 1786 statute. No state adopted truth as a defense during the period 1776–1789. If an objective of the Revolution was to repudiate the Blackstone exposition of the common law's restrictions on freedom of expression, how very strange that Americans of the revolutionary generation did not say so. Excepting a few dissident reactions to the Oswald prosecution in Pennsylvania in 1782, Americans accepted the justice of punishing false opinions or malicious scandals against the government.[33]

The history of the reception of the common law during the Revolution tends to establish the acceptance of the Blackstonian definition of liberty of press and speech. Twelve states, including all nine guaranteeing a free press, provided by constitution or statute that the common law of England before the Revolution was to operate with full force unless inconsistent with or repugnant to some other statutory provision.[34] New York, the home of Zenger's case, repudiated its principles. The state constitution of 1777 expressly adopted the common law as of the date of the outbreak of the war with England.[35] In the states where no protection to freedom of speech or press was afforded, there is not even the basis of an implication that it was the intention to get rid of the idea that a republican government may be criminally assaulted by the opinions of its citizens.

In 1787 Massachusetts, which had a free press clause, indicted several people who encouraged and supported Shays' Rebellion; among the defendants were George Brock and Gideon Pond, accused of having published "scandalous, seditious" libels against the government.[36] Although their cases never came to trial, the state did convict Captain Moses Harvey of "seditious and inflammatory words" because he called the legislature "thieves" and urged the closing of the courts. In April 1787 the most important of these cases was tried. A jury convicted Dr. William Whiting before the Supreme Judicial Court sitting in Great Barrington, which was the scene of Whiting's crime. No ordinary libeler, Whiting was Chief Justice of the Court of Common Pleas of Berkshire County. Shortly before the fall term of his court in 1786, he had written an article, signed Gracchus, in which he censured the government for unjust laws and recommended that a virtuous people who lacked redress of grievances should "disturb the government." When Shays' Rebellion broke out, armed men with whom he sympathized closed his court. After the defeat of Shays at Petersham, the government began its arrests. Whiting was dismissed from his judicial post and convicted of writing a seditious libel; his prison sentence was suspended but he had to pay a one-hundred pound fine and post sureties for good behavior for five years. No one claimed that the free press clause of the state constitution stood in the way of a prosecution for seditious libel.[37]

In 1791 Edmund Freeman, a newspaper editor, for having grossly libeled the private life of a member of the legislature, was criminally prosecuted on the theory that his words tended to breach the public peace of the Commonwealth. Attorney General James Sullivan, later Jeffersonian governor of the state, maintained that the constitutional guarantee of a free press meant only the absence of a licensing act; he quoted Blackstone at length to prove the point and urged that licentiousness must be distinguished from liberty. The defendant's attorneys did not challenge Sullivan's principles. Although not asking for a ruling that truth was a defense, they denied licentiousness or breach of peace on the part of Freeman and sought to prove the accuracy of his publication. Of the three judges who presided at the trial, none accepted truth as a defense.[38] The jury's verdict was not guilty, but as Clyde A. Duniway, the historian of *The Development of Freedom of the Press in Massachusetts*, concluded: "A judicial construction of liberty of the press in the state had been announced, differing in no wise from the opinions of Chief Justice Hutchinson in 1768 or of the Superior Court of Judicature in 1724. In effect, it was affirmed that the constitutional provision of 1780 was merely declaratory of the law as it had existed for nearly sixty years, with an added prohibition of any possible reestablishment of censorship." This observation has the substantiation of the prosecutions for seditious libel against the editor of the Boston *Independent Chronicle* and the paper's clerk and bookkeeper.[39]

Two states, in the midst of affording a constitutional guarantee to freedom of religion, provided that its exercise could not justify libeling the government. North Carolina's article on religious liberty (1776) contained this qualification: "Provided, that nothing herein contained shall be construed to exempt preachers of treasonable or *seditious discourses*, from legal trial and punishment."[40] If preachers were not exempt from the law of seditious libel, others were not either. South Carolina's equivalent clause (1778) stated: "No person whatever shall speak anything in their religious assembly irreverently or *seditiously* of the government of this State."[41] If one could not speak seditiously of the state in church, he could not do so elsewhere. To the same effect, though not as explicitly, are the qualifying clauses of the religious freedom provisions in the first constitutions of New York,[42] New Hampshire,[43] Massachusetts,[44] Georgia,[45] and Maryland.[46] The last, for example, provided (1776) that no one "under colour of religion . . . shall disturb the good order, peace, or safety of the State, or shall infringe the laws of morality." At common law, an utterance tending to disturb the peace of the state was seditious. New York, New Hampshire, Massachusetts, and Georgia used similar language, prohibiting exercises of religion repugnant to the public peace or safety.

Before 1798, the avant-garde among American libertarians staked everything on the principles of the Zenger case, which they thought beyond improvement. They believed that no greater liberty could be conceived than the right to publish without restriction, if only the defendant could plead truth as a defense in a criminal prosecution for libel, and if the criminality of his words might be determined by a jury of his peers rather than by a judge. The substantive law of criminal libels was unquestioned. But libertarians who accepted Zengerian principles painted themselves into a corner. If a jury returned a verdict of "guilty" despite a defense of truth, due process had been accorded and protests were groundless, because the substance of the law that made the trial possible—criminal responsibility for abuse of the press—had not been challenged.

American acquiescence in the common law definition of a free press was so widespread that even the frail Zengerian principles seemed daring, novel, and had few adherents. It was not until 1790 that the first state, Pennsylvania, took the then radical step of adopting those principles, which still left the crux of common law of seditious libel intact.[47] The Pennsylvania provision was drafted by James Wilson, who endorsed Blackstone's definition of liberty of the press.[48] The state constitutional provision of 1790 reflected this proposition, as did state trials before and after 1790.[49]

Delaware and Kentucky followed Pennsylvania's lead in 1792,[50] but elsewhere the status quo prevailed. In 1789 William Cushing and John Adams worried about whether the guarantee of a free press in Massachusetts ought to mean that truth was a good defense to a charge of criminal libel, but they agreed that false publications against the government were punishable.[51] In 1791, when a Massachusetts editor was prosecuted for a criminal libel against a state official, the Supreme Judicial Court divided on the question of truth as a defense, but agreed, like the Pennsylvania judges,[52] that the state constitutional guarantee of a free press accommodated common law crimes of libel.[53]

State pronouncements show no greater enlightenment. None of the first nine states to ratify the Constitution recommended an amendment guaranteeing freedom of speech or press. Indeed, the Pennsylvania ratifying convention, led by Wilson and Thomas McKean, rejected the minority's proposal for such an amendment, and the Maryland convention took no action on any of the amendments recommended by its committee on amendments, one of which declared, "That the freedom of the press be inviolably preserved." The committee had added this explanation: "In prosecutions in the federal courts for libels, the constitutional preservation of the great and fundamental right may prove invaluable."⁵⁴ The necessary implication of this is that prosecutions for criminal libel might be maintained in the federal courts under common if not statutory law, and that the free press guarantee would provide some advantage to the defendant—possibly truth as a defense or a general verdict by a jury.

Of the twelve states to ratify the Constitution before Congress drafted the First Amendment in 1789, only the last three, Virginia, North Carolina, and New York, sought to safeguard the expression of political opinion from violation by the new national government. Virginia urged that "among other essential rights the liberty of Conscience and of the Press cannot be cancelled abridged restrained or modified by any authority of the United States."⁵⁵ Virginia sought to prevent a concurrent jurisdiction in the national government on the subject of criminal libels. State sovereignty probably dominated Virginia's concern. New York accompanied its ratification of the Constitution in 1788 with the recommendation for an amendment worded, "That the Freedom of the Press ought not to be violated or restrained,"⁵⁶ although no comparable provision existed in that state's constitution. In 1799 New York court imprisoned a printer, David Frothingham, for four months and fined him for the crime of having copied from another newspaper the criminal innuendo that Alexander Hamilton opposed the republican form of government and worked with the British government to undermine it by trying to buy out the Philadelphia *Aurora*. Hamilton himself instigated the indictment on the theory that the calumny against him had the "dangerous tendency," he said, of destroying the confidence of the people in the leading defenders of the administration. At Frothingham's trial the court refused to allow evidence to prove the truth of his accusation, even though the prosecution consented to permit truth as a defense. Hamilton, the star witness for the state, testified that the Philadelphia *Aurora*, the source of the seditious libel and the country's foremost Jeffersonian newspaper, was hostile to the government of the United States.⁵⁷

As for the states that constitutionally protected freedom of speech or press, the evidence for the 1776–1791 period does not show an understanding that the crime of seditious libel and government by consent of the governed contradicted each other.

State recommendations that a free press clause be annexed to the Constitution did not signal a different theory about the compass of freedom of political expression. Whatever the Anti-Federalists meant in recommending a bill of rights with a free press clause, they transformed political opinion in the nation. In 1787 a consensus had existed to strengthen the national government. In 1788 a new consensus existed: ratify the Constitution with the understanding that a bill of rights be added to it. A failure to fulfill public expectations could easily have aborted the Constitution by turning public opinion in favor of a second constitutional convention that would have scrapped the Constitution and merely modified the Articles of Confederation. Madison prevented that. He saved the new system and his own political career by his successful struggle in the First Congress for the amendments that became the Bill of Rights.

He described freedom of the press as one of the "choicest" of the "great rights of mankind" and sought vainly to secure it against violation by the states as well as by the United States.[58] But he said nothing in 1789, or earlier, that revealed what he meant by a free press clause. Although he remarked that freedom of the press was unguarded by the British constitution,[59] he meant only that none of the great freedom documents, such as the English Bill of Rights of 1689, mentioned the press. Had he meant more than that and in any way implied a novel view, proof would have appeared in his private correspondence, if not his public speeches. He capitalized on existing public opinion; when he proposed his amendments he did not intend to reshape either the legal or the popular mind. He sought, rather, to satisfy the widespread clamor for protection of rights, rather than provoke fresh controversy. He said explicitly that Congress should "confine" itself to "an enumeration of simple, acknowledged principles."[60] The entire history of the framing and ratification of the free press clause, from 1789 through 1791, suggests nothing new about its meaning or the way in which it was understood. Madison did, however, contribute a crucially important verb to the free press clause by providing that it "shall" be inviolable. No state constitution and no state ratifying convention had used the imperative voice; previously the weaker "ought" prevailed.[61]

What import did the free press clause possess at the time of its adoption? Its meaning was surely not self-evident. The controversy in the states over the ratification of the Constitution without a bill of rights had revealed little about the substance and scope of a free press, and the debates by the First Congress, which framed the free press clause, illumined even less. Congress debated the clauses on religion, but on the remainder of the First Amendment it considered only whether the right of peaceable assembly vested the people with the power to instruct their representatives on how to vote. In the course of that discussion, Madison made the only recorded statement on the subject of speech or press. If by peaceable assembly, he said, "We mean nothing more than this, that the people have a right to express and communicate their sentiments and wishes, we have provided for it already. The right of freedom of speech is secured; the liberty of the press is expressly declared to be beyond the reach of this Government. . . ."[62] Any interpretation of the meaning and compass of the free press drawn from this vague statement would strain credulity.

The state legislatures that ratified the First Amendment offer no enlightenment either. Without the records of their legislative debates, we do not know what the state legislatures understood the free press clause to mean. Other contemporary materials do not help either. Most people undoubtedly cared about protecting freedom of the press, but no one seems to have cared enough to clarify what he meant by the subject upon which he lavished praise. If definition were unnecessary because of the existence of a tacit and widespread understanding of "liberty of the press," only the received or traditional understanding could have been possible. To assume the existence of a generally accepted latitudinarian understanding that veered substantially from the common law definition is warrantless, given the absence of evidence. Any novel definition expanding the scope of free expression or repudiating, even altering, the concept of seditious libel would have been the subject of public debate or comment. Not even the Anti-Federalists offered the argument that the clause on speech and press was unsatisfactory because it was insufficiently protective against prosecutions for criminal defamation of the government. Not even they urged that truth could be no libel.

Even if we assume that the Framers really intended to impose upon the national government "an absolute, unqualified prohibition"[63]—there shall be *no* law abridging freedom of the press—we should recognize that the Framers cared less about giving unqualified immunity to all discourse than they cared for states' rights and the federal principle. Granting, for the moment, an intention to render the national government utterly powerless to act in any way against oral, written, or printed utterances, the Framers meant the clause to reserve to the states an exclusive legislative authority in the field of speech and press. Thus, no matter what the Framers meant or understood by freedom of speech or press, the national government even under the unamended Constitution could not make speech or press a legitimate subject of restrictive statutory action. The Framers intended the First Amendment as an added assurance that Congress would be limited to the exercise of its enumerated powers and therefore they phrased it as an express prohibition against the possibility that Congress might use those powers to abridge freedom of speech or press. It goes without saying that an express prohibition on power did not vest or create a new power, previously nonexistent, to abridge speech or press, because, as Madison declared, the Bill of Rights was not framed "to imply powers not meant to be included in the enumeration."[64] Because the Senate rejected the House-approved amendment to prohibit state abridgment of freedom of speech, the First Amendment left the states free to act against individual expression, subject only to such restraints as might be laid down in state constitutions. The big question persists, however: Even had Congress passed, and the states ratified, an amendment imposing upon the states the same prohibition laid by the First Amendment upon the national government, what did the Framers understand by freedom of speech and freedom of press?

No one can say for certain what the Framers had in mind because there is not enough evidence to justify cocksure conclusions, even though all the evidence points in one direction. Whether the Framers themselves knew what they had in mind is uncertain. At the time of the drafting and ratification of the First Amendment, few among them clearly understood what they meant by the free press clause, and we cannot know that those few represented a consensus. Considerable disagreement existed, for example, on the question of whether freedom of expression meant the right to print the truth about government measures and officials if the truth was defamatory or was revealed for unworthy motives. Disagreement existed too about the function of juries in trials for criminal libel. Zengerian principles had few open advocates.

What is clear is that no evidence suggests an understanding that the concept of a free press conflicted with prosecutions of seditious utterances. Freedom of speech and press was not understood to include a right to broadcast sedition by words. The security of the state against libelous advocacy or attack outweighed any social interest in open expression, at least through the period of the adoption of the First Amendment. The thought and experience of a lifetime, indeed the taught traditions of law and politics extending back many generations, supplied an a priori belief that freedom of political discourse, however broadly conceived, stopped short of seditious libel.

The Sedition Act, passed less than seven years after the ratification of the First Amendment, suggests that the generation that framed the amendment did not consider the suppression of seditious libel to be an abridgment of freedom of speech or press. Yet the Framers themselves, whatever they understood freedom of the press to mean, had given the public specific assurances again and again that neither speech nor press could be the subject of repressive legislation by a government bereft of authority on that subject.

The injunction of the First Amendment, therefore, did not imply that a sedition act might be passed without abridging the freedom of the press. Even if a sedition act might not be an abridgment, that was not the main point of the amendment. To understand its framers' intentions, the amendment should not be read with the focus only on the meaning of "the freedom of the press." It should also be read with the stress on the opening clause: "Congress shall make no law. . . ." In part, the injunction was intended and understood to prohibit any congressional regulation of the press, whether by means of censorship, a licensing law, a tax, or a sedition act. The Framers meant Congress to be totally without power to enact legislation respecting the press, excepting copyright laws. They intended a federal system in which the central government could exercise only specifically enumerated powers, or powers necessary and proper to carry out the enumerated ones. Thus, no matter what was meant or understood by freedom of the press, the national government, even in the absence of the First Amendment, could not make the press a legitimate subject of regulation. The objective of the amendment was to quiet public apprehension by offering further assurance that Congress would be limited to the exercise of its delegated powers. The First Amendment could not possibly have enhanced the powers of Congress; it did not add to them a previously nonexisting power.

The amendment protected the *freedom* of the press, not the press. The freedom of the press and of political discourse generally had so widened in scope that seditious libel had become a rather narrow category of verbal offenses against government, government officials, and government policies. To be sure, the legal definition of seditious libel remained what it had been from the time of Hawkins to Mansfield: malicious, scandalous falsehoods of a political nature that tended to breach the peace, instill revulsion or contempt in the people against their government, or lower their esteem for their rulers. But prosecutions for criticism of government were infrequent, and the press was habitually scurrilous. Governments forbore, realizing that prosecutions might fail or backfire because critics represented strong factions and, often, influential men. Moreover, public opinion, except in times of crisis like Shays' Rebellion, tended to distrust an administration that sought to imprison its critics. The press could not have endured as aspersive and animadversive as it was without public support. For the most part people understood that scummy journalism unavoidably accompanied the benefits to be gained from a free press. People seem also to have understood that critics vented unfavorable opinions in order to excite a justifiable contempt for the government; to prosecute those critics seemed to immunize from criticism public officials who probably deserved to be disliked or distrusted.

The actual freedom of the press had slight relationship to the fact that, as a legal concept, freedom of the press was a cluster of constraints. The law threatened repression; yet the press conducted itself as if the law scarcely existed. In 1799 Madison observed that in England, despite the common law on the press and "the occasional punishment of those who use it with a freedom offensive to the government," all knew that "the freedom exercised by the press, and protected by the public opinion far exceeds the limits prescribed by the ordinary rules of law." The English press, said Madison, criticized the ministry "with peculiar freedom," and during elections for the House of Commons the calumnies of the press raged. The American press enjoyed at least as much freedom.[65]

When the Framers of the First Amendment provided that Congress shall not abridge the freedom of the press, they could only have meant to protect the press with which they were familiar and as it operated at the time. In effect, they constitutionally guaranteed the freedom of the press as it existed and was practiced at the time. They did not adopt the limited conception of it found in the law or in the views of libertarian theorists. By freedom of the press, the Framers meant a right to engage in rasping, corrosive, and offensive discussions on all topics of public interest. The English common law definition had become unsuitable, and American libertarian theory had not caught up with press practice. Government in the United States derived from the people, who reserved a right to alter it, and the government was accountable to the people. That required a broader legal concept of freedom of the press than existed in England, where the monarch was a hereditary ruler not accountable to the people and the House of Lords was also not elected or accountable. Glimmerings of a broader libertarian theory existed but did not systematically emerge until 1798.

In a sense, the constitutional guarantee of freedom of the press signified nothing new. It did not augment or expand freedom of the press. It recognized and perpetuated an existing condition. Freedom of the press meant, in part, an exemption from prior restraints and continued to mean that. The practical problem faced by writers and printers dealt with subsequent punishment for licentious use of the right to publish without prior restraint. The press remained subject to the common law despite a constitutional guarantee, but the threshold of public tolerance had significantly widened. Thus freedom of the press meant more than just freedom from prior restraint. It meant the right to criticize harshly the government, its officers, and its policies as well as to comment on any matters of public concern. The right to criticize and comment no longer implied a decent or temperate fashion. It meant a freedom for foul-tempered, mean-spirited expression. For practical purposes what the law called malice did not signify just a nasty disposition; it signified ill-will, an intention to provoke readers or listeners to hope for damage to the public weal or to the government. But this broad view of the matter rests on inference. Within a decade of the ratification of the First Amendment, merely mild criticism, certainly not scorching billingsgate, resulted in convictions under the Sedition Act, showing a wholly different understanding of freedom of the press. The public revulsion that shortly manifested itself in Jefferson's election suggests, however, that the Federalists of 1798–1800 misread the free press clause.

Freedom of the press signified not only freedom from prior restraints; if politics allowed, it also meant responsibility under the law for damaging publications. It meant, too, that the press enjoyed a preferred position in the American constitutional scheme because of its special relationship to popular government. The electoral process would have been a sham if voters did not have the assistance of the press in learning what candidates stood for and what their records showed about past performance and qualifications. A free press was becoming indispensable to the existence of a free and responsible government. Even Blackstone conceded, "The liberty of the press is indeed essential to the nature of a free state."[66] Its essentiality derived also from the fact that the press had become the tribune of the people by sitting in judgment on the conduct of public officials. A free press meant the press as the Fourth Estate, or, rather, in the American scheme, an informal or extraconstitutional fourth branch that functioned as part of the intricate system of checks and balances that exposed public mismanagement and kept power fragmented, manageable, and accountable. Freedom of the press had accrued still another function that intimately associated it with a free state, meriting its constitutional protection. The cliché that it was the bulwark of liberty, "essential," as the Massachusetts constitution asserted, "to the security of freedom in a state," meant that the existence of various personal liberties depended at least in part on the vigilance of the press in exposing unfairness, inequality, and injustice. Freedom of the press had become part of the matrix for the functioning of popular government and the protection of civil liberties.

It does not necessarily follow that the Framers desired to give the utmost latitude to expression. The First Amendment did not embody an absolute because not all speech is free speech, or, to put it another way, there are several classes of speech or of publication, some of which were not intended to be categorized under the rubric of "freedom of speech" or freedom of the press. Did the Framers intend that the federal mails should be open to pornographic materials or that a speaker should be free to incite violence directly and immediately against the United States? Did they intend that knowingly false, malicious, and damaging calumnies against the government should be free? Madison himself was "inclined to think that absolute restrictions in cases that are doubtful, or where emergencies may overrule them, ought to be avoided."[67] If the Framers did not intend that all speech, without exception, should be free without exception, the crucial question is, where did they intend to draw the line between speech that was constitutionally protected and speech that was not? The eighteenth century did not provide answers.

In 1798, however, a sudden breakthrough occurred in American libertarian thought on freedom of political expression. The change was abrupt, radical, and transforming. The Sedition Act, which was a thrust in the direction of a single-party press and a monolithic party system, triggered the libertarian surge among the Republicans. The result was the emergence of a new body of libertarian thought.

The Federalists in 1798 believed that true freedom of the press would benefit if truth—*their* truth—were the measure of freedom. Their infamous Sedition Act was, in the words of Gilbert and Sullivan, the true embodiment of everything excellent. It was, that is, the very epitome of libertarian thought since the time of Zenger's case. Everything that the libertarians had ever demanded was incorporated in the Sedition Act: a requirement that criminal intent be shown; the power of the jury to decide whether the accused's statement was libelous as a matter of law as well as of fact; and truth as a defense, which was an innovation not accepted in England until 1843.[68] By every standard the Sedition Act was a great victory for libertarian principles of freedom of the press—except that libertarian standards abruptly changed, because the Republicans immediately recognized a Pyrrhic victory.

The Sedition Act provoked them to develop a new libertarian theory. It began to emerge in 1798 when Congressmen Albert Gallatin, John Nicholas, Nathaniel Macon, and Edward Livingston argued against the enactment of the sedition bill.[69] It was further developed by defense counsel, most notably George Blake, in Sedition Act prosecutions.[70] It reached its most reflective and systematic expression in tracts and books that unfortunately became rare and little known. The main body of original Republican thought on the scope, meaning, and rationale of the First Amendment was expressed in George Hay's tract, *An Essay on the Liberty of the Press*[71]; in Madison's *Report* on the Virginia Resolutions for the Virginia House of Delegates[72]; in the book *A Treatise Concerning Political Enquiry, and the Liberty of the Press*, by Tunis Wortman of New York[73]; in John Thomson's book, *An Enquiry, Concerning the Liberty, and Licentiousness of the Press*[74]; and in St. George Tucker's appendix to his edition of Blackstone's *Commentaries*,[75] a most significant place for the repudiation of Blackstone on the liberty of the press. Of these works, Wortman's philosophical book is preeminent as the only equivalent on this side of the Atlantic to John Milton and John Stuart Mill.

The new libertarians abandoned the straitjacketing doctrines of Blackstone and the common law, including the recent concept of a federal common law of crimes. They scornfully denounced the no-prior-restraints definition. Said Madison: ". . . this idea of the freedom of the press can never be admitted to be the American idea of it," because a law inflicting penalties would have the same effect as a law authorizing a prior restraint. "It would seem a mockery to say that no laws shall be passed preventing publications from being made, but that laws might be passed for punishing them in case they should be made."[76] As Hay put it, the "British definition" meant that a man might be jailed or even put to death for what he published, provided that no notice was taken of him before he published.[77]

The old yardstick for measuring the scope of freedom was also rejected by the new libertarians. "Liberty" of the press, for example, had always been differentiated from its "licentiousness," which was the object of the criminal law's sanctions. "Truth" and "facts" had always divided the realm of lawfulness from "falsehoods," and a similar distinction had been made between "good motives" and "criminal intent." All such distinctions were now discarded, on the grounds that they did not distinguish and therefore were not meaningful standards that might guide a jury or a court in judging an alleged verbal crime. The term "licentiousness," wrote Thomson, "is destitute of any meaning"; it was used, according to him, by those who wished "nobody to enjoy the Liberty of the Press but such as were of their own opinion."[78] The term "malice," in Wortman's view, was invariably confused with mistaken zeal or prejudice.[79] It was merely an inference drawn from the supposed evil tendency of the publication itself, and just a further means of punishing the excitement of unfavorable sentiments against the government even when the people's contempt of the government was richly deserved. The punishment of "malice," or intent to defame the government, concluded Madison, necessarily struck at the right of free discussion, because critics intended to excite unfavorable sentiments.[80] Finding criminality in the tendency of words was merely an attempt to erect public "tranquility . . . upon the ruins of Civil Liberty," wrote Wortman.[81]

The wholesale abandonment of the common law's limitations on the press was accompanied by a withering onslaught against the constrictions and subjectivity of Zengerian principles. The Sedition Act, Hay charged, "appears to be directed against falsehood and malice only; in fact . . . there are many truths, important to society, which are not susceptible of that full, direct, and positive evidence, which alone can be exhibited before a court and a jury."[82] If, argued Gallatin, the administration prosecuted a citizen for his opinion that the Sedition Act itself was unconstitutional, would not a jury, composed of the friends of that administration, find the opinion "ungrounded, or, in other words, false and scandalous, and its publication malicious? And by what kind of argument or evidence, in the present temper of parties, could the accused convince them that his opinions were true?"[83] The truth of opinions, the new libertarians concluded, could not be proved. Allowing "truth" as a defense and thinking it to be a protection for freedom, Thomson declared, made as much sense as letting a jury decide which was "the most palatable food, agreeable drink, or beautiful color."[84] A jury, he asserted, could not give an impartial verdict in political trials. Madison agreed, commenting that the "baleful tendency" of prosecutions for seditious libel was "little diminished by the privilege of giving in evidence the truth of the matter contained in political writings."[85]

The renunciation of traditional concepts reached its climax in the assault on the idea that there was such a thing as a crime of seditious libel. That crime, Wortman concluded, could "never be reconciled to the genius and constitution of a Representative Commonwealth."[86] He and the others constructed a new libertarianism, genuinely radical because it broke sharply with the past and advocated an absolute freedom of political expression. One of the major tenets of this new libertarianism was that a free government cannot be criminally attacked by the opinions of its citizens. Hay, for example, insisted that freedom of the press, like chastity, was either "absolute"[87] or did not exist. Abhorring the very concept of verbal political crimes, he declared that a citizen should have a right to "say everything which his passions suggest; he may employ all his time, and all his talents, if he is wicked enough, to do so, in speaking against the government matters that are false, scandalous and malicious,"[88] and yet he should be "safe within the sanctuary of the press" even if he "condemns the principle of republican institutions . . . censures the measures of our government, and every department and officer thereof, and ascribes the measures of the former, however salutary, and conduct of the latter, however upright, to the basest motives; even if he ascribes to them measures and acts, which never had existence; thus violating at once, every principle of decency and truth."[89]

In brief, the new libertarians advocated that only "injurious conduct," as manifested by "overt acts" or deeds, rather than words, should be criminally redressable.[90] They did not refine this proposition except to recognize that the law of libel should continue to protect private reputations against malicious falsehoods. They did not even recognize that under certain circumstances words may immediately and directly incite criminal acts.

This absolutist interpretation of the First Amendment was based on the now familiar, but then novel and democratic, theory that free government depends for its very existence and security on freedom of political discourse. The scope of the amendment, according to his theory, is determined by the nature of the government and its relationship to the people. Because the government is the people's servant, exists by their consent and for their benefit, and is constitutionally limited, responsible, and elective, it cannot, said Thomson, tell the citizen: "You shall not think this, or that upon certain subjects; or if you do, it is at your peril."[91] The concept of seditiousness can exist only in a relationship based on inferiority, when people are subjects rather than sovereigns and their criticism implies contempt of their master. "In the United States," Madison declared, "the case is altogether different."[92] Coercion or abridgment of unlimited political opinion, Wortman explained, would violate the very "principles of the social state"— by which he meant a government of the people.[93] Because such a government depended upon popular elections, all the new libertarians agreed that the widest possible latitude must be maintained to keep the electorate free, informed, and capable of making intelligent choices. The citizen's freedom of political expression had the same scope as the legislator's, and had the same reasons behind it.[94] That freedom might be dangerously abused, but the people, if exposed to every opinion, would decide on men and measures wisely.

This brief summary of the new libertarianism barely does justice to its complexity and sophistication but suggests its boldness, originality, and democratic character.[95] The new libertarianism developed, to be sure, as an expediency of self-defense on the part of a besieged political minority that was struggling to maintain its existence and its right to function unfettered. But the new libertarians established, virtually all at once and in nearly perfect form, a theory justifying the rights of individual expression and of opposition parties. That the Jeffersonians in power did not always adhere to their new principles does not diminish the enduring nobility and rightness of those principles. It proves only that the Jeffersonians set the highest standards of freedom for themselves and posterity. Their legacy was the idea that there is an indispensable condition for the development of free men in a free society: the state must be bitted and bridled by a bill of rights that is to be construed in the most generous terms and whose protections are not to be the playthings of momentary majorities. That legacy deepened and enriched American libertarian theory, but it did not surmount the resistance of the law. Ultimate victory in the courts and statutes belongs to Alexander Hamilton's restatement of Zengerian principles.[96]

Hamilton, a supporter of the Sedition Act and of prosecutions for criminal libel, believed that the law of libel should be governed by the principles of the Zenger case, in order to protect the legitimate freedom of the press. In 1804 he was permitted by his Jeffersonian opponents in New York, who were then in power, to make political capital and legal history by advocating these old principles. The state indicted Harry Croswell, an obscure Federalist editor, for the common law crime of seditious libel against President Jefferson. Croswell's crime was his publishing of the accusation that Jefferson had paid to have Washington denounced as a traitor and Adams as an incendiary. Chief Justice Morgan Lewis, a Jeffersonian, refused Croswell the opportunity of introducing evidence to prove the truth of his statements. In instructing the jury, Lewis told the jurors that their only duty was to determine whether the defendant had in fact published the statements as charged; that they must leave to the court, as a matter of law, the determination of the statements' libelous character. Lewis, in other words, charged the jury that the law of New York was the law as laid down by Chief Justice DeLancey in the Zenger case.[97]

On the appeal of Croswell's conviction, before the highest court of the state, Alexander Hamilton championed the cause of freedom of the press. That freedom, he said (in words that were even more restrictive than those of the Sedition Act), "consists in the right to publish, with impunity, truth, with good motives, for justifiable ends, though reflecting on government, magistracy, or individuals." The Sedition Act itself did not require proof of "good motives, for justifiable ends," but Hamilton's position seemed a shining standard of libertarianism when compared with the reactionary views of Chief Justice Lewis—or of the prosecutor, Attorney General Ambrose Spencer, another Jeffersonian. Spencer argued from Blackstone (not Tucker's version), and declared that a libel, even if true, was punishable because of its dangerous tendency. The former prosecutor had become a member of the Supreme Court of Judicature by the time it decided the case. Had Spencer not been ineligible to participate in the decision, the repressive opinion reexpressed by Chief Justice Lewis would have commanded a majority. Instead, the court divided evenly, two against two. The opinion of Judge James Kent expressed Hamilton's position.[98]

In the following year, 1805, the state legislature enacted a bill that allowed the jury to decide the criminality of an alleged libel and that permitted truth as a defense, if published "with good motives and for justifiable ends." That standard prevailed in the United States until 1964.[99]

CHAPTER ELEVEN

The Fourth Amendment: Search and Seizure

We the People

*B*efore the American Revolution, the right to be secure against unreasonable searches and seizures had slight existence. British policies assaulted the privacy of dwellings and places of business, particularly when royal revenues were at stake. The right to be taxed only by the consent of representatives of one's choice was the great right whose violation helped cause the Revolution. British attempts to enforce tax measures by general searches also occasioned deeply felt resentments that damaged relations between England and the American colonies, and provoked anxious concerns that later sought expression in the Fourth Amendment. That amendment repudiates general warrants by recognizing a "right of the people to be secure in their persons, houses, papers, and effects, against unreasonable searches and seizures." Any warrant that is vague about the persons, places, or things to be searched violates the specificity required by the command of the amendment that warrants shall issue only "upon probable cause, supported by oath or affirmation, and particularly describing the place to be searched, and the persons or things to be seized."

The Fourth Amendment would not have been possible but for British legal theory, which Britons of North America inherited and cherished as their own. The Fourth Amendment emerged not only from the American Revolution; it was a constitutional embodiment of the extraordinary coupling of Magna Carta to the appealing fiction that a man's home is his castle. That is, the amendment resulted from embellishments on the insistence, which was rhetorically compelling, though historically without foundation, that government cannot encroach on the private premises of the individual subject. What mattered was not what Magna Carta actually said but what people thought it said or, rather, what it had come to mean. What also mattered was the inspiring imagery that swelled the sense of freedom in the ordinary subject. William Pitt expressed it best in a speech in Parliament in 1763, when he declaimed: "The poorest man may, in his cottage, bid defiance to all the forces of the Crown. It may be frail; its roof may shake; the wind may blow through it; the storm may enter; the rain may enter; but the King of England may not enter; all his force dares not cross the threshold of the ruined tenement."[1] The assertion that "a man's house is his castle" goes back at least to the early sixteenth century, and it was repeated with such frequency that it became a cliché.[2]

The first person to link the privacy of one's home to a right secured by Magna Carta seems to have been Robert Beale, clerk of the Privy Council, in 1589. Beale asked rhetorically what had happened to chapter 39 of the great charter when agents of a prerogative court, acting under its warrant, could "enter into mens houses, break up their chests and chambers" and carry off as evidence whatever they pleased.[3] That Beale's statement was historically unsound is unimportant compared to the fact that he took a feudal document, which protected the barons, and converted it into a constitution for everyone. Creative glosses like Beale's would make Magna Carta a talismanic symbol of freedom, subjecting all authority, including the royal prerogative, to the rule of law. Construing chapter 39 to be a ban on general warrants helped make a myth that would transform American thinking about privacy rights against government.

One of the most strategically significant places for the belief that a legal writ authorizing a legitimate search must be specific as to persons and places was Sir Edward Coke's *Institutes of the Laws of England*.[4] From the Puritans of Massachusetts Bay, who studied Coke, to Jefferson, who admiringly said of him that "a sounder Whig never wrote" nor one more learned "in the orthodox doctrines of British liberties," Americans regarded Coke as the foremost authority on English law.[5] Coke's authority legitimated the belief that Magna Carta outlawed general warrants based on mere surmise.

Sir Matthew Hale, another seventeenth-century legal luminary, more systematically analyzed the problem of search and seizure in his book, *History of Pleas of the Crown*.[6] Hale criticized warrants that failed to name the persons sought for crime or the places to be searched for evidence of theft. He even laid a basis for the concept of probable cause by maintaining that the person seeking a warrant should be examined judicially under oath so that the magistrate could determine whether he had grounds for his suspicions. Hale also asserted that an officer who made an illegal search and arrest was liable to a civil suit for false arrest.[7]

Beale, Coke, and Hale did not stand alone. They invented a rhetorical tradition against general searches, which Sergeant William Hawkins and Sir William Blackstone continued.[8] But the rhetoric was empty; the tradition had almost no practical effect. Beale's views leaked out through officially licensed publications that sought to refute him, but he did not dare publish his manuscript.[9] Coke's own report of *Semayne's Case* of 1604 refuted the accuracy of the propositions that he advanced in his *Institutes*, for in that case the court had held that although a man's house is his castle, his privacy did not extend to his guests or to "cases where the King is a party."[10] Coke's own experience shows best that the maxim represented only the frailest aspiration, not the law in cases involving the crown. In 1634, when Coke lay dying, the Privy Council's agents searched his home and law chambers for seditious papers and seized not only the manuscripts of his voluminous legal writings but also his personal valuables, including his money, keys, jewelry, will, and a poem addressed to his children.[11] Hale's book did not even get published until sixty years after his death. Pitt spoke in a losing cause; Parliament enacted the excise bill whose passage he so eloquently opposed as dangerous to the liberty of the subject. Blackstone made only a passing remark against general searches; his target, rather, was the general arrest warrant.

In fact, English law was honeycombed with parliamentary enactments that relied on warrantless general searches and on general warrants for their enforcement, including hue and cry methods, sumptuary legislation, and measures aimed at punishing theft, at governing crafts and guilds, bankruptcy, and military recruitment, as well as measures preventing illegal imports, manufactures, poaching, counterfeiting, unlicensed printing, seditious, heretical, or lewd publications, and nonpayment of taxes. Taxes extended to hearths and stoves, to estates, to intoxicating drinks, to a variety of consumer goods such as salt, candles, soap, glass, and paper, and to foreign goods. The king's customs office and his exchequer depended on both the general warrant and warrantless searches as ordinary means of collecting royal revenues, and Parliament passed dozens of pieces of legislation to provide the taxes and authorize general searches.[12] Promiscuously broad warrants allowed officers to search wherever they wanted and to seize whatever they wanted, with few exceptions. An eighteenth-century collection of warrants contains 108 authorized by secretaries of state or by the King's Bench for the period 1700–1763, all but two of which were general warrants.[13] The frequency in the use of general warrants substantially increased as time went by.[14]

General searches completely pervaded colonial law as well as Great Britain's. Colonial legislation on search and seizure either copied Britain's or derived from it; until 1750, all handbooks for justices of the peace, who issued warrants, contained or described only general warrants. William Cuddihy asserts that a "colonial epidemic of general searches" existed, indeed, that until the 1760s, "a man's house was even less of a legal castle in America than in England," because the Americans, when adapting English models, ignored exceptions.[15] As a result, warrants in America tended to give their enforcers every discretion. The Fourth Amendment would not emerge from colonial precedents; rather, it would repudiate them; or, as Cuddihy states, "The ideas comprising the Fourth Amendment reversed rather than formalized colonial precedents. Reasonable search and seizure in colonial America closely approximated whatever the searcher thought reasonable."[16]

Officers or their informants merely reported that an infraction of the law had occurred or that they had a suspicion, not that a particular person was suspected or that a particular place contained evidence of a crime; on the basis of such an assertion, a magistrate issued a warrant. Neither custom, judicial precedent, nor statutory law provided that he should interrogate the seeker of the warrant to determine the credibility of the suspicion or of his informant. The magistrate made no independent determination of his own whether a basis existed for the warrant other than the assertion that a crime had occurred or that a basis existed for some suspicion. Magistrates had an obligation to provide the warrant, rather than deny one or limit one to a particular person or place that was suspected. Probable cause in a modern sense did not exist; not even a reasonable basis for suspicion existed. Although an officer seeking a warrant more than likely would designate a particular person or place if known to him in advance, he need not do so to get a warrant.

Colonial documents contain no suggestion of a right against general warrants. Recommendations for them were common in the manuals that had been published in the colonies before 1763 for the use of justices of the peace. American legal writers even relied on the great authority of Coke and Hale as proof that an officer could forcibly enter a person's house.[17]

In 1756, however, the province of Massachusetts enacted extraordinary legislation that reversed the tide of practice by abandoning general warrants in favor of warrants founded on some elements of particularity. The legislation of 1756 marked a watershed in Massachusetts law, indeed in Anglo-American law. As Cuddihy states, beginning in 1756 "Massachusetts invented the statutory prototypes of the Fourth Amendment."[18] The new legislation resulted mainly from a vehement public clamor against provincial legislation of 1754. The excise act of that year authorized tax collectors to interrogate any subject, under oath, on the amount of rum, wine, and other spirits he had consumed in his private premises in the past year and taxed it by the gallon. Pamphleteers condemned the measure in hyperbolic language. John Lovell, a Boston schoolmaster whose pupils had included John Hancock and Samuel Adams, called it "the most pernicious attack upon *English Liberty* that was ever attempted," and the minister of the Brattle Church imagined that he saw a revival of the Inquisition, requiring people to incriminate themselves. One pamphlet, *The Monster of Monsters* (the excise act), so savagely attacked the legislature that it condemned the tract as a seditious libel, and imprisoned its seller and the suspected author.[19] That author warned of the danger of the tax collector having power to break chains, doors, locks, and bolts, and invade bedchambers and winecellars.[20] In the torrent of tracts against the excise, it was described as a violation of Magna Carta, of the sanctity of one's home as his castle, and of natural rights.

The provincial impost laws, which employed general warrants for enforcement, provoked such animosity that mobs threatened impost officers who tried to collect duties on uncustomed imports—foreign goods on which the duties had not been paid. The hostility to general searches further intensified as the result of two other practices. In 1755 the royal governor of Massachusetts issued ex officio writs of assistance, a type of general warrant that became enormously controversial. And, since 1745, British impressment gangs, operating under a general warrant provided by the governor, had been invading private premises as well as taverns and inns, seeking to kidnap able-bodied men for service in the royal navy.[21]

Enforcement of the excise and impost acts by general searches, the introduction into the province of writs of assistance, and the general warrants for impressment gangs produced a hullabaloo that the enactments of 1756 sought to allay. The excise and impost acts of that year required an element of probable cause only in the sense that the informant had the obligation to swear on oath that he knew that an infraction of the law had occurred in the place specified. The justices of the peace, who issued the warrants, had no discretion to deny a petition for one; magistrates made no independent judgment whether adequate grounds for the issuance of the warrant existed. But, the informant had to swear that he had "just cause" for his sworn statement. The officer conducted his search during the daytime, only in the designated location, and could seize only things or objects regulated by the statute that he enforced by his search and seizure. The statutes of 1756 also authorized warrants of arrest for named individuals.[22] "The British, in short," Cuddihy states, "introduced writs of assistance into Massachusetts just as the colony itself was rejecting the legal assumptions on which they were based."[23]

The writ of assistance was a type of general warrant deriving its name from the fact that a crown official possessed the legal

authority to command the assistance of a peace officer and the
assistance, if necessary, of all nearby subjects, in his execution of
the writ. Parliament authorized writs of assistance by an act of 1662
that empowered the Court of Exchequer to issue a writ to a customs
official who, with the assistance of a constable, could enter "any
House, shop, Cellar, Warehouse or Room or other Place, and in
Case of Resistance to break open Doors, Chests, Trunks and other
packages, there to seize" any uncustomed goods.[24] The writ, once
issued, lasted for the life of the sovereign, and therefore constituted
a long-term hunting license for customs officers on the lookout for
smugglers and articles imported in violation of the customs laws.
In 1696 Parliament extended the act of 1662 to the colonies, but
because the Court of Exchequer did not operate in America, no
way existed to enforce it. Massachusetts, however, had extended
the jurisdiction of its own high court to include the jurisdiction of
the Court of Exchequer, thus opening the possibility of enforcement in that colony and in New Hampshire, which copied Massachusetts.[25]

When George II died, the high court of Massachusetts, presided over by Chief Justice Thomas Hutchinson, heard *Paxton's
Case*, a petition by a customs officer for a new writ of assistance.[26]
James Otis Jr. appeared, he said, on behalf of the inhabitants of
Boston to oppose issuance of the writ. Any fastidious legal historian
must acknowledge that Otis's argument compounded mistakes and
misinterpretations. In effect, he reconstructed the fragmentary evidence buttressing the rhetorical tradition against general searches,
and he advocated that any warrant other than a specific one violated
the British constitution. That Otis distorted history is pedantic; he
was making history. By an old British technique, which Coke himself had practiced, Otis sought the creation of new rights while
asserting strenuously that they had existed nearly from time immemorial. His speech electrified young John Adams, who was present in the courtroom and took notes. As an old man, fifty-six years
later, he declared, "Otis was a flame of Fire! . . . Then and there
was the first scene of the first Act of Opposition to the arbitrary
Claims of Great Britain. Then and there the child Independance
[sic] was born." On the night before the Declaration of Independence, Adams asserted that he consider "the Argument concerning
Writs of Assistance . . . as the Commencement of the Controversy,

between Great Britain and America."[27] Adams's reaction to Otis's
speech is so important because a straight line of progression runs
from Otis's argument in 1761 to Adams's framing of Article XIV of
the Massachusetts Declaration of Rights of 1780 to Madison's introduction of the proposal that became the Fourth Amendment.[28]

We have Adams's brief notes of Otis's speech made at the time
of the speech and the fuller version made by Adams not long after.
The fuller version takes about twenty minutes to read by comparison with the original which took Otis four to five hours to deliver.[29]
He denounced the writ of assistance as an instrument of "slavery,"
of "villainy," of "arbitrary power, the most destructive of English
liberty and [of] the fundamental principles of the constitution. . . ."
The writ reminded him of the kind of power that had cost one
English king his head and another his throne. The only legal writ,
Otis asserted, was a "special warrant directed to specific officers,
and to search certain houses, &c. especially set forth in the writ
may be granted . . . upon oath made . . . by the person, who asks
[for the warrant], that he suspects such goods to be concealed in
those very places he desires to search."[30] In the recent past, Otis
alleged, only special warrants existed, authorizing search of particularly named houses, and they were issued only after the com-
plainant had taken an oath to support his suspicion; "special warrants only are legal," he concluded. He condemned writs of assistance
because they were perpetual, universal (addressed to every officer
and subject in the realm), and allowed anyone to conduct a search
in violation of the essential principle of English liberty that a peaceable man's house is his castle. A writ that allowed a customs officer
to enter private homes when he pleased, on bare suspicion, and
even to break locks to enter, was void. An act of Parliament authorizing such writs was void because it violated the British constitution, and courts should not issue an unconstitutional writ.[31]

Otis lost his case. The writs issued, but Americans found a
cause and a constitutional argument. In 1762 the Massachusetts
legislature passed a bill that would have required all writs to be as
specific as the warrants used by provincial officers to enforce the
excise and impost acts, but the royal governor vetoed the bill.
Thereafter, crowds frequently prevented enforcement or "rescued"
goods seized by customs agents. In a 1766 case a Boston merchant,
believing that in "Whig Boston Whig furies made Whig law," used

force to barricade his home, as a crowd gathered. Officers prudently decided that calling on bystanders to assist as a *posse comitatus* might result in a loss of life—their own—and abandoned efforts to enforce the writ. After a rescue in Falmouth (Portland), Maine, the governor conceded that public opposition had effectively paralyzed the use of writs to conduct searches and seizures. Britain's Attorney General William DeGrey decided that the act of Parliament that authorized the writ allowed them to issue only from the Court of Exchequer, whose writ did not run in America.[32] In London, far more than DeGrey's technical opinion damaged the principle of general warrants.

John Wilkes's studied insult of the king's speech in 1763, in the forty-fifth number of his journal *North Britain*, provoked massive retaliation by the government. One of the secretaries of state issued general search warrants for the arrest of everyone connected with *North Britain* #45. Crown agents enforcing the warrants had unfettered discretion to search, seize, and arrest anyone as they pleased. They ransacked printer's shops and houses, and arrested forty-nine persons including Wilkes, a member of Parliament, his printer, publisher, and booksellers. The officers seized his private papers for incriminating evidence after a thorough search; thousands of pages and scores of books belonging to persons associated with him were also seized. The House of Commons voted that *North Britain* #45 was a seditious libel and expelled Wilkes, and he was eventually convicted and jailed. The government found, however, that it had mounted a tiger; no one since the time of John Lilburne, more than a century earlier, had proved to be such a resourceful and pugnacious antagonist. Wilkes had quickly filed suits for trespass against everyone, from flunky to minister, connected with the warrant that had resulted in his undoing; others who had suffered searches and arrest filed similar suits. A legal donnybrook ensued. On the one hand, the government, based on about two hundred informations, had engaged in mass arrests and searches, and on the other, the victims filed a couple of dozen suits for trespass and false imprisonment. The Wilkes case became the subject of sensational controversies, angry tracts, and confusing trials. Wilkes would emerge from his prosecution a popular idol, the personification of constitutional liberty to Englishmen on both sides of the Atlantic. Although he focused mainly on the dangers of general warrants and the seizures of private papers, some of his supporters also championed freedom of the press and the right against self-incrimination.[33]

In the colonies, "Wilkes and Liberty" became a slogan that patriot leaders exploited in the service of American causes. In New York, for example, Alexander McDougall, a leader of the Sons of Liberty who had censured a bill to provision the king's troops, posed as an American Wilkes and turned his imprisonment into a theatrical triumph, as had Wilkes, while his supporters used the number 45, the seditious issue of *North Britain,* as a symbol of their cause. On the forty-fifth day of the year, for example, forty-five Liberty Boys dined on forty-five pounds of beef from a forty-five-month-old bull, drank forty-five toasts to liberty—liberty of the press, liberty from general warrants, liberty from compulsory self-accusation, liberty from seizure of private papers—and after dinner marched to the jail to salute McDougall with forty-five cheers. On another festive liberty day, forty-five songs were sung to him by forty-five virgins, every one of whom, according to some damned Tory, was forty-five years old.[34] The Fourth Amendment, as well as the First and the Fifth, owes something to the Wilkes cases. Unlike *Paxton's Case,* the Wilkes cases filled the columns of American newspapers from Boston to Charleston.

The first of these cases, *Huckle v. Money,* established the doctrine, traceable at least to Hale, that crown officers are liable to damage suits for trespass and false imprisonment resulting from unlawful search. Chief Justice Charles Pratt said, when charging the jury: "To enter a man's house by virtue of a nameless warrant, in order to procure evidence, is worse than the Spanish Inquisition, a law under which no Englishman would wish to live an hour." The jury awarded 300 pounds in damages, an excessive sum for the deprivation of a journeyman printer's liberty for six hours, but on appeal Pratt ruled that the small injury done to one of low rank meant nothing compared to the "great point of the law touching the liberty of the subject" invaded by a magistrate of the king in· an exercise of arbitrary power "violating Magna Carta, and attempting to destroy the liberty of the kingdom, by insisting on the legality of this general warrant. . . ."[35] In *Wilkes v. Wood* (1763), Pratt presided over a similar trial and engaged in similar rhetoric ("totally subversive of the liberty of the subject"); the jury awarded damages of 1,000 pounds to Wilkes, who later got an award of 4,000 pounds against the secretary of state who had issued the warrant.[36] In fact, the government paid a total of about 100,000 pounds in costs and judgments.[37]

In one of the Wilkes cases, the government appealed to England's highest criminal court, the King's Bench, and Lord Mansfield, the chief justice, agreed that the warrants in the Wilkes cases were illegal. Although the common law, he observed, authorized arrests without warrant and Parliament had often authorized searches and arrests on the basis of general warrants, in this case no circumstance existed justifying warrantless searches or arrests, and no act of Parliament was involved. Accordingly, a secretarial warrant, based on executive authority, leaving discretion to the endorsing officer, "is not fit." Mansfield thought that the "magistrate ought to judge; and should give certain directions to the officer"— a foundation for what later emerged as probable cause.[38]

The victories of the Wilkesites encouraged other victims of secretarial warrants in seditious libel cases to bring suits for damages. The most important of those cases, *Entick v. Carrington* (1765), resulted in an opinion by Chief Justice Pratt, now Lord Camden, which the Supreme Court of the United States would describe as "one of the landmarks of English liberty."[39] Victory for the government, Camden declared, would open the secret cabinets of every subject whenever the secretary of state suspected someone of seditious libel. The law required no one to incriminate himself, for that would be "cruel and unjust" to the innocent and guilty alike, "and it should seem, that search for evidence is disallowed upon the same principle." Camden held that neither arrests nor general warrants could issue on executive discretion, and he implied that evidence seized on the authority of such a warrant could not be used without violating the right against self-incrimination. Similarly, the Supreme Court in 1886 ruled that the Fourth and Fifth Amendments have an "intimate relation" and "throw great light on each other."[40]

In 1764 and 1765 the House of Commons irresolutely debated whether general warrants should be regarded as illegal, and in 1766 it repeated the debate. The upshot was the passage of three resolutions, not statutes, that revealed a victory for the narrow position of Mansfield rather than the broader one of Camden. The

Commons condemned general warrants in all cases involving arrests but condemned general warrants for searches only in cases where the warrants issued from the executive branch in connection with the crime of seditious libel. Secretarial search warrants in treason cases remained legal. The resolutions of 1766 left in place the elaborate system of warrantless searches when authorized by Parliament, and of general searches when undergirded by statutory authority. The House of Lords rejected a proposal from the Commons that would have restricted general search warrants to cases of treason and felony. Thus, the reforms resulting from the judicial decisions and parliamentary resolves of 1763 to 1766 conformed to the prime directive of England's law of search and seizure: even promiscuously general searches did not violate the liberty of the subject or infringe the maxim about a man's home so long as Parliament had laid down the law.[41]

On the other hand, the Wilkes cases and the parliamentary debates unleashed a lot of rhetoric that went far beyond the reality of actual judicial holdings and legislative resolves. Americans were practiced in making a highly selective use of authorities and other sources that suited their needs. They could even turn Blackstone, that spokesman for parliamentary supremacy, into an advocate of constitutional restraints. In Britain, Englishmen often spoke thunderously but thrashed about with a frail stick; in America they threw the stick away, contenting themselves with the thunder. They found a lot of it in Pitt, Camden, Wilkes, and in "Father of Candor," all of whom they knew well. Father of Candor was the author of a little book of 1764, "on libels, warrants, and the seizure of papers," which had gone through seven editions by 1771. He condemned general warrants as "excruciating torture,"[42] and he urged that search warrants should be specific as to persons, places, and things, and should be sworn on oath.[43] That was the sort of thing Americans could exploit when confronted by Parliament's determination to impose writs of assistance on the colonies.

Twenty years after the Townshend Acts of 1767, James Madison, speaking in the First Congress on the occasion of recommending the amendments to the Constitution that became the Bill of Rights, recalled that the legislative power constituted a great danger to liberty; in Britain, he noted, "they have gone no farther than to raise a barrier against the power of the Crown; the power of the Legislature is left altogether indefinite."[44] Notwithstanding grandiose rhetoric against general warrants, Parliament in 1767 superseded its act of 1696, which had extended writs of assistance to America without providing a mechanism for granting them under the seal of the Court of Exchequer. The Townshend Act of 1767 provided that the highest court in each colony possessed authority to issue writs of assistance to customs officers to search where they pleased for prohibited or uncustomed goods and to seize them.

The Townshend Acts, therefore, expanded the controversy over writs of assistance to all of the thirteen colonies. What had been a local controversy, centering mainly on Boston, spread continent-wide. Only the two colonies, Massachusetts and New Hampshire, that had previously experienced the writs, continued to issue them, although the mobs "liberated" seized goods as often as not. Elsewhere the provincial high courts stalled, compromised, or declined the writ. The New York court issued the writ but deviated from the exact language authorized by Parliament, with the result that the customs officers refused to execute the deviant writ and sought one in the correct form. It was not forthcoming; indeed, applications kept getting lost or mislaid. In 1773, five years after the first application, the New York court held that "it did not appear to them that such Writs according to the form now produced are warranted by law and therefore they could not grant the motion."[45]

Something like that happened in several colonies. In Connecticut, Chief Justice Jonathan Trumbull and Judge Roger Sherman refused to be rushed into making a decision on the application for a writ. Trumbull remarked privately that he and his associates were not clear "the thing was in itself constitutional."[46] Chief Justice William Allen of Pennsylvania was more forthcoming. In 1768 he declared that he had no legal authority to issue the writ. Customs officials sent Allen's statement to Attorney General William DeGrey in London for his opinion. He thought that Allen would see the error of his ways if confronted by a copy of the writ, a copy of the act of Parliament, and a copy of the opinion of England's attorney general.[47] On a new application for the writ backed by English legal artillery, Allen replied that he would grant "particular [not general] writs whenever they are applied for on oath." The customs agent must swear he knew or had reason to believe that prohibited or uncustomed goods were located in a particular place. Allen's groping toward a concept of probable cause as well as specific warrants became clearer as customs officials vainly persisted to engage his cooperation.[48]

In South Carolina a judge, explaining his court's refusal to issue the writ, stated that it "trenched too severely and unnecessarily upon the safety of the subject secured by Magna Charta." After five years of persistence, however, the customs officials got a writ of assistance in South Carolina.[49] In Georgia, where the judges declined to issue the writ, they said they would authorize a search warrant for a specific occasion if supported by an affidavit.[50]

Virginia issued writs of assistance in 1769 but undermined the process by annexing a degree of specificity obnoxious to the customs office. Its agent had to swear an oath in support of his suspicion and could obtain a writ only for a special occasion and for a limited duration of time. The Virginia judges alleged that the writ sought by the customs office under the Townshend Act was "unconstitutional" because it allowed the officer "to act under it according to his own arbitrary discretion." The customs office appealed to England for support against the Virginia court. Attorney General DeGrey had to acknowledge that he knew of "no direct and effective means" to compel a provincial court to award a writ of assistance. He asserted that judges might be impeached for contumacious refusal to execute an act of Parliament, but he did not know how to proceed in such a case. He preferred to believe that Virginia's judges had acted out of a mistaken understanding of the law. Virginia's court, however, remained contumacious.[51]

Between 1761 and 1776 a glacial drift in American legal opinion can be discerned toward increased reliance on specific warrants. Law books, including manuals of the justices of the peace, began to recommend specific warrants in some cases; most, however, relied on general warrants, as did American judges in actual practice. American rhetoric and reality diverged. John Dickinson's *Letters of a Pennsylvania Farmer*, which circulated in every colony, censured general warrants and repeated the cliché about a man's home being his castle; but Dickinson did not recommend specific warrants in their place or condemn any warrantless searches. Americans never spoke of a right to privacy as such, although they understood the concept, and like their British counterparts expressed outrage over the possibility that customs agents might "break the rights of domicil," "ransack houses," and "enter private cabinets" or "secret repositories."[52] The best known of such remarks, which received considerable publicity in the colonies, was that of the Boston Town Meeting of 1772, which complained:

> Thus our houses and even our bed chambers, are exposed to be ransacked, our boxes chests & trunks broke open ravaged and plundered by wretches, whom no prudent man would venture to employ even as menial servants; whenever they are pleased to say they suspect there are in the house wares &c for which the dutys have not been paid. Flagrant instances of the wanton exercise of this power, have frequently happened in this and other sea port Towns. By this we are cut off from that domestick security which renders the lives of the most unhappy in some measure agreeable. Those Officers may under colour of law and the cloak of a general warrant break thro' the sacred rights of the Domicil, ransack mens houses, destroy their securities, carry off their property, and with little danger to themselves commit the most horred murders.[53]

In all the American rhetoric, only one writer seems to have urged special warrants in place of warrantless searches and general warrants. Some writers revealed that their objection lay against a parliamentary empowerment, rather than one by their own assemblies.[54] General searches continued in the colonies as the prevailing standard, not the specific warrants used in Massachusetts. Nevertheless, some colonies became more familiar with specific warrants and even used them in various kinds of cases. Cuddihy states:

> The failure of colonial legislatures and courts to abandon general searches for domestic consumption locates the "American Revolution Against Writs of Assistance" in clearer perspective. Appeals to Magna Carta notwithstanding, the typical searches actually authorized by judges and legislators in the colonies had remained as general as those in the writs of assistance rejected by local judiciaries and intellectuals. Damning such searches under British auspices was one thing; renouncing them oneself was another matter. In Connecticut, where judicial resistance to those writs was most extreme in 1769, the local code of that year included an impost enforced by search warrants strongly resembling the writs. The same conclusion applied equally to Pennsylvania. Had Allen, Trumbull, or any of the Connecticut newspaper essayists wished to attack general searches on principle alone, they need have looked no further than Pennsylvania and Connecticut, for local session laws and judicial search warrants

had read like writs of assistance throughout the histories of those colonies. Only when those searches loomed from a foreign quarter and threatened political autonomy was the civil libertarian threat posed by them announced.[55]

In sum, one need only add that Otis's extraordinary forensic effort of 1761 on behalf of specific warrants, which a Boston newspaper printed in 1773, bore scarce fruit elsewhere, at least not until well after the Revolution.

The Declaration of Independence, however, spurred the definition of American ideals. Although that document, which itemized the king's perfidies, failed to say anything about search and seizure or even about general warrants, it inspired the making of the first state constitutions. In the midst of war, Americans engaged in the most important, creative, and dynamic constitutional achievements in history, among them the first written constitutions and the first bills of rights against all branches of government. Their provisions on search and seizure are significant because they distilled the best American thinking on the subject, constituted benchmarks to show the standard by which practise should be measured, and provided models for the Fourth Amendment.

Virginia, the oldest, largest, and most influential of the new states, anticipated the Declaration of Independence by adopting a Declaration of Rights on June 12, 1776, and completed its constitution before the month ended. Article 10 of the Declaration of Rights provided: "That general warrants, whereby any officer or messenger may be commanded to search suspected places without evidence of a fact committed, or to seize any person or persons not named, or whose offence is not particularly described and supported by evidence, are grievous and oppressive, and ought not to be granted."[56] Obviously this provision is a substantial step in the direction of specific warrants. Its force is weakened by the wishy-washy climax: certain warrants are grievous, not illegal, and "ought" not be granted, but the language imposes no prohibition against them. The concept of probable cause is stunted with respect to searches but considerably broader with respect to arrests. The search may be conducted, presumably under warrant, if the fact of a crime has been established, though no need exists to show a connection between the crime and the place to be searched, and there is no reference to a need for specificity with respect to the things to be seized. Moreover, the warrant need not be based on a sworn statement. Probable cause must be shown for the criminal involvement of the persons to be arrested; far more than mere suspicion is required for an arrest.

As the first search and seizure provision in any American con-stitution, Virginia's had egregious deficiencies as well as pioneering attainments. That the attainments might have been better still is evident from the fact that in a committee draft of May 27, the property to be seized had to be "particularly described." We do not know why that clause was omitted in the final draft.[57] We do know that the provision could have been far worse or altogether nonexistent. George Mason, who provided the original draft of the Declaration of Rights had omitted a search and seizure provision, and Thomas Jefferson's draft of a state constitution omitted one, too.[58] Edmund Randolph may have been right in recalling that his state's search and seizure provision "was dictated by the remembr-ance of the seizure of Wilkes's paper under a warrant from a Sec-retary of State,"[59] but Virginia went well beyond a condemnation of general warrants issued under executive authority.

In August 1776 Pennsylvania adopted its extraordinary con-stitution preceded by a Declaration of Rights influenced by Virginia yet original in major respects. Its tenth article provided:

> That the people have a right to hold themselves, their houses, papers, and possessions free from search and seizure, and therefore warrants without oaths or affirmations first made, affording a sufficient foun-dation for them, and whereby any officer or messenger may be com-manded or required to search suspected places, or to seize any person or persons, his or their property, not particularly described, are contrary to that right, and ought not to be granted.[60]

That provision is memorable because it recognizes a right of the people in affirmative terms rather than merely declaring against general warrants or grievous searches. And, the right of the people is broad, promiscuously so; there is no such thing as an absolute right to be free from search and seizure. The provision meant, rather, that searches and seizures made without specific warrants "ought"—that weak word again—not to be granted. Even that prop-

osition had to be subject to exceptions, because no evidence suggests that Pennsylvania intended to depart from common law exceptions to the need for a warrant if a peace officer was in hot
pursuit of a felon or had reason to believe that the felon might
escape if the officer called time out to obtain a warrant. Exigent
circumstances of various kinds always allowed warrantless arrests
and even warrantless searches and seizures of evidence of crime,
of weapons, or of contraband. The Pennsylvania provision had the
virtue of including a requirement for specificity with respect to the
things seized when a warrant was attainable. It was also the first
to require that the warrant be available only if the informant swore
or affirmed that he had "sufficient foundation" for specific information about the person, place, or things described. Probable cause,
attested to on oath, derives partly from Pennsylvania's contribution
to the constitutional law of search and seizure.

Delaware's Declaration of Rights of 1776 derived its search
and seizure provision partly from Maryland and partly from Pennsylvania, though the Delaware variant was truncated; it omitted
the clause recognizing the right of the people. It also omitted a
requirement for specificity respecting the property to be seized
under a warrant, yet deplored as grievous any warrant for the
seizure of property not based on a sworn statement. Delaware's
contribution consisted, rather, in the fact that its provision was the
first to declare "illegal" any warrants not meeting the constitutional
requirement of specificity.[61] In this respect, the Delaware provision
was based on a draft of the Maryland Declaration of Rights, not
yet adopted.[62] The texts of the search and seizure provisions of
these two states were nearly the same. As Delaware copied Maryland, North Carolina copied Virginia, and Vermont copied Pennsylvania.[63]

Similarly, New Hampshire in 1784 would copy Massachusetts,
which did not adopt its Declaration of Rights and Constitution until
1780. As a source of the Fourth Amendment, the Massachusetts
provision on search and seizure was the most important of all the
state models, because it was the one that the Fourth Amendment
most resembles. The Massachusetts provision was the work of John
Adams, the witness to and recorder of Otis's monumental speech
in Paxton's Case about twenty years earlier. Through Adams and

Article 14 of the Massachusetts Declaration of Rights, Otis's influence at last bore triumphant fruits. Article 14 declared:

> Every subject has a right to be secure from all unreasonable searches, and seizures of his person, his houses, his papers, and all his possessions. All warrants, therefore, are contrary to this right, if the cause or foundation of them be not previously supported by oath or affirmation; and if the order in the warrant to the civil officer, to make search in suspected places, to arrest one or more suspected persons, or to seize their property, be not accompanied with a special designation of the persons or objects of search, arrest, or seizure: and no warrant ought to be issued but in cases and with the formalities, prescribed by the laws.[64]

The detail of the provision is striking. No other right received such particularity in the Massachusetts constitution, and, like the provision of Pennsylvania, which Adams borrowed, it is a "right" that is protected. The right is to be secure against "unreasonable search, and seizures," the first use of the phrase that would become the prime principle of the Fourth Amendment. The warrant must be based on sworn statement providing "cause or foundation" for the warrant, but the provision omits, amazingly, a requirement that the search, arrest, or seizure occur within specifically designated premises.[65]

The war years were the worst possible for testing whether American practices matched American ideals or constitutional provisions. Search and seizure was a method of fighting the enemy and those suspected of adhering to his cause. Perhaps the grossest violation of a constitutional provision occurred in Pennsylvania in 1777. Three years earlier Congress had complained about customs officials breaking and entering without authority. In 1777, though, Congress urged Pennsylvania's executive council to search the homes of Philadelphians, mostly Quakers, whose loyalty to the American cause was suspect. Congress wanted to disarm such persons and to seize their political papers. Pennsylvania's executive council authorized a search of the homes of anyone who had not taken an oath of allegiance to the United States. The searches of at least six Quaker homes were conducted cruelly and violently, and all sorts of books, papers, and records were confiscated; over forty people were arrested and deported without trial, let alone conviction, to

Virginia, where they were detained until the next year.[66] Nothing that the British had done equaled the violation of privacy rights inflicted by Pennsylvania on its "Virginia Exiles," in defiance of the state constitution and a writ of habeas corpus by the state chief justice, but with the support of Congress.

American adherence to professed principles stands up far better and is more fairly tested after the shooting stopped. Between 1782 and the ratification of the Constitution, five states—Maryland, New York, North and South Carolina, and Georgia—employed general searches. The southern states conventionally employed warrantless searches without restriction against slaves, especially to detect vagrants and fugitives. But all five states used general warrants to enforce their impost laws. Although Maryland's constitution banned general warrants, Maryland used them to enforce excise laws and laws regulating bakers. Such laws, however, derived from past experience. More significant, perhaps, is the fact that the laws of Massachusetts kept faith with its commitment to specific warrants. Moreover, Rhode Island, which had no constitution, and New Jersey, which had one but did not include a search and seizure clause, enacted legislation that required the use of specific warrants. In the remaining states, general warrants continued to be used, but specific warrants were becoming more common, especially in cases of theft. In Virginia, the trend toward specificity was pronounced, if belated.[67]

In Connecticut, which, like Rhode Island, had no constitution, the state supreme court delivered an opinion of major consequence that voided a general warrant directed against every person and place suspected by the victim of a theft. The state chief justice ruled that a justice of peace, in granting a warrant, had an obligation "to limit the search to such particular place or places, as he, from the circumstances, shall judge there is reason to suspect," and he must limit the arrests under the warrant to those persons found with the stolen goods. The warrant before the court, the chief justice concluded, "is clearly illegal," because not specific. The case, *Frisbie v. Butler* (1787), shows that probable cause as determined independently by a magistrate was not an unknown concept.[68]

The failure of the Framers to include in the Constitution a bill of rights exposed it to the withering criticism of those who opposed ratification for any reason. Ten days after the Convention adjourned, Richard Henry Lee of Virginia, a member of Congress, sought to wreck the ratification process by moving that Congress adopt a bill of rights. Acting out of a genuine fear of the proposed national government, Lee had troubled to frame his own bill of rights rather than simply urging the famous one of his own state. He omitted numerous liberties of importance, but included a search and seizure clause of significance: ". . . the Citizens shall not be exposed to unreasonable searches, seizures of their papers, houses, persons, or property." Lee had constructed the clause from the Massachusetts Constitution of 1780. It was the broadest on the subject.

Lee's colleague from Virginia, James Madison, led the fight against Lee's motion. Madison observed that the Articles of Confederation required that all thirteen state legislatures would have to approve the Lee proposals if endorsed by Congress. That would cause confusion because of the Convention's rule that ratification by nine state conventions would put the Constitution into operation.[69] Lee's motion lost, but he did not quit. He wrote his *Federal Farmer* letters, the best of the Anti-Federalist tracts.[70]

In an early letter, Lee discoursed on the rights omitted from the proposed Constitution. The second one he mentioned was the right against unreasonable warrants, those not founded on oath or on cause for searching and seizing papers, property, and persons.[71] In another letter he included the term "effects," which would become part of the Fourth Amendment.[72] In his final word on the subject, he urged a constitutional provision "that all persons shall have a right to be secure from all unreasonable searches and seizures of their persons, houses, papers, or possessions; and that all warrants shall be deemed contrary to this right, if the foundation of them be not previously supported by oath, and there be not in them a special designation of persons or objects of search, arrest, or seizure."[73]

Other Anti-Federalists also popularized the demand for a provision on searches and seizures, and some used significant language. "Centinel" employed an extract from the Pennsylvania constitution. The "Dissent" of the Pennsylvania convention's Anti-Federalists, which also circulated throughout the country in newspapers and pamphlet form, used a truncated form of the same provision. "Brutus," another whose writings were reprinted almost everywhere, used his own formulation against warrants that were not specific.[74] Anti-Federalists who addressed the issue usually opposed general warrants in purple language, either reflecting fear or calculated to inspire it. Newspapers in the four largest states reprinted the rant of "A Son of Liberty," who depicted federal officers dragging people off to prison after brutal searches and confiscations that shocked "the most delicate part of our families."[75] No one could compete with the florid fears expressed by that first-rate demagogue, Patrick Henry.[76]

Virginia's convention ratified the Constitution with recommendations for amendments to be considered by the First Congress. Among them was a detailed provision on the right of every free person "to be secure from all unreasonable searches and seizures"; the provision also required sworn warrants to be based on "legal and sufficient cause." The Virginia recommendation of 1788, of unknown authorship, was moved by George Wythe on behalf of a powerful bipartisan committee which included James Madison.[77] The committee blended the precedents of the Pennsylvania and Massachusetts state constitutions and the recommendations of Richard Henry Lee. Virginia was the first state to ratify with a search and seizure recommendation. North Carolina copied it in her recommended amendments; New York and Rhode Island did so also, with slight changes.[78]

Without a single supporter when he began his fight in the House for amendments safeguarding personal liberties, Madison struggled to overcome apathy and opposition from members of his own party as well as the Anti-Federalists. He meant to win over the great body of people who withheld their support of the new government in the sincere belief that the Constitution should secure them against the abuse of powers by the United States. And, he meant to isolate the leaders of the opposition by depriving them of their supporters. But Madison could have achieved his goals and redeemed his campaign pledge by taking the least troublesome route. On the issue of search and seizure, for example, he might have shown up the Anti-Federalists by proposing that the United States would not enforce its laws by searches and seizures that violated the laws of the states, most of which still allowed general warrants. That would have put the burden on the states to bring about reforms securing the rights of citizens against unreasonable searches and seizures. Or, Madison might have simply proposed that the United States would not employ general warrants.[79] Or, he might have recommended the weak formulation of his own state's constitution, with its omission of specificity for the things to be seized, its failure to require a sworn statement, and its flabby assertion that "grievous" warrants "ought" not to be granted. Even Virginia's excellent 1788 recommendation for a search and seizure provision to be added to the federal Constitution employed the same "ought."

If Madison had chosen a formulation narrower than the one he offered, only the citizens of Massachusetts could consistently have criticized him. Facing a variety of minimal options, any of which would have been politically adequate, Madison chose the maximum protection conceivable at the time. He recommended:

> The rights of the people to be secured in their persons, their houses, and their other property, from all unreasonable searches and seizures, shall not be violated by warrants issued without probable cause, supported by oath or affirmation, or not particularly describing the places to be searched, or the persons or things to be seized.[80]

No one previously had proposed the imperative voice, "shall not be violated," rather than the wishful "ought not," which allowed for exceptions. "Probable cause" was also a significant contribution, or became so; it required more than mere suspicion or even reasonable suspicion, as had its antecedents such as "just cause" and "sufficient foundation." Above all, Madison used the positive assertion drawn from Pennsylvania and Massachusetts that the people have rights against "unreasonable searches and seizures"—John Adams's formulation for the Massachusetts constitution.

A House Committee of Eleven, composed of one member from each state, deleted the crucial phrase that establishes the general principle of the Fourth: no "unreasonable searches and seizures." Specificity in warrants is the lesser half of the amendment, because it provides the standard of reasonableness only when a search or seizure is conducted with a warrant. But the standard of reasonableness must also apply to warrantless searches according to the Fourth Amendment. The committee version initially declared that the "rights of the people to be secured in their persons,

houses, papers, and effects, shall not be violated by warrants issuing
without probable cause, supported by oath or affirmation, and not
particularly describing the places to be searched, and the persons
or things to be seized."[81] During the debate by the House acting
as the Committee of the Whole, Elbridge Gerry of Massachusetts
moved the restoration of "unreasonable seizures and searches."
Oddly, he said he did so on the presumption that a "mistake" had
been made in the wording of the clause, which he corrected by
changing "rights" to "right" and "secured" to "secure." The effect
was to provide security or, as we might say, privacy to the people;
Gerry's motion changed the meaning from a protection of the right
to a protection of individuals in their persons, homes, papers, and
effects. The Committee of the Whole adopted his motion but defeated others that were also important.[82] According to the House
Journal, the defeated motions of August 17 were reported as agreed
upon by the Committee of the Whole. Thus, the provision recommended to the House, in the articles arranged by a special
committee of three, read:

> The right of the people to be secure in their persons, houses, papers,
> and effects, against unreasonable searches and seizures, shall not be
> violated; and no warrants shall issue, but upon probable cause, sup-
> ported by oath or affirmation, and particularly describing the place
> to be searched, and the persons or things to be seized.[83]

The changes that seem to have been sneaked in did more than
eliminate a double negative. The entire provision was split into
two parts separated by a semicolon. The first part fixed the right
of the people and laid down the standard against unreasonable
searches and seizures. The second part required probable cause
for the issue of a specific warrant. No other changes were made
except in the number of the article. Its text remained the same as
adopted by the House and accepted by the Senate. Thus, Otis and
Adams finally had a belated but cardinal impact on the making of
the Fourth Amendment, even though Madison was immediately
influenced by Lee and Virginia's recommendation. Lee, whom
Virginia's legislature had elected to the United States Senate instead of Madison, bitterly complained to Patrick Henry that the
idea of recommending amendments to the Constitution turned out
to be political suicide; the Bill of Rights made impossible the

amendments most desired by the Anti-Federalists limiting national powers concerning taxes, treaties, and commerce.[84]

When Madison had first recommended to the House that it consider amendments to the Constitution, some Anti-Federalists thought the House should not neglect the more important business of passing a law for the collection of duties. That law, which passed seven weeks before the amendments were adopted for state consideration, contained a clause on search and seizure. It allowed collectors and naval officers to enter and search any ships suspected of having uncustomed goods and to seize such goods. That is, Congress authorized general searches for the search and seizure of ships—warrantless, general searches. By contrast, if an officer suspected the concealment of uncustomed goods in a building on land, he must apply for a specific warrant before a magistrate and under oath state the cause of his suspicion, and he "shall . . . be entitled to a warrant to enter such house, store, or any place (in the day time only)" and to conduct the search for and seizure of uncustomed goods.[85] Thus, the statute enacted before the framing of the Fourth Amendment required magistrates to issue the warrant on the basis of the officer's suspicion, not on the magistrate's independent judgment of the question of whether probable cause existed.

Allowing the officer who executed a warrant to determine its specificity put the fox in charge of the chicken coop. The magistrate in effect accepted the officer's sworn statement that he was acting in good faith. That is difficult to reconcile with the fact that the good faith execution of a general warrant by a customs officer in the years before the Revolution did not, to American whigs, validate the warrant or the seizures under it.

The adoption of the Fourth Amendment changed the situation drastically. In March 1791, before the amendment had been formally ratified but after approval by nine state legislatures, Congress enacted a tax on liquor, whether imported or distilled in the United States. The statute reflected the meaning of the Fourth Amendment. Unlike the collections act of 1789, the act of 1791 explicitly empowered magistrates to decide for themselves whether an officer had probable cause. Any judge with jurisdiction might issue a "special warrant" for the detection of fraudulently concealed spirits, but the warrant was lawful only "upon reasonable cause of suspicion, to be made out to the satisfaction of such judge or justice of the peace" and sworn under oath. That became the basis in federal law for the determination of probable cause.[86]

The amendment constituted a swift liberalization of the law of search and seizure. Its language was the broadest known at the time. It provided no remedy, however, for an illegal search or seizure, or for the introduction in evidence of illegally seized items. It contained principles that were as vague as they might be comprehensive; "probable" and "unreasonable," even if judicially determined, remained uncertain in meaning, and Congress made no provision for the liability, civil or criminal, of federal officers who violated the amendment. Moreover, no exclusionary rule existed. Consequently, the right of privacy created by the amendment, while better secured by the fundamental law in comparison to previous practices and standards, depended on congressional and judicial adherence to the spirit of the amendment. In effect, the meaning of the right to privacy depended then, as now, upon the interpretation of the "probable cause" that justified a specific warrant and, above all, on the reasonableness of searches and seizures.

CHAPTER TWELVE

The Fifth Amendment: The Right Against Self-Incrimination

$\mathscr{A}$s originally proposed by James Madison, when he introduced the recommendations that became the Bill of Rights, the Fifth Amendment's self-incrimination clause was part of a miscellaneous article that read: "No person shall be subject, except in cases of impeachment, to more than one punishment or trial for the same offense; nor shall be compelled to be a witness against himself; nor be deprived of life, liberty, or property, without due process of law; nor be obliged to relinquish his property, where it may be necessary for public use, without a just compensation."[1] That hodgepodge reflects the industriousness and creativity of Madison's work. He stated that he merely sought to satisfy a widespread conviction that the United States should be restrained from violating personal rights. But no state, either in its own constitution or in its recommended amendments, had a self-incrimination clause phrased as generously as that introduced by Madison: "no person . . . shall be compelled to be a witness against himself."

Not only was Madison's phrasing original; his placement of the clause was also unusual. In the widely imitated model of his own state, the clause appeared in the midst of an enumeration of the procedural rights of the criminally accused at his trial. Only Delaware and Maryland had departed from this precedent by giving the clause independent status and applicability in all courts, thereby extending it to witnesses as well as parties and to civil as well as criminal proceedings. In presenting his amendment, Madison said nothing whatever that explained his intentions concerning the self-incrimination clause. Nor do his papers or correspondence illuminate his meaning. We have only the language of his proposal, and that revealed an intent to incorporate into the Constitution the whole scope of the common law right.

Madison's proposal certainly applied to civil as well as criminal proceedings, and in principle to any stage of a legal inquiry, including the initial interrogation in a criminal case and the swearing of a deposition in a civil one. It extended to any kind of governmental inquiry, judicial or otherwise. Moreover, the unique phrasing, that no one could be compelled to be a *witness* against himself, was far more comprehensive than a prohibition against self-incrimination. But the conventional phrasing, that no one should be compelled to *accuse* oneself or *furnish evidence* against oneself, also comprehended more than self-incrimination. By its terms the clause could also apply to any testimony that fell short of making one vulnerable to criminal jeopardy or civil penalty or forfeiture but that nevertheless exposed him to public disgrace or obloquy, or other injury to name and reputation. Finally, Madison's phrasing protected third parties, those who were merely witnesses called to give testimony for one side or the other, whether in civil, criminal, or equity proceedings. According to customary procedure, witnesses, unlike parties, could in fact be compelled to give evidence, under oath, although they were safeguarded against the necessity of testifying against themselves in any manner that might open them to prosecution for a criminal offense or subject them to a forfeiture or civil penalties. By contrast, neither the criminal defendant nor the parties to a civil suit could be compelled to give testimony at all. They could furnish evidence neither for nor against themselves. The law did require mere witnesses to give evidence for or against the parties but not against themselves. Madison, going beyond the recommendations of the states and the constitution of his own state, phrased his own proposal to make it coextensive with the broadest practice.

Comparing his proposal with its precedents is revealing. To George Mason of Virginia belongs the credit for initiating the constitutionalization of the old English rule of evidence that a person, in Mason's words, "cannot be compelled to give evidence against himself." That was the language adopted by Virginia in Section 8 of its Declaration of Rights of 1776, prefacing its first state constitution. But the guarantee appeared in the context of an enumeration of the rights of the criminally accused. Therefore, Virginia's constitutional right against self-incrimination did not extend to anyone but the accused, nor apply to any proceedings other than a criminal prosecution. As a matter of actual practice, however, Virginia's courts allowed a right against self-incrimination in all stages of equity and common law proceedings, and also allowed witnesses as well as defendants to invoke the right. Indeed, it could be claimed by a criminal suspect at his preliminary examination before a justice of the peace; by a person testifying at a grand jury investigation into crime; by anyone giving evidence in a suit between private parties; and, above all perhaps, by the subject of an inquisitorial proceeding before any governmental or nonjudicial tribunal, such as a legislative committee or the governor and council, seeking to discover criminal culpability. If one's disclosures could make him vulnerable to legal peril, he could invoke his right to silence. He might even do so if his answers revealed infamy or disgrace yet could not be used against him in a subsequent prosecution. The law of Virginia at this time, as in England, shielded witnesses against mere exposure to public obloquy. The right against self-incrimination incorporated a protection against self-infamy and was as broad as the jeopardy against which it sought to guard. Yet the Virginia Declaration of Rights, though vesting a testimonial rule with the impregnability of a constitutional guarantee, provided only a stunted version of the common law.[2]

Read literally and in context, the right seemed to apply only to a criminal defendant at his trial. If that was its meaning, it was a superfluous guarantee, because the defendant at his trial was not even permitted to testify. If he had not confessed, the prosecution had to prove its case against him by the testimony of witnesses and

other evidence; the prisoner, in turn, made his defense by witnesses, if he had them, by cross-examining the prosecution's witnesses, and by commenting on the evidence against him. If he
could afford counsel, he need never open his mouth during the
trial. With or without counsel, he could neither be placed on the
stand by the prosecution nor take the stand if he wished. Consequently, neither George Mason nor his colleagues in the legislature, who were acting as a constitutional convention, could have
meant what they said. More likely, they failed to say what they
meant. The provision against self-incrimination was the product of
bad draftsmanship, which the Virginia convention failed to remedy.
But no evidence exists to show that it was taken literally or regarded
as anything but a sonorous declamation of the common law right
of long standing. Other common law rights that had been entirely
overlooked by Virginia's constitution makers, including such vital
rights as habeas corpus, grand jury indictment, and representation
by counsel, continued to be observed in daily practice. Thus the
great Declaration of Rights did not alter Virginia's system of criminal procedure nor express the totality of rights that actually flourished. The practice of the courts was simply unaffected by the
restrictions inadvertently or unknowingly inserted into Section 8.
Thus, the language of a constitutional text does not necessarily
reveal original intent or contemporaneous practice.

Section 8, nevertheless, became a model for other states and
for the United States Bill of Rights. Indeed, the Virginia Declaration of Rights became one of the most influential constitutional
documents in our history. The committee draft was reprinted in
the Philadelphia newspapers even before Independence, making
it available to the delegates from all the states assembled in the
Second Continental Congress. That committee draft was republished all over America, and even in England and on the Continent,
in time to be a shaping force in the framing of other state constitutions. Except for the corporate colonies of Rhode Island and
Connecticut, which stood pat with their old colonial charter, the
other states followed Virginia's example of framing a state constitution. Eight states, including Vermont, which was technically an
independent republic from 1776 until admitted to the Union in
1791, annexed separate bills of rights to their constitutions.[3]

Every one of the eight states protected the right against self-incrimination, and every one in essentially the language of Virginia's Section 8, because each followed the basic formulation that no man can be "compelled to give evidence against himself." In 1776, Pennsylvania adopted Section 8 in entirety, adding only the right to be represented by counsel and retaining the self-incrimination clause verbatim. In 1776 Delaware introduced a subtle but crucial change by making that clause an independent section instead of inserting it among the enumerated rights of the criminally accused. Moreover, Delaware's guarantee, "That no Man in the Courts of common Law ought to be compelled to give evidence against himself," extended the right against self-incrimination to witnesses as well as parties, in civil as well as criminal cases. Maryland in the same year also placed the self-incrimination clause in a section by itself and broadened it, as did Delaware, extending it not only to "a common court of law" but also to "any other court," meaning courts of equity. But Maryland simultaneously qualified the right by providing for exceptions to it "in such cases as have been usually practised in this State, or may hereafter be directed by the Legislature." That qualification, in effect, required a man to give evidence against himself if a pardon or a grant of immunity against prosecution exempted him from the penal consequences of his disclosures. North Carolina in 1776 followed Virginia's Section 8, as did Vermont in 1777. In 1780 Massachusetts slightly modified the Virginia phraseology. Referring to a criminal defendant, Massachusetts provided that he should not be compelled "to accuse, or furnish"—instead of "give"—evidence against himself. In 1784 New Hampshire followed suit. George Mason's observation that his Declaration of Rights was "closely imitated" was certainly accurate with respect to the self-incrimination clause.[4]

Of the four states—New Jersey, New York, Georgia, and South Carolina—that did not preface their constitutions with a separate bill of rights, none secured the right against self-incrimination. All, however, guaranteed some rights, even if only a few, at various points in their constitutions. New Jersey, for example, had an omnibus clause that kept the common law of England in force, thereby protecting the right against self-incrimination. Superfluously, New Jersey specifically protected the right to counsel and trial by jury. New York also provided that the common law should continue as the law of the state, yet the right to indictment and trial by jury, which were expressly mentioned in New York's con-stitution, were secured by the common law. Why those two were singled out above all other common law rights is inexplicable, especially because the courts were enjoined to "proceed according to the course of the common law," and citizens were additionally protected by the standard "law of the land" clause, the equivalent of a due process of law clause. The constitution also protected the right to vote, the free exercise of religion, representation by coun-sel, and a qualified freedom from bills of attainder. Perhaps these rights were singled out because they were either unprotected or, at best, inadequately protected by the common law. Yet, other rights in the same category were ignored, while trial by jury was superfluously secured. The whole process of selection in New York was baffling. No reasoned explanation nor any drawn from the evidence is available.[5]

Although the right against self-incrimination was not men-tioned in New York's constitution, neither were the rights to free-dom of speech and press—shade of Zenger!—nor the writ of habeas corpus. New York also ignored protections against unreasonable searches and seizures, ex post facto laws, and double jeopardy. The absence of express guarantees simply cannot be construed to indicate that these rights were not present in practice. One could no more reasonably argue that the omission of a ban against com-pulsory self-incrimination proved that it did not exist or was re-garded without respect than he could argue that the right to the writ of habeas corpus was illusory because it, too, was not consti-tutionally protected. In its enumeration of rights, New York's con-stitution was framed in an incredibly haphazard fashion, like New Jersey's, with no discernible principle of selection. The same ob-servation applied to the constitutions of South Carolina and Geor-gia, neither of which protected the right against self-incrimination.[6]

The history of the writing of the first American bills of rights and constitutions simply does not bear out the presupposition that the process was a diligent or systematic one. Those documents, which we uncritically exalt, were imitative, deficient, and irration-ally selective. In the glorious act of framing a social compact ex-pressive of the supreme law, Americans tended simply to draw up a random catalogue of rights that seemed to satisfy their urge for a statement of first principles—or for some of them. That task was executed in a disordered fashion that verged on ineptness. Original intent as the basis for constitutional jurisprudence seems, therefore, equally disordered or irrational, for its premises are based on illusions. At any rate, the inclusion or exclusion of any particular right neither proved nor disproved its existence in a state's colonial history.

In the First Congress, there was no debate on the self-incrimination clause. Only one speaker, John Laurence, a Federalist lawyer of New York, addressed himself to what he called the proposal that "a person shall not be compelled to give evidence against himself." Interestingly, he restated Madison's phrasing in the language of the more familiar clause deriving from Section 8 of the Virginia Declaration of Rights, as if they were the same. Calling it "a general declaration in some degree contrary to laws passed," Laurence thought that it should "be confined to criminal cases," and he moved an amendment for that purpose. The House adopted Laurence's motion for an amendment without discussion; the clause as amended was adopted unanimously. The speed with which the House seems to have acted, without the record showing any controversy over the significant restriction of the scope of the clause, is bewildering. Simply respect for the House's own distinguished select committee, a nonpartisan group that included one member from each state, five of whom had been delegates to the Philadelphia Constitutional Convention of 1787, ought to have required some explanation. The select committee, following Madison, had intended what Laurence rightly called "a general declaration." Taken literally, the amended clause, "No person shall . . . be compelled in any criminal case, to be a witness against himself," excluded from its protection parties and witnesses in civil and equity suits as well as witnesses before nonjudicial governmental proceedings such as legislative investigations. As amended it applied only to parties and witnesses in criminal cases, presumably to all stages of proceedings from arrest and examination to indictment and trial.[7]

Laurence's passing remark that the committee proposal was "in some degree contrary to laws passed" was inaccurate yet illuminated the purpose of his motion to amend. Exactly a month earlier, on July 17, the Senate had passed and sent to the House the bill that became the Judiciary Act of 1789. Thanks to Madison's efforts, the House tabled the judiciary bill while it attended to the matter of amending the Constitution. Not until the House approved of the proposed amendments and sent them to the Senate on August 24 did the Committee of the Whole take up the judiciary bill. Its provisions contained a section to which Laurence may have alluded when referring to "laws passed." Section 15 in the original Senate draft empowered the federal courts to compel civil parties to produce their books or papers containing relevant evidence. It also provided that a plaintiff might require a defendant, on proving to the satisfaction of a court that the defendant had deprived him of evidence to support his cause, "to disclose on oath his or her knowledge in the cause in cases and under circumstances where a respondent might be compelled to make such a disclosure on oath by the aforesaid rules of chancery." Opponents of that final clause described it as an authorization for "inquisitorial powers." Senator William Maclay of Pennsylvania argued that "extorting evidence from any person was a species of torture. . . . [H]ere was an attempt to exercise a tyranny of the same kind over the mind. The conscience was to be put on the rack; that forcing oaths or evidence from men, I consider equally tyrannical as extorting evidence by torture." The clause, he concluded, would offend his constituents, whose state bill of rights provided that no person could be compelled to give evidence against himself. As a result of such opposition the oath provision was stricken from the bill as adopted by the Senate. Nevertheless, it retained the clause forcing the production of books or papers that contained pertinent evidence in civil cases "under circumstances where they might be compelled to produce the same by the ordinary rules of proceeding in Chancery," that is, in courts of equity.[8]

According to an early federal court ruling, this provision was intended to prevent the necessity of instituting equity suits to obtain from an adverse party the production of documents related to a litigated issue.[9] The provision did not suspend or supersede the right against self-incrimination, but it did limit the reach of the general principle that no one could be compelled to be a witness against himself. The documents in question could be *against* the party without incriminating him. He might, for example, be forced to produce a deed proving plaintiff's ownership, thereby exposing himself to a civil, but not a criminal, liability. Thus Laurence, with this pending legislation in mind, may have moved the insertion of the words "in any criminal case" in order to retain the customary equity rule that compelled evidence of civil liability. To compel a civil defendant to produce records or papers "against himself," harming his case, in no way infringed his traditional right not to produce them if they could harm him criminally. The House, incidentally, passed the judiciary bill with Section 15 unchanged.[10]

In the Senate, the House's proposed amendments to the Constitution underwent further change. However, the Senate accepted the self-incrimination clause without change. The double jeopardy clause in the same article was rephrased and a clause on the grand jury, which the House had coupled with guarantees relating to the trial of crimes, was transferred to the beginning of what became the Fifth Amendment. In what was to be the Sixth Amendment the Senate clustered together the procedural rights of the criminally accused after indictment.[11] That the self-incrimination clause did not fall into the Sixth Amendment indicated that the Senate, like the House, did not intend to follow the implication of Virginia's Section 8, the original model, that the right not to give evidence against oneself applied merely to the defendant on trial. The Sixth Amendment, referring explicitly to the accused, protected him alone. Indeed, the Sixth Amendment, with the right of counsel added, was the equivalent of Virginia's Section 8 and included all of its rights except that against self-incrimination. Thus, the location of the self-incrimination clause in the Fifth Amendment rather than the Sixth proves that the Senate, like the House, did not intend to restrict that clause only to the criminal defendant nor only to his trial. The Fifth Amendment, even with the self-incrimination clause restricted to criminal cases, still expressed its principle broadly enough to apply to witnesses and to any phase of the proceedings.

The clause also protected against more than just "self-incrimination," a phrase that had never been used in the long history of its origins and development. The "right against self-incrimination" is a shorthand gloss of modern origin that implies a restriction not in the constitutional clause. The right not to be a witness against oneself imports a principle of wider reach, applicable, at least in criminal cases, to the self-production of any adverse evidence, including evidence that made one the herald of his own infamy, thereby publicly disgracing him. The clause extended, in other words, to all the injurious as well as incriminating consequences of disclosure by witness or party. Clearly, to speak merely of a right against self-incrimination stunts the wider right not to give evidence against oneself, as the Virginia model put it, or not to be a witness against oneself, as the Fifth Amendment stated. The previous history of the right, both in England and in America, proves that it was not bound by rigid definition. After the adoption of the Fifth Amendment, the earliest state and federal cases were in accord with that previous history, which suggests that whatever the wording of the constitutional formulation, it did not supersede or even limit the common law right.

Pennsylvania's experience is to the point. The state constitution of 1776 had followed the Virginia model by placing in the context of criminal prosecutions the principle that "no man" should be compelled to give evidence against himself. In 1790 Pennsylvania, in a new constitution, replaced the "no man" formulation with a specific reference to "the accused." Nevertheless, in the first Pennsylvania case involving this clause, the state supreme court ignored the restriction introduced in 1790, or rather, interpreted it as expressing the historic maxim that no person is obliged to accuse himself. The case involved a prosecution for violating an election law that required answers on oath to questions concerning loyalty during the American Revolution. Counsel for defense argued that the constitutional clause of 1790 protected against questions the answers to which might tend to result in a prosecution or bring the party into disgrace or infamy. Chief Justice Edward Shippen, who had studied at Middle Temple and had begun his legal practice in Pennsylvania way back in 1750, delivered the following opinion:

> It has been objected that the questions propounded to the electors contravene an established principle of law. The maxim is, 'Nemo tenetur seipsum accusare (sen prodere).' It is founded on the best policy, and runs throughout our whole system of jurisprudence. It is the uniform practice of courts of justice as to witnesses and jurors. It is considered cruel and unjust to propose questions which may tend to criminate the party. And so jealous have the legislatures of this commonwealth been of this mode of discovery of facts that they have refused their assent to a bill brought in to compel persons to disclose on oath papers as well as facts relating to questions of mere

property. And may we not justly suppose, that they would not be less jealous of securing our citizens against this mode of self-accusation? The words 'accusare' and 'prodere' are general terms, and their sense is not confined to cases where the answers to the questions proposed would induce to the punishment of the party. If they would involve him in shame or reproach, he is under no obligation to answer them.

The same court applied a similar rule in a purely civil case, holding that no one could be forced to take the oath of a witness if his testimony "tends to accuse himself of an immoral act."[12]

The state courts of the Framers' generation endorsed the extension of the right to cover self-infamy as well as self-incrimination, although the self-infamy rule eventually fell into disuse. Both federal and state courts followed in all other respects Shippen's far-reaching interpretation of what on its face and in context was a narrow clause. In the earliest federal case on the right against self-incrimination, Justice James Iredell of the Supreme Court, on circuit duty, ruled that a *witness* was not bound to answer a question that might tend to "implicate" or criminate himself.[13] In one of the most famous cases in our constitutional history, *Marbury v. Madison*, Attorney General Levi Lincoln balked at a question relating to his conduct as acting secretary of state when Jefferson first became President. Marbury's commission as a justice of the peace for the District of Columbia had been signed by the outgoing President and affixed with the seal of the United States by the then secretary of state, John Marshall, who had had no time to deliver it. What, asked Chief Justice Marshall, had Lincoln done with that commission? Lincoln, who probably had burned it, replied that he did not think that he was bound to disclose his official transactions while acting as secretary of state, nor should he "be compelled to answer any thing which might tend to criminate himself." Marbury's counsel, Charles Lee, who was himself a former attorney general of the United States, and Chief Justice Marshall were in agreement: Lincoln, who was in the peculiar position of being both a witness and counsel for the government in a civil suit, was not obliged to disclose anything that might incriminate him.[14] In Aaron Burr's trial, Chief Justice Marshall, without referring to the constitutional clause, again sustained the right of a witness to refuse answer to an incriminating question.[15] The courts have always assumed that the meaning of the constitutional clause is determined by the common law.[16]

Whether the Framers of the Fifth Amendment intended it to be fully co-extensive with the common law cannot be proved—or disproved. The language of the clause and its Framers' understanding of it may not have been synonymous. The difficulty is that its Framers, from Mason to Madison and Laurence, left too few clues. Slight explication emerged during the process of state ratification of the Bill of Rights from 1789 through 1791. Indeed, in legislative and convention proceedings, in letters, newspapers, and tracts, in judicial opinions, and law books, the whole period from 1776 to 1791 reveals neither sufficient explanation of the scope of such a clause nor the reasons for it. That it was a ban on torture and a security for the criminally accused were the most important of its functions, but these were not all of its functions. Still, nothing can be found of a theoretical nature expressing a rationale or underlying policy for the right in question or its reach.

The probable reason is that by 1776 the right against self-incrimination was simply taken for granted and was so deeply accepted that its constitutional expression had the mechanical quality of a ritualistic gesture in favor of a self-evident truth needing no explanation. The clause itself, whether in Virginia's Section 8 or the Fifth Amendment, might have been so imprecisely stated, or misstated, as to raise vital questions of intent, meaning, and purpose. But constitution makers, in that day at least, did not explain themselves and did not regard themselves as framers of detailed codes. To them the statement of a bare principle was sufficient, and they were content to put it spaciously, if ambiguously, in order to allow for its expansion as the need might arise, and in order to avoid the controversy that detail or explanation might provoke.

By stating the principle in the Bill of Rights, which was also a bill of restraints upon government, the Framers were once again sounding the tocsin against the dangers of government oppression of the individual; they were also voicing their conviction that the right against self-incrimination was a legitimate defense possessed by every individual against government. Tough-minded revolutionists, the equal of any in history in the art of self-government, they were willing to risk lives and fortunes in support of their belief that government is but an instrument of man, its sovereignty held in subordination to his rights. They cannot justly be accused of having been naive, or disregardful of the claims of law and order. They were mindful, nevertheless, that the enduring interests of the community required justice to be done as fairly as possible. The Constitution with its amendments was an embodiment of their political morality, an ever-present reminder of their view that the citizen is the master of his government, not its subject. As Abe Fortas observed, "The principle that a man is not obliged to furnish the state with ammunition to use against him is basic to this conception." The state, he acknowledged, must defend itself and, "within the limits of accepted procedure," punish lawbreakers. "But it has no right to compel the sovereign individual to surrender or impair his right of self-defense." The fundamental value reflected by the Fifth Amendment "is intangible, it is true; but so is liberty, and so is man's immortal soul. A man may be punished, even put to death, by the state; but . . . he should not be made to prostrate himself before its majesty. Mea culpa belongs to a man and his God. It is a plea that cannot be exacted from free men by human authority. To require it is to insist that the state is the superior of the individuals who compose it, instead of their instrument."[17]

The same point underlay the statement of another distinguished federal judge, who observed, "Our forefathers, when they wrote this provision into the Fifth Amendment of the Constitution, had in mind a lot of history which has been largely forgotten today."[18] The remark applies with equal force, of course, to the right of representation by counsel, trial by jury, or any of the other, related procedural rights that are constitutionally sanctified. With good reason the Bill of Rights showed a preoccupation with the subject of criminal justice. The Framers understood that without fair and regularized procedures to protect the criminally accused, liberty could not exist. They knew that from time immemorial, the tyrant's first step was to use the criminal law to crush his opposition. Vicious and ad hoc procedures had always been used to victimize nonconformists and minorities of differing religious, racial, or political persuasions. The Fifth Amendment was part and parcel of the procedures that were so crucial, in the minds of the Framers, to the survival of the most treasured rights. One's home could not be his "castle," his property be his own, his right to express his opinions or to worship his God be secure, if he could be searched, arrested, tried, or imprisoned in some arbitrary or ignoble manner.

The Framers of the Bill of Rights saw their injunction, that no man should be a witness against himself in a criminal case, as a central feature of the accusatory system of criminal justice. While deeply committed to perpetuating a system that minimized the possibilities of convicting the innocent, they were no less concerned about the humanity that the fundamental law should show even to the offender. Above all, the Fifth Amendment reflected their judgment that in a free society, based on respect for the individual, the determination of guilt or innocence by just procedures, in which the accused made no unwilling contribution to his conviction, was more important than punishing the guilty.

As Justice Felix Frankfurter declared, "The privilege against self-incrimination is a specific provision of which it is peculiarly true that 'a page of history is worth a volume of logic.' "[19] That page of history begins with the origins of the right against self-incrimination. Frederic William Maitland's epigram, that the "seamless web" of history is torn by telling a piece of it, is borne out by any effort to explain the origins of that right.[20] The American origins derive largely from the inherited English common law system of criminal justice. But the English origins, so much more complex, spill over legal boundaries and reflect the many-sided religious, political, and constitutional issues that racked England during the sixteenth and seventeenth centuries: the struggles between Anglicanism and Puritanism, between Parliament and king, between limited government and arbitrary rule, and between freedom of conscience and suppression of heresy and sedition. Even within the more immediate confines of law, the history of the right against self-incrimination is enmeshed in broad issues: the contests for supremacy between the accusatory and the inquisitional systems of procedure, between the common law and the royal prerogative, and between the common law and its canon and civil law rivals. Against this broad background the origins of the concept that "no man is bound to accuse himself" (*nemo tenetur seipsum prodere*) must be understood and the concept's legal development traced.

The right against self-incrimination originated as an indirect product of the common law's accusatory system and of its opposition to rival systems that employed inquisitorial procedures. Toward the close of the sixteenth century, just before the concept first appeared in England on a sustained basis, all courts of criminal jurisdiction habitually sought to exact self-incriminatory admission from persons suspected of or charged with crime. Although defendants in crown cases suffered from this and many other harsh procedures, even in common law courts, the accusatory system afforded a degree of fair play not available under the inquisitional system. Moreover, torture was never sanctioned by the common law, although it was employed as an instrument of royal prerogative until 1641.[21]

By contrast, torture for the purpose of detecting crime and inducing confession was regularly authorized by the Roman codes of the canon and civil law. "Abandon all hope, ye who enter here" well describes the chances of an accused person under inquisitorial procedures characterized by presentment based on mere rumor or suspicion, indefiniteness of accusation, the oath *ex officio*, secrecy, lack of confrontation, coerced confessions, and magistrates acting as accusers and prosecutors as well as "judges." This system of procedure, by which heresy was most efficiently combated, was introduced into England by ecclesiastical courts.[22]

The use of the oath *ex officio* by prerogative courts, particularly by the ecclesiastical Court of High Commission, which Elizabeth I reconstituted, resulted in the defensive claim that "no man is bound to accuse himself." The High Commission, an instrument of the Crown for maintaining religious uniformity under the Anglican establishment, used the canon law inquisitorial process, but made the oath *ex officio*, rather than torture, the crux of its procedure. Men suspected of "heretical opinions," "seditious books," or "conspiracies" were summoned before the High Commission without being informed of the accusation against them or the identity of their accusers. Denied due process of law by common law standards, suspects were required to take an oath to answer truthfully to interrogatories that sought to establish guilt for crimes neither charged nor disclosed.[23]

A nonconformist victim of the High Commission found himself thrust between hammer and anvil: refusal to take the oath, or having taken it, refusal to answer the interrogatories, meant a sentence for contempt and invited Star Chamber proceedings; to take the oath and respond truthfully to questioning often meant to convict oneself of religious or political crimes and, moreover, to supply evidence against nonconformist accomplices; to take the oath and then lie meant to sin against the Scriptures and risk conviction for perjury. Common lawyers of the Puritan party developed the daring argument that the oath, although sanctioned by the Crown, was unconstitutional because it violated Magna Carta, which limited even the royal prerogative.[24]

The argument had myth-making qualities, for it was one of the earliest to exalt Magna Carta as the symbol and source of English constitutional liberty. As yet there was no contention that one need not answer incriminating questions after accusation by due process according to common law. But a later generation would use substantially the same argument—"that by the Statues of Magna Carta . . . for a man to accuse himself was and is utterlie inhibited"[25]— on behalf of the contention that one need not involuntarily answer questions even after he had been properly accused.

Under Chief Justice Edward Coke the common law courts, with the sympathy of the House of Commons, vindicated the Puritan tactic of litigious opposition to the High Commission. The deep hostility between the canon and common law systems expressed itself in a series of writs of prohibition issued by Coke and his colleagues, staying the commission's proceedings. Coke, adept at creating legal fictions which he clothed with the authority of resurrected "precedents" and inferences from Magna Carta, grounded twenty of these prohibitions on the allegedly ancient common law rule that no man is bound to accuse himself criminally.[26]

In the 1630s the High Commission and the Star Chamber, which employed similar procedures, reached the zenith of their powers. But in 1637 a flinty Puritan agitator, John Lilburne, refused the oath. His well-publicized opposition to incriminatory questioning focused England's attention upon the injustice and illegality of such practices. In 1641 the Long Parliament, dominated by Puritans and common lawyers, condemned the sentences against Lilburne and others, abolished the Star Chamber and the High Commission, and prohibited ecclesiastical authorities from administering any oath obliging one "to confess or to accuse himself or herself of any crime."[27]

Common law courts, however, continued to ask incriminating questions and to bully witnesses into answering them. The rudimentary idea of a right against self-incrimination was nevertheless lodged in the imperishable opinions of Coke, publicized by Lilburne and the Levellers, and firmly associated with Magna Carta. The idea was beginning to take hold of men's minds. Lilburne was again the catalytic agent. At his various trials for his life, in his testimony before investigating committees of Parliament, and in his ceaseless tracts, he dramatically popularized the demand that a right against self-incrimination be accorded general legal recognition. His career illustrates how the right against self-incrimination developed not only in conjunction with a whole gamut of fair procedures associated with "due process of law" but also with demands for freedom of conscience and expression. After Lilburne's time the right became entrenched in English jurisprudence, even under the judicial tyrants of the Restoration. As the state became more secure and as fairer treatment of the criminally accused became possible, the old practice of bullying the prisoner for answers gradually died out. By the early eighteenth century the accused was no longer put on the stand at all; he could not give evidence in his own behalf even if he wished to, although he was permitted to tell his story, unsworn. The prisoner was regarded as incompetent to be a witness for himself.[28]

After the first quarter of the eighteenth century, the English history of the right centered primarily upon the preliminary examination of the suspect and the legality of placing in evidence various types of involuntary confessions. Incriminating statements made by suspects at the preliminary examination could be used against them at their trials; a confession, even though not made under oath, sufficed to convict. Yet suspects could not be interrogated under oath. One might be ensnared into a confession by the sharp and intimidating tactics of the examining magistrate; but there was no legal obligation to answer an incriminating question—nor, until 1848, to notify the suspect or prisoner of his right to refuse answer. One's answers, given in ignorance of his right, might be used against him. However, the courts excluded confessions that had been made under duress. Only involuntary confessions were seen as a violation of the right. Lord Chief Baron Geoffrey Gilbert in his *Law of Evidence* (1756) declared that although a confession was the best evidence of guilt, "this Confession must be voluntary and without compulsion; for our Law . . . will not force any Man to accuse himself; and in this we do certainly follow that Law of Nature" which commands self-preservation.[29]

Thus, opposition to the oath *ex officio* ended in the common law right to refuse to furnish incriminating evidence against oneself even when all formalities of common law accusation had first been fulfilled. The prisoner demanded that the state prove its case against him, and he confronted the witnesses who testified against him. The Levellers, led by Lilburne, even claimed a right not to answer any questions concerning themselves, if life, liberty, or property might be jeopardized, regardless of the tribunal or government agency directing the examination, be it judicial, legislative, or executive. The Leveller claim to a right against self-incrimination raised the generic problem of the nature of sovereignty in England and spurred the transmutation of Magna Carta from a feudal relic of baronial reaction into a modern bulwark of the rule of law and regularized restraints upon government power.

The claim to this right also emerged in the context of a cluster of criminal procedures whose object was to ensure fair play for the criminally accused. It harmonized with the principles that the accused was innocent until proven guilty and that the burden of proof was on the prosecution. It was related to the idea that a man's home should not be promiscuously broken into and rifled for evidence of his reading and writing. It was intimately connected to the belief that torture or any cruelty in forcing a man to expose his guilt was unfair and illegal. It was indirectly associated with the right to counsel and the right to have witnesses on behalf of the defendant, so that his lips could remain sealed against the government's questions or accusations. It was at first a privilege of the guilty, given the nature of the substantive law of religious and political crimes. But the right became neither a privilege of the guilty nor a protection of the innocent. It became merely one of the ways of fairly determining guilt or innocence, like trial by jury itself; it became part of due process of the law, a fundamental principle of the accusatorial system. It reflected the view that society benefited by seeking the defendant's conviction without the aid of his involuntary admissions. Forcing self-incrimination was thought to brutalize the system of criminal justice and to produce untrustworthy evidence.

Above all, the right was closely linked to freedom of speech and religious liberty. It was, in its origins, unquestionably an invention of those who were guilty of religious crimes like heresy, schism, and nonconformity, and later, of political crimes like treason, seditious libel, and breach of parliamentary privilege. More often than not, the offense was merely criticism of the government, its policies, or its officers. The right was associated, then, with guilt for crimes of conscience, of belief, and of association. In the broadest sense it was not so much a protection of the guilty, or even the innocent, but a protection of freedom of expression, of political liberty, and of the right to worship as one pleased. The symbolic importance and practical function of the right was certainly settled matters, taken for granted, in the eighteenth century. And it was part of the heritage of liberty which the common law bequeathed to the English settlers in America.

Yet, the right had to be won in every colony, invariably under conditions similar to those that generated it in England. The first glimmer of the right in America was evident in the heresy case of John Wheelwright, tried in 1637 in Massachusetts. In colony after colony people exposed to the inquisitorial tactics of the prerogative court of the governor and council refused to answer to incriminating interrogatories in cases heavy with political implications. By the end of the seventeenth century the right was unevenly recognized in the colonies.[30]

As the English common law increasingly became American law and the legal profession grew in size, competence, and influence, Americans developed a greater familiarity with the right. English law books and English criminal procedure provided a model. From Edmond Wingate's *Maxims of Reason* (1658), which included the earliest discussion of the maxim, "*Nemo tenetur accusare seipsum*," to Gilbert's *Evidence*, law books praised the right.[31] It grew so in popularity that in 1735 Benjamin Franklin, hearing that a church wanted to examine the sermons of an unorthodox minister could declare: "It was contrary to the common Rights of Mankind, no Man being obliged to furnish Matter of Accusation against himself." In 1754 a witness parried a Massachusetts legislative investigation into seditious libel by quoting the well-known Latin maxim, which he freely translated as "A Right of Silence as the Priviledge of every Englishman." In 1770 the attorney general of Pennsylvania ruled that an admiralty court could not oblige people to answer interrogatories "which may have a tendency to criminate them-selves, or subject them to a penalty, it being contrary to any prin-ciple of Reason and the Laws of England." When a right becomes so profoundly accepted that it has been hallowed by its association with Magna Carta and has been ranked as one of the common rights of man deriving from the law of nature, it receives genuflection and praise, not critical analysis; and it gets exalted as a fundamental liberty that receives constitutional expression.[32]

CHAPTER THIRTEEN

The Ninth Amendment: Unenumerated Rights

We the People

For 175 years, from 1791 to 1965, the Ninth Amendment lay dormant, a constitutional curiosity comparable in vitality to the Third Amendment (no quartering of troops in private homes) or to the privileges and immunities clause of the Fourteenth Amendment after the Supreme Court had "interpreted" the meaning out of it in the *Slaughterhouse Cases*.[1] Obscurity shrouded the meaning of the Ninth Amendment. One member of the Supreme Court, in a speech made after some reflection, acknowledged that the rights secured by the Ninth Amendment were "still a mystery."[2]

The year 1965 marks the beginning of Ninth Amendment jurisprudence. For the first time the Court mentioned the amendment, at least in part, as a basis for holding a government measure unconstitutional. Justice William O. Douglas for the Court confronted a state act that made the use of contraceptives criminal, even when counseled by a physician treating a married couple. From the First, Third, Fourth, and Fifth Amendments and in part from the Ninth Amendment, Douglas derived a "right of privacy older than the Bill of Rights" with respect to the "sacred precincts of marital bedrooms," and three Justices believed that the Ninth Amendment, unfortified by the "penumbras" and "emanations" of other provisions of the Bill of Rights, supported the voiding of the offensive state act. Justice Arthur Goldberg for the three wrote a concurring opinion based on the Ninth Amendment, buttressed by the "liberty" guaranteed by the Fourteenth Amendment.[3]

Within fifteen years the Ninth Amendment, once the subject of only incidental references, was invoked in over 1,200 state and federal cases in the most astonishing variety of matters.[4] After the Court had resuscitated the amendment, litigants found its charms compelling precisely because of its utter lack of specificity with respect to the rights that it protects. It says: "The enumeration in the Constitution, of certain rights, shall not be construed to deny or disparage others retained by the people." Those who have relied on this amendment for constitutional armament include schoolboys and police officers seeking relief from regulations that govern the length of their hair, citizens eager to preserve the purity of water and air against environmental polluters, and homosexuals claiming a right to be married. The question whether the Ninth Amendment was intended to be a cornucopia of unenumerated rights produces as many answers as there are points of view.

Oddly enough, those who advocate a constitutional "jurisprudence of original intention" and assert that the Constitution "said what it meant and meant what it said,"[5] are the ones who most vigorously deny content to the Ninth Amendment and to the concept of a "living Constitution." Presumably they would not swear fealty to a dead Constitution, not even to a static one of the sort endorsed by Chief Justice Roger Taney in the *Dred Scott* case.[6] Nevertheless they reject as absurd the idea that the Ninth Amendment could have been intended as a repository for newly discovered rights that activist judges embrace.

The fact that the Framers did not intend most, if any, of the rights that litigants read into the Ninth and would have found bizarre the notion that the Constitution protects any of those rights is really of no significance. We must remember, after all, that the Framers would have found absurd and bizarre most features of our constitutional law as well as of our politics, cities, industries, and society. Justice Hugo L. Black, in the very case of 1965 that breathed life into the Ninth Amendment, could not find much justification for the discovery of a right to privacy anywhere in the Constitution, let alone in the Ninth Amendment. The judicial reading of rights into it or out of it, he cautioned, "would make of this Court's members a day-to-day constitutional convention."[7] Figuratively, however, that is what the Supreme Court is—a continuous constitutional convention. The Court has functioned as if it were that since John Marshall's time, if not earlier, and few Justices in the history of the Court have contributed so much to the Court's effectiveness as a constitutional convention as Justice Black, especially in his First and Fifth Amendment opinions.

To say that the Framers did not intend the Court to act as a constitutional convention or to shape public policies by interpreting the Constitution is, again, to assert historical truth. However, that truth does not invalidate judicial decisions that the Framers failed to foresee; it reveals, rather, their human incapacity to predict how the system that they designed would work. They did not expect the development of a judicial power that influenced public policies. They did not expect judicial activism whether conservative or liberal. Nor did they foresee political parties, administrative agencies, overwhelming executive domination of foreign policy, national governance of the economy, foreign policy made without knowledge of any elected members of the government, or management of fiscal policies by the Federal Reserve Board. The argument for or against some judicial interpretation of the Constitution progresses not at all by the allegation, even if verifiable, that the Framers would have been shocked or surprised by such an interpretation.

The starting points for interpreting the Ninth Amendment are the text itself and the rule of construction which holds that if a plain meaning exists, it should be followed. As Justice Joseph Story said, "The first and fundamental rule in the interpretation of all instruments is, to construe them according to the sense of the terms, and the intention of the parties." If a plain meaning does not exist, the language of the text must be construed so as not to contradict the document at any point, and meaning must be sought in its purposes or in the principles that it embodies as understood from "its nature and objects, its scope and design."[8] We know enough about the making of the Ninth Amendment and about its historical context to apply these rules with considerable confidence, wherever they might lead. They lead first to the indisputable fact that the amendment by force of its terms protects unenumerated rights of the people. That opens the question, What are those rights? The answer depends on a preliminary question: Why would the Framers have included an amendment that acknowledges the existence of unenumerated rights that are no more subject to abridgment than the rights that are specified in the first eight amendments?

We must remember, by way of an answer, that ratificationists, including the most sophisticated of Framers, had made the enormously unpopular and weak argument that a bill of rights was superfluous in the United States, because government derived from the people and had only delegated powers. Alexander Hamilton, James Wilson, Oliver Ellsworth, and James Madison, among others, also argued that no need for a bill of rights existed because the government could not use its limited powers to encroach on reserved rights; no powers extended, for example, to religion or the press. That argument shriveled against contentions that Congress might exercise its delegated powers in such a way that abridged unprotected rights. The power to tax, implemented by the ominous necessary and proper clause, could be used to destroy a critical press and might be enforced by general warrants enabling the government to ransack homes and businesses for evidence of criminal evasion of the revenue laws or for evidence of seditious publications.

The Federalist #84 argued that particularizing rights was "not only unnecessary in the proposed Constitution but would even be dangerous. They would contain various exceptions to powers which are not granted; and, in this very account, would afford a colorable pretext to claim more than were granted." If no power had been granted to restrict the press, Hamilton reasoned, no need existed to declare that the liberty of the press ought not be restricted. To make such a declaration furnished "a plausible pretense for claiming that power" to violate the press. A provision "against restraining the liberty of the press afforded a clear implication that a power to prescribe proper regulations concerning it was intended to be vested in the national government." Ratificationists had also argued unconvincingly that a bill of rights would be "dangerous" because any right omitted from it might be presumed to be lost.

This argument proved far too much. First, it proved that the particular rights that the Constitution already protected—no religious test, no bills of attainder, trials by jury in criminal cases, *inter* alia—stood in grave jeopardy: specifying a right implied a power to violate it. Second, the inclusion of some rights in the original text of the constitution implied that all unenumerated ones were relinquished.

James Wilson, in the course of arguing that a bill of rights was not only unsuitable for the United States but dangerous as well, made another well-publicized statement of the ratificationist position: "A bill of rights annexed to a constitution is an enumeration of the powers reserved. If we attempt an enumeration, everything that is not enumerated is presumed to be given. The consequence is, that an imperfect enumeration would throw all implied powers into the scale of government; and the rights of the people would be rendered incomplete." Oliver Ellsworth advocated the same position.[9] Madison more carefully declared in his state's ratifying convention, "If an enumeration be made of all our rights, will it not be implied that everything omitted is given to the general government?" He too thought that "an imperfect enumeration," that is, an incomplete one, "is dangerous."[10]

Madison switched to the cause of adding amendments to the Constitution that would protect individual liberties and allay the fears of people who would likely support the Constitution, if given a sense of security about their rights. When he proposed his amendments to the House, he was mindful that proponents of ratification had warned that a bill of rights might be dangerous because the government could violate any right omitted. During the course of his great speech of June 8, 1789, Madison repeatedly reminded Congress of the need to satisfy the legitimate fears of "the great number of our constituents who are dissatisfied" with the Constitution because it seemed to put their rights in jeopardy. We must, he added, "expressly declare the great rights of mankind secured under this constitution."[11] The "great object in view," Madison declared, "is to limit and qualify the powers of Government, by excepting out of the grant of power those cases in which the Government ought not to act, or to act only in a particular mode. They [state recommendations] point these exceptions sometimes against the abuse of the executive power, sometimes against the legislative, and in some cases, against the community itself; or, in other words, against the majority in favor of the minority." Clearly, Madison was referring to constitutional prohibitions upon government to protect not only the rights of the people but even unpopular rights, such as those exercised by a minority that needed protection.[12]

Defending his recommendation that became the Ninth Amendment, Madison acknowledged that a major objection against a bill of rights consisted of the argument that "by enumerating particular exceptions to the grant of power, it would disparage those rights which were not placed in that enumeration; and it might follow, by implication, that those rights which were not singled out, were intended to be assigned into the hands of the General Government, and were consequently insecure." He called that "one of the most plausible arguments" he had even heard against the inclusion of a bill of rights. It was an argument that he himself had made, and it had become a Federalist cliché, although it self-destructed by virtue of the fact that the Constitution explicitly protected several rights, exposing all those omitted—including, by Madison's description, "the great rights of mankind"—to governmental violation.[13] He was, therefore, answering his own previous objection, not one that had been advanced by Anti-Federalists, when he devised the simple proposal that became the Ninth Amendment. It was, he said, meant to guard against the possibility that unenumerated rights might be imperiled by the enumeration of particular rights.[14] By excepting many rights from the grant of powers, no implication was intended, and no inference should be drawn, that rights not excepted from the grant of powers fell within those powers. As Madison phrased his proposal, it declared:

> The exceptions [to power] here or elsewhere in the constitution made in favor of particular rights, shall not be so construed as to diminish the just importance of other rights retained by the people, or as to enlarge the powers delegated by the constitution; but either as actual limitations on such powers, or as inserted merely for greater caution.[15]

Madison devised that proposal. No precedent for it existed. It was one of several proposals by Madison that stamped the Bill of Rights with his own creativity. Changing the flaccid verb "ought" to "shall" fell into the same category. So did his selection of particular rights for inclusion. No state, for example, had a due process of law clause in its own constitution, and only New York had recommended such a clause in place of the more familiar "law of the land" clause. Either phrasing carried the majesty and prestige of Magna Carta. Sir Edward Coke had taught, and Americans believed, that due process of law meant accordance with regularized common law procedures, especially grand jury accusation and trial by jury, both of which Madison provided for.[16] Madison also provided the basis for a radical alteration of the law of search and seizure by his choice of the broadest possible language available at the time.[17] Madison enumerated several rights whose constitutional protection was uncommon. Only New Hampshire by its state constitution provided against double jeopardy, and only Massachusetts and Vermont had constitutionally guaranteed just compensation when private property is taken for a public use. Madison's personal choice of the phrasing of several provisions of the Bill of Rights also became significant. Instead of saying that a person could not be compelled to give evidence against himself, Madison preferred to say that he could not be compelled to be a witness against himself, thereby laying the basis for a future distinction between testimonial and nontestimonial compulsion.[18] Notwithstanding the personal touch Madison imposed on his proposed amendments, he claimed that he had recommended only the familiar and avoided the controversial. He warned against enumerating anything except "simple, acknowledged principles," saying that amendments of a "doubtful nature" might damage the constitutional system.[19]

The House did not take the time or trouble to review his recommended amendments with the attention they deserved. In committee or as a result of debate, the House added only one important right to Madison's list, freedom of speech, which Pennsylvania had constitutionally protected. Some major principles, which appropriately prefaced a bill of rights, were deleted, despite their commonplaceness. Madison, for example, had urged a statement that power derives from and rests with the people, that government should be exercised for their benefit, and that they have a right to change that government when inadequate to its purposes. He had lifted his statement of those purposes from his own state's 1776 constitution and from its 1788 recommendations for inclusion in a national bill of rights. Those purposes expressed the idea that governments are instituted to secure the people, said Madison, "in the enjoyment of life and liberty, with the right of acquiring and using property, and generally of pursuing and obtaining happiness and safety."[20] The Declaration of Independence had made the points more concisely and felicitously, but not with such generosity: The Virginia version proposed by Madison (and adopted in numerous state constitutions) spoke not only about the pursuit of happiness but of obtaining it. Conceivably, the committee that eliminated Madison's prefatory principles believed them to be implicit in its streamlined version of what became the Ninth Amendment: "The enumeration in this Constitution of certain rights shall not be construed to deny or disparage others retained by the people." Both houses approved.[21]

The Ninth Amendment served as a definitive solution to the ratificationists' problem of how to enumerate the rights of the people without endangering those that might be omitted. The amendment served also as a device for Congress to avoid making a systematic enumeration when framing the Bill of Rights. Framing it was not high on Congress's agenda and, except for Madison's nagging insistence, might not have been attempted at all or, perhaps, would have been disposed of in an even more perfunctory fashion. The Ninth Amendment functioned as a sweep-it-under-the-rug means of disposing as swiftly as possible of a task embarrassing to both parties and delaying the organization of the government and providing for its revenues. And the Ninth Amendment could also serve to draw the sting from any criticism that the catalogue of personal freedoms was incomplete. Another conclusion one must draw from the text of the amendment is that the enumeration of rights in the preceding text was not meant to be exhaustive.

What rights did the Ninth Amendment protect? They had to be either "natural rights" or "positive rights," to use the terms Madison employed in the notes for the great speech of June 8 advocating amendments.[22] In that speech he distinguished "the pre-existent rights of nature" from those "resulting from a social compact."[23] In his notes, he mentioned freedom of "speach" as a natural right, yet he failed to provide for it in his recommended amendments. That is an example of Madison having acknowledged the existence of important rights that he had not enumerated or believed to be included within the unenumerated category. Freedom of speech was a right that preexisted government; it was inherent in human nature and did not depend for its existence on organized society. In 1775, Alexander Hamilton wrote that "the sacred rights of mankind are not to be rummaged for among old parchments or musty records. They are written, as with a sunbeam, in the whole volume of human nature, by the hand of the divinity itself, and can never be erased or obscured by mortal power."[24] Another tough-minded American materialist had led the way to such thinking. John Dickinson, speaking of "the rights essential to happiness," rhapsodized:

> We claim them from a higher source—from the King of kings, and Lord of all the earth. They are not annexed to use by parchments and seals. They are created in us by the decrees of Providence, which establish the laws of our nature. They are born with us; exist with us; and cannot be taken from us by any human power without taking our lives. In short, they are founded on the immutable maxims of reason and justice.[25]

Such opinions were commonplace.

So, too, the directly related views expressed by Jefferson in the preamble of the Declaration of Independence reflected commonly held principles. In 1822 John Adams, who had been a member of the committee of Congress that Jefferson had chaired in 1776, observed that there was "not an idea in it [the Declaration] but what had been hackneyed."[26] Jefferson asserted that "All American whigs thought alike" on those matters. The purpose of the Declaration, he wrote, was not "to find out new principles, or new arguments . . . but to place before mankind the common sense of the subject. . . ."[27] These views are central to the meaning of the Ninth Amendment. Contrary to cynical legal scholars of today, the ideas of the preamble to the Declaration did not go out of fashion in a decade and a half; and those ideas were as appropriate for writing a frame of government as for writing a "brief."[28]

The proof derives from both text and context. The text of the Ninth Amendment does protect the unenumerated rights of the people, and no reason exists to believe that it does not mean what it says. The context consists of Madison's remarks about natural rights during the legislative history of the amendment and also the references to natural rights in the opinion of the time, or what Madison called "contemporaneous interpretations." The last of the state constitutions that came out of the Revolution, that of New

Hampshire, began with a bill of rights of 1783 whose language
Madison might have used in his first proposed amendment, the
one that included the pursuit and obtaining of happiness.[29] Virginia's
1788 recommendations for amendments to the Constitution
began similarly, as had New York's and North Carolina's.[30] At the
Pennsylvania ratifying convention, James Wilson, who had been
second only to Madison as an architect of the Constitution, quoted
the preamble of the Declaration of Independence, and he added:
"This is the broad basis on which our independence was placed;
on the same certain and solid foundation this system [the Constitution]
is erected."[31]

The pursuit of happiness, a phrase used by Locke for a concept
that underlay his political ethics, subsumed the great rights of
liberty and property, which were inextricably related. Lockean
thought, to which the Framers subscribed, included within the
pursuit of happiness that which delighted and contented the mind,
and a belief that indispensable to it were good health, reputation,
and knowledge.[32] There was nothing radical in the idea of the right
to the pursuit of happiness. The anti-American Tory, Dr. Samuel
Johnson, had used the phrase, and Sir William Blackstone, also a
Tory, employed a close equivalent in his *Commentaries* in 1765,
when remarking "that man should pursue his own happiness. This
is the foundation of what we call ethics, or natural law."[33]

In the eighteenth century property did not mean merely the
ownership of material things. Locke himself had not used the word
to denote merely a right to things; he meant a right to rights. In
his *Second Treatise on Government,* he remarked that people "united
for the general preservation of their lives, liberties, and estates,
which I call by the general name—property." And, he added, "by
property I must be understood here as in other places to mean
that property which men have in their persons as well as goods."
At least four times in his *Second Treatise,* Locke used the word
"property" to mean all that belongs to a person, especially the rights
he wished to preserve.[34] Americans of the founding generation
understood property in this general Lockean sense, which we have
lost.

This view of property as a human right is the theme of a 1792
essay by Madison on *Property*. He described what he called the
"larger and juster meaning" of the term "property." It "embraces,"

he said, "every thing to which a man may attach a value and have a right." In the narrow sense it meant one's land, merchandise, or money; in the broader sense, it meant that

> a man has property in his opinions and the free communication of them. He has a property of peculiar value in his religious opinions, and in the profession and practices dictated by them. He has property very dear to him in the safety and liberty of his person. He has an equal property in the free use of his faculties and free choice of the objects on which to employ them. In a word, as a man is said to have a right to his property, he may be equally said to have a property in his rights.[35]

If the Fifth Amendment incorporated this broad meaning of "property" in the due process clause (no person shall be deprived of life, liberty, or property without due process of law), then "property" had a dual meaning in that clause but only the narrower, materialistic meaning in the eminent domain or takings clause (private property shall not be taken for a public use except at a just compensation). This inconsistency in the different uses of the same word in the same amendment seems baffling. But, no matter how defined, property rights nourished individual autonomy.

Not only were liberty, property, and the pursuit of happiness deeply linked in the thought of the Framers. They also believed in the principle that all people had a right to equal justice and to equality of rights. When Lincoln at Gettysburg described the creation of a new nation "conceived in liberty and dedicated to the proposition that all men are created equal," he reminded the nation that it could not achieve freedom without equal rights for all nor could it maintain equality without keeping society free. Liberty and equality constituted the master principles of the founding, which the Framers perpetuated as constitutional ideals, even if slyly. In a society that inherited a system of human slavery, the Framers compromised by accepting political reality; they could not abolish slavery and still form a stronger Union, but they did what was feasible. Nowhere in the Constitution is any person described in derogatory terms. Nowhere is slavery even acknowledged as a human condition. The Framers in effect spoke to the future by using circumlocutions that acknowledged only the status of "persons held to service"—a term that could be applied to white indentured servants. Race was not mentioned in the Constitution, not until the Fifteenth Amendment. The three-fifths rule, which applied to both direct taxation and to representation, was a device by which the Convention tied southern voting strength in Congress to southern liability for direct taxes on land and people. The Framers did not intentionally insult the humanity of blacks held to service. The same Constitution authorized Congress to extinguish the slave trade in twenty years, and thus prevented untold tens of thousands of people from being enslaved, but the authorization refers only to the "importation of such persons" as some states had thought proper to admit. The point is that the Constitution as amended by the Ninth Amendment provided a subsequent foun-dation for equal justice to all persons, regardless of race, sex, or religion. The Reconstruction amendments did not require the deletion or alteration of any part of the Constitution.

The Ninth Amendment is the repository for natural rights, including the right to pursue happiness and the right to equality of treatment before the law. Madison, presenting his proposed amendments, spoke of "the perfect equality of mankind."[36] Other natural rights come within the protection of the amendment as well, among them the right, then important, to hunt and fish, the right to travel, and very likely the right to intimate association or privacy in matters concerning family and sex, at least within the bounds of marriage. Such rights were fundamental to the pursuit of happiness.[37] But no evidence exists to prove that the Framers intended the Ninth Amendment to protect any particular natural rights. The text expressly protects unenumerated rights, but we can only guess what the Framers had in mind. On the basis of tantalizing hints and a general philosophy of natural rights, which then prevailed, conclusions emerge that bear slight relation to the racial, sexual, or political realities of that generation.

In addition to natural rights, the unenumerated rights of the people included positive rights, those deriving from the social com-pact that creates government. What positive rights were familiar, when the Ninth became part of the Constitution, yet were not enumerated in the original text or the first eight amendments? The right to vote and hold office, the right to free elections, the right not to be taxed except by consent through representatives of one's choice, the right to be free from monopolies, the right to be free from standing armies in time of peace, the right to refuse military service on grounds of religious conscience, the right to bail, the right of an accused person to be presumed innocent, and the person's right to have the prosecution shoulder the responsibility of proving guilt beyond a reasonable doubt—all these were among existing positive rights protected by various state laws, state constitutions, and the common law. Any of these, among others, could legitimately be regarded as rights of the people before which the power of government must be exercised in subordination.

In addition to rights then known, the Ninth Amendment might have had the purpose of providing the basis for rights then unknown, which time alone might disclose. Nothing in the thought of the Framers foreclosed the possibility that new rights might claim the loyalties of succeeding generations. As the chief justice of Virginia's highest court mused when the Bill of Rights was being framed, "May we not in the progress of things, discover some great and important [right], which we don't now think of?"[38]

To argue that the Framers had used natural rights as a means of escaping obligations of obedience to the king but did not use natural rights "as a source for rules of decision" is hogwash.[39] One has only to read the state recommendations for a bill of rights to know that the natural rights philosophy seized the minds of the Framers as it had the minds of the rebellious patriots of 1776. One can also read natural rights opinions by members of the early Supreme Court to arrive at the same conclusion.[40] Without doubt, natural rights, if read into the Ninth Amendment, "do not lend themselves to principled *judicial* enforcement,"[41] but neither do positive rights. That is, the enumerated rights such as freedom of speech and the right to due process of law have resulted in some of the most subjective result-oriented jurisprudence in our history. That judicial decisions can be unprincipled does not detract from the principle expressed in a right, whether or not enumerated. If the Ninth Amendment instructs us to look beyond its four corners for unenumerated rights of the people, as it does, it must have some content, contrary to its detractors. Some cannot stomach the thought of such indefiniteness, and they disapprove of a license for judicial subjectivity; so they draw conclusions that violate the commonsensical premises with which they begin. John Hart Ely, for example, initially suggests that the amendment should be read for what it says and that it is the provision of the Constitution that applies the principle of equal protection against the federal government. "In fact," he wrote, "the conclusion that the Ninth Amendment was intended to signal the existence of federal constitutional rights beyond those specifically enumerated in the Constitution is the only conclusion its language seems comfortably able to support." Yet Ely ridicules natural rights theory and believes that it swiftly became passé. He ends by leaving the amendment an empty provision, significant only as a lure to judicial activism.[42]

Raoul Berger is an even more hostile critic of the amendment, but he is so eager to keep it the feckless provision that was a mystery to Justice Jackson that he confuses the Ninth and and Tenth Amendments. For example, he speaks of "the ninth's retention of rights by the states or the people," when in fact it is the Tenth Amendment, not its predecessor, that speaks of states' rights, that is, of powers retained by the states or the people. "The ninth amendment," added Berger, ". . . was merely declaratory of a basic presupposition: all powers not 'positively' granted are reserved to the people. It added no unspecified rights to the Bill of Rights. . . ."[43] But an explicit declaration of the existence of unenumerated rights *is* an addition of unspecified rights to the Bill of Rights, whose Tenth Amendment, not Ninth, reserved powers not granted.[44]

Confusion between the Ninth and Tenth Amendments seems to originate with two amendments proposed by Virginia in 1788. One in modified terms was modeled after Article II of the Articles of Confederation, retaining to each state every power not delegated to the United States. The second amendment concerned clauses in the Constitution declaring that Congress shall not exercise certain powers (e.g., no bills of attainder). The second proposed that such clauses should not be construed to extend the powers of Congress; rather, they should be construed "as making exceptions to the specified powers where this shall be the case, or otherwise, as inserted merely for greater caution."[45] Neither proposal addressed the issue of reserving to the people unenumerated rights. Yet the Virginia Assembly, in 1789, when debating whether to ratify the amendments proposed by Congress, initially rejected what became the Ninth and Tenth Amendments. The Assembly preferred instead its two proposals of 1788. The reasoning behind the Assembly's action was confused and gave rise to the confusion between the Ninth and Tenth Amendments.

According to Hardin Burnley, a member of the Assembly who kept Madison informed about the progress of his amendments in the state legislature, Edmund Randolph, who led the opposition to the Ninth Amendment (then the eleventh), objected to the word "retained" because it was too indefinite. Randolph had argued that the rights declared in the preceding amendments (our First through Eighth) "were not all that a free people would require the exercise of; and that there was no criterion by which it could be determined whether any other particular right was retained or not." Thus Randolph argued that the Ninth was not sufficiently comprehensive and explicit. From that point he concluded, illogically, that the course of safety lay not in retaining unenumerated rights but in providing against an extension of the powers of Congress. Randolph believed that the Ninth Amendment did not reduce rights to a "definitive certainty."[46]

Madison soon after sent to Washington Burnley's information (and language) as if his own. The letter, as construed by those who find the Ninth Amendment an empty vehicle, became a means of putting Madison's authority behind the proposition that the Ninth Amendment means no more than the Tenth. Plagiarizing Burnley, Madison informed Washington that he found Randolph's distinction to be without force, because "by protecting the rights of the people & of the States, an improper extension of power will be prevented & safety made equally certain."[47] Madison did not challenge Randolph's assertion that the amendments preceding the Ninth and Tenth did not exhaust the rights of the people that needed protection against government. Nor did he challenge the assertion that the Ninth was too vague. Rather, Madison disagreed that adoption of the Virginia proposals of 1788 more effectively secured the rights deserving of protection.

In the only part of his letter that did not repeat Burnley's, Madison expressed regret that the confusion had come from Randolph, "a friend to the Constitution," and he added: "It is a still greater cause of regret, if the distinction [made by Randolph] be, as it appears to me, altogether fanciful. If a line can be drawn between the powers granted and the rights retained, it would seem to be the same thing, whether the latter be secured, by declaring that they shall not be abridged, or that the former shall not be extended. If no line can be drawn, a declaration in either form would amount to nothing."[48] The reference to "whether the latter be secured" meant the retention of a specific right. In effect, Madison argued that the line between a power granted and a right retained amounted to the same thing if a right were named. Thus, to say that the government may not abridge the freedom of the press is the equivalent of saying that the government shall not abridge the freedom of the press. If, as Madison said, a line cannot be drawn between rights retained and powers denied, retaining unenumerated rights would be useless against a power of government to violate them. Whether the formulation of the First Amendment is used—"Congress shall make no law"—or whether that of the Fourth Amendment is used—"The right of the people to be secure . . . against unreasonable searches and seizures, shall not be violated"—the effect is the same. In the case of unenumerated rights, however, one can only argue that no affirmative power has been granted to regulate.

Randolph had identified a problem that remains without a solution. Madison's response was by no means a satisfactory one in all respects. Although both houses of Virginia's legislature finally ratified the Bill of Rights, the Ninth Amendment continues to bedevil its interpreters. Courts keep discovering rights that have no literal textual existence, that is, rights not enumerated, only to meet howls of denunciation from those who deplore the result— whether the right of a woman to an abortion, a right of privacy against electronic eavesdropping, or a right to engage in nude dancing.[49] Opponents have another string to their bow, which they find in a declaration by Madison in the First Congress, when he proposed his amendments. Adding a bill of rights to the Constitution, he argued, would enable courts to become "the guardians of those rights; they will be an impenetrable bulwark against every assumption of power in the legislative or executive; they will be naturally led to resist every encroachment upon rights *expressly* stipulated for in the constitution by the declaration of rights."[50] "Expressly stipulated" can be read to mean that Madison either opposed or failed to predict judicial review in cases involving unenumerated rights. And, without doubt he was not referring to the desirability of giving courts what Raoul Berger calls "a roving commission to enforce a catalog of unenumerated rights against the will of the states."[51]

Madison might well, however, have approved of courts' enforcing against the states the amendment that he thought "the most valuable amendment in the whole list"—one that prohibited the states from infringing upon the equal rights of conscience, the freedom of speech or press, and the right to trial by jury in criminal cases.[52] The House passed but the Senate defeated that proposal, making enforcement by the federal courts against the states impossible. The incorporation doctrine, drawn from the Fourteenth Amendment, superseded whatever limitations the Framers of the Bill of Rights had in mind concerning judicial review over state acts.

So long as we continue to believe that government is instituted for the sake of securing the rights of the people, and must exercise powers in subordination to those rights, the Ninth Amendment should have the vitality intended for it. The problem is not whether the rights it guarantees are as worthy of enforcement as the enumerated rights; the problem, rather, is whether our courts should read out of the amendment rights worthy of our respect, which the Framers might conceivably have meant to safeguard, at least in principle.

CHAPTER FOURTEEN

History and Original Intent

We the People of the E

A constitutional jurisprudence of original intent would be a sham and an illusion if it lacked historical foundation. The very concept of original intent depends upon history, in two senses. Without records of the past that permit a reconstruction of it, we would have no way of ascertaining original intent. We cannot answer any question concerning the intent of the Framers without first determining whether evidence exists that will provide an answer. Ascertaining the existence and authenticity of the primary sources, which establish the record for interpretation, is a job for the historian. Ascertaining the accuracy, completeness, and meaning of the historical evidence is also a task at which the historian is most proficient. Justice Horace Gray maintained that the question in a particular case, "like all questions of constitutional construction, is largely a historical question. . . ."[1] Unlike most Justices, Gray was an able, amateur historian. Few lawyers or judges are good historians. But only lawyers have ever been appointed to the Supreme Court.

If history is so crucial to constitutional interpretation, at least with respect to questions that have a historical dimension, Congress should create the Office of Historian to the Supreme Court. The official historian and his staff would tell the Court not how to decide cases but how to answer questions of history asked by the Justices: Did the Framers intend to vest any inherent powers in the President in matters of foreign policy or concerning the involvement of the armed forces in military or naval conflicts? Did the Constitutional Convention intend the contract clause to extend to contracts to which a state is a party? Did the states that ratified the Constitution understand the two ex post facto clauses to apply only to criminal cases? Did the First Amendment have as an objective the elimination of prosecutions for seditious libel? Did those who framed and ratified the self-incrimination clause of the Fifth Amendment understand that it could be superseded by a statute providing immunity against prosecution based on compelled testimony or its fruits? Did the Congress that proposed the Fourteenth Amendment mean to eliminate racial discrimination in public schools or places of public accommodation? Did the states that ratified the amendment understand that it extended the prohibitions of the first ten amendments to the states? Did the Congress that enacted the Sherman Anti-Trust Act mean to make criminal only unreasonable conspiracies in restraint of trade, and did it mean to include trade unions within the compass of the act? These are all historical questions that a constitutional historian can probably answer more accurately than the members of the Supreme Court, even though historians are also subjective in their judgments.

Whether Supreme Court cases ought to be decided on the basis of historical evidence or original intent, even if that intent is discernible, is a different question. The extent to which the past should govern the present constitutes a separate issue from the question whether the opinions of the past can be determined. Whether the records are ample enough to warrant a judgment about original intent forms still another question.

The extant records are simply not sufficiently ample, a fact rendering a jurisprudence of original intent quite impossible. Assume, for the time being, that original intent is the meaning ascribed to the Constitution by its Framers and ratifiers, as if they were all of one mind. Do we possess the records that tell us what they meant? We have the official *Journal* of the Convention, first published in 1819,[2] which Max Farrand, who edited the definitive edition of *The Records of the Federal Convention*[3] judged to have been "carelessly" kept by William Jackson, the secretary of the

Constitutional Convention. According to Farrand, the *Journal* "cannot be relied upon absolutely."[4] Absolute reliability, however, is a standard far in excess of the need for an accurate record of motions and votes. That is all the *Journal* provides. It is more than adequate for motions and votes but utterly inadequate for the purpose of determining original intent.

Apart from the text of the Constitution, the determination of that intent depends entirely upon Madison's Notes, first published in 1840. Despite some jaundiced accounts challenging the integrity of Madison's record,[5] it is an accurate account composed from notes made daily by Madison throughout the life of the Convention, with some corrections introduced in 1789, when Madison had access to Jackson's manuscript Journal; in 1819, Madison revised the Notes slightly to improve the accuracy of motions and resolves after publication of the *Journal* and of the short record kept by Robert Yates of New York.[6] The peculiar value of Madison's Notes consists in the fact that it is the only reliable and systematic record of the debates. In effect, it is the sole basis for determining original intent at the Convention.

Some extremely sketchy records made by other participants exist, mainly by Robert Yates, John Lansing, and Rufus King, plus some tidbits by others, such as character sketches by William Pierce and notes by William Paterson and Alexander Hamilton of their own speeches. Of these the most important is the record kept by Yates, an Anti-Federalist who left the Convention in a huff on July 10, five days after he had ceased his record-keeping. Yates's six-week record is therefore very incomplete; it does not report the last ten weeks of the Convention. It is also an unreliable account. When Yates's notes were published in 1821,[7] Madison spoke of Yates's "extreme incorrectness" and "strong prejudices."[8] James H. Hutson, chief of the Manuscripts Division of the Library of Congress, has observed that the sheets of Yates's manuscript that have survived show that Edmond C. Genet, the anonymous editor of the 1821 publication of Yates's notes, butchered the document. He "omitted half of the material on the sheets and altered every sentence that he published." As a result, Hutson added, our record of what Yates wrote is untrustworthy "and cannot be consulted as a source of the intentions of the Framers."[9]

Thus, in the near-absence of anything else, Madison's Notes

stand as the source for a jurisprudence of original intent based on what the Framers said in Philadelphia—aside from the Constitution, of course. Even if we assume the accuracy of Madison's Notes, they do not support a confident determination of original intent simply because they omit too much. Madison was not adept at stenography; he invented his own system of note-taking. An authority on the history of shorthand has declared, "Eighteenth-century shorthand was inadequate to the task of recording verbatim."[10] We know that Madison spent his evenings writing up his notes of the day. He doubtless exaggerated his role at the Convention by reporting his own speeches at a greater length than the speeches of others. He could not take notes as he spoke, and he never spoke from prepared speeches. He probably embellished what he said. But he sought to record faithfully what others said. The trouble is that the task exceeded his talents; he was not up to the labors that he said "almost killed" him.[11] In an undated document that Madison said he wrote "nearly half a century" after the Convention, he declared that he had not been absent a single day "nor more than a casual fraction of an hour in any day, so that I could not have lost a single speech, unless a very short one."[12] In fact, however, he recorded considerably less than half of what was said.

James H. Hutson has described an experiment conducted in the Library of Congress, in which a verbatim transcript of a scholarly symposium showed that the remarks of the thirty speakers amounted to about 8,400 words an hour. In June of 1787, when Madison was at his freshest and recorded more than he did in succeeding months, his Notes yielded, according to Hutson, an average of 548 words hourly, less than seven percent of the 8,400. Hutson rounds out the figures by allowing Madison 600 words per hour, which is more than he actually recorded, and by assuming that 6,000 words an hour would be a fairer standard. Hutson's conclusion: "Even if the possible words per hour are reduced to 6,000, Madison recorded only ten percent of each hour's proceedings."[13]

Hutson's estimates are unfair, because people engaged in a political discussion, which is for the most part conducted extemporaneously, cannot speak as swiftly and as steadily as individuals giving prepared statements. Anyone speaking at a rate of 8,000 or even 6,000 words an hour is firing a verbal machine gun; also, he is probably reading with his head down, rather than thinking aloud and speaking to his audience. Members of the Constitutional Convention probably hemmed and hawed, paused a lot, repeated themselves, and proceeded at a slow tempo; they stopped talking altogether when state delegations caucused and when votes were counted.

Still, Madison probably missed much more than half of what was said. He averaged 2,740 words on a June *day*. If the Convention produced 2,740 words an *hour*, instead of the 6,000 words assumed by Hutson, we more nearly approximate the rate of speech at the Convention. From the testimony of George Washington, we know that the daily session of the Convention lasted "not less than five, for a large part of the time Six, and sometimes 7 hours sitting every day. . . ."[14] If we use only five hours as the basis of calculation, the figure most favorable to Madison, and disregard the extra space he gave to his own speeches, we conclude that at best he reported only one-fifth of what was said. If that is a fact, a jurisprudence of original intent must rest on an extremely shaky and incomplete foundation. The members of the Convention would have had to speak in slow motion for Madison to have recorded as much as fifty percent of what was said. We are left with a record that is only half complete if Madison caught 600 words an hour of a discussion that proceeded at the yawning pace of 1,200 words an hour. Nevertheless the very real possibility exists that Madison consistently and accurately caught the gist of the debates: But an original jurisprudence based on the gist of what was said is an uncertain basis for resolving questions of constitutional law in real cases, especially in the presence of dissenting opinions.

The reliability of the records degenerates with a shift of focus from Philadelphia to the state ratifying conventions. The National Historical Publications Commission, in a report of 1954, declared that the reporters of the ratification period took notes on the debates "and rephrased those notes for publication. The short hand in use at that time was too slow to permit verbatim transcription of all speeches, with the result that a reporter, in preparing his copy for the press, frequently relied upon his memory as well as his notes and gave what seemed to him the substance, but not necessarily the actual phraseology, of speeches. Different reportings of the same speech exhibited at times only a general similarity, and details often recorded by one reporter were frequently omitted by another."[15] A reporter used his hastily taken notes to spur his memory, "and his report was as good as his understanding plus his memory."[16]

When Jonathan Elliot started the publication of his *Debates* in 1827, he collected the previously published records of the state ratifying conventions. He misleadingly called his collection *The Debates in the Several State Conventions, on the Adoption of the Federal Constitution*. In fact Elliot's *Debates* unreliably report the proceedings of only five states, plus some fragments from others. Elliot acknowledged that the debates that he reported "may, in some instances, have been inaccurately taken down, and, in others, probably, too faintly sketched. . . ."[17] Of the five states, Elliot's *Debates* reported Pennsylvania most inadequately, because the reporter, Thomas Lloyd, who had been in the pay of the Federalists, published only speeches by their two leaders, James Wilson and Thomas McKean, ignoring all opponents of ratification. One hundred years after the Pennsylvania ratification convention had met, a scholarly edition of the Pennsylvania debates appeared, which included substantial records that had been made by other reporters as well as a variety of out-of-convention statements.[18] A still fuller edition of the debates in Pennsylvania, in and out of state convention, appeared in 1976.[19] All of Pennsylvania's Anti-Federalist pamphlets and editorials have now been republished.[20] No other states' debates have yet been so fully reported, or, rather, reconstructed from newspapers and tracts. Elbridge Gerry, a member of the Philadelphia Convention who refused to sign the Constitution and became a leader of the Anti-Federalists, complained on the floor of Congress in 1791 that the "debates of the State Conventions, as published by the short-hand writers were generally partial and mutilated. . . ."[21] Gerry's remark no longer has any validity with respect to Pennsylvania.

The editor of the debates for Gerry's own state, Massachusetts, apologized for the existence of "some inaccuracies, and many omissions," the result, he said, of "inexperience." He also doctored some speeches, altering the meaning of the speakers, and provided some spurious speeches as well.[22] Without doubt, the University of Wisconsin scholars who are presently editing *The Documentary History of the Ratification of the Constitution* will add very measurably to the records for Massachusetts, where ratification was long and closely contested. On the other hand, they are not likely to be able to remedy the deficiencies of the records for New York. Elliot published the report of the debates by Francis Childs, a novice reporter who apologized for his "imperfect" presentation of the debates. "Not long accustomed to the business," he wrote of himself, "he cannot pretend to as much accuracy as might be expected from a more experienced hand;—and it will easily be comprehended how difficult it must be to follow a copious and rapid Speaker, in the train of his reasoning, much more in the turn of his expression."[23] Childs kept a record of the debates for only the first half of the state convention's proceedings and thereafter merely confined himself to a skeletal journal of motions. From the description of the extant sources of the debates in New York by a senior editor of *The Documentary History of the Ratification of the Constitution*, the records for the second half of the convention will remain skimpily reported, despite the fierceness of the controversy in that state.[24]

Although the debates in Virginia's ratification convention were reported in greater detail than the debates of any other state convention, by a reporter sympathetic to the Federalists, James Madison and John Marshall expressed dissatisfaction with the results. Madison informed Jonathan Elliot that he found passages that were "defective," "obscure," "unintelligible," and "more or less erroneous."[25] Marshall complained that if he had not seen his name prefixed to his speeches, he would not have recognized them as his own. Impartially, he also said that the speeches of Patrick Henry had been reported worst of all.[26] North Carolina's debates were also poorly reported by an amateur in the employ of Federalist leaders, and though the record seems ample, it covers only North Carolina's first convention, which failed to ratify the Constitution. The second convention has not been reported. Those are the five states (Pennsylvania, Massachusetts, New York, Virginia, and North Carolina) whose records provide a basis, however, incomplete and inaccurate, for determining ratifier intent.

Although *The Documentary History of the Ratification of the Constitution* has published every scrap of material surrounding the ratification controversy in Delaware, New Jersey, Georgia, and

Connecticut, the results are meager. No report of debates exists for the state ratifying conventions in any of these four states, and their journals either do not exist or too inadequately describe motions and votes. The newspapers of Connecticut opened their columns only to Federalist opinions. The newspapers of the other three states published scarcely any local productions but reprinted essays from out-of-state presses.[27] The records of New Hampshire, Maryland, and South Carolina are so fragmentary as to be useless. Rhode Island, the thirteenth state to ratify, took action so late that its records scarcely matter. The Constitution had already been ratified, the new government had been formed, and the First Congress had, eight months earlier, recommended the Bill of Rights to the state legislatures for adoption.

James Hutson's remark has force. Speaking of the records of the state ratification convention debates, he said, "Documents as corrupt as these cannot be relied upon to reveal the intentions of the Framers." He should have added that records for four or five states, even if not deficient with respect to accuracy and completeness, can hardly support serious original intent analysis or ratifier intent analysis. Although we cannot and do not know what the ratifiers understood the various provisions of the Constitution to mean, the ratifiers, we should remember, adopted the Constitution, not the original intent at Philadelphia, which the ratifiers did not likely know or agree about. Ratification legitimated the text that the Convention recommended. The Convention did not recommend its intention, only its text. The authority of the state conventions to ratify and legitimate should not be confused with ratifier intent. Madison conflated authority and intent. The one does not show the other.

The history of the framing and ratification of the Bill of Rights, which must be considered as if part of the original Constitution, adds no dimension of solidity to a jurisprudence of original intent. The principal sources for an inquiry into the meaning of the various provisions of the first ten amendments should be the records of the First Congress, which framed and submitted them for ratification to the states, and the records of the state legislatures that engaged in the process of ratification. But the records of the state legislatures do not exist, leaving an enormous gap in our knowledge of the ways the Framers' generation understood the Bill of Rights. Moreover, the sources for a study of the congressional history of its framing are incomplete and yield few definite answers.

No official records were kept of the debates in either the Senate or the House. Because the Senate met in secret session during the First Congress, no reporters were present to make unofficial notes of the proceedings. A useful account of the Senate's deliberations at this time is *The Journal of William Maclay*.[28] Unfortunately, Senator Maclay was absent during most of the time the Senate debated the Bill of Rights, and he mentioned the subject only in passing. No account of the Senate debate exists, and the only Senate document that we have is the meager record of action taken on motions and bills.[29]

The situation for the House is considerably better, but unsatisfactory. In addition to a House Journal comparable to that of the Senate,[30] we have a version of the House debates because the House, unlike the Senate, permitted entry to reporters, who took notes of the proceedings in what then passed for shorthand. "According to contemporary critics, the reports were defective, full of error, seldom seen or revised by the speakers, and biased."[31] Volume One of *The Debates and Proceedings in the Congress of the United States*, commonly known as the *Annals of Congress*, was published in 1834. The information that it contains about Senate proceedings was merely abstracted from the Senate's scanty Journal. The House debates for the First Congress as recorded in the *Annals of Congress* derive wholly from a weekly periodical known as Lloyd's *Congressional Register*—the same Lloyd whom the Federalists bought in Pennsylvania and Maryland to report only their side, and only part of that.

Despite the official sounding name, Lloyd's *Congressional Register* was a private venture, not an official publication. According to the National Historical Publications Commission, the reports of the proceedings of the First Congress were "so condensed" by Lloyd "that much information about the debates was omitted entirely or was presented only in garbled form."[32] Another authority, who has compared Lloyd's notes with the record in the *Annals of Congress*, stated that what he published "bears only slight resemblance to the literal transcript of his own notes. Sometimes a speech is printed for which no notes or only very brief notes exist; sometimes a long speech reported in the manuscript is printed very briefly or not at all."[33] Lloyd used few connectives or articles, and he embellished considerably. He took down "skeleton" versions of speeches, which he could make intelligible only by imaginative and understanding editing. But at the time of the First Congress, he seems to have resorted more to imagination than to understanding, because his deficient technique of note-taking was aggravated by drunkenness. Madison, a severe critic of Lloyd, remembered years later that he had not only been "indolent" and filled up the blanks of his notes "from memory or *imagination*" but also that he had become "a votary of the bottle and perhaps made too free use of it sometimes at the period of his printed debates [on the Bill of Rights]."[34] Madison condemned his "mutilation & perversion," and his "illiteracy," and wrote that his reports "abound in errors; some of them very gross."[35]

Thus, our record of the legislative history of the framing of the Bill of Rights in the House fails to include all that was said, includes remarks not made, and does not report accurately what it does include. And, we have no records, official or otherwise, except the final report, of the deliberations of the special House committee on amendments, which drafted the amendments that became the Bill of Rights, from proposals advanced by Madison. Nor is there any record of the joint Senate–House conference committee, which worked out a compromise draft of the differing House and Senate proposals that became the Bill of Rights.

Other sources do not offer much enlightenment, either. Knowledge of the fact that Congress was drafting the Bill of Rights during the summer of 1789 prompted no analytical discussions by the press, nothing remotely comparable to the outpourings of opinion during the controversy over the ratification of the unamended Constitution. Moreover, as a historian who scoured the sources has pointed out, "The finished amendments were not the subject of any special newspaper comment, and there is little comment in the available correspondence."[36] As for the records of the state legislatures that ratified the Bill of Rights, the situation is hopeless. Because no records were kept of the debates, we do not know what the legislators of the various states understood to be the meanings of the various parts of the Bill of Rights. Nor has any scholar who has read the contemporary newspapers uncovered anything revealing as to these meanings. Public interest in the proposed amendments was desultory, and public discussion of them was largely confined to generalities.

A constitutional jurisprudence of original intent is insupportable for reasons other than the fact that the records of the framing and ratification of both the Constitution and the Bill of Rights are inadequate because they are incomplete and inaccurate. Original intent also fails as a concept that can decide real cases. Original intent is an unreliable concept because it assumes the existence of one intent on a particular issue such as the meaning of executive powers or of the necessary and proper clause, the scope of the commerce clause, or the definition of the obligation of contracts. The entity we call "the Framers" did not have a collective mind, think in one groove, or possess the same convictions.

In fact, they disagreed on many crucial matters, such as the question whether they meant Congress to have the power to charter a bank. In 1789 Hamilton and Washington thought Congress had that power, but Madison and Randolph believed that it did not. Although the Journal of the Convention, except as read by Hamilton, supports Madison's view, all senators who had been at the Convention upheld the power,[37] and Madison later changed his mind about the constitutionality of a bank. Clearly the Convention's "intent" on this matter lacks clarity; revelation is hard to come by when the Framers squabbled about what they meant. They often did, as political controversies during the first score of years under the Constitution revealed.

Sometimes Framers who voted the same way held contradictory opinions on the meaning of a particular clause. Each believed that his understanding constituted the truth of the matter. James Wilson, for example, believed that the ex post facto clause extended to civil matters, while John Dickinson held the view that it applied only to criminal cases, and both voted for the clause. George Mason opposed the same clause because he wanted the states to be free to enact ex post facto laws in civil cases, and he believed that the clause was not clearly confined to criminal cases; but Elbridge Gerry, who wanted to impose on the states a prohibition against retroactive civil legislation, opposed the clause because he thought it seemed limited to criminal cases. William Paterson changed his mind about the scope of the ex post facto clause.[38] Seeking original intent in the opinions of the Framers is seeking a unanimity that did not exist on complex and divisive issues contested by strong-minded men. Madison was right when he spoke of the difficulty of verifying the intention of the Convention.

A serious problem even exists as to the identity of the Framers and as to the question whether the opinions of all are of equal importance in the determination of original intent. Who, indeed, were the Framers? Were they the fifty-five who were delegates at Philadelphia or only the thirty-nine who signed? If fathoming original intent is the objective, should we not also be concerned about the opinions of those who ratified the Constitution, giving it legitimacy? About 1,600 men attended the various state ratifying conventions, for which the surviving records are so inadequate. No way exists to determine their intent as a guide for judicial decisions; we surely cannot fathom the intent of the members of eight states for which no state convention records exist. The deficiencies of the records of the other five permit few confident conclusions and no basis for believing that a group mind can be located. Understanding ratifier intent is impossible except on the broadest kind of question: Did the people of the states favor scrapping the Articles of Confederation and favor, instead, the stronger Union proposed by the Constitution? Even as to that question, the evidence, which does not exist for a majority of the states, is unsatisfactorily incomplete, and it allows only rough estimates of the answers to questions concerning popular understanding of the meaning of specific clauses of the Constitution.

Even if the state ratification records were complete and accurate, original intent might still be elusive for the reasons given by Thomas M. Cooley, the illustrious nineteenth-century commentator on the Constitution. His statement, which applies with equal force to the Philadelphia Convention, referred to a situation common in any constitutional convention. Cooley said:

> Every member of such a convention acts upon such motives and reasons as influence him personally, and the motions and debates do not necessarily indicate the purpose of a majority of a convention in adopting a particular clause. It is quite possible for a clause to appear so clear and unambiguous to the members of a convention as to require neither discussion nor illustration; and the few remarks made concerning it in the convention might have a plain tendency to lead

directly away from the meaning in the minds of the majority. It is equally possible for a part of the members to accept a clause in one sense and a part in another. And even if we were certain we had attained to the meaning of the convention, it is by no means to be allowed a controlling force, especially if that meaning appears not to be the one which the words would most naturally and obviously convey.[39]

Justice Joseph Story, the foremost constitutional commentator, had expressed similar observations in an earlier generation.[40]

That will o' the wisp of constitutional history, original intent, cannot be captured even if we focus on only the fifty-five men who attended the Constitutional Convention in Philadelphia. We know remarkably little about the constitutional views of many of them. Indeed, we know with some confidence the constitutional views of only a distinct minority of the Framers. The fifty-five included sixteen who did not sign the Constitution, several of whom actively opposed its ratification. Some of the opponents stayed throughout the Convention's proceedings, or were present most of the time, and significantly influenced the actual framing by their participation. Edmund Randolph, George Mason, and Elbridge Gerry refused to sign the Constitution, yet had a greater impact on its making than about half of the thirty-nine signers. Luther Martin quit the Convention in disgust two weeks before its conclusion and bitterly opposed its ratification, yet had actively participated in its making. The Constitution can hardly express their intent, however, because they opposed it. Some delegates who opposed ratification had almost no role in the framing of the Constitution. Robert Yates and John Lansing of New York outvoted Hamilton while they were present in June and kept useful notes of the early proceedings.[41] They huffed and they puffed, and they departed Philadelphia without doing much damage, although during the ratification controversy they produced Anti-Federalist tracts that misrepresented the Constitution. To include John F. Mercer of Maryland as a Framer is also unjustifiable. He attended the Convention for eleven days, having turned up midway in the proceedings to denounce the decisions that had been made, and he shortly departed.

Some other nonsigners, who supported ratification, had little if anything to do with the framing of the Constitution, and the inclusion of their names on the list of fifty-five misleads. George

Wythe of Virginia, a great law teacher (Jefferson and Marshall were pupils) left after the first week because of family illness. William Pierce of Georgia wrote insightful sketches of the delegates but became an early dropout, as did William C. Houston of New Jersey. The obscurity of some of the fifty-five is remarkable. Few scholars of our constitutional history can differentiate William Houston of New Jersey from William Houstoun of Georgia, let alone describe their constitutional opinions in relation to original intent. James McClurg of Virginia was another Framer of no importance.

Constitutional scholars might be hard pressed to derive original intent from the constitutional views espoused at the Convention by a batch of Framers who signed the Constitution but did little more than warm their seats. They include Richard Bassett and Jacob Broom of Delaware; William Blount and Alexander Martin of North Carolina; George Clymer, Thomas FitzSimons, Jared Ingersoll, and Robert Morris of Pennsylvania; Abraham Baldwin and William Few of Georgia; Daniel of St. Thomas Jenifer and James McHenry of Maryland; and Jonathan Dayton of New Jersey. Some of these men, all signers, were political titans in their states but had slight or no influence at Philadelphia. John Blair of Virginia, who became a member of the first Supreme Court, exercised influence because he frequently cast the decisive vote of the Virginia delegation. Without his vote Mason and Randolph would have canceled out Madison and Washington; but Blair never spoke to an issue or served on a committee. Robert Morris of Pennsylvania, the former superintendent of finance during the American Revolution, was one of the most famous men at the Convention but he was a do-nothing, say-nothing. Caleb Strong of Massachusetts was another nonsigner whose opinions at Philadelphia are not readily perceived. As a matter of fact, of the thirty-nine signers, only about half actively participated in the proceedings by serving on a committee and speaking with some regularity. But some nonsigners, including Oliver Ellsworth of Connecticut, were significant forces at Philadelphia. William R. Davie of North Carolina, a nonsigner, was far more constructive than Alexander Hamilton, who had been a major influence before the Convention and would become an influence nearly beyond compare after it. As a Framer at Philadelphia, however, Hamilton was less important than David Brearly of New Jersey, Hugh Williamson and Richard Dobbs Spaight of

North Carolina, or William Samuel Johnson of Connecticut. Moreover, Hamilton's Convention intent on most issues was shared by
no one.

When seeking original intent, we must recognize that not all
opinions were equal. Without Washington, the Convention would
not have succeeded and perhaps the Constitution would not have
been ratified. The fact that he presided made an enormous difference. He usually cast his vote with Madison, but he spoke on an
issue only once. Old Benjamin Franklin, the other internationally
famous American who was present at the Convention, attended
daily, spoke often, and cast votes that had clout. James Wilson and
Gouverneur Morris, Franklin's Pennsylvania colleagues, were movers
and shakers second in importance only to Madison in framing the
Constitution. Nathaniel Gorham of Massachusetts presided over
the Committee of the Whole, served on the Committee of Detail,
and entered the debate effectively. John Rutledge of South Carolina, Rufus King of Massachusetts, and Ellsworth were also among
the most important Framers. William Paterson ranked with the
most influential while he was present, but he missed the last seven
weeks; George Read of Delaware signed the Constitution for Paterson. Read was one of several Framers who had a minor if constructive influence at Philadelphia, like John Dickinson of Delaware, Pierce Butler of South Carolina, and William Livingston of
New Jersey. What Wilson or Rutledge meant mattered greatly;
what Thomas FitzSimons or Richard Bassett meant hardly mattered
at all or cannot be determined. Madison correctly observed that
many members of the Convention did not reveal their minds or
open their mouths on issue after issue. In sum, the intent of some
of the fifty-five or thirty-nine should weigh considerably more than
the intent of most, and the intent of most remains shrouded.

None of this means that original intent did not exist at all or
that it is at all unascertainable. It means, rather, that original intent
is not a viable foundation for a jurisprudence of constitutional law.
It means, in short, that in real cases, which pose particular controversies, original intent cannot provide a decision. It means that
the Framers and ratifiers cannot speak from their graves to run our
lives by settling the constitutional issues of our time. We live in a
world of supersonic aircraft, recombinant DNA, robots, com-
puters, microwaves, a global village ecology, interplanetary explo-

ration, and an interdependent world economy. Our particular problems of constitutional law cannot be settled by the wisdom and insight of those who framed and ratified the Constitution, even though we observe their intent on many crucial and fundamental matters.

We still live by the Constitution, a federal system, representative government, separation of powers, checks and balances, elections at fixed intervals, tripartite government, and a political ideology based on liberty and equality. We can also discern with ease many matters of overweening importance on which the Framers agreed. Consensus existed to such an extent on fundamentals that it outweighed in importance the conflicts, compromises, and ambiguities. The generation of the Framers without doubt intended to establish a stronger Union with its own sources of revenue and with authority to impose certain limitations on state powers. They meant to limit powers, distribute powers, fragment powers, separate powers, and stymie powers. They believed in measuring the powers of government, not the rights of the people. They assumed a natural rights philosophy. They concurred on the supremacy clause, on the enumeration of congressional powers, on the need for adding to that enumeration the necessary and proper clause, and speedily concurred on the need to add the Bill of Rights to the Constitution. The Constitution is certainly a principled document that reflects a coherent political philosophy. All this bespeaks of an ascertainable and enormously important original intent as to which one might almost say that a collective mind existed.[42] But none of this requires or enables judges to reach a decision favoring one side of an issue rather than another in real cases that come before the Supreme Court.

Throughout its existence, however, that Court, especially after the publication of Madison's Notes, has sought for the elusive yeti of our constitutional history: original intent. The Court has attempted whenever possible to veil its lawmaking role by giving the impression that its judgments correspond with the wisdom of our sages, the Framers. But the Court's principles, which tend to overarch the Constitution, do not and cannot dictate most decisions. The Justices tend to reason backward from their decisions. They reach results first and then find reasons, precedents, and historical support. In effect, their principles are not to be found in the Constitution but in their results. History is just a means to an end for the Court.

Two centuries of Court history should bring us to understand what really is a notorious fact: the Court has flunked history. The Justices stand censured for abusing historical evidence in a way that reflects adversely on their intellectual rectitude as well as on their historical competence. Scholars of constitutional history charge that the Justices frequently use "law office history," which is merely a function of *ex parte* advocacy. The Court artfully selects historical facts from one side only, ignoring contrary data, in order to support, rationalize, or give the appearance of respectability to judgments resting on other grounds. Alfred H. Kelly, who aimed his sharpest barbs at the liberal activists, claimed that the Court's historical scholarship is simplistic, manipulative, and devoid of balance or impartiality. He referred to the Court's "historical felony," "amateurish historical solecism," "mangled constitutional history," and its practice of confusing the writing of briefs with the writing of history—all of which "runs wild" in the Court's opinions. Kelly also questioned whether history as written by the Court is reconcilable with historians' history.[43]

Ever since Jacobus tenBroek's path-breaking article on the Court's use of "Extrinsic Aids on Constitutional Construction," scholars have regularly criticized the Court's use of history.[44] Charles Fairman demolished Justice Hugo L. Black's opinion in the *Adamson* case[45] on the question whether the Fourteenth Amendment was intended to incorporate the Bill of Rights as limitations on the states.[46] Paul L. Murphy preceded Kelly in condemning "law office history" and described one opinion as having relied on "a shockingly inaccurate use of historical data," a charge demonstrated by Charles A. Lofgren.[47] Alexander M. Bickel negated the Court's reading of the history of the first section of the Fourteenth Amendment on the question of racial segregation.[48] Historical evidence has also been mustered to disprove the Court's assertion that the free speech clause of the First Amendment was intended to supersede the common law of seditious libel.[49] The Court's use of history in cases on the Fifth Amendment's self-incrimination clause also fits a pattern that might charitably be described as historical incompetence, uncharitably as law office history.

The most historically minded opinion on the Fifth Amendment was Justice William Moody's in *Twining v. New Jersey*, decided in 1908.[50] *Twining*, which the Court abandoned in 1964,[51] runs counter to the trend of decisions favoring a broad construction of the Fifth Amendment. But the Court's use of history in *Twining* is representative, not of its viewpoint but of its historical knowledge. The question was whether the right against self-incrimination was "a fundamental principle of liberty and justice which inheres in the very idea of free government" and therefore ought to be included within the concept of the due process of law safeguarded from state abridgment.[52] Relying on its own version of history, the Court decided against the right. Justice Moody said that he had resorted to "every historical test by which the meaning of the phrase [of the Fifth Amendment] can be tried,"[53] although he had to "pass by the meager records of early colonial time, so far as they have come to our attention, as affording light too uncertain for guidance."[54] But Moody did not pass by the 1637 trial of Anne Hutchinson, which proved, he alleged, that the Massachusetts authorities were "not aware of any privilege against self-incrimination or any duty to respect it."[55] Four decades later Justice Hugo Black, in his famous *Adamson* dissent, exclaimed, "Of course not," because the court that tried Anne Hutchinson for heresy, believing that its religious convictions must be forced upon others, could not believe that dissenters had any rights worth respecting.[56] Black's outraged explanation was misleading. Incriminating interrogation was routine in 1637 on both sides of the Atlantic in all criminal cases. Nevertheless, the Hutchinson case did not reveal that the judges were unaware of the right against self-incrimination or of a duty to respect it, because she did not claim it. She welcomed incriminating questions as an opportunity to reveal God's word as she saw it. What was significant is not that the court sought her incrimination but, rather, that she freely and voluntarily incriminated herself. Justice Moody did not know that the same Massachusetts court a few months earlier, when trying her brother-in-law John Wheelwright on similar charges, was put on the defensive by objections to its procedure and questioning. Governor John Winthrop explained that his court neither meant to examine the defendant by compulsory means, such as by using an incriminating oath, nor sought to "draw matter from himselfe whereupon to proceed against him."[57] The maxim *nemo tenetur seipsum prodere*—no one is bound to accuse himself—was familiar to the Massachusetts Puritans.[58]

Moody said in *Twining* that the right was not in Magna Carta and that the practice of self-incriminatory examinations had continued for more than four centuries after 1215. That was true, but far short of the whole truth. As early as 1246, when the church introduced its inquisitional oath procedure into England, a procedure that required self-incrimination, Henry II condemned it as "repugnant to the antient Customs of his Realm" and to "his peoples Liberties."[59] In the early fourteenth century Parliament outlawed the church's incriminatory oath procedure,[60] and when the King's Council emulated that procedure, Parliament protested and reenacted section 29 of Magna Carta.[61] One such reenactment, in 1354, for the first time used the phrase "by due process of law."[62] On its face the statute said nothing about self-incrimination. Seen in its context the statute condemned incriminating examinations, when conducted outside the common law courts, as violations of Magna Carta or denials of due process. In *Twining* the Supreme Court failed to recognize that Magna Carta grew in meaning. Originally a feudal document protecting the barons, it became the talismanic symbol and source of the expanding liberties of the subject. Thus, in 1590 Robert Beale, the clerk of the Privy Council, declared that "by the Statute of Magna Carta and the olde lawes of this realme, this othe [oath] for a man to accuse himself was and is utterlie inhibited."[63] This became the view of other common-lawyers, of Chief Justice Edward Coke, and of Parliament.[64] To allege that Magna Carta did not outlaw compulsory self-incrimination is a mischievous oversimplification, a half-truth. The same can be said of the Court's *Twining* statement that the Petition of Right of 1628 did not address itself to the evil of compulsory self-incrimination. It did, in the passage censuring "an oath . . . not warrantable by the laws or statutes of this realm. . . ." That oath, which preceded interrogation, operated to coerce confessions from the opponents of the king's forced loan of 1626.[65]

The Court in *Twining* also found significance in the fact that compulsory self-incrimination was not condemned by the Stamp Act Congress, the First Continental Congress, or the Northwest Ordinance.[66] But the Stamp Act Congress mentioned only trial by jury among the many well-established rights of the criminally accused; failure to enumerate them all proved nothing. The Court failed to note that the First Continental Congress did claim that the colonists were "entitled to the common law of England," which had long protected the right against self-incrimination, nor did the Court note, or know, that Congress in 1778, in an investigation of its own, did respect that right.[67] The Northwest Ordinance did contain a guarantee of "judicial proceedings according to the court of the common law."[68] Indeed, the Supreme Court itself said in *Twining*, though without proof, that by 1776 the courts recognized the right even in the states whose constitutions did not protect it. Justice Moody mentioned six states whose constitutions provided such protection; but he neglected a seventh, Delaware, and an eighth, Vermont, not then a member of the Union.[69] What Moody did not recognize was that every state that had a separate bill of rights protected the right against self-incrimination. He noted that only four of the original thirteen states insisted that the right be incorporated in the new national Constitution, but he failed to note that these were the only states that ratified the Constitution with comprehensive recommendations for a national bill of rights.[70] Using Moody's yardstick, one could argue that the fundamental concept of due process of law was not fundamental at all because it did not appear in any of the thirteen state constitutions and was recommended by only one state ratifying convention. Moody remarked, inaccurately, that the principle that no person could be compelled to be a witness against himself "distinguished the common law from all other systems of jurisprudence."[71] If so, and if that principle was first elevated to constitutional status in America, and if it was safeguarded by every state having a bill of rights, and if it fit the several definitions of due process that Moody offered, there is no explaining the Court's finding that the right came into existence as a rule of evidence that was not "an essential part of due process."[72]

There were many other misleading or mistaken statements of history in *Twining*, but the point has been made: the opinion was founded on inaccurate and insufficient data. Contrary to the Court's assertion, the right against self-incrimination did evolve as an essential part of due process and as a fundamental principle of liberty and justice. Thus, Ben Franklin in 1735 called it a natural right ("the common Right of Mankind"), and Baron Geoffrey Gilbert, the foremost English authority on evidence at the time, called it part of the "Law of Nature."[73]

Other cases reveal the Justices to be equally inept as historians even when conscripting the past into service for the defense and expansion of the Fifth Amendment. The most historically minded opinion of this kind was Justice William Douglas's dissent in *Ullmann v. United States*, decided in 1956.[74] The seven-man majority, speaking through Justice Felix Frankfurter, sustained the constitutionality of Congress's Immunity Act of 1954. That act required that in certain cases involving national security, a federal court, on application approved by the attorney general, might require a witness to testify or produce records that might otherwise incriminate him, on condition that his revelations could not be used as evidence against him in any criminal proceeding. Frankfurter's opinion for the majority stressed the importance of history in interpreting the Fifth. History, he said, showed that it should be construed broadly, though he construed it narrowly, and he quoted Chief Judge Calvert Magruder's remark that "Our forefathers, when they wrote this provision into the Fifth Amendment of the Constitution, had in mind a lot of history which has been largely forgotten today."[75] Frankfurter himself observed that "the privilege against self-incrimination is a specific provision of which it is peculiarly true that 'a page of history is worth a volume of logic'."[76] But Frankfurter did not provide that page of history despite his rhetorical stress on its importance. He offered only the brief line that the Fifth was aimed against a recurrence of the Inquisition and of the Star Chamber. Though Frankfurter was the best and most historically minded scholar on the Court, he was apparently unaware of the several colonial precedents in support of his argument that the right cannot be claimed if the legal peril, which is the reason for its existence, ceases. As early as 1698 a Connecticut statute required testimony by providing immunity against prosecution for self-incriminatory disclosures.[77] Among the later colonial precedents are cases of 1758, when the Pennsylvania Assembly granted a witness immunity in exchange for his testimony, [78] and of 1763, when the Supreme Court of Judicature of New York offered pardons to some ships' captains in order to force them to testify about illicit trading with the enemy.[79]

Douglas's dissent, in which Black joined, is a splendid specimen of law office history, yet most of his history was not even relevant to his conclusion that the Immunity Act violated the Fifth Amendment. Douglas's relevant data, which dealt with the concept of infamy, were unsound. He claimed that the act was unconstitutional because it was not broad enough: it did not protect against infamy or public disgrace. In support of this proposition he had to prove that the Framers of the Fifth meant it to protect against disclosures resulting in public disgrace accompanied by noncriminal penalties such as the loss of employment. Such evidence as history provides to support his proposition was unknown to Douglas.

Douglas did not know the early state cases showing that neither witnesses nor parties were required to answer against themselves if to do so would expose them to public disgrace or infamy.[80] Douglas did not know that the origins of so broad a right of silence can be traced as far back as sixteenth-century claims by Protestant reformers like William Tyndale and Thomas Cartwright in connection with their argument that no man should be compelled to accuse himself.[81] Douglas did not know that the idea passed to the common-lawyers, including Coke,[82] was accepted even in the Star Chamber as well as English case law,[83] and found expression in Blackstone[84] and the American manuals of practice.[85]

The evidence produced by Douglas was far-fetched, for he based his argument on the fact that protection against infamy is found in the ideas of Beccaria and The Encyclopedistes, whom Jefferson read. But the Fifth Amendment was exclusively the product of English and American colonial experience. The influence of continental theorists was nonexistent. As for Jefferson, he had nothing to do with the making of the Fifth. Indeed, he omitted protections against self-incrimination in two model constitutions that he proposed for Virginia.[86]

Douglas's other evidence dealt not with the issue in question, immunity, but with the general origins of the Fifth. He referred to the Puritan hatred of the self-incriminatory oath *ex officio* used by the Star Chamber and its ecclesiastical counterpart, the High Commission. The hatred existed, but there were significant differences between the Star Chamber's use of the oath and the High Commission's. The High Commission required the suspect to take

that oath to tell the truth as the first step of the examination, and
then interrogated him orally without telling him the charges against
him or the identity of his accusers. By contrast, the Star Chamber
normally provided a bill of complaint, as specific as a common law
indictment, and permitted the accused to have plenty of time to
answer the charges in writing and with the advice of counsel; only
then did the accused have to take the oath and be interrogated.[87]
However, in Archbishop Laud's time, the power of examining parties under oath, as a Star Chamber lawyer recorded, "was used
like Spanish inquisition to rack men's consciences."[88] But that was
exceptional in the Star Chamber, routine in the High Commission.
The same Star Chamber lawyer stated that if "the matter in charge
tendeth to accuse the defendant of some crime which may be
capital; in which case *nemo tenetur prodere seipsum* [no man is
bound to accuse himself]. . . ." And, "neither must it question the
party to accuse him of crime."[89] The same rule applied to witnesses.
In the High Commission, however, the inquisitional procedure
conformed to a quite different rule: any person suspected, even if
only by rumor, must answer the interrogatories, however incriminating. The maxim *nemo tenetur seipsum prodere,* from which the
right against self-incrimination derived, did not operate in the High
Commission.[90] For these reasons common-lawyers led by Robert
Beale, James Morice, and Coke, who supported that maxim and
assaulted the oath *ex officio,* did not attack the use of the oath by
the Star Chamber.[91] The Star Chamber is too loosely identified as
the symbol of arbitrary, inquisitorial procedure, the opposition to
which gave rise to the right against self-incrimination. Thus Justice
Black in his *Adamson* dissent spoke of the Star Chamber practice
of compelling people to testify against themselves, and the same
thought is in Chief Justice Earl Warren's opinion for the Court in
the 1966 *Miranda* case, which extended the right against self-
incrimination to the police station.[92]

Black in *Adamson,* Douglas in *Ullmann,* and Warren in *Miranda* referred to John Lilburne's Star Chamber trial of 1637 and
his refusal to take the oath.[93] As these Justices imply, Lilburne was
more responsible than any other single individual for the recognition by the common law courts of the right against self-incrimination. If any one man deserves to be remembered as the father
of the right, it was he. But not because of his opposition to the

oath in 1637. He said then, "Before I swear, I will know to what I must swear," and the court examiner replied, "As soon as you have sworn, you shall, but not before."[94] The fact is that in this case the Star Chamber had abandoned its normal procedure. Rather, it followed High Commission procedure, demanding the oath first instead of providing the written complaint first. As a result Lilburne refused the oath, claiming that he was the first ever to have done so before the Star Chamber[95]—proof that its procedure in that 1637 case was exceptional. Moreover, Lilburne remained silent only to incriminating questions that were not germane to the issue.[96] Justice Douglas's quotations from Lilburne in 1648 and 1653 against the oath were redundant. Douglas should have quoted statements by Lilburne that even in the absence of the oath and after common law indictment, Magna Carta and the Petition of Right protected a man from being examined on interrogatories concerning himself—"concerning," which is far broader than "incriminating."[97] Douglas should also have quoted Lilburne's claim, made during his trial for treason in 1649, that even after common law indictment and without oath, he did not have to answer questions "against or concerning myself."[98] At that trial Lilburne placed the right against self-incrimination squarely in the context of what he called "fair play," "fair trial," "the due process of the law," and "the good old laws of England."[99] Justice Douglas gave to John Lilburne a page of his opinion in *Ullmann*, straining the evidence and never knowing that history provided him with stronger facts with which to construct his one-sided argument.

Douglas's respect for evidence, particularly historical evidence, had frequently been minimal when he had a libertarian theme to defend. In his *Ullmann* opinion he grossly distorted the evidence concerning an important episode in the colonial history of the right against self-incrimination. He mentioned that Governor William Bradford of Plymouth sought the advice of his ministers on the question, "How farr a magistrate may extracte a confession from a delinquente, to acuse himselfe of a capitall crime, seeing *Nemo tenetur prodere seipsum*."[100] Inexplicably, Douglas omitted the Latin phrase that both supported his argument and invalidated the generalization in *Twining*, based on the Anne Hutchinson case, that the right against self-incrimination was unknown. Three Plymouth ministers, Douglas said, were unanimous in concluding that

the oath was illegal, and he quoted as "typical" only the answer of
Ralph Partrich that the magistrate might not extract a confession
"by any violent means," whether by oath or "punishment."[101] Douglas concealed the answer of Charles Chauncy who said,

> But now, if the question be mente of inflicting bodly torments to
> extract a confession from a mallefactor, I conceive that in matters of
> highest consequence, such as doe conceirne the saftie or ruine of
> stats or countries, magistrats may proceede so farr to bodily torments,
> as racks, hote-irons, &c. to extracte a confession, espetially wher
> presumptions are strounge; but otherwise by no means.[102]

Chauncy would not force self-incrimination by oath, but he would
employ torture in matters such as sedition or treason and perhaps
heresy. Douglas's account also omits the fact that John Winthrop,
who received the opinions of the elders and magistrates of Massachusetts Bay, New Haven, and Connecticut, as well as of Plymouth, recorded that "most" answered that in a capital case if one
witness or "strong presumtions" pointed to the suspect, the judge
could examine him "strictly, and he is bound to answer directly,
though to the peril of his life."[103] Douglas stressed the Puritan
opposition to the oath, yet Samuel Maverick, when petitioning the
General Court of Massachusetts in 1649 for a remission of the fines
imposed on him for his part in the Robert Child Remonstrance,
declared, "your whole proceeding against us seemes to depend on
our refusall to answer Interrogatories upon oath."[104]

   Another instance of the Court's abuse of history in connection
with the Fifth Amendment arose in *Kastigar v. United States*,
decided in 1972.[105] The question in that case was whether the
statutory provision of "use immunity" had the same function as the
Fifth Amendment's guarantee that no person shall be compelled
to be a witness against himself in a criminal case. If a grant of use
immunity serves to displace the Fifth Amendment, one may be
compelled to testify against himself. Use immunity is a form of
partial immunity against prosecution for a particular criminal involvement. Full immunity or "transactional immunity," immunity
from prosecution for the particular criminal transaction, is far broader
than use immunity. Use immunity guarantees only that the compelled evidence and its fruits, which is evidence derived directly
or indirectly from it, cannot be used in a subsequent criminal

prosecution. But government may resort to such a prosecution if it is based on evidence independently derived or unrelated to the compelled testimony. Under a grant of use immunity, for example, a person might confess to a crime secure in the knowledge that his confession could not be used against him. However, should the prosecution discover evidence of his guilt without having used any leads drawn from his confession, he can be tried for the crime. By contrast, transactional immunity insures absolute protection against prosecution for the crime concerning which one's testimony is compelled. In *Kastigar,* the Court sustained the constitutionality of a use-immunity grant and rejected the claim that such a grant was not the equivalent of the provision of the Fifth Amendment.

Justice Lewis Powell, writing for the Court, cited several colonial examples of immunity that he found in my book *Origins of the Fifth Amendment,*[106] but he neglected to observe that all, in today's language, exemplified transactional immunity; all had the effect of making the compelled confession a purging of the offense. Those grants of immunity operated like a pardon or amnesty, so that the individuals whose testimony was required stood to the offense as if they had never committed it. A grant of transactional immunity and nothing short of that displaced the protection of the Fifth Amendment until 1972. The law paid a price for exacting information otherwise criminally actionable but constitutionally protected. The right not to give evidence against oneself criminally put one beyond the peril of penal sanctions if the government sought to make a deal that forced one to testify against himself.

Powell's *Kastigar* opinion employed historical evidence not for what it revealed but merely as a grace note to give the impression that the past and scholarship buttressed his opinion. Powell was wrong. Use immunity not only preserved the state's right to prosecute for the transaction; such a grant of immunity increased the original jeopardy by exposing one to a conviction for contempt if he refused to talk, and exposing him to a conviction for perjury if he spoke falsely. In England the House of Lords in 1742 even rejected a bill granting transactional immunity because it might lead to perjury and perjury charges; the Lords also believed that the bill diminished the voluntary character of the only sort of confession that the law could accept. The *Kastigar* Court cited the episode but misunderstood and misrepresented it.[107] By ruling that a mere statute can displace a constitutional provision, the Supreme Court repudiated the very fundament of having a written Constitution that is superior to statute.[108] For those interested in original intent, the Fifth Amendment became part of the Constitution at a time when the right not to give evidence against oneself extended even to evidence that exposed a person to public obloquy or disgrace, as well as criminal jeopardy.

On one occasion the Court acknowledged its abuse of history by admitting error and overruling itself—not, however, until long after it had endorsed the "two sovereignties" rule as historically authorized. The rule was that a person could not refuse to testify on the grounds that his disclosures would subject him to prosecution in another sovereignty or jurisdiction. Thus he could be convicted of a federal crime on the basis of testimony that he was compelled to give in a state proceeding, or vice versa. In matters involving national supremacy, Congress at its discretion could grant immunity against state prosecution, but not vice versa, and one state could not immunize against a prosecution in another. When the Court established the rule in 1931, it alleged that history supported the rule.[109] The Court did not know that one English precedent upon which it had based its opinion had been distinguished away, if not overruled, and that the other supposed precedent upon which it relied was not in point. Worse, the Court did not even know the English case that established a contrary rule, where the English court had ruled that an individual did not have to answer a question that exposed him to criminal jeopardy in another jurisdiction.[110] After a legal historian published his work on the subject of the two sovereignties rule, the Court's historical mistakes rotted in the sun like dead mackerels for all to see.[111] In 1964, when the issue arose again, the Court confessed its errors, demonstrated that history belied the two sovereignties rule, and scrapped it completely.[112]

The credit due to the Court for acknowledging its mistake does not lead to a sense of confidence that the Court knows how to use historical evidence responsibly. A court that frequently cannot get its facts right or even understand precedents cannot be trusted to expound a jurisprudence of original intent, which relies completely upon history. Justices of the Supreme Court are not particularly at fault. They think along lines that members of the bench and bar tend to share as people trained in the adversarial process. Despite their knowledge of the law of evidence, they are for the most part advocates—practitioners of the art of argumentation in the interest of a client or cause. They believe, or act, as if truth is best revealed by the clash of formidable statements on both sides of a question, and they know only two sides, as if no question were more than two-dimensional. The adversarial process is antagonistic to truth-finding, regardless of the legal fiction that truth emerges from a trial or from opposing arguments. Jonathan Swift spoke of "a society of men among us, bred up from their youth in the art of proving by words multiplied for their purpose, that White is Black and Black is White, according as they are paid."[113] As a great satirist, Swift naturally exaggerated. Yet, no doubt exists that lawyers are keen on promoting their clients' interests. That is their job, not the disinterested pursuit of knowledge wherever the evidence may lead. A scholar who has no stake in the outcome of a question is more likely to answer it correctly, if the evidence will allow, than the advocate. The adversarial system, by contrast with historical scholarship, invites the manipulation of evidence and distorted interpretations.

In *Brown v. Board of Education*, one of the foremost cases in our constitutional history, the Supreme Court, revealing that it had no capacity of its own to discover historical facts and that it thinks that client-oriented presentations advance truth, asked the parties to prepare briefs and engage in oral arguments on the following question: "What evidence is there that the Congress which submitted and the State legislatures and conventions which ratified the Fourteenth Amendment, contemplated or did not contemplate, understood or did not understand, that it would abolish segregation in public schools?"[114] The cumbersome language, which mistakenly assumed that some state conventions had ratified the amendment, in effect invited the two sides to cook the facts on a question of original intent; as Alfred H. Kelly wrote, the Court welcomed law-office history. Kelly, who had helped to mastermind the NAACP's answer to the Court's question, later acknowledged that its brief marshaled every scrap of evidence on behalf of the desired interpretation, "just as carefully doctoring all the evidence to the contrary, either by suppressing it when that seemed plausible, or by distorting it when suppression was not possible." The brief for the southern school boards "was no less law-office history. It, too, doctored, distorted, twisted, and suppressed historical evidence in as competent a fashion as did the NAACP." The results, which canceled each other out, "exposed too grossly . . . the entire fallacy of law-office history," and so the Court in this instance avoided a decision based on original intent.[115]

Yet it could have easily held, in conformance with the preponderance of evidence, that the framers of the Fourteenth Amendment and the state legislatures that ratified it, intended the amendment to establish the principle of racial equality before the law. The Court should have restricted itself to an exposition of that principle, which is implicit in the text and explicit in original intent. The principle sufficed to show that Jim Crow statutes violated equal protection of the laws by discriminating on the grounds of race. How blacks and whites felt about inferiority and superiority had nothing whatever to do with the objective right of human beings of one color to be treated by the law as it treats those of another color. Having lost its historical foundation and having bumbled on the principle of racial equality, the Court played with sociological notions that properly exposed it to an avalanche of criticism. In other cases the use of law-office history possessed a cosmetic appearance of truth as if based on historical evidence. Here, however, the Court fled from original intent because it did not adequately support the case against state-compelled racial segregation in the public schools. The briefs showed that law-office history is not reconcilable with history as employed by professional historians who are comparatively disinterested scholars. Montaigne presented the problem long ago when he wrote:

> You recite a case simply to a lawyer, he answers you wavering and doubtful, you feel that it is a matter of indifference to him whether he undertakes to support one party or the other. Have you paid him well to get his teeth into it and get excited about it, is he beginning to be involved in it, has he got his will warmed up about it? His reason and his knowledge are warmed up at the same time. Behold an evident and indubitable truth that appears to his intelligence. He discovers a wholly new light on your case, and believes it in all conscience, and persuades himself that it is so.[116]

Judges are freer than lawyers to decide as scholars might. But appellate judges are restricted by the evidence presented to them.

And, unlike scholars, judges must decide that the law or Constitution comes down on one side rather than the other. In law, one party is right, the other wrong. No middle ground exists. One side *must* win. That is the function of the adversary process: to produce a winner in a sort of peaceable trial by combat before judges. The judges are freer than lawyers to decide as scholars might but can decide only for one party or the other, regardless of how complicated truth may be. Unlike scholars, who can see a full spectrum of color but usually stare at shades of gray, judges are permitted to see only black or white.

Judges, moreover, do not look at the past as historians are supposed to. Judges do not try to understand the past on its own terms, for its own sake, and as if they did not know how things turned out. Judges always *use* history. They turn to it only because they think it might help decide some issue posed in a case. They look for something to confirm a hunch or to illustrate a point that they have already decided on other grounds. They hardly ever decide a case on the basis of original intent or because historical evidence requires a particular judgment. The intent that they find invariably bears out the result they seek. In short, judges exploit history by making it serve the present and by making it yield results that are not historically founded.

Mark DeWolfe Howe, an excellent legal historian who was known for his judiciousness, complained that the Supreme Court has too often "pretended that the dictates of the nation's history, rather than the mandates of its own will, compelled a particular decision," and he added: "By superficial and purposive interpretations of the past, the Court has dishonored the arts of the historian and degraded the talents of the lawyer."[117] The Justices of the Supreme Court, one must add, do not knowingly dishonor or degrade. They are, rather, bad historians; they are simply naive, biased, and incompetent. They are also victims of their training as lawyers. The adversarial process is inherently hostile to the process of discovering and ordering facts in the way that historians perform those tasks. The adversarial process also seems to have an adverse impact on the Court's capability of reasoning its way toward convincing explanations of how it reaches results.

A decision based on an unsound rationale is not likely to survive or be respected. A rationale may be unsound because it plays fast and loose with relevant precedents or with truth; it may be overbroad, illogical, or biased, or, it may be one-sided because it ignores opposing arguments. Far too often in its intellectually unconvincing explanations, the Court issues edicts without foundation. It also fails to give fair and serious consideration to arguments advanced by those who disagree, especially by dissenters on the Court. The Court has a long history of turning away from rather than facing opposing views. There is too little debate in majority opinions and far too little effort to attain the degree of objectivity and disinterestedness that is humanly attainable. The Justices seem, lawyerlike, first to choose what the outcome should be and then reason backward to supply a rationalization, replete with the appropriate rules and precedents, of which there are enough on any side of an issue to make any argument seem to respect tradition and professional expertise. Howe's criticism has truth because the members of the Court do not with some regularity reach judgments that conflict with their private policy preferences. If their opinions on more occasions than are fitting lack cogency, rigor, and even intellectual rectitude, they cannot also be expected to employ historical evidence responsibly.

Look, for example, at the way Chief Justice John Marshall, speaking for the Court in the *Dartmouth College* case, mishandled historical facts.[118] His strategy was to extend the protection of the contract clause to corporate charters, even though, as he conceded, original intent provided no support. The text of the Constitution did not prohibit the inclusion of corporate charters within the protection of the contract clause. So Marshall saw no reason to exclude them. He merely had to show that the college's charter created a private corporation. By his recitation of the facts, the crown had granted the charter of the college because the college had received private gifts and had a proper mission. Reading Marshall, however, one could not know that the monies had been given to a different institution, Moore's Charity School for Indians, that its grantors had vehemently objected to the transference of those monies to Dartmouth College, that most of the college's property came from grants of public lands, and that the donors, private and public, believed the college to be performing public functions. Whether Dartmouth's charter had "every ingredient" of a private contract, as Marshall alleged, was a question that mainly concerned the college, but it was a question that Marshall debauched to reach the doctrine that had such consequences in the economy and in constitutional law, namely, that the charter of a private corporation has the protection of Article I, section 10, of the Constitution.[119]

Chief Justice Roger B. Taney's opinion in the *Dred Scott* case, which is the classic exposition of the doctrine of original intent (the Constitution means what the Framers intended), constitutes another prize example of the Court's mangling of historical evidence.[120] The Court held that Scott was not a free man entitled to bring a suit in a federal court, but rather belonged to that "degraded class" which lacked the rights of citizenship. The holding rested on history. If free blacks possessed no rights worthy of constitutional respect in 1789, Taney reasoned, they possessed none in 1857. Don E. Fehrenbacher, the historian of the case, having asked whether Taney's historical narrative, which was the basis of his legal judgment, was honest and accurate, answered, "As 'historical narrative,' it was a gross perversion of the facts."[121]

Another extraordinary abuse of history occurred in the *Slaughterhouse Cases* of 1873, which transformed American constitutional law. Justice Samuel F. Miller's opinion for the Court rendered the privileges and immunities clause of the Fourteenth Amendment "a vain and idle enactment, which accomplished nothing, and most unnecessarily excited Congress and the people on its passage." to quote Justice Stephen Field's dissenting opinion.[122] By making that clause a nullity, the Court in effect amended the Constitution, doomed a comprehensive federal program for the protection of civil rights, and paved the constitutional way for Jim Crow.

These results of the decision hinged on the Court's finding that the Fourteenth Amendment was intended to protect only the rights of citizens of the United States but not the rights of state citizenship, which included most rights of importance. The Court entrusted the rights of black Americans to southern white supremacists and left to state protection all significant rights, ranging from the freedoms of speech and religion to the rights of the criminally accused.

What then, were the rights of United States citizenship? Miller declared that they derived from the existence of the United States government. Thus, one's federal rights included the right to use the federal mails and federal courts, the right to use the navigable waterways and seaports, the right to be protected on the high seas, and the right to petition Congress for redress of grievances. The Fourteenth Amendment left all other rights as they were before the amendment—at the mercy of state laws. A state might institute a religious inquisition, suppress political dissidents, and torture suspects to extort confessions, without violating the United States Constitution. The amendment, construed by the Court for the first time in this case, did not have as its purpose the transference of "the security and protection of all the civil rights . . . from the states to the Federal government" nor "was it intended to bring within the power of Congress the entire domain of civil rights" previously belonging to the states.[123] Thus, the Court relied on history by speaking of the purpose and intent of the amendment. Yet the Court settled the matter on its own *ipse dixit*, without ever having consulted the *Congressional Globe* or the state records that would show historical purpose and intent.[124]

In the *Civil Rights Cases* of 1883 the Court held unconstitutional an act of Congress that prohibited racial discrimination in transportation facilities, inns and hotels, and theaters.[125] Congress, exercising powers seemingly granted by the Thirteenth and Fourteenth Amendments, had sought to institute equality of civil rights for all citizens in places of public accommodation. The Court found that the statute was unauthorized by those amendments and was repugnant to the Tenth Amendment. Justice John Marshall Harlan, dissenting, in effect invoked original intent against the majority of the Court by stressing the forgotten purpose that unified the Civil War amendments. In the *Slaughterhouse Cases*, the Court had declared that the one pervading purpose of each of the Civil War amendments was the freedom of black Americans, the establishment and security of that freedom, and their protection against oppression from those who once held dominion over them.[126] Harlan additionally accused the majority of having betrayed history by ruling that because the parties who had engaged in racial discrimination were private, they did not come within the terms of the Fourteenth Amendment. Private parties, Harlan answered, might be exempt from the Fourteenth, which applied to state action. Private parties were not, however, exempt from the Thirteenth, which he construed broadly enough to prohibit the imposition of badges of servitude or discrimination based on race. In these cases, the Court ignored the fact that the parties—inns, theaters, and railroads—were not merely private. All were businesses affected with a public interest and subject to special regulation. They exercised public functions under public charters for the use and benefit of the public and, in return, received special privileges. In effect their action constituted state action. Harlan had history on his side.[127]

Another path-breaking case that revealed the Court's easy use of history was *Hurtado v. California,* decided in 1884. In that case the Court displayed magisterial disdain for original intent, as it construed the meaning of the due process clause of the Fourteenth Amendment. It held that the guarantee of due process of law did not require that a capital defendant must be indicted by a grand jury and that prosecuting him by way of an information, an accusation of crime proferred by a prosecutor before a magistrate, did not violate due process of law.[128] Sir Edward Coke's commentaries on Magna Carta equated due process of law with indictment by grand jury,[129] but the Court reasoned that other forms of justice, not merely those known to the Framers, could provide due process of law. To make due process dependent on old forms for its essential meaning would "stamp upon our jurisprudence the unchangeableness attributed to the laws of the Medes and the Persians."[130] That led to a whittling away of the rights of the criminally accused for the next four decades.[131]

Plessy v. Ferguson, decided in 1896, also displayed the Court's disastrous use of history. In this case the Court sustained the constitutionality of state laws compelling racial segregation by alleging that although the Fourteenth Amendment's purpose was "to enforce the absolute equality of the two races," the amendment "could not have been intended to abolish distinctions based upon color." The Court invoked precedents from case law to prove that dubious assertion. The Court did not bother to examine the intent of the Congress that framed the amendment nor the understanding of the state legislatures that ratified it. The Court also asserted that laws requiring segregation "do not necessarily imply the inferiority of either race to the other" and that the "fallacy" of the argument against segregation was the "assumption" that it imposed upon blacks a badge of inferiority. "If this be so, it is not by reason of anything found in the act, but solely because the colored race chooses to put that construction upon it."[132] The Court ignored massive evidence heard in the trumpetings of white racists from the pulpits, the press, and public platforms, that the purpose of Jim Crow laws was to uphold white supremacy and keep the blacks in their places of inferiority. The point is significant because the Court conceded that if segregation was discriminatory, if it implied inferiority of one race to the other, or if it violated the "absolute equality" demanded by the Fourteenth Amendment, it would be unconstitutional.

In the two *Income Tax Cases* of 1895, the Court first held that a tax on the income from land was unconstitutional because it had not been apportioned among the states as the Constitution requires of direct taxes. Because a tax on land itself is a direct tax, a tax on the income earned from its use—rents, agriculture, mining, or drilling—constituted a special case: it too was a direct tax. Having held that, the Court then somersaulted by finding that because a tax on the income from land was a direct tax, so too must be a tax on income from other sources.[133] The trouble with these important decisions, which were finally superseded by an amendment to the Constitution, was that the Court relied heavily on a misreading of history with respect to the clause of the Constitution empowering Congress to impose direct taxes. The Court completely misstated the purpose of the clause and alleged, wrongly, that "the distinction between 'direct' and 'indirect' taxation was well understood by the Framers of the Constitution and those who adopted it."[134]

The Court missed the fact that the vague clause on "capitation and other direct taxes" was a concession to the South, not, as the Court generalized, a bulwark of "inequality" imposed "to prevent an attack upon accumulated property by mere force of numbers."[135] Moreover, the Court drew the wrong conclusion after quoting Madison's Notes: "Mr. King asked what was the precise meaning of direct taxation. No one answered." The right conclusion is that the Framers were unsure or did not know.[136] In his argument as counsel for the government in the *Carriage Tax Case* of 1795,[137] Hamilton had asked what the distinction was between direct and indirect taxes, and he began his response by stating, "It is a matter of regret that terms so uncertain and vague, on so important a point, are to be found in the Constitution. We shall seek in vain for any *antecedent* settled legal maxim to the respective terms.

There is none."[138] In the *Income Tax Cases*, the Court imposed its own views of history in order to deliver an opinion that seemed to have the paternity of original intent; in effect the Court sought to rely on the wisdom of the Framers to get around encumbering precedents.

Another example of the Court's felonious use of historical evidence is a 1965 case in which Justice Hugo L. Black for the Court decided that "construed in its historical context, the command of Article I, Sec. 2, that Representatives be chosen 'by People of the several States' means that as nearly as practicable one man's vote in a congressional election is to be worth as much as another's."[139] The statement is absurd, despite all the evidence that Black relied on for his twistory. That evidence, which derived from Madison's Notes, concerned the issue that the Convention's Great Compromise settled: proportionate representation in the House of Representatives and equal state representation in the Senate. The compromise reflected a battle between large-state and small-state interests. It had nothing to do with the principle of one person, one vote. Representation in the House benefited large states by ensuring that the size of their delegation would reflect their population. Equality of size of congressional districts within a state or equality of votes was simply irrelevant. Black also distorted the evidence from the ratification controversy, including the quotation out of context by Madison from *The Federalist* #54.[140]

In a case involving the establishment clause of the First Amendment, decided in 1983, Chief Justice Warren Burger for the Court jettisoned establishment clause jurisprudence in favor of a decision wholly based on history. The question was whether the practice of having a publicly paid chaplain open the legislature's day with a prayer violated the First Amendment.[141] Historical custom settled the matter for the Court. Burger pointed out that the First Congress had provided for legislative chaplains, proof that the Framers of the establishment clause did not understand it to prohibit the practice. Madison himself, Burger observed, had served on the committee that recommended chaplaincies "and voted for the bill authorizing payment of chaplains."[142] But the *Annals of Congress* does not record the vote or say how any member voted, and Madison himself years later declared that he thought chaplains for Congress constituted a "national religion" in violation of the establishment clause and that "it was not with my approbation that the deviation from it [the establishment clause] took place in Congress when they appointed Chaplains. . . ."[143] In the case before the Court, the state legislature had retained the same Presbyterian chaplain for over eighteen years, a fact that Burger believed made no difference. He did not mention that the First Congress, which he relied on as a historical model, had required that "two Chaplains of different denominations . . . shall interchange weekly."[144]

Of a similar character was a dissenting opinion that Burger's successor, Chief Justice William Rehnquist, wrote in the Alabama School Prayer case. He passed fiction off as history when he converted Madison's argument in the First Congress against a "national religion" into meaning merely that Congress cannot promote a national church or prefer one sect over another. The establishment clause, Rehnquist urged, did not prohibit Congress "from providing nondiscriminatory aid to religion."[145] Rehnquist was flat wrong, as wrong as his proposition that among the establishments of religion that existed in the late eighteenth and early nineteenth centuries was the one created by the Rhode Island charter of 1633 and lasting until 1842.[146] Rhode Island's charter of 1663, not 1633, guaranteed religious liberty and neither as a colony nor as a state did Rhode Island ever have an establishment of religion.

These examples of the historical illiteracy of the Supreme Court can be multiplied *ad nauseam*. The Court rarely gets its history right. Chief Justice Richard Neely of West Virginia, a judge of some wit and learning, has observed that people who take seriously the Supreme Court's "historical scholarship as applied to the Constitution also probably believe in the Tooth Fairy and the Easter Bunny."[147] From the time of John Jay and John Marshall, members of the Supreme Court have been shrewd enough to grasp a principle later promulgated in the slogan of the Party in George Orwell's *1984*: "Who controls the past controls the future; who controls the present controls the past."[148] Perhaps, however, the Court's search for original intent has been a noble one, though a failure. The Framers may have made mistakes, but they were in fact a lot wiser than we are. They gave us a magnificent Constitution. Its words remain the same and mean something. We might be better off if judges were cabined and contained by those words, rather than deciding on the basis of their own agendas. Sir William S.

Holdsworth, the master historian of English law, believed that "a little bad history" might not be too high a price to pay for certainty in the law.[149] That would be especially true of the supreme law of the land expressed in a written Constitution. It is equally true, however, that over two centuries, the Court has failed to show that original intent can serve as the foundation of a constitutional jurisprudence. And the Court has given us far more than just a little bad history. It has given us an enormous amount of bad history, not always in a bad cause, but far more than enough to merit restatement of the fact that good causes should not triumph by use of a stacked deck. History ought to be more than a way to prettify a desired result. Persistent misuse of history by the Court demeans its intellectual probity and capability.

CHAPTER FIFTEEN

A Constitutional Jurisprudence of Original Intent? Part One

A constitutional jurisprudence of original intent would be as viable and sound as Mr. Dooley's understanding of it. Mr. Dooley, Finley Peter Dunne's philosophical Irish bartender, believed that original intent was "what some dead Englishman thought Thomas Jefferson was goin' to mean whin he wrote th' Constitution."[1] Acceptance of original intent as the foundation of constitutional interpretation is unrealistic beyond belief. It obligates us, even if we could grasp that intent, to interpret the Constitution in the way the Framers did in the context of conditions that existed in their time. Those conditions for the most part no longer exist and cannot be recalled with the historical arts and limited time available to the Supreme Court. Anyway, the Court resorts to history for a quick fix, a substantiation, a confirmation, an illustration, or a grace note; it does not really look for the historical conditions and meanings of a time long gone in order to determine the evidence that will persuade it to decide a case in one way rather than another.

The Court, moreover, cannot engage in the sort of sustained historical analysis that takes professional historians some years to accomplish. In any case, for many reasons already described, concerning the inadequacies of the historical record and the fact that we cannot in most instances find a collective mind of the Framers, original intent analysis is not really possible, however desirable.

We must keep reminding ourselves that the most outspoken Framers disagreed with each other and did not necessarily reflect the opinions of the many who did not enter the debates. A point that Justice Rufus Peckham made for the Court in an 1897 case about legislative intent carries force with respect to the original intent of the Constitutional Convention. In reference to the difficulty of understanding an act by analyzing the speeches of the members of the body that passed it, Peckham remarked: "Those who did not speak may not have agreed with those who did; and those who spoke might differ from each other; the result being that the only proper way to construe a legislative act is from the language used in the act, and, upon occasion, by a resort to the history of the times when it was passed."[2] We must keep reminding ourselves, too, that the country was deeply divided during the ratification controversy. And we must keep reminding ourselves that the Framers who remained active in national politics divided intensely on one constitutional issue after another—the removal power, the power to charter a corporation, the power to declare neutrality, the executive power, the power to enact excise and use taxes without apportioning them on population, the power of a treaty to obligate the House of Representatives, the power of judicial review, the power to deport aliens, the power to pass an act against seditious libel, the power of the federal courts to decide on federal common law grounds, the power to abolish judicial offices of life tenure, and the jurisdiction of the Supreme Court to decide suits against states without their consent or to issue writs of mandamus against executive officers. This list is not exhaustive; it is a point of departure. The Framers, who did not agree on their own constitutional issues, would not likely speak to us about ours with a single loud, clear voice.

Adherence to original intent requires that we construe the Constitution as the Framers did. That means that if the Court could discover original intent, it would freeze the meaning of the Constitution as it was two centuries ago. A frozen or sclerotic Constitution would lose its character as a document intended to serve for ages to come. We cannot transform ourselves into the Framers or transport ourselves into their time; we cannot see with their eyes or understand with their minds in order to comprehend the Constitution as they did. If we could perform such miracles and could discover a single predominant meaning applicable to the issue of a particular case, we would be relying on 1789 to provide answers. We would be charging the Framers and ratifiers with a burden they could not bear. Their advice is the most we can hope for, but it cannot be dispositive; it is most likely to be irrelevant or uncomprehending. "When we are dealing with words that are also a constituent act, like the Constitution of the United States," Justice Oliver Wendell Holmes wisely observed, "we must realize that they have called into life a being the development of which could not have been foreseen completely by the most gifted of its begetters. . . . The case before us must be considered in the light of our whole experience and not merely in the light of what was said a hundred years ago"—or two hundred years ago. "We must consider what this country has become," he added.[3]

The idea of a fixed Constitution with unchanging meaning is an old one that constitutional commentators have advanced. In 1793 Nathaniel Chipman, the chief justice of Vermont, a Hamiltonian Federalist, wrote one of the first commentaries on the Constitution. Even if the meanings of words change, "the meaning of the constitution is not therefore changed," he declared. "In such a case it is necessary to seek and learn the meaning intended by the framers." But he later added, following James Madison, that if a particular construction has prevailed for a reasonable length of time and has received judicial endorsement, "it has then acquired all the sanction" as true meaning.[4]

Chief Justice Thomas M. Cooley, whose commentaries of 1868 dominated until about 1937, devoted much space on the rules for interpreting a constitution. One "cardinal rule" was that it should receive an unvarying, uniform interpretation, so that it is not "made to mean one thing at one time, and another at some subsequent time when the circumstances may have changed as perhaps to make a different rule in the case seem desirable." A constitution, Cooley believed, would lose the benefit of its being written if it became "so flexible as to bend to circumstances or be modified by public opinion." Given such a view, Cooley concluded, "The meaning is fixed when it is adopted, and it is not different at any subsequent time when a court has to pass upon it." The object of construction, he asserted, is to honor the intention of the Constitution's Framers and give effect to the intent of the people in adopting it. Cooley also advocated that judges should find the rule in the text of the document, if possible.[5]

The Supreme Court has intermittently endorsed such views about the unchanging meaning of the Constitution. The definitive statement on a constitutional jurisprudence of original intent was made by Chief Justice Roger B. Taney in the *Dred Scott* case:

> No one, we presume, supposes that any change in public opinion or feeling, in relation to this unfortunate race . . . should induce the Court to give to the words of the Constitution a more liberal construction in their favor than they were intended to bear when the instrument was framed and adopted. Such an argument would be altogether inadmissible in any tribunal called on to interpret it. If any of its provisions are deemed unjust, there is a mode prescribed in the instrument itself by which it may be amended; but while it remains unaltered, it must be construed now as it was understood at the time of its adoption. It is not only the same in words, but the same in meaning, and delegates the same powers to the government, and reserves and secures the same rights and privileges to the citizen; and as long as it continues to exist in its present form, it speaks not only in the same words, but with the same meaning and intent with which it spoke when it came from the hands of its framers, and was voted on and adopted by the people of the United States. Any other rule of construction would abrogate the judicial character of this court, and make it the mere reflex of the popular opinion or passion of the day. This court was not created by the Constitution for such purposes.[6]

In a case decided in the centennial year of the Constitution's framing, the Court again claimed to believe in a Constitution of fixed meaning. Justice Samuel F. Miller for the Court advised that no one ought ever forget that when construing the Constitution, "we are to place ourselves as nearly as possible in the condition of the men who framed that instrument."[7] In 1905 the Court, speaking through Justice David Brewer, approvingly quoted Taney's *Dred*

Scott statement to support the view that because the Constitution is written, "its meaning does not alter. That which it meant when adopted, it means now."[8] Brewer had earlier explained, however, that the unchangeability of the Constitution did not make it a static document. As he explained:

> Constitutional provisions do not change, but their operation extends to new matters, as the modes of business and the habits of life of the people vary with each succeeding generation. The law of the common carrier is the same today as when transportation on land was by coach and wagon, and on water by canal boat and sailing vessel; yet in its actual operation it touches and regulates transportation by modes then unknown,—the railroad train and the steamship. Just so is it with the grant to the national government of power over interstate commerce. The constitution has not changed. The power is the same. But it operates to-day upon modes of interstate commerce unknown to the fathers, and it will operate with equal force upon any new modes of such commerce which the future may develop.[9]

In 1926, when the Court restated that view, Justice George Sutherland emphasized that "while the meaning of constitutional guaranties never varies, the scope of their application must expand or contract to meet the new and different conditions which are constantly coming within their field of operation." This note of realism was even accompanied by a recognition that change is ceaseless. There was little realism, however, in the distinction between the meaning of the Constitution and its application. Sutherland acknowledged the need to impart "elasticity . . . not to the *meaning*, but to the *application* of constitutional principles."[10] The Court seemed intoxicated by the fiction that it was clinging to original intent, even as it construed the Constitution to apply to a situation unforeseeable by the Framers and as to which original intent was meaningless.

When the make-believe seemed too forced eight years later, Sutherland spoke for the dissenters as he asserted that the Constitution had a fixed meaning that could not change from case to case. He quoted Taney, Cooley, and Brewer in the course of an argument that insisted on the fact that meaning is "changeless," even if its application "is extensible." The entire aim of interpreting the Constitution, he maintained, was "to discover the meaning, to ascertain and give effect to the intent of its framers and the people who adopted it."[11]

The *Blaisdell* case in which Sutherland dissented in 1934 ranks as one of the most important in which the Court has ever construed the contract clause. The case seemed to be exactly the sort for which the clause had been designed. A state enacted a stay law that prevented foreclosures on unpaid mortgages, and thus impaired the obligation of private executory contracts. But if small businessmen, independent farmers, and homeowners symbolized the American way, it was going down the drain during the Great Depression, and the emergency statute constituted an attempt to stay financial corporations from engorging themselves at the expense of the institution of individual ownership. Chief Justice Charles Evans Hughes for the Court reasoned that the prohibition in the contract clause "is not an absolute one and is not to be read with literal exactness like a mathematical formula."[12] The state might prevent its immediate and literal enforcement by a temporary and reasonable restraint "where vital public interests would otherwise suffer." Hughes refused to consider "that what the provision of the Constitution meant to the vision of that day it must mean to the vision of our time." The statement that the Constitution means today what it meant originally to its Framers "carries its own refutation," if its point is that the interpretation of the Constitution must be confined to the interpretation of its Framers. So narrow a conception, Hughes reminded, was the mischief that Chief Justice Marshall had sought to guard against in his imperishable remark, "We must never forget that it is a Constitution we are expounding."[13]

Hughes found no help in the distinction between the intended meaning of the Constitution's text and its application. Nor did he find a reason for believing, as the four dissenters did, that the contract clause had been warped by the Court's rule in favor of the state acts. In Hughes's opinion, which was based on divination, if the Framers had been confronted by the conditions of the depression of the 1930s, they would have decided as the Court did. They too would believe that although an economic emergency did not create power, it provided the opportunity for its exercise in a way that would in ordinary times have been prohibited.[14] Clearly some confusion existed in this remarkable interpretation by Hughes of the contract clause. In effect the Court added to the contract clause the words "except in emergencies." But Hughes pretended that the Court had decided as the Framers would have, if only they could have sat on the Court in 1934 and could have seen the application of the clause in the context of the conditions then existing.

The majority and minority opinions in *Blaisdell* offered two different theories of a constitutional jurisprudence based on original intent. Choosing the least spooky is not easy. In the majority opinion we have the ectoplasmic theory of original intent that summons the spirits of the Framers to give spectral evidence on how they would decide cases of the present. In the time-travel theory of original intent, the Justices imagine themselves returning to the past so that they can stand in the shoes of the Framers and pretend to know what they knew in order to apply that knowledge to decide current issues. Whether either view makes any sense is best determined by posing some twentieth-century issues and trying to decide them by both theories. Does the commerce power extend to control the production of a farmer who uses his own seed to plant a crop and consumes the entire crop on his own farm? Must government respect a woman's right to obtain an abortion in a manner prescribed by her doctor even if the unborn child might have been saved by a different surgical procedure that posed no significant health risk to the mother? Does a state violate the establishment clause if it imposes on public school pupils a moment of silence for meditation or if it gives to parochial schools instructional aids, such as movie projectors, globes, and wordprocessors, for use by the students? Is the separation of powers doctrine violated by administrative agencies that combine legislative, executive, and judicial powers? Does requiring a motorist to submit to a sobriety test, which may result in criminal penalties, violate the right of a person not to be a witness against himself in a criminal case? These cases and almost any constitutional cases decided by the Supreme Court do not lend themselves to any form of mechanical or historical jurisprudence that will crank out decisions or even guides to decisions so likely true or convincing that all the Justices will agree. Simply to state real questions undermines the validity of both the ectoplasmic theory and the time-travel theory.

By whatever theory the Justices look for original intent, whether by construing the fixed Constitution by the past's standards or by conscripting the Framers into service as contemporary expositors, the Justices lack a T-square to measure the constitutionality of a government act by holding it up against original intent to see if the act and the intent square. Justice Robert H. Jackson, evincing frustration after a search for original intent, concluded with some disillusionment: "Just what our forefathers did envision, or would have envisioned had they foreseen modern conditions, must be divined from materials almost as enigmatic as the dreams Joseph was called upon to interpret for Pharaoh. A century and a half [now 200 years] of partisan debate and scholarly speculation yields no net result but only supplies more or less apt quotations from respected sources on each side of any question. They largely cancel each other."[15]

The notion that the Constitution does not change but that its application does is a product of judges schooled in the common law. Ours is a common law Constitution. Common-lawyers shun detailed codes, which become obsolete as conditions and practices and public opinion change. Chief Justice Marshall, when reminding us that the Court expounds "a *constitution*," observed that a constitution should not have the prolixity of a legal code but, rather, requires "only" that "its great outlines should be marked, its important objects designated."[16] The Constitution is a brief, elliptical document framed by men trained to believe that a few comprehensive and expansive principles, supplementing a structural description, will be infinitely adaptable and will provide a guide that can serve to answer virtually any question that might arise on a case-to-case basis. As Nathaniel Chipman stated, the principles, rules, and maxims of the English common law, as corrected by experience and adapted to American needs, was the inheritance of the Framers. "Such was the language, and such the habits of thinking, both of those who framed, and of those who ratified the constitution. To the common law we must resort to learn what is meant by a legislative, an executive, and a judicial power in government, by an impeachment, by a court of law, a jury, a Grand Jury, and indictment, and a trial by jury. The same observation will be found applicable to almost every clause of the constitution."[17]

When the Committee of Detail met to frame a document that incorporated all decisions that had been made from late May to late July, Edmund Randolph prepared guidelines. In the draft of "a fundamental constitution," he wrote, two matters deserved attention:

> 1. To insert essential principles only, lest the operations of government be clogged by rendering those provisions permanent and unalterable, which ought to be accomodated [sic] to times and events, and
> 2. To use simple and precise language, and general propositions. . . .[18]

John Marshall seized the truth when he said that the Constitution marked only the great outlines and designated only the important objectives, leaving the rest to be deduced.

Chief Justice Lemuel Shaw of Massachusetts, whom Oliver Wendell Holmes described as "our greatest magistrate,"[19] might just as well have been describing the growth of constitutional law, when he made his classic statement on the growth of the common law:

> It is one of the great merits and advantages of the common law, that, instead of a series of detailed practical rules, established by positive provisions, and adapted to the precise circumstances of particular cases, which would become obsolete and fail, when the practice and course of business, to which they apply, should cease or change, the common law consists of a few broad and comprehensive principles, founded on reason, natural justice, and enlightened public policy, modified and adapted to the circumstances of all the particular cases which fall within it. These general principles of equity and policy are rendered precise, specific, and adapted to practical use, by usage, which is the proof of their general fitness and common convenience, but still more by judicial exposition; so that, when in a course of judicial proceeding, by tribunals of the highest authority, the general rule has been modified, limited and applied, according to particular cases, such judicial exposition, when well settled and acquiesced in, becomes itself a precedent, and forms a rule of law for future cases, under like circumstances.[20]

The Constitution grows similarly, which is why it is regarded as a "living" Constitution.

To the extent that original intent analysis is static, it is hostile to the common law, which is evolutionary. Theoretically, however, in both common law and original intent analysis, every case has a preexisting law that governs its decision; the task of the judge is to find and apply that law, not make it. Judges, according to such views, merely declare what the law *is* rather than legislate or fashion public policy. The law is already there; the judges simply have to ascertain it. The law of the Constitution, especially if based on original intent, is like America before the voyages of discovery and exploration. It was there, awaiting to be discovered. Similarly, judges draw a pre-Columbian map, a false description of reality, when they draw the wrong conclusions to a question of law. If they were good judicial cartographers, they would draw the right map. In cases where they draw it wrongly, the right law remains to be discovered and likely will be sooner or later. Advocates of original intent analysis believe original intent describes the right map. They position themselves to make a powerful appeal to the wisdom of the Framers as the only creditable basis for overruling important Supreme Court decisions that they despise. They blame judicial activism, but only when it conflicts with their policy preferences.

That judges should merely declare but not make law is one of the tritest of the legal fictions that clutter our thinking about the Constitution and judicial review. People who condemn judicial activism because it reflects judge-made law usually dislike particular results of judge-made law. They fail to understand that common-lawyers framed and ratified the Constitution and that common law is judge-made law. They unrealistically assume that the members of the Supreme Court can merely declare and not make law. They think that because the Constitution is written and must mean something, the prejudices and preconceptions of the Justices will supplant the Constitution, for practical purposes, if the text of the document is not construed in the light of original intent.

The text *is* what counts, but the notion that it must be construed according to original intent is itself a prejudice. It is, moreover, a notion that lacks original intent. That is, no evidence, not a shred, exists to show that the Framers meant, wanted, or expected future generations to construe the Constitution as they, the Framers, had. Nor is there any evidence to show that they expected the future to be bound by the past. Rather, they expected the future to interpret the Constitution as best it could, just as the development of the common law was left open. The text of the Constitution declares it to be the supreme law of the land together with treaties and laws made in pursuance of the Constitution. By binding state courts to follow the supreme law and by extending the judicial power of the United States to that law, the Constitution obligates courts to expound its meaning. In that regard the intention of the Convention clearly appears in the Constitution itself. As Hamilton wrote in *The Federalist* #22, the "true import" of treaties and laws that constitute the supreme law of the land must "be ascertained by judicial determination."[21] Madison, who blew hot and cold on judicial review and defended the right of the President and Congress to decide constitutional questions for themselves, acknowledged that "in the ordinary course of government, . . . the exposition of the laws and Constitution devolves upon the judicial."[22]

Unlike John Locke, an inept constitution-maker who believed that written statements of the fundamental law must, like the laws of the universe, be immutable to be eternal, the Framers of the Constitution recognized the need for plasticity and the inevitability of change. Locke once wrote a constitution for the Carolinas expressly providing that "every part thereof, shall be and remains the sacred and unalterable form and rule of government, for Carolina forever." As insurance he prohibited "all manner of comments and expositions."[23]

For the most part the Convention designed the Constitution with the utmost diligence and attention to detail. Almost always the Constitution is explicit. The Convention chose words with craft and craftsmanship, on the whole. That is the reason that constitutional law does not involve the bulk of the Constitution. It does not have to be litigated because it is clear and understandable. Consequently, one who carefully reads the Constitution finds startling the occasional vagueness and ambiguities, such as the provision requiring no "capitation, and other direct tax" unless apportioned among the states on the basis of population. Although we believe that the Framers regarded as direct taxes only taxes imposed on people per capita and on land,[24] they did not say so. Because the Constitution is overwhelmingly a model of precision and pithiness, an open-ended phrase like "other direct tax" must have been deliberate.

That phrase appears in the midst of a list of prohibitions. The Constitution clearly describes the three branches of the national government but seems to waffle when describing some prohibitions, some powers, and some rights. As to them we find ambiguities and vagueness. During the ratification controversy, Anti-Federalists lambasted the Constitution because of its lack of clarity in crucial respects. They feared that uncertainty in meaning would sap states' rights and civil rights. The "necessary and proper" clause was their particular *bête noire*. Even Edmund Randolph, who had introduced the Virginia Plan at the Convention (Congress "ought to be impowered to . . . legislate in all cases to which the separate States are incompetent, or in which the harmony of the United States may be interrupted" by state acts[25]), stated during the ratification controversy that he objected to the necessary and proper clause because "the clause is ambiguous."[26] In *The Federalist #37*, Madison sought to answer the ambiguity charge leveled at many clauses when he wrote:

> All new laws, though penned with the greatest technical skill and passed on the fullest and most mature deliberation, are considered as more or less obscure and equivocal, until their meaning be liquidated and ascertained by a series of particular discussions and adjudications. Besides the obscurity arising from the complexity of objects and the imperfection of the human faculties, the medium through which the conceptions of men are conveyed to each other adds a fresh embarrassment. The use of words is to express ideas. Perspicuity, therefore, requires not only that the ideas should be distinctly formed, but that they should be expressed by words distinctly and exclusively appropriate to them. But no language is so copious as to supply words and phrases for every complex idea, or so correct as not to include many equivocally denoting different ideas. Hence it must happen that however accurately objects may be discriminated in themselves, and however accurately the discrimination may be considered, the definition of them may be rendered inaccurate by the inaccuracy of the terms in which it is delivered. And this unavoidable inaccuracy must be greater or less, according to the complexity and novelty of the objects defined. When the Almighty himself condescends to address mankind in their own language, his meaning, luminous as it must be, is rendered dim and doubtful by the cloudy medium through which it is communicated.

Here, then, are three sources of vague and incorrect definitions:

indistinctness of the object, imperfection of the organ of conception, inadequateness of the vehicle of ideas. Any one of these must produce a certain degree of obscurity. The convention, in delineating the boundary between the federal and State jurisdictions, must have experienced the full effect of them all.

To the difficulties already mentioned may be added the interfering pretentions of the larger and smaller States. . . . The real wonder is that so many difficulties should have been surmounted, and surmounted with a unanimity almost as unprecedented as it must have been unexpected.[27]

Another signer of the Constitution, Abraham Baldwin of Georgia, confronted the issue of ambiguity as a member of the Congress that debated Jay's Treaty. Baldwin declared:

He would begin it by the assertion, that those few words in the Constitution on this subject, were not those apt, precise, definite expressions, which irresistibly brought upon them the meaning which he had been above considering. He said it was not to disparage the instrument, to say that it had not definitely, and with precision, absolutely settled everything on which it had spoken. He had sufficient evidence to satisfy his own mind that it was not supposed by the makers of it at the time, but that some subjects were left a little ambiguous and uncertain. It was a great thing to get so many difficult subjects definitely settled at once. If they could all be agreed in, it would compact the Government. The few that were left a little unsettled might, without any great risk, be settled by practice or by amendments in the progress of the Government. He believed this subject of the rival powers of legislation and Treaty was one of them; the subject of the Militia was another, and some question respecting the Judiciary another. When he reflected on the immense difficulties and dangers of that trying occasion—the old Government prostrated, and a chance whether a new one could be agreed on—the recollection recalled to him nothing but the most joyful sensations that so many things had been so well settled, and that experience had shown there was very little difficulty or danger in settling the rest.[28]

Although the Framers were masters of the art of the possible, sometimes their compromises led to cloudy language; sometimes they could not compromise and deliberately left the phrasing of a proposition open-ended to avoid still greater offense by spelling out something better left only partially said.

Ambiguity and vagueness crop up in the nonstructural sections of the Constitution. Ambiguous words permit different understandings, while vague words do not allow for much understanding. The exceptions clause of Article III is a good example of the Constitution's ambiguity. Does it mean that Congress may switch appellate jurisdiction to original jurisdiction, as counsel for Marbury thought, thereby adding to the Court's original jurisdiction, or does it mean, as Marshall thought, that the original jurisdiction is fixed? If Congress may diminish the Court's appellate jurisdiction, how far may Congress go, and how can the Court exercise the jurisdiction specified in Article III as belonging to the judicial power of the United States?[29]

Another illustration of ambiguity is in Article I, section 8, on the tax power. Is that power limited by the specified purposes of paying the debts and providing for the common defense and general welfare? Does the clause authorize a spending power? What are the limitations, if any, on the spending power? What, indeed, does "general welfare" mean? Nothing in the Constitution is more ambiguous in meaning than the "general welfare."

The term "in pursuance of" in Article VI, the supremacy clause, is also ambiguous. That term is usually taken to mean that for acts of Congress to be constitutional, they must be consistent with the Constitution; but at the time of the Framers, the term, as appears from the text of the Articles of Confederation also suggested "under authority of" or "done in prosecution of."[30]

A good example of ambiguity is the term "establishment of religion," which its author, James Madison, used interchangeably with "religious establishment." That connotes an institution of religion such as a church or sectarian school, which carries no implication of government aid to or involvement with religion. When Madison quoted the clause as if it outlawed religious establishments, he meant that the government had no authority to legislate on religion or its institutions.[31] Whatever he and Congress meant, the phrase "establishment of religion" has no self-evident meaning. History supplies its meaning, yet historians differ.[32]

The term "freedom of the press" constitutes another ambiguity. In Anglo-American thought and law it meant an exemption from prior restraints and did not exclude liability under the criminal law for seditious, obscene, or blasphemous libels. On the other hand, the Framers, who did not adopt or reject the definition of the common law, knew only a rasping, corrosive, and licentious press. They did not likely use the term "freedom of the press" without intending to protect the freedom that in fact existed and that they knew.[33] The text itself surely lacks clarity. It declares in absolute terms that Congress shall make no law abridging the freedom of speech or press, but the copyright clause authorizes Congress to make laws that do abridge the freedom of speech and press of those who would infringe copyrights.

In some instances an opposite kind of problem occurs: The text is utterly clear but because of its inappropriate specificity, it does not mean what it says. It cannot be taken literally because it was not meant literally. Some advocates of original intent assert that the Justices should not "depart from the literal provisions of the Constitution."[34] But the Justices cannot perpetuate the Constitution by a literal interpretation of its provisions, even if it meant what it says, because it does not say nearly enough to be applied literally. An example of its inadequacy as a document to be taken literally is the copyright clause in Article I, section 8, which empowers Congress "to promote the progress of science and useful arts, by securing for limited times to authors and inventors the exclusive right to their respective writings and discoveries." Only "authors and inventors"? Original intent analysis leads nowhere, because the records of the Convention show nothing, and the ratification debates do not assist either. A literal interpretation of the text would deny copyright protection to artists, sculptors, cartographers, composers, industrial designers, and photographers, and would deny protection to theatrical productions, TV and radio programming, and computer software systems. If the only people to receive the protection of the clause were authors and inventors, they could not assign a copyright to others.

The Fifth Amendment's self-incrimination clause cannot be taken literally, either, for three reasons. First, if it meant what it said, it meant little when it was framed, because defendants had no right to give sworn testimony for or against themselves; they were regarded as incompetent because of the temptation to perjury. Second, the clause protected the right only in criminal cases, but the right existed in civil as well as criminal cases, and in nonjudicial proceedings such as grand jury and legislative investigations. Third, a person may be compelled to be a witness against himself in noncriminal ways; at the time of the adoption of the Bill of Rights, the right protected a person from being forced to expose himself to public infamy. In 1892 the Supreme Court acknowledged that the constitutional clause does not mean what it says; the Court declared, "It is impossible that the meaning of the constitutional provision can only be that a person shall not be compelled to be a witness against himself in a criminal prosecution against himself."[35]

Another example of the Framers not having meant what they said appears in the Sixth Amendment, which enumerated a variety of rights of the criminally accused, available to them "in all criminal prosecutions." "All" is an absolute that admits no exceptions. Yet, the Framers did not intend to extend the right to trial by jury to misdemeanants; persons accused of petty crimes were tried in a more summary manner than trial by jury. As Felix Frankfurter and Thomas G. Corcoran wrote, "Certain it is that the framers did not mean to provide for jury trials in criminal cases under the new government beyond the established practice in their various states. The exclusion of 'petty offense' had been, as we have seen, the accepted doctrine of the colonies and thereafter in the states"— and, thereafter, under the Constitution.[36] Yet the Sixth Amendment is not the only provision of the Constitution that guarantees trial by jury in "all" criminal cases. Article III, section 2, of the original text (without the Bill of Rights) does so, too: "The trial of all crimes, except in cases of impeachment, shall be by jury. . . ." Misdemeanants are still not entitled to trial by jury unless they can be imprisoned for more than six months.[37]

Still another Sixth Amendment guarantee, the right to the assistance of counsel in all criminal prosecutions, does not mean what it says: "In all criminal prosecutions, the accused . . . shall have the assistance of counsel." "Shall" conveys an imperative. But the amendment merely meant that one might have counsel if he could afford it. Nevertheless, an act of Congress passed in 1790 required the appointment of counsel on request in all capital cases.[38] It was not until 1932 that indigents received the benefit of court-appointed counsel in capital cases in the state courts.[39] In 1938 all federal defendants received that right to court-appointed counsel in any criminal prosecution.[40] In 1963 the Supreme Court extended that right to all felony defendants in state prosecutions and in 1972

338   Constitutional Jurisprudence of Original Intent—I

to misdemeanants, if they could be imprisoned on conviction.[41] Juveniles have long been deprived of the right to trial by jury, and no one may be represented by counsel before a grand jury, which initiates a criminal prosecution.

Inappropriate specificity appears also in the double jeopardy clause of the Fifth Amendment: "Nor shall any person be subject for the same offense to be twice put in jeopardy of life or limb." In this clause the Framers neither said what they meant nor meant what they said. They should have said "life or liberty," for one cannot be imprisoned if tried by the same jurisdiction for the same offense, after having been acquitted. The reference to jeopardy of limb is a dead letter. We have long ceased to tear people apart. One cannot be put in jeopardy of the loss of limb even if convicted by due process of law. The double jeopardy clause is framed in such a way, however, as to imply that conviction can result in loss of limb. That would surely constitute a violation of the Eighth Amendment's guarantee against "cruel and unusual punishment." Those who favor the constitutionality of the death penalty against claims based on the Eight Amendment base their reasoning on the Fifth Amendment. It implies that capital punishment may be inflicted. If one is not exposed to double jeopardy, his life may be taken. If he received due process his life may be taken. But, even if he is not exposed to double jeopardy, his limb cannot be taken. But if his limb cannot be taken, why can his life be taken? Perhaps because the Fifth Amendment also provides for indictment by grand jury if a person may be tried for a capital crime. One cannot be sure, however, because the text of the Fifth Amendment, even when seemingly explicit, is not really clear. Nevertheless, the text aside, overwhelming evidence shows that the Framers and ratifiers approved of the death penalty for certain offenses.[42]

In addition to ambiguity and inappropriate specificity, the Constitution is vague or indefinite at significant points. Consider the term "executive power" with which the President is endowed. We know unmistakably the minimum age for a candidate, the method of election, the tenure of office, and the powers the President exercises with respect to appointments, pardons, and, for the most part, the negotiation of treaties and the command of the armed forces. But we do not know what is meant by the executive power apart from an obligation to execute the laws faithfully. We know the President can call on the armed forces to suppress rebellions or repel attacks, but doubts linger whether or not the executive power comprehends his authority to mine Nicaraguan harbors, conduct an undeclared war in Grenada, send the marines to a war zone in Lebanon, "reflag" Kuwaiti vessels, and dispatch some forty naval vessels to the Persian Gulf in combat readiness—without congressional support or a congressional declaration of war. The power of the commander-in-chief is not unlimited in the absence of hostile attack or a declaration of war; original intent analysis demonstrates that the executive power did not mean to the Framers whatever the President could get away with politically. The Constitution, which clearly delineates structure, only roughly maps the contours of power because of vagueness of its expression.

In the case of executive agreements, we do not have even a vague provision of the Constitution to construe. Nothing in the document authorizes treaty-making by the President without the advice and consent of the Senate. Nothing in the document authorizes the Congress to empower the President to make international agreements that have the force of the supreme law of the land, or authorizes them to have that force when both branches of Congress retroactively or subsequently approve of an international agreement made by the President on his own initiative. The Constitution simply does not provide for a power of the President to make international agreements on his own authority or with the approval of Congress, whether in advance of or after the fact. Nevertheless, Presidents have been making executive agreements with foreign nations throughout our history and on major matters, without successful constitutional challenge.[43] Neither the text of the Constitution nor original intent allows for an understanding of executive agreements or, for that matter, of the device of the Joint Congressional Resolution. By that device, Congress has considerably augmented its powers in foreign affairs, as when it annexed Texas and then Hawaii to circumvent the requirement of a two-thirds vote of the Senate to approve of treaties.

Congress has the power to regulate commerce among the states. Neither the national government nor a state may take life, liberty, or property without due process of law. And no state may deny to any person the equal protection of the laws. Those are the most litigated clauses in our constitutional history, because they are among the vaguest and most important. The proofs can easily be book-length as to each of the three. Learned Hand, who was one of the few truly great federal judges, believed that judges called upon to pass on questions of constitutional law should be broadly educated in history, literature, and philosophy, because in constitutional matters "everything turns upon the spirit in which he approaches the questions before him. The words he must construe are empty vessels into which he can pour nearly anything he will."[44] Similarly, Professor Felix Frankfurter observed that the Supreme Court confronts tremendous and delicate problems as its staple business. "But," he added, "the words of the Constitution on which their solution is based are so unrestricted by their intrinsic meaning or by their history or by tradition or by prior decisions that they leave the individual Justice free, if indeed they do not compel him, to gather meaning, not from reading the Constitution, but from reading life."[45] Later, Justice Frankfurter remarked, "Judicial exegesis is unavoidable with reference to an organic act like our Constitution, drawn in many particulars with purposed vagueness so as to leave room for the unfolding future."[46]

Even the seemingly specific injunctions and provisions of the Bill of Rights are vague, requiring much interpretation. The meaning of an establishment of religion may be discerned from history but not from the First Amendment. That is a fact equally true of freedom of speech and press, neither of which may be abridged. What constitutes an abridgment is not self-evidently clear. The actual problems confronted by the Court in the cases that arise are difficult enough: Does the free speech clause cover desecration of the flag, movies, picketing, filthy language, corporations, or nude dancing? The trouble begins not with the actual problems but with the text. It says "no law" shall be passed against the freedom of the press. However, copyright laws abridge that freedom; so do laws against libels, obscenity, and pornography. So do laws that punish direct and successful verbal incitements to crime. "No law"—another of the Constitution's absolutes—does not really mean no law. The First Amendment also puzzles us because it says that freedom of the press may not be abridged, but about religion it merely says that the free exercise thereof shall not be prohibited. If any part of the Bill of Rights is cherished more than freedom of speech and press, it is religious liberty. We cannot explain why the Framers failed to say that it too cannot be abridged or why the prohibitions in the two clauses are differently expressed. If taken literally, the free exercise of religion may be abridged in some ways short of a prohibition.

The Second Amendment is as vague as it is ambiguous. Some think it upholds the collective right of state militias to bear arms, while others, probably more accurate in so far as original intent is concerned, argue that it protects the right of individuals to keep arms.[47] Vagueness, not ambiguity, saturates the Fourth Amendment, which prohibits "unreasonable" searches and seizures and provides that no warrants shall issue "but on probable cause." "Unreasonable" and "probable" rank high on a list of indefinite terms. The amendment offers no indication whether there may be searches and seizures without warrants, and it does not suggest a remedy for violation of its terms. It is quite specific, however, with respect to its coverage: "persons, houses, papers, and effects." The Framers were familiar with eavesdropping, but made no provision for protection against it by government agents. The text does not seem to support protection against unauthorized wiretapping or electronic eavesdropping, to which the Court has extended the amendment.[48]

What is the meaning of "infamous crimes" referred to by the Fifth Amendment, and what is the meaning of its provision that no person can be compelled to be a witness against himself in a criminal case? When does a criminal case begin? What about civil cases and nonjudicial cases such as legislative investigations? What is the meaning of "limb" in the Fifth Amendment? What is the process of law that is "due" to anyone who might be denied life, liberty, or property? What is a "public use" and "just compensation"? Do the many rights of the Sixth Amendment really extend to "all" criminal prosecutions? What is a criminal prosecution and at what point do Sixth Amendment rights come into play? What is a "speedy" trial or an "impartial" jury, and what does the assistance of counsel mean? What is "excessive" bail or an "excessive" fine? Is there a right to bail? What punishments are "cruel and unusual"? What are the unenumerated rights protected by the Ninth Amendment? What are the "privileges and immunities" of United States citizenship? What is the meaning of "the equal protection of the law"?

All these provisions of the Bill of Rights and of the Fourteenth Amendment are vague. Judge Learned Hand remarked:

> Here, history is only a feeble light, for these rubrics were meant to answer future problems unimagined and unimaginable. Nothing which by the utmost liberality can be called interpretation describes the process by which they must be applied. Indeed if law be a command for specific conduct, they are not law at all; they are cautionary warnings against intemperance of faction and the first approaches of despotism. The answer to the questions which they raise demand the approach and balancing of human values which there are no scales to weigh.[49]

The imprecision of the text of the Constitution's litigated provisions makes "strict construction" a faintly ridiculous concept. Ambiguity cannot be strictly construed. The Constitution is indeed, as Jefferson said in exasperation, "merely a thing of wax that the Judiciary may twist and shape into any form they please."[50] Unlike Humpty Dumpty, the Framers could not make words mean what they wanted them to mean. "When *I* use a word," Humpty Dumpty said, in rather a scornful tone, "it means just what I choose it to mean—neither more nor less." "The question is," said Alice, "whether you *can* make words mean so many different things." "The question is," said Humpty Dumpty, "which is to be master—that's all."[51] The Framers sensed that America would change beyond their grasp. They did not think that they could master the future. At the Pennsylvania ratifying convention, James Wilson announced, "We are representatives, sir, not merely of he present age, but of future times; not merely of the territory along the sea-coast, but of regions immensely extended westward."[52] That is the reason that the Convention accepted the advice of Edmund Randolph and kept the Constitution focused on "essential principles . . . which ought to be accomodated [sic] to times and events."[53]

The Framers were not perfect. They made mistakes or, perhaps, did not really expect to be taken literally, when they provided for jury trial in "all" cases of crime, or when they referred to "limb" in the double jeopardy clause, or when they used "no prohibition thereof" instead of "no abridgment thereof," or when they said "Congress shall make no law," or when they ineptly phrased the self-incrimination clause. But they did not make many mistakes of draftsmanship. They were capable of using words with extraordinary care and of spelling out what could not be left to deduction or to the future, as in the state imposts clause. Note first that they authorized Congress to make all laws "necessary and proper" for carrying into execution the delegated powers. If by "necessary" they had meant "indispensable" or something without which the delegated power would have been rendered nugatory, they could have used more exact language. Compare, for example, the specificity of the exception in the clause banning state imposts: "No state shall, without the consent of the Congress, lay any imposts, or duties on imports or exports, except what may be absolutely necessary for executing its inspection law. . . ." The distinction between "necessary" and "absolutely necessary" shows a capacity for precise qualification. A comparison between the detailed treason clause and the brief free press clause shows that the Framers meant to govern the subject of treason as closely as possible, keeping the crime tightly constrained and emancipated from its loose common law usage, but they were content merely to endorse the principle of a free press, making its emancipation from common law restraints possible but not inevitable. They knew what they were doing.

Edward S. Corwin offered an explanation of the reason they seemed so clear in some respects and not in others. But it was not a reason grounded in original intent analysis; it was not based on historical evidence at all. Corwin deduced his theory from the pattern of Supreme Court opinions. He wrote:

> [I]t will be generally found that words which refer to governing institutions, like "jury," "legislature," "election," have been given their strictly historical meaning, while words defining the subject-matter of power and of rights like "commerce," "liberty," "property," have been deliberately moulded to the views of contemporary [the date of decision] society. Nor is the reason for this difference hard to discover. Not only are the words of the former category apt to have the more definite, and so more easily ascertainable, historical denotation, but the Court may even warrantably feel that if the people wish to have their governmental institutions altered, they should go about the business in accordance with the forms laid down by the basic institution [amendment process]. Questions of power or right, on the other hand, are apt to confront the Court with problems that are importunate for solution.[54]

Although Corwin did not advance the theory as historically founded on the intent of the Framers, it might seem to be a plausible theory if only it also indicated why history should stop in 1789. The theory does not explain why the terms in the Constitution that had a historical meaning should possess in perpetuity only the historical meaning known to the Framers. That seems as arbitrary as saying that Magna Carta must mean only what it meant to its framers in view of the fact that we can assess the historical meanings of its terms.

Finding proof that an "adaptive interpretation," in Corwin's phrase, should be followed for terms dealing with powers and rights is difficult. Finding proof that the Framers "deliberately" provided those terms so that future generations might mold them to their needs is still more difficult to demonstrate, even if true. But, of course, Corwin meant that the Court, not the Framers, employed an "adaptive interpretation" and "deliberately moulded" rights and powers to suit those needs. In fact, at the time that Corwin wrote in 1926, proof that the Court had molded or even protected rights would have been difficult to establish, depending on the rights chosen for illustration. Even today, when the incorporation doctrine has achieved unshakable acceptance by the Court, so that the states are obligated to observe most provisions of the Bill of Rights, the Court still employs double standards. It requires the United States to observe the Sixth Amendment right to trial by jury as meaning a unanimous verdict of twelve jurors, while it allows the states to use nonunanimous verdicts by juries of less than twelve.[55] Similarly, the Seventh Amendment and the grand jury provision of the Fifth Amendment apply to the United States only, not to the states.[56] Nor is it clear that all terms of the Constitution with a "strictly historical meaning" continue to have a fixed meaning. Still less is it clear why the amendment process is appropriate for altering the meaning of such terms but should give way to judicial revision of the meaning of some rights and powers in the face of "problems that are importunate for solution."

Justice Frankfurter advanced a theory similar to Corwin's to explain decisions that retained a static Constitution in some respects and an evolutionary one in others. In a 1946 opinion, he wrote:

> Broadly speaking, two types of constitutional claims come before this Court. Most constitutional issues derive from the broad standard of

fairness written into the Constitution (e.g., "due process," "equal protection of the laws," "just compensation"), and the division of power as between States and Nation. Such questions, by their very nature, allow a relatively wide play for individual legal judgment. The other class gives no such scope. For this second class of constitutional issues derives from very specific provisions of the Constitution. These had their source in definite grievances and led the Fathers to proscribe against recurrence of their experience. These specific grievances and the safeguards against their recurrence were defined by the Constitution. They were defined by history. Their meaning was so settled by history that definition was superfluous. Judicial enforcement of the Constitution must respect these historic limits. The prohibition of bills of attainder falls of course among these very specific constitutional provisions.[57]

The trouble with Frankfurter's theory is that it assumes, wrongly, that the second class of terms had a meaning so settled by history that their definition was superfluous. On the contrary, the definition of some, such as the right of a person not to give evidence against himself, was nearly impossible because they were still evolving in meaning.[58] Despite Frankfurter's remark about federal relations allowing an open-endedness or wide play in interpretation, the right to trial by jury, as indicated, remains rigidly fixed in federal cases but not in state cases.

Bills of attainder, which Frankfurter instanced as a specific and unchanging provision of the Constitution, had changed in meaning, as shown by the very case in which Frankfurter described his theory.[59] In that case, Congress had passed a rider to an appropriations bill, prohibiting the payment to three named federal officials who were suspected of being "subversives." The Court found that rider to be an unconstitutional bill of attainder, because it "accomplishes the punishment of named individuals without a judicial trial."[60] Frankfurter's opinion sounded like that of the dissenters in the 1867 *Test Oath Cases*, where the Court defined a bill of attainder as a legislative act that inflicted punishment without a judicial trial and held unconstitutional state and federal acts imposing loyalty oaths that disqualified persons who had been pro-Confederate from pursuing their professions. The offensive statutes named no individuals as guilty, did not designate their conduct as criminal, and did not inflict a punishment known to the common law, which recognized as a punishment only loss of life, limb, liberty, or property.[61] Yet, the history of bills of attainder suggested no reason that it had come to a static meaning as of 1789.

Blackstone's *Commentaries* had suggested that punishments might include exile, deportation, and even "a disability of holding offices . . ."[62] Hamilton, in an essay of 1783, had also laid a basis for the expansion of the concept of a bill of attainder (or bill of pains and penalties in cases less than death) when protesting against New York legislation that penalized Loyalists. He condemned exculpatory test oaths as obligating a citizen to establish his own innocence to avoid the penalty imposed for failure or inability to take the test oath. The oath had been invented, he argued, to disqualify persons; he called it "an inquisition into mens [sic] consciences," a violation of the presumption of innocence and of the right to trial by jury. The oath also subverted the spirit of the constitution of a free society by declaring classes of people disfranchised and disqualified from the rights enjoyed by others. No person "should lose his rights without a hearing and conviction before a proper tribunal," Hamilton asserted.[63] The evidence drawn from him and Blackstone shows that bills of attainder were still evolving in meaning when the Constitution was framed. Its framing, contrary to Corwin and Frankfurter, did not hold the sun and moon at pause with respect to changing meanings of its historical or common law terms.

Frankfurter relied again on his two-clause theory in a case of 1949, which involved federal court jurisdiction. He took note of the fact that Article III, describing federal jurisdiction, is "explicit and specific" to the point of precision, in "striking contrast to the imprecision" of other provisions of the Constitution. The difference between the two types of clauses was not the result of "chance or ineptitude on the part of the Framers," he explained:

> The differences in subject-matter account for the drastic differences in treatment. Great concepts like "Commerce . . . among the several States," "due process of law," "liberty," "property," were purposely left to gather meaning from experience. For they relate to the whole domain of social and economic fact, and the statesmen who founded this Nation knew too well that only a stagnant society remains unchanged. But when the Constitution in turn gives strict definition of power or specific limitations upon it we cannot extend the definition

or remove the translation. Precisely because "it is *a constitution* we are expounding," we ought not to take liberties with it.[64]

Madison's Notes of the Convention contain no hint that the Framers designed two types of clauses, nor do his Notes suggest that the Framers were composing "strict definitions" that would make the Constitution freeze the past rather than allow it to serve as a guide for the future. In the case before the Court in which Frankfurter, dissenting, repeated his two-clause theory, the issue of jurisdiction that he thought was so clearly governed by the specificity of the words in Article III dealt with suits between citizens of different states. The District of Columbia is not a state, but the Court majority sustained an act of Congress extending the jurisdiction of the federal courts to such suits if one party was a citizen living in the District of Columbia.

Frankfurter could not accept the constitutionality of the act of Congress, although the people of the District possessed various constitutional rights even if they were not citizens of a state. Moreover, other terms as specific as "state" had evolved in meaning. The Court had long ago extended the word "citizen" to include corporations in diversity suits.[65] Corporations had also become "persons" for the purpose of benefiting from the due process and equal protection clauses of the Fourteenth Amendment and from the Fourth Amendment.[66] Given the flexibility of such supposedly specific words, few words in the Constitution seem exempt from changes in their meaning, just as few seem bound by the meaning of 1789. Zechariah Chafee observed that the Constitution is not what its Framers knew; it is, rather, "the words they gave us for meeting the needs of our own time. The bill of attainder clause is not imprisoned by the past any more than the power to regulate 'Commerce.' Congress is not obliged to let railroads alone because the only transportation in 1787 was by oxen, horses, and breezes."[67]

Constitutional terms that were very specific and had historical definitions, like "citizen," "jury," and "bill of attainder," took on the deposit of new meaning. Still others, specific and historical, also possessed a dynamism. They included habeas corpus, ex post facto laws, impeachment, cruel and unusual punishment, and the right not to have to give evidence against oneself. The historian of habeas corpus, William F. Duker, noted that many of his predecessors made the mistake (like Frankfurter) of viewing history "as an event rather than as a process and therefore have failed to take note of the most striking characteristic of the writ of habeas corpus: like liberty itself, the writ is the product of continuous creation."[68] It was changing when the Convention met in Philadelphia; it has changed since. Blackstone described how the idea of cruel punishment had undergone substantial change, from the infliction of death by disemboweling, beheading, and quartering to the imposition of merely ignominious punishment such as the stocks and ducking stool.[69] In noncapital cases, the ban on cruel and unusual punishments has extended to disproportionate or excessive punishments for a particular crime,[70] to depriving a person of citizenship,[71] and to punishing a person for being a drug addict.[72] The arguments made by Blackstone and Hamilton against legislative declarations of guilt and punishment apply with equal force to the concept of ex post facto laws when the attainder, or bill of pains and penalties, deprived people of rights for conduct not criminal at the time engaged in or for past opinions. Further proof that ex post facto laws lacked one fixed meaning at the time of the adoption of the Constitution consists of the fact that during the Framers' generation, many people thought that retroactive civil laws also constituted ex post facto laws.[73] Finally, the common law by no means controlled the meaning of impeachment in America. The American meaning was dynamic, not static, and the history that influenced it was not British but American. Peter Charles Hoffer and N. E. H. Hull, in their splendid book on impeachment, have conclusively demonstrated that "its American shape" not only restricted impeachment for crimes committed in office; it also reformed the definition of impeachable offenses, restricted the penalty on conviction to removal and disqualification from office, and required a two-thirds majority vote for conviction. The United States "republicanized" the impeachment process. Moreover, the meaning of impeachment was still fluid when the Constitution was adopted.[74]

The two-clause theory simply buckles under critical scrutiny. The words and phrases of the Constitution, especially if derived from the common law, have been evolutionary, like the common law itself, and were in process of changing at the time of the framing. In a bill of attainder case of 1910, Justice Joseph McKenna for the Court stated that the attainder clause could not have been intended to prohibit only practices known to the Stuarts or "to prevent only an exact repetition of history." McKenna added:

> Time works changes, brings into existence new conditions and purposes. Therefore a principle, to be vital, must be capable of wider application than the mischief which gave it birth. This is peculiarly true of constitutions. They are not ephemeral enactments, designed to meet passing occasions. They are, to use the words of Chief Justice Marshall, "designed to approach immortality as nearly human institutions can approach it." The future is their care, and provision for events of good and bad tendencies of which no prophecy can be made. In the application of a constitution therefore, our contemplation cannot be only of what had been but of what *may be*. Under any other rule a constitution would indeed be as easy of application as it would be deficient in efficacy and power. Its general principles would have little value, and be converted by precedent into impotent and lifeless formulas. Rights declared in words might be lost in reality. And this has been recognized. The meaning and vitality of the Constitution have developed against narrow and restrictive construction.[75]

When the Framers were ambiguous or vague, the likely reason is that they meant to be. They intended their ambiguity and vagueness to be pregnant with meaning for unborn generations, rather than be restricted to whatever meaning then existed. We must look for the purpose they sought to achieve in a clause, not in their application of it. We must look for the principle implicit in their text, not for something to be revealed in an analysis of their practices. The Constitution defines and limits power, not rights. It is a point of departure for fulfilling the fundamental maxim of the preamble of the Declaration of Rights: "governments are instituted among men to secure these rights." The Constitution also is a point of departure for fulfilling the ends mentioned in its own Preamble. Thus, when the Framers left a crucial term wide open, as in "unreasonable search," "probable cause," "freedom of speech," "excessive bail," and "cruel and unusual punishment," they probably chose words deliberatively, leaving room for the widest possible interpretation.

CHAPTER SIXTEEN

A Constitutional Jurisprudence of Original Intent? Part Two

*I*n crucial respects, the Constitution resembles Martin Chuzzlewit's grandnephew who, Dickens said, "had no more than the first idea and sketchy notion of a face." The Framers had a genius for studied imprecision and calculated ambiguity. They relied on generalized terms because common-lawyers expressed themselves that way out of conviction, because politics required compromise, and because compromise required ambiguity. The Framers formulated principles and they expressed purposes. Those principles and purposes, both explicit and implied, were meant to endure, not their Framers' understanding of them. The murkiest parts of the Constitution express principles and purposes. That is the reason that the Constitution provides very little guidance for judgment in real cases of constitutional law. And that is the reason the Supreme Court can interpret the Constitution in any way that it pleases.

The document itself, with all twenty-six amendments that have been added in two centuries, is scarcely 7,000 words long, and only about two percent of the verbiage possesses any significance in constitutional law. Almost without exception these are the ambiguous and vague terms, perhaps the purposefully or unavoidably general terms: commerce among the states, obligation of contracts, necessary and proper, bills of credit, republican form of government, due process, privileges and immunities, direct taxes, general welfare, liberty, unreasonable searches, equal protection, and the like. When the Constitution is compared with the actual cases that the Supreme Court must decide, what seems striking is the fact the document says nothing decisive, if not next to nothing, about so many subjects, the very subjects of constitutional law, which consists of the body of decisions made by the Court. What counts in constitutional law is what the Court has said about the Constitution, in nearly 500 volumes thus far. Words of crucial importance in constitutional law are not even in the Constitution, including fair trial, executive agreement, beyond reasonable doubt, the spending power, clear and present danger, cross-examination, separation of church and state, war powers, exigent circumstances, public purpose, discrete and insular minorities, separate but equal, presumption of innocence, liberty of contract, equal justice, the right to privacy, the right to travel, the right to silence, the right against self-incrimination, strict scrutiny, interstate commerce, fair return, community standards, and the police power. They are judicial glosses.

In large measure we have an unwritten constitution whose history is the history of judicial review. Commentators have made the point by comparing the work of the Supreme Court to that of a continuous constitutional convention that adapts the original charter by reinterpretation, "making its duties political in the highest sense of the word, as well as judicial."[1] Members of the Court, too, usually in dissent, have objected that the Court majority has acted like a superlegislature or a continuous constitutional convention.[2] The Court does indeed behave in some respects like a superlegislature or a continuous constitutional convention, figuratively speaking. It has no alternative. The American people prefer letting the Court adapt the Constitution rather than amending it themselves. Constitutional amendment, except occasionally, is simply an unrealistic and cumbersome if not impossible way of refreshing the Constitution.

The Constitution plays a secondary role in constitutional law because it is so concise and ambiguous, and therefore it is merely a point of departure for judicial analysis. Consider, for example, the remarks of Justices who have been nonplussed when searching for original intent in the establishment clause of the First Amendment. In 1948 Justice Robert H. Jackson wrote of the difficulty of separating the secular from the religious: "It is idle to pretend that this task is one for which we can find in the Constitution one word to help us as judges to decide where the secular ends and the sectarian begins in education. Nor can we find guidance in any other legal source. It is a matter on which we can find no law but our own presuppositions."[3] Similarly, Justice Byron R. White later declared:

> No one contends that he can discern from the sparse language of the Establishment Clause that a State is forbidden to aid religion in any manner or, if it does not mean that, what kind or how much aid is permissible. And one cannot seriously believe that the history of the First Amendment furnishes unequivocal answers to many of the fundamental issues of church–state relations. In the end, the courts have fashioned answers to these questions as best they can, the language of the Constitution and its history having left them a wide range of choice among many alternatives. But decision has been unavoidable; and in choosing, the courts necessarily have carved out what they deemed to be the most desirable national policy governing various aspects of church–state relationships.[4]

Whether or not Jackson and White were right about the guidance available from the Constitution or from history, the reality is that the Court exercises a freedom almost legislative in character. The Court finds itself obligated to behave like Humpty Dumpty, making words mean whatever it pleases.

Justices who look to the Constitution for more than a puzzling if majestic phrase might just as well turn to the comic strips for all the practical guidance they will find on how to decide most of the great cases that involve national public policy, whether the question relates to legislative apportionment, use immunity, pornography, nonunanimous jury verdicts, racial segregation, affirmative action, electronic eavesdropping, the regulation of utility rates, child labor, subversive activities, warrantless searches, the curtailment of crop production, the seizure of steel mills, a lawyer at lineups, places of public accommodation, the legislative veto, the length of freight trains, the exclusionary rule, government aid to parochial schools, custodial interrogation, the public's right to know, sodomy, prisoner's rights, school prayers, motion pictures, stock frauds, stop and frisk, environmental protection, commercial speech, the gold standard, abortion, sovereign immunity, cable television, social security, administrative searches, sex discrimination, agricultural production, greenbacks, mental health, Medicaid, pretrial publicity, commodity futures—the list goes on and on. The Constitution contains not one word about these or most of the subjects of considerable import with which the Court must deal. That fact, paradoxically, is a great strength of the Constitution, accounting in part for its longevity and vitality, because it allows for evolutionary adaptation to new needs.

The Court itself has explained the point on numerous occasions. In an 1877 case dealing with the telegraph, it said, in an opinion by Chief Justice Morrison R. Waite:

> The powers thus granted are not confined to the instrumentalities of commerce, or the post service known or in use when the Constitution was adopted, but they keep pace with the progress of the country, and adapt themselves to the new developments of time and circumstance. They extend from the horse with its rider to the stagecoach, from the sailing vessel to the steamboat, from the coach and the steamboat to the railroad, and from the railroad to the telegraph, as these new agencies are successively brought into use to meet the demands of increasing population and wealth. They were intended for the government of the business to which they relate at all times and under all circumstances. As they were intrusted to the General Government for the good of the nation, it is not only the right but the duty of Congress to see to it that the intercourse among the States and the transition of intelligence are not obstructed or unnecessarily incumbered by state legislation.
>
> The electric telegraph marks an epoch in the progress of time.[5]

In another case, dealing with primary elections, Justice Harlan Fiske Stone spoke for the Court, saying:

> But we are now concerned with the question whether the right to choose at a primary election, a candidate for election as representative, is embraced in the right to choose representatives secured by Article I § 2. We may assume that the framers of the Constitution

in adopting that section, did not have specifically in mind the selection and elimination of candidates for Congress by the direct primary any more than they contemplated the application of the commerce clause to interstate telephone, telegraph and wireless communication which are concededly within it. But in determining whether a provision of the Constitution applies to a new subject matter, it is of little significance that it is one with which the framers were not familiar. For in setting up an enduring framework of government they undertook to carry out for the indefinite future and in all the vicissitudes of the changing affairs of men, those fundamental purposes which the instrument itself discloses. Hence we read its words, not as we read legislative codes which are subject to continuous revision with the changing course of events, but as the revelation of the great purposes which were intended to be achieved by the Constitution as a continuing instrument of government. . . . If we remember that "it is a Constitution we are expounding," we cannot rightly prefer, of the possible meanings of its words, that which will defeat rather than effectuate the Constitutional purpose.[6]

The broad statements by Waite and Stone raise the question whether any statable limits exist to the adaptability of the Constitution. Are the rules of construction limiting? Alexander Hamilton, James Madison, and Elbridge Gerry, Framers of diverse constitutional opinions, agreed that the Constitution should be construed by the usual rules of interpreting documents such as statutes. Similarly, Thomas Jefferson and John Marshall, Founding Fathers who had not been at the Philadelphia Convention, also agreed that the Constitution should be interpreted that way.[7] That people of such different opinions agreed on how to construe the Constitution seems like an extraordinary fact, until one realizes that in the application of the ordinary rules of construction they reached strikingly different results. That fact suggests that in constitutional law there are simply no legal rules that are objective, or neutral, or value free, enabling judges to apply those rules in the same way to reach the same decisions. The rules themselves, as Oliver Wendell Holmes explained, reflect considerations of public policy and social advantage.[8] At the very least those rules are slippery and contradictory, allowing for diverse constructions. The rules do not govern judicial choice.

Karl N. Llewellyn stated forty-seven rules for each of which he provided an opposite.[9] Llewellyn focused on the common law rules governing the interpretation of statutes, which are generally the same rules governing interpretation of the Constitution. The rules governing the interpretation of statutes have produced some significant constitutional decisions.

For example, the Court has held that an act of Congress authorizing the Court to issue writs of mandamus in cases warranted by the principles and usages of the law means that Congress has added to the Court's original jurisdiction, which the statute did not mention.[10] The Court has also held that a statute making criminal "all" combinations and conspiracies in restraint of trade applies only to "unreasonable" combinations and conspiracies, though "unreasonable" does not appear in the statute, which makes no exceptions.[11] The Court has additionally ruled that the Clayton Act of 1914, which trade unions proclaimed to be organized labor's Magna Carta because it exempted unions from the Sherman Anti-Trust Act, did not exempt labor from the Sherman Anti-Trust Act.[12] And, the Court held unconstitutional an entire statute because one of its parts was unconstitutional, despite the fact that the act of Congress explicitly provided for wholly different administrative mechanisms for its different parts and stated that the unconstitutionality of one part should not taint the other part.[13] The Court has construed the Constitution with the same fidelity that it has demonstrated for the language of acts of Congress, despite rules of construction that mandate observance of the plain meaning of words. In effect, the rules emancipate the judges from the Constitution in the sense of giving them an opportunity to interpret the Constitution as they wish. Rules free; they do not fetter.

One rule of particular relevance here is that the text, not the intent of its authors, should govern, especially if the text is clear. We must remember that the Framers rejected original intent interpretation.[14] Original intent is a fallback position for a judge who is construing the meaning of a statute. Presumably its framers might explain its meaning and objective, although James Kent, Joseph Story, and Thomas M. Cooley laid down caveats in that regard.[15] In the case of the Constitution, however, unlike that of a statute, its ratifiers could not know original intent, except as revealed by participants, and they radically differed, as was shown by the positions of Madison, George Mason, and Edmund Randolph during the Virginia ratifying convention. The Convention proposed no more than a text, and the ratifiers adopted only that text, not original intent. As we have seen, the text creates enormous problems. Not even the basic rule—follow the text when it is plain— can be relied on. Consider, once more, that "writings and inventions" include more than that, that "no law" does not always mean "no law" in the First Amendment, that "criminal case" in the Fifth Amendment can mean a civil case or a legislative hearing, and that "all" in the Sixth Amendment has exceptions. Consider, too, that for decades the Court construed "commerce among the states" to mean "commerce between the states" or "commerce crossing state lines," rather than "commerce within the states."[16] The text cannot be a reliable anchor if the Constitution does not necessarily mean what it plainly says.

Plainly it says that no state shall impair the obligation of a contract, and equally plain is the fact that the Framers omitted a comparable ban on the United States. However, the Court has tried to sneak the substance of the contract clause into the due process clause of the Fifth Amendment, in order to prevent the United States from impairing the obligation of a contract. The Court did not care or know that Elbridge Gerry could not even get a second to his motion to include a contract clause against the United States.[17] To the same effect is a case of 1935, although the Court did not then mention the contract clause. Rather, it made the bankruptcy clause subject to the limitations of the eminent domain clause of the Fifth Amendment.[18] Either way, whether the Fifth Amendment's eminent domain or due process clause is relied on, the Court limited the plain meaning of the original Constitution by applying the subsequent amendment. No proof can be mustered to show that the Bill of Rights restricted or diminished the delegated powers. And in the eminent domain case, the Court ignored the words of the clause of the Fifth Amendment that referred to just compensation when the property is actually taken for a public use, which did not happen in the 1935 case.

In much the same way, the Court construed the due process clause of the Fifth Amendment to mean the same as, or have the same effect as, the equal protection clause of the Fourteenth Amendment.[19] The Court's construction turns the text to fungible hash and defies the meaning of words. Moreover, if the due process clause of the Fourteenth Amendment guarantees equal protection, the equal protection clause of the same amendment is superfluous. Or, the equal protection clause is redundant because it means what the due process clause of the Fifth Amendment protects. Either option is silly. If due process means equal protection and also means no law impairing the obligation of contracts, the rule against the redundancy of any part of the Constitution is meaningless.

The rules simply do not settle cases. Legal rules, legal logic, legal erudition, legal research, and legal precedents do not decide questions involving the ambiguous or vague clauses of the Constitution, the very clauses usually at issue in those cases whose outcome helps to determine justice, shape public policy, and measure the degree of liberty or equality that exists in this country. A proponent of a constitutional jurisprudence of original intent stated that original intent must make "important concessions . . . to the claims of stare decisis"—standing by precedents.[20] The magic that legal reasoning performs on precedents fascinated Mr. Dooley. He heard his advocate argue his case and learned that the decisions "were all on my side. Be hivens it looked as though they were all written with an eye to this partickler case. It didn't make anny diff'rence whether th' decision was about the capture iv fugutive slaves or consarvin' th' goold standard, it fitted onto my case as though it had been measured f'r it."[21]

Although some judges can intoxicate themselves into believing that precedents control their decisions, Justices of the Supreme Court are intellectually supple enough to find their way around encumbering precedents. They usually avoid dramatic overruling of precedents, especially if overruling might appear to be the act of personal will. No matter how subjective, decisions must not seem to look like the result of personal choice. In the art of judging, a proper regard for appearances counts. Accordingly, precedents, like rules, get their day in court. No member of the Court has ever wanted to give the impression that he did not appreciate the values of coherence, stability, and continuity with the past. Any person who reaches the highest court is sophisticated enough to understand the strategic and political values of achieving desired objectives by following rules and giving precedents their due. Overruling is a device of last resort, employed when other alternatives have failed. The Court can alter the meaning of the Constitution by reinterpreting precedents, distinguishing them away, blunting them, distorting them, even ignoring them, and thus make constitutional law over without the need of being bound by the past or of overruling. By citing precedent, the Court nourishes the impression that it is standing pat; it cultivates the illusion that it respects precedent, even when leaving precedents meaningless or moribund. Moreover, the Court always has available to it alternative principles of constitutional interpretation, broad or narrow, as well as alternative and even conflicting lines of precedent, with the result that it can draw on the rules and the precedents as needed and still have nearly complete freedom to read the Constitution.

In his poem "Law Like Love," W. H. Auden wrote:

> Law, says the judge as he looks down his nose,
> Speaking clearly and most severely,
> Law is as I've told you before,
> Law is as you know I suppose,
> Law is but let me explain it once more,
> Law is The Law.[22]

The Lord High Chancellor in *Iolanthe* might have characterized the Constitution and the Supreme Court's relation to it when he asserted, "The Law is the embodiment of everything that's excellent. It has no kind of fault or flaw, and I, my Lords, embody the Law. The constitutional guardian I. . . ."[23]

Ever since *Marbury v. Madison*, the Supreme Court has assumed that it embodies the Constitution and is its especially consecrated protector and expounder. One of the Court's prime tasks is to protect the Constitution against the unchaste or contaminating advances of government that cannot be squared with the Constitution. That task supposedly pits the Court against the principle that the will of the people is sovereign. Advocates of a constitutional jurisprudence of original intent pass themselves off as dedicated democrats who subordinate their personal policy preferences to the decisions of the people and who find judicial legislation offensive to democratic theory. They assume that departures from original intent betray the will of the people as it is expressed in the Constitution and laws made in pursuance of it. They regard judicial review as undemocratic and contrary to the will of the people. What they think of as judicial activism—subjectivity on the part of judges—is particularly repugnant to them. Indeed, they present a jurisprudence of original intent as a reflection of hostility to judicial activism. They consider themselves as exponents of judicial self-restraint. The ongoing controversy about original intent is, as a matter of fact, the latest phase of an old controversy over judicial review, matching advocates of judicial self-restraint against exponents of judicial activism.[24]

The advocates of a jurisprudence of original intent are the latest carriers of the Hoadly syndrome, *genus Americanus*. Its principal symptom is a conviction that the judgments of the representative branches of the government, which are the elected branches, should not be thwarted or superseded by the judgments of Platonic guardians who are not responsible to the electoral batallions. Related symptoms are a chronic commitment to majority rule, a trusting faith that the majority will not infringe individual or minority rights, a belief that a people with a demonstrated capacity for self-government will correct their own errors if left alone, and a sure sense that political salvation may be earned but can never be imposed from above, certainly not by the oligarchic branch of government.

The Hoadly syndrome, which is deeply Jeffersonian in its American context, may be traced to a celebrated remark by Benjamin Hoadly, the bishop of Bangor, who in 1717 observed, "Whoever hath an absolute authority to interpret any written or spoken laws, it is he who is truly the lawgiver, to all intents and purposes, and not the person who first wrote or spoke them."[25] So far as our constitutional literature is concerned, this statement was discovered by Oliver Wendell Holmes and handed down in a sort of apostolic succession to some of our greatest jurists, including Louis D. Brandeis, Learned Hand, and Felix Frankfurter, and to a distinguished succession of constitutional scholars beginning with James Bradley Thayer at the turn of this century.

Jefferson had transmitted the Hoadly syndrome. From his time and example, perceptive if jaundiced critics have advanced the grand paradox that at the very apex of our system of a government of laws and not of men, to a considerable degree we have a government by judicial supremacy. The Supreme Court, said Jefferson, is "the subtle corps of sappers and miners constantly working to undermine" the Constitution; the Court, he alleged, is "an irresponsible body," "usurping legislation . . . practicing on the

Constitution by inferences, analogies and sophisms. . . ."[26] Some of our greatest presidents have remarked on the estrangement between the Court and the popular will. Lincoln, for example, declared in his First Inaugural Address that "the candid citizen must confess that if the policy of the Government upon vital questions affecting the whole people is to be irrevocably fixed by decisions of the Supreme Court . . . the people will have ceased to be their own rulers, having to that extent practically resigned their Government into the hands of that eminent tribunal."[27]

Those who quote that statement neglect to state that Lincoln began the paragraph in which it occurs by saying that "constitutional decisions are to be decided by the Supreme Court" and that its decisions are binding. Nor do those who quote the First Inaugural Address quote the Springfield speech, made after the decision of *Dred Scott* case, when Lincoln endorsed the need to obey and respect the Court, and he added, "We think its decisions on Constitutional questions, when fully settled, should control, not only the particular cases decided, but the *general policy of the country,* subject to be disturbed only by amendments to the Constitution as provided in that instrument itself."[28] Attorney General Robert H. Jackson, who quoted Lincoln's First Inaugural out of context, argued that the Court was "anti-democratic."[29] Attorney General Edwin Meese III also conscripted Lincoln into service, quoting him out of context when making an argument that Court decisions on constitutional questions are not the supreme law of the land and do not bind anyone but the parties; any proposition to the contrary, Meese claimed in an anti-Lincolnian statement, is "at war with the Constitution, at war with the basic principles of democratic government, and at war with the very meaning of the rule of law."[30] Justice Felix Frankfurter, who perpetuated the Hoadly syndrome, described the Court's power of judicial review as "a limitation on popular government" and therefore "an undemocratic aspect" of our system; in opinions from the bench, he also called the Court's powers "uncontrollable" and "inherently oligarchic," the Court itself "the nondemocratic organ of our Government."[31]

Judicial review, according to its critics and to original intent theorists, sabotages the objectives of the electoral process, which is at the center of democratic theory and practice. Judicial review frustrates the policymaking power of the representative institutions that are the product of the electoral process. Former U.S. Court of Appeals Judge Robert H. Bork, probably the foremost theorist of a constitutional jurisprudence of original intent, has argued that "a Court that makes rather than implements value choices [of the Framers or of legislators] cannot be squared with the presuppositions of a democratic society." He concludes that the judiciary "must accept any value choice the legislature makes unless it clearly runs contrary to a choice made in the framing of the Constitution."[32]

Similarly the Chief Justice of the United States, William H. Rehnquist, the preeminent exponent of a jurisprudence of original intent, asserted that "judicial review has basically antidemocratic and antimajoritarian facets," which is the reason that the Constitution "was designed to enable the popularly elected branches of government, not the judicial branch, to keep the country abreast of the times." In a democratic society, he stated, for the nonelected judiciary to be "freewheeling" and to "second guess Congress, state legislatures, and state and federal administrative officers concerning what is best for the country" is "quite unacceptable."[33] When the Court invalidates an act of Congress, the one nonelective and nonremovable element in the government rejects the conclusions of the two elective and removable branches. But it is the Court itself, whose appointed members hold office for life and are not accountable to the electorate, that is undemocratic by comparison with the political branches and not necessarily its exercise of judicial review. Not every act of the political branches is democratic merely because they are democratic when compared to the Court. The executive order commanding the relocation and internment of American citizens of Japanese ancestry was not democratic, nor was the McCarran Internal Security Act of 1950. Never mind that the political branches may win office in elections in which a minority of eligible voters participate, or that election districts may be gerrymandered, or that people are likely to vote on the basis of personality rather than issues, or that equality of state representation in the Senate means that about 15 percent of the population can outvote the rest, or that lobbyists with big money and narrow interests influence public policy. Regardless of the imperfections of the political branches, the Court is less democratic.[34]

Although not politically responsible, the Court is hardly beyond the checks of the political branches. The President nominates and the Senate confirms appointments to the Court. Congress controls the Court's size, its funds, its staff, and even its rules of procedure. The President and Congress also control the enforcement agencies by which the Court's decisions may have to be carried out. Congress also possesses the impeachment powers and the power to diminish the Court's appellate jurisdiction. These facts make irresponsible the frequent references to "judicial supremacy" and to "government by judiciary" as characteristics of our system of government. Advocates of a jurisprudence of original intent exaggerate the powers of an undemocratic Court.

Despite the Court's supposedly prescriptive powers to compel the President, Congress, and the states to do its bidding, it cannot enforce its own decisions against lower courts, state or federal, that choose to misunderstand or be evasive, and it cannot make war, influence foreign relations, tax, spend, or do anything warranting a justification for calling it "supreme" in the sphere of policymaking. It can order racial integration of schools or reapportionment of legislatures, but its authority is moral and depends upon backup by the other branches of the government. The Court cannot prevail against their wishes or against a sustained opposition by public opinion. The very power of judicial review is itself subject to abolition or modification by constitutional amendment. But judicial puissance or faineance neither adds nor detracts from the democratic character of judicial review. Nor does judicial review become democratic because the people of this nation have acquiesced in its exercise for almost two centuries. Popular acquiescence may signify popular consent, but consent freely given, whether by referendum, legislation, or amendment, is simply not the same as the failure of the people to abolish or impair judicial review.

The strongest argument against judicial review as an undemocratic power is that when the Court checks the majority it has sapped the capacity of the people to learn from experience and to correct their own mistakes. Democracy's battles are not won in the Supreme Court; they are won in the legislatures and in the arena of public opinion. The impatient, confronted by some legislative stupidity or injustice, may scream for intervention by the judiciary, but the effect of resolving issues, in the judicial arena, even those issues concerning minority rights or personal liberty, is to lull the people into apathy on matters that are fundamentally their concern.

Comforted by the notion that courts will take care of personal and minority rights, the people are effectively deprived of the inestimable benefit of vindicating self-government by taking sober second thought. As James Bradley Thayer pointed out, in a passage quoted by Henry Steele Commager, the exercise of judicial review, "even when unavoidable is always attended with serious evil, namely, that the correction of legislative mistakes comes from the outside, and the people thus lose the political experience and the moral education and stimulus that come from fighting the question out in the ordinary way, and correcting their own errors. The tendency of a common and easy resort to this great function, now lamentably too common, is to dwarf the political capacity of the people, and to deaden its sense of moral responsibility." Commager, relying on Frankfurter, added that "education in the abandonment of foolish legislation is itself a training in liberty."[35] If courts did not exercise judicial review, majority rule would not be unbridled because our constitutional system provides for many checks and balances, as does our political system. They pit various branches and governments against each other, and various classes, sections, interests, and other groups against each other, too, at the ballot box and in the legislative halls. The resulting compromises and shifting majorities yield to public opinion. Majority rule in the United States does not mean unlimited government.

Even if judicial review is utterly undemocratic, the argument against it as thwarting popular will is almost irrelevant so far as validating a jurisprudence of original intent is concerned. Original intent is not necessarily democratic or majoritarian. A court that follows the meaning of the Framers on a contract clause or commerce clause issue neither advances nor inhibits democracy. However, following original intent on some vitally important matters, including race and sex, would likely subvert democracy. In any case, democracy should not be confounded with majority rule, which is an essential aspect of democracy but only half the equation; the other half requires obedience to minority rights and to democratic procedures. Most of the Framers probably feared and deplored democracy as a sort of direct, participatory government verging on mob rule. They did not favor government by a majority of *all* the people, but they did believe in constitutional restraints that limit the power of government and protect the rights of dissident individuals and minorities. The Constitution is chock full of limitations on majority rule. The Court can be countermajoritarian without being undemocratic.

Not even Jefferson, despite all his frothings against the Marshall Court when he was an aged, crabby localist, opposed judicial review in all respects. In 1787, after he first read the proposed Constitution, he told Madison that he liked the executive veto and would have liked it even more if the judiciary had "been associated for that purpose, or invested separately with a similar power." In 1789, Jefferson wrote to Madison, "In the arguments in favor of a declaration of rights, you omit one which has great weight with me; the legal check which it puts into the hands of the judiciary." In the same letter he warned of the "tyranny of the legislatures." His First Inaugural Address rejected legislative omnipotence where civil liberties were concerned.[36] Similarly, Madison, when proposing the amendments that became the Bill of Rights, favored and expected judicial review on behalf of the rights that would be protected. Arguing that the greatest danger to liberty derived from "the body of the people, operating by the majority against the minority," Madison said that after the adoption of the Bill of Rights, "independent tribunals of justice will consider themselves in a peculiar manner the guardians of those rights; they will be an impenetrable bulwark against every assumption of power in the legislative or executive; they will be naturally led to resist every encroachment upon rights expressly stipulated for in the Constitution by the declaration of rights."[37]

The Bill of Rights and other constitutional limitations do exist and must be honored; they are self-imposed by the people but are not self-enforcing. The checks of democratic politics as well as the formal checks and balances of the Constitution itself do not have the same operation in the states as in the nation, and no one can sensibly argue that judicial review over the states is illegitimate or in defiance of popular will—not after the Judiciary Act of 1789 and surely not after Appomattox. Whether as a harmonizer of the federal system, securing a uniform interpretation of the supreme law of the land throughout the Union, or as an enforcement device to secure constitutional rights against state abridgment, judicial review over the states should be beyond dispute, whatever the Framers intended and however undemocratic judicial review may be.

At a national level, judicial review over the political, military, and administrative branches or agencies of government is equally indispensable as a way "to secure these rights," which are integral to democracy. Any government measure restricting the democratic political process or directed against discrete and insular minorities, whether racial, national, or religious, calls for the most searching and skeptical judicial scrutiny.[38] In the *Second Flag Salute Case*, in 1943, Justice Robert H. Jackson for the Court made an imperishable statement that provides the bedrock justification for judicial review: "The very purpose of the Bill of Rights was to withdraw certain subjects from the vicissitudes of political controversy, to place them beyond the reach of majorities and officials, and to establish them as legal principles to be applied by the courts."[39]

Precisely because the members of the Court are not elected, are not politically responsible, and hold office for life, they are best suited for the task of deciding constitutional issues; for the same reason they are considered by the electorate as more trustworthy than the political branches. The people sometimes dislike Court decisions that protect obnoxious practices or despised members of society, but the people usually respect the Court's appeal to their ideals, and they comply with decisions that can be explained by the Court as upholding the Bill of Rights or any part of the Constitution protecting some historic principle of liberty, equality, or justice. The people seem to regard the Court as their conscience. The Court's restraining power, as Justice Benjamin N. Cardozo noted, holds "the standard aloft and visible to those who must run the race and keep the faith."[40] The country, as Woodrow Wilson put it, looks to the Court for "statesmanship," because the Constitution, which the Court expounds, is the "vehicle of the nation's life."[41] If the people accept the Court's will it is because it has no political constituency and is beholden to no majority or minority; it is comparatively trustworthy. The political branches cannot be expected to do the right thing, because of political considerations from which the Court is comparatively immune. Congress, for example, never enforced section 2 of the Fourteenth Amendment by reducing the South's representation in proportion to the number of blacks that the South disfranchised.

Contrary to proponents of a jurisprudence of original intent, judicial review can be democratic in its results. A pluperfect democratic theorist like Frankfurter may complain that the Court does not lose its oligarchic character when it serves humane ends, and a Hand may object to being "ruled by a bevy of Platonic Guardians,"[42] but our historical experience reveals that the Court saps or deadens popular responsibility when it reaches undemocratic results, and it quickens public responsibility when it reaches democratic results. In a dazzling essay on "The Democratic Character of Judicial Review," Eugene V. Rostow argued that the Court's precepts constitute a vital element in the making of policy. "The Supreme Court is, among other things," he wrote, "an educational body, and the Justices are inevitably teachers in a vital national seminar. The prestige of the Supreme Court as an institution is high . . . and the members of the Court speak with a powerful voice." By way of proof Rostow offered the "immensely constructive influence" of the decisions in favor of equal rights for black Americans. Those decisions "have not paralyzed or supplanted legislative and community action. They have precipitated it. They have not created bigotry. They have helped to fight it . . . and . . . have played a crucial role in leading public opinion and encouraging public action towards meeting the challenge and burden of the Negro problem as a constitutional—that is, as a moral—obligation."[43] Rostow was completely right in this most important of all examples that might be adduced. He was also right in another example, the Court's reformation of state criminal procedures. The Court has wrought still other changes that can be described only, in Rostow's words, as "releasing and encouraging the dominantly democratic forces of American life."[44] The series of decisions on reapportionment did as much as the Fifteenth and Nineteenth Amendments to democratize the political process. One could not be more wrong in saying of the modern Court, as Thayer did of the Court long ago, that the necessary effect of judicial review is "to dwarf the political capacity of the people and to deaden its sense of moral responsibility." Thayer was right at the time that he wrote, because of undemocratic opinions such as those in the *Civil Rights Cases* of 1883[45] and *Plessy v. Ferguson*.[46]

Not a single case of judicial review in favor of the Bill of Rights has been hurtful in any way to the democratic process, to popular responsibility, or to the moral sense of the community. The cases proving that judicial review has stunted the growth of the people or had undemocratic effects are those in which the Court sustained undemocratic measures, such as Jim Crow laws, or checked efforts, state and federal, to defend minorities or the underprivileged, but never those in which the Court has defended minorities or unpopular people against legislative majorities. The *Flag Salute Cases* are illustrative. The issue in those cases was whether a local school board could compel a flag salute from pupils who were members of Jehovah's Witnesses, to whom the salute was an obnoxious act of blasphemy that violated their consciences and forced them to bear false witness to their religion. In the *First Flag Salute Case*, the Court sustained the school board.[47] J. Skelly Wright, one of our finest federal judges, has written:

> But without guidance from the Supreme Court, the people misread their responsiblities. From the standpoint of religious freedom and respect for human rights, the effect of that Supreme Court decision in the First Flag Salute case was disastrous. School board after school board adopted new requirements commanding the flag salute, on pain of expulsion or other penalties. And often the school boards would quote the very words of the Supreme Court opinion in justification of their action. In many cases the salute to the flag was used simply as a device to expel the unpopular Jehovah's Witnesses. The words of the Supreme Court, that the protection of freedom could best be left to the responsibility of local authorities, were perverted and used as an excuse for what was in effect religious persecution by the local school boards. At the same time, and worse than the official action against the Jehovah's Witnesses, was the nation-wide wave of mob violence, attempts in the name of patriotism and support for the Supreme Court opinion.[48]

Within three years the Court reversed itself, striking down as unconstitutional the flag-salute requirement when imposed against religious conscience. The Court acted on behalf of the freedom of a very small, unpopular minority not to salute the flag during time of war, yet the opinion in the *Second Flag Salute Case* was honored by the nation's school boards and persecution of the Witnesses petered out. When the Court legitimizes a Smith Act or a Taft-Hartley Non-Communist Affidavit or a Subversive Activities Control Act, it gives constitutional sanction to much that is pernicious or repressive.[49] The Court may offer highly technical reasons for its decisions, but the public, which has little understanding and less patience with constitutional niceties, assumes that the Court has also given its seal of approval to the wisdom or policy of the legislation. Decisions that sustain legislation tend to end further debate; the remedial channels for public reconsiderations may remain open, but those who have had their "day in court" no longer have the public's ear.

By contrast, when the Court holds a congressional measure unconstitutional, public controversy is stimulated by fresh debate on the merits of the controverted legislation as well as on the merits of the Court's opinion. It enters into the people's education in the abandonment of foolish legislation by encouraging, rather than discouraging, their active interest in these matters. Invalidation on constitutional grounds is not always conclusive. Although the political branches will not override the Court by ignoring its constitutional objections, legislation can often be redrawn to achieve substantially the same end by constitutional means. The majority can still achieve its goal. By contrast, validation by the Court of legislation adversely affecting civil liberties ends debate without stimulating the democratic process; judicial review can promote the debate and the process. To argue that experience will teach the people to correct their mistakes of policy by remedial legislation, without a lead from the Court, ignores the high probability that they cannot learn in time to prevent irremediable injustice or damage. Pardoning victims of the Sedition Act could not reestablish lost presses or restore time spent in prison, just as the American-Japanese Evacuation Claims Act of 1948, which provided reparations for property losses, could not restore broken homes or the time spent behind barbed wire enclosures.

A swift historical review provides the basis for understanding the emergence of the case for the potentially democratic character of judicial review and for the emergence of demands for a constitutional jurisprudence of original intent. In the period between the Civil War and the 1890s, state regulatory powers enjoyed their greatest triumphs, despite threatening judicial language that laid the groundwork for new doctrines of constitutional limitations on government power when it trenched on property rights, especially corporate rights. During this time, too, the Court struck down or emasculated most of a comprehensive congressional program for the protection of civil rights, making corporations rather than black citizens the chief beneficiary of the Fourteenth Amendment. Judicial interpretation eroded the historic meanings of due process of law as a protection of the rights of the criminally accused, and engrafted a new economic substance to due process, making it a device for keeping man's relationship to his gold as private as possible.

From 1895 to 1936, the period of relative "judicial supremacy," the Court acted as if it were a superlegislature or third chamber, and the due process clause became the most formidable weapon in the armory of judicial review. Brooks Adams tartly observed that the historic purpose of the federal judiciary seemed to be to "dislocate any comprehensive body of legislation, whose effect would be to change the social status." This same patrician, with his contempt for the profit-hungry captains of industry, remarked: "The capitalist, as I infer, regards the constitutional form of government which exists in the United States, as a convenient method of obtaining his own way against a majority."[50] The Supreme Court arrogantly, artlessly, and inconsistently manipulated doctrines of constitutional law against an array of statutory reforms that sought to protect consumers, trade unions, farmers, unorganized workers, women, and children from the exploitation and abuses of economic enterprise. The high point of the Court's attempt to control public policy was reached during seventeen months of 1935–1936 in a massive and unprecedented judicial assault against a single administration. No less than twelve acts of Congress, parts of a systematic program to combat economic and social disaster, were held unconstitutional. Public opinion, though opposed to packing the Court, was outraged. The Court-packing plan failed largely because the Court, in the spring of 1937, made a timely, strategic retreat, validating the observation that it could read election returns, even if belatedly. During this long era from 1895 to 1936, critics of the Court, liberals and democrats of both parties, lambasted it for its activism and propounded arguments that the reactionary Court was oligarchic; they contended that it should devote itself to self-restraint, so that popular government might have its way.

President Franklin D. Roosevelt reconstructed the Court by placing it in the control of its critics, including Hugo L. Black, Felix Frankfurter, Robert H. Jackson, and William O. Douglas, who remade constitutional law from the dissenting opinions of Oliver

Wendell Holmes, Louis D. Brandeis, and Harlan F. Stone. The great issues of the 1930s were quickly settled. Outworn and reprehensible precedents fell like cold clinkers through an open grate. The new Court also junked economic due process and doctrines constricting government powers. At the same time that the Court emancipated both federal and state governmental powers, it vitalized the constitutional law of human rights. Cases involving free speech, the claims of the criminally accused, equality, racial justice, and expansion of the political process dominated, then overwhelmed, the Court's docket. The supreme tribunal at last caught up with folklore: it became the protector of civil rights and civil liberties, sometimes anticipating rather than following the election returns. Liberal intellectuals and scholars as well as spokesmen for racial, religious and ethnic minorities, and women, warmed themselves in the glowing approval that the Court's opinions provided to them. People who had once castigated the Court for its undemocratic propensities discovered that it stood, in many respects, in the vanguard of social revolution. The political branches, by default as in the cases involving the rights of the criminally accused, reapportionment, and racial discrimination, took their leads from the Court. Once conservative activist, it had become liberal activist. Judicial review possessed new attractions.[51]

While liberals welcomed the new trend of decision, conservatives found it repugnant, leveling charges that the Court had coddled communists and criminals, outlawed God from the public schools, legislated morality and sociology in its desegregation decisions, and intruded into the "political thicket" of legislative apportionment. Liberals rushed to the Court's protection, defending it against such charges as irresponsible, misleading, and misunderstanding. By no coincidence the argument harmonizing judicial review and democracy seems to have originated during the McCarthy period, when majoritarian excesses invited thoughtful but overwrought liberals to reconsider the benefits of judicial intervention. Then *Brown v. Board of Education* (1954) became the watershed case in modern history, and modern constitutional law developed feverishly under the aegis of the Warren Court.

The Burger Court deeply disappointed ultraconservatives.[52] It sniped at the Warren Court but carried on in much the same way. It did not overturn *Miranda v. Arizona*[53] or the exclusionary rule.[54]

It extended the principle of one person, one vote, even when racial criteria served as the basis for reapportionment.[55] It backed enforced school busing to achieve integration in the public schools.[56] It advanced the cause of sexual equality by invalidating a variety of sexual classifications.[57] It rejected the principle of racial colorblindness and supported racial quotas as well as affirmative action.[58] It did little to permit the censorship of blatant, commercialized pornography.[59] It disallowed publicly financed field trips, instructional aids, and specialized auxiliary services for parochial school children.[60] It denied the constitutionality of a state act requiring the posting in every public school room of an enlargement of the Ten Commandments.[61] It disapproved of inherent executive power to eavesdrop electronically on domestic "subversives."[62] It sharply restricted the use of capital punishment and reversed the death sentences of hundreds of convicted murderers by finding that the death penalty, though not unconstitutional per se, was inflicted arbitrarily and capriciously when the juries received inadequate judicial guidance.[63] Even worse than its softness on the death penalty, according to ultraconservatives, the Burger Court made a most heinous decision in *Roe v. Wade* (1973), one doubtlessly saturated with judicial activism, and wholly unforgivable: the Court sustained the right of a woman to an abortion in the early stages of pregnancy.[64]

Under the leadership of Attorney General Edwin Meese III, the Reagan administration, backed by increasingly vehement religious fundamentalists and a curious mix of other social conservatives and political rightwingers, maintained a sustained assault on the Court. Disapproval of the Court's decisions on policy grounds led conservatives to a reevaluation of its role in our government, a reassessment of judicial review, and a search for a way to contain the Supreme Court. Distinguished scholars, deeply resentful of the Court and concerned that its activism might discredit it seriously, engaged in a parallel search for a theory of judicial review that preserved the Court's constructive influence in constitutional law but sought reasonable limits to a judicial activism that seemed overly subjective in character. Two splendid books, both extraordinarily insightful and reflective, deserve mention here rather than be consigned to an unread footnote. They are Jesse H. Choper's *Judicial Review and the National Political Process*[65] and John Hart

Ely's *Democracy and Distrust: A Theory of Judicial Review*.[66] Another group of scholars, generally younger and inclined leftward,
argued the impossibility of judging in cases of constitutional law,
because the Justices necessarily find in the text only what they
want; these scholars believe that the text is contradictory and meaningless, and that the judges are necessarily biased. Some eminent
scholars passingly advocated that the Court should be aggressively
activist and read into the Constitution fresh moral insights, derived
in part from natural law, but not necessarily shackled to history.[67]
A preeminent constitutional lawyer proposed that the Court must
supply a constitutional "vacuum" with "a substantive vision of the
needs of human personality."[68]

Justice William J. Brennan, Jr., who will rank with Brandeis
and Douglas in leadership and ability as a liberal member of the
Court, supplies that vacuum with such a vision in cases dealing
with capital punishment. On that issue, Brennan's humanistic activism runs amok and he evinces an arrogance beyond belief. His
profound conviction that the death penalty violates the very essence
of human dignity, as indeed it does, goes out of control, as is true
of Justice Thurgood Marshall. In a position that Brennan described
as "fixed and immune" (since 1971),[69] he declared, in a famous and
controversial speech of 1985, "As I interpret the Constitution, capital punishment is under all circumstances cruel and unusual punishment prohibited by the Eighth and Fourteenth Amendments."
He believed the ban on cruel and unusual punishments embodies
uniquely "moral principles" that prevent the state from inflicting
the death penalty because it irreversibly degrades "the very essence
of human dignity." What makes this humane opinion so arrogant
is that Brennan knows that the Fifth Amendment three times assumes the legitimacy of the death penalty as does the Fourteenth
Amendment (no denial of life without due process). Moreover, he
also understands that a majority of his countrymen and his fellow
Justices disagree with his opinion, yet he holds it, he said, because
he perceives their interpretation of the text "to have departed from
its essential meaning," making him "bound, by a larger constitutional duty to the community, to expose the departure and point
toward a different path."[70] No one has a right to veto the Constitution because his moral reasoning leads him to disagree with it in

so clear a case. Brennan and Thurgood Marshall corrupt the judicial process and discredit it.

Conservatives grasp the point that if the virtues of judicial review depend largely upon the results that it achieves, the way to reduce the subjectivity of judicial decisions will be to condemn a result-oriented jurisprudence in favor of a jurisprudence that prescribes a fairly rigid way of ascertaining the meaning of the constitutional text. Original intent jurisprudence, according to its advocates, satisifies the method of finding out what the text means; at the same time, it imposes substantive limitations on the interpretation of the Constitution. A jurisprudence of original intent also has the virtue of giving protective cover to results that might otherwise seem to have been reached on the basis of personal discretion. Result-oriented jurisprudence disgraces the judicial process, while original intent jurisprudence has the pleasing aspect of resting on the wisdom of the Founding Fathers. Excepting the scholarly theorists who want the Court to reach results of which they approve, no matter whether related to what the Constitution says or what it meant to its Framers, most scholars and probably all judges believe that the task of judging should be as impersonal and objective as humanly possible. In constitutional cases, as in any others, the judge who first chooses what the outcome should be and then reasons backward to supply a rationalization replete with rules and precedents has betrayed his calling; he has decided on the basis of prejudice or prejudgment, and he has made constitutional law little more than the embodiment of his policy preferences, reflecting his personal predilections. Result-oriented jurisprudence, whether liberal or conservative, is a gross abuse of judicial office.

By comparison, original intent analysis seems seductively attractive to its proponents as an escape from liberal activism. The integrity of the Constitution and of the judicial process would be far better preserved if the Framers' intent guided decision rather than its being guided by the hopes, hearts, and souls of the members of the Court or of its self-professed "noninterpretivist" critics, those who claim not to believe in the Constitution as supreme law and disdain interpreting it because it is irrelevant to constitutional law. Original intent analysis is far more preferable than the surrealistic visions, moral reasoning, and noninterpretivism that abandon the text, its historical origins, its Framers' intent, and the expositions of it in their time. But it does not follow that the "only way in which the Constitution can constrain judges," in the words of Judge Robert H. Bork, "is if the judges interpret the document's words according to the intentions of those who drafted, proposed, and ratified its provisions and various amendments."[71] That remark occurred in the midst of a speech repudiating the notion that judges should create new rights. Bork's propositions are no more justifiable than an earlier proposition that he advanced in a different incarnation, when he said, like most proponents of liberal activism, that "working in the method familiar to lawyers trained in the common law, the judge can construct principles that explain existing constitutional rights and extrapolate from them to define new natural rights."[72]

Although a jurisprudence of original intent need not be conservative in its political coloration, and, in fact, has been resorted to by liberal Justices,[73] liberals have, for the most part, abandoned it, and conservatives now monopolize it. As they understand a jurisprudence of original intent, it allows no room for the right to an abortion, it validates the death penalty, it repudiates the *Miranda* warnings, it provides no protection to pornography, it disallows desecration of the flag, it prevents reverse discrimination, it permits government aid to religion on a nonpreferential basis, and it safeguards nearly every plank in the conservative platform that might become involved in litigation. A constitutional jurisprudence of original intent, according to its advocates, would prevent the federal courts from making policy or legislating in any way; it would confine the courts to carrying out policies made by the political branches. They also intoxicate themselves in the hope that it might end the expansion of judicial responsibility in the United States and reinstitute the old proscriptive character of judicial review in place of the new prescriptive judicial review. The new review prescribes what government must do, such as merge school districts and bus children across town, empty prisons of prisoners denied a "speedy" trial, and redraw election districts. Over a decade ago, Donald L. Horowitz described the phenomenal expansion of the business of the federal courts as follows:

Judicial activity has extended to welfare administration, prison administration, and mental hospital administration, to education policy and employment policy, to road building and bridge building, to automotive safety standards, and to natural resource management. In just the past few years, courts have struck down laws requiring a period of in-state residence as a condition of eligibility for welfare. They have invalidated presumptions of child support arising from the presence in the home of a "substitute father." Federal district courts have laid down elaborate standards for food handling, hospital operations, recreation facilities, inmate employment and education, sanitation, and laundry, painting, lighting, plumbing, and renovation in some prisons; they have ordered other prisons closed. Courts have established equally comprehensive programs of care and treatment for the mentally ill confined in hospitals. They have ordered the equalization of school expenditures on teachers' salaries, established hearing procedures for public school discipline cases, decided that bilingual education must be provided for Mexican-American children, and suspended the use by school boards of the National Teacher Examination and of comparable tests for school supervisors. They have eliminated a high school diploma as a requirement for a fireman's job. They have enjoined the construction of roads and bridges on environmental grounds and suspended performance requirements for automobile tires and air bags. They have told the Farmers Home Administration to restore a disaster loan program, the Forest Service to stop the clear-cutting of timber, and the Corps of Engineers to maintain the nation's non-navigable waterways. They have been, to put it mildly, very busy, laboring in unfamiliar territory.[74]

They have been prescribing remedies that trench on the functions of legislatures, administrative agencies, and executive officers.

Presumably, a jurisprudence of original intent would restore courts to the role envisaged for them by the Framers. The Framers did not expect that judicial review would go beyond enforcement of clear prohibitions; they did not expect judicial innovations of public policy. For an "originalist," *The Federalist* #81 speaks the wisdom of the Framers. Hamilton in that essay rejected an Anti-Federalist contention that under the Constitution the Supreme Court would become superior to Congress as a result of its power to construe laws according to the "spirit" of the Constitution. That would enable the Court to "mould" laws "into whatever shape it may think proper."[75] This contention appeared in *The Essays of*

Brutus, quite probably by Judge Robert Yates of New York, a Framer who walked out of the Constitutional Convention. Hamilton responded by observing that not a word in the Constitution authorizes the federal courts to construe laws according to its spirit, and that the laws would give way to the Constitution only when in "evident opposition."[76] Because Brutus was in part more accurate in his forecast than Hamilton, an objective of original intent analysis is to restore the Hamiltonian understanding.

A peculiar charm of original intent analysis is that the judge employing it seems to escape the subjectivity as well as the creativity that otherwise would color the judicial process in constitutional litigation. The judge becomes an impersonal time traveler who reports what the Framers intended, or, absent clarity on that point, restricts his opinion to a construction of the principle or purpose clearly discernible in their intent and applied it to the issue in the case at hand. Norms or standards outside of that intent or outside of the Constitution itself would be, or should be, off limits. So conceived, the judicial process based on original intent analysis is similar to the old view that judges should discover and declare preexisting law but not make it. Thus, an originalist judge supposedly rises above criticism if he is nothing but an intermediary for transmitting and applying the wishes of the Framers. A sophisticated conservative, United States Court of Appeals Judge Richard A. Posner, rejected that proposition in an article entitled, "What Am I? A Potted Plant?" He repudiated the belief that in constitutional law judges should speak the Framers' mind, that judicial review and democracy are incompatible, and that no place exists for judicial creativity or policymaking. "There has never been a time," Posner accurately wrote, "when the courts of the United States, state or federal, behaved consistently in accordance with this idea. Nor could they," he argued.[77]

The constitutional historian Alfred H. Kelly criticized "historical adjudication," a term synonomous with a jurisprudence of original intent, as the creature of people whose historical scholarship is simplistic, naive, and distorted. He found that the assumption that judges should rely on original intent

> supplies an apparent rationale for politically inspired activism that can be indulged in the name of constitutional continuity. The return

to historically discovered "original meaning" is . . . an almost perfect excuse for breaking precedent. After all, if the Fathers proclaimed the truth and the Court merely "rediscovers" it, who can gainsay the new revelation? The discovery may, upon examination, prove to be illusory or to involve distinct elements of law-office history in its creation, or even prove to be profoundly naive, but it will have served its purpose in supplying an activist rationale. . . .[78]

Kelly added that a critic of the Court could assault its rationale in such a case only by writing counterhistory.

Kelly's statement contains several insights, one of which is that original intent is a device of judicial activism, another that it serves to rationalize the overruling of precedents that an originalist judge dislikes, and a third that it provides the judge with a seemingly objective way of doing so. At the time Kelly wrote, in the mid-1960s, the Warren Court was using original intent to scrap precedents. Now, in a more systematic manner, some conservatives on and off the courts, expound original intent jurisprudence as a way of scrapping the work of the Warren Court. In that connection, consider the statement by Harry Jaffa, the illustrious political theorist, a conservative who sternly believes in "the laws of nature and of nature's God":

All that Ed Meese has done is to espouse what he thinks are "conservative" interpretations of the Constitution and dubbed them "original intent." While denouncing result oriented jurisprudence he has in fact merely substituted conservative result oriented jurisprudence for liberal result oriented jurisprudence. Calling it "original intent" is what Lincoln would say is calling the sheep's tail a leg. A tail is not a leg, no matter what you call it![79]

What Jaffa said of Meese may be said of Chief Justice William H. Rehnquist and Robert H. Bork, the two leading advocates of a constitutional jurisprudence of original intent Both are conservative activists who clad themselves in the sheep's garb of judicial self-restraintsmanship. Each would radically change American constitutional law to make it conform to his idealized projection of it. Their subjective choices are strikingly similar. Each prefers business over government, government over the individual, and the states over the nation.[80] With pizzazz and passion, Rehnquist and Bork vehemently condemn a cluster of Court-invented rights, especially the right to privacy and its offshoot, the right to an abortion.

Bork claims that whenever he speaks of original intent someone asks why we should be ruled by men long dead, but that the question is always asked about the clauses that guarantee individual freedom, never about the main body of the Constitution as to the powers of the three branches, "where we really are ruled by men long dead." The objection, he added, is not to the rule of the dead "but to the rule of living majorities," and it is made in the hope that judges, not the majorities, will protect newly claimed freedoms.[81] Similarly, Rehnquist accepts "the notion of a living constitution," which he says "only a necrophile" would reject, but he energetically repudiates the notion that the Court is the voice and conscience of contemporary society and that it is a measure of human dignity. He rejects any "end run around popular government," and therefore renounces judicial endorsement of any right not "within the four corners" of the Constitution.[82] Rehnquist argues that the Court should limit itself to original intent, whether or not difficult to determine, and should not use its authority "to make the Constitution relevant and useful in solving the problems of modern society."[83]

Bork and Rehnquist are moral relativists and legal positivists; they believe that in the absence of the sanction of law no position based on natural law, morality, or conscience can be proved superior or should be the basis of constitutional judgment. Bork asked why sexual gratification (the right of a married couple to use contraceptives) was "nobler" than economic gratification (the right of an industrial polluter to magnify profits). "There is no way of deciding these matters," he declared, "other than by reference to some system of moral or ethical values that has no objective or intrinsic validity of its own and about which men can and do differ."[84] The only reason Rehnquist finds for believing in the "moral rightness or goodness" of individual liberty is that the Constitution, adopted by a democratic society, safeguards it and not because of any "intrinsic worth" or "someone's idea of natural justice."[85] Rehnquist emphasizes, instead, what he has called "the original understanding at Philadelphia."[86] Rehnquist's dissenting opinion in a 1985 establishment clause case in which he spoke only for himself starkly reveals his judicial activism. When he speaks for himself alone, he does not need to temper his opinions in order to retain the votes of others. "It is impossible," he wrote in that 1985 case, "to build a sound constitutional doctrine upon a mistaken understanding of constitutional history," but, he added, "unfortunately" the constitutional law of the establishment clause has been founded on Jefferson's "metaphor" of the wall of separation between church and state.

If Rehnquist was right in believing that sound constitutional doctrine must rest on accurate constitutional history, his pernicious opinion in that case, endorsing the power of the United States to support religion financially, is utterly baseless. Rehnquist quite literally does not know the facts relating to the constitutional history of the establishment clause, let alone understand them rightly. He wrongly asserted that when Madison proposed the establishment clause, he meant only to prohibit a "national church" and "perhaps to prevent discrimination among sects." "He did not see it," Rehnquist wrongly stated, "as requiring neutrality on the part of government between religion and irreligion." Rehnquist was wrong, too, when he declared that the Court had been "demonstrably incorrect as a matter of history" in an earlier case in saying that the First Amendment incorporated the position of Roger Williams, Madison, and Jefferson. He was also wrong when he said that the Constitution, including the First Amendment, was not designed to "prohibit the federal government from providing non-discriminatory aid to religion."[87]

Only an activist judge on a rampage would recommend the abandonment of the Court's entire jurisprudence on the establishment clause, as Rehnquist did. He declared that the Court should "frankly and explicitly" abandon its earlier decisions based on the principle of separation of church and state, because that principle is based on "bad history." He would also abandon the so-called *Lemon* test, which the Court regularly employs to determine the constitutionality of government action under the establishment clause. That test, which he described as a buttress of the "wall metaphor," provides that if an act of government has no secular purpose, advances or inhibits religion, or unduly entangles the state with religion, it is unconstitutional as a violation of the First Amendment.[88] "The true meaning of the Establishment Clause," Rehnquist argued, "can only be seen in its history. . . . Any deviation from their [the Framers'] intentions frustrates the permanence of that Charter [the Bill of Rights] and will only lead to the type of unprincipled decisionmaking that has plagued our Establishment Clause cases since *Everson*"[89] (1947)—this from a Justice who thinks that Madison, the sponsor of Jefferson's Statute of Religious Freedom, did not support neutrality between religion and irreligion, and who thinks that an establishment of religion existed in Rhode Island from 1633 to 1842. Rhode Island, founded in 1636 by Roger Williams, a separatist, never had an establishment of religion.[90] The man who makes such mistakes and passes fiction off as history makes historical judgments about the First Amendment that he would like to use as the anchor to a new establishment clause jurisprudence.

In accord with Alfred H. Kelly's analysis, Rehnquist seeks to overrule precedents and end separation of church and state, or, at least, end government neutrality and no aid to religion, by relying on history, very bad history at that. He is reputedly a minimalist on the powers of the United States, and he is also supposed to be devoted to a theory of judicial review that finds limitations in the structure of the Constitution.[91] How he derives from the structure an unenumerated power of Congress to pass laws on the subject of religion is a mystery explicable only by black magic—or sheer bias, distorted history, and arbitrary construction. A scholar who analyzed his views on federalism concluded:

> Therefore, Rehnquist's attempt to use the intention of the Framers as an objective basis for constitutional law fails at its most fundamental and crucial point—its connection to history. The power of his argument rests on the claim that his position is derived from objectively determinable historical facts about the Framers' purposes. But his reconstruction of the Framers' intention not only fails to convince, it in fact seems susceptible to objective refutation. The evidence is strong that the Framers intended to establish a vigorous national government for the purpose of securing the liberties of the sovereign people. Justice Rehnquist offers us instead an alliance of sovereign state governments dedicated to the preservation of their parochial autonomy. By so misreading the Constitution's text and history, Rehnquist commits the precise emotivist error that he sets out to avoid: the erection of a judge's personal values and opinions into constitutional norms.[92]

Robert Bork, who has the distinction of being the most sophisticated theorist among exponents of original intent jurisprudence, managed to use the judicial process to reach opinions congenial to his personal preferences with extraordinary regularity. Bork's views are important because despite the Senate's rejection of his nomination for the Supreme Court and his resignation from the federal bench, he is the intellectual role model for scores of federal judges appointed by President Ronald Reagan; they will be serving for decades to come. Bork disarmingly acknowledged that the judicial process is complicated, and he disclaimed as useless a narrow belief that an originalist judge may apply a constitutional provision only to circumstances specifically contemplated by the Framers. He declared reasonable that "all"—notice the word—"all the intentionalist [a judge applying original intent analysis] requires is the text, structure, and history of the Constitution" to provide him "not with a conclusion but with a premise. The premise states the core value that the framers intended to protect."[93] So armed the judge can apply the Constitution to circumstances the Framers could not foresee.

Whether the Framers saw what Bork may see as a "core value," and whether he can see their core values is not at all certain or clear. Did the Framers of the Bill of Rights intend to protect a right to privacy? No such right receives explicit recognition in the Constitution. Justice William O. Douglas, however, in a plurality opinion for the Court in 1965 understood a right to privacy to exist as a result of various "penumbras" and "emanations" from several provisions of the Bill of Rights. In the First Amendment's peripheral right to association, he said, the Court had found "a penumbra where privacy is protected from government intrusion." Government has no legitimate authority, for example, to inquire into one's religious beliefs or political associations. The Third Amendment bans the quartering of soldiers in homes during peacetime without the consent of the owners, "another facet of privacy." The Fourth Amendment's protection against unreasonable searches and seizures doubtlessly protects privacy, as does the self-incrimination clause of the Fifth Amendment, which the Court has referred to as a "right to silence." Finally, Douglas observed, the Ninth Amendment acknowledges the existence of rights other than those enumerated. Three Justices in the 1965 case believed that the

Ninth Amendment comprehends a right to privacy, and the entire majority of seven Justices believed that the Fourteenth Amendment's protection of "liberty" includes a right to privacy.[94]

Robert Bork, however, ridicules such reasoning about the right to privacy, which he denies that the Constitution protects. Douglas, he wrote, "performed a miracle of transubstantiation" by reasoning that "was utterly specious" and constituted "an unprincipled decision."[95] Bork believes that nonenumerated or nonspecific rights do not exist and cannot be derived from the Constitution, because the judges who find such rights are "enforcing their own morality upon us and calling it the Constitution."[96] To Bork a general right to privacy is a judicial invention that thwarts majority rule in matters of sexual privacy. He did not explain why he thought a right to privacy had to be an absolute in order to exist at all; he showed, rather, that it could not be inclusive enough to protect the right to shoot heroin in private or the right to have sex with a minor. He then concluded that it does not exist as a recognizable and independent right, unconnected with an enumerated right. Consequently, the state may deny a physician a right to counsel married couples on methods of contraception. Similarly, no right to an abortion exists for Bork.

Bork used to reject all of the substantive due process decisions of the Court, including decisions of the 1920s that championed the right to be taught in languages other than English and the right to send children to private sectarian schools instead of public schools. He also found intellectually and constitutionally empty those decisions that in effect recognized a right not to be sterilized, a right to receive welfare benefits without meeting a state's residence requirements, and a right to sue for the wrongful death of illegitimate, as well as legitimate, children. He found no "principled" way to define the spheres of "liberty" or of "equality." "These," he said, "are matters of morality, of judgment, of prudence. They therefore belong to the political community." In addition to leaving the meaning of liberty and equality to the ballot box he found no right against restrictive covenants; no right to be represented on the principle of one person, one vote; and no right for any speech other than political speech, thus excluding from First Amendment protection free speech for education, philosophy, religion, art, literature, science, music, sociology, and drama, as well as for pornography. Even as to political speech, he found surprising limits; he excluded speech protected by the clear and present danger test, which he thought erected "a barrier to legislative rule where none should exist." In 1971 and for long after he saw only "specified" or enumerated rights, which he construed narrowly, and "derivative rights" or privileges delegated by government and revocable by it.[97]

In 1985 Bork recognized "core value" rights, but still conceived of them narrowly by seeking a low "level of generality" for determining their scope. He found it possible to apply the free press clause to electronic media and the Fourth Amendment to electronic surveillance. He could not, however, find in the equal protection clause anything but a ban on invidious racial classification; "equality on matters such as sexual orientation was not under discussion" by the authors of the Fourteenth Amendment. Nor did they have in mind equality of the sexes, or for persons of different national origins, or of religion, or of mental or physical abilities, or anything but race. When a judge chooses "a higher level of generality" than Bork discerned, that judge "reaches a result far beyond anything that the Framers intended . . . and creates a concept without limits, thus ensuring erratic judicial enforcement."[98] Similarly, Bork recently declared that "once the function of searching for the Framers' intent is abandoned," judicial opinions "are rooted only in the judges' moral predilections."[99]

Thus, Bork's jurisprudence of original intent erodes or vaporizes most rights, including the right not to be discriminated against on sexual grounds and the right to marital intimacy. How he discerns a right to be electronically free from unreasonable search and seizure but not a right to privacy is explicable, in his terms, by the fact that the first derives from a specified right and the other does not. But anyone who thinks that the Framers did not believe in sexual privacy, at least with respect to marital relations, has the historical imagination of a toad. What Bork's theory of jurisprudence adds up to is that in his opinion, any right with which he disagrees is not a right derived from original intent.

His jurisprudence also leads him to exalt original intent over the text of the Constitution. Despite his talk about discerning core values, principles, and purposes in the Framers' text, he ignores the text when it does not coincide with his assumptions, which he never tries to prove, about the intent of the Framers. For practical purposes, original intent analysis emancipates him from the Constitution. The First Amendment, notwithstanding Bork's view, guarantees the freedom of speech and press; it makes no exceptions, certainly not for various classes of nonpolitical speech. The Fourteenth Amendment protects against denial of the equal protection of the laws. It does not speak of race at all. Its principle is as applicable to women as to men and to atheists as well as to believers; it makes no distinction or exceptions; it applies to everyone. Does original intent analysis free judges from the text of the Constitution? During the Senate hearings on his nomination as a member of the Supreme Court in 1987, Bork was said to have experienced "confirmation conversion" and wishy-washily shifted his opinions. He said he accepted civil rights, equal protection for everyone, and free speech for more than political speech. Men in public life, in any branch of government, are entitled to change their opinions. But when the reigning grand theorist of original intent jurisprudence who is a federal judge changes his mind, what happens to the theory that he had so insistently claimed yielded impersonal results? What happens to the theory that constituted the only escape from judicial subjectivity, the only way to maintain a principled judicial process, the only way to avoid moral reasoning that puts the judge's heart and soul in place of the Constitution?

The fact is, and it is a fact, that Bork and Rehnquist, like any other originalist judges, are every bit as subjective as Brennan and Marshall. Their manipulation of the rules of construction achieves whatever result they seek. What they attribute to the Framers derives from their own moral reasoning. No credence can be given to Bork's contention that "only by limiting themselves to the historic intentions underlying each clause of the Constitution [where is that to be found?] can judges avoid becoming legislators, avoid enforcing their own moral predilections, and ensure that the Constitution is law."[100]

Rehnquist and Bork, the heaviest guns of the original intent analysts, do not support a thesis that modern judicial review is qualitatively different from the old "interpretive" review that was merely proscriptive in nature.[101] Judicial review now is supposed to be far more sweeping and controlling because it has become prescriptive. It does not simply thwart public will; it compels government to behave contrary to its wishes. Even if validity saturated that supposed distinction between the old proscriptive or prohibitive review and the new prescriptive or compulsive review, the distinction has no merit as evidence that the Court is more activist or more influential than it used to be. As shown in earlier chapters of this book, the Court was extremely activist and influential from its beginnings. And consider the activism involved in telling the nation that it cannot regulate slavery in the territories; cannot regulate railroad and utility rates; cannot enact income tax laws; cannot prohibit child labor; cannot fix maximum hours or minimum wage laws; cannot regulate agricultural, mining, or industrial production; and cannot promote trade unionism.

Consider also the activism and influence of the Court in the area of civil rights a century ago, when its lead severly inhibited and weakened popular responsibility in the areas of liberty, equality, and justice. Given the fact that the Court is an institution of enormous prestige whose declaration of principles teaches and leads the nation, its series of decisions crippling and voiding most of the comprehensive programs for the protection of civil rights after the Civil War was most pernicious. Those decisions paralyzed or supplanted legislative and community action, created bigotry, and played a crucial role in destroying public opinion that favored meeting the challenge of the race problem as a constitutional—that is, as a moral—obligation.

The process began when the Court cut the heart out of the principal clause of the Fourteenth Amendment, the privileges and immunities clause. What is more activist than judicial emasculation of a clause of the Constitution itself? In the *Slaughterhouse Case* of 1873, the Court ruled that with few exceptions civil rights were not attributes of United States citizenship and therefore were not constitutionally protected by the privileges and immunities clause against state violation.[102] The principle of the *Slaughterhouse Case* doomed federal civil rights legislation and heralded the triumph of white supremacy in American constitutional law. That principle bore first fruit in the *Cruikshank Case*, which grew out of the infamous Colfax Massacre. The ringleaders of a band of armed whites who slaughtered fifty-nine Negroes, having been acquitted by a local Louisiana jury on a charge of murder, were convicted in a federal court for having conspired to interfere with the free exercise of rights granted or secured by the Constitution or laws of the United States. The Supreme Court unanimously decided that the rights in question—to assemble (unless for the purpose of petitioning Congress), to bear arms, not to be deprived of life or liberty without due process of law, and to vote—were not federal rights and therefore depended upon the states for their protection. The act of Congress was not voided, but its usefulness was drastically impaired and the convictions were reversed.[103] In another case of 1876, the Court struck down the section of the Civil Rights Act of 1870 by which Congress made it a federal crime for state or local election officials to refuse to receive or count the vote of persons qualified to vote under state law.[104] This decision permitted the white South to circumvent the Fifteenth Amendment by denying Negroes the right to vote on any ground other than race, that is, by poll taxes, literacy tests, understanding clauses, good character tests, and other devices that resulted in mass disfranchisement.

In 1880 the Court ruled that in the absence of official state action excluding blacks from jury service on explicitly racial grounds, black defendants would have to prove deliberate discrimination and the proof would have to consist of more than the fact that there had never been a black person on the jury lists of the county.[105] This rule made possible the systematic exclusion of black citizens from jury service in the South. In one case of 1883, a banner year for white supremacy, the Court sustained state miscegenation laws, thereby giving constitutional sanction to poisonous notions of racial purity.[106] In another case of the same year the Court reversed the convictions of a mob of twenty whites who captured four black men from the custody of a sheriff, beat them, and lynched one. The ruling was that the defendants had been convicted under an unconstitutional act of Congress, the 1871 Anti-Lynching Act, which made it a federal crime to conspire for the purpose of depriving anyone of the equal protection of the laws.[107] Finally, in 1883, the Court held unconstitutional the great Civil Rights Act of 1875 by which Congress had outlawed segregation or any form of racial discrimination in all public transportation facilities, hotels and inns, and theaters and other places of public amusement.[108] In 1878 the Court had held unconstitutional, as a burden on interstate commerce, a Louisiana law requiring carriers to provide equal facilities without regard to race.[109] Following this decision, nine southern states passed laws requiring Jim Crow in local transportation facilities, and in 1896, in the notorious *Plessy* case, the Court upheld this legislation.[110] Thus Congress and the states could not prohibit racial segregation, but the states could compel it. These nineteenth-century decisions most certainly dammed up and discouraged the democratic values of American life, stunted the political and moral capacity of the people, and released and energized the most unworthy forces. One might also analyze early decisions on state criminal procedures and come to similar conclusions.[111]

Later decisions, both in the field of state criminal procedures and civil rights, in nature and effect enhanced popular responsibility and democratic values, but they began at about the time of the Hughes Court and gained in both breadth and impact only under the Warren Court. Meanwhile millions of black Americans suffered lives of humiliation for five or six or more decades under a Jim Crow, white supremacist Constitution, because the Court had betrayed the intent of the Reconstruction Amendments, enfeebling the privileges and immunities clause of the Fourteenth Amendment, and had rendered meaningless the enabling clauses in those amendments—"Congress shall have power to enforce, by appropriate legislation, the provisions of this article." And no one knows how many thousands of cases of miscarriages of justice occurred for both black and white defendants in criminal cases, because the Court took half a century to begin reforming and civilizing state criminal procedures under the Fourteenth Amendment.

Thus, no credit can be extended to the view that the Court has exercised a new role in the past three decades by deciding "fundamental issues of social policy"—as if it had not been doing so for much of its history—and no credit whatever attaches to the assertion that interpreting the Constitution "simply means to determine the intent of its framers, those who wrote and ratified it."[112]

CHAPTER SEVENTEEN

Conclusions

$\mathcal{F}$ifty years ago, in his fine study of how the Supreme Court used original intent (not what the Framers and ratifiers believed), Jacobus tenBroek asserted, rightly, that "the intent theory," as he called it, "inverts the judicial process." It described decisions of the Court as having been reached as a result of a judicial search for Framers' intent, "whereas, in fact, the intent discovered by the Court is most likely to be determined by the conclusion that the Court wishes to reach." Original intent analysis involves what tenBroek called "fundamental misconceptions of the nature of the judicial process." It makes the judge "a mindless robot whose task is the utterly mechanical function" of using original intent as a measure of constitutionality. In the entire history of the Supreme Court, as tenBroek should have added, no Justice employing the intent theory has ever written a convincing and reliable study. Lawyers making a historical point will cite a Court opinion as proof, but no competent historian would do that. He knows that judges cannot do their own research or do the right kind of research and that they turn to history to prove some point they have in mind. To paraphrase tenBroek, Justices mistakenly use original intent theory to depict a nearly fixed Constitution, to give the misleading impression that they have decided an issue of constitutionality by finding original intent, and to make a constitutional issue merely a historical question. The entire theory, tenBroek asserted, "falsely describes what the Court actually does," and it "hypothesizes a mathematically exact technique of discovery and a practically ines-capable conclusion." That all added up, said tenBroek, to "judicial hokum."[1]

If we could ascertain original intent, one may add, cases would not arise concerning that intent. They arise because the intent is and likely will remain uncertain; they arise because the Framers either had no discernible intent to govern the issue or their intent cannot control it because the problem before the Court would have been so alien to the Framers that only the spirit of some principle implied by them can be of assistance. The Framers were certainly vaguer on powers than on structure and vaguer still on rights.

If, as Robert H. Bork noticed,[2] people rarely raise questions about original intent on issues involving powers or structure, the reason is likely that the Constitution provides the answer, or it has been settled conclusively by the Court, making inquiry futile or unnecessary. For example, the question of constitutional powers to regulate the economy has overwhelmingly been put beyond question by the 1937 "constitutional revolution, limited," in Ed-ward S. Corwin's phrase.[3] Not even the most conservative Justices on today's Court question the constitutionality of government con-trols. Congress has the constitutional authority under Court de-cisions to initiate a socialist economy; political restraints, not con-stitutional ones, prevent that. There are no longer any serious limits on the commerce powers of Congress.[4] The government can take apart the greatest corporations, like Ma Bell; if it does not proceed against them, the reason is to be found in national defense needs and in politics, not in the Constitution.

The states are supplicants before the United States govern-ment, beneficiaries of its largesse like so many welfare recipients, unable to control their own policies, serving instead as adminis-trative agencies of federal policies. Those federal policies extend to realms not remotely within the federal power to govern under the Constitution, except for the fact that the spending power, so called, the power to spend for national defense and general welfare can be exercised through programs of grants-in-aid to states and to over 75,000 substate governmental entities; they take federal tax money and obediently enforce the conditions laid down by Congress and by federal agencies for control of the expenditures.

Federalism as we knew it has been replaced by a new federalism that even conservative Republican administrations enforce.[5] The government today makes the New Deal look like a backer of Adam Smith's legendary free enterprise and a respecter of John C. Calhoun's state sovereignty.

Even conservative Justices on the Supreme Court accept the new order of things. William H. Rehnquist spoke for the Court in *PruneYard*, Sandra Day O'Connor in *Hawaii Housing Authority*, and the Court was unanimous in both.[6] In the first of these cases, decided in 1980, the Court held that a state does not violate the property rights of a shopping center owner by authorizing the solicitation of petitions in places of business open to the public. Rehnquist, finding a reasonable police power regulation of private property, asserted that the public right to regulate the use of property is as fundamental as the right to property itself. One might have thought that as a matter of constitutional theory and of original intent, the property right was fundamental and the regulatory power was an exception to it that had to be justified. Rehnquist did not explain why the regulation was justifiable or reasonable; under its rational basis test the Court has no obligation to explain anything. It need merely believe that the legislature had some rational basis for its regulation.

In the *Hawaii Housing Authority* case of 1984, the Court unanimously held that the state could do the very thing that Justice William Paterson had said in 1795 that it could not do—take property from one citizen, even at a just compensation, and give it to another at that price.[7] Landownership in Hawaii was concentrated in a few people; to break the oligopoly of ownership the state fixed on a scheme whereby it took private property by eminent domain, lent tenants up to 90 percent of the purchase price, and arranged for transfer of titles. But the Constitution states that property may be taken at a just price only for a public use. Anyone who thinks that means for an arsenal, a courthouse, a school, a road, a firestation, or some such, is as naive as was Justice Paterson.

Justice O'Connor for the Court identified a public use with a public purpose. She added to the misreasoning by equating the power of eminent domain with the police power. She proclaimed the need for judicial deference to legislatures, because legislatures are better able than courts to assess what public purposes should be promoted by eminent domain. Granted, an appropriation or taking of property for a public use may have a public purpose, like satisfying the need for an airfield or for a public dump, but vesting the title of land in private parties does not constitute a *public* purpose or a public *use*. The public use requirement, O'Connor said, is "coterminous with the scope of the sovereign's police powers." That is law because the Court says so, just as the Court says that the power to regulate is the same as the power to transfer private title. Humpty Dumpty wins again.

This case teaches that wherever an oligopoly exists, whether in the making of automobiles or of disposable diapers, the voters can decide to transfer ownership to the workers in the industry by taking the property, selling it to the employees, and financing the loan they need to make the purchase. Such an outcome is bizarre given the fact that the Constitution itself at several points explicitly shows respect for property rights, and that its text speaks of taking for a "public use," not for a public purpose.

No real questions of structure are likely to arise, except perhaps for questions involving the separation of powers, a perennial hardy for those who like their structure as it is described in elementary textbooks. In 1986 the Court held unconstitutional a provision of the Gramm-Rudman-Hollings Balanced Budget Act, on ground that it violated the doctrine of separation of powers by vesting in the comptroller general, a creature of Congress, a role in the execution of laws.[8] Chief Justice Warren Burger larded his simplistic opinion with irrelevant references to Montesquieu and to a debate in the First Congress on removal powers, but ignored *The Federalist's* explanation of the reason that the system of checks and balances allows for shared powers and purposefully fails to keep the separation distinct. The three branches are separate, not necessarily their powers.[9] The Court seems not to have known that the First Congress, which established the President's cabinet officers, required the secretary of the treasury to "make report and give information to either branch of the legislature, in person or in writing (as he may be required), respecting all matters referred to him by the Senate or House of Representatives. . . ." Secretary Alexander Hamilton's four great reports on the American economy were made to Congress, not to President Washington.[10] No Court that cared a fig for original intent and had any historical competence

would have declared the Gramm-Rudman-Hollings Act unconstitutional on separation-of-powers grounds.

If much of contemporary constitutional law is about rights, the
reason is that as government gets larger, more complex, more
powerful, and more intrusive, the need to stay Caesar's hand in-
creases. If government exists to protect the individual, as the
preamble of the Declaration of Independence suggests, and as the
provisions of the Constitution suggest as strongly, then the Court
must fortify our rights. Rehnquist and Bork mislead when they
insist that because particular rights are not specified they have no
constitutional existence. The Constitution exists to describe and
limit the government, not to describe and limit rights. Government
power must be exercised in subordination to the right of the individual, as much as possible. The fact that nothing in the Constitution refers to the rights of homosexuals or a woman's right to
an abortion is of considerably less importance than the fact that
nothing in the Constitution militates against those rights (so long
as a fetus is not regarded as a person). Chief Justice John Marshall's
rule of construction was that if the Constitution does not prohibit,
it can permit and protect.[11] The burden of proof should always be
on government to show that rights claimed must be denied lest
legitimate ends go unfulfilled because no alternative means are
possible and the needs of the government are compelling.

The historic mission of judicial review is supposed to be the
vindication of individual freedoms. To acknowledge that yet to
understand and protect only the most obvious and conventional
freedoms cancels two centuries of democratic growth by returning
us to the world of the Framers. But even in that lost world of two
centuries ago, rights were still in evolution, people understood that
new rights might emerge, and the Ninth Amendment put the
Framers' thumbs down on the "rights" side of the scales that weigh
rights against powers. Those who measure individual rights against
the rights of society forget that society has a profound stake in the
rights of the individual; we possess rights as individuals not only
because they inhere in us and serve to fulfill us as individuals but
because we function as a free society and maintain its openness by
respecting personal differences. The Framers were deeply concerned about the humanity that the fundamental law should show
even to the criminal offender not because they wanted to coddle

criminals but because they were tough-minded enough to understand that the enduring interests of society require justice to be done as fairly as possible.

No apostle of original intent jurisprudence advocates it with consistency or in a thoroughgoing manner. Rehnquist and Bork have not disparaged juries of less than twelve or nonunanimous verdicts as departures from original intent. To the Framers a jury in a criminal trial consisted of twelve men who rendered a unanimous verdict. President Reagan's Department of Justice did not engage in a campaign to eliminate use immunity from our statutes, and the original intent jurists have not declared that use immunity statutes fall short of the constitutional provision that no person shall be compelled to be a witness against himself criminally. No originalist has explained how a constitutional provision can be superseded by a mere statute, let alone one that requires people to be witnesses against themselves and be subject to criminal penalties of perjury unavailable to the prosecution in the absence of a grant of immunity, whether use or transactional. Attorney General Meese campaigned against the *Miranda* decision, supposedly because the Framers would not have recognized the requirement of the *Miranda* warnings, but he did not campaign against use immunity, which would have been equally alien to them.

Meese also campaigned against the Boland Amendment, which prohibited the expenditure of funds on behalf of the Contras in Nicaragua, and he offered as his explanation that the amendment inhibited the President's inherent powers in the field of foreign affairs; Meese showed no appreciation of the fact that the Framers believed that Congress controls appropriations and expenditures. Indeed, the Constitution provides that money bills should originate in the House of Representatives. If we returned to original intent, money bills would no longer originate, as they do nowadays, in the White House or its Bureau of the Budget, despite the provision in Article I, section 7. Two sections further the Constitution also says that no money shall be expended except in accordance with appropriations made by law, but the Reagan administration encouraged or tolerated the payment of monies to the Contras— monies that belonged in the Treasury, had not been appropriated, and whose payment defied the Boland Amendment, which the President had signed. Article I, section 9, requires "from time to time" a public accounting of all receipts and expenditures. The Central Intelligence Agency receives and expends monies that are never publicly accounted for.

Originalists in Reagan's Department of Justice and on the federal courts insisted on a return to the pristine meanings of 1789, but never with respect to executive powers. The administration that backed original intent analysis allowed "The Enterprise," a secret government within the government, consisting of National Security Administration officers, to make foreign policy without the knowledge of the President (preserving "plausible deniability" for him), or of the secretary of state, or of the secretary of defense, or of any elected officials. The concept of inherent executive powers was foreign to the Philadelphia Convention and if known would have been vehemently opposed by those who ratified the Constitution. The same administration that supported original intent as the basis of constitutional jurisprudence also contended that the War Powers Resolution of 1973 is unconstitutional because it checks the President's inherent executive powers in the realm of foreign policy and with respect to his command of the armed services. The Framers intended that the President should have discretion to repel attacks and suppress insurrections, but they would have thought it was stretching the letter of the law somewhat to engage in foreign adventures on the basis of unmentioned inherent powers. Rehnquist and Bork, who are so tight with rights that they require them to be specified and familiar before according them recognition, are extravagant in recognizing inherent as well as implied executive powers. The administration that supported original intent made war in Libya, Lebanon, Nicaragua, and Grenada, and sent a powerful navy to a war zone in the Persian Gulf, but cried "unconstitutional" when Congress sought to keep it accountable and asked the President to execute the laws faithfully. The more one looks at a jurisprudence of original intent, the more it seems politically motivated as a disguise for political objectives. The more one scrutinizes it, the more it seems to be a pose for reasoning from unquestioned subjective assumptions to foregone subjective conclusions.

The Constitution of the United States is our national covenant, and the Supreme Court is its special keeper. The Constitution's power of survival derives in part from the fact that it incorporates and symbolizes the political values of a free people. It creates a representative, responsible government empowered to serve the great objectives specified in the Preamble, while at the same time it keeps government bitted and bridled. Through the Bill of Rights and the great Reconstruction amendments, the Constitution requires that the government respect the freedom of its citizens, whom it must treat fairly. Courts supervise the process, and the Supreme Court is the final tribunal. "The great ideals of liberty and equality," wrote Justice Benjamin N. Cardozo, "are preserved against the assaults of opportunism, the expediency of the passing hour, the scorn and derision of those who have no patience with general principles, by enshrining them in constitutions, and consecrating to the task of their protection a body of defenders."[12] Similarly, Justice Hugo L. Black once wrote for the Court, "Under our constitutional system, courts stand against any winds that blow, as havens of refuge for those who might otherwise suffer because they are helpless, weak, outnumbered, or because they are nonconforming victims of prejudice and public excitement."[13]

The Court should have no choice but to err on the side of the constitutional liberty and equality of the individual, whenever doubt exists as to which side requires endorsement. Ours is so secure a system, precisely because it is free and dedicated to principles of justice, that it can afford to prefer the individual over the state. To interpose original intent against an individual's claim defeats the purpose of having systematic and regularized restraints on power; limitations exist for the minority against the majority, as Madison said. Original intent analysis becomes a treacherous pursuit when it turns the Constitution and the Court away from assisting the development of a still freer and more just society.

The history of Magna Carta throws dazzling light on a jurisprudence of original intent. Magna Carta approaches its 800th anniversary. It was originally "reactionary as hell," to quote the chief justice of West Virginia.[14] But the feudal barons who framed it could not control its evolution. It eventually came to signify many things that are not in it and were not intended. Magna Carta is not remotely important for what it intended but for what it has become. It stands now for government by contract of the people, for fundamental law, for the rule of law, for no taxation without representation, for due process of law, for habeas corpus, for equality before the law, for representative government, and for a cluster of the rights of the criminally accused. No one cares, or should, that the original document signifies none of this. The Constitution is comparably dynamic.

The Court has the responsibility of helping regenerate and fulfill the noblest aspirations for which this nation stands. It must keep constitutional law constantly rooted in the great ideals of the past yet in a state of evolution in order to realize them. Something should happen to a person who dons the black robe of a Justice of the Supreme Court of the United States. He or she comes under an obligation to strive for as much objectivity as is humanly attainable by putting aside personal opinions and preferences. Yet even the best and most impartial of Justices, those in whom the judicial temperament is most finely cultivated, cannot escape the influences that have tugged at them all their lives and inescapably color their judgment. Personality, the beliefs that make the person, has always made a difference in the Court's constitutional adjudication. There never has been a constitutional case before the Court in which there was no room for personal discretion to express itself.

We may not want judges who start with the answer rather than the problem, but so long as mere mortals sit on the Court and construe its majestic but murky words, we will not likely get any other kind. Not that the Justices knowingly or deliberately read their presuppositions into law. There probably has never been a member of the Court who consciously decided against the Constitution or was unable in his own mind to square his opinions with it. Most judges convince themselves that they respond to the words on parchment, illuminated, of course, by historical and social imperatives. The illusion may be good for their psyches or the public's need to know that the nine who sit on the nation's's highest tribunal really become Olympians, untainted by considerations that move lesser beings in political office.

Even those Justices who start with the problem rather than the result cannot transcend themselves or transmogrify the obscure or inexact into impersonal truth. At bottom, constitutional law reflects great public policies enshrined in the form of supreme and fundamental commands. It is truer of constitutional law than of any other branch that "what the courts declare to have always been the law," as Holmes put it, "is in fact new. It is legislative in its grounds.

The very considerations which judges most rarely mention, and always with an apology, are the secret root from which the law draws all the juices of life. I mean, of course, consideration of what is expedient for the community concerned."[15] Result-oriented jurisprudence or, at the least, judicial activism is nearly inevitable— not praiseworthy, or desirable, but inescapable when the Constitution must be construed. Robert H. Bork correctly said that the best way to cope with the problem "is the selection of intellectually honest judges."[16] One dimension of such honesty is capacity to recognize at the propitious moment a need for constitutional evolution, rather than keep the Constitution in a deepfreeze.

Sometimes the Framers have to be ignored. The Babylonian Talmud tells a story about a rabbi who, unable to convince his brethren, declared that if the law agreed with his interpretation, a tree would prove it, whereupon the tree was torn from its roots. The other rabbis retorted that no proof could come from a tree. The first rabbi then declared that if he were right, the stream would prove it, and the stream suddenly flowed backward. The others replied that nothing could be proved from a stream. Still other miracles occurred, yet the others remained unconvinced. Finally the first rabbi declared that Heaven would prove that he had the right interpretation of the law. A Heavenly Voice then demanded to know why the others did not agree with the first rabbi in view of the fact that he was correct about the rule of law. The others replied that because the Law had already been given by God at Mount Sinai, they would pay no attention to a Heavenly Voice. Later the rabbi met a friend who asked, "What did the Holy One, Blessed be He, do in that hour," and the rabbi said, "He laughed with joy; he replied, saying, "My sons have defeated Me, My sons have defeated Me."[17] The story illustrates that the text, not its Framers' intent, should be followed, and that reinterpretation is sometimes necessary.

Holmes said, in one of his Olympian moments, "The present has a right to govern itself, so far as it can. . . . Historical continuity with the past is not a duty, only a necessity."[18] The same man, warning against the "pitfall of antiquarianism," declared that he looked forward to a time when history would not be so important "and instead of ingenious research we shall spend our energy on the study of the ends sought to be attained and the reasons for desiring them."[19] Holmes meant that although we cannot escape history, because it has shaped us and explains how we have come to be where we are, we are not obliged to be static or be bound by original intent.

Two hundred years of expanding the meaning of democracy and of becoming a heterogeneous nation of nations in which the citizens have the remarkable duty and the right to keep the government from falling into error, must have tremendous constitutional impact. History can only be a guide, not a controlling force. How the Supreme Court uses history, origins, and evolution as well as original intent depends on those who serve on the Court, because in the end, we must face up to the fact stated by Chief Justice Earl Warren on his retirement in 1969. Speaking of the Court he declared, "We serve only the public interest as we see it, guided only by the Constitution and our own consciences."[20] That, not the original intent of the Framers, is our reality.

Notes

Preface

1. Jacobus tenBroek, "Use by the United States Supreme Court of Extrinsic Aids in Constitutional Construction," *California Law Review* 27 (1939): 399.
2. Clinton Rossiter, *1787: The Grand Convention* (New York: Macmillan, 1966), pp. 333 and p. 424 N. 14.
3. Edwin Meese III, Speech before the American Bar Association, July 9, 1985, Washington, D.C., in *The Great Debate: Interpreting Our Written Constitution,* booklet published by The Federalist Society (Washington, D.C., 1986), p. 9.
4. Robert H. Bork, "Original Intent and the Constitution," *Humanities* 7 (1986), p. 26.
5. Richard Neely, *How Courts Govern America* (New Haven, Conn.: Yale University Press, 1981), p. 18.
6. Samuel L. Clemens, *Adventures of Huckleberry Finn* (New York: W. W. Norton, 1977), p. 194.
7. *The Babylonian Talmud*, ed. I. Epstein (London: Soncino Press, 1948), *Menahoth* 29b (trans. Eli Cashdan), p. 190.
8. E. L. Doctorow, "A Citizen Reads the Constitution," *The Nation*, Feb. 21, 1987, p. 214.

Chapter 1 The Framers and Original Intent

1. Letter to Thomas Ritchie, Sept. 15, 1821, in *Letters and Other Writings of James Madison,* ed. William C. Rives and Philip R. Fendall (New York: Worthington, 1884, 4 vols.), III, p. 228.
2. *The Papers of James Madison,* ed. Henry D. Gilpin (Washington, 1840, 3 vols.).
3. *Journal, Acts and Proceedings, of the Convention . . . Which Formed the Constitution of the United States* (Boston, 1819), reprinted in Jonathan Elliot, ed., *The Debates in the Several State Conventions, on the Adoption of the Federal Constitution* (Washington, 1827–1830, 4 vols.), as vol. 4, and again reprinted by Elliot in his definitive 2nd ed. (Washington, 1836–1840, 5 vols.), in I, pp. 139–318.
4. Four tracts, by Elbridge Gerry (1787), George Mason (1787), Robert Yates and John Lansing (1788), and Luther Martin (1788), all dissident members of the Convention, are conveniently reprinted in Herbert J. Storing, ed., *The Complete Anti-Federalist* (Chicago: University of Chicago Press, 1981, 7 vols.), II, Part I, Objections of Non-Signers, pp. 3–98. Elliot, ed., *Debates,* I, includes the same documents and "The Notes of the Secret Debates of the Federal Convention of 1787 Taken by the late Hon. Robert Yates," pp. 389–479, published originally as *Secret Proceedings and Debates of the Convention Assembled at Philadelphia (Albany, N.Y., 1821). Yates's Notes* or *Secret Proceedings* cover only the period through July 5 and, aside from their incompleteness, are untrustworthy. Madison deplored Yates's "egregious errors." To John G. Jackson, Dec. 27, 1821, in *The Writings of James Madison,* ed. Gaillard Hunt (New York: Putnam's, 1900–1910, 9 vols.), VIII, p. 71.
5. Mason and Henry are quoted in Charles Warren, *The Making of the Constitution* (Boston: Little, Brown, 1928), pp. 67–68.
6. Jefferson to John Adams, Aug. 30, 1787, in *The Papers of Thomas Jefferson,* ed. Julian Boyd (Princeton, N.J.: Princeton University Press, 1950–   ), XII, p. 69.
7. Trimble v. Gordon, 430 U.S. 762, 778 (1977).
8. Madison, "Preface to the Debates in the Convention of 1787," in Max Farrand, ed., *The Records of the Federal Convention* (New Haven: Yale University Press, 1911, 3 vols.), III, pp. 539–51; "nearly half a century" is at p. 551; the remaining material is at p. 550.
9. Ibid., p. 550.
10. Ibid., note 1 citing Madison to Edward Coles, quoted in Hugh Blair Grigsby, *History of the Virginia Federal Convention of 1788,* I, p. 95 note.

11. Farrand, ed., *Records*, I, p. 15, Journal of May 29, 1787.
12. Mason to Mason, May 27, 1787, in ibid., III. p. 28.
13. Farrand, ed., *Records*, II, p. 648, Sept. 17, 1787.
14. Elliot, ed., *Debates*, IV, pp. 191–92.
15. Ibid., II, p. 148.
16. Ibid., III, pp. 436, 448–49.
17. On this subject see infra, chap. 8, on "The Bill of Rights."
18. *The Federalist* #37, ed. Jacob E. Cooke (Cleveland, Ohio: Meridian Books, 1961), pp. 234, 237, and 239 for "must have."
19. See, e.g., his letters to James Monroe, Dec. 27, 1817, in *Writings of Madison*, ed. Hunt, VIII, p. 406, and to T. Jefferson, June 27, 1823, in ibid., IX, p. 142, both supporting the supremacy of the Supreme Court in cases of constitutional law.
20. To Andrew Stevenson, March 25, 1826, in *Letters and Other Writings*, ed. Rives and Fendall, III, p. 522.
21. To Prof. Davis, 1832 or 1833, not sent, in ibid., IV, p. 242. Later in the same letter Madison referred to "the intention of its authors."
22. To Prof. Davis, in ibid., p. 247. The other congressmen who had been Framers were Nicholas Gilman of New Hampshire, Elbridge Gerry of Massachusetts, Roger Sherman of Connecticut, George Clymer and Thomas FitzSimons of Pennsylvania, Daniel Carroll of Maryland, and Abraham Baldwin of Georgia.
23. *The Debates and Proceedings of the Congress of the United States (Annals of Congress)*, comp. Joseph Gales (Washington, 1834), 1st Cong., 1st sess., I, pp. 514–15, June 17, 1789.
24. The debate is in the *Annals of Congress*, 1st Cong., 1st sess., I, pp. 473–608; Elliot, ed., *Debates*, IV, pp. 350–404, reproduced the entire debate. Passing, unsubstantial references to the Convention are in ibid., pp. 490, 559, 566, 588.
25. Farrand, ed., *Records*, II, p. 325, Aug. 18, 1787.
26. In 1798, Jefferson recorded in his *Anas* an anecdote by Abraham Baldwin, who had been at the Convention and the First Congress. The point of the anecdote is that Baldwin reminded Wilson, at the time of the bank bill, that the Convention had defeated "a power to establish a national bank," partly because the bank with which Wilson had been connected in Pennsylvania had provoked such political dissension that granting the power in question would have enlisted the state's anti-bank party against the Constitution. "Wilson agreed to the fact." Farrand, ed., *Records*, III, pp. 375–76.
27. Ibid., II, pp. 615–16, Sept. 14, 1787.
28. *Annals of Congress*, 1st Cong., 3rd sess., II, p. 1896, Feb. 2, 1791. Madison's argument is conveniently available in *The Papers of James*

Madison, ed. William T. Hutchinson et al. (Chicago: University of Chicago Press, 1962, and from vol. XI in 1977, Charlottesville: University Press of Virginia, series in progress), XIII, pp. 372–88.

29. *Annals of Congress,* 4th Cong., 1st sess., V, pp. 775–76, April 6, 1796.
30. Ibid., 1st Cong., 3rd sess., II, p. 1952, Feb. 7, 1791.
31. Ibid., II, p. 1955, Feb. 8, 1791.
32. *Papers of Jefferson,* ed. Boyd, XIX, pp. 277–78.
33. "Opinion on Constitutionality of an Act to Establish a Bank," *The Papers of Alexander Hamilton,* ed. Harold C. Syrett (New York: Columbia University Press, 1961–81, 26 vols.), VIII, p. 110.
34. Ibid., VIII, p. 111.
35. *Papers of Madison,* ed. Hutchinson et al., XII, p. 92, and XIII, p. 348. See also *Annals of Congress,* 1st Cong., 1st sess., I, pp. 178–80, April 20, 1789.
36. "Madison's 'Detached Memoranda'," ed. Elizabeth Fleet, *William and Mary Quarterly,* 3rd ser., III, pp. 534, 542–43 (1946), and for the veto message, *Papers of James Madison,* ed. Hutchinson et al., XIII, p. 395.
37. McCulloch v. Maryland, 4 Wheaton 316 (1819).
38. Madison to Spencer Roane, Sept. 2, 1819, in *Writings of Madison,* ed. Hunt, VIII, pp. 447–53.
39. Jefferson to Spencer Roane, Sept. 6, 1819, in *Writings of Thomas Jefferson,* ed. Albert Ellery Bergh (Washington: Jefferson Memorial Association, 1907, 20 vols.), XV, p. 213.
40. Boston, 1833, 3 vols., I, pp. 382–442.
41. Frank H. Easterbrook, "Legal Interpretation and the Power of the Judiciary," *Harvard Journal of Law and Public Policy,* VII (1981), p. 91. See Karl Llewellyn, *The Common Law Tradition* (Boston: Little, Brown, 1960), pp. 521–35.
42. Corwin, *Twilight of the Supreme Court* (New Haven: Yale University Press, 1933), p. 117.
43. See Charles Grove Haines, *The Role of the Supreme Court in American Government and Politics, 1789–1835* (Berkeley: University of California Press, 1944), pp. 187–219, 357–68, 514–23.
44. *Annals of Congress,* 4th Cong., 1st sess., V, p. 701, March 23, 1796.
45. Ibid., 4th Cong., 1st sess., V, p. 734, March 24, 1796.
46. Ibid., pp. 734–35.
47. Ibid., 4th Cong., 1st sess., V, pp. 760–61, for Washington's message of March 30, 1796; or see Farrand, ed., *Records,* III, p. 371.
48. To Jefferson, April 4, 1796, in Farrand, ed., *Records,* III, p. 372.
49. Ibid., II, p. 648, Sept. 17, 1787.

50. Ibid., I, pp. xii–xiii.
51. *Annals of Congress*, 4th Cong., 1st sess., V, p. 775, April 6, 1796.
52. Ibid.
53. Ibid., pp. 775–76.
54. 2 Dallas 419 (1793).
55. In his "Detached Memoranda," cited above, note 36, pp. 543–44, Madison elaborated his criticism of Washington's use of the Journal. He also believed that unexplained votes recorded in the Journal could be misleading. See his letter to Prof. Davis, 1832 or 1833, unsent, in *Letters and Other Writings of Madison*, IV, pp. 253–54.
56. *Annals of Congress*, 4th Cong., 1st sess., V, p. 776, April 6, 1796.
57. Ibid., pp. 777–78. Madison knew nothing about the proceedings of the second North Carolina Convention, which ratified the Constitution. To Jonathan Elliot, Feb. 14, 1827, in *Writings of Madison*, ed. Hunt, IX, p. 271. The publication of Elliot's *Debates* (1827–1830, 1st ed.) did not much improve the situation. Elliot added some fragmentary material from New Hampshire, Connecticut, and Maryland, and noted that his reports of debates "may, in some instances, have been inaccurately taken down, and, in others, probably, too faintly sketched," in Preface to the First Edition (1830).
58. Merrill Jensen, *The Documentary History of the Ratification of the Constitution*. Vol. I. *Constitutional Documents and Records, 1776–1787*. (Madison: State Historical Society of Wisconsin, 1976), p. 34.
59. To J. Elliot, Nov. 1827, in ibid., pp. 291–92.
60. *Annals of Congress*, 1st Cong., 3rd sess., II, pp. 1952–53, Feb. 7, 1791.
61. Joseph Story, *Commentaries on the Constitution of the United States* (Boston, 1833, 1st ed., 3 vols.), I, pp. 388–89.
62. Ibid., p. 391.
63. To N. P. Trist, Dec. 1831, in *Writings of Madison*, ed. Hunt, IX, p. 477, Madison's emphasis.
64. To Henry Lee, June 25, 1824, in ibid., IX, p. 191.
65. Ibid., IX, facing p. 610, Madison's emphasis.
66. To Spencer Roane, May 6, 1821, in ibid., IX, p. 59.
67. To Henry St. George Tucker, Dec. 23, 1817, in ibid., VIII, p. 403.
68. To Prof. Davis, 1832 or 1833, not sent, in *Letters and Other Writings of Madison*, ed. Rives and Fendall, IV, p. 249; compare ibid., IV, p. 242.
69. To Thomas Ritchie, Sept. 15, 1821, in ibid., III, p. 228.
70. To M. L. Hurlbert, May 1830, in *Writings of Madison*, ed. Hunt, IX, p. 372. The sentence is ambiguous: did Madison mean the

understanding of the language? If not, the phrase "of the language used" seems superfluous.

71. "Proceedings of Commissioners to Remedy Defects of the Federal Government," Sept. 11, 1786, in *Documents Illustrative of the Formation of the Union of the American States,* ed. Charles C. Tansill (Washington: Government Printing Office, 1927), p. 43, and "Report of Proceedings in Congress," Feb. 21, 1787, in ibid., p. 46.

72. Resolution of Congress, Sept. 28, 1787, in ibid., p. 1007.

73. To Thomas Richie, Sept. 15, 1821, in *Letters and Other Writings of Madison,* ed. Rives and Fendall, III, p. 228.

74. Farrand, ed., *Records,* II, p. 91, July 23, 1787.

75. See Leonard W. Levy, articles on Concord Town Meeting Resolutions, Constitution, Constitutional Convention, and Social Compact Theory, in Leonard W. Levy, Kenneth L. Karst, and Dennis J. Mahoney, eds., *Encyclopedia of the American Constitution* (New York: Macmillan, 1986, 4 vols.).

76. Jensen et al., *Documentary History.Vol. II. Ratification of the Constitution by States: Pennsylvania* pp. 483–84, Dec. 4, 1787.

77. To M. L. Hurlbert, May 1830, in *Writings of Madison,* ed. Hunt, IX, p. 372.

78. To John G. Jackson, Dec. 27, 1821, in ibid., IX, p. 74, Madison's emphasis.

79. To Henry Lee, June 25, 1824, in ibid., IX, p. 191.

80. "Detached Memoranda" cited above, note 36, at p. 544.

81. *The Federalist* #37, ed. Cooke, pp. 236–37.

82. To J. G. Jackson, Sept. 27, 1821, in *Writings of Madison,* ed. Hunt, IX, p. 74. For his criticism of McCulloch v. Maryland, 4 Wheaton 316 (1819), see letter to Roane, Sept. 2, 1819, in ibid., VIII, pp. 450–51; of Cohens v. Virginia, 6 Wheaton 264 (1821), see letter to Roane, May 6, 1821, in ibid., IX, pp. 61–62.

83. To Roane, May 6, 1821, in ibid., IX, p. 59.

84. To Roane, Sept. 2, 1819, in ibid., VIII, pp. 447 and 450.

85. To M. L. Hurlbert, May 1830, in ibid., IX, p. 372; to C. E. Haynes, Feb. 25, 1831, in ibid., IX, p. 443; and to Joseph C. Cabell, March 22, 1827, in ibid., IX, p. 286, item #11.

86. To Henry Lee, in ibid., June 25, 1824, IX, p. 191.

87. To Prof. Davis, 1832 or 1833, not sent, in *Letters and Other Writings of Madison,* ed. Rives and Fendall, IV, p. 249.

88. Veto Message, March 3, 1817, in *Writings of Madison,* ed. Hunt, VIII, pp. 386–88.

89. For "final resort," see letter to Jefferson, June 27, 1823, in ibid., IX, p. 142.

90. To James Monroe, Dec. 27, 1817, in ibid., p. 406.
91. Ibid., pp. 405–406. For Madison's opposition to excises and the carriage tax, see *Papers of Madison,* ed. Hutchinson et al., XV, pp. 320–22, 327. The Supreme Court sustained the carriage tax in *Hylton v. United States,* 3 Dallas 171 (1796).
92. To Roane, May 6, 1821, in *Writings of Madison,* ed. Hunt, IX, pp. 57–61.
93. To Monroe, Dec. 27, 1817, in ibid., VIII, pp. 406–407.
94. To Roane, Sept. 2, 1819, in ibid., IX, pp. 448–49.
95. To M. L. Hurlbert, May 1830, in ibid., p. 374.
96. To Jefferson, June 27, 1823, in ibid., IX, pp. 141–43. See also Madison's entitled essay of 1829, in ibid., pp. 351–53, for an exposition of his views on the Court. For Jefferson's views, see Charles Grove Haines, *The Role of The Supreme Court in American Government and Politics, 1789–1835* (Berkeley, 1944), pp. 514–20.
97. To N. Trist, Feb. 15, 1830, in *Writings of Madison,* ed. Hunt, IX, p. 355. See also letter to Roane, June 29, 1821, on the dangers of variant interpretations of the supreme law, in ibid., p. 66.
98. To Edward Everett, Aug. 29, 1830, in ibid., IX, p. 397.
99. To N. Trist, Dec. 1831, in ibid., IX, p. 476.
100. To Jefferson, June 27, 1823, in ibid., IX, p. 143; to Martin Van Buren, Sept. 30, 1826, in ibid., IX, p. 254; to Martin Van Buren, June 3, 1830, in ibid., IX, p. 374; to Edward Everett, Aug. 28, 1830, in ibid., IX, pp. 397–98.
101. To Jefferson, June 27, 1823, in ibid., IX, pp. 140–41.
102. To N. P. Trist, Dec. 1831, in ibid., IX, p. 477.
103. To Henry Lee, June 25, 1824, in ibid., IX, p. 191.
104. Veto Message, March 3, 1817, in ibid., IX, pp. 386–88.
105. *Writings of Madison,* ed. Hunt VIII, pp. 386–88, 406, and IX, pp. 66, 142, 254, 351, 374, 471, and 476.
106. To Prof. Davis, in *Letters and Other Writings of Madison,* ed. Rives and Fendall; IV, p. 249.
107. See letter to M. L. Hurlbert, May 1830, in *Writings of Madison,* ed. Hunt, IX, p. 372. For earlier versions of the argument, see Madison's letter to Joseph C. Cabell, March 22, 1827, in ibid., IX, pp. 284–86, where he also recommended the use of the Journal of the Convention, and his letter to Cabell, Sept. 18, 1828, in ibid., IX, pp. 316–40.
108. Farrand, ed., *Records,* II, p. 316, Aug. 21, 1787.
109. To Samuel H. Smith, Feb. 2, 1827, in *Writings of Madison,* ed. Hunt, IX, p. 270.

110. To Thomas Ritchie, Sept. 15, 1821, in *Letters and Other Writings of Madison*, ed. Rives and Fendall, III, p. 228.
111. To John G. Jackson, Dec. 27, 1821, in *Writings of Madison*, ed. Hunt, IX, p. 70.

Chapter 2 President and Congress: Foreign Policy and War Powers

1. Alexander Hamilton, James Madison, and John Jay, *The Federalist*, ed. Jacob E. Cooke (New York: Meridian Books, 1961), #64, 69, and 75, discussed below.
2. Ibid., p. 340.
3. Ibid.
4. Ibid., #47, p. 331.
5. Ibid.
6. Ibid., #48, p. 332.
7. Ibid., pp. 333, 334.
8. Ibid., #51, p. 350.
9. Max Farrand, ed., *The Records of the Federal Convention* (New Haven, Conn.: Yale University Press, 1937, rev. ed., 4 vols.), I, p. 21, Resolve No. 7 of Virginia Plan, proposed May 29, 1787, by Edmund Randolph.
10. Articles of Confederation, Article IX reprinted in Merrill Jensen, *The Articles of Confederation* (Madison: University of Wisconsin Press, 1940), p. 266.
11. Farrand, ed, *Records*, pp. 64–65.
12. Ibid., p. 65.
13. Ibid., pp. 65–66, Madison's Notes. Madison's own remark is from notes kept by Rufus King, ibid., p. 70.
14. William Blackstone, *Commentaries on the Laws of England* (London, 1765–1769, 4 vols.), I, p. 250.
15. Ibid., pp. 252–62.
16. Farrand, ed., *Records, I*, pp. 288–89, 293.
17. *Papers of Alexander Hamilton*, ed. Harold C. Syrett (New York: Columbia University Press, 1961–1981), IV, p. 211, document entitled "Constitutional Convention. Remarks on the Abolition of the States," June 19, 1789. Hamilton's speech was reported by Madison, Robert Yates, John Lansing, and Rufus King, and, we have Hamilton's own notes of his speech, in ibid., pp. 178–211. I have relied mainly on Madison's report, checked against Yates's statement of the provisions of the plan for a constitution suggested by Hamilton. Compare

Farrand, ed., *Records*, I, pp. 291–93, Madison's version of that plan, and pp. 300–301, Yates's version.
18. Farrand, ed., *Records*, I, p. 292.
19. Ibid., II, p. 132.
20. Ibid., p. 134.
21. Ibid., I, p. 21.
22. Ibid., pp. 244–45. For the various drafts by the Committee of Detail, ibid., II, pp. 137–75, especially pp. 145, 158, and 171.
23. Ibid., p. 185.
24. Ibid., pp. 182, 183.
25. Ibid., pp. 318–19. The 4–5 vote is recorded in the Journal of the Convention, p. 313. Madison's Notes show only that the motion passed.
26. See letter by Sherman, Dec. 8, 1787, in James H. Hutson, ed., *Supplement to Max Farrand's The Records of the Federal Convention* (New Haven, Conn.: Yale University Press, 1987), p. 288.
27. The best treatment of the subject is Charles Lofgren, *"Government from Reflection and Choice": Constitutional Essays on War, Foreign Relations, and Federalism* (New York: Oxford University Press, 1986), pp. 3–38, reprinting his *Yale Law Journal* essay, "War-Making Under the Constitution."
28. See Ernest May, ed., *The Ultimate Decision* (New York: Braziller, 1960), p. 19, essay by May, "The President Shall Be Commander-in-Chief (1787–1789)."
29. Farrand, ed., *Records*, II, p. 392.
30. Lawrence A. Kaplan, *Colonies into States: American Diplomacy, 1763–1801* (New York: Macmillan, 1972), chap. VI, "Diplomacy and the Confederation."
31. Ibid.
32. Farrand, ed., *Records*, II, p. 15.
33. Ibid., p. 393.
34. Ibid., p. 394.
35. Ibid., p. 482, by James McHenry of Maryland.
36. Ibid., p. 481.
37. Ibid., pp. 498–99.
38. Ibid., pp. 508–509.
39. Blackstone, *Commentaries*, I, p. 258. See Lofgren, *Government from Reflection and Choice*, pp. 23–32.
40. Farrand, ed., *Records*, II, p. 392.
41. *The Federalist*, No. 64, ed. Cooke, p. 436.
42. Ibid., p. 304.
43. New York constitution of 1777, section XXIII, in Francis N. Thorpe,

ed., *The Federal and State Constitutions* (Washington, D.C.: Government Printing Office, 1909, 7 vols.), V, p. 2633.

44. Massachusetts constitution of 1780, chap. 2, sect. IX, in ibid., V, p. 1902.

45. Farrand, ed., *Records*, II, pp. 522–23.

46. Ibid., p. 538.

47. Ibid., p. 540.

48. Ibid., pp. 540–41.

49. Ibid.

50. Ibid., p. 543.

51. Ibid., p. 549.

52. Charles Warren, *The Making of the Constitution* (Boston: Little, Brown, 1928), pp. 686–88.

53. Report of Committee of Style, in Farrand, ed., *Records*, II, p. 599, presented Sept. 12.

54. Ibid., pp. 626–27.

55. Pp. 432–36 of *The Federalist*, ed. Cooke, #64. Emphasis added.

56. For expressions of this view, see Herbert J. Storing, *The Complete Anti-Federalist* (Chicago: University of Chicago Press, 1981, 7 vols.), II, p. 67 (L. Martin: the President "was a KING, in everything but the name"); II, p. 16 (Letters of Cato: "these powers, in both president and king, are substantially the same"); III, p. 37 (Old Whig: The President "is in reality to be a KING as much a King as the King of Great-Britain"); III, p. 137 (Philadelphiensis: "that dangerous and uncontrouled officer, the *President General*, or more properly, our new KING").

57. *The Federalist*, ed. Cooke, #69, pp. 462–70.

58. Ibid., #75, pp. 503–506. Emphasis added.

59. Jonathan Elliot, ed., *The Debates in the Several State Conventions* (Philadelphia: Lippincott, 1836–1845, rev. ed., 5 vols.), II, p. 278.

60. Merrill Jensen, John Kaminski, and Gaspare Saladino, eds., *The Documentary History of the Ratification of the Constitution. Ratification of the Constitution by the States. Pennsylvania* (Madison: State Historical Society of Wisconsin, 1976–   ), II, pp. 480, 491.

61. Elliot, ed., *Debates*, IV, pp. 107–108.

62. Ibid., IV, p. 120.

63. Ibid., IV, p. 263.

64. Ibid., p. 265.

65. Farrand, ed., *Records*, II, pp. 205, 212 (Aug. 7), and 297 (Aug. 15).

66. One of the Anti-Federalists who made such an argument was the future diplomat and President, James Monroe. See Elliott, ed., *Debates*, III, p. 221, June 10, 1788, Virginia ratifying convention.

67. Lofgren, *Government from Reflection and Choice*, p. 16.
68. Charles C. Tansill, ed., *Documents Illustrative of the Formation of the Union* (Washington, D.C.: Government Printing Office, 1927), 69th Congress, 1st Sess., House Doc. No. 398, pp. 1032, 1051.
69. See Storing, *Complete Anti-Federalist*, I, separately entitled *What the Anti-Federalists Were* For; Cecilia M. Kenyon, *The Anti-Federalists* (Indianapolis: Bobbs-Merrill, 1966), pp. xxi–cxxiii.
70. See above, text connected with note 60.
71. *Pacificus* No. 1, June 29, 1793, in *Papers of Alexander Hamilton*, XV, pp. 33–43.
72. Letters of Helvidius, Aug. 24 and Sept. 14, 1793, in *The Writings of James Madison*, ed. Gaillard Hunt (New York: Putnam's, 1900–1910, 9 vols.), VI, pp. 138–51, 171–77.
73. Opinion on the Powers of the Senate Respecting Diplomatic Appointments, April 24, 1790, in *Papers of Thomas Jefferson*, ed. Julian Boyd (Princeton, N.J.: Princeton University Press, 1950–ᅠ), XVI, p. 379.
74. Quoted in Abraham D. Sofaer, *War, Foreign Affairs and Constitutional Power: The Origins* (Cambridge, Mass.: Ballinger, 1976), p. 137, and in Louis Henkin, *Foreign Affairs and the Constitution* (Mineola, N.Y.: Foundation Press, 1972), p. 45, both citing *Annals of Congress*, X, p. 610.
75. United States v. Curtiss-Wright Export Corp., 299 U.S. 304, 319 (1936). For a demolition of the opinion of the Court, see Lofgren, *Government from Reflection and Choice*, pp. 167–205.
76. 1 Cranch 1, 28 (1801).
77. Joseph Story, *Commentaries on the Constitution* (Boston, 1833, reprinted New York: Da Capo Press, 1970, 3 vols.), III, pp. 355–66, sections 1501–13.
78. In the preparation of this chapter, I have been instructed by several outstanding essays. They include, most important, two by Arthur Bestor: "Separation of Powers in the Domain of Foreign Affairs: the Intent of the Constitution Historically Examined," *Seton Hall Law Review*, V (1974): 527–666, and "Respective Roles of Senate and President in the Making and Abrogation of Treaties—The Original Intent of the Framers of the Constitution Historically Examined," *Washington Law Review*, LV (1979), pp. 1–136. Charles Lofgren's essays in his *Government from Choice and Reflection*, especially the first one on the power to declare war, cited above, note 27, and his "War Powers, Treaties, and the Constitution," in Leonard W. Levy and Dennis J. Mahoney, eds., *The Framing and Ratification of the Constitution* (New York: Macmillan, 1987), pp. 242–58, are also

splendid. So is Jack N. Rakove, "Solving a Constitutional Puzzle: The Treatymaking Clause as a Case Study," *Perspectives in American History*, new ser., I (1984), pp. 233–81.

Chapter 3 Judicial Review and Judicial Activism

1. Osborne v. Bank of the United States, 9 Wheaton 738, 866 (1824).
2. See Gary L. McDowell, *The Constitution and Contemporary Constitutional Theory* (Cumberland, Va.: Center for Judicial Studies, 1985); Christopher Wolfe, *The Rise of Modern Judicial Review: From Constitutional Interpretation to Judge-Made Law* (New York: Basic Books, 1986).
3. Fletcher v. Peck, 6 Cranch 87 (1810); New Jersey v. Wilson, 7 Cranch 164 (1812); Piqua Branch Bank v. Knoop, 16 Howard 369 (1853); Dodge v. Woolsey, 18 Howard 331 (1856). Benjamin F. Wright, Jr., *The Contract Clause of the Constitution* (Cambridge, Mass.: Harvard University Press, 1938), which is still the authoritative study, discusses these cases and contract clause doctrines.
4. Civil Rights Cases, 109 U.S. 3 (1883).
5. Pollock v. Farmers Loan & Trust Co., 158 U.S. 601 (1895).
6. Standard Oil Co. v. United States, 221 U.S. 1, 58–64 (1911), for the rule of reason; United States v. United Shoe Machinery Co., 247 U.S. 32 (1918); United States v. U.S. Steel Corp., 251 U.S. 417 (1920); United States v. International Harvester Co., 274 U.S. 693 (1927).
7. Panama Refining Co. v. Ryan, 293 U.S. 388 (1935).
8. Quoted by James Bradley Thayer, "The Origin and Scope of the American Doctrine of Constitutional Law," *Harvard Law Review*, 7 (1893):129, at p. 152.
9. Message to Congress, Dec. 8, 1908, in *The Congressional Record*, XLIII, Part I, 60th Cong., 2nd sess., p. 21.
10. *Letters of Brutus*, No. 13, Feb. 21, 1788, in Herbert J. Storing, ed., *The Complete Anti-Federalist* (Chicago: University of Chicago Press, 1981, 7 vols.), II, p. 429.
11. *Letters of Agrippa*, No. 12, Jan. 14, 1788, in ibid., II, p. 97, and *Letters from the Federal Farmer to the Republican*, No. 3, Oct. 10, 1787, in ibid., II, p. 245.
12. *Federalist* #81, in Cooke, ed., pp. 548–49.
13. Elliot, ed., *Debates*, III, p. 527.
14. Ibid., III, p. 533.
15. Ibid., III, p. 543.
16. Ibid., III, p. 549.

17. Ibid., V, p. 554.
18. Ibid., p. 452.
19. Ibid., pp. 453–66.
20. Jensen et al., eds., *Documentary History*, II, p. 518.
21. *Independent Chronicle* (Boston), April 4, 1793, quoted in Charles Warren, *The Supreme Court in United States History* (Boston: Little, Brown, 1923, 3 vols.), I, p. 96.
22. *The Debates and Proceedings of the Congress of the United States* (Annals of Congress), comp. Joseph Gales (Washington, D.C., 1834), 4th Cong., 1st sess., V, p. 539, March 14, 1796.
23. Warren, *Supreme Court*, I, p. 100.
24. See Cohens v. Virginia, 6 Wheaton 264 (1821).
25. Hans v. Louisiana, 134 U.S. 1, 12–16 (1889).
26. 3 Dallas 171 (1796).
27. *Annals of Congress*, 3rd Cong., 1st sess., IV, p. 730, May 29, 1794.
28. 3 Dallas 171, 173.
29. Farrand, ed., *Records*, II, p. 350, Aug. 20, 1787.
30. Ibid., II, p. 618.
31. Ibid.
32. Ibid., III, p. 628, June 18, 1787.
33. William Blount, Richard D. Spaight, and Hugh Williamson to Gov. Richard Caswell, Sept. 18, 1787, in ibid., III, pp. 83–84.
34. *Federalist* #12, 21, 38, 40, and 53.
35. *Federalist* #21, ed. Cooke, p. 134.
36. Ibid., p. 225.
37. 3 Dallas 171, 175 (1796).
38. Ibid., pp. 181–83.
39. Ibid., pp. 175–81.
40. Ware v. Hylton, 3 Dallas 199 (1796).
41. Ibid., p. 211.
42. Ibid., p. 236.
43. Samuel Chase, Notes of Speeches Delivered to the Maryland Ratifying Convention, April 1788, in Storing, ed., *Complete Anti-Federalist*, V, p. 84.
44. Ibid., V, pp. 88–89.
45. James Morton Smith, *Freedom's Fetters: The Alien and Sedition Laws and American Civil Liberties* (Ithaca, N.Y.: Cornell University Press, 1956).
46. Calder v. Bull, 3 Dallas 386 (1798).
47. Louise I. Trenholme, *The Ratification of the Federal Constitution in North Carolina* (New York: Columbia University Press, 1932), pp. 119, 120.

48. William Cushing of Massachusetts, the fourth Justice, did not address the issue.

49. 3 Dallas 386, 397.

50. Ibid., p. 390.

51. William Blackstone, *Commentaries on the Laws of England* (London, 1765–1769, 4 vols.), I, p. 46, as quoted in 3 Dallas 386 (1798).

52. Chase added, without offering a quotation or even a citation, that Blackstone's opinion that ex post facto laws applied only to criminal matters was "confirmed by his successor, Mr. Wooddeson . . . " [3 Dallas at p. 391]. But Richard Wooddeson's Vinerian lectures, *A Systematical View of the Laws of England* (London, 1792, 3 vols.) II, p. 641, merely stated that "justice wears her sternest aspect" when penal statutes are passed ex post facto, and that is all that Blackstone's passage showed.

53. See Calder v. Bull, 3 Dallas 386, 391–92 and 396–97. Delaware's statement was: "That retrospective laws punishing offenses committed before the existence of such laws, are oppressive and unjust, and ought not to be made." The statement should have referred to actions or conduct instead of offenses. Massachusetts declared: "Laws made to punish for actions done before the existence of such laws, and which have not been declared crimes by preceding laws, are unjust, oppressive, and inconsistent with the fundamental principles of a free government."

54. "That no *ex post facto* law, nor any law impairing the obligation of contracts, shall be made." Francis N. Thorpe, ed., *The Federal and State Constitutions, Colonial Charters, and Other Organic Laws* (Washington, 1909, 7 vols.), V, p. 3101 (Pennsylvania). South Carolina had a similar provision, which included a ban on bills of attainder. Ibid., VI, p. 3264.

55. Ibid., IV, p. 2456.

56. Jonathan Elliot, ed., *The Debates in the Several State Conventions on the Adoption of the Federal Constitution* (Philadelphia: Lippincott, 1836–1845, rev. ed., 5 vols.), IV, p. 184.

57. Ibid.

58. Ibid., p. 185.

59. Ibid., p. 181.

60. Van Horne's Lessee v. Dorrance, 2 Dallas 304, 319–20 (1795).

61. *Annals of Congress*, 5th Cong., 2nd sess., IX, pp. 2577–79, Jan. 8, 1799; *ibid.*, 7th Cong., 2nd sess., XII, pp. 377–78, Jan. 13, 1803, and XII, p. 551, Feb. 18, 1803. Charles Warren, *Bankruptcy in the United States* (Cambridge, Mass.: Harvard University Press, 1935), p. 14. William W. Crosskey, *Politics and the Constitution* (Chicago: University of Chicago Press, 1953, 2 vols.), I, pp. 248–49.

62. Fletcher v. Peck, 6 Cranch 87 (1810).
63. See Ogden v. Saunders, 12 Wheaton 266, 303, 329, 330, 335 (1827); Satterlee v. Matthewson, 2 Peters 380, memorandum by Justice William Johnson in Appendix No. 1, at pp. 681–87; Joseph Story, *Commentaries on the Constitution of the United States* (Boston, 1833, 3 vols.), I, p. 211, sect. 1339.
64. Carpenter v. Pennsylvania, 17 Howard 456, 463 (1854).
65. Farrand, ed. *Records*, II, p. 375, Aug. 22, 1787.
66. Ibid., p. 376.
67. Ibid., p. 440.
68. Ibid. Madison was confused, because no motion had yet been passed or even proposed that banned state ex post facto laws.
69. Ibid., p. 435, Journal of Convention.
70. Ibid., pp. 448–49, Aug. 29.
71. Ibid., p. 617, Sept. 14.
72. To Governor Samuel Huntington, Sept. 26, 1787, in Merrill Jensen, John P. Kaminski, and Gaspare J. Saladino, eds., *The Documentary History of the Ratification of the Constitution* (Madison: State Historical Society of Wisconsin, 1981), XIII, p. 471.
73. Crosskey, *Politics and the Constitution*, I, pp. 327–38.
74. Ibid., pp. 325–29.
75. "Letters of Centinel." No. 16, Feb. 23, 1788, originally published in *Independent Gazetteer* (Philadelphia), reprinted in Storing, ed., *Complete Anti-Federalist*, II, p. 198.
76. *Massachusetts Centinel* (Boston), Nov. 28, 1787. Crosskey, *Politics and the Constitution*, I, p. 328, also quotes *The* (Boston) *Independent Chronicle*, May 31, 1787, criticizing the legislature's enactment of a legal tender law that was based on "a power to dispose by an ex post facto law, of the private contracts between man and man."
77. Elliot, ed., *Debates*, I, p. 328, and II, p. 407.
78. Ibid., III, pp. 461, 471–73, 474–75, 479–80, 481.
79. Ibid., p. 465.
80. Ibid., p. 473.
81. Ibid., p. 479.
82. Turner v. Turner's Executrix, 4 Call. (Va.) 234, 237 (1792).

Chapter 4 *Marbury v. Madison:* Judicial Activism Run Amok

1. Marbury v. Madison, 1 Cranch 137 (1803).
2. The Holmes Devise, Vol. II, says Marshall was "statesmanlike" on "the sensitive issues that *Marbury* raised." George Lee Haskins and

Herbert Johnson, *Foundations of Power: John Marshall 1801-15.* (New York: Macmillan, 1981), p. 203, Vol. II of Oliver Wendell Homes Devise *History of the Supreme Court,* ed. Paul A. Freund.

3. Robert L. Stern and Eugene Gressman, *Supreme Court Practice* (Washington, D.C.: Bureau of National Affairs, 1969, 4th ed.), p. 411, citing 28 U.S.C. sect. 1651.

4. See Charles Warren, "New Light on the History of the Federal Judiciary Act of 1789," *Harvard Law Review* 37 (1923): 49–132.

5. The eleven were John Langdon of New Hampshire, Caleb Strong of Massachusetts, Oliver Ellsworth and William S. Johnson of Connecticut, William Paterson of New Jersey, Robert Morris of Pennsylvania, Richard Bassett and George Read of Delaware, Daniel Carroll of Maryland, Pierce Butler of South Carolina, and William Few of Georgia.

6. The list of fifty-one is in *Congressional Record,* 68th Cong., 1st sess., speech of Henry St. George Tucker, Jan. 23, 1924, LXV, p. 51.

7. Myers v. United States, 272 U.S. 52, 174 (1926).

8. Albert J. Beveridge, *The Life of John Marshall* (Boston: Houghton Mifflin, 1916–1919, 4 vols.), III, pp. 50 and 75.

9. For an excellent account of the enforcement of the Sedition Act, see James Morton Smith, *Freedom's Fetters: The Alien and Sedition Laws and American Civil Liberties* (Ithaca, N.Y.: Cornell University Press, 1956).

10. Haskins and Johnson, *Foundations of Power,* pp. 135, 183; Charles Warren, *The Supreme Court in United States History* (Boston: Little, Brown, 1923, 3 vols.), I, pp. 200–201; Beveridge, *Life of Marshall,* III, p. 110. See also the splendid accounts by Kathryn Turner, "Federalist Policy and the Judiciary Act of 1801," *William and Mary Quarterly,* 3rd ser., 22 (1965): 3–22, and "The Midnight Judges," *University of Pennsylvania Law Review,* 109 (1961): 494–523.

11. Jefferson to John Dickinson, Dec. 19, 1801, in *the Writings of Thomas Jefferson,* ed. Albert Ellery Bergh (Washington: Jefferson Memorial Association, 1905, 20 vols.), X, p. 302.

12. Waren, *Supreme Court,* I, pp. 195–97.

13. On the repeal act, see Richard E. Ellis, *The Jeffersonian Crisis: Courts and Politics in the Young Republic* (New York: Oxford University Press, 1971), pp. 45–60; Haskins and Johnson, *Foundations of Power,* pp. 163–81; Beveridge, *Life of Marshall,* III, pp. 68–97.

14. Warren, *Supreme Court,* I, pp. 200–201; Haskins and Johnson, *Foundations of Power,* pp. 183–84; Beveridge, *Life of Marshall,* III, p. 124.

15. The best treatments of Marbury v. Madison include William W. Van

Alstyne, "A Critical Guide to Marbury v. Madison," *Duke Law Journal*, 169 (1969):1–45; Beveridge, *Life of Marshall*, III, pp. 101–156; and Haskins and Johnson, *Foundations of Power*, pp. 182–204.

16. S. T. Mason to J. Monroe, Dec. 21, 1801, and J. Breckenridge to J. Monroe, Dec. 24, 1801, both quoted in Warren, *Supreme Court*, I, pp. 203, 204.

17. In addition to the sources cited in note 13 above, see Charles Grove Haines, *The Role of the Supreme Court in American Government and Politics: 1789–1835* (Berkeley: University of California Press, 1944), pp. 227–42.

18. Warren, *Supreme Court*, I, p. 205, quoting *Salem* (Mass.) *Register*, Jan. 28, 1802.

19. Beveridge, *Life of Marshall*, III, pp. 94–97, and Warren, *Supreme Court*, I, pp. 222–23.

20. Quoted in Warren, *Supreme Court*, I, p. 233.

21. Ellis, *Jeffersonian Crisis*, pp. 69–75, and Haskins and Johnson, *Foundations of Power*, pp. 211–15, 234–38.

22. Beveridge, *Life of Marshall*, III, pp. 112–13, citing *Independent Chronicle* (Boston), March 10, 1803.

23. Warren, *Supreme Court*, I, pp. 247–48.

24. Stuart v. Laird, 1 Cranch 299 (1803).

25. Marbury v Madison, 1 Cranch 137, 149 and 171–72, opinion by Marshall reporting Chandler's case arising under an act of Congress of 1793. The fullest discussion is in Gordon E. Sherman, "The Case of John Chandler v. the Secretary of War," *Yale Law Journal*, 14 (1905):431–51, whose conclusions are unreliable.

26. Farrand, ed., *Records*, II, p. 147, draft of a constitution in the writing of Edmund Randolph with emendations by John Rutledge, both members of the committee.

27. 1 Cranch 137, 146.

28. Ibid., p. 148.

29. On the impeachment of Chase, see Haskins and Johnson, *Foundations of Power*, pp. 215–45, and Beveridge, *Life of Marshall*, III, pp. 157–222.

30. Beveridge, *Life of Marshall*, III, p. 177.

31. Dred Scott v. Sandford, 19 Howard 393 (1857).

32. Turner, "Federalist Policy and the Judiciary Act of 1801," pp. 3–32.

33. Turner, "The Midnight Judges," pp. 494–523.

34. Warren, *Supreme Court*, I, pp. 195–97.

35. Haskins and Johnson, *Foundations of Power*, pp. 170–77.

36. Letter of May 3, 1802, reprinted in ibid., pp. 169–70.

37. Ibid., pp. 170–77, and Ellis, *Jeffersonian Crisis*, pp. 61–65.

38. 1 Cranch 299, 302–304 (1803).

39. Ibid., p. 309.

Chapter 5 Was Judicial Review Intended? The State Precedents

1. William Blackstone, *Commentaries on the Laws of England* (London, 1766–1769, 4 vols.), I, p. 91.

2. Andrew C. McLaughlin, *A Constitutional History of the United States* (New York: Appleton Century Crofts, 1935), p. 310.

3. Edward S. Corwin, *Doctrine of Judicial Review* (Princeton, N.J.: Princeton University Press, 1914), pp. 2 and 17. See also Charles Grove Haines, *The American Doctrine of Judicial Supremacy* (Los Angeles: University of California, 1932, 2nd ed.), p. 66.

4. In addition to Charles Warren's *Making of the Constitution* (Boston: Little, Brown, 1928), p. 332, see his *Congress, the Constitution, and the Supreme Court* (Boston: Little, Brown, 1925), pp. 41–57, 64–74, and 91–93. Charles Grove Haines's *American Doctrine of Judicial Supremacy* (New York: Russell & Russell, 1932), is discussed below. Raoul Berger, *Congress v. the Supreme Court* (Cambridge, Mass.: Harvard University Press, 1969), p. 49.

5. David John Mays, *Edmund Pendleton* (Cambridge, Mass.: Harvard University Press, 1952), II, pp. 169–72.

6. Haines, *American Doctrine*, p. 73 of the 1st ed. At p. 88 of the 2nd ed., Haines repeated only the last sentence; he eliminated the preceding lines without altering his opinion and without correcting numerous misrepresentations of the cases he described, and at p. 95 of the 2nd ed. he repeated the thought that a "series of precedents with a cumulative effect, along with a common sentiment in practically all of the states, led men to accept certain ideas which made review of legislative acts by the courts seem necessary." See also Max Farrand, *The Framing of the Constitution of the United States* (New Haven, Conn.: Yale University Press, 1913), p. 156.

7. William James, *Memories and Studies*, quoted by Jerome Frank, *Fate and Freedom* (New York: Simon & Schuster, 1945), p. 181.

8. Rutgers v. Waddington, 1784, Mayor's Court of New York City, opinion by James Duane, mayor and chief justice, reprinted in entirety by Julius Goebel Jr., ed., *The Law Practice of Alexander Hamilton: Documents and Commentary* (New York, 1964), I, chap. 3; the quotation is at p. 415; emphasis in original.

9. See Louis B. Boudin, *Government by Judiciary* (New York: William

Godwin, 1932, 2 vols.), I, 536–55; William W. Crosskey, *Politics and the Constitution in the History of the United States* (Chicago: University of Chicago Press, 1953, 3 vols.), II, pp. 948–52; and Haines, *American Doctrine*, pp. 80–83.

10. Holmes v. Walton, which was unreported, is referred to in State v. Parkhurst, 4 Halsted (N.J.) 427, supposedly decided in 1802 but not reported until 1828; in State v. Parkhurst the state court said that in Holmes the court had held a state act unconstitutional.

11. 4 Call's Virginia Reports 5 (1782), discussed in Mays, *Edmund Pendleton*, I, pp. 196–201 and 387 n. 65; Crosskey, *Politics and the Constitution*, II, pp. 952–60; Haines, *American Doctrine*, pp. 83–85.

12. Documents by Pendleton providing contemporary information on the *Caton* case are in David John Mays, ed., *The Letters and Papers of Edmund Pendleton* (Charlottesville: University Press of Virginia, 1967, 2 vols.), II, pp. 417–35.

13. See note 8 above for citation; discussed by Crosskey, *Politics and the Constitution*, II, pp. 965–68; Boudin, *Government by Judiciary*, I, pp. 58–62; Haines, *American Doctrine*, pp. 85–88.

14. Discussed in Crosskey, *Politics and the Constitution*, II, pp. 965–68; Haines, *American Doctrine*, pp. 88–92; Boudin, *Government by Judiciary*, I, 58–62.

15. Crosskey, *Politics and the Constitution*, II, pp. 968–70.

16. 1 Martin (N. Car.) 42 (1787), discussed in Crosskey, *Politics and the Constitution*, II, pp. 971–73; Boudin, *Government by Judiciary*, I, pp. 63–66; Haines, *American Doctrine*, pp. 92–94.

17. Griffith J. McRee, *Life and Correspondence of James Iredell* (New York: D. Appleton & Co., 2 vols.), II, pp. 145–76.

18. Edward S. Corwin, *Court over Constitution* (Princeton, N.J.: Princeton University Press, 1950), p. 25. Henry M. Hart, Jr., "Professor Crosskey and Judicial Review," *Harvard Law Review* 67 (June 1954): 1456–86, at 1463, disputed Crosskey's contention that the precedents emerged in cases of legislative invasion of judicial prerogatives. His article is a running critique, generally sound but overstated, on the point that Crosskey's evidence is suspect. Hart believed that the Constitutional Convention "repeatedly and with complete consistency" showed its understanding that the Court should have the power of judicial review over Congress, thus indicating that his own use of the evidence is also suspect. On the matter of the precedents Hart counted Trevett v. Weeden among the "square holdings" in favor of judicial review, despite the denial by the judges in that case.

Chapter 6 Development of Judicial Review

1. Richard Dobbs Spaight to James Iredell, Aug. 12, 1787, in Griffith J. McRee, *Life and Correspondence of James Iredell* (New York, 1858), II, p. 168.
2. Felix Frankfurter, "A Note on Advisory Opinions," *Harvard Law Review* 36 (1924):1003, note 4.
3. Charles A. Beard, *The Supreme Court and the Constitution*, Spectrum edition (Englewood Cliffs, N.J., 1962), with an introduction by Alan F. Westin. Beard's introduction to the 1938 edition is at pp. 35–36; the quote from Westin is at p. 2.
4. *Reorganization of the Federal Judiciary*. Hearings before the Committee on the Judiciary, United States Senate, 75th Congress, 1st Session, on S. 1392, Part 2, March 17 to 20, 1937, p. 184.
5. Beard, *Supreme Court and Constitution*, pp. 95, 96, and 117.
6. Edward S. Corwin, book review in *American Political Science Review* 7 (May 1913):330.
7. Edward S. Corwin, *The Doctrine of Judicial Review* (Princeton, N.J.: Princeton University Press, 1914), p. 10.
8. *Reorganization of the Federal Judiciary*, pp. 175, 176, 172.
9. Raoul Berger, *Congress v. The Supreme Court* (Cambridge, Mass.: Harvard University Press, 1969), p. 112. "The primary evidence, of course," Berger wrote, "is what was said on the Convention floor," ibid., p. 48. However, when Berger made a complete tally of the fifty-five members by counting their statements made at any time in favor of any kind or semblance of judicial review, not just over acts of Congress, and without regard to whether the statements were made before or after the Convention, he claimed a gross total of twenty-six, a significant figure. Ibid., p. 104. Even if accurate it does not purport to be the number who at the Convention supported judicial review over *Congress*. That figure remains "possibly thirteen," which is more than twice the actual number. Berger not only used far-fetched evidence (the belief that judges expound law becomes sufficient proof) to include some members (N. Gorham, C. Strong, J. Rutledge, and C. Pinckney); Berger also included those who favored review by the Supreme Court over state acts and review by state courts over state acts; and he counted opponents of the Constitution as well as proponents. Original intent, in my opinion, should be sought primarily in the opinions of those who supported the Constitution; the views of Luther Martin, Elbridge Gerry, and George Mason, among others, carry slight weight as evidence of what "the Framers" intended. What was meant by those who voted against

the Constitution and who distorted its meaning does not show what was meant by those who voted for it.

10. Louis B. Boudin, *Government by Judiciary* (New York: William Godwin, Inc., 1932), 2 vols.

11. William W. *Politics and the Constitution in the History of the United States* (Chicago: University of Chicago Press, 1953), 2 vols.

12. Max Farrand, ed., *The Records of the Federal Convention* (New Haven, Conn., 1911), II, p. 93. Beard neither quoted nor misused this statement. Among those who did were Farrand, *The Framing of the Constitution* (New Haven, 1913), pp. 156–57; Charles Warren, *The Making of the Constitution* (Boston: Little, Brown, 1928), pp. 333–34; Raoul Berger, *Congress v. The Supreme Court* (Cambridge, Mass.: Harvard University Press, 1969), p. 75; and Corwin, *Doctrine of Judicial Review*, p. 43. Corwin did not repeat the error in his *Court over Constitution*, p. 32.

13. Farrand, ed., *Records of the Federal Convention*, II, p. 430.

14. *Federalist #44*, Cooke ed., p. 305; emphasis added.

15. "Remarks on Mr. Jefferson's Draft of a Constitution," Oct. 1788, in Gaillard Hunt, ed., *The Writings of James Madison* (New York, 1900–1910, 9 vols.), V, p. 294.

16. *The Debates and Proceedings of the Congress of the United States* (Annals of Congress), comp. Joseph Gales (Washington, 1834), 1st Cong., 1st sess., I, p. 439.

17. Ibid., I, p. 500.

18. Ibid., I, pp. 514–15, June 17, 1789.

19. Beard, *Supreme Court and Constitution*, p. 55.

20. Corwin, *Doctrine*, p. 47.

21. Corwin, *Court over Constitution*, p. 31.

22. Berger, *Congress v. Court*, p. 81.

23. Ibid, p. 108; emphasis added.

24. Farrand, ed., *Records*, II, p. 74, July 21, 1787.

25. Farrand, *Records*, II, p. 440. Berger, *Congress v. Court*, p. 265 n. 195, quotes Madison without indicating that he spoke about the ban on *state* ex post facto laws.

26. Five versions of Hamilton's speech of presentation and his "Plan of Government," all dated June 18, 1787, are in *The Papers of Alexander Hamilton*, ed. Harold C. Syrett and Jacob E. Cooke (New York: Columbia University Press, 1962–1981, 26 vols.), IV, pp. 178–211.

27. *The Federalist #16* and #33, ed. Cooke, pp. 104, 206–208.

28. The three "Letters of Brutus" on judicial review are reprinted in the Appendix to Corwin's *Court over Constitution*, pp. 231–262. The complete essays of Brutus are in Herbert J. Storing, ed., *The Com-*

plete Anti-Federalist (Chicago: University of Chicago Press, 1981, 7 vols.), II, pp. 358–452.

29. Berger systematically combed the state ratifying convention debates and found less than a dozen statements endorsing judicial review over Congress, not many from hundreds of delegates. He acknowledged that he found only a "scattering of remarks" but considered them to be representative of a widely held viewpoint. He did not explain how or why they were representative. Berger, *Congress v. Court*, pp. 120–42; "scattering" is at p. 123.

30. Farrand, ed., *Records*, II. p. 73, and Elliot, ed., *Debates*, II, p. 489.

31. To Messrs. Eddy, Russel, Thurber, Wheaton, and Smith, March 27, 1801, in *The Writings of Jefferson*, ed. Albert Ellery Bergh (Washington, D.C.: Jefferson Memorial Association, 1907, 20 vols.), X, p. 248.

32. Wilson in Pennsylvania, in Elliot, ed., *Debates*, II, p. 489; Pendleton and Marshall in Virginia, in ibid., III, pp. 548 and 553. Berger, *Congress v. Court*, pp. 198–222, presents the most sustained argument for deriving judicial review from Article III.

33. Farrand, ed., *Records*, II, pp. 423, 430.

34. *Federalist* #80; Elliot, ed., *Debates*, III, pp. 484–85, 532, and IV, pp. 156–57, 165–66.

35. Berger, *Congress v. Court*, pp. 223–47, presents a detailed discussion of judicial review in connection with Article VI.

36. James Iredell, William Davie, and Samuel Johnson, of North Carolina, in Elliot, ed., *Debates*, IV, pp. 28, 178, 179, 182, 188; Edmund Pendleton of Virginia, in ibid., III, p. 548. Berger also included Robert Whitehall of Pennsylvania, but his remark shows the opposite of what Berger sought to prove, because Whitehall declared that "Laws might be made in *Pursuance* of the Constitution tho' not agreeably to it," and he added, "The laws may be unconstitutional." The argument, rather, supposedly proves that a law is unconstitutional because it is not in pursuance of the Constitution.

37. Crosskey, *Politics and the Constitution*, II, pp. 990–94. Whitehall's statement in the preceding note illustrates this use of "in pursuance."

38. U.S. Statutes at Large, I, pp. 73–77.

39. Beard, *Supreme Court*, p. 65; Corwin, *Doctrine*, pp. 10, 11, 17; Haines, *Judicial Supremacy*, pp. 143, 145; Charles Warren, *Congress, the Constitution, and the Supreme Court* (Boston: Little, Brown, 1925), p. 104; and Berger, *Congress v. Court*, pp. 49, 101, 258–74. Berger found, in addition to Ellsworth, nine others voting for the Judiciary Act who had been Framers, whom he added to his tally of Framers supporting judicial review of acts of Congress.

40. Corwin, *Doctrine*, p. 62.

41. Ibid., p. 63; emphasis in original.

42. Corwin, "The Progress of Constitutional Theory Between the Declaration of Independence and the Philadelphia Convention," *American Historical Review*, April 1925, reprinted in *American Constitutional History, Essays by Edward S. Corwin*, ed. A. T. Mason and G. Garvey (New York: Harper Torchbooks, 1964), pp. 1–24.

43. Massachusetts Constitution of 1789, in Thorpe, ed., *Constitutions*, Art. IV of Frame of Governfment, III, p. 1894. For the statement on separation of powers, see Art. 30 of Declaration of Rights, ibid., p. 1893. The justices of the state's high court held office for life; the government had a veto, extensive appointment powers, and commanded the state's armed forces. The provisions on the "Judiciary Power" did not mention judicial review.

44. See Leonard W. Levy, *The Law of the Commonwealth and Chief Justice Shaw* (Cambridge, Mass.: Harvard University Press, 1957), pp. 266–69. However, in an unreported and forgotten case of 1799, the Massachusetts court invoked the contract clause of the federal Constitution to hold void the act of the Georgia legislature repealing the Yazoo land grants, thus anticipating Fletcher v. Peck by more than a decade. The case, Derby v. Blake, discussed in *Columbia Centinel* (Boston), Oct. 9, 1799, reprinted in 226 Mass. 618-25, Supplement (1927), was rediscovered and first cited by Charles Warren, *A History of the American Bar* (Boston: Little, Brown, 1909), p. 269 note.

45. Charles Warren, *The Supreme Court in United States History* (Boston: Little, Brown, 1923, 3 vols.) I, pp. 65–66.

46. Ware v. Hylton, 3 Dallas 199 (1796).

47. June 16, 1792, quoted in Warren, *Supreme Court*, pp. 1–67. The fullest account is by Warren in "Earliest Cases of Judicial Review of State Legislation by Federal Courts," *Yale Law Journal*, 32 (1922):15–28.

48. Ibid., p. 25.

49. Ibid., p. 28.

50. Hayburn's Case, 2 Dallas 409 (1792), as reported in 1 Law. Ed. 436–38, reprints in a note all three of the letters addressed to Pres. Washington by the judges; Warren, *Supreme Court*, I, pp. 69–71; Julius Goebel, Jr., *Antecedents and Beginnings to 1801* (New York: Macmillan, 1971), pp. 560–62.

51. *Annals of Congress*, 2d Cong., 1st sess., III, pp. 556–57, April 13, 1792.

52. Hayburn's Case, 2 Dallas 409 (1792) involved a mandamus to compel

the circuit court to grant a pension to Hayburn, but the Court did not decide the matter and, after a postponement the case became moot as a result of the 1793 Act of Congress.

53. Letter of April 15, 1792 in *The Papers of James Madison*, ed. William T. Hutchinson et al. (Chicago: University of Chicago Press, 1962, and from vol. XI in 1977, Charlottesville, Va.: University Press of Virginia, series in progress), XIV, p. 288.

54. Ames to Thomas Dwight, April 25, 1792, in *Works of Fisher Ames*, ed. Seth Ames (New York: Da Capo reprint, 1969, of 1854 ed., 2 vols.), II, p. 117.

55. *National Gazette* (Philadelphia), April 16, 1792.

56. *General Advertiser* (Philadelphia), April 20, 1792. See Donald H. Stewart, *The Opposition Press of the Federalist Period* (Albany: State University of New York Press, 1969), pp. 454–55, and Warren, *Supreme Court*, I, p. 73.

57. *Annals of Congress*, 1st Cong., 1st sess., p. 477. See also Warren, *Congress the Constitution, and the Court*, pp. 101–103.

58. Quoted in Warren, *Congress, Constitution, and Court*, p. 99 n.1. Warren's citation for the quotation is wrong. I could not verify it or find the quotation elsewhere in the *Annals of Congress*, 3rd Cong.

59. Ibid., 1st Cong., 3rd sess., 1944, Feb. 7, 1791.

60. Ibid., 3rd Cong., 2nd sess., p. 1203, Feb. 11, 1795.

61. Warren, *Congress, the Constitution, and the Court*, p. 115.

62. *Annals of Congress*, 5th Cong., 2nd sess., VIII, p. 2152, July 10, 1798.

63. Ibid., 6th Cong., 2nd sess., X, p. 965, Jan. 23, 1801.

64. James Morton Smith, *Freedom's Fetters: The Alien and Sedition Laws and American Civil Liberties* (Ithaca, N.Y.: Cornell University Press, 1956), is the definitive study.

65. Albert J. Beveridge, *The Life of John Marshall* (Boston: Houghton Mifflin, 1916–1919, 4 vols.), I, pp. 58–92, reviews the party debate, the first in our history, on national judicial review in 1802; the *Annals of Congress*, 7th Cong., 1st sess., records the extensive debate from Jan. 2–March 3, 1802, in XII, pp. 31–983.

66. Madison to Jefferson, Oct. 17, 1788, in *Papers of Madison*, XI, pp. 295–300, "parchment barriers" at p. 197.

67. Jefferson to Madison, March 15, 1789, in *The Papers of Thomas Jefferson*, ed. Julian Boyd et al. (Princeton, N.J.: Princeton University Press, 1950– , series in progress, 21 vols. to date), XIV, pp. 659–61.

68. Speech of June 8, 1789, reprinted in *Papers of Madison*, XII, p. 198 (great rights) and pp. 206–207 (judicial review).

69. Warren, *Congress, the Constitution, and the Court*, pp. 91–93. See also Berger, *Congress v. Court*, pp. 120–43.
70. Warren, *Congress, the Constitution, and the Court*, pp. 97–127, reviews the first decade of Congress in relation to judicial review. The quotation is at p. 99.
71. Warren, *Supreme Court*, I, pp. 82–83.
72. Cooper v. Telfair, 4 Dallas 14, 19 (1800).
73. Charles L. Black, *The People and the Court: Judicial Review in a Democracy* (New York: Macmillan, 1960), p. 178.
74. Ex part McCardle, 7 Wallace 700 (1869), discussed in Warren, *Supreme Court*, III, pp. 187–210; Stanley I. Kutler, *Judicial Power and Reconstruction Politics* (Chicago: University of Chicago Press, 1968), pp. 100–108; and Charles Fairman, *Reconstruction and Reunion, 1864–88*, Part One (New York: Macmillan, 1971), pp. 433–514.
75. Hepburn v. Griswold, 8 Wallace 603 (1870); United States v. De Witt, 9 Wallace 41 (1870); and Collector v. Day, 11 Wallace 113 (1871).

Chapter 7 The Contract Clause

1. James Madison, Preface to Debates in the Convention of 1787, written near the end of his life, in Max Farrand, ed., *The Records of the Federal Convention of 1787* (New Haven, Conn.: Yale University Press, 1911, 3 vols.), III, p. 548.
2. Charles Warren, *The Making of the Constitution* (Boston: Little, Brown, 1928), pp. 550–51.
3. *The Papers of James Madison*, ed. William T. Hutchinson et al. (Chicago and Charlottesville, University of Chicago Press and University Press of Virginia, 1962–   ), Oct. 24, 1787, X, p. 212. Madison believed that in addition to the contract clause and the prohibition on state paper money laws, Congress should have a veto on state laws.
4. Ogden v. Saunders, 12 Wheaton 213, 354–55 (1827), dissenting.
5. Francis Newton Thorpe, ed., *Federal and State Constitutions* (Washington, D.C.: Government Printing Office, 1909, 7 vols.), II, p. 961–62.
6. Farrand, ed., *Records*, II, p. 439.
7. Ibid.
8. Ibid., II, p. 440. Emphasis added.
9. Ibid., II, p. 597.
10. Ibid., II, p. 588.

11. Ibid., II, pp. 617–19.
12. Herbert J. Storing, ed., *Complete Anti-Federalist* (Chicago: University of Chicago Press, 1981, 7 vols.), II, pp. 64–65.
13. See above, pp. 71–72.
14. Ogden v. Saunders, 12 Wheaton 213, 354 (1827).
15. Elliot, ed., *Debates*, IV, p. 173.
16. Ibid., III, p. 174.
17. Ibid., III, p. 178.
18. Ibid., IV, pp. 190–91.
19. Ibid., IV, p. 191.
20. Similarly, in a letter to his father, Dec. 12, 1786, Madison condemned "interposition of the law in private contracts," *Papers of James Madison*, IX, p. 205.
21. *Essays of Brutus*, No. 14, in Storing, ed., *The Complete Anti-Federalist*, II, p. 436. "Brutus," who was a member of the New York ratifying convention, might have been Robert Yates, who had left the Constitutional Convention in a huff. Storing uncertainly observed that others have identified "Brutus" as Yates; William Jeffrey, Jr., "The Letters of 'Brutus'," *University of Cincinnati Law Rev.* 40 (1971): 643, 645–46, surmised his identity as Melancthon Smith, an Anti-Federalist who switched his vote at the end and voted to ratify the Constitution.
22. Merrill Jensen, John P. Kaminski, and Gaspar J. Saladino, eds., *The Documentary History of the Ratification of the Constitution* (Madison: State Historical Society of Wisconsin, 1976–   ), III, pp. 286, 300–307.
23. Elliot, ed., *Debates*, IV, p. 345; *Address to the Freemen of South Carolina on the Subject of the Federal Constitution*, in Paul Leicester Ford, ed., *Pamphlets on the Constitution of the United States* (Brooklyn, 1888), pp. 371, 379.
24. Jensen et al., eds., *Documentary History*, XIII, p. 302, reprinting "A Citizen of Philadelphia," *Remarks on the Address of Sixteen Members*. See also the widely reprinted statement from Northampton County, Pa., in ibid., III, p. 648.
25. E.g., Sturges v. Crowninshield, 4 Wheaton 122 (1819); Ogden v. Saunders, 12 Wheaton 213 (1827); Bronson v. Kinzie, 1 Howard 311 (1843); Home Building & Loan Assoc. v. Blaisdell, 290 U.S. 398 (1934).
26. Benjamin F. Wright, *The Contract Clause of the Constitution* (Cambridge, Mass.: Harvard University Press, 1938), p. 243.
27. Max Lerner, "The Supreme Court and American Capitalism," *Yale Law Journal* 42 (1933): 668–701.

28. Brooks Adams, *The Theory of Social Revolutions* (New York: Macmillan, 1914), p. 214.
29. 6 Cranch 87 (1810).
30. Fletcher v. Peck, 6 Cranch 87 (1810).
31. New Jersey v. Wilson, 6 Cranch 164 (1812).
32. Dartmouth College v. Woodward, 4 Wheaton 518 (1819).
33. 2 Dallas 304 (1795).
34. See above, pp. 66–72, 125–30.
35. 6 Cranch 87, 137.
36. For precursors, not cited by Marshall, see Van Horne's Lessee v. Dorrance, 2 Dallas (U.S. District Court of Pennsylvania) 304 (1795), and Hamilton's opinion, in Julius Goebel, Jr., ed., *The Law Practice of Alexander Hamilton: Documents and Commentary* (New York: Columbia University Press, 1980), IV, pp. 420–35.
37. 6 Cranch 87.
38. New Jersey v. Wilson, 7 Cranch 164 (1812).
39. Dartmouth College v. Woodward, 4 Wheaton 518, 608 (1819).
40. Ibid., pp. 644–45.
41. 1 Cranch 137 (1803).
42. Cooper v. Telfair, 4 Dallas 14, 15, 19 (1800).
43. Calder v. Bull, 3 Dallas 386, 399 (1798).
44. Ibid., pp. 388–89.
45. Ibid., p. 399.
46. Terrett v. Taylor, 9 Cranch 43, 52 (1815).

Chapter 8 Why We Have the Bill of Rights

1. Ralph Waldo Emerson, "Fortune of the Republic" (1874), in *The Complete Works of Ralph Waldo Emerson*, ed. Edward W. Emerson (Boston: Houghton Mifflin, 1903–1904, 12 vols.), XI, p. 528.
2. Richard L. Perry, ed., *Sources of Our Liberties: Documentary Origins of Individual Liberties in the United States Constitution and Bill of Rights* (Chicago: American Bar Foundation, 1959), includes the Virginia charter provision, p. 44. Perry also reprints the first charters of all the other colonies. The Declaration of Rights and Resolves of the First Continental Congress 1774, in ibid., p. 287.
3. Emerson, "Fortune of the Republic," p. 528. See also Louis Hartz, *The Liberal Tradition in America* (New York: Harcourt Brace, 1955), pp. 3–56.
4. The best short survey of the development of the American constitutional position in the controversy with Great Britain is Andrew

C. McLaughlin, *Constitutional History of the United States* (New York: Appleton Century, 1935), pp. 3–106. Burke himself regarded taxation of the colonies by Parliament as "perfect uncompensated slavery," ibid., p. 29.

5. *The Papers of James Madison*, ed. William T. Hutchinson et al. (Chicago and Charlottesville, 1962–   ), I, p. 106, letter of Madison to William Bradford, Jan. 24, 1774.

6. Rufus Jones, *The Quakers in the American Colonies* (New York: W. W. Norton, 1966), pp. 63–89. For Zenger's case, see *A Brief Narrative of the Case and Trial of John Peter Zenger*, ed. Stanley Nider Katz (Cambridge: Harvard University Press, 1972, 2nd ed.).

7. See Leonard W. Levy, *Emergence of a Free Press* (New York: Oxford University Press, 1985), which covers the colonial period to the end of the eighteenth century.

8. On the social compact theory, see Andrew C. McLaughlin, *The Foundations of American Constitutionalism* (New York: New York University Press, 1932), pp. 63–84.

9. John Dickinson, *An Address to the Committee of Correspondence in Barbados* (1766), in Paul L. Ford, ed., *Writings of John Dickinson* (Philadelphia, 1895), p. 261 (Memoirs of the Historical Society of Pennsylvania, XIV).

10. McLaughlin, *Foundations*, p. 66.

11. Arthur E. Sutherland, *Constitutionalism in America: Origin and Evolution of Its Fundamental Ideas* (New York: Blaisdell, 1965), is the best book on the British background of American constitutionalism. All documents mentioned are in Perry, ed., *Sources of Our Liberties*.

12. Perry, ed., *Sources of Our Liberties*, pp. 62–75; Frances H. Relf, *The Petition of Right* (Minneapolis: University of Minnesota Press, 1917).

13. See Perry, ed., *Sources of Our Liberties*, pp. 189–203, for the Habeas Corpus Act, and pp. 222–50 for the Bill of Rights. See also Lois G. Schwoerer, *The Declaration of Rights, 1689* (Baltimore: Johns Hopkins University Press, 1981).

14. For the Toleration Act, see Henry Gee and W. J. Hardy, eds., *Documents Illustrative of English Church History* (London, 1896), pp. 654–64. A. A. Seaton, *The Theory of Toleration Under the Later Stuarts* (New York: Octagon, 1972), is excellent.

15. For Madison, see Jonathan Elliot, ed., *The Debates in the Several State Conventions on the Adoption of the Federal Constitution* (Philadelphia: Lippincott, 1941 reprint of rev. 2nd ed., 5 vols.), III, p. 330.

16. On the Maryland Toleration Act of 1649, see Thomas O'Brien Hanley, *Their Rights and Liberties: The Beginnings of Religious and Political Freedom in Maryland* (Westminster, Md.: Newman Press, 1959); Thomas J. Curry, *The First Freedoms: Church and State in America to the Passage of the First Amendment* (New York: Oxford University Press, 1986), pp. 30–41, an outstanding book.
17. See Perry, ed., *Sources of Our Liberties*, pp. 162–79, for the document, prefaced by commentary.
18. Ibid., pp. 143–61, reprints the Body of Liberties and at p. 143 quotes Winthrop. George Lee Haskins, *Law and Authority in Early Massachusetts* (New York: Macmillan, 1960), covers the subject best.
19. Perry, ed., *Sources of Our Liberties*, pp. 180–88.
20. Ibid, pp. 204–221.
21. Leonard W. Levy, *Origins of the Fifth Amendment: The Right Against Self-Incrimination* (New York: Oxford University Press, 1968), pp. 364–65.
22. See Leonard W. Levy, "Constitution," in Levy, Kenneth L. Karst, and Dennis J. Mahoney, eds., *Encyclopedia of the American Constitution* (New York: Macmillan, 1986, 4 vols.), I, pp. 355–57. For the town orator, see McLaughlin, *Foundations*, p. 77. Jefferson's statement is from the Declaration of Independence.
23. Bernard Schwartz, ed., *The Bill of Rights: A Documentary History* (New York: Chelsea House, 1971, 2 vols.), I, pp. 234–36, reprints the Virginia Declaration of 1776. This easily available collection of primary sources is comprehensive; I have relied on it for most documents related to bills of rights from 1776–1791. For the Virginia act of 1786, see Anson Phelps Stokes, *Church and State in the United States* (New York: Harper, 1950, 3 vols.), I, pp. 366–97, which includes a reprint of the act.
24. Schwartz, ed., *The Bill of Rights*, I, pp. 262–75.
25. Ibid., pp. 276–89.
26. Ibid., pp. 319–24.
27. Ibid., pp. 337–74. See Levy, "Constitutional Convention," in Levy et al., eds., *Encyclopedia of the American Constitution*, I, pp. 358–60.
28. Thomas Jefferson, *Notes on the State of Virginia*, ed. Thomas Perkins Abernathy (New York: Harper Torchbooks, 1964), Query XIII, sect. 5, pp. 115–119.
29. Schwartz, ed., *Bill of Rights*, I, pp. 374–82.
30. Ibid., reproduces all state recommendations for amendments to the Constitution, as well as the first state declarations of rights. See also Edward Dumbauld, *The Bill of Rights and What It Means*

Today (Norman: University of Oklahoma Press, 1957), pp. 10–33, Appendix I, Table for Sources of Provisions of the Bill of Rights, and Appendix 4, State Proposals. See also Dumbauld's "State Precedents for the Bill of Rights," *Journal of Public Law* 7 (1958):323–44.

31. Schwartz, ed., *Bill of Rights,* I, pp. 385–402, reprints the document with commentary.
32. Madison to Richard Peters, Aug. 1, 1789, in Hutchinson et al., eds., *Papers of James Madison,* XII, pp. 346–47.
33. March 1, 1792, letter to state governors, in Schwartz, ed., *Bill of Rights,* II, p. 1203.
34. Max Farrand, ed., *The Records of the Federal Convention* (New Haven, Conn.: Yale University Press, 1911, 3 vols.), II, pp. 587–88.
35. Ibid., II, pp. 617–18. The vote may have been 6–5. See ibid., p. 618 n. 15.
36. Ibid, III, p. 143.
37. For Lee's proposals and Madison opposition, see Jensen et al., eds., I, pp. 337–39, 343–44.
38. See Farrand, ed., *Records,* II, p. 479, for the statement of Aug. 31, 1787, and II, p. 640, for "insuperable objection."
39. Charles Warren, *The Making of the Constitution* (Boston: Little, Brown, 1928), p. 508 (Washington), pp. 67–68 (praising makeup); Jefferson to J. Adams, Aug. 30, 1787, in Lester Cappon, ed., *The Adams–Jefferson Letters* (Chapel Hill: University of North Carolina Press, 1959, 2 vols.), I, p. 196.
40. Farrand, ed., *Records,* II, p. 137.
41. Schwartz, ed., *Bill of Rights,* I, p. 234.
42. Farrand, ed., *Records,* II, pp. 177–89.
43. Ibid., II, pp. 340–42.
44. Ibid., II, pp. 375–76, 435, 440, 448–49. Calder v. Bull, 3 Dallas 386 (1798).
45. Farrand, ed., *Records,* II, pp. 314, 438.
46. Ibid., II, pp. 342, 468; III, p. 78, for letter of Jonas Phillips. For the Pennsylvania religious test, see state constitution of 1776, sec. 9, in Schwartz, ed., *Bill of Rights,* I, p. 267. Schwartz's preface at p. 262 is incorrect.
47. *The Federalist,* ed. Jacob E. Cooke (New York: Meridian Books, 1961), #84, pp. 579–80.
48. Jensen et al., eds., *Documentary History,* II, pp. 387–90.
49. *Federalist,* #84.
50. On the Philips attainder, see Leonard W. Levy, *Jefferson and Civil*

Liberties: The Darker Side (Cambridge, Mass.: Harvard University Press, 1963), pp. 33–41.

51. Madison to Jefferson, Oct. 17, 1788, in Hutchinson et al., *Papers of Madison*, XI, pp. 297–98. For illustrations of a similar sentiment expressed only by Virginians, see Elliot, ed., *Debates*, III, p. 70 (Randolph), p. 298 (Pendleton), and p. 561 (Marshall).
52. Thomas E. Buckley, *Church and State in Revolutionary Virginia, 1776–1787* (Charlottesville: University Press of Virginia, 1977), pp. 70–172, is the best study.
53. Jensen et al., eds., *Documentary History*, II, p. 383.
54. Elliot, ed., *Debates*, III, p. 191.
55. Herbert J. Storing, ed., *The Complete Anti-Federalist* (Chicago: University of Chicago Press, 1981, 7 vols.), II, p. 144.
56. Adams to Jefferson, Nov. 10, 1787, in Cappon, ed., *Adams–Jefferson Letters*, I, p. 210.
57. Jefferson to Madison, Dec. 20, 1787, in *The Papers of Thomas Jefferson*, ed. Julian P. Boyd et al. (Princeton, N.J.: Princeton University Press, 1950), XII, pp. 339–42.
58. John Locke, *Two Treatises of Government*, ed. Peter Laslett (Cambridge: At the University Press, 1963), Book II, chap. 2, sec. 14, pp. 317–18.
59. Farrand, ed., *Records*, I, p. 446.
60. Massachusetts Constitution of 1780, Preamble, in Schwartz, ed., *Bill of Rights*, I, p. 339.
61. 1 Dallas 419, 471.
62. Storing, ed., *Complete Anti-Federalist*, V, p. 185.
63. Ibid., II, p. 330.
64. Elliot, ed., *Debates*, III, pp. 448–49.
65. Storing, ed., *Complete Anti-Federalist*, III, p. 37.
66. Ibid., III, p. 59.
67. Elliot, ed., *Debates*, III, p. 448.
68. Jensen et al., eds., *Documentary History*, II, p. 427.
69. Elliot, ed., *Debates*, III, p. 461.
70. Storing, ed., *Complete Anti-Federalist*, II, p. 326.
71. Ibid., III, p. 86.
72. Ibid., II, pp. 324–25.
73. Ibid., IV, p. 111.
74. Washington to Madison, Oct. 10, 1787, quoted in Robert Allen Rutland, *The Birth of the Bill of Rights, 1776–1791* (Chapel Hill: University of North Carolina Press, 1955), pp. 122–23.
75. Hamilton's "Caesar" letters, Oct. 1788, in Paul L. Ford, ed., *Essays on the Constitution of the United States* (Brooklyn, 1892), p. 289.

76. All state documents related to ratification are reprinted in Schwartz, ed., *Bill of Rights*, II.

77. On Madison and a bill of rights at the Virginia convention, see, for example, *Papers of Madison*, ed. Hutchinson et al., XI, p. 130, for speech of June 12, 1788; see ibid., XI, pp. 301–304, Editorial Note, on Madison in Virginia politics.

78. Ibid., XI, pp. 295–300, letter to Jefferson.

79. Farrand, ed., *Records*, II, p. 440.

80. Jefferson to Madison, March 15, 1789, in *Papers of Jefferson*, ed. Boyd, XIV, pp. 659–61.

81. *Papers of Madison*, ed. Hutchinson et al., XI, pp. 12, 238, 330–31. See also p. 307.

82. Schwartz, ed., *Bill of Rights*, II, pp. 1023–34, reprints Madison's speech of June 8, 1789.

83. Ibid., II, pp. 1027, 1033, 1113.

84. Ibid., II, p. 1031.

85. Davie to Iredell, June 4, 1789, quoted in Griffith J. McRee, *Life and Correspondence of James Iredell* (New York, 1857–1858, 2 vols.), II, p. 260. Williamson to Madison, May 24, 1789, *Papers of James Madison*, ed. Hutchinson et al., XII, pp. 183–84. Pendleton to Madison, Sept. 2, 1789, in ibid., XII, p. 368; Coxe to Madison, June 18, 1789, in ibid., XII, p. 239.

86. Schwartz, ed., *Bill of Rights*, II, pp. 1034–42, 1050, 1054–57, 1062.

87. Ibid., II, pp. 1062–77, 1126.

88. Ibid., II, pp. 1088–1114, 1121–38.

89. Madison to Richard Peters, Aug. 19, 1789, in *Papers of Madison*, ed. Hutchinson et al., XII, pp. 346–47.

90. Schwartz, ed., *Bill of Rights*, II, p. 1103; Grayson to Henry, June 12, 1789, quoted in William Wirt Henry, *Patrick Henry: Life, Correspondence and Speeches* (New York, 1891), III, p. 391; Lee to Henry, Sept. 14, 1789, ibid., III, p. 399; Grayson to Henry, Sept. 29, 1789, ibid., III, p. 406.

91. See ibid., II, pp. 1145–58, for the Bill of Rights in the Senate.

92. Ibid., II, pp. 1159–66.

93. David M. Matteson, "The Organization of the Government under the Constitution," in Sol Bloom, *History of the Formation of the Union Under the Constitution* (Washington: Government Printing Office, 1943), pp. 316–19; Rutland, *Birth of Bill of Rights*, pp. 213–18; Schwartz, ed., *Bill of Rights*, II, pp. 1171–1203.

94. Matteson, "Organization of the Government," pp. 325–27; Schwartz, ed., *Bill of Rights*, II, pp. 1173–76.

95. Jefferson to Christopher Gore, Aug. 8, 1791, in *Papers of Jefferson*,

NOTES FOR PAGES 171-176   431

ed. Boyd, XXII, p. 15; Matteson, "Organization of the Government," pp. 327–28.

96. Rutland, *Birth of the Bill of Rights*, p. 217.

97. On Grayson and Lee, see Schwartz, ed., *Bill of Rights*, II, pp. 1186–88; on Mason, see *Papers of George Mason*, ed. Robert A. Rutland (Chapel Hill: University of North Carolina Press, 1970, 3 vols.), III, pp. 1164, 1172, letters of July 31, 1789, and Sept. 8, 1789.

98. Randolph to Washington, Dec. 6, 1789, in Schwartz, ed., *Bill of Rights*, II, p. 1190; Hardin Burnley to Madison, Nov. 5, 1789, quoted in ibid., pp. 1184–85. See also Irving Brant, *James Madison, Father of the Constitution* (Indianapolis: Bobbs-Merrill, 1941–1961, 6 vols.), pp. 286 and 491 n. 15.

99. Randolph to Washington, Dec. 15, 1789, in Schwartz, ed., *Bill of Rights*, II, p. 1191; E. Carrington to Madison, Dec. 20, 1789, in ibid., II, pp. 1191–93; Madison to Washington, Jan. 4, 1790, in ibid., II, p. 1193. See also, Matteson, "Organization of the Government," p. 232, and Brant, *Madison, Father of the Constitution*, pp. 286–87, and p. 491 n. 16 for the voting records.

100. To Lafayette, April 2, 1790, in *Papers of Jefferson*, ed. Boyd, XVI, p. 293.

Chapter 9 The First Amendment: The Establishment Clause

1. Wallace v. Jaffree, 472 U.S. 38, 110 (1985).

2. For example, Jonathan Elliot, ed., *The Debates in the Several State Conventions* (Philadelphia: Lippincott, 1941, 2nd ed. rev., 5 vols.), III, pp. 203–204, 450, 600 (Randolph and Nicholas in Virginia); IV, p. 149 (Iredell in North Carolina); IV, pp. 315–16 (C. C. Pinckney in South Carolina); and II, p. 78 (Varnum in Massachusetts). For the very influential statements by Wilson of Pennsylvania, see ibid., II, pp. 436 and 453; see also John Bach McMaster and Frederick D. Stone, eds., *Pennsylvania and the Federal Constitution, 1787–1788* (Lancaster, Pa., 1888), pp. 313–14. See also McKean in ibid., p. 337; Ellsworth in Paul L. Ford, ed., *Essays on the Constitution of the United States* (Brooklyn, N.Y., 1892), pp. 163–64; Williamson, "Remarks," ibid., p. 398 (North Carolina); and Hanson, "Remarks on the Proposed Plan," in Paul L. Ford, ed., *Pamphlets on the Constitution of the United States* (Brooklyn, N.Y., 1888), pp. 241–42 (Maryland).

3. *The Federalist* #84, any edition.

4. Elliot, ed., *Debates*, II, p. 455.

5. Ibid., III, p. 204; see also ibid., p. 469.

6. Ibid., III, p. 330.
7. Ibid., IV, p. 208.
8. Speech in Congress, Feb. 2, 1790, in William T. Hutchinson et al., eds., *The Papers of James Madison* (Chicago and Charlottesville, 1962–), XIII, p. 16.
9. Charles C. Tansill, ed., *Documents Illustrative of the Formation of the Union* (Washington, D.C.: Government Printing Office, 1927), p. 1027.
10. Ibid., pp. 1031, 1035, 1053.
11. Thomas C. Buckley, *Church and State in Revolutionary Virginia, 1776–1787* (Charlottesville: University Press of Virginia, 1977), is a model study.
12. Thomas J. Curry, *The First Freedoms: Church and State in America to the Passage of the First Amendment* (New York: Oxford University Press, 1986), most reliably surveys all the states.
13. Oscar and Mary Handlin, eds., *The Popular Sources of Political Authority* (Cambridge, Mass., 1966), p. 819, for the town of Charlton. See also ibid., pp. 618–19 (West Springfield), p. 674 (Sherborn), pp. 727–28 (Berwick), p. 785 (Medway), and p. 855 (Petersham). Art. III is in ibid., pp. 442–43. See also Leonard W. Levy, *The Establishment Clause: Religion and the First Amendment* (New York: Macmillan, 1986), pp. 27–28.
14. L. F. Greene, ed., *Writings of John Leland* (New York: Arno Press, 1969 reprint), p. 229, and Levy, *Establishment Clause*, pp. 111–13.
15. Speech of June 8, 1789, in Bernard Schwartz, ed., *The Bill of Rights: A Documentary History* (New York: Chelsea House, 1971, 2 vols.), II, pp. 1025, 1029, 1031.
16. Madison to Jefferson, Oct. 17, 1788, in *Papers of Madison*, XI, p. 297.
17. *Annals of Congress*, 1st Cong., 1st sess., I, p. 451; in Schwartz, ed., *Bill of Rights*, II, p. 1026, June 8, 1789.
18. *Papers of Madison*, VIII, pp. 298–304. For discussion, see Buckley, *Church and State*, pp. 131–36.
19. For an examination of Madison's views on church and state, especially in connection with the concept of "national religion," see Levy, *Establishment Clause*, pp. 93–108.
20. *Annals of Congress*, I, 1st Cong., 1st sess., 1789, pp. 757–59, 796; Schwartz, ed., *Bill of Rights*, II, pp. 1088–89, reprints the debate of Aug. 15, 1789; ibid., p. 1122 for the recommendation of The Committee of the Whole, and p. 1126 for Ames.
21. *Journal of the First Session of the Senate of the United States* (Wash-

ington, 1820), p. 70, Schwartz, ed., *Bill of Rights*, II, p. 1148, has the Senate motions of Sept. 2, 1789.

22. Levy, *Establishment Clause*, p. 112.

23. *Journal of the First Session of the Senate*, p. 77, or Schwartz, ed., *Bill of Rights*, II, p. 1153.

24. Levy, *Establishment Clause*, pp. 49–51.

25. William G. McLoughlin, *New England Dissent, 1630–1833* (Cambridge, Mass.: Harvard University Press, 1971, 2 vols.), II, pp. 783–84.

26. Curry, *First Freedoms*, p. 211.

27. Levy, *Establishment Clause*, pp. 85–87.

28. Newton B. Jones, ed., "Writings of the Reverend William Tennent, 1740–1777," *South Carolina Historical Magazine* 61 (July–October 1960):197–202, reprinting "Mr. Tennent's speech on The Dissenting Petition, Delivered in the House of Assembly, Charles-Town, January 11, 1777."

29. Sanford Cobb, *The Rise of Religious Liberty in America* (New York: Macmillan, 1902), p. 236. John Webb Pratt, *Religion, Politics, and Diversity: The Church–State Theme in New York History* (Ithaca, N.Y.: Cornell University Press, 1967), pp. 27–29. Hugh Hastings and Edward T. Corwin, eds., *Ecclesiastical Records of the State of New York*, 7 vols. (Albany, N.Y.: J. B. Lyon, State Printer, 1901–1906), I, p. 571.

30. Pratt, *Religion*, p. 39.

31. *Ecclesiastical Records*, II, pp. 1073–78. Pratt, *Religion*, pp. 40–42. Carl Bridenbaugh, *Mitre and Sceptre: Transatlantic Faiths, Ideas, Personalities, and Politics 1689–1775* (New York: Oxford University Press, 1962), pp. 117–18.

32. *Ecclesiastical Records*, II, p. 1114.

33. E. B. O'Callaghan, ed., *Documents Relative to the Colonial History of the State of New York*, ed. E. B. O'Callaghan (Albany, N.Y.: Weed, Parsons, Printers, 1853–1887, 15 vols.), V, p. 323. Bridenbaugh, *Mitre and Septre*, p. 118.

34. *The Documentary History of the State of New York*, ed. E. B. O'Callaghan, (Albany, N.Y.: Weed, Parsons, Printers, 1848–1849, 4 vols.), III, p. 278.

35. Ibid., pp. 309–311. The Jamaica controversy can be followed in this work, pp. 205–302. See also Pratt, *Religion*, pp. 54, 61–62.

36. O'Callaghan, ed., *Documentary History*, III, pp. 311, 330. Pratt, *Religion*, p. 62.

37. *Ecclesiastical Records*, II, p. 1392, III, pp. 1589, 1591, 1695, 2141.

38. William Smith, *A General Idea of the College of Mirania* (New York,

1753). Charles Evans, *American Bibliography: Early American Imprints*. Microcard Collection (Chicago, 1903–1959), #7121, microcard, p. 84, hereafter cited as Evans, *Early American Imprints*. Pratt, *Religion*, pp. 67–71.

39. Milton Klein ed., *The Independent Reflector* (Cambridge, Mass.: Harvard University Press, 1963), pp. 171–78; *New York Mercury*, May 26, 1755; William Livingston, *Address to Sir Charles Hardy* (New York, 1755), pp. vii–viii.

40. *Acts and Resolves, Public and Private of the Province of Massachusetts Bay (1692–1786)* (Boston: Wright and Potter, 1869–1922, 21 vols.), I, p. 62. Susan M. Reed, *Church and State in Massachusetts 1691–1740* (Urbana: University of Illinois Press, 1914), pp. 19–35. McLoughlin, *New England Dissent*, I, pp. 113–27.

41. Levy, *Establishment Clause*, pp. 15–17.

42. Reed, *Church and State*, p. 180. McLoughlin, *New England Dissent*, I. p. 221.

43. M. Louise Greene, *The Development of Religious Liberty in Connecticut* (Boston: Houghton Mifflin, 1905), pp. 200–201; McLoughlin, *New England Dissent*, I, p. 269.

44. McLoughlin, *New England Dissent*, I, pp. 225–43.

45. Cotton Mather, *Ratio Discipline*, Boston, 1726 (Evans, *Early American Imprints* #2775, microcard), p. 20.

46. Ebenezer Turell, *The Life and Character of Benjamin Colman*, Boston, 1749 (Evans, *Early American Imprints* #6434, microcard), p. 138.

47. Jonathan Mayhew, *A Defense of the Observations*, Boston, 1763 (Evans, *Early American Imprints*, #9442), pp. 46–47.

48. Charles B. Kinney, *Church and State: The Struggle for Separation in New Hampshire, 1630–1900* (New York: Teachers College, Columbia University, 1955), pp. 58–62, 72–82. McLoughlin, *New England Dissent*, II, p. 833–43.

49. Thorpe, *Federal and State Constitutions*, II, pp. 1890–91.

50. See Jacob Meyer, *Church and State in Massachusetts to 1833* (Cleveland, Ohio: Western Reserve University Press, 1930), for details, beginning with chap. 4. McLoughlin, *New England Dissent*, II, pp. 697–722.

51. Thorpe, *Federal and State Constitutions*, IV, p. 2454. See Kinney, *Separation*, pp. 83–108. McLoughlin, *New England Dissent*, II, pp. 833–911, is most reliable on New Hampshire.

52. McLoughlin, *New England Dissent*, II, pp. 915–1072, is best on Connecticut.

53. Thorpe, *Federal and State Constitutions*, III, p. 1689.

54. Allan Nevins, *The American States During and After the Revolution* (New York: Macmillan, 1927), p. 431; Werline, *Problems of Church and State*, pp. 169–86. John C. Rainbolt, "The Struggle to Define 'Religious Liberty' in Maryland, 1776–1785," *Journal of Church and State* 17 (1975):448.

55. Thorpe, *Federal and State Constitutions*, III, p. 1705.

56. Ibid., II, p. 784.

57. Reba C. Strickland, *Religion and the State in Georgia in the Eighteenth Century* (New York: Columbia University Press, 1939), pp. 164, 166.

58. Thorpe, *Federal and State Constitutions*, II, p. 789.

59. Ibid., II, p. 801. Evans, *Early American Imprints*, microcards: #19750, p. 8; #19998, p. 43; #20715, p. 48; #22895, pp. 11–12. John Wesley Brinsfield, *Religion and Politics in South Carolina* (Easley, S.C.: Southern Historical Press, 1983), pp. 122–27.

60. Thorpe, *Federal and State Constitutions*, VI, pp. 3253–57. Brinsfield, *Religion and Politics*, p. 134.

61. Thorpe, *Federal and State Constitutions*, VI, p. 3264.

62. Buckley, *Church and State*, contains appendices that reprint the important documents.

63. Levy, *Establishment Clause*, pp. 51–59, and Buckley, *Church and State*, pp. 147–52.

64. Levy, *Establishment Clause*, pp. 44–46. For Vermont's establishment of religion, see McLoughlin, *New England Dissent*, II, 789–832.

Chapter 10 The First Amendment: The Free Press Clause

1. Max Farrand, ed., *The Records of the Federal Convention* (New Haven, Conn.: Yale University Press, 1911, 3 vols.), pp. 177–89, for the Committee of Detail; pp. 340–42 for Pinckney's proposals.

2. Ibid., pp. 587–88.

3. Jonathan Elliot, ed., *The Debates in the Several State Conventions* (Philadelphia, 1836–1845, 5 vols.), II, p. 148; III, pp. 436, 448–49; IV, p. 192. Herbert Storing, ed., *The Complete Anti-Federalist* (Chicago: University of Chicago Press, 1981, 7 vols.), II, pp. 229–30; III, pp. 81, 85.

4. Storing, ed., *Complete Anti-Federalist*, II, pp. 9, 13. See generally Leonard W. Levy, *Emergence of a Free Press* (New York: Oxford University Press, 1985).

5. Storing, ed., *Complete Anti-Federalist*, II, pp. 15–18, 358–452.

6. *Commentaries on the Laws of England* (London, 1765–1769), bk. 4, chap. 11, p. 152.
7. Levy, *Emergence,* pp. 204–213. McKean, a signer of the Declaration of Independence, was the Constitution's foremost protagonist in Pennsylvania, after James Wilson.
8. "Trial of William Cobbett," Nov. 1797, in Francis Wharton, ed., *State Trials of the United States During the Administration of Washington and Adams* (Philadelphia, 1849), pp. 323–24.
9. Levy, *Emergence,* p. 214.
10. Merrill Jensen, ed., *The Documentary History of the Ratification of the Constitution. Vol. II. Ratification of the Constitution by States. Pennsylvania* (Madison: State Historical Society of Wisconsin, 1976–), pp. 454–55.
11. Storing, ed., *Complete Anti-Federalist,* VI, p. 145.
12. Melanchton Smith, "Address . . . by a Plebian," 1788, in ibid., VI, p. 145; "Federal Farmer," No. 6, 1788, in ibid., II, p. 271.
13. Ibid., V, pp. 249–50.
14. *The Papers of Benjamin Franklin,* ed. Leonard W. Labaree et al. (New Haven, Conn.: Yale University Press, 1959–), VIII, pp. 28–40, 87–88; Levy, *Emergence,* pp. 51–58.
15. Levy, *Emergence,* p. 192.
16. *The Independent Reflector* (New York), Aug. 30, 1753, reprinted in Leonard W. Levy, ed., *Freedom of the Press from Zenger to Jefferson* (Indianapolis: Bobbs-Merrill, 1966), pp. 75–82, the quotation at p. 81; pp. 138–40.
17. Richard F. Hixon, *Isaac Collins: A Quaker Printer* (New Brunswick, N.J.: Rutgers University Press, 1968), pp. 95–96.
18. *New York Times,* July 29, 1987, 1st section, p. 20, for the text of Sherman's proposal, recently discovered in the Library of Congress. See also Levy, *Emergence,* pp. 13, 121.
19. "Lectures on the Law," 1791, in *The Works of James Wilson,* ed. Robert G. McCloskey (Cambridge, Mass.: Harvard University Press, 1967, 2 vols.), II, p. 652.
20. "Remarks on the New Plan of Government," 1788, in Ford, ed., *Essays on the Constitution,* p. 394.
21. Paul L. Ford, ed., *Pamphlets on the Constitution of the United States* (Brooklyn, N.Y.: 1888), p. 361.
22. Levy, *Emergence,* pp. 293–94, 306–307, 315–25.
23. Query XVII, "Religion," in *Notes on the State of Virginia,* William Peden, ed. (Chapel Hill: University of North Carolina Press, 1955), p. 159.
24. "A Bill for new modelling the form of government and for establishing

the Fundamental principles of our future Constitution," in *The Papers of Thomas Jefferson*, ed. Julian P. Boyd (Princeton, N.J.: Princeton University Press, 1950–), I, p. 353. Jefferson copied this provision from a similar one in an earlier draft, then bracketed it out, and omitted it from a third draft; ibid., p. 347.

25. Willard Hurst, "Treason in the United States," *Harvard Law Review* 58 (1944):267, quoting *The Statutes at Large Being a Collection of All The Laws of Virginia (1619–1792)*, ed. William W. Hening (1821), IX, p. 170. For Jefferson, see ibid., p. 251, and *Papers of Jefferson*, ed. Boyd, I, p. 598.

26. Boyd, ed., *Papers of Jefferson*, VI, p. 304.

27. Jefferson to Madison, July 31, 1788, in ibid., XIII, pp. 442–43.

28. Jefferson to Madison, Aug. 28, 1789, in ibid., XV, p. 367.

29. Ibid., II, pp. 545–53.

30. Virginia Code, 1803, chap. CXXXVI, quoted in *Dennis v. United States:* 341 U.S. 494, 521 n. 3 (1951). Hening, ed., *Statutes of Virginia*, XII, pp. 41–43.

31. Chapter CXII, in *A Collection of all such Acts of the General Assembly . . . as are now in Force* (Richmond, Va., 1794), Evans #27999, p. 219.

32. Archibald Magill in *The Virginia Report of 1799–1800 . . . Including the Debates and Proceedings Thereon in the House of Delegates of Virginia* (Richmond, Va., 1850), p. 75.

33. Levy, *Emergence*, pp. 207–210.

34. Ford W. Hall, "The Common Law: An Account of Its Reception in the United States," *Vanderbilt Law Review* 4 (June 1951):797–800.

35. Article XXXV, in Francis N. Thorpe, ed., *The Federal and State Constitutions* (Washington, D.C.: Government Printing Office, 1909, 7 vols.), V, p. 2637.

36. Clyde A. Duniway, *The Development of Freedom of the Press in Massachusetts* (New York: Longmans, Green, 1906), p. 142 n. 1, citing *Suffolk Court (Mass.) Files*, Nos. 104616, 104618, 106011.

37. Stephen T. Riley, "Dr. William Whiting and Shays' Rebellion," *Proceedings of American Antiquarian Society* 66 (1956):119–31; pp. 131–66 include Whiting's essays and letters.

38. The case is reported in the Boston *Independent Chronicle*, Feb. 24, March 3, 10, 17, and 24 (1791).

39. Ibid., Feb. 14–18, 1799.

40. Section XXXIV, North Carolina Constitution of 1776, in Thorpe, ed., *Federal and State Constitutions*, V, p. 2793. Emphasis added.

41. Section XXXVIII, South Carolina Constitution of 1778, in ibid., VI, p. 3257. Emphasis added.

42. Section XXXVIII, New York Constitution of 1777, in ibid., V, p. 2637.
43. Article V, Bill of Rights, New Hampshire Constitution of 1784, in ibid., IV, p. 2454.
44. Article II, Declaration of Rights, Massachusetts Constitution of 1780, in ibid., III, p. 1889.
45. Article LVI, Georgia Constitution of 1777, in ibid., II, p. 784.
46. Article XXXIII, Declaration of Rights, Maryland Constitution of 1776, in ibid., III, p. 1689.
47. "Pennsylvania Constitution of 1790," Article IX, Section 7, in ibid., V, p. 3100.
48. See note 13 above.
49. *Respublica v. Oswald*, 1 Dallas (Penn.) Reports 319 (1788); "Trial of William Cobbett," Nov. 1797, in *State Trials of the United States*, ed. Wharton, pp. 323–24; *Respublica v. Dennie*, 4 Yeates' (Penn.) Reports 267 (1805).
50. "Delaware Constitution of 1792," Article I, Section 5, in *Federal and State Constitutions*, ed. Thorpe, I, p. 569; and "Kentucky Constitution of 1792," Article XII, sections 7–8, ibid., III, p. 1274.
51. "Hitherto Unpublished Correspondence Between Chief Justice Cushing and John Adams in 1789," Frank W. Grinnell, ed., *Massachusetts Law Quarterly* 27 (1942):12–16. Adams signed the Sedition Act into law and urged its enforcement; and Cushing, as a Supreme Court judge on circuit duty presided over some of the Sedition Act trials and charged juries on the act's constitutionality. See James Morton Smith, *Freedom's Fetters: The Alien and Sedition Laws and American Civil Liberties* (Ithaca, N.Y.: Cornell University Press, 1950), pp. 97–98, 152, 242, 267, 268, 271, 284, 311, 363, and 371.
52. See cases cited above at note 51. The judges in Oswald's case included Thomas McKean, then a Federalist but subsequently a Republican, and George Bryan, an Anti-Federalist and libertarian advocate of a national bill of rights.
53. *Commonwealth v. Freeman*, reported in the *Independent Chronicle* (Boston), Feb. 24 and March 3, 10, 17, 24 (1791).
54. Ibid., II, p. 552.
55. Charles C. Tansill, ed., *Documents Illustrative of the Formation of the Union of the American States* (Washington, D.C.: Government Printing Office, 1927), p. 1027.
56. Ibid., p. 1037.
57. "Trial of David Frothingham, for a Libel on General Hamilton," New York, 1799, in Wharton, ed., *State Trials*, pp. 649–51. Frothingham's case is narrated in Smith, *Freedom's Fetters*, pp. 400–414.

58. Speech of June 8, 1789, in First Congress, reprinted in Bernard Schwartz, ed., *The Bill of Rights: A Documentary History* (New York: Chelsea House, 1971, 2 vols.), II, pp. 1024, 1028.
59. Ibid., p. 1028.
60. Ibid., p. 1096.
61. Ibid., p. 1026.
62. Ibid., p. 1096.
63. Alexander Meiklejohn, *Free Speech and Its Relation to Self-Government* (New York: Harper, 1948), p. 17.
64. Madison to Jefferson, Oct. 17, 1788, in *The Papers of James Madison*, William T. Hutchinson et al. (Chicago and Charlottesville, 1962–   ), II, p. 297.
65. "Report on the Resolutions" (*The Virginia Report of 1799–1800*), in The Writings of James Madison, ed. Gaillard Hunt (New York, 1906) VI, p. 388.
66. William Blackstone, *Commentaries*, Bk. 4, chap. II, p. 153.
67. Madison to Jefferson, Oct. 17, 1788, *Papers of Madison*, ed. Hutchinson et al., II, p. 299.
68. Sir James Fitzjames Stephen, *A History of the Criminal Law of England* (London, 1883, 3 vols.), II, p. 383; and Frank Thayer, *Legal Control of the Press* (Brooklyn, N.Y., 1950), pp. 17, 25, and 178.
69. *Annals of Congress*, 5th Cong., 2nd sess., VIII, July 5, pp. 2102–2111, July 10, 1798, pp. 2139–43, 2153–54, and 2160–66.
70. *Independent Chronicle* (Boston), issues of March 4–7, April 8–11, April 11–15, and April 29–May 2, 1799, reporting the trial of Abijah Adams, editor of the *Chronicle*, for seditious libel against the state legislature of Massachusetts.
71. "Hortensius," *An Essay on the Liberty of the Press. Respectfully Inscribed to the Republican Printers Throughout the United States* (Philadelphia, 1799), 51 pp. Reprinted in Richmond, Va., in 1803 by Samuel Pleasants, Jr., but set in small type, in an edition of 30 pages, cited here. Hay also published, in 1803, a different tract with a similar title, *An Essay on the Liberty of the Press, Shewing, That the Requisition of Security for Good Behavior from Libellers, is Perfectly Compatible with the Constitution and Laws of Virginia* (Richmond, Va., 1803), 48 pp. Both of Hay's tracts were reprinted as *Two Essays on the Liberty of the Press* (New York: Da Capo Press, 1970), a facsimile edition.
72. The *Report* originally appeared as a tract of over 80 pages and was adopted on January 11, 1800, by the Virginia legislature, which immediately published it. It is reproduced in Elliot, ed., *Debates*, IV, pp. 546–80, under the title, "Madison's Report on the Virginia Res-

olutions." The *Report* is also available in *Writings of Madison*, ed. Hunt, VI, pp. 341–406. The edition cited here is *The Virginia Report of 1799–1800, Touching the Alien and Sedition Laws; together with the Virginia Resolutions of December 21, 1798, The Debates and Proceedings thereon, in the House of Delegates in Virginia* (Richmond, Va., 1850); see pp. 189–237. This book, which includes the Virginia debates on the Sedition Act, at pp. 22–161, was reprinted by Da Capo Press of New York in 1970.

73. New York, 1800, 296 pp. Reprinted by Da Capo Press, 1970.

74. New York, 1801, 84 pp. Reprinted by Da Capo Press, 1970.

75. Five vols. (Philadelphia, 1803), Vol. I, Part II, Note G, pp. 11–30 of Appendix.

76. *The Virginia Report of 1799–1800*, p. 220.

77. *An Essay on the Liberty of the Press* (1803 ed. of 1799 tract), p. 29; and *An Essay on the Liberty of the Press, Shewing . . .* (1803), p. 32. See note 71, above.

78. *An Enquiry, Concerning the Liberty, and Licentiousness of the Press*, pp. 6–7.

79. *A Treatise Concerning Political Enquiry*, p. 173.

80. *The Virginia Report of 1799–1800*, pp. 226–27.

81. *A Treatise Concerning Political Enquiry*, p. 253.

82. *An Essay on the Liberty of the Press* (1803 ed. of 1799 tract), p. 28.

83. *Annals of Congress*, VIII, 5th Cong., 2nd sess., p. 2162, July 10, 1798.

84. *An Enquiry, Concerning the Liberty, and Licentiousness of the Press*, p. 68.

85. *The Virginia Report of 1799–1800*, p. 226.

86. *A Treatise Concerning Political Enquiry*, p. 262.

87. *An Essay on the Liberty of the Press* (1803 ed. of 1799 tract), pp. 23–24.

88. Ibid., p. 25.

89. *An Essay on the Liberty of the Press* (1803 tract), p. 29.

90. Wortman, *A Treatise Concerning Political Enquiry*, pp. 140, 253; Thomson, *An Enquiry, Concerning the Liberty, and Licentiousness of the Press*, p. 79.

91. *An Enquiry, Concerning the Liberty, and Licentiousness of the Press*, p. 22.

92. *The Virginia Report of 1799–1800*, p. 222.

93. *A Treatise Concerning Political Enquiry*, p. 29.

94. *An Enquiry, Concerning the Liberty, and Licentiousness of the Press*, pp. 20, 22; *An Essay on the Liberty of the Press* (1803 ed. of 1799 tract), p. 26.

95. For further detail, see Levy, *Emergence,* pp. 282–349.
96. See *People v. Croswell,* 3 Johnson's (N.Y.) Cases 336 (1804).
97. Ibid., p. 341.
98. The best discussion of Croswell's case is in Julius Goebel, Jr., *The Law Practice of Alexander Hamilton* (New York: Columbia University Press, 1964), I, pp. 775–806.
99. *New York Times v. Sullivan,* 376 U.S. 254 (1964).

Chapter 11 The Fourth Amendment: Search and Seizure

1. Quoted in Nelson B. Lasson, *The History and Development of the Fourth Amendment to the United States Constitution* (Baltimore: Johns Hopkins University Press, 1937), pp. 49–50. Variations of the statement exist, and its date is not certain. 1766 is the commonly used date. The earliest report of the statement, according to William Cuddihy, is from a tract of 1783. Cuddihy, "The Fourth Amendment: Origins and Original Meaning," Ph.D. dissertation, Claremont Graduate School, manuscript-in-progress, citing William Godwin, *The History . . . of William Pitt* (London, 1783), pp. 152–53. Cuddihy believes that Pitt made the statement in connection with an excise act of 1763, not on a question involving general warrants. Cuddihy is the best authority on the origins of the Fourth Amendment. However, I have minimized citations to his work, which is still being radically revised and lacks a fixed pagination, especially if I can cite a printed source instead. This note is by way of acknowledging my debt to him even when I cite others. I am responsible, however, for interpretations that I put on the data.
2. Cuddihy, "The Fourth Amendment," introduction, citing a 1505 opinion of Chief Justice John Fineux in a King's Bench case reported in the Year Books.
3. Leonard W. Levy, *Origins of the Fifth Amendment* (New York: Oxford University Press, 1968), pp. 170–71, 466.
4. Sir Edward Coke, *Institutes of the Laws of England* (London, 1628–1644, 4 vols.), IV, pp. 176–77.
5. Francis R. Aumann, *The Changing American Legal System* (Columbus: Ohio State University Press, 1940), pp. 46–47, and Charles Warren, *A History of the American Bar* (Boston: Little, Brown, 1911), p. 174.
6. Sir Matthew Hale, *History of Pleas of the Crown,* ed. Solom Emlyn (London, 2 vols., 1st ed., 1736), I, pp. 577–83; II, pp. 107–11, 149–52.

7. See Lasson, *History of the Fourth,* pp. 35–36, for discussion of Hale.

8. Serjeant William Hawkins, *A Treatise of the Pleas of the Crown* (London, 1724, 2nd ed., 2 vols.), II, pp. 81–82, and William Blackstone, *Commentaries on the Laws of England* (Oxford, 1766–1769, 4 vols.), I, pp. 288, 308. Blackstone, we are told, "wrote boldly . . . against discretionary search and seizure." William Cuddihy and B. Carmon Hardy, "A Man's House Was Not His Castle: Origins of the Fourth Amendment," *William and Mary Quarterly,* 3rd ser., 38 (July 1980):385. The entire comment by Blackstone on search and seizure, in vol. I, p. 308, is: "the rigour and arbitrary proceedings of excise-laws seem hardly compatible with the temper of a free nation. For the frauds that might be committed in this branch of the revenue, unless a strict watch is kept, make it necessary, wherever it is established, to give the officers a power of entering and searching the houses of such as deal in excisable commodities, at any hour of the day, and, in many cases, of the night likewise."

9. Levy, *Origins,* p. 171.

10. 5 Coke Reports 91a, 91b, 93a, 78 English Reports 194-95, 198.

11. Lasson, *History of the Fourth,* pp. 31–32, and Catherine Drinker Bowen, *The Lion and the Throne: The Life and Times of Sir Edward Coke* (Boston: Little, Brown, 1956), pp. 533–34.

12. Cuddihy, "The Fourth Amendment," chaps. 1–4, discusses search and seizure in Great Britain prior to 1763.

13. Philip Carteret Webb, ed., *Copies of Warrants Taken from the Records Office Books of the Kings Bench at Westminster; The Original Office Books of the Secretaries of State* . . . (London, 1763), pp. 10–72.

14. Cuddihy and Hardy, "A Man's House," p. 382.

15. Cuddihy, "The Fourth Amendment," chap. 7 on American colonies to 1761. Cuddihy and Hardy, "A Man's House," p. 388.

16. Cuddihy, "Fourth Amendment," chap. 7.

17. Ibid.

18. Ibid., chap. 10.

19. Levy, *Origins,* pp. 386–87. See Paul S. Boyer, "Borrowed Rhetoric: The Massachusetts Excise Controversy of 1754," *William and Mary Quarterly,* 3rd ser., 21 (1964):328–51.

20. M. H. Smith, *The Writs of Assistance Case* (Berkeley: University of California, 1978), pp. 113–14.

21. Cuddihy and Hardy, "A Man's House," pp. 396–97. Cuddihy informs me that the governors of most colonies with major ports denied the royal navy's request for impressment warrants, and that in New York,

naval officers conducted warrantless searches in defiance of the governor, with the result that they were imprisoned.

22. Act of Feb. 28, 1756, chap. 31, sect. 24, *Acts and Resolves . . . of the Province of Massachusetts Bay* (Boston, 1869–1922, 21 vols.), III, p. 109. Ibid., III, pp. 936–37, for the impost act of April 20, 1756.

23. Cuddihy and Hardy, "A Man's House," p. 397.

24. 13 & 14 Car. 2, chap. 11, sect. 5, as quoted by the crown attorney Jeremiah Gridley in Paxton's Case, reported in L. Kinvin Wroth and Hiller B. Zobel, eds., *Legal Papers of John Adams* (Cambridge, Mass.: Harvard University Press, 1965, 3 vols.), II, p. 131; Smith, *Writs of Assistance Case*, pp. 17–50, contains a detailed account of the originating legislation. On the writs, see also the documents and annotations by Justice Horace Gray, Jr., in Josiah Quincy, Jr., ed., *Reports of Cases Argued and Adjudged in the Superior Court of Judicature of the Massachusetts Bay Between 1761 and 1772* (Boston, 1865), Appendix I, pp. 395–540.

25. Wroth and Zobel, *Legal Papers of Adams*, II, p. 132.

26. Smith, *Writs of Assistance Case*, is a massive study of Paxton's Case.

27. Both statements by Adams quoted in Wroth and Zobel, *Legal Papers of Adams*, II, p. 107.

28. For the Massachusetts Declaration, see Bernard Schwartz, ed., *The Bill of Rights: A Documentary History* (New York: Chelsea House, 1971, 2 vols.), I, p. 342, sect. XIV. Madison's proposal in his speech of June 8, 1789, in the First Congress is in ibid., II, p. 1027.

29. Wroth and Zobel, *Legal Papers of Adams*, reprinted both versions of the speech, II, pp. 125–29, 139–44, with elaborate annotations. The longer version was first published by the *Massachusetts Spy* (Boston), April 29, 1773, p. 3. In John Kukla, ed., *The Bill of Rights: A Lively Heritage* (Richmond: Virginia State Library, 1978), pp. 85–97, William Cuddihy, "From General to Specific Search Warrants," at p. 93, alleges that Otis "cited Sir Edward Coke's exaggeration of Magna Carta, incorrectly asserted that Coke required all search warrants to be specific, and appealed to 'higher law'." Cuddihy cites Wroth and Zobel as his source for Otis's remarks, but that source does not show any reference by Otis to Coke's use of Magna Carta to condemn general warrants or to any reliance by Otis on Coke as an authority for specific warrants. Quincy, ed., *Reports of Cases*, pp. 51–57, includes a fourteen-line extract from Otis, in which Otis's claim that a writ of assistance is illegal is backed by these citations: "1 Inst. 464. 29M." Vol. I of Coke's *Institutes* is on feudal tenures. "29M," a reference to the famous judgment-of-peers or by-law-of-

the-land clause, seems to support the point. However, Gray's discussion of "Otis's quotations from Coke on Magna Carta, cap. XXIX," in Quincy's *Reports*, pp. 483–85, has nothing to do with search and seizure.

30. Wroth and Zobel, *Legal Papers of Adams*, II, p. 141; I have not followed the capitalization of the original.

31. Ibid., p. 144. Curiously, in the briefer version of the speech, Otis relied more fully on Coke's decision in Dr. Bonham's Case, 8 Coke's Reports 113b, 118a (C.P. 1610), and more clearly asked the court to hold the act unconstitutional, Wroth and Zobel, *Legal Papers of Adams*, II, pp. 127–28.

32. Smith, *Writs of Assistance Case*, pp. 442–47, 542–43; Quincy, ed., *Reports of Cases*, pp. 437–38, 446, 495–99; John Phillip Reid, *In Rebellious Spirit* (University Park: Pennsylvania State University Press, 1979), pp. 1–35.

33. See Robert R. Rea, *The English Press in Politics, 1760–1774* (Lincoln: University of Nebraska press, 1963), pp. 40–85; Raymond Postgate, *That Devil Wilkes* (New York: Vanguard Press, 1929); George Nobbe, *The North Briton: A Study in Political Propaganda* (New York: Columbia University Press, 1939), chap. 16; and George Rude, *Wilkes and Liberty* (Oxford: Oxford University Press, 1962).

34. Leonard W. Levy, *Emergence of a Free Press* (New York: Oxford University Press, 1985), p. 79. For the fallout of the Wilkes cases in America, see Patricia Bonomi, *A Factious People: Politics and Society in Colonial New York* (New York: Columbia University Press, 1971), pp. 267–76; Pauline Maier, *From Resistance to Revolution* (New York: Knopf, 1972), pp. 162–77; Jack P. Greene, "Bridge to Revolution: The Wilkes Fund Controversy in South Carolina 1769–1775," *Journal of Southern History* 27 (1963):19–52.

35. Huckle v. Money, 95 Eng. Rep. 768 (C.P. 1763), in Philip B. Kurland and Ralph Lerner, eds., *The Founders' Constitution* (Chicago: University of Chicago Press, 1987, 5 vols.), V, p. 230.

36. 98 Eng. Rep. 489 (C.P. 1763), in ibid., pp. 230–31.

37. Thomas Erskine May, *Constitutional History of England Since the Accession of George III* (New York, 1880, 2 vols.), p. 249. May is the source for the earlier statement that the government filed 200 informations in these cases; ibid., II, p. 112.

38. Money v. Leach, 97 Eng. Rep. 1075 (K.B. 1765), in Kurland and Lerner, eds. *Founders' Constitution*, V, p. 235.

39. Boyd v. United States, 116 U.S. 616, 626 (1886), citing Entick v. Carrington, 95 Eng. Rep. 807 (K.B.), most easily available in Kurland and Lerner, eds., *Founders' Constitution*, V, pp. 233–35.

40. 19 Howell's *State Trials* at pp. 1038, 1041, 1063, 1073. Boyd v. United States, 116 U.S. 616, 633 (1886).

41. My generalizations are based on the discussion in the dissertation by Cuddihy, "The Fourth Amendment," which cites contemporary sources and recommends as the best summary of the accounts [Robert Bisset], *History of the Reign of George III* (London, 1782–1783, 2 vols.), I, pp. 182–88, and John Adolphus, *History of England* (London, 1802, 3 vols.), I, pp. 152–54, 191–92, and 235–36.

42. Father of Candor, *An Enquiry Into the Doctrine Lately Propagated Concerning Libels, Warrants, and the Seizure of Papers* (London, 1764, reprinted by Da Capo Press of New York, 1970), p. 55.

43. Ibid., pp. 55–56.

44. Speech by Madison, June 8, 1789, in Schwartz, ed., *Bill of Rights*, II, p. 1028.

45. Oliver Dickerson, "Writs of Assistance as a Cause of the American Revolution," in Richard B. Morris, ed., *Era of the American Revolution* (New York: Columbia University Press, 1939), pp. 54–58.

46. Cuddihy, "Fourth Amendment," citing a manuscript letter. Dickerson, "Writs of Assistance," pp. 52–54.

47. Quincy, ed., *Reports*, pp. 453–54, for De Grey's opinion, dated Aug. 20, 1768.

48. Dickerson, "Writs of Assistance," pp. 59–60.

49. Cuddihy, "Fourth Amendment," citing William Henry Drayton, *A Letter from Freeman of South-Carolina* (Charles Town, 1774), pp. 19–20; Dickerson, "Writs of Assistance," p 67.

50. Dickerson, "Writs of Assistance," p. 66.

51. Ibid., pp. 68–71.

52. Cuddihy, "Fourth Amendment," collects many of such statements from newspapers and tracts of the time.

53. "The Rights of the Colonies," 1772, in Schwartz, ed., *Bill of Rights*, I, p. 206.

54. William Henry Drayton, cited above, n. 49, seems to have been the exception.

55. Cuddihy, "Fourth Amendment," chap. 15 on "Writs of Assistance."

56. Schwartz, ed., *Bill of Rights*, I, p. 235.

57. Ibid., p. 238, Article 12.

58. Ibid., pp. 232, 243–46.

59. Ibid., p. 248.

60. Ibid., p. 265.

61. Ibid., p. 278, Article 17.

62. Ibid., pp. 279, 283, Article 23.

63. Ibid., pp. 287, 323.

64. ibid., p. 342.

65. For New Hampshire, see ibid., p. 377, Article 19.

66. Isaac Sharpless, *A History of Quaker Government in Pennsylvania* (Philadelphia, 1900, 2 vols.), II, pp. 151–68.

67. Cuddihy, "Fourth Amendment," chap. 17, which covers the states in the 1780s.

68. 1 Kirby (Conn.) 231–35 (1787), excerpted in Kurland and Lerner, eds., *Founders' Constitution*, V, p. 237.

69. Lee's Proposed Amendments, Sept. 27, 1787, in Merrill Jensen, ed., *The Documentary History of the Ratification of the Constitution. Constitutional Documents and Records, 1776–1787* (Madison: State Historical Society of Wisconsin, 1976), I, pp. 325–40; the quotation from Lee is at p. 338.

70. *Observations . . . in a Number of Letters from the Federal Farmer* (New York, 1787), a tract that sold several thousand copies in a few months. Reprinted in Herbert J. Storing, ed., *The Complete Anti-Federalist* (Chicago: University of Chicago Press, 1981, 7 vols.), II, pp. 214–357. Lee's authorship is not certain, but the author's remarks on search and seizure accord with Lee's motion in Congress and with his letter of Dec. 22, 1787, in ibid., V, p. 117.

71. Ibid., II, p. 249, Letter IV, Oct. 12, 1787.

72. Ibid., II, p. 262, Letter VI, Dec. 25, 1787.

73. Ibid., II, Letter XVI, Jan. 20, 1788.

74. Ibid., II, pp. 136 and 153 for Centinel (Samuel Bryan of Pennsylvania); ibid., III, p. 151, for the Pennsylvania minority; and ibid., II, p. 375, for Brutus (Robert Yates of New York).

75. Ibid., VI, p. 35. See also John DeWitt, in ibid., IV, p. 33, and Mercy Otis Warren, in ibid., p. 279.

76. Jonathan Elliot, ed., *The Debates in the Several State Conventions* (Philadelphia, 1836–1845, 5 vols.), III, pp. 58, 412, 448–49, and 588, for Henry's oratory on the despoliations of hearth and home by tyrannical federal agents unrestricted by a requirement of specific warrants.

77. Lee was not a member of the Virginia convention. Mason, a member of the Wythe committee, had omitted from his draft of the Virginia Declaration of Rights a search and seizure provision. The Wythe committee ignored the weak provision in their own state's constitution. See Robert A. Rutland, ed., *The Papers of George Mason* (Chapel Hill: University of North Carolina Press, 1979, 3 vols.), III, note on p. 1071.

78. Charles Tansill, ed., *Documents Illustrative of the Formation of the Union of the American States* (Washington, D.C.: Government Print-

ing Office, 1927), pp. 1030, 1036, 1046, and 1054. The recommendations of North Carolina and Rhode Island were made too late to be of influence; Congress had already recommended the Bill of Rights.

79. In his speech of June 8, 1789, urging amendments, Madison took note of the fact that one argument against the Constitution was that the government, under the necessary and proper clause, might enforce the collection of its revenue laws by issuing general warrants. Schwartz, ed., *Bill of Rights,* II, pp. 1030–31.

80. Ibid., p. 1027.

81. Ibid., p. 1061, and p. 1112, Aug. 17.

82. Ibid., p. 1112, Aug. 17. Cuddihy, relying on newspaper accounts rather than on Thomas Lloyd's *Congressional Register,* which is the source of the debates of the First Congress in *Annals of Congress,* declares that Egbert Benson of New York, not Gerry, made the motion to reintroduce the standard of no unreasonable searches and seizures.

83. Schwartz, ed., *Bill of Rights,* p. 1123.

84. Lee to Henry, Sept. 14, 1789, in William Wirt Henry, *Patrick Henry* (New York, 1891, 3 vols.), III, p. 399.

85. Statutes at Large, 1st Cong., sess. I, chap. 5, sec. 24, July 31, 1789, An Act to Regulate the Collection of Duties, vol. I, p. 43.

86. Statutes at Large, 1st Cong., sess. III, chap. XV, sec. 32, March 3, 1791, vol. I, p. 207.

Chapter 12 The Fifth Amendment: The Right Against Self-Incrimination

1. Speech of June 8, 1789, *Annals of Congress,* 1st Cong., 1st sess., I, p. 434. The speech is reprinted in Bernard Schwartz, ed., *The Bill of Rights: A Documentary History* (New York: Chelsea House, 1971, 2 vols.), II, pp. 1023–34.

2. Sect. 8, Virginia Declaration of Rights, in Francis N. Thorpe, ed., *The Federal and State Constitutions* (Washington, D.C.: Government Printing Office, 1909, 7 vols.), VII, p. 3813. William Waller Hening, ed., *The Statutes at Large Being a Collection of All the Laws of Virginia (1619–1792)* (Richmond, 1809–1823, 13 vols.), II, p. 442, for an act of 1677 protecting one against the need to expose himself to criminal jeopardy. Richard Starke, *Office and Authority of Justice of the Peace* (Williamsburg, Va., 1774), pp. 141, 146. See also Hugh F. Rankin, *Criminal Trial Proceedings in the General Court of Virginia* (Charlottesville: University of Virginia Press, 1965), p. 99, and

Arthur P. Scott, *Criminal Law in Colonial Virginia* (Chicago: University of Chicago Press, 1930), p. 100. Parties in civil, as well as criminal, cases were incompetent by reason of "interest" to be witnesses in their own behalf. John H. Wigmore, *A Treatise on the Anglo-American System of Evidence in Trials at Common Law* (Boston: Little, Brown, 1940, 3rd ed., 10 vols.), II, pp. 681–82, 693–95. Sir William Blackstone wrote that "no man is to be examined to prove his own infamy" and said that not even a juror could be examined as to "anything which tends to his disgrace or disadvantage." *Commentaries on the Law of England* (Oxford, 1765–1769, 4 vols.), III, pp. 364, 370. In their descriptions of criminal procedure in colonial Virginia, neither Scott, pp. 50–101, nor Rankin, pp. 67–103, makes mention of the defendant's testifying, even unsworn, or being questioned by the prosecution, or saying anything.

3. On the committee draft, which is printed in Kate Mason Rowland, *The Life of George Mason, 1725–1792* (New York: G. P. Putnam's Sons, 1892, 2 vols.), I, pp. 436–38, see William T. Hutchinson et al., *The Papers of James Madison* (Chicago: University of Chicago Press, 1962–   ), I, p. 171. The final draft is in Thorpe, ed., *Federal and State Constitutions*, VII, pp. 3812–14.

4. Thorpe, ed., *Federal and State Constitutions*, III, p. 1688 (Maryland); III, p. 1891 (Massachusetts): IV, p. 2455 (New Hampshire); V, p. 2787 (North Carolina); V, p. 3083 (Pennsylvania); VII, p. 3471 (Vermont). Thorpe did not include the Delaware Declaration of Rights of 1776; it is available in *Proceedings of the Convention of the Delaware State Held at New-Castle on Tuesday the Twenty-Seventh of August, 1776* (1776, reprinted Wilmington, Del, 1927), p. 19. Schwartz, ed., *Bill of Rights*, reprints it, I, p. 278. Mason to George Mercer, Oct. 2, 1778, quoted in Rowland, *Life of Mason*, I, p. 237.

5. Thorpe, ed., *Federal and State Constitutions*, V, pp. 2594–98 (New Jersey); V, pp. 2623–38 (New York). Julius Goebel, Jr., and T. Raymond Naughton, *Law Enforcement in Colonial New York: A Study in Criminal Procedure (1664–1776)* (New York: Commonwealth Fund, 1944), xvii; see also ibid., pp. 57, 325.

6. Thorpe, ed., *Federal and State Constitutions*, II, pp. 777–85 (Georgia); VI, pp. 3248–57 (South Carolina).

7. The amendments reported by the House Select Committee, July 28, 1789, are printed in Schwartz, ed., *Bill of Rights*, II, pp. 1055–56; pp. 1122–23 for the amendments as passed by the House Committee of the Whole; ibid., p. 1111, for Laurence's remarks of Aug. 17, 1789. The members of the House Select Committee who had been members of the Federal Convention were Madison, Roger Sherman of Con-

necticut, Abraham Baldwin of Georgia, Nicholas Gilman of New Hampshire, and George Clymer of Pennsylvania.

8. Charles Warren, "New Light on the History of the Federal Judiciary Act of 1789," *Harvard Law Review* 37 (Nov. 1923): 111, 116, 118, 120, 122, 130 n. 177. [Edgar S. Maclay, ed.], *The Journal of William Maclay, United States Senator from Pennsylvania, 1789–1791*, intro. by Charles Beard (New York: A & C. Boni, 1927), pp. 90–92, entries for June 29 and June 30, 1789. Richard Peters, eds., *The Public Statutes at Large of the United States of America* (Boston, 1861ff.), I, p. 82, for the Judiciary Act of 1789, sect. 15.

9. Geyger's Lessee v. Geyger, 2 Dallas (Circ. Ct., Pa.) 332, at 333 (1795).

10. On the noncompellability of the party opponent in a civil suit at common law and his compellability, by bill of discovery, to testify and produce documents in chancery cases, see Wigmore, *Evidence*, VIII, pp. 168–74.

11. For the Senate proceedings, see Schwartz, ed., *Bill of Rights*, II, pp. 1149, 1154.

12. Respublica v. Gibbs, 3 Yeats (Pa.) 429, at 437 (1802). See also Galbreath v. Eichelberger, 3 Yeates (Pa.) 515 (1803); Bell's Case, 1 Browne (Pa.) 376 (1811).

13. United States v. Goosley, Case No. 15,230, in 25 Fed. Cases (Circ. Ct., Va.) 1363, 1364 (undated but in 1790s).

14. Marbury v. Madison, 1 Cranch 137, 144 (1803).

15. United States v. Burr, In re Willie, Case No. 14,692e, in 25 Fed. Cases (Circ. Ct., Va.) 38, 39–41 (1807).

16. For state cases showing that the common law right protected against self-infamy, as in the Pennsylvania cases cited in note 15 above, see State v. Bailly, 2 N.J. 396 (1807); Vaughn v. Perrine, 3 N.J. 299, 303 (1811); Miller v. Crayon, 2 Brevard (S.C.) 108 (1806); and People v. Herrick, 13 Johnson (N.Y.) 82 (1816). For English cases, early federal cases, and other state cases broadly construing the right, see the elaborate footnote 35, pp. 515–17, in Leonard W. Levy, *Origins of the Fifth Amendment: The Right Against Self-Incrimination* (New York: Oxford University Press, 1969).

17. Abe Fortas, "The Fifth Amendment: Nemo Tenetur Prodere Seipsum," Cleveland Bar Association, *The Journal* 25 (April 1954): 91, at 98–100, passim.

18. Chief Judge Calvert Magruder, in Maffie v. United States, 209 Fed. 2nd 225, 237 (1954).

19. Justice Felix Frankfurter, in Ullmann v. United States, 350 U.S. 422, 427 (1956). See also, to the same effect, Quinn v. United States, 349 United States 155, 161 (1955).

20. Frederic William Maitland, "A Prologue to a History of English Law," in *Select Essays in Anglo-American Legal History* (Boston: Little, Brown, 1907, 3 vols.), I, p. 7.

21. Sir James Fitzjames Stephen, *A History of the Criminal Law of England* (London, 1883, 3 vols.), I, pp. 319–57. On torture, see David Jardine, *A Reading on the Use of Torture in the Criminal Law of England* . . . (London, 1837), and John H. Langbein, *Torture and the Law of Proof* (Chicago: University of Chicago Press, 1977), pp. 73–139.

22. See A[dhemar] Esmein, *A History of Continental Criminal Procedure*, trans. John Simpson (London, 1914), pp. 3–12, 78–94; Wigmore, *Evidence* (1923 ed.), IV, sec. 2250, pp. 795–803; Levy, *Origins*, pp. 3–82.

23. See Roland G. Usher, *The Rise and Fall of the High Commission* (Oxford, 1913), and Levy, *Origins*, pp. 109–35.

24. Mary Hume Maguire, "Attack of the Common Lawyers on the Oath *Ex Officio* as Administered in the Ecclesiastical Courts in England," in *Essays in History and Political Theory in Honor of Charles Howard McIlwain* (Cambridge, Mass.: Harvard University, 1936), pp. 199–229. See also Faith Thompson, *Magna Carta: Its Role in the Making of the English Constitution, 1300–1629* (Minneapolis: University of Minnesota Press, 1948), pp. 205–230; Levy, *Origins*, pp. 136–204.

25. Robert Beale, "A Collection Shewinge what Jurisdiction the Clergie Hathe Heretofore Lawfully Used" (c.1590), quoted in Levy, *Origins*, p. 171.

26. Ibid., pp. 229–65.

27. M. A. Gibb, *John Lilburne, The Leveller: A Christian Democrat* (London, 1947), pp. 42–54; St. 16 Car. I, c. II, sec. 4 (1641); Levy, *Origins*, pp. 266–300.

28. Proceedings against the Twelve Bishops, 1642, in T. B. Howell, ed., *Cobbett's Complete Collection of State Trials* . . . (London, 1809–1826), IV, 76. See also The Trial of the King, 1649, in ibid., IV, 1101, where Holder objected to his having to give evidence against Charles I, and the court, "finding him [Holder] already a Prisoner, and perceiving that the Questions intended to be asked him, tended to accuse himself, thought fit to wave his Examination." This is the first time the right against self-incrimination was extended to a witness as well as the accused; Levy, *Origins*, pp. 301–326.

29. Levy, *Origins*, pp. 326–32; [Geoffrey Gilbert], *The Law of Evidence by a Late Learned Judge* (London, 1756), pp. 139–40. A fifth edition, published in Philadelphia in 1788, contains the identical passage at p. 137.

30. Levy, *Origins*, pp. 333–67.
31. Ibid., pp. 371–73, 505–506.
32. Ibid., pp. 381–404; Benjamin Franklin, "Some Observations on the Proceedings against the Rev. Mr. Hemphill" (1735), in *The Papers of Benjamin Franklin*, ed. Leonard W. Labaree et al. (New Haven, Conn.: Yale University Press, 1959–   ), II, pp. 37, 44, 45, 49, 90, 99. Daniel Fowle, *A Total Eclipse of Liberty* (Boston, 1755), pp. 11–14, 16–20. For the Pennsylvania declaration, see Oliver Dickerson, *The Navigation Acts & The American Revolution* (Philadelphia: University of Pennsylvania Press, 1954), pp. 246–47.

Chapter 13 The Ninth Amendment: Unenumerated Rights

1. 16 Wallace 36 (1873).
2. Robert H. Jackson, *The Supreme Court in the American System of Government* (Cambridge, Mass.: Harvard University Press, 1958), pp. 74–75.
3. Griswold v. Connecticut, 381 U.S. 479, 484–86 (1965). Only a plurality agreed with the Ninth Amendment grounds. Chief Justice Earl Warren and Justice William Brennan were the others.
4. Raoul Berger, "The Ninth Amendment," *Cornell Law Review* 61 (1980):1, note 2, relying on a computer study.
5. Edwin Meese III, Address before the American Bar Association, Washington, D.C., July 9, 1985, Dept. of Justice typescript, pp. 13, 15.
6. Dred Scott v. Sandford, 19 Howard 393 (1857).
7. Griswold v. Connecticut, p. 520.
8. Joseph Story, *Commentaries on the Constitution of the United States* (Boston, 1833, 1st ed., 3 vols.), I, pp. 383, 387.
9. Merrill Jensen, ed., *The Documentary History of the Ratification of the Constitution*. Vol. II, *Ratification of the Constitution by States*. *Pennsylvania* (Madison: State Historical Society of Wisconsin, 1976–   ), p. 388, for Wilson. See the sixth "Landholder" essay by Ellsworth in Paul L. Ford, ed., *Essays on the Constitution of the United States . . . 1787–1789* (Brooklyn, N.Y.: 1892), p. 163.
10. Jonathan Elliot, ed., *The Debates in the Several State Conventions* (Philadelphia: Lippincott, 1941, 5 vols., reprinting the final, rev. ed.), III, p. 620.
11. Speech of June 8, 1789, reprinted in Bernard Schwartz, ed., *The Bill of Rights: A Documentary History* (New York: Chelsea House, 1971, 2 vols.), II. pp. 1023–34, quoted material at p. 1024.

12. Ibid., II, p. 1029.
13. Ibid., II, p. 1024.
14. Ibid., II, p. 1031.
15. Ibid., II, p. 1027.
16. Coke, *The Second Part of the Institutes of the Laws of England* (London, 1681, 6th ed.) chap. XXIX, p. 50. See Rodney L. Mott, *Due Process of Law* (Indianapolis: Bobbs-Merrill, 1926), pp. 75–80, and Charles H. McIlwain, "Due Process of Law in Magna Carta," *Columbia Law Review* 14 (1914):27–51. Keith Jurow, "Untimely Thoughts: A Reconsideration of the Origins of Due Process of Law," *American Journal of Legal History* 19 (1975): 265–79, straightens out the history of the matter but does not alter the fact that a tradition existed, even if ill-founded, equating due process with the law of the land and, in particular, with proceedings by grand and petty juries in criminal cases.
17. See supra, chap. 11, text connected with notes 79–80.
18. See supra, chap. 12, text connected with notes 1–2.
19. Schwartz, ed., Bill of Rights, II, p. 1096.
20. Ibid., II, p. 1026.
21. Ibid, II, pp. 1112, 1123.
22. Ibid., p. 1042.
23. Ibid., p. 1029.
24. Hamilton, "The Farmer Refuted," in *Papers of Alexander Hamilton*, ed. Harold C. Syrett et al. (New York: Columbia University Press, 1961–1981, 26 vols.), I, p. 122.
25. Dickinson, "An Address to the Committee of Correspondence in Barbados (1766), in Paul L. Ford, ed., *Writings of John Dickinson* (Philadelphia, 1895), vol. XIV of *Memoirs of the Historical Society of Pennsylvania*, p. 261.
26. John Adams to Timothy Pickering, Aug. 6, 1822, in *Works of John Adams*, ed. Charles F. Adams (Boston, 1850–1859, 10 vols.), II, p. 512.
27. Jefferson to Henry Lee, May 8, 1825, in *The Writings of Thomas Jefferson*, ed. Albert E. Bergh (Washington: Jefferson Memorial Association, 1907, 20 vols), XVI, pp. 118–19.
28. See John Hart Ely, *Democracy and Distrust: A Theory of Judicial Review* (Cambridge, Mass.: Harvard University Press, 1980), p. 49.
29. Schwartz, ed., *Bill of Rights*, I, p. 375.
30. Ibid, II, pp. 840, 911, 966.
31. Dec. 4, 1787, in Jensen, ed., *Documentary History of Ratification*, II, p. 473.
32. Locke's note on happiness in Maurice Cranston, *John Locke, a Bi-*

ography (London: Longmans, Green, 1957), p. 123. For Locke's use of "pursuit of happiness," see his *Essays Concerning Human Understanding,* ed. Alexander Campbell Fraser (Oxford: Clarendon Press, 1894, 2 vols.), I, pp. 342, 345, 348, 352.

33. Herbert L. Ganter, "Jefferson's 'Pursuit of Happiness' and Some Forgotten Men," *William and Mary Quarterly,* 2nd ser. 16 (1936), pp. 558–85, traces the pre-1776 uses of "pursuit of happiness," and quotes Johnson and Blackstone.

34. See Locke, *Second Treatise,* sections 27, 87, 123, 173; see also Laslett, ed., *Two Treatises,* p. 367, note for lines 5–6.

35. *National Gazette* (Philadelphia), March 29, 1792, reprinted in *Papers of Madison,* ed. Hutchinson et al., XIV, p. 266.

36. Ibid., XII, p. 203.

37. See Kenneth L. Karst, "Freedom of Intimate Association," in Leonard W. Levy, Kenneth L. Karst, and Dennis J. Mahoney, eds., *Encyclopedia of the American Constitution* (New York: Macmillan, 1986, 4 vols.), II, pp. 782–89, and Karst's lengthy article of the same title in *Yale Law Journal,* 89 (1980): 624–92. See also David H. Flaherty, *Privacy in Colonial New England* (Charlottesville: University Press of Virginia, 1967), chap. 2, "The Family," chap. 3, "The Neighborhood," and chap. 6, "Government and the Law." The right to travel and the right to hunt and fish are old; precedents can be found in the Massachusetts Body of Liberties of 1641, the source, also, of equal protection of the laws and many other rights. See Richard L. Perry, ed., *Sources of Our Liberties: Documentary Origins of Individual Liberties* (Chicago: American Bar Foundation, 1959), pp. 143–61, for the document prefaced by commentary, and, especially, pp. 148 and 150.

38. Edmund Pendleton to Richard Henry Lee, June 14, 1788, in David Mayes, ed., *Letters and Papers of Edmund Pendleton* (Cambridge, Mass.: Harvard University Press, 1967, 2 vols.), II, p. 533.

39. Ely, *Democracy and Distrust,* p. 39, so argues. He relies on Robert Cover, *Justice Accused: Antislavery and the Judicial Process* (New Haven, Conn.: Yale University Press, 1975), p. 27; but Cover refers to the period before 1776. Ely extended Cover's point to the time of the Framers and later.

40. Van Horne's Lessee v. Dorrance, 2 Dallas 304 (1795); Calder v. Bull, 3 Dallas 386 (1798); Fletcher v. Peck, 6 Cranch 87 (1810); and Terrett v. Taylor, 9 Cranch 43 (1815); all discussed in chapters below; see index.

41. Ely, *Democracy and Distrust,* p. 39.

42. Ibid., pp. 49–52.

43. Berger, "Ninth Amendment," p. 16 note 95 and p. 23.
44. Russell L. Caplan, "The History and Meaning of the Ninth Amendment," *Virginia Law Review* 69 (1983): 223–68, is a desperately confused article. Most of it is a sprawling collection of historical data of no relevance. The thesis is that the Ninth Amendment derived from a provision of the Articles of Confederation, which spoke of state sovereignty and the retention by the states of all rights and powers not "expressly" delegated to the United States. Not even the Tenth Amendment, with which Caplan confuses the Ninth, speaks of powers not "expressly" delegated. Lawrence E. Mitchell, "The Ninth Amendment and the Jurisprudence of Original Intention," *Georgetown Law Journal* 74 (1986): 1719–42, focuses wholly on contemporary issues, after endorsing as good history the article by Caplan and the remarkably bad little book, Bennett Patterson's *The Forgotten Ninth Amendment* (Indianapolis: Bobbs-Merrill, 1955), which advocates that the Ninth Amendment's natural rights philosophy protects God, corporations, and patriotism. Mitchell's article is otherwise worth reading. A better article on the subject, though outdated in some respects, is Norman Redlich, "Are There Certain Rights . . . Retained by the People," *New York University Law Review* 37 (1961): 787–808. Charles L. Black, *Decision According to Law* (New York: W. W. Norton, 1981), is an 83-page essay whose principal theme is that the Ninth Amendment should be the basis for judicial decisions in favor of women's rights. Black's thesis does not rest on history or original intent.
45. Articles 1 and 17, Virginia's recommended amendments, 1788, in Schwartz, ed., *Bill of Rights*, II, pp. 842, 844.
46. Burnley to Madison, Nov. 28, 1789, in *Papers of Madison*, ed. Hutchinson et al., XII, p. 456.
47. Madison to Washington, Dec. 5, 1789, in ibid., p. 459.
48. Ibid.
49. Roe v. Wade, 410 U.S. 113 (1973); Katz v. United States, 389 U.S. 347 (1967); Schad v. Borough of Mt. Ephraim, 452 U.S. 61 (1981).
50. Speech of June 8, 1789, in Schwartz, ed., *Bill of Rights*, II, p. 1031, my emphasis.
51. Berger, "Ninth Amendment," p. 9.
52. Ibid., pp. 1112–13.

Chapter 14 History and Original Intent

1. Sparf v. United States, 156 U.S. 51, 169 (1895).
2. *Journal, Acts and Proceedings of the Convention, . . . which formed the Constitution of the United States* (Boston, 1819).

3. Max Farrand, ed., *The Records of the Federal Convention* (New Haven, Conn.: Yale University Press, 1911, 3 vols.; rev. ed. 1937, 4 vols.). Vol. 4 of Farrand has been superseded by *Supplement to Max Farrand's The Records of the Federal Convention*, ed. James H. Huston (New Haven, Conn.: Yale University Press, 1987).

4. Farrand, ed., *Records*, I, p. xiii.

5. See especially William Winslow Crosskey, *Politics and the Constitution in the History of the United States* (Chicago: University of Chicago Press, 1953, 2 vols.), I, p. 313, and II, pp. 1009, 1012, where Crosskey accused Madison of inventing spurious dialogue and falsely presenting the opinions of others in order to further his later political views. Max Farrand, who did not question Madison's integrity or the enormous value of his Notes, grumbled about the fact that Madison later altered his Notes after seeing the *Journal* and the published records kept by Robert Yates of New York. See note 7, below. As a result, according to Farrand, Madison introduced errors into his Notes. In most instances, however, the alterations are discernible so that we can distinguish, as Farrand did, between the original version and its subsequent "correction." Farrand complained that in some instances the ink had so faded that he could not make that distinction. Farrand, ed., *Records*, I, pp. xvi-xviii.

6. See next note, below.

7. *Secret Proceedings and Debates of the Convention Assembled at Philadelphia in the year 1787, . . . From Notes taken by the late Robert Yates* (Albany, N.Y., 1821). Reprinted in Elliot, ed., *Debates*, I, pp. 389–479.

8. Madison to Joseph Gales, Aug. 26, 1821, in Farrand, ed., *Records*, III, pp. 446–47.

9. James Hutson, "The Creation of the Constitution: The Integrity of the Documentary Record, *Texas Law Review* 65 (1986):12. I have found this excellent article to be most useful.

10. Marion Tinling, "Thomas Lloyd's Reports of the First Federal Congress," *William and Mary Quarterly*, 3rd ser., 18 (1961):530. Mrs. Tinling was also an editor for the National Historical Publications Commission.

11. Madison to Gov. Edward Coles, as quoted in Farrand, *Records*, III, p. 550 n. 1, citing H. B. Grigsby, *History of Virginia Federal Convention of 1788*, I, p. 95 note.

12. Undated Preface to Madison's Notes, in Farrand, ed., *Records*, III, pp. 550, 551.

13. Hutson, "Creation of the Constitution," p. 34.

14. Washington's Diary, Sept. 17, 1787, quoted in Hutson, ed., *Supplement to Farrand*, p. 276.
15. *A National Program for the Publication of Historical Documents*. A Report to the President by the National Historical Publications Commission (Washington, D.C.: Government Printing Office, 1954), p. 92.
16. Tinling, "Thomas Lloyd's Reports," p. 530.
17. Elliot, ed., *Debates*, I, preface to 1st ed.
18. John Bach McMaster and Frederick D. Stone, eds., *Pennsylvania and the Federal Constitution, 1787–1788* (Lancaster: Historical Society of Pennsylvania, 1888), p. 212.
19. Merrill Jensen, ed., *The Documentary History of the Ratification of the Constitution*. Vol. II, *Ratification of the Constitution by the States. Pennsylvania* (Madison: State Historical Society of Wisconsin, 1976).
20. Herbert Storing, ed., *The Complete Anti-Federalist* (Chicago: University of Chicago Press, 1981, 7 vols.), III.
21. *Annals of Congress*, 1st Cong. 3rd sess., II, pp. 1952–53, Feb. 7, 1791.
22. Samuel B. Harding, *The Contest over Ratification of the Federal Constitution in the State of Massachusetts* (New York: Da Capo Press, 1970 reprint of 1896 book), p. 177.
23. Quoted in Harold C. Syrett et al., eds. *The Papers of Alexander Hamilton* (New York: Columbia University Press, 1961–1981, 26 vols.), V, note on pp. 11–12.
24. Gaspare J. Saladino, "A Guide to Sources for Studying the Ratification of the Constitution by New York State," in Stephen L. Schechter, ed., *The Reluctant Pillar: New York and the Adoption of the Federal Constitution* (Troy, N.Y.: Russell Sage College, 1985), pp. 132–33.
25. Letter of Nov. 1827, in *The Writings of James Madison*, ed. Gaillard Hunt (New York: G. P. Putnam, 1900–1910, 9 vols.), IX, p. 291. See also Madison to Elliot, Feb. 14, 1827, in ibid., pp. 270–71.
26. Marshall to Thomas H. Bayly, 1832, quoted in *The Papers of John Marshall*, ed. Herbert A. Johnson et al. (Chapel Hill: University of North Carolina Press, 1974–   ), I, p. 256 n. 7.
27. Jensen, ed., *Documentary History*, III, p. 7.
28. Edgar S. Maclay, ed., *Journal of William Maclay* (New York, 1890).
29. *The Journal of the First Session of the Senate of the United States of America* (New York, 1789), reprinted in Linda Grand De Pauw, ed., *Documentary History of the First Federal Congress of the*

United States of America, 1789–1791 (Baltimore: Johns Hopkins University Press, 1972, 4 vols.), I, pp. 3–210.

30. Ibid., III, pp. 3–246.
31. Tinling, "Thomas Lloyd's Reports of the First Federal Congress," p. 521.
32. *A National Program,* p. 93.
33. Tinling, "Thomas Lloyd's Reports," p. 530.
34. Madison to Edward Everett, Jan. 7, 1832, quoted in ibid., p. 538; emphasis in original.
35. Madison to Jefferson, May 9, 1789, quoted in ibid., p. 533, available in *Papers of James Madison,* ed. William T. Hutchinson et al. (Chicago and Charlottesville: University of Chicago Press and University Press of Virginia, 1962–), XII, p. 142. See also Tinling's article, pp. 531, 537. At p. 536 Tinling quotes the 1792 remark of Elbridge Gerry that Lloyd put into people's mouths "arguments directly the reverse of what they had advanced."
36. David M. Matteson, "The Organization of the Government Under the Constitution," in Sol Broom, ed., *History of the Formation of the Union Under the Constitution* (Washington, D.C. U.S. Constitution Sesquicentennial Commission, 1943), p. 316.
37. See above, chap. 1, text connected with notes 25–36.
38. See above, chap. 2, text connected with notes 60 and 71.
39. Thomas M. Cooley, *A Treatise on the Constitutional Limitations Which Rest upon the Legislative Power* (Boston, 1868, 1st ed. reprinted New York: Da Capo Press, 1972), chap. IV, p. 66.
40. Joseph Story, *Commentaries on the Constitution of the United States* (Boston, 1833, 3 vols., 1st ed., reprinted New York: Da Capo Press, 1970), I, pp. 388–90, of Bk. 3, chap. V, sect. 406. Discussed above, chap. 1, text associated with note 61.
41. Joseph Strayer, ed., *The Delegates from New York, or, Proceedings of the Federal Convention of 1787 from the Notes of John Lansing, Jr.* (Princeton, N.J.: Princeton University Press, 1939).
42. See Leonard W. Levy, "The Making of the Constitution, 1776–1789," in Levy, ed., *Essays on the Making of the Constitution* (New York: Oxford University Press, 1987, 2nd ed.), ix–xl.
43. Alfred H. Kelly, "Clio and the Court: An Illicit Love Affair," in Philip B. Kurland, ed., *Supreme Court Review: 1965* (Chicago, 1965), pp. 119–58.
44. Jacobus tenBroek, "Admissibility and Use by the United States Supreme Court of Extrinsic Aids in Constitutional Construction," *California Law Review* 26 (1938):287–308, 437–54, 664–81; 27 (1939):157–81, 399–421.

45. Adamson v. California, 332 U.S. 46 (1947).
46. Charles Fairman, "Does the Fourteenth Amendment Incorporate the Bill of Rights? The Original Understanding," *Stanford Law Review* 2 (1949):5–139.
47. Paul L. Murphy, "Time to Reclaim: The Current Challenge of American Constitutional History," *American Historical Review* 69 (1963):64–79. Murphy referred to United States v. Curtiss-Wright Export Corp., 299 U.S. 304 (1936). He credited Howard J. Graham for the phrase "law office history." Charles A. Lofgren proved that the Court's history in Curtiss-Wright was "shockingly inaccurate," in his intensive study of that case published as a *Yale Law Journal* article, reprinted in his book, *Government from Reflection and Choice* (New York: Oxford University Press, 1986), pp. 167–205.
48. Alexander M. Bickel, "The Original Understanding and the Segregation Decision," *Harvard Law Review* 69 (1955):1–43.
49. Leonard W. Levy, *Legacy of Suppression: Freedom of Speech and Press in Early American History* (Cambridge, Mass.: Harvard University Press, 1960). For a lucid discussion of the problem generally, see John Wofford, "The Blinding Light: The Uses of History in Constitutional Interpretation," *University of Chicago Law Review* 31 (1964):502–533. See also Charles Miller, *The Supreme Court and the Uses of History* (Cambridge, Mass.: Harvard University Press, 1969); H. Jefferson Powell, "The Original Understanding of Original Intent," *Harvard Law Review* 98 (1985):885–948, and Powell, "Rules for Originalists," *Virginia Law Review* 73 (1987):659–99.
50. Twining v. New Jersey, 211 U.S. 78 (1908).
51. Malloy v. Hogan, 378 U.S. 1 (1964).
52. Twining v. New Jersey, 211 U.S. 78, 106.
53. Ibid., p. 110.
54. Ibid., p. 108.
55. Ibid., pp. 103–104.
56. Adamson v. California, 332 U.S. 46, 88 (1947).
57. *A Short Story of the Rise, Reign, and Ruine of the Antinomians, Familists and Libertines, that Infected the Churches of New England* (London, 1649), reprinted in Charles Francis Adams, ed., *Antinomianism in the Colony of Massachusetts Bay, 1636–1638* (Boston, 1894), pp. 194, 195.
58. (William Bradford), *Bradford's History "Of Plimoth Plantation"* (Boston, 1898), p. 465.
59. E. G. Atkinson, ed., *Close Rolls of the Reign of Henry III, 1247–51* (London: H.M. Stationery Office, 1922), pp. 221–22.

60. Prohibition Formata de Statuto Articuli Cleri, in A. Luders et al., eds., *Statutes of the Realm* (London, 1810), I, p. 209.

61. I. S. Leadam and J. F. Baldwin, eds., *Select Cases Before the King's Council, 1243–1482* (Cambridge, Mass.: Harvard University Press, 1918), pp. xxvi–xxvii, xliii, 33, 40, 74, 79–80, 94, 103, 105–106; James Fosdick Baldwin, *The King's Council in England during the Middle Ages* (Oxford: Clarendon Press, 1913), pp. 296–97.

62. *Statutes of the Realm*, I, p. 345, 28 Edw. III, chap. 3 (1354). On Magna Carta in the fourteenth century, see Faith Thompson, *Magna Carta, Its Role in the Making of the English Constitution, 1300–1629* (Minneapolis: University of Minnesota Press, 1948), chap. 3.

63. Robert Beale, "A Collection Shewinge what Jurisdiction the Clergie Hathe Heretofore Lawfully Used," British Museum, Cotton MSS, Cleopatra F. I., no. 1, folio 18, recto.

64. James Morice, *A brief treatise of Oathes exacted by Ordinaries and Ecclesiasticall Judges* (n.p., 1600), pp. 8–10, 11–18, 22, 26–31, 32, 37, 47; (Nicholas Fuller), *The Argument of Master Nicholas Fuller* (London, 1607), pp. 7–13, 23, 28–29. Stowe MSS #424, folios 158a–164b (British Museum) contains seventeen unreported cases of 1609–1611 in most of which Coke invoked Magna Carta to rule on the illegality of the incriminatory oath *ex officio;* for reported decisions, see Edward's Case, 13 Coke's Reports 9 (1609); Huntley v. Cage, 2 Brownlow & Goldesborough 14 (1611); and Burrowes, Cox, Dyton et al. v. High Commission, 3 Bulstrode 48 (1616). See also "Of Oaths before an Ecclesiastical Judge Ex Officio," 12 Coke's Reports 26 (1607). For Parliament, see the bill passed by Commons against the oath *ex officio* on June 25, 1610, in Maurice F. Bond, ed., *Manuscripts of the House of Lords, Addenda 1514–1714,* Historical Manuscripts Commission, new series (London: H.M. Stationery Office, 1962), XI, pp. 125–26. The claim that Magna Carta vested a right against self-incrimination, wholly apart from the oath issue, originated with the Levellers. In 1645, John Lilburne, relying on chap. 29 of Magna Carta and the 1628 Petition of Right, claimed that "it is contrary to Law, to force a man to answer to Questions concerning himself . . ."; Lilburne, *England's Birth-Right Justified Against all Arbitrary usurpation, whether Regall or Parliamentary* (1645), in William Haller, ed., *Tracts on Liberty in the Puritan Revolution, 1638–1647* (New York: Columbia University Press, 1933), III, p. 263.

65. On the use of the incriminatory oath procedure by Charles I, see "The Commission and Instructions for Raising the Forced Loan," Sept. 23, 1626, in Samuel Rawson Gardiner, ed., *The Constitutional*

Documents of the Puritan Revolution, 1625–1660 (3rd ed., Oxford: Clarendon Press, 1906), p. 55; for the Petition of Right, see ibid., p. 69.

66. Twining v. New Jersey, 211 U.S. 78, 108 (1908).
67. For the action of Congress in 1778, in the case of Silas Deane, see letter of Gouverneur Morris, in *The Freeman's Journal, or North-American Intelligencer* (Philadelphia), June 14, 1781; see also the statement by Henry Laurens, president of the Continental Congress, April 21, 1779, in Edmund C. Burnett, ed., *Letters of the Members of the Continental Congress* (Washington, 1928), IV, pp. 166 n. 12, 168. For the Resolutions of the Stamp Act Congress and the Declaration and Resolves of the First Continental Congress, see Richard L. Perry (ed.), *Sources of Our Liberties: Documentary Origins of Individual Liberties in the United States Constitution and Bill of Rights* (Chicago: American Bar Foundation, 1959), pp. 270, 288.
68. Northwest Ordinance, Art. 2, in ibid., p. 395.
69. Delaware Declaration of Rights, 1776, Sect. 15, in ibid., p. 339; Constitution of Vermont, 1777, Sect. 10, in ibid., p. 366. The six states named by Justice Moody were North Carolina, Pennsylvania, Virginia, Massachusetts, New Hampshire, and Maryland, in Twining v. New Jersey, 211 U.S. 78, 91 (1908).
70. For the amendments proposed by Virginia, New York, North Carolina, and Rhode Island, see Moody's summary, in *Twining*, at p. 109.
71. Ibid., p. 91. For a similar remark, see John H. Wigmore, *A Treatise on the Anglo-American System of Evidence* (2nd ed., Boston: Little, Brown, 1923), IV, p. 819. See Leonard W. Levy, *Origins of the Fifth Amendment: The Right Against Self-Incrimination* (New York: Oxford University Press, 1968), pp. 433–41 on ancient Jewish law.
72. Twining v. New Jersey, 211 U.S. 78, 106 (1908). New York was the only state to recommend a due process of law clause; see Jonathan Elliot, ed., *The Debates in the Several State Conventions on the Adoption of the Federal Constitution* (2nd rev. ed., Philadelphia, 1941, 5 vols.), I, p. 328. Although no state had a due process of law clause in its constitution before the Fifth Amendment, several states had a "law of the land" clause which was a historical equivalent.
73. The *Twining* decision was reaffirmed in Palko v. Connecticut, 302 U.S. 319, 324, 325 (1937); Adamson v. California, 332 U.S. 46 (1947); and Cohen v. Hurley, 366 U.S. 117, 128–129 n. 7 (1961). For earlier cases, arising in the federal courts, in which the Supreme Court treated the right against self-incrimination as a fundamental right, see Boyd v. United States, 116 U.S. 616 (1886); Counselman v. Hitchcock, 142

U.S. 547 (1892); Brown v. Walker, 161 U.S. 596 (1896); and Bram v. United States, 168 U.S. 532 (1897). The Court first held the right to be fundamental in state cases, too, in Malloy v. Hogan, 378 U.S. 1 (1964). Franklin's remark is in his pamphlet, "Some Observations on the Proceedings against Mr. Hemphill" (1735), in Leonard W. Labaree et al., eds., *Papers of Benjamin Franklin* (New Haven, Conn.: Yale University Press, 1959–   ), I, p. 44. For Gilbert, see *The Law of Evidence by a Late Learned Judge* (London, 1756), pp. 139–40.
74. 350 U.S. 422 (1956).
75. Ibid., pp. 426, 427.
76. Ibid., p. 438.
77. J. Hammond Trumbull and Charles J. Hoadly, eds., *The Public Records of the Colony of Connecticut* (Hartford, 1850–1890), IV, p. 236.
78. Gertrude MacKinney and Charles F. Hoban, eds., *Votes and Proceedings of the House of Representatives of the Province of Pennsylvania (1682–1776)*, in *Pennsylvania Archives* (n.p., 1931–1935), 8th Series, VI, p. 4679.
79. MS Minute Book of the Supreme Court of Judicature, Oct. 19, 1762, to April 28, 1764, entries for Oct. 28, 1763, pp. 273, 289. Engrossed Minutes, Hall of Records, New York County, N.Y.
80. See Republica v. Gibbs, 3 Yeates (Pa.) 429, 473 (1802); Republica v. Gibbs, 3 Yeates (Pa.) 515 (1803); State v. Bailly, 2 N.J. 396 (1807); Vaughn v. Perrine, 3 N.J. 299, 300 (1811); Miller v. Crayon, 2 Brevard (S. Car.) 108 (1806); People v. Herrick, 13 Johnson (N.Y.) 82 (1816). The English courts at this time were still applying the same rule.
81. William Tyndale, *The Obedience of a Christian Man* (1528), reprinted in Henry Walter, ed., *Doctrinal Treatises and Introductions to Different Portions of the Holy Scriptures. By William Tyndale* (Cambridge, 1848), p. 355, where Tyndale said it was "a crule thing to break up into a man's heart, and to compel him to put either soul or body in jeopardy, or to shame himself." In 1584 Archbishop John Whitgift referred to a Puritan claim that "nemo tenetur seipsum prodere, aut propriam turpitudinem revelare" (no man is bound to accuse himself, or to reveal his own infamy); in John Strype, *The Life and Acts of John Whitgift* (Oxford, 1822, 2 vols.) I, p. 319. See also the document of 1590 by Thomas Cartwright and others in Albert Peel and Leland H. Carlson, eds. *Cartwrightiana* (London, 1951), 38 ff., and a document of about the same date in Thomas Fuller, *The Church History of Britain*, ed. J. S. Brewer (Oxford, 1845), V, pp. 107–12.

82. Morice, *A briefe treatise,* p. 8; 1 Coke's Institutes 158b, and 4 ibid. 279.

83. William Hudson, *A Treatise of the Court of Star Chamber* (ante 1635), in Francis Hargrave, ed., *Collectanea Juridica. Consisting of Tracts Relating to the Laws and Constitution of England* (London, 1791), I, pp. 208–209; Trial of Nathanael Reading, *State Trials,* VIII, pp. 259, 296–97 (1679); Trial of Peter Cook, ibid., XIII, pp. 311, 334–35 (1696); Trial of Jonathan Freind, ibid., XIII, pp. 1, 17 (1696); East India Co. v. Campbell, 1 Vesey Sr. 246 (1749); Rex v. Lewis, 4 Espinasse 225, 226 (1802); Macbride v. Macbride, 4 Espinasse 242, 243 (1802).

84. Blackstone, *Commentaries,* III, pp. 363, 370.

85. For American manuals of practice, see (James Parker), *Conductor Generalis, Or the Office, Duty and Authority of Justices of the Peace* (New York, 1764), p. 167; (Richard Burn), *An Abridgment of Burn's Justice of the Peace* (Boston, 1773), p. 123; J. Davis, *The Officer and Authority of a Justice of the Peace* (Newbern, No. Car., 1774), p. 159; Richard Starke, *The Office and Authority of Justice of the Peace* (Williamsburg, Va., 1774), p. 146; (John F. Grimke), *The South-Carolina Justice of the Peace* (Philadelphia, 1788), p. 191; William W. Hening, *The New Virginia Justice* (Richmond, Va., 1795), p. 177. All these include a standardized quotation from Coke that a "witness alledging [sic] his own infamy or turpitude, is not to be heard."

86. Douglas relied on Mitchell Franklin, "The Encyclopediste Origin and Meaning of the Fifth Amendment," *Lawyers Guild Review* 15 (1955):41–62, an article without merit as an explanation of the historical origins of the Fifth Amendment. For Jefferson's proposed constitutions of Virginia, in 1776 and 1783, see Julian Boyd et al., eds., *The Papers of Thomas Jefferson* (Princeton, 1950–   ), I, pp. 341, 348, 359; VI, p. 298. At the pages cited, Jefferson recommended a ban against torture. Jefferson made no reference to the right against self-incrimination in his letters of 1787–1789, when he recommended provisions that should be included in a national bill of rights.

87. For the procedure of Star Chamber, contrasting it with that of the High Commission, see Morice, *A briefe treatise of Oathes,* pp. 38–39. For a similar contrast by Robert Beale, see Strype, *John Whitgift,* II, p. 138. The best contemporary work is Hudson, *Court of Star Chamber,* I, pp. 1–240.

88. Hudson, *Court of Star Chamber,* p. 169.

89. Ibid., pp. 208–209; see also ibid., pp. 64, 164.

90. On High Commission procedure and the practice of compulsory

self-incrimination, see the book by a member of that court, Richard Cosin, *An Apologie for Sundrie Proceedings Ecclesiasticall* (London, 1593), Part II, pp. 51–52, 57–58, 104; Part III, pp. 43, 113–16. See also Strype, *John Whitgift*, I, pp. 321–22.

91. For Beale and Morice, see notes 63 and 64 above. For a similar distinction by Coke on the use of the oath by the Star Chamber and the High Commission, see 12 Coke's Reports 26 (1607). Wigmore, *Treatise on Evidence* (McNaughton rev.), VIII, p. 281, incorrectly traced the Star Chamber and its oath procedure to a statute of 1487, misstated that procedure, and charged Coke with inconsistency in opposing the use of the oath in the High Commission. The best study of the Star Chamber is the introduction by C. G. Bayne in Bayne and W. H. Dunham, eds., *Select Cases in the Council of Henry VII* (London, 1958, Selden Society Publications), LXXV, which corrects the common error concerning that statute of 1487.

92. Adamson v. California, 332 U.S. 46, 88 n. 14 (1947); Miranda v. Arizona, 384 U.S. 436, 459 (1966).

93. See citations in preceding note for the remarks by Black and Warren; for Douglas, see Ullmann v. United States, 350 U.S. 422, 446–47 (1956).

94. Trial of Lilburne, Howell (comp.), *State Trials*, III, pp. 1315, 1318 (1637).

95. Lilburne, *The Christian Mans Triall* (2nd ed., London, 1641), p. 6.

96. Trial of Lilburne, *State Trials*, III, p. 1318.

97. Lilburne, *A Copy of a Letter from Lieutenant-Colonel John Lilburne to a friend* (London, 1645), pp. 2, 14; Lilburne, *England's Birth-Right Justified Against all Arbitrary Usurpations* (London, 1645), in Haller, ed., *Tracts on Liberty*, III, p. 263. The Presbyterians made a similar claim. Thus, Clement Walker declared, ". . . and our accusation beginneth with the examination of our persons, to make us state a charge against ourselves, to betray ourselves, and cut our owne throats with our tongues, contrary to Magna Carta, the Petition of Right," in Verax, *Anarchia Anglicana*, p. 57.

98. Trial of Lilburne, *State Trials*, IV, pp. 1269, 1292, 1340, 1341 (1649).

99. Ibid., pp. 1292, 1340, 1341.

100. *Bradford's History*, p. 465.

101. Douglas said, "Partrich's answer is typical"; Ullmann v. United States, p. 448, and he cited the book by Bradford.

102. *Bradford's History*, pp. 472–73.

103. James Savage, ed., *The History of New England from 1630 to 1649. By John Winthrop* (Boston, 1853), II, p. 56.

104. Maverick's petition is quoted in George Lyman Kittredge, "Dr.

Robert Child the Remonstrant," *Publications of the Colonial Society of Massachusetts*, XXI, Transactions, 1919, pp. 58–59, no. 5, citing Massachusetts Archives (MS) B xxviii, 228a, dated May 8, 1649.

105. Kastigar v. United States, 406 U.S. 441 (1972).
106. Ibid., pp. 445–46 and note 13. Levy, *Origins*, covers the subject at pp. 328, 359, 365–66, 384–85, 389, 402–403, and 495.
107. 406 U.S. 441, 443 n. 5 Cf. Levy, *Origins*, pp. 328–29, 495.
108. Brown v. Walker, 161 U.S. 591 (1896).
109. United States v. Murdock, 284 U.S. 141 (1931).
110. The misused cases were King of the Two Sicilies v. Willcox, 7 St. Tr. (N.S.) 1050, 1068 (1851), distinguished in United States of America v. McRae, L.R. 3 Ch. 79 (1867), and Queen v. Blyes, 1 B. & S. 311, 330. The case in point unknown to the Court was East India Co. v. Campbell, 1 Vesey Sr. 246 (1749).
111. J. A. C. Grant, "Immunity from Compulsory Self-Incrimination in a Federal System of Government," *Temple Law Quarterly* 9 (1935); 57–58; Grant, "Federalism and Self-Incrimination," *UCLA Law Review* 4 (1957):549–82, and ibid., V (1958):1–25.
112. Murphy v. Waterfront Commission of New York, 378 U.S. 79 (1964).
113. Swift, *Gulliver's Travels* (1726), intro. Jacques Barzun (New York: Crown Publishers, 1947), Part IV, chap. 5, pp. 295–96.
114. 345 U.S. 972 (1953).
115. Kelly, "Clio and the Court," *Supreme Court Review 1965*, pp. 142–45.
116. Michel de Montaigne, Bk. II, chap. 12, "Apology for Raymond Sebond," in *The Complete Essays of Montaigne*, ed. Donald M. Frame (Stanford, Calif.: Stanford University Press, 1958), p. 426.
117. Mark DeWolfe Howe, *The Garden and the Wilderness: Religion and Government in American Constitutional History* (Chicago: University of Chicago Press, 1965), p. 4. I agree with Howe's statement but believe that Howe misread the evidence on the church–state issues that he addressed. For a contrast to his views, see my book, *The Establishment Clause: Religion and the First Amendment* (New York: Macmillan, 1986).
118. Dartmouth College v. Woodward, 4 Wheaton 518 (1819).
119. John M. Shirley, *The Dartmouth College Causes and the Supreme Court of the United States* (Chicago, 1895, reprinted New York: Da Capo Press, 1971), pp. 20–65. See also Frederick Chase, *A History of Dartmouth College and the Town of Hanover*, ed. John K. Lord (Cambridge, 1891), pp. 8–58, 116–17, 121–55, 228, 243–45, 277. In *The Constitutional Decisions of John Marshall*, ed. Joseph P. Cotton (New York: G. P. Putnam's Sons, 1905, 2 vols., reprinted

New York: Da Capo Press, 1969), I, p. 347, the editor stated that Marshall's Dartmouth College opinion was especially "argumentative, combative. . . . There is bias in the statement of facts, a bias in the statement of premises; and surely, what seems now to us the main issue of the case, the assumption that the charter of the college was a 'contract,' as that term is used in the Constitution, is too hasty and too barely supported."

120. Dred Scott v. Sandford, 19 Howard 393 (1857).
121. Don E. Fehrenbacher, *The Dred Scott Case: Its Significance in American Law and Politics* (New York: Oxford University Press, 1978), pp. 348–49.
122. Slaughterhouse Cases, 16 Wallace 36, 96 (1873).
123. Ibid., p. 77.
124. The literature on the framing and ratification of the Fourteenth Amendment in voluminous. The best recent works include Harold M. Hyman and William M. Wiecek, *Equal Justice Under Law: Constitutional Development 1835–75* (New York: Harper, 1982); Charles Fairman, *History of the Supreme Court, Vol. VI. Reconstruction and Reunion, 1864–88, Part One* (New York: Macmillan, 1971); and Michael Kent Curtis, *No State Shall Abridge: The Fourteenth Amendment and the Bill of Rights* (Durham, N.C.: Duke University Press, 1968).
125. Civil Rights Cases, 109 U.S. 3 (1883).
126. Slaughterhouse Cases, 16 Wallace 36, 71 (1873).
127. Leonard W. Levy, *Chief Justice Shaw and the Law of the Commonwealth* (Cambridge, Mass.: Harvard University Press, 1957, reprinted 1987), chap. 8 on the public works doctrine.
128. Hurtado v. California, 110 U.S. 516 (1884).
129. Coke, *The Second Part of the Institutes of the Laws of England* (London, 1681, 6th ed.), p. 50.
130. Hurtado v. California, p. 529.
131. Leonard W. Levy, ed., *The Fourteenth Amendment and the Bill of Rights* (New York: Da Capo Press, 1970), pp. 225–52, reprints Stanley Morrison, "Does the Fourteenth Amendment Incorporate the Bill of Rights: the Judicial Interpretation," which reviews the cases from the standpoint of a scholar hostile to judicial expansion of the rights of the criminally accused.
132. Plessy v. Ferguson, 163 U.S. 537, 544, 551 (1896).
133. Pollock v. Farmers Loan and Trust Co., 157 U.S. 429 (1895), and 158 U.S. 601 (1895).
134. 157 U.S. 429, 573.
135. Ibid., p. 582.

136. Ibid., p. 563.
137. Hylton v. United States, 3 Dallas 171 (1796).
138. Julius Goebel, Jr., and Joseph H. Smith, eds., *The Law Practice of Alexander Hamilton* (New York: Columbia University Press, 1964–1980, 4 vols.), IV, p. 351.
139. Wesberry v. Sanders, 376 U.S. 1, 7–8 (1964).
140. Ibid., p. 17, for Wilson; on Madison, compare Black at p. 15 with Justice John Marshall Harlan, p. 31 note 15.
141. Marsh v. Chambers, 463 U.S. 783 (1983).
142. Ibid., p. 788 note 8.
143. "Madison's Detached Memoranda" (post-1817), ed. Elizabeth Fleet, *William and Mary Quarterly*, 3rd ser. III (1946):554. Madison to E. Livingston, July 10, 1822, in *The Writings of James Madison*, ed. Gaillard Hunt (New York: G. P. Putnam's 1900–10, 9 vols.), IX, p. 100.
144. *Annals of Congress*, 1st Cong., 1st sess., I, p. 1077, Jan. 7, 1790. Burger gave a different date for the act of Congress and a different citation.
145. Wallace v. Jaffree, 105 S. Ct. 2479, 2516, 2520 (1985).
146. Ibid., footnote 4. For a sustained refutation of Rehnquist, see Levy, *The Establishment Clause: Religion and the First Amendment* (New York: Macmillan, (1986), especially chap. 5.
147. Richard Neely, *How Courts Govern America* (New Haven, Conn.: Yale University Press, 1981), p. 18.
148. George Orwell, *1984* (New York: Harcourt Brace, 1949), p. 35.
149. Holdsworth, *Essays in Law and History* (Oxford: Clarendon Press, 1946), p. 24.

Chapter 15 A Constitutional Jurisprudence of Original Intent? Part One

1. "Freedom of the Press," in [Finley Peter Dunnel], *Mr. Dooley on the Choice of Law*, ed. Edward J. Bander (Charlottesville, Va.: Mitchie Co., 1963), p. 65.
2. United States v. Trans-Missouri Freight Assoc., 166 U.S. 290, 318–19 (1897).
3. Missouri v. Holland, 252 U.S. 416, 433 (1920).
4. Nathaniel Chipman, *Principles of Government: A Treatise on Free Institutions. Including the Constitution of the United States* (1793, revised Burlington, Vt., 1833, reprinted New York: Da Capo Press, 1970), pp. 254–55. In his appendices, Chipman reprinted several

long letters by Madison on constitutional interpretation, written between 1828 and 1832.

5. Thomas M. Cooley, *A Treatise on the Constitutional Limitations Which Rest Upon the Legislative Power* (Boston, 1868, reprinted New York: Da Capo Press, 1972), pp. 54–55.
6. Dred Scott v. Sandford, 19 Howard 393, 426 (1857).
7. Ex parte Bain, 121 U.S. 1, 12 (1887).
8. South Carolina v. United States, 199 U.S. 437, 448 (1905).
9. In re Debs, 158 U.S. 564, 591 (1895).
10. Euclid v. Ambler Realty Co., 272 U.S. 365, 387 (1926).
11. Home Building and Loan Association v. Blaisdell, 290 U.S. 398, 449–53 *passim*.
12. Ibid., p. 436.
13. McCulloch v. Maryland, 4 Wheaton 316, 497 (1819).
14. Ibid., pp. 443–44.
15. Youngstown Steel v. Sawyer, 343 U.S. 579, 634–35 (1952).
16. McCulloch v. Maryland, 4 Wheaton 316, 407 (1819).
17. Chipman, *Principles of Government*, p. 254. See also Cooley, *Constitutional Limitations*, p. 60, on the point that American constitutions "are to be construed in the light of the common law. . . ."
18. Max Farrand, ed., *The Records of the Federal Convention of 1787* (New Haven, Conn.: Yale University Press, 1911, 3 vols.), I, p. 137.
19. Holmes, *The Common Law* (Boston, 1881), p. 106.
20. Norway Plains Co. v. Boston and Maine Railroad, 1 Gray (Mass.) 263, 267 (1854).
21. *The Federalist*, ed. Jacob E. Cooke (Cleveland: Meridian Books, 1961), p. 143.
22. *Annals of Congress*, 1st Cong., 1st sess., I, p. 500, June 17, 1789.
23. Fundamental Constitutions of Carolina, 1669, Sections 80 and 120, in Francis Newton Thorpe, ed., *The Federal and State Constitutions, Colonial Charters, and Other Organic Laws* (Washington, D.C.: Government printing Office, 1909, 7 vols.), V, pp. 2782 and 2786.
24. See above, chap. 2, text associated with notes 28–39.
25. Farrand, ed., *Records*, II, p. 21, May 29, 1787.
26. Jonathan Elliot, ed., *The Debates in the Several State Conventions* (Philadelphia: Lippincott, 1941 reprint ed., 5 vols.), III, 470, Va. ratifying convention, June 15, 1788.
27. *The Federalist*, ed. Cooke, pp. 236–37, 238.
28. *Annals of Congress*, 4th Cong., 1st Sess., March 14, 1796, quoted in Farrand, ed., *Records*, III, pp. 369–70.
29. Marbury v. Madison, 1 Cranch 137 (1803).
30. See Articles 6 and 12 of the Articles of Confederation.

31. Leonard W. Levy, *The Establishment Clause: Religion and the First Amendment* (New York: Macmillan, 1986), pp. 79, 96–109.
32. Compare Levy, *Establishment Clause*, with Thomas J. Curry, *The First Freedoms* (New York: Oxford University Press, 1986).
33. See Leonard W. Levy, *Emergence of a Free Press* (New York: Oxford University Press, 1985).
34. Address of Edwin Meese III . . . before the American Bar Association, Washington, D.C., July 9, 1985, in *The Great Debate: Interpreting Our Written Constitution* (pamphlet published by the Federalist Society, Washington, D.C., 1986), p. 1.
35. Counselman v. Hitchcock, 142 U.S. 547, 562 (1892).
36. Felix Frankfurter and Thomas G. Corcoran, "Petty Offenses and the Constitutional Guaranty of Trial by Jury," *Harvard Law Review* 39 (1926):917–1017; the quotation is from p. 969.
37. Baldwin v. New York, 399 U.S. 66 (1970).
38. Felix Rackow, "The Right to Counsel: English and American Precedents," *William and Mary Quarterly*, 3rd ser., 11 (1954):3–27, and William M. Beaney, *The Right to Counsel in American Courts* (Ann Arbor: University of Michigan Press, 1955), pp. 8–29.
39. Powell v. Alabama, 287 U.S. 45 (1932).
40. Johnson v. Zerbst, 304 U.S. 458 (1938).
41. Gideon v. Wainwright, 372 U.S. 335 (1963); Argersinger v. Hamlin, 407 U.S. 25 (1972).
42. See Martin L. Friedland, *Double Jeopardy* (Oxford: Clarendon Press, 1969), pp. 1–15, and Jay Sigler, *Double Jeopardy* (Ithaca, N.Y.: Cornell University Press, 1969), pp. 1–37; Raoul Berger, *Death Penalties* (Cambridge, Mass.: Harvard University Press, 1982), pp. 1–76, and Anthony Granucci, "Nor Cruel and Unusual Punishments Inflicted: The Original Meaning," *California Law Review* 67 (1969):839–65.
43. United States v. Belmont, 301 U.S. 324 (1937); United States v. Pink, 315 U.S. 203 (1942). See Edward S. Corwin, *The President: Office and Powers, 1787–1984* (New York: New York University Press, 1984, 5th rev. ed.), pp. 242–47, 259–60; Louis Henkin, *Foreign Affairs and the Constitution* (Mineola, N.Y.: Foundation Press, 1972), pp. 173–88.
44. Learned Hand, "Sources of Toleration," *University of Pennsylvania Law Review* 79 (1930):12.
45. Felix Frankfurter, "The Supreme Court of the United States," in *Law and Politics: Occasional Papers of Felix Frankfurter, 1913–1938*, ed. Archibald MacLeish and E. F. Prichard, Jr. (New York: Harcourt, Brace, 1939), p. 30.
46. Graves v. O'Keefe, 306 U.S. 466, 491–92 (1939).

47. Robert E. Shalhope, "The Ideological Origins of the Second Amendment," *Journal of American History* 69 (1982):599–614; Stephen P. Halbrook, *That Every Man Be Armed: The Evolution of a Constitutional Right* (Albuquerque: University of New Mexico Press, 1984).
48. Katz v. United States, 389 U.S. 347(1967). See also United States v. White, 392 U.S. 1 (1968), and United States v. United States District Court, 407 U.S. 297 (1972).
49. Learned Hand, "The Contribution of an Independent Judiciary to Civilization," in *The Spirit of Liberty: Papers and Addresses of Learned Hand,* ed. Irving Dilliard (New York: Knopf, 1953), pp. 122–23.
50. Jefferson to Spencer Roane, Sept. 6, 1819, in Paul L. Ford, ed., *The Writings of Thomas Jefferson* (New York: G. P. Putnam's, 1892–1899, 10 vols.), X, p. 401.
51. Lewis Carroll, *Through the Looking Glass and What Alice Found There* (1865) (New York: Heritage Press, 1941), p. 112.
52. Elliot, ed., *Debates,* II, p. 462.
53. Farrand, ed., *Records,* I, p. 137.
54. Edward S. Corwin, "Judicial Review in Action," *University of Pennsylvania Law Review* 124 (1926):659–60.
55. Williams v. Florida, 399 U.S. 78 (1970); Apodaca v. Oregon, 406 U.S. 404 (1972); Johnson v. Louisiana, 406 U.S. 356 (1972).
56. On grand juries, see Hurtado v. California, 110 U.S. 516 (1884); Sparf v. United States, 156 U.S. 51 (1895). On the Seventh Amendment, see Minneapolis & St. Louis Ry. Co. v. Bombolis, 241 U.S. 211 (1916), and Charles W. Wolfram, "The Constitutional History of the Seventh Amendment," *Minnesota Law Review* 57 (1973):639–747.
57. United States v. Lovett, 328 U.S. 303, 321 (1946), concurring.
58. Leonard W. Levy, *Origins of the Fifth Amendment: The Right Against Self-Incrimination* (New York: Oxford University Press, 1968, reprinted by Macmillan, 1987), pp. 422–32.
59. On bills of attainder, see Zechariah Chafee, Jr., *Three Human Rights in the Constitution* (Lawrence: University of Kansas Press, 1956), pp. 90–161.
60. Lovett v. United States, 328 U.S. 303, 316 (1946).
61. Test Oath Cases (Cummings v. Missouri and Ex parte Garland), 4 Wallace 277 and 331 (1867).
62. Sir William Blackstone, *Commentaries on the Laws of England* (London, 1765–1769, 4 vols.), IV, p. 377.
63. "Second Letter from Phocion," April 1784, in *The Papers of Alexander Hamilton* ed. Harold C. Syrett et al. (New York: Columbia University Press, 1962–1981), III, pp. 543–51.

64. National Mutual Insurance Co. v. Tidewater Transfer Co., 337 U.S. 582, 646–47 (1949), dissenting.
65. Louisville, C.&C. Ry v. Letson, 2 Howard 497 (1844).
66. Granger Cases, 94 U.S. 113 (1877); Santa Clara Co. v. Southern Pacific Ry., 118 U.S. 394 (1886); Silverthorne Lumber Co. v. United States, 251 U.S. 385 (1920).
67. Chafee, *Three Human Rights*, p. 154.
68. William F. Duker, *A Constitutional History of Habeas Corpus* (Westport, Conn.: Greenwood Press, 1980), p. 7.
69. Blackstone, *Commentaries*, IV, p. 377.
70. Weems v. United States, 217 U.S. 349 (1910); Solem v. Helm, 459 U.S. 986 (1983).
71. Trop v. Dulles, 356 U.S. 86 (1958).
72. Robinson v. California, 370 U.S. 660 (1962).
73. See above, chap. 3, text associated with notes 46–82.
74. Hoffer and Hull, *Impeachment in America, 1635–1805* (New Haven, Conn.: Yale University Press, 1980), pp. 96–106, 264–70. The entire book, a work of superb scholarship, proves the point.
75. Weems v. United States, 217 U.S. 349 (1910), emphasis added.

Chapter 16 A Constitutional Jurisprudence of Original Intent? Part Two

1. James M. Beck, *The Constitution of the United States, Yesterday, Today—and Tomorrow?* (New York: George H. Doran Co., 1924), p. 221. The phrase "continuous constitutional convention" has been used to describe the work of the Court in constitutional law by many, including Henry Steele Commager, "Constitutional History and the Higher Law," in Conyers Read, ed., *The Constitution Reconsidered* (New York: Columbia University Press, 1938), p. 231, and Robert H. Jackson, *The Struggle for Judicial Supremacy* (New York: Knopf, 1941), pp. x–xi.
2. The roll call here would produce a long string of citations, including opinions by Louis D. Brandeis, Felix Frankfurter, Hugo L. Black, Byron R. White, and Warren Burger.
3. McCollum v. Board of Education, 333 U.S. 203, 237–38 (1948).
4. Committee of Public Education v. Nyquist, 413 U.S. 756, 820 (1973), dissenting.
5. Pensacola Telegraph Co. v. Western Union Telegraph Co., 96 U.S. 1, 9 (1877).
6. United States v. Classic, 313 U.S. 299, 315–16 (1941).

7. See above, chap. 1.
8. Oliver Wendell Holmes, *The Common Law* and "The Path of the Law," reprinted in Max Lerner, ed., *The Mind and Faith of Justice Holmes* (New York: Modern Library, 1943), pp. 51, 54, 81–82.
9. Karl N. Llewellyn, *The Common Law Tradition* (Boston: Little, Brown, 1960), pp. 520–35. See also Frank H. Easterbrook, "Legal Interpretation and the Power of the Judiciary," *Harvard Journal of Law and Public Policy* 7 (1981):87–99.
10. Marbury v. Madison, 1 Cranch 137 (1803).
11. Standard Oil v. United States, 221 U.S. 1 (1911).
12. Duplex Printing Press v. Deering, 254 U.S. 443 (1921).
13. Carter v. Carter Coal Co., 298 U.S. 238 (1936).
14. See above, chap. 1.
15. James Kent, *Commentaries on American Law* (Boston: Little, Brown, 1826, rev. 10th ed. in 1860, 4 vols.), I, pp. 460–68; Joseph Story, *Commentaries on the Constitution of the United States* (Boston: Little, Brown, 1833, 3 vols.), I. pp. 389–91; Thomas M. Cooley, *Constitutional Limitations*, pp. 66–67.
16. Marshall's opinion in Gibbons v. Ogden, 9 Wheaton 1 (1824), which at p. 196 referred to "commerce within the states," did not achieve acceptance by the Court until 1937. William W. Crosskey, *Politics and the Constitution in the History of the United States* (Chicago: University of Chicago Press, 1953, 2 vols.), I, pp. 50–292, developed an eighteenth-century lexicon to prove that the commerce clause as understood by the generation that produced it meant that Congress had the power to regulate all commerce without regard to distinctions between interstate commerce and intrastate commerce. Original intent analysis of the commerce clause should begin with Crosskey, whose work I have never seen cited by proponents of a jurisprudence of original intent.
17. Max Farrand, ed., *The Records of the Federal Convention* (New Haven, Conn.: Yale University Press, 1911, 3 vols.), II, p. 619. The cases are Hepburn v. Griswold, 8 Wallace 603 (1870), and Sinking Fund Cases, 99 U.S. 700 (1879).
18. Louisville Joint Stock Land Bank v. Radford, 295 U.S. 555 (1935).
19. Bolling v. Sharpe, 347 U.S. 497 (1954), preceded, by implication, in Hurd v. Hodge, 334 U.S. 224 (1948).
20. Henry P. Monaghan, "Our Perfect Constitution," *New York University Law Review* 56 (1981):360.
21. "The Art of Advocacy," in *Mr. Dooley on the Choice of Law*, ed. Bander, p. 34.

22. *The Collected Poetry of W. H. Auden* (New York: Random House, 1945), p. 75. Reprinted by permission.
23. *Iolanthe*, in *The Complete Operas of W. S. Gilbert* (New York: Dorset Press, n.d.), p. 245.
24. For a sampling of the literature on the original intent controversy, see the Bibliography, infra.
25. Quoted in James Bradley Thayer, "The Origin and Scope of the American Doctrine of Constitutional Law," *Harvard Law Review* 7 (1893):152.
26. Jefferson to Thomas Richie, Dec. 25, 1820, in *The Writings of Thomas Jefferson*, ed. Albert Ellery Bergh (Washington: Thomas Jefferson Memorial Association, 1907, 20 vols.), XV, p. 297; to Charles Hammond, Aug. 18, 1821, in ibid., XV, p. 331; to Edward Livingston, March 25, 1825, in ibid., XVI, p. 113.
27. March 4, 1861, in *The Collected Works of Abraham Lincoln*, ed. Roy P. Basler (New Brunswick, N.J.: Rutgers University Press, 1953, 8 vols.), IV, p. 268.
28. Speech at Springfield, Ill., June 26, 1857, in ibid., III, p. 401 (emphasis added).
29. Robert H. Jackson, *The Struggle for Judicial Supremacy* (New York: Knopf, 1941), p. 311. See also Jackson's preface, which develops the same theme and describes the Court as a "continuous constitutional convention."
30. Edwin Meese III, "The Law of the Constitution." A Bicentennial Lecture, Tulane University, Oct. 21, 1986, distributed by the Department of Justice, pp. 12–13, and for his quotation from Lincoln, pp. 14–15.
31. Minersville School District v. Gobitis, 310 U.S. 586, 600 (1940); West Virginia Bd. of Ed. v. Barnette, 319 U.S. 624, 650, 666 (1943); and AFL v. American Sash and Door Co., 335 U.S. 538, 555 (1949).
32. Robert H. Bork, "Neutral Principles and Some First Amendment Problems," *Indiana Law Journal* 47 (1971): 6, 11.
33. William H. Rehnquist, "The Notion of a Living Constitution," *Texas Law Review* 54 (1976):695, 699.
34. For an excellent discussion, see Jesse H. Choper, *Judicial Review and the National Political Process* (Chicago: University of Chicago Press, 1980), pp. 4–59.
35. James Bradley Thayer, *John Marshall* (Boston: Houghton Mifflin, 1901), pp. 106, 107; Henry Steele Commager, *Majority Rule and Minority Rights* (New York: Oxford University Press, 1943), pp. 71–77, quoting Thayer at pp. 73–74; Frankfurter, "Can the Supreme Court Guarantee Toleration," from his *Law and Politics*, p. 197, and

Frankfurter, in Minersville School District v. Gobitis, 310 U.S. 586, 600 (1940).

36. Jefferson to Madison, Dec. 20, 1787, in *The Papers of Thomas Jefferson*, ed. Julian P. Boyd (Princeton, N.J.: Princeton University Press, 1959–   ), XII, p. 440; Jefferson to Madison, March 15, 1789, in ibid., XIV, pp. 659, 661.

37. Speech of June 8, 1789, 1st Cong., 1st sess., reprinted in Bernard Schwartz, ed., *The Bill of Rights: A Documentary History* (New York: Chelsea House, 1971, 2 vols.), II, pp. 1029, 1031.

38. United States v. Carolene Products Co., 304 U.S. 144, 152 n. 4 (1938).

39. West Virginia State Bd. of Ed. v. Barnette, 319 U.S. 624, 638 (1943).

40. Benjamin N. Cardozo, *The Nature of the Judicial Process* (New Haven, Conn.: Yale University Press, 1921), p. 93.

41. Woodrow Wilson, *Constitutional Government in the United States* (New York: Columbia University Press, 1908), p. 157.

42. AFL v. American Sash and Door Co., 335 U.S. 538, 555–56 (1949), and Learned Hand, *The Bill of Rights* (Cambridge, Mass.: Harvard University Press, 1958), p. 73.

43. Eugene V. Rostow, *The Sovereign Prerogative: The Supreme Court and the Quest for Law* (New Haven, Conn.: Yale University Press, 1962), pp. 168–69.

44. Ibid., p. 170.

45. 109 U.S. 3 (1883).

46. 163 U.S. 537 (1896).

47. Minersville School District v. Gobitis, 310 U.S. 586 (1940).

48. J. Skelly Wright, "The Role of the Courts: Conscience of a Sovereign People," *The Reporter Magazine* 29 (September 26, 1963):28. See also the outstanding study by David R. Manwaring, *Render unto Caesar: The Flag Salute Controversy* (Chicago: University of Chicago Press, 1962).

49. American Communications Assoc. v. Douds, 339 U.S. 94 (1950); Dennis v. United States 341 U.S. 494 (1951); and Communist Party v. Subversive Activities Control Board, 367 U.S. 1 (1961).

50. Brooks Adams, *The Theory of Social Revolutions* (New York: Macmillan, 1914), pp. 214, 218.

51. Compare Henry Steele Commager's *Majority Rule and Minority Rights* (1943) with his lectures seventeen years later on "Democracy and Judicial Review," in his *Freedom and Order* (New York: Braziller, 1966), pp. 3–51, which conclude, like Rostow, "It is as an educational institution that the Court may have its greatest contribution to make to the understanding and preservation of liberty."

52. Vincent Blasi, ed., *The Burger Court: The Counter-Revolution That Wasn't* (New Haven, Conn.: Yale University Press, 1983), is a good account by various constitutional scholars. For ultraconservative accounts, see Christopher Wolfe, *The Rise of Modern Judicial Review: From Constitutional Interpretation to Judge-made Law* (New York: Basic Books, 1968), pp. 258–322, and Lino A. Graglia, "Constitutional Theory: The Attempted Justification for the Supreme Court's Liberal Political Program," *Texas Law Review* 65 (1987):789–98.

53. Miranda v. Arizona, 384 U.S. 436 (1966).

54. Harris v. New York, 401 U.S. 222 (1971); United States v. Calandra, 414 U.S. 338 (1974); United States v. Leon, 468 U.S. 897 (1984).

55. United Jewish Organizations v. Carey, 430 U.S. 144 (1977).

56. Columbus Bd. of Ed. v. Penick, 443 U.S. 449 (1979); Dayton Bd. of Ed. v. Brinkman, 443 U.S. 526 (1979).

57. Califano v. Goldfarb, 430 U.S. 199 (1977), and Califano v. Westcott, 433 U.S. 76 (1979).

58. United Steelworkers Union v. Weber, 443 U.S. 193 (1979), and Fullilove v. Klutznick, 448 U.S. 448 (1980).

59. Miller v. California, 413 U.S. 15 (1973), and Young v. American Mini Theatres, 427 U.S. 50 (1976).

60. Meek v. Pittenger, 421 U.S. 349 (1975); Wolman v. Walter, 433 U.S. 229 (1977).

61. Stone v. Graham, 449 U.S. 39 (1980).

62. United States v. United States District Court, 407 U.S. 297 (1972).

63. Furman v. Georgia, 408 U.S. 238 (1972).

64. Roe v. Wade, 410 U.S. 113 (1973).

65. Jesse H. Choper, *Judicial Review and the National Political Process* (Chicago: University of Chicago Press, 1980).

66. John Hart Ely, *Democracy and Distrust: A Theory of Judicial Review* (Cambridge, Mass.: Harvard Univeristy Press, 1980).

67. See Ronald Dworkin, *Taking Rights Seriously* (Cambridge, Mass.: Harvard University Press, 1977), pp. 131–49.

68. Laurence H. Tribe, *American Constitutional Law* (Mineola, N.Y.: Foundation Press, 1978), p. 889.

69. McGautha v. California, 402 U.S. 183 (1971); Furman v. Georgia, 408 U.S. 238 (1972).

70. William J. Brennan, Jr., Speech of Oct. 12, 1985, Georgetown University, in Federalist Society, *The Great Debate: Interpreting Our Written Constitution* (Washington, D.C., 1986), pp. 23–24.

71. Robert H. Bork, Speech of Nov. 18, 1985, University of San Diego Law School, in ibid., p. 45.

72. Robert H. Bork, "The Supreme Court Needs a New Philosophy," *Fortune* 58 (Dec. 1968), p. 170.

73. E.g., Brandeis in Whitney v. California, 274 U.S. 357 (1927), concurring; Black in Adamson v. California, 332 U.S. 46 (1947), dissenting, and in Wesberry v. Sanders, 376 U.S. 1 (1964); Rutledge in Everson v. Bd. of Ed., 330 U.S. 1 (1947), dissenting; Douglas in Ullmann v. United States, 350 U.S. 422 (1956), dissenting; Brennan in New York Times v. Sullivan, 376 U.S. 254 (1964).

74. Donald L. Horowitz, *The Courts and Social Policy* (Washington, D.C.: The Brookings Institution, 1977), pp. 4–5.

75. Essay No. 15, March 20, 1788, in Herbert J. Storing, ed., *The Complete Anti-Federalist* (Chicago: University of Chicago Press, 1981, 7 vols.), II. p. 440. Brutus's essays on the judiciary, Nos. 12–15, in ibid., pp. 422–42, have proved to be far more perceptive than Hamilton's.

76. *The Federalist*, ed. Jacob E. Cooke (Cleveland: Meridian Books, 1961), pp. 542–53.

77. Richard A. Posner, "What Am I?" *The New Republic*, Sept. 28, 1987, pp. 23–25.

78. Alfred H. Kelly, "Clio and the Court: An Illicit Love Affair," *1965 Supreme Court Review*, ed. Philip B. Kurland (Chicago: University of Chicago Press, 1965), pp. 131–32.

79. Harry Jaffa to William A. Rusher, Publisher, *National Review*, March 15, 1986, photocopy of letter provided by Professor Jaffa to me. See also Jaffa's "What Were the 'Original Intentions' of the Framers of the Constitution of the United States:" *University of Puget Sound Law Review* 10 (1987):343–448.

80. For a similar opinion of Rehnquist, see David L. Shapiro, "Mr. Justice Rehnquist: A Preliminary View," *Harvard Law Review* 90 (1976):293–357.

81. Robert H. Bork, Speech of Nov. 18, 1985, in Federalist Society, *The Great Debate*, p. 47.

82. Rehnquist, "Living Constitution," p. 706. For a perceptive discussion, see Jeff Powell, "The Complete Jeffersonian: Justice Rehnquist and Federalism," *Yale Law Journal* 91 (1982):1317–70. The Jefferson with whom Powell associates Rehnquist is not Jefferson the champion of civil liberties or Jefferson the nationalist (when President), but Jefferson the states' rights supporter (when out of federal power); Powell should have compared Rehnquist with Calhoun. For a dazzling analysis of the Calhounian thought of Meese, Bork, and Rehnquist, see Jaffa, "Original Intentions of the Framers," pp. 351–448.

83. Rehnquist, "Living Constitution," pp. 693–706 *passim*.

84. Robert H. Bork, "Neutral Principles and Some First Amendment Problems," *Indiana Law Journal* 47 (1971):10.
85. Rehnquist, "Living Constitution," pp. 698, 704.
86. Rehnquist in Trimble v. Gordon, 430 U.S. 762, 778 (1977), dissenting opinion not joined by other dissenters.
87. Wallace v. Jaffree, 105 Sup. Ct. 2479, 2508 (1985), at pp. 2509 (understanding history), p. 2512 (discriminating against sects and referring to Williams et al.), p. 2516 (on federal aid), and p. 2520 (on national church).
88. Lemon v. Kurtzman, 403 U.S. 602 (1971).
89. Everson v. Board of Education, 330 U.S. 1 (1947).
90. Wallace v. Jaffree, 2520; see ibid., p. 2512 n. 4 for the gaffes on Rhode Island.
91. See Frank H. Easterbrook, "William H. Rehnquist," in Leonard W. Levy, Kenneth L. Karst, and Dennis J. Mahoney, eds., *Encyclopedia of the American Constitution* (New York: Macmillan, 1986, 4 vols.), III, pp. 1533–35.
92. Powell, "Compleat Jeffersonian," pp. 1369–70.
93. Speech of Nov. 18, 1985, in Federalist Society, *The Great Debate*, p. 46.
94. Griswold v. Connecticut, 381 U.S. 479, 483–84 (1965).
95. Bork, "Neutral Principles," pp. 8–9. In 1986 Bork reexpressed belief that a constitutional right to privacy did not exist. Bork, "Judicial Review and Democracy," in Levy et al., eds., *Encyclopedia of the American Constitution*, III, p. 1063.
96. Bork, "Original Intent and the Constitution," *Humanities* 7 (1986):26.
97. Bork, "Neutral Principles," pp. 11–33, passim.
98. Robert H. Bork, Foreword to Gary L. McDowell, *The Constitution and Contemporary Constitutional Theory* (Cumberland, Va.: Center for Judicial Studies, 1985), p. x.
99. Bork, "Judicial Review and Democracy," p. 1063.
100. Bork, Speech of Nov. 18, 1985, p. 52.
101. That is a thesis of Christopher Wolfe, *Rise of Modern Judicial Review*, a book of slight merit.
102. Slaughterhouse Cases, 16 Wallace 36 (1873).
103. United States v. Cruikshank, 92 U.S. 542 (1876).
104. United States v. Reece, 92 U.S. 214 (1876).
105. Virginia v. Rives, 100 U.S. 313 (1880).
106. Pace v. Alabama, 106 U.S. 583 (1883).
107. United States v. Harris, 106 U.S. 629 (1883).
108. Civil Rights Cases, 109 U.S. 3 (1883).
109. Hall v. DeCuir, 95 U.S. 485 (1878).

110. Plessy v. Ferguson, 163 U.S. 537 (1896).

111. See Stanley Morrison, "Does the Fourteenth Amendment Incorporate the Bill of Rights? The Judicial Interpretation," *Stanford Law Review* 2 (1949):140–173 and cases there cited.

112. Graglia, "Constitutional Theory," p. 792.

Chapter 17 Conclusions

1. Jacobus tenBroek, "Use by the United States Supreme Court of Extrinsic Aids in Constitutional Construction: The Intent Theory," *California Law Review* 27 (1939):404–406, 410.

2. Robert H. Bork, Speech of Nov. 18, 1985, in the Federal Society, *The Great Debate: Interpreting Our Written Constitution* (Washington, 1986), p. 47.

3. Edward S. Corwin, *Constitutional Revolution, Ltd.* (Claremont, Calif.: Claremont Colleges, 1941).

4. Robert L. Stern, "The Commerce Clause Revisited—The Federalization of Intrastate Crime," *Arizona Law Review* 15 (1973):271–85.

5. Arnold M. Howitt, *Managing Federalism: Studies in Intergovernmental Relations* (Washington: C.Q. Press, 1984); David B. Walker, *Toward a Functioning Federalism* (Cambridge, Mass.: Winthrop, 1981); Michael D. Reagan, *The New Federalism* (New York: Oxford University Press, 2nd ed., 1981). These works supply the facts; the generalizations are mine.

6. PruneYard Shopping Center v. Robins, 447 U.S. 74 (1980). Hawaii Housing Authority v. Midkiff, 467 U.S. 229 (1984).

7. Van Horne's Lessee v. Dorrance, 2 Dallas 304 (1795).

8. Bowsher v. Synar, 106 Sup. Ct. 3181 (1986).

9. *The Federalist*, ed. Jacob E. Cooke (Cleveland: Meridian Books, 1961), Nos. 47–48, especially at p. 332.

10. *The Public Statutes at Large of the United States of America* (Boston: Little, Brown, 1861), I, p. 66, Sept. 2, 1789, chap. XII—An Act to Establish the Treasury Department.

11. Dartmouth College v. Woodward, 4 Wheaton 518, 644–45 (1819).

12. Benjamin N. Cardozo, *The Nature of the Judicial Process* (New Haven, Conn.: Yale University Press, 1921), pp. 92–93.

13. Chambers v. Florida, 309 U.S. 227, 241 (1940).

14. Richard Neely, *How Courts Govern America* (New Haven, Conn.: Yale University Press, 1981), p. 203, n. 8.

15. Oliver Wendell Holmes, *The Common Law* (Boston: Little, Brown, 1881), p. 35.

16. Bork, "Original Intent and the Constitution," *Humanities* 7 (1986):26.
17. *The Babylonian Talmud,* ed. I. Epstein (London: Soncino Press, 1935 ff.), *Seder Nezikin,* P. 59B (p. 353).
18. Oliver Wendell Holmes, "Learning and Science," in Holmes's *Speeches* (1913), reprinted in Julius J. Marke, ed., *The Holmes Reader* (Dobbs Ferry, N.Y.: Oceana Press, 1955), p. 106.
19. Holmes, "The Path of the Law" (1897), in Holmes's *Collected Legal Papers* (New York: Harcourt Brace, 1920), pp. 194–95.
20. Earl Warren, Speech on retirement, June 23, 1969, in 89 Sup. Ct. 20.

Bibliography

Adams, John. *Works of John Adams*, 10 vols., ed. Charles F. Adams. Boston, 1850–1859.

Agresto, John. *The Supreme Court and Constitutional Democracy*. Ithaca, N.Y.: Cornell University Press, 1984.

Alfange, Dean, Jr. "On Judicial Policymaking and Constitutional Change: Another Look at the 'Original Intent' Theory of Constitutional Interpretation," *Hastings Constitutional Law Quarterly* 5 (1978):603–638.

Barber, Soterios A. *On What the Constitution Means*. Baltimore: Johns Hopkins University Press, 1984.

Beaney, William M. *The Right to Counsel in American Courts*. Ann Arbor: University of Michigan Press, 1955.

Beard, Charles A. *The Supreme Court and the Constitution*. Englewood Cliffs, N.J.: Spectrum, 1962.

Bennett, Robert W. "Objectivity in Constitutional Law," *University of Pennsylvania Law Review* 132 (1984):445–96.

——. "The Mission of Moral Reasoning in Constitutional Law," *Southern California Law Review* 58 (1985):647–59.

Berger, Raoul. *Congress v. The Supreme Court*. Cambridge, Mass.: Harvard University Press, 1969.

————. *Government by Judiciary*. Cambridge, Mass.: Harvard University Press, 1977.

————. "'Original Intention' in Historical Perspective," *The George Washington Law Review* 54(1986):296–337.

————. "The Ninth Amendment," *Cornell Law Review* 61 (1980):1–26.

Bestor, Arthur. "Respective Roles of Senate and President in the Making and Abrogation of Treaties—The Original Intent of the Framers of the Constitution Historically Examined," *Washington Law Review* 55 (1979):1–136.

————. "Separation of Powers in the Domain of Foreign Affairs: The Intent of the Constitution Historically Examined," *Seton Hall Law Review* 5 (1974):527–666.

Beveridge, Albert J. *The Life of John Marshall*, 4 vols. Boston: Houghton Mifflin, 1916–1919.

Bickel, Alexander M. *The Least Dangerous Branch*. Indianapolis: Bobbs-Merrill, 1962.

———— "The Original Understanding and the Segregation Decision," *Harvard Law Review* 69 (1955):1–43.

Black, Charles L. *The People and the Court: Judicial Review in a Democracy*. New York: Macmillan, 1960.

Blackstone, Sir William. *Commentaries on the Laws of England*, 4 vols. London, 1766–1769.

Bork, Robert H. "Judicial Review and Democracy," *Encyclopedia of the American Constitution*, 4 vols., ed. Leonard W. Levy et al. New York: Macmillan, 1986, 3:1061–64.

————. "Neutral Principles and Some First Amendment Problems," *Indiana Law Journal* 47 (1971):1–35.

————. "Original Intent and the Constitution," *Humanities* 7 (1986):22, 26–27.

————. "The Supreme Court Needs a New Philosophy," *Fortune* 78 (1968):138–41, 166–71.

————. Foreword to Gary L. McDowell, *The Constitution and Contemporary Constitutional Theory*. Cumberland, Va.: Center for Judicial Studies, 1985.

————. Speech of Nov. 18, 1985, in the Federal Society, *The Great Debate: Interpreting Our Written Constitution*. Washington, D.C., 1986.

Boudin, Louis B. *Government by Judiciary*, 2 vols. New York: William Godwin, Inc., 1932.

Brant, Irving. *James Madison, Father of the Constitution*. Indianapolis: Bobbs-Merrill, 1950.

Brest, Paul. "The Fundamental Rights Controversy: The Essential Contradictions of Normative Constitutional Scholarship," *Yale Law Journal* 90 (1981):1063–1109.

———. "Who Decides," *Southern California Law Review* 58 (1985):661–71.

———. "The Misconceived Quest for the Original Understanding," *Boston University Law Review* 60 (1980):204–254.

Buckley, Thomas C. *Church and State in Revolutionary Virginia, 1776–1787*. Charlottesville: University Press of Virginia, 1977.

Caplan, Russell L. "The History and Meaning of the Ninth Amendment," *Virginia Law Review* 69 (1983):223–68.

Cappon, Lester, ed. *The Adams–Jefferson Letters*, 2 vols. Chapel Hill: University of North Carolina Press, 1959.

Cardozo, Benjamin N. *The Nature of the Judicial Process*. New Haven, Conn.: Yale University Press, 1921.

Chafee, Zechariah, Jr. *Three Human Rights in the Constitution*. Lawrence: University of Kansas Press, 1956.

Chase, Frederick. *A History of Dartmouth College and the Town of Hanover*, ed. John K. Lord. Cambridge, Mass. 1891.

Chipman, Nathaniel. *Principles of Government: A Treatise on Free Institutions. Including the Constitution of the United States*, 1793, revised Burlington, Vt., 1883, reprinted New York: Da Capo Press, 1970.

Choper, Jesse H. *Judicial Review and the National Political Process*. Chicago: University of Chicago Press, 1980.

Cobb, Sanford. *The Rise of Religious Liberty in America*. New York: Macmillan, 1902.

Coke, Sir Edward. *The Second Part of the Institutes of the Laws of England*, 6th ed. London, 1681.

Commager, Henry Steele. *Majority Rule and Minority Rights*. New York: Oxford University Press, 1943.

———. "Constitutional History and the Higher Law," in Conyers Read, ed., *The Constitution Reconsidered*. New York: Columbia University Press, 1938.

———. "Democracy and Judicial Review," in Commager, *Freedom and Order*. New York: George Braziller, 1966.

———. "The Constitution and Original Intent," *The Center Magazine:*

A Publication of the Center for the Study of Democratic Institutions 19 (1986):4–17.

Cooley, Thomas M. *A Treatise on the Constitutional Limitations Which Rest Upon the Legislative Power*. Boston, 1868, 1st ed. reprinted New York: Da Capo Press, 1972.

Cooper, Charles, and Nelson Lund. "Landmarks of Constitutional Interpretation: Seven Lessons in the Rule of Law for Justice Brennan," *Policy Review* 40 (1987):10–24.

Corwin, Edward S. *The Doctrine of Judicial Review*. Princeton, N.J.: Princeton University Press, 1914.

———. *The President: Office and Powers, 1787–1984*, 5th rev. ed. New York: New York University Press, 1984.

———. "Judicial Review in Action," *University of Pennsylvania Law Review* 74 (1926):639–71.

———. "The Progress of Constitutional Theory Between and Declaration of Independence and the Philadelphia Convention," *American Historical Review*, April 1925, reprinted in *American Constitutional History, Essays by Edward S. Corwin*, ed. A. T. Mason and G. Garvey. New York: Harper Torchbooks, 1964.

Crosskey, William Winslow. *Politics and the Constitution in the History of the United States*, 2 vols. Chicago: University of Chicago Press, 1953.

Cuddihy, William, and B. Carmon Hardy. "A Man's House Was Not His Castle: Origins of the Fourth Amendment," *William and Mary Quarterly*, 3rd ser., 37 (1980):371–400.

Cuddihy, William. "From General to Specific Search Warrants," in John Kukla, ed., *The Bill of Rights: A Lively Heritage*. Richmond: Virginia State Library, 1987.

———. "The Fourth Amendment: Origins and Original Meaning," Ph.D. dissertation, Claremont, Calif.: Claremont Graduate School, manuscript-in-progress.

Currie, David P. *The Constitution in the Supreme Court: The First Hundred Years*. Chicago: University of Chicago Press, 1985.

Curry, Thomas J. *The First Freedoms: Church and State in America to the Passage of the First Amendment*. New York: Oxford University Press, 1986.

Curtis, Michael Kent. *No State Shall Abridge: The Fourteenth Amendment and the Bill of Rights*. Durham, N.C.: Duke University Press, 1968.

De Pauw, Linda Grant, ed. *Documentary History of the First Federal*

Congress of the United States of America, 1789–1791, 4 vols. Baltimore: Johns Hopkins University Press, 1972.

Dickerson, Oliver. *The Navigation Acts & The American Revolution*. Philadelphia: University of Pennsylvania Press, 1954.

———. "Writs of Assistance as a Cause of the American Revolution," in Richard B. Morris, ed., *Era of the American Revolution*. New York: Columbia University Press, 1939.

Dickinson, John. *Writings of John Dickinson*, ed. Paul L. Ford. Philadelphia: Historical Society of Pennsylvania. Memoirs. Vol. 14, 1895.

Doctorow, E. L. "A Citizen Reads the Constitution," *The Nation*, Feb. 21, 1987, pp. 208–217.

Duker, William F. *A Constitutional History of Habeas Corpus*. Westport, Conn.: Greenwood Press, 1980.

Dumbauld, Edward. "State Precedents for the Bill of Rights," *Journal of Public Law*, 7 (1958):323–44.

Dunne, Finley Peter. *Mr. Dooley on the Choice of Law*, ed. Edward J. Bander. Charlottesville, Virginia: Michie Co., 1963.

Dworkin, Ronald. *A Matter of Principle*. Cambridge, Mass.: Harvard University Press, 1985.

———. *Taking Rights Seriously*. Cambridge, Mass.: Harvard University Press, 1977.

Easterbrook, Frank H. "Legal Interpretation and the Power of the Judiciary," *Harvard Journal of Law and Public Policy* 7 (1981):87–99.

Elliot, Jonathan, ed. *The Debates in the Several State Conventions on the Adoption of the Federal Constitution*, 5 vols. Philadelphia, Pa.: J. B. Lippincott Co., 1836–1845, rev. ed.

Ely, John Hart. *Democracy and Distrust: A Theory of Judicial Review*. Cambridge, Mass.: Harvard University Press, 1980.

Fairman, Charles. "Does the Fourteenth Amendment Incorporate the Bill of Rights? The Original Understanding," *Stanford Law Review* 2 (1949):5–139.

Farrand, Max, ed. *The Records of the Federal Convention*, 4 vols., rev. ed. New Haven, Conn.: Yale University Press, 1937.

———. *The Framing of the Constitution of the United States*. New Haven, Conn.: Yale University Press, 1913.

Fehrenbacher, Don E. *The Dred Scott Case: Its Significance in American Law and Politics*. New York: Oxford University Press, 1978.

Flaherty, David H. *Privacy in Colonial New England*. Charlottesville: University Press of Virginia, 1972.

Ford, Paul L., ed. *Pamphlets on the Constitution of the United States*. Brooklyn: New York Historical Printing Club, 1888.

———. *Essays on the Constitution of the United States*. Brooklyn: New York Historical Printing Club, 1892.

Framer's Intent: An Exchange. Symposium issue of *University of Puget Sound Law Review* 10 (1987):343–569.

Frankfurter, Felix, and Thomas G. Corcoran. "Petty Offenses and the Constitutional Guaranty of Trial by Jury," *Harvard Law Review* 39 (1926):917–1017.

Frankfurter, Felix. *Law and Politics: Occasional Papers of Felix Frankfurther, 1913–1938*, ed. Archibald MacLeish and E. F. Prichard, Jr. New York: Harcourt, Brace, 1939.

Franklin, Benjamin. *The Papers of Benjamin Franklin*, ed. Leonard W. Labaree et al. New Haven, Conn.: Yale University Press, 1959–

Franklin, Mitchell. "The *Encyclopediste* Origin and Meaning of the Fifth Amendment," *Lawyers Guild Review* 15 (1955):41–62.

Friedland, Martin L. *Double Jeopardy*. Oxford: Clarendon Press, 1969.

Gales, Joseph, and W. W. Seaton, comps. *The Debates and Proceedings of the Congress of the United States (Annals of Congress)*, 42 vols. Washington, 1834–1856.

Ganter, Herbert L. "Jefferson's 'Pursuit of Happiness' and Some Forgotten Men," *William and Mary Quarterly*, 2nd ser., 16 (1936):558–85.

Gilbert, Geoffrey. *The Law of Evidence by a Late Learned Judge*. London, 1756.

Gilpin, Henry D., ed. *The Papers of James Madison*, 3 vols. Washington, 1840.

Goebel, Julius, Jr., and Joseph H. Smith, eds. *The Law Practice of Alexander Hamilton*, 4 vols. New York: Columbia University Press, 1964–1980.

Goebel, Julius, Jr., and T. Raymond Naughton. *Law Enforcement in Colonial New York: A Study in Criminal Procedure (1664–1776)*. New York: The Commonwealth Fund, 1944.

Graglia, Lino A. "Constitutional Theory: The Attempted Justification for the Supreme Court's Liberal Political Program," *Texas Law Review* 65 (1987):789–98.

———. "How the Constitution Disappeared," *Commentary* 81 (1986):19–27.

Grant, J. A. C. "Federalism and Self-Incrimination," *UCLA Law Review* 4 (1957):549–82.

Granucci, Anthony. "Nor Cruel and Unusual Punishments Inflicted: The Original Meaning," *California Law Review* 57 (1969):839–65.

Greene, M. Louise. *The Development of Religious Liberty in Connecticut*. Boston: Houghton Mifflin, 1905.

Grey, Thomas C. "Do We Have an Unwritten Constitution?" *Stanford Law Review*, 27 (1975):703–718.

———. "The Constitution as Scripture," *Stanford Law Review* 37 (1984):1–25.

Grinnell, Frank W. ed. "Hitherto Unpublished Correspondence Between Chief Justice Cushing and John Adams in 1789," *Massachusetts Law Quarterly* 27 (1942):12–16.

Haines, Charles Grove. *The American Doctrine of Judicial Supremacy*, 2nd ed. Los Angeles: University of California at Los Angeles, 1932.

———. *The Role of the Supreme Court in American Government and Politics, 1789–1835*. Berkeley: University of California Press, 1944.

Hale, Sir Matthew. *History of Pleas of the Crown*, 2 vols., ed. Solom Emlyn. London, 1st ed., 1736.

Hamilton, Alexander, James Madison, and John Jay. *The Federalist*, ed. Jacob E. Cooke. Cleveland, Ohio: Meridian Books, 1961.

Hand, Learned. *The Bill of Rights*. Cambridge, Mass.: Harvard University Press, 1958.

———. "Sources of Tolerance," *University of Pennsylvania Law Review* 79 (1930):1–14.

———. "The Contribution of an Independent Judiciary to Civilization," in *The Spirit of Liberty: Papers and Addresses of Learned Hand*, ed. Irving Dilliard. New York: Knopf, 1953.

Handlin, Oscar and Mary, eds. *The Popular Sources of Political Authority*. Cambridge, Mass., 1966.

Hart, Henry M., Jr. "Professor Crosskey and Judicial Review," *Harvard Law Review* 67 (1954):1456–86.

Hartz, Louis. *The Liberal Tradition in America*. New York: Harcourt, Brace, 1955.

Haskins, George Lee, and Herbert Johnson. *Foundations of Power: John Marshall 1801–1815*. New York: Macmillan, 1981.

Haskins, George Lee. *Law and Authority in Early Massachusetts*. New York: Macmillan, 1960.

Hawkins, William. *A Treatise of the Pleas of the Crown*, 2nd ed., 2 vols. London, 1724.

Hay, George. *Two Essays on the Liberty of the Press*. New York: Da Capo Press, 1970, facsimile edition of tracts of 1799 and 1803.

Henkin, Louis. *Foreign Affairs and the Constitution*. Mineola, N.Y.: Foundation Press, 1972.

Henry, William Wirt. *Patrick Henry: Life, Correspondence and Speeches*. New York, 1891.

Hoffer, Peter Charles, and N. E. H. Hull. *Impeachment in America, 1635–1805*. New Haven, Conn.: Yale University Press, 1980.

Holmes, Oliver Wendell. *Collected Legal Papers*. New York: Harcourt, Brace, 1920.

———. *The Common Law*. Boston: Little, Brown, 1881.

Hurst, Willard. "Treason in the United States," *Harvard Law Review* 58 (1944–1945):226–72, 395–44, 806–857.

Hutson, James H. "The Creation of the Constitution: The Integrity of the Documentary Record," *Texas Law Review* 65 (1986):1–39.

———. *Supplement to Max Farrand's The Records of the Federal Convention*. New Haven, Conn.: Yale University Press, 1987.

Hyman, Harold M., and William M. Wiecek. *Equal Justice Under Law: Constitutional Development 1835–1875*. New York: Harper & Row, 1982.

Jackson, Robert H. *The Struggle for Judicial Supremacy*. New York: Knopf, 1941.

———. *The Supreme Court in the American System of Government*. Cambridge, Mass.: Harvard University Press, 1958.

Jaffa, Harry. "What Were the 'Original Intentions' of the Framers of the Constitution of the United States?" *University of Puget Sound Law Review* 10 (1987):343–448.

Jefferson, Thomas. *Notes on the State of Virginia*, ed. William Peden. Chapel Hill: University of North Carolina Press, 1955.

———. *The Papers of Thomas Jefferson*, ed. Julian Boyd et al. Princeton, N.J.: Princeton University Press, 1950–

———. *The Writings of Thomas Jefferson*, 20 vols., ed. Albert Bergh. Washington, D.C.: Thomas Jefferson Memorial Association, 1907.

Jeffrey, William Jr., ed. "The Letters of 'Brutus'," *University of Cincinnati Law Review* 40 (1971):643–777.

Jensen, Merrill, John P. Kaminski, and Gasper J. Saladino, eds. *The Documentary History of the Ratification of the Constitution*. Madison: State Historical Society of Wisconsin, 1976–

Journal, Acts and Proceedings of the Convention, . . . which formed the Constitution of the United States. Boston, 1819.

Jurow, Keith. "Untimely Thoughts: A Reconsideration of the Origins of

Due Process of Law," *American Journal of Legal History* 19 (1975):265–79.

Kammen, Michael. *A Machine That Would Go of Itself: The Constitution in American Culture*. New York: Knopf, 1986.

————. *Constitutional Pluralism: Conflicting Interpretations of the Founders' Intentions*. Address before American Jewish Committee, New York City, May 15, 1987.

Karst, Kenneth L. "Freedom of Intimate Association," *Yale Law Journal* 89 (1980):624–92.

Katz, Stanley Nider, ed. *A Brief Narrative of the Case and Trial of John Peter Zenger*, 2nd ed. Cambridge, Mass.: Harvard University Press, 1972.

Kay, Richard S. "The Illegality of the Constitution," *Constitutional Commentary* 4 (1987):57–80.

Kelly, Alfred H. "Clio and the Court: An Illicit Love Affair," in Philip B. Kurland, ed., *Supreme Court Review: 1965*. Chicago: University of Chicago Press, 1965.

Kent, James. *Commentaries on American Law*, 4 vols. Boston: Little, Brown, 1826, rev. 10th ed. in 1860.

Kenyon, Cecilia M. *The Anti-Federalists*. Indianapolis: Bobbs-Merrill, 1966.

Klein, Milton, ed. *The Independent Reflector*. Cambridge, Mass.: Harvard University Press, 1963.

Kurland, Philip B., and Ralph Lerner, eds. *The Founders' Constitution*, 5 vols. Chicago: University of Chicago Press, 1987.

Lasson, Nelson B. *The History and Development of the Fourth Amendment to the United States Constitution*. Baltimore: Johns Hopkins University Press, 1937.

Lerner, Max, ed. *The Mind and Faith of Justice Holmes*. New York: Modern Library, 1943.

Levy, Leonard W. *Emergence of a Free Press*. New York: Oxford University Press, 1985.

————. *Jefferson and Civil Liberties: The Darker Side*. Cambridge, Mass.: Harvard University Press, 1963.

————. *Origins of the Fifth Amendment: The Right Against Self-Incrimination*. New York: Oxford University Press, 1968.

————. *The Establishment Clause: Religion and the First Amendment*. New York: Macmillan, 1986.

————. "The Making of the Constitution, 1776–1789," in Levy, ed.,

Essays on the Making of the Constitution, 2nd ed. New York: Oxford University Press, 1987.

————, ed. *The Fourteenth Amendment and the Bill of Rights*. New York: Da Capo Press, 1970.

————, Kenneth L. Karst, and Dennis J. Mahoney, eds. *Encyclopedia of the American Constitution*, 4 vols. New York: Macmillan, 1986.

————, and Dennis J. Mahoney, eds. *The Framing and Ratification of the Constitution*. New York: Macmillan, 1987.

Llewellyn, Karl N. *The Common Law Tradition*. Boston: Little, Brown, 1960.

Locke, John. *Essay Concerning Human Understanding*, 2 vols., ed. Alexander Campbell Fraser. Oxford: Clarendon Press, 1894.

————. *Two Treatises of Government*, ed. Peter Laslett. Cambridge: At the University Press, 1963.

Lofgren, Charles A. "The Original Understanding of Original Intent?" *Constitutional Commentary* 5 (1988):77–113.

————. *"Government from Reflection and Choice": Constitutional Essays on War, Foreign Relations, and Federalism*. New York: Oxford University Press, 1986.

Macedo, Stephen. *The New Right v. the Constitution*. Washington, D.C.: Cato Institute, 1987.

Madison, James. *The Papers of James Madison*, ed. William T. Hutchinson et al. Chicago: University of Chicago Press, 1962–

————. *The Writings of James Madison*, 9 vols., ed. Gaillard Hunt. New York: Putnam's, 1900–1910.

————. "Madison's Detached Memoranda," ed. Elizabeth Fleet, *William and Mary Quarterly*, 3rd ser., III (1946):534–68.

Maltz, Earl M. "Some New Thoughts on an Old Problem: The Role of the Intent of the Framers in Constitutional Theory," *Boston University Law Review* 63 (1983):811–36.

————. "The Failure of Attacks on Constitutionalism," *Constitutional Commentary* 4 (1987):43–56.

Marcus, Maeva, and James R. Perry, eds. *The Documentary History of the Supreme Court of the United States, 1789–1800*. New York: Columbia University Press, 1985.

Matteson, David M. "The Organization of the Government under the Constitution," in Sol Bloom, ed., *History of the Formation of the Union under the Constitution*. Washington, D.C.: U.S. Constitution Sesquicentennial Commission, 1943.

Mays, David John, ed. *The Letters and Papers of Edmund Pendleton*, 2 vols. Charlottesville: University Press of Virginia, 1967.

McDowell, Gary L. *The Constitution and Contemporary Constitutional Theory*. Cumberland, Va.: Center for Judicial Studies, 1985.

McLaughlin, Andrew C. *A Constitutional History of the United States*. New York: Appleton-Century-Crofts, 1935.

——. *The Foundations of American Constitutionalism*. New York: New York University Press, 1932.

McLoughlin, William G. *New England Dissent, 1630–1833*, 2 vols. Cambridge, Mass.: Harvard University Press, 1971.

McMaster, John Bach, and Frederick D. Stone, eds. *Pennsylvania and the Federal Constitution, 1787–1788*. Lancaster: Historical Society of Pennsylvania, 1888.

McRee, Griffith J. *Life and Correspondence of James Iredell*, 2 vols. New York: D. Appleton & Co., 1857–1858.

Meese, Edwin III. *The Constitution as a Bill of Rights: Separation of Powers and Individual Liberty*. Speech delivered on February 27, 1986, and published as a Bicentennial Essay. Irving, Texas: University of Dallas, 1986.

——. "The Battle for the Constitution: The Attorney General Replies to His Critics," *Policy Review* (1986):32–35.

——. Address of Edwin Meese III . . . before the American Bar Association, Washington, D.C., July 9, 1985, in *The Great Debate: Interpreting Our Written Constitution*. Pamphlet published by the Federalist Society, Washington, D.C., 1986.

——. "The Law of the Constitution." A Bicentennial Lecture, Tulane University, Oct. 21, 1986, distributed by the Department of Justice.

Miller, Arthur S. *Social Change and Fundamental Law: America's Evolving Constitution*. Westport, Conn.: Greenwood Press, 1979.

——. *Toward Increased Judicial Activism*. Westport, Conn.: Greenwood Press, 1982.

Miller, Charles. *The Supreme Court and the Uses of History*. Cambridge, Mass.: Harvard University Press, 1969.

Mitchell, Lawrence E. "The Ninth Amendment and the Jurisprudence of Original Intention," *Georgetown Law Journal* 74 (1986):1719–42.

Monaghan, Henry P. "Our Perfect Constitution," *New York University Law Review* 56 (1981):353–77.

Mott, Rodney L. *Due Process of Law*. Indianapolis: Bobbs-Merrill, 1926.

Munzer, Stephen R., and James W. Nickel, "Does the Constitution Mean What It Always Meant?" *Columbia Law Review* 77 (1977):1029–62.

Murphy, Paul L. "Time to Reclaim: The Current Challenge of American Constitutional History," *American Historical Review* 69 (1963):64–79.

A National Program for the Publication of Historical Documents. A Report to the President by the National Historical Publications Commission. Washington, D.C.: Government Printing Office, 1954.

Neely, Richard. *How Courts Govern America.* New Haven, Conn.: Yale University Press, 1981.

Patterson, Bennett. *The Forgotten Ninth Amendment.* Indianapolis: Bobbs-Merrill, 1955.

Peel, Alfred, and Leland H. Carlson, eds. *Cartwrightiana.* London, 1951.

Perry, Michael J. *The Court, the Constitution, and Human Rights.* New Haven, Conn.: Yale University Press, 1982.

———. "Interpretivism, Freedom of Expression, and Equal Protection," *Ohio State Law Journal* 42 (1981):261–317.

———. "Noninterpretive Review in Human Rights Cases: A Functional Justification," *New York University Law Review* 56 (1981):278–352.

———. "The Authority of Text, Tradition, and Reason: A Theory of Constitutional 'Interpretation'," *Southern California Law Review* 58 (1985):551–602.

Perry, Richard L., ed. *Sources of Our Liberties: Documentary Origins of Individual Liberties in the United States Constitution and Bill of Rights.* Chicago: American Bar Foundation, 1959.

Peters, Richard, ed. *The Public Statutes at Large of the United States of America.* Boston, 1861ff.

Posner, Richard A. "What Am I? A Potted Plant?" *The New Republic,* Sept. 28, 1987, pp. 23–25.

Powell, H. Jefferson. "Parchment Matters: A Meditation on the Constitution," *Iowa Law Review* 71 (1986):1427–35.

———. "Rules for Originalists," *Virginia Law Review* 73 (1987):659–99.

———. "The Complete Jeffersonian: Justice Rehnquist and Federalism," *Yale Law Journal* 91 (1982):1317–70.

———. "The Original Understanding of Original Intent," *Harvard Law Review* 98 (1985):885–948.

Quincy, Josiah Jr., ed. *Reports of Cases Argued and Adjudged in the Superior Court of Judicature of the Massachusetts Bay Between 1761 and 1772.* Boston, 1865.

Rackow, Felix. "The Right to Counsel: English and American Precedents," *William and Mary Quarterly,* 3rd ser., 11 (1954):3–27.

Rakove, Jack N. "Mr. Meese, Meet Mr. Madison," *The Atlantic Monthly (1986):77–86.*

———. "Solving a Constitutional Puzzle: The Treatymaking Clause as a Case Study," *Perspectives in American History,* new ser., 1 (1984):233–81.

Redlich, Norman. "Are There Certain Rights . . . Retained by the People," *New York University Law Review* 37 (1961):787–808.

Rehnquist, William H. "The Notion of a Living Constitution," *Texas Law Review* 54 (1976):693–706.

Relf, Frances H. *The Petition of Right.* Minneapolis: University of Minnesota Press, 1917.

Reorganization of the Federal Judiciary. Hearings before the Committee on the Judiciary, United States Senate, 75th Congress, 1st Session, on S. 1392, Part 2, March 17–20, 1937.

Rives, William C., and Philip R. Fendall, eds. *Letters and Other Writings of James Madison,* 4 vols. New York: Worthington, 1884.

Rossiter, Clinton. *1787: The Grand Convention.* New York: Macmillan, 1966.

Rostow, Eugene V. *The Sovereign Prerogative: The Supreme Court and the Quest for Law.* New Haven, Conn.: Yale University Press, 1962.

Rowland, Kate Mason. *The Life of George Mason, 1725–1792,* 2 vols. New York: G. P. Putnam's Sons, 1892.

Rutland, Robert Allen, ed. *The Papers of George Mason,* 3 vols. Chapel Hill: University of North Carolina Press, 1970.

———. *The Birth of the Bill of Rights, 1776–1791.* Chapel Hill: University of North Carolina Press, 1955.

Saladino, Gaspare J. "A Guide to Sources for Studying the Ratification of the Constitution by New York State," in Stephen L. Schechter, ed., *The Reluctant Pillar: New York and the Adoption of the Federal Constitution.* Troy, N.Y.: Russell Sage College, 1985.

Schlag, Pierre. "Framer's Intent: The Illegitimate Uses of History," *University of Puget Sound Law Review* 8 (1985):283–330.

Schwartz, Bernard, ed. *The Bill of Rights: A Documentary History,* 2 vols. New York: Chelsea House, 1971.

Schwoerer, Lois G. *The Declaration of Rights, 1689.* Baltimore: Johns Hopkins University Press, 1981.

Shalhope, Robert E. "The Ideological Origins of the Second Amendment," *Journal of American History* 69 (1982):599–614.

Shapiro, David L. "Mr. Justice Rehnquist: A Preliminary View," *Harvard Law Review* 90 (1976):293–357.

Shirley, John M. *The Dartmouth College Causes and the Supreme Court of the United States*. Chicago, 1895, reprinted New York: Da Capo Press, 1971.

Sigler, Jay. *Double Jeopardy*. Ithaca, N.Y.: Cornell University Press, 1969.

Simon, Larry G. "The Authority of the Framers of the Constitution: Can Originalist Interpretation Be Justified?" *California Law Review* 73 (1985):1482–1539.

Smith, James Morton. *Freedom's Fetters: The Alien and Sedition Laws and American Civil Liberties*. Ithaca, N.Y.: Cornell University Press, 1956.

Smith, M. H. *The Writs of Assistance Case*. Berkeley: University of California Press, 1978.

Sofaer, Abraham, D. *War, Foreign Affairs and Constitutional Power: The Origins*. Cambridge, Mass.: Ballinger, 1976.

Stephen, Sir James Fitzjames. *A History of the Criminal Law of England*, 3 vols. London, 1883.

Stevens, John Paul. "Judicial Restraint." The Nathaniel L. Nathanson Memorial Lecture Series, The University of San Diego School of Law, October 18, 1984, San Diego, California.

Stewart, Donald H. *The Opposition Press of the Federalist Period*. Albany: State University of New York Press, 1969.

Stokes, Anson Phelps. *Church and State in the United States*, 3 vols. New York: Harper, 1950.

Storing, Herbert J., ed. *The Complete Anti-Federalist*, 7 vols. Chicago: University of Chicago Press, 1981.

Story, Joseph. *Commentaries on the Constitution of the United States*, 3 vols. Boston: Little, Brown, 1833.

Strayer, Joseph, ed. *The Delegates from New York, or, Proceedings of the Federal Convention of 1787 from the Notes of John Lansing, Jr*. Princeton, N.J.: Princeton University Press, 1939.

Sutherland, Arthur E. *Constitutionalism in America: Origin and Evolution of Its Fundamental Ideas*. New York: Blaisdell, 1965.

Syrett, Harold C., and Jacob E. Cooke, eds. *The Papers of Alexander Hamilton*, 26 vols. New York: Columbia University Press, 1962–1981.

Tansill, Charles C., ed. *Documents Illustrative of the Formation of the Union of the American States*. Washington, D.C.: Government Printing Office, 1927.

tenBroek, Jacobus. "Admissibility and Use by the United State Supreme

Court of Extrinsic Aids in Constitutional Construction," *California Law Review* 26 (1938):287–308, 437–54, 664–81, and 27 (1939):157–81, 399–421.

Thayer, James Bradley. "The Origin and Scope of the American Doctrine of Constitutional Law," *Harvard Law Review* 7(1893):129–52.

Thompson, Faith. *Magna Carta: Its Role in the Making of the English Constitution, 1300–1629.* Minneapolis: University of Minnesota Press, 1948.

Thomson, John. *An Enquiry, Concerning the Liberty, and Licentiousness of the Press.* New York, 1801. Reprinted New York: Da Capo Press, 1970.

Thorpe, Francis Newton, ed. *The Federal and State Constitutions, Colonial Charters, and Other Organic Laws,* 7 vols. Washington, D.C.: Government Printing Office, 1909.

Tinling, Marion. "Thomas Lloyd's Reports of the First Federal Congress," *William and Mary Quarterly,* 3rd ser., 18 (1961):519–45.

Tribe, Laurence H. *American Constitutional Law.* Mineola, N.Y.: Foundation Press, 1978.

———. *Constitutional Choices.* Cambridge, Mass.: Harvard University Press, 1985.

———. "The Holy Grail of Original Intent," *Humanities* 7 (1986):23–25.

Tucker, St. George. *Blackstone's Commentaries. With Notes of Reference to the Constitution and Laws of the Federal Government of the United States and of the Commonwealth of Virginia,* 5 vols. Philadelphia, 1803.

Turner, Kathryn. "Federalist Policy and the Judiciary Act of 1801," *William and Mary Quarterly,* 3rd ser., 22 (1965):3–22.

———. "The Midnight Judges," *University of Pennsylvania Law Review* 109 (1961):494–523.

Tushnet, Mark V. "Following the Rules Laid Down: A Critique of Interpretivism and Neutral Principles," *Harvard Law Review* 96 (1983):781–827.

VanAlstyne, William W. "A Critical Guide to Marbury v. Madison," *Duke Law Journal* 169 (1969):1–45.

The Virginia Report of 1799–1800, Touching the Alien and Sedition Laws; Together with the Virginia Resolutions of December 21, 1798, the Debates and Proceedings Thereon, in the House of Delegates in Virginia. Richmond, Va., 1850.

Warren, Charles. *Congress, the Constitution, and the Supreme Court.* Boston: Little, Brown, 1925.

————. *The Making of the Constitution*. Boston: Little, Brown, 1928.

————. *The Supreme Court in United States History*, 3 vols. Boston: Little, Brown, 1923.

————. "Earliest Cases of Judicial Review of State Legislation by Federal Courts," *Yale Law Journal* 32 (1922):15–28.

————. "New Light on the History of the Federal Judiciary Act of 1789," *Harvard Law Review* 37 (1923):49–132.

Webb, Philip Carteret, ed. *Copies of Warrants from the Records Office Books of the Kings Bench at Westminster; the Original Office Books of the Secretaries of State* . . . London, 1763.

Wechsler, Herbert. "Toward Neutral Principles of Constitutional Law," *Harvard Law Review* 73 (1959):1–35.

Wharton, Francis, ed. *State Trials of the United States during the Administration of Washington and Adams*. Philadelphia, Pa., 1849.

Wilson, James G. "The Most Sacred Text: The Supreme Court's Use of *The Federalist Papers*," *Brigham Young Law Review* 1 (1985):65–135.

Wilson, James. *The Works of James Wilson*, 2 vols. ed. Robert G. McCloskey. Cambridge, Mass.: Harvard University Press, 1967.

Wofford, John G. "The Blinding Light: The Uses of History in Constitutional Interpretation," *University of Chicago Law Review* 31 (1964):502–533.

Wolfe, Christopher. *The Rise of Modern Judicial Review: From Constitutional Interpretation to Judge-Made Law*. New York: Basic Books, 1986.

Wolfram, Charles W. "The Constitutional History of the Seventh Amendment," *Minnesota Law Review* 57 (1973):639–747.

Wortman, Tunis. *A Treatise Concerning Political Enquiry, and the Liberty of the Press*. New York, 1800. Reprinted New York: Da Capo Press, 1970.

Wright, Benjamin F., Jr. *The Contract Clause of the Constitution*. Cambridge, Mass.: Harvard University Press, 1938.

Wright, J. Skelly. "Professor Bickel, the Scholarly Tradition, and the Supreme Court," *Harvard Law Review* 84 (1971):769–805.

————. "The Role of the Courts: Conscience of a Sovereign People," *The Reporter Magazine*, 29 (1963):24–29.

————. "The Role of the Supreme Court in a Democratic Society: Judicial Activism or Restraint?" *Cornell Law Review* 54 (1968):1–28.

Wroth, L. Kinvin, and Hiller B. Zobel, eds. *Legal Papers of John Adams*, 3 vols. Cambridge, Mass.: Harvard University Press, 1965.

INDEX

276; right not to be witness against
oneself, 256; and right of privacy, 267,
381; and self-incrimination clause, xii,
255, 258, 300, 301; and Supreme
Court's use of history, 300, 301, 304,
308; taking clause, 66, 67, 276; and
transactional immunity, 308; in *Twining
v. New Jersey*, 301; in *Ullmann v.
United States*, 304, and use immunity,

religion, 187; as Framer, 298; on
freedom of the press, 199
Llewellyn, Karl, 11, 354–55
Lloyd, Thomas, 289, 292, 293, 457
Locke, John, on contract, 158; and fixed
meaning of constitution, 332; on
property, 276; on pursuit of happiness,
276; *Second Treatise*, 139, 158, 276
Lofgren, Charles, 51, 300, 458
Louisiana Purchase, 201
Lusk, William, 4

Maclaine, Archibald, on contract clause,
128; on ex post facto laws, 69
Maclay, William, 254, 292
Macon, Nathaniel, 119–20, 215
Madison, James, "Advice to my
Country," 17; on ambiguity of
Constitution, 333–34; on "arising
under" clause, 109; on assembly, 208;
on Bank charter, 118, 294; Berger on,
105; Bill of Rights, 146, 165–70, 172,
178, 207, 232; on bill of rights, need
for, 121, 154, 163–64, 166, 196, 270;
on carriage tax, 22, 59; on chaplains,
319–20; charters of incorporation,
proposal re, 7; checks and balances,
31; Committee of Style member, 45,
126; Committee on Postponed Parts,
39; on Congress's review of
constitutionality, 105; on conscience,
freedom of, 178; on consent of the
governed, 273; constitutional
interpretation based on textual
interpretation and experience, 5, 16,
20, 21, 26, 27, 28, 58; on contract
clause, 126, 129; Democratic Party
head in House, 117; "Detached
Memoranda," 19–20, 403; on direct
taxes, 62; disliked amendments to
Constitution, 25; disliked Hamilton's
economic measures, 117; and double
jeopardy, 273; and due process, 273;
election to House, 163; on enumerated
powers, 209; on enumerated rights,
271, 273; on executive powers, 33, 52;
on ex post facto laws, 70–71, 73, 74,
164; Father of the Bill of Rights, 1,

146, 165; Father of the Constitution,
1, 165; in *The Federalist*, 4–5, 20, 27,
62, 87, 105, 129, 333–34; and Fifth
Amendment, 247; First Amendment,
joint committee on, 182; on freedom
of speech, 214; on freedom of the
press, 166, 199, 207, 211–12; on
general welfare clause, 9; on House
review of constitutionality, 105; on
independent judiciary, 121; in
indictment by grand jury, 273; on
judicial interpretation of Constitution,
21, 24, 25, 106; on judicial review,
103–105, 106, 108, 117–18, 364; on
judicial tenure, 87; on jury trial right,
166, 273; on just compensation, 273;
on Lee bill of rights, 241;legislative
power, concern *re*, 32; on legitimacy
of Constitution, 18; on limited powers
of government, 271; on Lloyd's
records, 293; in *Marbury v. Madison*,
80, 82; on *McCulloch v. Maryland*, 10;
"magnetic theory," 9; on malice, 216;
"Memorial and Remonstrance against
Religious Assessments, 179–80, 192;
and national roads and canals bill, 21–
22, 26; and natural rights, 275; on
necessary and proper clause, 9, 447;
new libertarian, 215; on Ninth
Amendment, 281–82; "Notes of
Debates in the Federal Convention,"
ix, 1, 5, 6, 14, 27, 28, 29, 61, 70, 71,
286–88, 299, 318, 319; and original
intent, 355; prepared message *re* veto
of Bank bill for Washington, 10; and
probable cause, 243; *Property*, 276; on
property as human right, 276–77;
proposal *re* charters of incorporation,
7; on protective tariff, 27; ratification
conventions, use of, 14; on ratifiers'
intent, 16, 19; reads Gerry's remarks
to House, 7–8; rejected original intent,
1, 14, 16; on religion, 141, 176, 178–
79, 379; on removal power, 6; *Report
on Virginia Resolutions*, 215; response
to Spencer Roane, 23; on rules of
construction, 354; and search and
seizure, 242–44, 273; as secretary of

Jefferson on, 158, 199–200; and juries
in seditious libel cases, 206; Lee on,
198; and libertarian theory, 212;
Madison on, 166, 199, 207, 208, 211–
12; in Massachusetts, 203; meaning of,
207; and necessary and proper clause,
196; original intent and, 179; in
Oswald's case, 197; Pinckney on, 147,
151, 195; and popular government,
213; and prior restraints, 212–13; at
ratification conventions, 208; right to
criticize, 212–13; scope of, 208; and
Sedition Act of 1798, 132, 210, 213,
214; and seditious libel, 210, 211; and
seditious libel prosecutions in
Massachusetts, 198; Senate defeated
proposal on, 170; "shall," 207; Sherman
on need for clause, 195; Smith on, 198;
and stamp tax in Massachusetts, 198;
and states' rights, 209; and truth as
defense, 206; in Virginia Declaration of
Rights, 144; Virginia free press clause,
200, 202; and Wilkes' case, 230;
Williamson on, 199; Wilson on, 153,
198, 199; and Zenger prosecution, 138,
216
Principles of construction: see rules of
construction; Constitution,
interpretation of
Prior restraints, 197, 198, 200, 212,
335
Privacy, right of, 234, 244, 246, 267, 268–
69, 381–82; Black on, 268–69; Bork on,
382; Douglas on, 267, 381; Fourteenth
Amendment, 382; Ninth Amendment,
381–82; penumbras, 381; right of
association, 381; and search and
seizure, 244, 246, 381; self-
incrimination clause, 381
Privileges and immunities clause: see
Fourteenth Amendment
Probable cause, 221, 223, 226, 236–37,
245–46; in collection of duties law, 245;
in Connecticut, 240; and excise acts,
226; in Frisbie v. Butler, 240; and
Hale, 223; and liquor tax, 245–46;
Madison's formulation of, 243;
Mansfield's influence on, 231; in

Pennsylvania, 238; in Virginia, 236–37;
and warrants, 225
Property rights, Beard on, 101–102;
checks and balances protect, 101–102;
in Fifth Amendment, 276; as a human
right, 276; and judicial activism, 136;
Locke on, 276; and original intent, 390;
and pursuit of happiness, 276; and Van
Horne's Lessee v. Dorrance, 130–31,
132
Protective tariff acts, 26, 27
Prune Yard Case, 390
"In Pursuance of" clause: see Constitution
Pursuit of happiness, 276 (see also
Declaration of Independence)

Quakers, 239–40
Quartering of troops, in Delaware bill of
rights, 144; Pinckney recommended,
151; Third Amendment, 381

Race, 278
Racial discrimination, 316–17
Racial segregation, 300, 311, 317–18
Ramsay, David, 129
Randolph, Edmund, on Bank bill, 8, 294;
on Bill of Rights in Virginia senate,
172; Committee of Detail member, 35,
149, 156, 330; on Constitution's
structure, 330, 342; on contract clause,
128, 129; on ex post facto laws, 74;
influence as Framer, 296, 297; on
judicial review, 103; on necessary and
proper clause, 333; on Ninth
Amendment, 281; and original intent,
355; on religion, Congress' power over,
176; on religious tests, 151; and search
and seizure, 237; on treaty power, 39;
and unenumerated rights, 281; on
Virginia bill of attainder and outlawry,
154; on Virginia Declaration of Rights,
157; and Virginia Plan, 333
Ratification controversy, 4, 49, 50, 56, 62,
72, 104, 109, 120, 121, 124, 128, 148,
150, 158, 159, 176, 208, 290–91, 293,
296, 319, 323, 333; Abbott on, 4;
absence of bill of rights major issue,
148, 150, 158, 208; Anti-Federalists on,